The Ultimate Book of
Herbs

The Ultimate Book of
Herbs

Consultants

Deni Bown

The National Institute of Medical Herbalists

Reader's
Digest

Published by The Reader's Digest Association Limited
London • New York • Sydney • Montreal

Contents

Introduction

Herbs have been used for thousands of years to flavour and preserve food, treat ailments, ward off pests and diseases, freshen the air, and decorate and enhance our lives. Over the centuries, they have also become associated with fascinating myths, legends and folklore.

In general terms, a herb is a plant that is valued for its flavour, aroma or medicinal properties, and different parts of a herb – such as the stalks, flowers, fruits, seeds, roots or leaves – may have important applications. From small herbs growing beside our highways to bushy shrubs in mountain areas to tall trees in lush tropical rainforests, there are literally thousands of plants all over the world that belong to the herb family.

In *The Ultimate Book of Herbs*, we have combined traditional knowledge and herbal wisdom with up-to-date advice from gardening experts, herbalists, natural therapists, cleaning specialists, craft experts and cooks to show you how to grow herbs successfully and make the best use of them in your daily life. The comprehensive information on more than 100 herbs in the A to Z directory, together with the chapters on how to use them, will enable you to improve your health, save money and use fewer chemicals in your home.

With gardening know-how, safe herbal remedies, natural beauty products, innovative craft ideas, herbal cleaning items and delicious recipes, this practical reference guide to herbs is packed with information and illustrated with beautiful photographs. We hope you will find it a source of inspiration.

The editors

IMPORTANT

Growing herbs Some herbs can become invasive and may be toxic to livestock. This information has been given where possible, but regulations do change from time to time. Readers are advised to consult local plant services if they have any concerns.

Herbal medicine While the creators of this book have made every effort to be as accurate and up-to-date as possible, medical and pharmacological knowledge is constantly changing. Readers are advised to consult a qualified medical specialist for individual advice. Moreover, even though they are natural, herbs contain chemical substances that can sometimes have marked side-effects. They can also cause allergic reactions and may interact with prescription drugs and over-the-counter medicines. If used unwisely, herbs can be toxic. The writers, researchers, editors and publishers of this book cannot be held liable for any harm or actions that may be taken as a consequence of information contained in this book.

Herb directory

The history of herbs, their uses and methods of cultivation are fascinating, rewarding topics. This practical guide to more than 100 herbs, most of which can be grown in a home garden, tells you how to cultivate, use and store herbs.

Herb directory

Aloe vera

Aloe vera syn. *A. barbadensis*, Aloeaceae

The ancient Egyptians called it the 'plant of immortality', and Cleopatra used its juices to help preserve her beauty. The clear gel from the cut leaves has soothing and healing properties. Keep some in the kitchen to treat minor burns.

OTHER COMMON NAMES Barbados aloe, bitter aloe, Curaçao aloe
PART USED Leaves

Aloe vera

▉ Gardening

Aloe vera is a succulent plant with very fleshy light green leaves that create a fan from the stemless base. In warm climates, it produces narrow tubular yellow flowers. Cape aloe (*A. ferox*) is a much larger species that has long, greyish, spiny succulent leaves and tall, handsome spikes of orange-red flowers.
Position Aloes requires a sunny position and a very well-drained soil.
Propagation *Aloe vera* rarely sets seed in cool climates so it is usually propagated from offsets that form at the base of the plant. Allow these plantlets to dry for 2 days before planting them into small pots filled with a gritty, free-draining potting mix. Once they are well established, transfer them to their permanent position.
Maintenance Aloe is sensitive to temperatures below 10°C. Pot plants may be stood outside in summer only, as night-time temperatures in spring and autumn are often too chilly. Take care that plants on windowsills are not damaged by cold on winter nights. Keep dry at low temperatures but water regularly in the growing season, allowing to dry out between waterings.
Pests and diseases Mealybug and scale insects may prove a problem for plants grown indoors. Spray with insecticidal soap, which is non-toxic to animals and leaves no residue. Apply it late in the afternoon, as it can burn sensitive plants in full sun or at high temperatures.
Harvesting and storing Harvest leaves as needed, using only as much leaf as required. Cut the used end back to undamaged tissue, then wrap in cling film and store in fridge for further use.

▉ Herbal medicine

Aloe spp., including *Aloe vera* syn. *A. barbadensis* and *A. ferox*. Part used: leaves. The clear mucilaginous gel from the centre of the aloe vera leaf has anti-inflammatory and healing properties. Probably best known for its ability to encourage the healing of burns, aloe vera gel can also be applied to wounds, abrasions, eczema, psoriasis and ulcers. The exudate from the cut aloe vera leaf acts as an extremely cathartic laxative and, consequently, homemade preparations of aloe vera should not be consumed. Commercial preparations (without the laxative constituents) are available, and preliminary research indicates that they may be beneficial in a range of conditions, including non-insulin-dependent diabetes mellitus and high blood lipid levels.

For the safe and appropriate use of aloe vera, see *First aid*, page 226. Do not take aloe vera internally if you are pregnant or breastfeeding. Topical application is considered safe during these times.

▉ Natural beauty

Ultra-soothing and nourishing for even the most parched and dehydrated skin, aloe vera is also a mild exfoliant, gently removing dead skin cells and stimulating cell regeneration, helping to prevent scarring and diminish wrinkles. For specific treatments, see *Sunburn*, page 261, and *Hands and nails*, page 264. To treat your cat or dog, see *Herbal pet care*, page 303.

Cape aloe (*Aloe ferox*) in bloom. Its leaves can be used in the same way as aloe vera.

Angelica

Angelica archangelica Apiaceae

A showy, aromatic herb, angelica has both medicinal and culinary uses. Angelica's name honours the archangel Raphael, who is said to have revealed to a monk that the plant could cure the plague.

PARTS USED Leaves, stems, seeds, roots

Angelica (*Angelica archangelica*)

 Gardening

Native to northern Europe, *Angelica archangelica* is a hardy biennial that grows to 1.2m. It has ribbed, hollow stems, compound leaves and a flowering stem that appears in the second or third year, reaching 2m or more. The variety 'Corinne Tremaine' has ornamental white-variegated leaves and comes true from seed.

Wild angelica (*A. sylvestris*) and American angelica (*A. atropurpurea*) have similar uses to Chinese angelica or dong quai (*A. polymorpha* var. *sinensis*). American angelica is particularly ornamental, reaching 3m, with dark purple stems and pale green to white flowers. Also strikingly beautiful is *A. gigas*, which grows to 2m, with deep garnet buds opening to large umbels of red-purple flowers.

Position Angelica requires a shady position in well-drained but moist and slightly acidic soil that has been enriched with compost. Allow a distance of at least 1m between plants.

Propagation Plant angelica seed soon after collection. Mix the seed with damp, but not wet, vermiculite and place the mixture in a sealed plastic bag (see also page 50). Store in the crisper section of the refrigerator for 6 to 8 weeks before planting into seed trays. Barely cover the seed, and keep the soil moist. Transplant seedlings when 10cm high or when the fifth and sixth leaves emerge.

Maintenance Plants die once the seed has matured. You can delay this by removing emerging flower stems. First-year plants die-back in winter but will grow readily in spring. Water regularly.

Pests and diseases Angelicas are prone to leaf miners, which damage the leaves, but are otherwise generally trouble free. In warm dry conditions, powdery mildew may be a problem. The flowers attract many beneficial insects, including hoverflies and lacewings.

Harvesting and storing Harvest the leaves and flowering stalks in the second year. Dig the roots at the end of the second year, then wash and dry them. Gather the seed when brown and dry.

Herbal medicine

Angelica archangelica. Part used: roots. Angelica is an important digestive tonic in European herbal medicine. It stimulates the production of gastric juices and can relieve symptoms of poor appetite, dyspepsia and nausea. Angelica can also reduce the discomfort of flatulence, stomach cramps and bloating. It is a warming herb and suited to individuals who feel or are suffering from the effects of the cold.

For the safe and appropriate use of angelica and dong quai (see box below), consult your doctor or medical herbalist. Do not use angelica in greater than culinary quantities and do not use dong quai if pregnant or breastfeeding.

Cooking

Angelica is a popular boiled or steamed vegetable dish in some Scandinavian countries; it has a musky, bittersweet taste. The dried seeds and stems are used (in maceration or via the essential oil) in vermouth and liqueurs such as Chartreuse and Benedictine. Crystallised leaves and young stems are a popular decoration for cakes and sweets.

Blanch young shoots for use in salads. Use leaves and stalks in marinades and in poaching liquids for seafood. Add leaves to recipes for tart fruits, such as rhubarb. They cut the acidity, and their sweetness means that you can use less sugar.

Dong quai

Angelica polymorpha var. *sinensis*. Part used: roots. Indigenous to China, dong quai is found in damp meadows, moist valleys and on riverbanks. It grows to about 1.9m and has greenish white flowers. Worldwide, dong quai is one of the most commonly used herbs for women's health. In traditional Chinese medicine, it is considered a valuable tonic for the female reproductive system and is used to treat many menstrual and menopausal symptoms.

Anise

Pimpinella anisum Apiaceae

Anise is responsible for much of the 'liquorice' flavouring in bakery goods, liqueurs and teas. The unrelated Chinese star anise and aniseed myrtle also have a similar flavour.

OTHER COMMON NAMES Aniseed, common anise
PARTS USED Leaves (anise, aniseed myrtle), seeds/fruits (anise, star anise)

Gardening

Anise is an aromatic annual with stalked, toothed leaves that may be simple or lobed. The slender flowering stems bear compound umbels of white flowers followed by ridged grey seeds.

Chinese star anise (*Illicium verum*, family Illiciaceae), an evergreen tree, bears fruits that open to an 8-pointed star containing several hard shiny seeds. Do not confuse it with the neurotoxic Japanese star anise (*I. anisatum*) or the inedible Florida anise (*I. floridanum*).

Position Anise prefers an enriched, light, well-drained and fairly neutral soil. Star anise and aniseed myrtle need humus-rich, lime-free soil. Star anise is frost-hardy (minimum -5°C) and aniseed myrtle is tender (minimum 5-7°C).

Propagation Sow anise seed directly in late spring. Propagate Chinese star anise and aniseed myrtle by semi-ripe cuttings in summer and leave to root for several weeks in lime-free, sandy compost and a warm humid atmosphere.

Maintenance Keep anise free of weeds. Prune star anise and aniseed myrtle lightly in spring to remove crossing branches and maintain an open bushy shape.

Pests and diseases Anise repels aphids and attracts beneficial insects, such as hoverflies and wasps.

Harvesting and storing Cut anise when the seeds are fully developed. Tie bunches inside paper bags and hang them upside down to dry and catch the seed. Harvest leaves as required, and dig up roots in autumn. Harvest star anise fruits just before ripening and harvest firm leaves of aniseed myrtle at any time.

Herbal medicine

Pimpinella anisum, Illicium verum. Part used: dried ripe seeds/fruits. Anise and star anise are used medicinally for similar purposes. Despite belonging to different plant families, the essential oils derived from the seeds of each plant both contain a high percentage of a compound called anethole, which imparts the liquorice-like flavour. They both possess calming and antispasmodic properties, making them good remedies for alleviating flatulence, intestinal colic and bloating. Do not give star anise to infants and young children, as it may have serious side effects including vomiting and seizures.

Backhousia anisata. Part used: leaves. The essential oil of aniseed myrtle is similar to that of anise. Little is known of its medicinal use, though studies suggest that it may have certain antimicrobial properties.

Anise (*Pimpinella anisum*)

For the safe and appropriate use of anise and star anise, see *Indigestion*, page 210, and *Wind, bloating and flatulence*, page 212. Do not use these herbs in greater than culinary quantities if you are pregnant or breastfeeding.

Cooking

Anise seeds and oil are used in drinks such as French pastis, Greek ouzo and Turkish raki. Use whole or crushed, but for the best flavour, grind as required. They work well in baked and sweet foods, vegetable and seafood dishes, curries, pickles, soups and herb teas. Add young leaves sparingly to green salads, light fish dishes, fruit salads and cooked vegetables. Star anise fruits are very hard and need grinding or prolonged soaking in hot liquid to release their flavour.

A culinary star

Star anise is an essential ingredient in many Asian cuisines. In Vietnamese cookery, it is used to flavour the noodle soup known as pho. Along with Sichuan pepper, cloves, cassia and fennel seeds, it is a component in Chinese five-spice mix (ingredients pictured below) and in Indian garam masala.

You can use star anise whole, broken or ground. Add it to pork, chicken or duck stews. Insert a whole star anise into the cavity of a chicken or duck before roasting.

1 Sichuan pepper **2** Cassia **3** Cloves
4 Star anise **5** Fennel seeds

Anise hyssop

Agastache foeniculum syn. *A. anethiodora* Lamiaceae

Many agastaches have fragrant foliage, their scents ranging from anise to mint and citrus. The leaves are used for herbal tea, flavouring and in medicines, while the ornamental flower spikes, which attract beneficial insects, make a pretty addition to the herb garden.

OTHER COMMON NAMES Anise mint, blue giant hyssop, liquorice mint
PARTS USED Leaves, flowers

Korean mint (*A. rugosa*), with its purple blue flowers, is also known as wrinkled giant hyssop.

■ Gardening

Anise hyssop (*A. foeniculum*) is a hardy perennial with a sweet anise scent. Both balsamic and peppermint-pennyroyal scented forms are available.

Varieties Two varieties are 'Golden Jubilee', with golden foliage, and white-flowered 'Alabaster'. Other species include giant hyssop (*A. urticifolia*) and **Korean mint** (*A. rugosa*), which are both similar in appearance to anise hyssop. Korean mint is a short-lived perennial, that is rather more robust but slightly more frost-tender than anise hyssop, with purple flowers and mint-scented foliage.

Liquorice mint (*A. rupestris*) is a perennial with small liquorice-scented leaves and spikes of nectar-rich apricot flowers. Hummingbird mint (*A. cana*) is a spectacular perennial species that grows to 90cm with long, dense spikes of large rosy pink flowers and intensely aromatic foliage.

Position *A. foeniculum*, *A. rugosa* and *A. urticifolia* prefer light shade, and slightly acid to neutral soil. Most other species are from areas with a dry climate and are drought-tolerant. They prefer light, well-drained soil and a sunny position, and are well-suited to cultivation in a pot.

Propagation Sow agastache seed in spring; just cover the seed with soil. It usually takes 6 to 8 weeks to germinate. Pot on when large enough. Established plants produce many basal shoots in spring. Propagate these as softwood cuttings and plant out in summer, or multiply plants by root division.

Maintenance Agastaches are usually hardy but may be short-lived in cool damp areas. Anise hyssop and Korean mint will self-sow prolifically in these conditions.

Pests and diseases Leaves may be affected by powdery mildew in hot dry conditions.

Harvesting and storing Use the leaves and flowers freshly picked, or dry by hanging stems upside down in small bunches away from direct sunlight. They will retain their colour and scent.

■ Cooking

The flowers of anise hyssop yield large quantities of nectar, which was popular with North American beekeepers in the 19th century for producing a faintly aniseed-flavoured honey. Native Americans used it as a tea and a sweetener. Infuse the dried leaves to make a hot or cold drink. Also, use them to season lamb, chicken or salmon. Add the seeds to cakes and muffins. Use the flowers or fresh leaves of anise hyssop or Korean mint in salads. Korean mint has a peppermint and aniseed flavour and aroma and is a good substitute for mint.

Anise hyssop
(*Agastache
foeniculum*
syn. *A. anethiodora*)

Agastache is from the Greek words for 'very much' and 'ear of wheat', describing the appearance of the flower spikes.

Arnica

Arnica montana Asteraceae

There are about 30 species of *Arnica*, and all of them are perennials that spread by rhizomes and bear cheerful golden flowers. Arnica has long been used in ointments for the relief of sprains and bruises and aching muscles as well as for homeopathic treatments.

OTHER COMMON NAMES Leopard's bane, mountain tobacco
PART USED Flowers

Arnica (*Arnica montana*)

Gardening

Arnica montana is a hardy perennial that forms a basal rosette of aromatic leaves. From late spring to late summer it produces flowering stems up to 60cm high, each bearing 1–3 golden-yellow, daisy-like flowers.

Varieties Most species of *Arnica* are native to subalpine areas. European arnica (*A. montana*) is also known as mountain tobacco and leopard's bane (not to be confused with the ornamental perennial leopard's bane, *Doronicum orientale*, which is similar in appearance).

Arnica is toxic in all but the tiniest doses. In some countries, it is restricted to external use only.

Native to the northern Iberian peninsula northward to Scandinavia, its natural habitat is low fertility meadows to an altitude of about 3000m. *Arnica montana* is becoming rare, due to over-collection and agricultural practices, and is protected in many areas.

Consequently, the American species *A. chamissonis*, which has similar properties, is sometimes used in its place in herbal treatment.

Position Arnica requires a cool climate and full sun as well as slightly acid to slightly alkaline free-draining soil. In areas with wet winters, grow it in raised beds to prevent fungal attack.

Propagation You can raise arnica from seed but it will need a period of moist cold. In climates with cold winters, sow the seed outside in autumn or in containers in a cold frame. In milder winter areas, stratify the seed by mixing it with a little damp vermiculite or sterile sand. Seal it in a plastic bag, and place it in the crisper tray of the refrigerator for about 12 weeks before sowing (see also page 50). Propagate mature plants by division in spring.

Maintenance Arnica is a slow grower and resents competition from surrounding plants. Mulch well and weed regularly, or surround plants with weed matting.

Pests and diseases Fungal rots may occur in wet winters.

Harvesting and storing Gather the flowers when fully open and dry them.

Herbal medicine

Arnica montana, *A. chamissonis*. Part used: flowers. Arnica flowers have significant anti-inflammatory and mild analgesic properties. They are applied topically in the form of infused oils, ointments and creams to bruises, sprains and strains to encourage healing and to reduce the discomfort of pain and swelling. The pain-relieving effects of arnica also make this a suitable topical remedy for the treatment of sore and aching muscles and rheumatic joint problems.

Internally, *Arnica montana* is taken as a homeopathic remedy, in a very dilute preparation of the herb. It may help with the emotional effects of trauma as well as shock. It may also help to alleviate the physical complaints described above.

Arnica has been ruled unsafe in some countries. Do not use arnica preparations internally except in homeopathic dilutions and do not use if you are pregnant or breastfeeding.

The name 'arnica' probably derives from the Greek 'arnakis', meaning 'lamb's skin', due to the soft texture of the leaves.

Artemisia

Artemisia spp. Asteraceae

Named for Artemis, the Greek goddess of light and protector of the vulnerable, *Artemisia* is a genus that contains about 300 species, although few are grown in gardens. Some species produce chemicals that inhibit the growth of neighbouring plants.

OTHER COMMON NAMES Wormwood, sagebrush
PARTS USED Aerial parts, roots

 Gardening

Wormwood or absinth (*A. absinthium*) forms a woody shrub to about 80cm with a bittersweet smell. Its deeply incised grey-green leaves are densely covered in fine hairs.

Chinese Artemisia, sweet Annie or qing hao (*A. annua*) is a fast-growing hardy annual with bright green, finely divided leaves and a strong, chamomile-like fragrance. It reaches 1.5m and self-sows freely.

Tree wormwood (*A. arborescens*) resembles wormwood but grows upright to about 1.5 to 1.8m, with narrower leaf segments; it smells less strongly.

Roman wormwood or old warrior (*A. pontica*) is a low-growing plant to about 40cm, with finely cut, scented leaves. It spreads vigorously by rhizomes.

White prairie sage or western mugwort (*A. ludoviciana*) has silver-green foliage. It is an aromatic upright subshrub to 1.2m that spreads by stolons. The variety 'Silver Queen' is smaller and more ornamental.

Mugwort (*A. vulgaris*) is a perennial that spreads by rhizomes. It grows to about 90cm, with deeply incised leaves that are deep green above and greyish white below.

Southernwood or lad's love (*A. abrotanum*) forms an upward-growing bush to about 90cm with thread-like, finely divided leaves that have a lemon-camphor smell.

Varieties Some excellent ornamental forms include *A. absinthium* 'Lambrook Silver' and the hybrid 'Powis Castle'.
Position Most species are drought-tolerant and prefer full sun, good drainage and almost neutral soil, although mugwort tolerates partial shade. Rhizomatous species are often very invasive.
Propagation Propagate shrubby artemisias by greenwood, semi-ripe or heel cuttings taken in summer. Propagate rhizomatous species by root division in autumn. Directly sow the annual species *A. annua* in spring, or raise as seedlings in pots and transplant at 6 weeks.
Maintenance Lightly prune and shape shrubby artemisias in spring. Prune Southernwood heavily in spring. Remove surplus new growths from invasive species in the growing season.

Wormwood (*Artemisia absinthium*)

Tree wormwood (*Artemisia arborescens*)

Pests and diseases New growths are prone to attack by aphids and blackfly. Spray with soft soap solution or a selective insecticide that controls aphids but does not harm bees and other beneficial insects.
Harvesting and storing Harvest the leaves as required to use fresh or dried.

Herbal medicine

A. absinthium. Parts used: aerial parts. Wormwood is used to treat symptoms associated with poor digestion, including wind. In many cultures it is regarded as a valuable remedy for worm infestations and other parasitic infections of the gut. It is also used as a nerve tonic and to treat fever and menstrual complaints.

A. vulgaris. Parts used: aerial parts. Mugwort is used as a digestive stimulant and nerve tonic, and is also used to treat menstrual problems.

A. annua. Parts used: aerial parts. According to traditional Chinese medicine, Chinese wormwood (qing hao) is a bitter and cold remedy, used for treating fevers, rashes and nosebleeds. It is increasingly used in medicines to control and prevent malaria. See *Herbs in the future*, page 193, for more details.

For the safe and appropriate use of these herbs, consult a doctor or medical herbalist. Do not use these herbs if you are pregnant or breastfeeding.

Basil

Ocimum spp. Lamiaceae

While sweet basil, with its savoury clove fragrance, is the quintessential Italian culinary herb, it is in fact native to tropical Asia. Basils are available in an amazing range of forms and fragrances, from lemon, lime, anise, spice, cinnamon and thyme to incense and sweet camphor.

PARTS USED Leaves, flower spikes

Sweet basil
(*Ocimum basilicum*)

■ Gardening

There are 64 basil species, occurring in the subtropics and tropics, especially in Asia and Africa. They can be annuals, evergreen perennials or shrubs, with simple aromatic leaves and spikes of small white or pink thyme-like flowers. All interbreed readily and most varieties are complex hybrids. Tarragon-like scents are preferred in Mediterranean cooking, while Asian cuisine favours spicy aromas similar to cinnamon and anise. The first citrus-scented basil reached the United States from Thailand in around 1940. Some basils have a camphor-like scent which is not suitable for flavouring.

Varieties

The main culinary basil is sweet basil (*O. basilicum*). There are many varieties which fall into several categories.

Compact small-leafed forms of sweet basil, often referred to as bush basil or *O. minimum*, are popular in Greece and for pots. They include 'Green Globe' which forms a tight mound about 20cm across.

Large-leafed sweet basils include 'Napolitano' which also goes under the names 'Lettuce Leaf' and 'Italian'. It has large, crinkly, light green leaves and is excellent for pesto. 'Genovese' ('Perfume Basil') is another Italian variety, perfect with tomatoes and garlic. 'Mammoth' has leaves up to 15cm long that are large enough to use as food wraps.

Coloured-leaf forms, largely derived from the old varieties 'Purpurascens' and 'Dark Opal, are widely used as ornamentals as well as for culinary purposes. They include 'Red Rubin', the frilly-leafed 'Purple Ruffles' and 'Ararat' with green, purple-mottled leaves and a liquorice flavour.

Citrus-flavoured varieties are mostly crosses between sweet basil and lemon basil or kemangi (*O. americanum*). These hybrids, known as *O.* x *citriodorum* include 'Lime', 'Sweet Dani' and 'Mrs Burns' Lemon'. The variety 'Lesbos' or 'Greek Column' contains heady spice, floral and citrus notes. A similar variety, known as 'Aussie Sweetie' in Australia, is a separate introduction from Greece. Another columnar basil, grown mainly as an ornamental is 'Pesto Perpetuo'.

Spice-scented varieties of *O. basilicum* include 'Oriental Breeze', a purple-flowered form that is both attractive and well-flavoured; 'Cinnamon', a vigorous plant with purple-veined leaves and dark

Lemon basil (*Ocimum* x *citriodorum*) has a fresh lemon scent with undertones of sweet basil.

'A man taking basil from a woman will love her always.'

Sir Thomas More
Tudor statesman and philosopher,
1478–1535

pink flowers; 'Spice' has a heady, almost incense-like fragrance; and 'Horapha' (also known as 'Thai', 'Anise' and 'Liquorice'), with a liquorice-anise aroma, purple-flushed, toothed leaves and pale pink flowers with purple bracts. **Sacred or holy basil** (*O. tenuiflorum* syn. *O. sanctum*) has a mild spice scent and is available in a purple-flushed form known as 'Purple Tulsi'. It is important as a ritual and medicinal plant in India and is often planted around temples.

Some of the **handsome perennial** basils are the result of hybridisation between sweet basil and camphor basil (*O. kilimandscharicum*), an African species named after Mount Kilimanjaro in Tanzania They have a spicy clove fragrance, with a hint of balsam. They include the beautiful purple-suffused 'African Blue'.

Position Basils require a protected, warm, sunny site with well-drained soil. Plants grown indoors need good ventilation. Don't be tempted to put basil plants out in the garden unless night temperatures reliably reach 10°C.

Propagation With the exception of the perennial basils mentioned above, basils are generally treated as annuals and propagated from seed. For an early start, sow seeds thinly in pots or trays in a warm place. Prick out seedlings when large enough to handle, finally spacing plants about 30cm apart for small-

'Dark Opal', an old variety of *O. basilicum*, has cerise flowers and a delicate scent.

growing kinds and about 45cm apart for larger types. It is not worth saving your own seed from basils, unless you particularly want to experiment, as named varieties are unlikely to come true. Perennial and columnar basils are best propagated by softwood cuttings. They root easily, even in water.

Maintenance Water regularly but carefully as basils are sensitive to over watering. Being tropical, basil grows rapidly at temperatures above 16°C but is sensitive to damp, cool, cloudy conditions which rapidly cause plants to deteriorate. Pinch out flowerheads to promote bushy plant growth and prolong the plant's productive life.

Classically Italian

Insalata Caprese ('salad in the style of Capri'), represents the colours of the Italian flag. It is a light, summery salad that showcases the flavour of basil and ripe tomatoes. Arrange tomato slices on a plate. Intersperse with slices of fresh bocconcini (baby mozzarella). Season well. Add a dash of olive oil and a scattering of fresh basil.

Pests and diseases Basils are prone to fungal diseases, including fusarium wilt, which causes sudden wilting, and grey mould (*Botrytis*). Remove and destroy affected plants (do not compost them), and do not replant basil in the contaminated soil. Improve growing conditions by raising the temperature and increasing ventilation. The variety 'Nuphar', a Genovese type, has some resistance to fusarium wilt. Basil can also be attacked by aphids.

Harvesting and storing Harvest shoot tips, mature leaves and flower spikes at any time. To dry the leaves, cut bushes at the base and hang out of direct light, then crumble and store in glass (not plastic) containers in a cool dark place. However, basil freezes better than it dries. Frozen basil discolours though, so it is only suitable for use in cooked dishes. Freeze leaves whole, not chopped, as they crumble easily when still frozen.

Aromatic basil oil

Preserve basil the Italian way by layering the leaves in a jar and sprinkling each layer with salt. Then top up the jar with good-quality olive oil. Seal the jar securely and store in the refrigerator, allowing several days for the oil to be infused with the flavour of the basil. Use the leaves and the oil with pine nuts for making your own pesto (see recipe, page 340). Drizzle a little oil over pizzas or salads. Also, try adding a dash to a marinade.

Basil continued

■ Herbal medicine

Ocimum basilicum. Part used: leaves. Sweet basil is known more for its pleasant taste than for its medicinal effects. Due to its mild sedative properties, herbalists traditionally prescribed basil as a tea for easing nervous irritability.

Ocimum tenuiflorum syn. *O. sanctum.* Part used: leaves. Holy basil, an important herb in Ayurvedic medicine, is used for a range of complaints. Scientific research supports its role in the management of diabetes (due to a hypoglycaemic effect) and as a supportive herb during times of stress. It may also improve concentration and memory and, due to an antiallergic effect, may be beneficial in treating hay fever and asthma.

For the safe and appropriate use of basils, consult a doctor or medical herbalist. Do not use these herbs in greater than culinary quantities if you are pregnant or breastfeeding.

■ Around the home

Basil is a natural disinfectant. Use the essential oil in combination with other antiseptic herbal oils to make natural disinfectant sprays for cleaning household surfaces. Plant basil in a pot close to the back door to deter flies. Cut a bunch of basil as an aromatic table

centrepiece when you eat outdoors. The dried flowerheads add a sweet and spicy note to a potpourri.

■ Cooking

Basil is one of the great culinary herbs; different varieties are used extensively in both European and Asian cooking. If a recipe specifies simply 'basil', sweet or common basil (*O. basilicum*) is the type generally meant. Fresh sweet basil is highly aromatic, with a distinctive scent and flavour reminiscent of tarragon and aniseed. Using a knife to cut basil can bruise and darken the leaves. For salads and pasta sauces where appearance matters, shred the leaves with your fingers. Young leaves have the best flavour, while old ones have a coarser, stronger taste. In cooked dishes, basil quickly loses its aroma and the leaves

Herb of contradictions

Basil has both positive and negative associations that include love and fear, danger and protection, and life and death. The negative connotations probably come from basil's Latin epithet *basilicum*, which links it to the basilisk (left), the mythical serpent with a deadly gaze. The ancient Greeks and Romans believed that uttering a curse when sowing basil would ensure its germination.

In Greece, pots of small-leaved basil are placed on tables to deter flies.

tend to darken, so add it to give depth of flavour during cooking and then, for fragrance and visual appeal, stir in a little more just before serving. Basil goes especially well with tomato dishes, chicken, egg and rice dishes, pasta sauces, and vegetables such as beans, peppers and aubergines.

See Vegetarian spring rolls recipe, page 360. Basil is a good addition to stuffings. The most famous use of basil is in pesto (or *pistou* in French). Citrus-scented and spice-flavoured basils work well in a range of Asian recipes.

The word basil may come from the Greek *basilicon*, meaning kingly.

Sweet basil is sometimes called the 'Royal Herb'.

Bay

Laurus nobilis Lauraceae

The bay is a long-lived and slow-growing, pyramid-shaped evergreen tree or large shrub with crisp, glossy green leaves. According to folklore, a bay tree in the garden or placed in a pot at the front door will keep away evil as well as ward off thunder and lightning.

OTHER COMMON NAMES Bay laurel, Grecian bay, sweet bay
PARTS USED Leaves, flower buds, fruits, bark, roots

◼ Gardening

While a bay tree can reach about 15m over a long period, its slow, dense upright growth habit makes it an ideal specimen for a large pot, whether it is allowed to grow into its natural form or shaped into an ornamental topiary or standard. In this form, a small garden can accommodate a bay without concern; its growth is even slower when cultivated in a pot. Bay trees flower when quite young, producing, small fragrant cream flowers. In warm climates, these are followed by blue-black berries.

Varieties There are two species of bay, the Mediterranean *L. nobilis* and *L. azorica* from the Azores and Canary Islands; the latter is less hardy but similar in appearance, but has broader leaves which have downy undersides. There is a golden-leafed form of *L. nobilis* called 'Aurea', as well as a willow-leaf form, 'Angustifolia'.

Several other unrelated species are known as bay. They have similar flavours and uses to sweet bay and include American red bays (*Persea* spp.), typical of Creole cuisine, and Mexican bay (*Litsea glaucescens*) which is used in Mexican cooking.

Position Bay trees prefer well-drained soil, full sun and, in areas with cold winters, a sheltered position. Golden bays are particularly sensitive to severe frost and cold, drying winds which cause browning of the leaves. Bays tolerate relatively small pots for their size and hard pruning, so they make excellent container plants. Plants tend to become top heavy, so use heavy, broad-based pots and position them out of the wind.

Bay (*Laurus nobilis*)

History and myth

The bay tree was sacred to the sun god Apollo, and later his son Asclepius, the Greek god of medicine. According to myth, Apollo fell in love with Daphne, a beautiful nymph who, rather than returning his affection, appealed to the gods to rescue her from him. They changed her into a bay tree; Apollo thereafter declared the tree sacred and wore a bay laurel wreath in Daphne's honour.

Bay was believed to attract good fortune and wealth, and to repel evil. The death of bay trees was a portent of evil times; when Rome fell to invaders in the 4th century, all the bay trees are reputed to have died. During outbreaks of plague, Romans burned bay leaves in the public squares, and it was still used for this purpose in the 16th century.

Used in quantity, the leaves are mildly narcotic; it is said that the Oracle of Delphi in Greece chewed bay leaves before she entered a prophetic trance. The temple at Delphi was roofed with protective branches of bay.

The gods turned the nymph Daphne into a bay tree so that Apollo would stop pursuing her.

Bay continued

Propagation Seed may take 6 months to germinate. Cuttings are slow to root. Standing semi-ripe tip cuttings in water for about a month and changing the water regularly, encourages rooting. After soaking, dip the cuttings in hormone rooting powder and insert in gritty compost in a warm humid place. Faster rooting can also be obtained by using suckers that appear at the base of the plant and need removing anyway.

Maintenance In areas with very cold winters, sweet bay is best grown in pots and brought inside during the winter months or if the temperature is likely to drop below −15°C. Re-pot potted specimens into larger containers with fresh additional soil as required; when transplanting, disturb the root system as little as possible. Large specimens should be top-dressed in spring by removing a few centimetres of compost and replacing it with John Innes No3 Compost enriched with well-rotted compost and some slow-release fertiliser.

Pests and diseases Bay is prone to scale insects, which may infest the underneath of leaves and stems. To remove these, blend 2 cloves of garlic with a cup of water, filter, and add a little soft soap. Apply to the insects with cotton buds. Or apply horticultural neem oil in the same way. Plants grown without adequate ventilation and light can develop powdery mildew, which should be treated with sulphur while the plant is wet with morning dew.

Harvesting and storing Pick green leaves for use at any time. Dry leaves out of direct sunshine and store in an airtight glass jar. Also see *Harvesting, preserving and storing*, page 178.

Bouquet garni, a bundle of classic herbs, usually includes bay, thyme, parsley and peppercorns.

Vanilla bay custard

Bay complements fish, meat and poultry dishes, sauces such as béarnaise (see recipe, page 345), and, surprisingly, perhaps, sweet custards such as this, where it imparts a slightly spicy taste.

Place 150ml milk, 150ml double cream, 1 split vanilla pod and 1 bay leaf in a saucepan. Bring to a simmer, remove from heat and leave to infuse for 15 minutes. Remove pod and leaf. Beat 3 egg yolks and 1 tablespoon soft brown sugar in a bowl. Add infused milk, mixing thoroughly. Return mixture to a clean saucepan. Cook over a low heat, stirring, until custard thickens; do not let it boil. Serve warm with hot fruit pies and steamed puddings.

▓ Cooking

Sweet bay is indispensable in French and other Mediterranean cookery. The tough leaves withstand long cooking in soups and stews. Apart from meat and fish, they go well in lentil or bean dishes. Two leaves are enough in a dish that serves six people. Bay is essential in bouquet garni and is also used in pickling spice and garam masala. Fresh leaves tend to be bitter, but the taste will diminish if they are left to wilt for a few days. Fresh sprigs stripped of a few leaves make aromatic skewers for meat or fish cooked on the barbecue. Dried leaves retain their flavour for about a year. Remove dried leaves from dishes before serving.

To deter weevils in your pantry, add bay leaves to jars of flour and rice.

Crowning glory

Bay's botanical name, *Laurus*, stems from the Latin word, *laus*, or 'praise', in reference to the crown of bay leaves worn by the ancient Romans to celebrate victory. Other herbs were often incorporated into wreaths. The Roman emperor Tiberius always wore a wreath of bay laurel when thunderstorms were raging as he believed that it would provide protection from the gods of thunder and lightning.

Wild bergamot (*Monarda fistulosa*)

Bergamot

Monarda sp. Lamiaceae

Native Americans used Monarda to make medicinal tisanes. Following the Boston Tea Party of 1773, when American colonists dumped tea shipped by the East India Company, to protest against British rule, the bergamot tea of the Oswego Indians became a popular substitute.

OTHER COMMON NAMES Bee balm, Oswego tea
PART USED Leaves

Gardening

Bergamot obtained its English common name because the scent of its foliage resembled that of bergamot orange (*Citrus bergamia*), see page 41. There are about a dozen species of Monarda, with aromas ranging from mint and thyme to lemon and rose geranium. In the wild, the spectacular flowers attract humming birds, but bees also find them attractive.

Varieties Oswego tea (*M. didyma*) is a hardy perennial from rich moist woodland areas, growing to 1.2m, with several stems terminating in heads surrounded by dense whorls of long-tubed, scarlet flowers. The leaves have a very pleasant citrus scent.

Wild bergamot or horsemint (*M. fistulosa*) is another hardy perennial found on well-drained hillsides and in light woodland. It has whorled heads of lilac to pink flowers. There are several distinct varieties originating from different parts of North America, each slightly different in appearance and aroma. The variety known as oregano de la Sierra (*M. fistulosa* var. *menthifolia* syn. *M. menthifolia*) has lavender flowers and a true oregano scent and flavour.

Spotted bergamot (*M. punctata*) is an annual or short-lived perennial. It has densely whorled heads of cream flowers speckled purple and lavender bracts.

Lemon bergamot (*M. citriodora*) is a tall annual species from dry grasslands with heads of large, lipped, pink or lavender flowers. In the southwest USA and western Mexico a variety known as orégano in Spanish (*M. citriodora* var, *austromontana* syn. *M. austromontana*) has lavender flowers and an aroma like Greek oregano.

Most garden bergamots are hybrids (*M.* x *media*) including: 'Beauty of Cobham' with light pink flowers and purplish bracts; 'Blaustrumpf (syn. 'Blue Stocking') with dark violet-purple flowers and purple bracts; 'Cambridge Scarlet' with bright red flowers and red-brown bracts; 'Snow Queen' with large heads of white flowers; and a group of tall hybrids (160-180cm) developed by the Dutch garden designer Piet Oudolf and named after Indian tribes, such as 'Mohawk'.

Position As a rule, red-flowered bergamots need rich moist soil and some shade, whereas those with pink, mauve and white flowers are more drought-resistant and prefer a sunny position with well-drained soil.

Propagation Propagate annuals and species by seed. Hybrids do not come true from seed. Divide perennials in early spring. You can also take cuttings of new shoots in spring.

Maintenance Clear dead material in winter. Divide plants every 3 years.

Pests and diseases Some garden varieties are susceptible to powdery mildew, which, although it is disfiguring, does not appear to cause any permanent damage. Enriching the soil and regular watering may help to prevent this.

Harvesting and storing Harvest the edible flowers as required. Collect leaves in late spring and dry them.

Herbal medicine

Monarda didyma, *M. fistulosa*. Part used: leaves. Both species have been used medicinally to ease flatulence and colic, relieve colds and reduce fevers. *M. fistulosa* is known to contain thymol, an essential oil also found in thyme and marjoram, which may explain the calming effect on the digestive system. Do not confuse extracts of bergamot with essential oil of bergamot from *Citrus bergamia* (see page 41). For the safe and appropriate use of bergamot, consult your doctor or medical herbalist.

New World plant

Monarda is named after a Spanish physician and botanist, Nicholas Monardes, who was the first European to write a book about Native American medicinal plants. It was translated into English in 1577 with the title *Joyfull News out of the newe founde Worlde*. This may have been the origin of the term 'New World' as a way of distinguishing the colonial discoveries of North and South America from the 'Old World' of Europe, Africa and Asia.

Bilberry, blueberry and **cranberry**

Vaccinium myrtillus, V. corymbosum, V macrocarpon Ericaceae

Though many medicinal plants do not taste good, these berries are safe and delicious to eat, as well as providing potent beneficial effects on health. North American Indians used to grind cranberries with meat and melted fat as a staple winter food known as pemmican.

Cranberries (*Vaccinium corymbosum*)

OTHER COMMON NAMES Huckleberry, whortleberry
PART USED Fruits

Bilberries (*Vaccinium myrtillus*).

Gardening

Bilberry (*Vaccinium myrtillus*) is a creeping deciduous shrub up to 30cm tall, with upright stems, and small, oval, finely toothed leaves. In late spring and early summer, tiny pink bell-shaped flowers appear, followed by small, round, blue-black berries.

Blueberry (*V. corymbosum*) is larger, up to 1.8m with white flowers and large sweet berries. Highbush or swamp blueberry (*V. corymbosum*) has many commercial varieties and has been hybridised with other cold-tolerant species, such as the lowbush blueberry (*V. angustifolium*).

Cranberry (*V. macrocarpum*) is a prostrate mat-forming evergreen shrub with tiny dark green leaves and bell-shaped pale pink flowers in summer, followed by red fruits. Commercial varieties have larger berries and different cropping times.

Varieties 'Northland' gives heavy crops of good-sized bilberries. 'Earliblue' gives huge crops of blueberries from early July; 'Brigitta' is a vigorous late variety, cropping in August and September. 'Pilgrim' is the most widely grown cranberry for gardens, tolerating drier conditions with large, dark red berries.

Position *Vaccinium* species are very hardy. They need moist acid, peaty or sandy soil in sun or partial shade, and can be grown in large pots in lime-free (ericaceous) compost. Blueberries reach 1.5-1.8m in the ground but less in containers. Cranberries do well in low, wide containers.

Propagation Deciduous species are grown from greenwood cuttings taken in summer. Take semi-ripe cuttings of cranberries or weigh down long stems with large stones to encourage rooting. Cuttings need lime-free sandy compost for rooting. *Vaccinium* species can also be grown from seed sown in containers in autumn and left outdoors to stratify before germinating in spring. Named varieties do not come true from seed.

Maintenance Tidy deciduous shrubs in late winter when dormant, removing old, unproductive growth from the base and any crossing branches to give an open, balanced shape. Trim cranberries after fruiting; remove old straggly stems.

Pests and diseases Birds and mice find them irresistible. Either plant them in a fruit cage or cover individual plants with fine netting as fruits start to ripen.

Harvesting and storing Berries last well on the plants and keep for several weeks in the fridge. Wait until fully coloured before picking as unripe fruits are sour. Freeze berries on trays before packing in freezer bags or boxes. Dry berries on trays lined with kitchen paper in an airing cupboard or in the oven at the lowest setting.

Herbal medicine

Vaccinium myrtillus. Part used: fruit. Compounds in bilberries called anthocyanosides have potent anti-oxidant properties which lower blood sugar and improve blood supply to veins and capillaries. These effects can help to relieve mild diabetes in the elderly and are effective in maintaining eye health.

V. corymbosum. Part used: fruit. Rich in antioxidants, including vitamin C, cranberries are an important remedy for treating and preventing cystitis; the main effect is to protect tissues in the urinary tract from invasion by harmful bacteria.

Cooking

Fruits can be used in tarts, cheesecakes, mousses, sauces, compotes, coulis, juices, jams and jellies. Blueberry muffins are a favourite for breakfast. Dried fruits are a nutritious addition to breakfast cereals. Bilberries and blueberries are good on their own with yoghurt, or with other berries or fruits in desserts. Cranberry sauce is traditional with turkey.

Borage

Borago officinalis Boraginaceae

An ancient cure for 'melancholia', this hardy herb is also very attractive to bees and has often been planted by beekeepers as a forage crop for their hives. Today, borage is more likely to be grown for the seeds, which yield starflower oil. It is an excellent companion plant, helping to deter certain pests and benefiting strawberries.

OTHER COMMON NAME Starflower
PARTS USED Leaves, flowers

Borage
(*Borago officinalis*)

In the first century CE, Pliny declared that borage made men merry and glad.

Gardening

Borage is a robust hardy annual. It forms a rosette of large ovate leaves before sending up hollow, often sprawling flowering stems to 90cm. The plant has a cucumber scent and is bristly, making it unpleasant to handle and causing irritation to sensitive skin. The flower is five petalled and bright blue with a white centre and cone of black stamens. As the flowers age, they turn pink.

Varieties There are three species of *Borago*, but only *B. officinalis* has herbal uses. Although the occasional seedling shows white variegation, there is only one reliable colour variant of borage. It is called 'Alba', has white flowers and comes fairly true from seed.

Position Borage requires a sunny, well-drained position and prefers a well-dug and composted soil.

Propagation Sow plants directly into the ground in spring and in autumn. You can sow them in pots, but transplant when young, as they develop a large taproot. Borage germinates readily, in 3 to 5 days. Thin the plants to a spacing of 45cm. In good conditions, borage self sows freely.

Maintenance Keep the soil moist, and fertilise in spring.

Pests and diseases Generally pest and disease-free.

Harvesting and storing Harvest borage leaves and flowers as required. Both parts are used fresh. When using flowers, make sure to remove the bristly green sepals, which are unpalatable. Borage leaves used to be dried to make tea but this is no longer considered safe due to the presence of pyrrolizidine alkaloids that in excess can cause liver damage.

Herbal medicine

Borago officinalis. Part used: seed oil. Starflower or borage seed oil is a rich source of gamma-linolenic acid (GLA), an omega-6 fatty acid that is also found in evening primrose oil. GLA exhibits anti-inflammatory properties; some research suggests that it may be of therapeutic value in the treatment of dry and itching skin conditions, including eczema and psoriasis. The latest evidence suggests that better therapeutic results may be achieved when GLA and other omega-6 oils are taken in combination with omega-3 essential fatty acids, such as those found in flax seed and fish. The leaves are used as a poultice for sprains, bruises and inflammation, and in facial steams for dry skin.

The actual seeds of borage contain pyrrolizidine alkaloids. For this reason, consumption of raw borage seeds is not recommended. Commercially extracted borage seed oil is alkaloid free. For the safe and appropriate use of starflower oil, consult your doctor or medical herbalist.

Do not use starflower oil if you are pregnant or breastfeeding.

Cooking

The flowers can be added to salads but avoid contact with fruit juices and vinegar as the acids make them turn pink. The flowers can be preserved in the short term by freezing in ice cubes for using in cold drinks, or by crystallising as cake decorations (see page 386). A small leaf of borage is the traditional garnish for a glass of Pimm's and it also makes a good substitute for cucumber in other chilled summer drinks.

Brahmi

Bacopa monnieri Scrophulariaceae

This tropical herb is reputed to improve both brain function and memory, and the dried plant is used in many traditional Ayurvedic formulations. It is closely related to *Sutera*, a genus which has recently been hybridised to give small-flowered trailing or creeping plants for containers.

OTHER COMMON NAMES Bacopa, thyme-leafed gratiola, water hyssop
PARTS USED Whole plant above ground

Brahmi (*Bacopa monnieri*)

■ Gardening

Bright green brahmi is a modest ground-hugging perennial plant that grows in wetland environments. Leaves are simple, oval, arranged in opposite pairs, smooth-edged and bitter-tasting. Slightly succulent, it bears small five-petalled flowers that are white, with a faint blue tinge on the back, over many months. Fruits are small, flat capsules.
Position Brahmi needs constantly moist soil and light shade. It grows well in wide shallow containers, or as a trailing plant in pots or hanging baskets of summer bedding. You can also grow it in a heated aquarium or garden pond in summer. It is frost tender, so give protection in winter.
Propagation You can grow brahmi from seed, but it is much easier from

The name 'brahmi' comes from Brahma, the Hindu god of creation.

cuttings as it forms adventitious roots on creeping shoots, and the detached shoots quickly grow into new plants when potted up separately. Unrooted tip cuttings also strike quickly.
Maintenance As it has very shallow roots, water brahmi regularly, especially if exposed to direct hot sunshine. Promote rapid growth with liquid seaweed fertiliser diluted to the recommended strength. Keep at a minimum temperature of 15°C in winter, and above 20°C for optimum growth.
Pests and diseases Trouble free.
Harvesting and storing Harvest stems and leaves when plant is 5 months old, leaving 5cm stems so that plant can regenerate for further harvesting. Dry leaves in the shade at room temperature and store in airtight containers.

■ Herbal medicine

Bacopa monnieri. Parts used: whole herb. In Ayurvedic medicine, brahmi is prescribed by herbalists to improve memory, learning and concentration. Scientific research has provided

Food for the brain

Keeping our brains healthy is as important as keeping our bodies in shape. Brahmi has been used as a 'brain workout' herb in the Ayurvedic tradition of medicine for about 500 years. Researchers hypothesise that it may help by improving the way the nervous system transmits messages in the brain. Gotu kola (*Centella asiatica* syn. *Hydrocotyle asiatica*) is also sometimes confusingly referred to by the common name brahmi and is a 'brain' herb in its own right. The two plants are easily distinguished by their different leaf shapes (see Gotu kola, page 65).

encouraging evidence for some of these effects, but suggests improvements take around 3 months to occur. Brahmi is also renowned as an exceptional nerve tonic, so it is notable that a reduction in anxiety levels was also observed in some clinical studies, supporting its use during times of anxiety and nervous exhaustion.

For the safe and appropriate use of brahmi, see *Memory and concentration*, page 219. Do not use brahmi if you are pregnant or breastfeeding.

In its natural environment, brahmi thrives in and around wetland areas.

Burdock

Arctium lappa Asteraceae

Burdock is enjoying a resurgence in popularity, both as a vegetable and a traditional medicinal plant. It is a common wild plant of hedgerows and woodland that many people remember from childhood games of throwing the burrs (bristly fruits) so that they stick to clothing.

OTHER COMMON NAMES Beggar's buttons, great burdock
PARTS USED Leaves, roots, seeds

Burdock (*Arctium lappa*)

Gardening

Burdock is a very hardy biennial with large oval leaves and stout branched stems of purple thistle-like flowers. Burdock can grow as high as 2.4m.

Varieties Some Japanese varieties are grown as a vegetable for their slender, crisp-textured taproots, that can reach up to 1m long. They include 'Takinogawa Long' and 'Watanabe Early'. They are non-fibrous and have a flavour between that of parsnip and Jerusalem artichoke.

Lesser burdock (*Arctium minus*) is a widespread weed in the Northern Hemisphere. It can be used in similar ways but is more bitter.

Position Burdock requires moist, well-drained, humus-rich soil and full sun or light shade. It dies back in winter.

Propagation Propagate from seed sown in spring or late autumn. Thin seedlings to about 15cm apart when grown in rows as a vegetable. To produce long straight roots, dig the soil to a depth of 60cm and incorporate well-rotted compost before sowing.

Maintenance Keep the soil moist and weed the crop regularly, particularly when the plants are young.

Pests and diseases Burdock is rarely affected by pests and diseases, other than leaf miner which spoils the appearance of the leaves but does no other harm.

Harvesting and storing For cooking as a green vegetable, collect young shoots and leaves in spring. Leaf stems of larger leaves can be also be eaten when cooked. To prepare, scrape them first to remove downy layer. Lift the roots in autumn, 120-150 days after planting, according to the variety, when they are at least 30cm long. For medicinal purposes, clean, chop and dry the roots.

Herbal medicine

Arctium lappa. Part used: roots. In Western herbal medicine, burdock root is used as an alterative or blood purifier. These terms describe its gentle detoxifying effect on the body and stimulation of the body's eliminatory channels, namely the lymphatic, digestive and urinary systems. It is commonly prescribed for chronic inflammatory skin and joint conditions, which traditional herbalists regard as the result of a build-up of unwanted toxins in the body. When used over a long period of time, burdock root can be particularly effective in clearing dry, scaly skin complaints, including eczema and psoriasis, and improving rheumatic joint conditions.

For the safe and appropriate use of burdock, consult your doctor or medical herbalist. Do not use burdock if you are pregnant or breastfeeding.

Cooking

In Japan burdock is known as gobo. It is used as a vegetable and also in various pickles and a miso-based condiment. It is also eaten as a vegetable in Korea. Tender young roots and leaf stalks can be steamed or stir-fried and served with soy sauce and sesame seeds. Use the roots raw as a salad vegetable. To reduce bitterness, soak prepared roots and stems in water before cooking.

Making it stick

The evenly distributed hooks on the burdock burrs, which kept sticking to his clothes on walks in the countryside, inspired George de Mestral to invent Velcro in 1945. The name comes from the French words velour, meaning 'velvet' and crochet or 'hook'. The invention has been applied to a wide range of items, from fasteners on clothes, bags and shoes to stainless-steel hook and loop fasteners that are used to attach car parts.

Calamint

Calamintha grandiflora, C. menthifolia syn. *C. sylvatica,*
C. nepeta syn. *C. nepetoides* Lamiaceae

Calamints are native to grasslands and scrub in Europe and
central Asia. They belong to the mint family, *Lamiaceae*,
and are closely related to savory. A few species are grown
in herb gardens for their aromatic foliage and thyme-like,
nectar-rich flowers that attract pollinating insects such
as bees and butterflies.

PARTS USED Leaves, flowering sprigs

Lesser calamint (*Calamintha nepeta*)

 Gardening

Calamints are undemanding plants that
are ideal as 'fillers' in herb gardens and
mixed borders. Though not showy, they
complement many other more striking
plants. Lesser calamint (*C. nepeta*) is
popular for its clouds of tiny flowers and
very long-flowering period throughout
most of summer and autumn. Long-
lived, it self-sows modestly when
conditions are right.

Varieties Common calamint
(*C. menthifolia*) is a rhizomatous
perennial with shiny toothed mint-
scented leaves and spotted, lilac-pink
flowers. It reaches about 60cm.

Mint savory or showy calamint
(*C. grandiflora*) is a bushy plant reaching
30-45cm tall, with ovate toothed, mint-
scented leaves and relatively large pink
flowers. It has an attractive variegated
form ('Variegata').

Lesser calamint (*C. nepeta*) is a lax,
bushy perennial, up to 75cm tall, with
small, hairy, peppermint-scented leaves
and tiny pale lilac to white flowers.
There are some attractive subspecies,
including *C. nepeta* subsp. *nepetoides*,
which is large all round, often up to
90cm tall, and varieties with lilac-blue
and white flowers ('Blue Cloud' and
'White Cloud' respectively). Another is
emperor's mint (*C. nepeta* subsp.
glandulosa), with larger, strongly mint-
scented leaves and tiny white flowers.

Position Calamints thrive in most soils
but happiest in well-drained conditions
in sun or dappled shade. They are
drought and lime-tolerant, making good
subjects for dry chalky soils.

Propagation Sow seeds of species
varieties in spring in pots of well-
drained compost in gentle warmth.
Named varieties, which do not come
true from seed, should either be divided
in early spring or propagated by
softwood cuttings in summer. Given
some warmth and humidity, they will
root quite easily.

Maintenance Cut back in spring to
encourage strong new growth.

Common calamint (*Calamintha menthifolia*
syn. *C. sylvatica*)

Pests and diseases Generally
calamints are trouble free but in very
dry conditions foliage may be affected
by powdery mildew.

Harvesting and storing Leaves can
be picked throughout spring and
summer. Cut flowering sprigs when they
first come into bloom. Use both leaves
and flowering sprigs fresh for flavouring
and herb teas, or dry for winter use.

Herbal medicine

Calamints were used medicinally in
medieval times but are seldom used by
medical herbalists today. The 17th-
century herbalist Nicholas Culpeper
noted that calamint 'hinders conception
in women', and an 18th-century Irish
herbal recommended it 'to expel dead
child from womb'. These uses indicate
that calamints contain pulegone, a toxic
compound found in pennyroyal (*Mentha
pulegium*, see page 91) which in large
quantities cause uterine contractions.

Cooking

The leaves of calamint can be added in
very small quantities to add flavour to
roast meats, especially game, and
vegetables such as courgettes and
mushrooms. In Italy calamint is known
as nepetella and listed in a number of
recipes as an ingredient in sauces.

Calendula

Calendula officinalis Asteraceae

Calendula produces large daisy-like flowers in vivid golden yellow or orange. In ancient Rome, the herb was used to make a broth that was said to uplift the spirits. In India, the bright flowers decorate the altars in Hindu temples. Calendula has a range of useful medicinal properties.

OTHER COMMON NAMES Golds, marigold, pot marigold, ruddles
PART USED Petals

Calendula (*Calendula officinalis*)

Gardening

Native to Central Europe and the Mediterranean, calendula is a hardy annual that forms a dense clump of simple lance-shaped aromatic leaves. The flowers are up to 7cm across.

Varieties The original wild calendula has single flowers but over the centuries numerous double-flowered forms have been bred for their showier, longer lasting flowers. These include the dwarf 'Fiesta Gitana', reaching 20cm, and 'Princess', up to 60cm tall, with long-stemmed blooms that make good cut flowers. The german variety 'Erfürter Orangefarbigen' is used for commercial medicinal flower production in Europe. A remarkable heirloom single variety from the Elizabethan period, *C. officinalis* 'Prolifera', is still grown. It is known as 'hen and chickens' as the main flower is encircled by a number of smaller flowers from its base.

During the Middle Ages, many plants were renamed 'Mary's gold' in honour of the Virgin Mary.

Position Calendula needs full sun and moderately fertile, well-drained soil.
Propagation The large seeds of calendula are easy to handle and quick to germinate, making them ideal for children's gardens. They can be sown directly into the ground in spring or, for early flowering, in autumn.
Maintenance Regular deadheading will help to prolong flowering.
Pests and diseases Plants are prone to mildew in autumn. The variety 'Orange King' has good resistance.
Harvesting and storing Gather petals after the dew has dried and spread them very thinly over paper on racks, out of direct sunlight, in a well-ventilated place. When they are dried, store them in airtight containers. For optimum medicinal value, dry whole flowerheads, checking carefully that they are completely dry before packing away.

Herbal medicine

Calendula officinalis. Part used: flowers. Calendula flowers have significant wound-healing and local anti-inflammatory properties. With wounds, cuts and burns, apply topically as an ointment, cream or infused oil. The slight astringency may help to staunch bleeding, while its antimicrobial effects keep the injury free from infection. Use calendula tincture as a mouthwash against gum infections and mouth ulcers and also as a topical antifungal agent for fungal skin conditions.

Traditionally, calendula flowers are taken internally for infections and inflammation of the gut, including stomach and duodenal ulcers, and also as a lymphatic remedy for the treatment of swollen lymph nodes.

For the safe and appropriate external use of calendula, see *First aid*, page 226. For internal use, consult a doctor or medical herbalist. Do not take calendula internally if you are pregnant or breast-feeding. Topical application is considered safe at these times.

Globetrotting

This kind of marigold should not be confused with the so-called African and French marigolds which were developed by hybridising several Mexican species of the genus *Tagetes*. Some *Tagetes* are herbs in their own right, including the lemon marigold, *T. tenuifolia*, which has lemon-scented foliage and yellow flowers, and Mexican tarragon (*T. lucida*), see page 132.

Caraway

Carum carvi Apiaceae

Caraway was a popular Middle Eastern herb before being introduced into western Europe in the 12th century. It is named after Caria, a region of Asia Minor, now part of Anatolia in Turkey. Only a few species have herbal uses.

PARTS USED Leaves, roots, dried ripe fruits (known as seeds), essential oil

■ Gardening

Caraway is a hardy annual or biennial with divided fern-like leaves and a spindle-shaped taproot, which can be cooked as a root vegetable. The flowering stem, about 60cm tall, bears umbels of tiny white flowers touched with pink that are followed by crescent-shaped ridged seeds. As caraway is undistinguished in appearance, it is best grown among vegetables and other herbs than as an ornamental. Label plants carefully as the foliage of caraway looks similar to that of parsley and carrots.

Varieties 'Sprinter' is high-yielding and the seeds don't drop as soon as they ripen, making it easier to harvest them. There are several European varieties too, such as 'Arterner' which produces heavy crops of large smooth seeds.

Ajmud (*C. roxburghianum*) is a popular Indian spice with a celery-caraway flavour, and ajowan (*Trachyspermum ammi* syn. *Carum copticum*) with a peppery thyme-anise scent are closely related.

Position Caraway requires fertile soil and a warm sunny position.

Propagation Caraway does not transplant well so sow seed directly into the soil in either spring or early autumn. Thin plants to 15cm apart.

Maintenance Regularly weed and water, as seed is often slow to germinate.

Pests and diseases Caraway is rarely troubled by pests.

Harvesting and storing Gather leaves at any time. Harvest roots before plants start to flower. Cut flowering stems when the seeds begin to ripen. Hang them upside down over sheets of paper to catch the seeds when they dry.

■ Herbal medicine

Carum carvi. Part used: fruits (seeds). Caraway's ability to dispel wind and exert a calming, antispasmodic effect on the gastrointestinal tract makes it a reliable remedy for flatulence, intestinal colic and bloating. Due to its slightly drying nature, it is also prescribed with other suitable herbs to relieve diarrhoea.

For the safe and appropriate use of caraway, see *Wind, bloating and flatulence*, page 212. Do not use caraway in greater than culinary quantities if you are pregnant or breastfeeding.

■ Cooking

Caraway seeds flavour rye bread, soups, sausages, cabbage dishes, cheeses, pork dishes, goulash and cooked apples, as well as liqueurs and spirits such as Kümmel. Use the feathery caraway leaves in salads and soups. Their taste resembles a mixture of parsley and dill.

Caraway (*Carum carvi*)

Cardamom

Elettaria cardamomum Zingiberaceae

Cardamom is native to India and belongs to the same family as ginger, *Zingiberaceae*. Its strongly scented pods and seeds are redolent of its oriental origins. In ancient times it was traded overland in camel caravans along the Spice Route to Europe and was highly prized as an ingredient of perfumes as well as a spice.

PART USED Seeds

◾ Gardening

Cardamom is an evergreen, clump-forming perennial, up to 3m tall, with canes of aromatic, pointed leaves, 50cm long and 4-5cm wide. Loose, rather straggly spikes of orchid-like white flowers with pink-striped lips appear at the base of the plant in summer, followed by angular pale green pods. Each pod contains 5-7 highly aromatic black seeds. Cardamom plants are tropical but not particularly difficult to grow in large containers in a warm greenhouse or sun room. Only a very green-fingered gardener is likely to succeed in producing cardamom pods.

Varieties Closely related to cardamom are two other members of the ginger family with similar uses. One is *Afromomum*, including *A. angustifolium* (Madagascar cardamom) and *A. korarima* (Ethiopian cardamom). The other is *Amomum*, which has a number of cardamom substitutes. These include round cardamom (*A. compactum*), greater cardamom (*A. subulatum*) and bastard cardamom (*A. xanthioides*). Although they are interesting in their own way, the seeds of these cardamom-like plants are not as pleasant as those of true cardamom, having a more eucalyptus or camphoraceous aroma.

Position To thrive, cardamom needs rich, moist, well-drained soil in sun or dappled shade, along with high temperatures and humidity.

Propagation Sow seed as soon after harvesting as possible in pots of seed compost in a propagator, maintaining a temperature of 24°C. Plants grow rapidly into dense clumps which can be divided in spring.

Maintenance Water regularly and feed every two weeks during the growing season. In winter, keep on the dry side and at a minimum temperature of 10°C.

Pests and diseases The tips of the leaves tend to turn brown from under or over watering. In hot dry conditions, red spider mites may be a problem. This appears as yellowing leaves and fine spider-like webbing.

Harvesting and storing Cardamom pods are harvested when ripe but still fresh and green as they split open and eject the seeds if left to turn yellow and dry. The pods ripen at different times, which makes harvesting a slow process. It is done by cutting individual pods with scissors. The pods store well in jars in a cool dry place.

◾ Cooking

The flavour of ground cardamom deteriorates rapidly, so cardamom seeds are best bought as whole dried pods. Simply split open the shell, remove the seeds and grind in a pestle and mortar when you need them. Cardamom is used to flavour coffee in the Middle East and is a popular spice in baking in northern Europe. It is also an important ingredient in curries and works well in milk desserts. Locally, the aromatic leaves are used for wrapping foods to impart a delicious flavour when cooking.

The Spice Trade

Cardamom and other spices were precious commodities to the earliest traders. Spices were traded in the Middle East at least 4000 years ago and sellers spun tales of their exotic origins to increase their desirability. Arab traders, the Chinese and the Romans all profited from spices but by the Middle Ages, Venice had monopolised the trade; a situation that sent Europeans west for an alternative route to the spice islands – leading to the colonisation of America.

Cardamom pods
(*Elettaria cardamomum*)

Catnip

Nepeta cataria Lamiaceae

Many cats that encounter this velvety, curiously scented perennial react by rolling in it, rubbing against it, chewing it, and generally behaving as though it is quite irresistible. The chemicals responsible for this amazing response are nepetalactones. Not all cats exhibit such reactions: young kittens and older cats may show almost no response.

PART USED Leaves

Catnip (*Nepeta cataria*)

■ Gardening

A short-lived perennial native to Asia and warmer parts of Europe, catnip grows to 1m. It has soft, hairy, aromatic grey-green leaves, like those of nettles in shape, and small, white, lipped flowers.

Varieties There are some 250 species of *Nepeta*, including two common garden perennials that are both called catmints, namely *N. mussinii* and *N. x faassenii*. These ornamental catmints have no herbal uses but they can also attract cats, though less so than catnip. The lemon-scented variety of catnip, *N. cataria* 'Citriodora', is a rather smaller plant, just as attractive to cats, but with a nicer scent and flavour for teas.

Position Catnip needs a well-drained soil, and preferably full sun.

Propagation Catnip seed may be slow to germinate so sow in pots or trays between 20 and 30°C. You can also propagate it easily by tip or softwood cuttings, and by root division in early spring.

Maintenance Cover young transplants in wire netting to protect them from felines. Plants may need staking and further protection as they grow.

Pests and diseases Leaves may be affected by leafhoppers and powdery mildew but generally catnip is trouble free. The nepetalactones are reputed to have insect repellent effects.

Harvesting and storing Harvest bunches of catnip in the morning after the dew has dried. Hang stems upside down in a well-aired place. When dry, strip the foliage and store it in an airtight container.

■ Herbal medicine

Nepeta cataria. Parts used: leaves, flowers. Catnip can help to reduce fever in children. It is a mild sedative and can relieve irritability and teething pain. Its antispasmodic properties also alleviate flatulence and colic. It can be used to treat the symptoms of colds, flu, digestive bloating, nausea and cramp in adults, and is effective when stress is a factor.

For the safe and appropriate use of catnip, consult a doctor or medical herbalist. Do not use catnip if you are pregnant or breastfeeding.

■ Cooking

Catnip has a minty aroma (or lemon-mint in the case of 'Citriodora') that makes a pleasant herb tea or flavouring.

■ Around the home

Catnip is a useful herb to have on hand in the home as the nepetalactones may deter ants and other insect invaders.

Catnip cat toy

YOU WILL NEED
- thin cardboard
- soft pencil
- two 12 x 16cm rectangles fabric
- sewing thread
- dried catnip
- small bell

1 Trace a fish outline onto some thin cardboard and cut out a template. Place the fabric rectangles right sides together. Trace the fish onto the wrong side of one rectangle, remembering to add 6mm seam allowance all round.

2 Stitch the two shapes together, leaving a small opening for turning. Trim seam, clip curves and turn right side out. Fill with dried catnip and stitch opening closed. Stitch a small bell to the head of the fish.

Celery

Apium graveolens Apiaceae

Rich in vitamins and minerals, wild celery has been used as a food and flavouring since ancient Egyptian times. Milder cultivated celery was developed in Italy in the 17th century. Stems are blanched by earthing up or enclosing in collars of newspaper to make them pale and tender.

OTHER COMMON NAMES Cutting leaf celery, smallage
PARTS USED Leaves, seeds, roots

Gardening

The deep green leaves of wild celery may reach 50cm, while the flowering stem, bearing umbels of inconspicuous white-tinged green flowers, is 80-100cm tall. All parts, including the tiny brown seeds, are very aromatic.

Varieties Chinese celery or kin tsai ('Heung Kunn') produces crisp young stems, excellent in stir-fries. 'Zwolsche Krul' is a Dutch variety with curly leaves that can be used for flavouring or garnish. Celtuce (*Lactuca sativa* var. *augustana*) is a kind of lettuce with celery-like stems. 'Par-Cel' is a hybrid, mid-way between parsley and celery in flavour.

Position Celery prefers rich, moist, well-drained soil and a sunny, protected position. It is tolerant of saline soils.

Propagation Sow wild celery seed in spring. Plants grown in rows should be thinned to about 40cm apart.

Maintenance Water regularly in dry conditions.

Pests and diseases Wild celery is more disease tolerant than cultivated varieties, but leaves may be damaged by celery leaf miner and *Septoria* leaf spot. Remove damaged leaves to control the problem, and do not save seed from plants infected with leaf spot.

Harvesting and storing Harvest leaves as required. Pick ripe seed heads and place in paper bags until they dry and release seeds, then store in an airtight container.

Herbal medicine

Apium graveolens. Part used: dried ripe fruits (seeds). Celery seed has a strong diuretic effect and enhances elimination of uric acid and other toxins from the body via the urinary system. It is used as a specific remedy for the treatment of painful joint conditions, such as gout and arthritis, in which an accumulation of toxins in the joint area may lead to the characteristic symptoms of pain and swelling. As a result of its diuretic properties, celery seed can also be used to treat fluid retention. Due to its slightly antiseptic nature, it can help in treating urinary tract infections.

For the safe and appropriate use of celery seed, see *Arthritis and gout*, page 231. Do not use celery seed in greater than culinary quantities if you are pregnant or breastfeeding.

Cooking

Celery's tiny edible seeds have a concentrated celery flavour. Grind a

Celery
(*Apium graveolens*)

pinch of celery seed with sea salt to serve with quails' eggs, or use whole or crushed in small amounts in pickles and relishes, soups, stews, breads and savoury biscuits. The leaves give a celery flavour to stock, soups, casseroles and vegetable juices, especially in winter.

Celeriac

Celeriac (*Apium graveolens* var. *rapaceum*) is similar in appearance to wild celery but with a large rounded taproot, which is grown as a root vegetable. Slice off the rough, tough outer skin, then cook as a vegetable or use raw, grated or cut into thin strips in salads. It is particularly good as a puree or mashed with potato. The leaves and stems have a celery flavour and can be used in the same ways as wild celery. They make an excellent garnish for Bloody Marys.

Chamomile

Chamaemelum nobile syn. *Anthemis nobilis* and *Matricaria recutita* Asteraceae

Two kinds of chamomile are used in herbal medicine: Roman or perennial chamomile (*Chamaemelum nobile*) and the annual German chamomile (*Matricaria recutita*). The flowers of both species have similar properties but those of German chamomile are less bitter so they make a more palatable herb tea. Chamomile may be spelt 'camomile'.

PARTS USED Flowers, leaves

Roman chamomile (*Chamaemelum nobile*), foreground; German chamomile (*Matricaria recutita*), background

■ Gardening

Roman chamomile is a densely carpeting hardy perennial with feathery green leaves which have a very strong, apple-like aroma, and small single white daisies. It is an attractive low-growing plant that is ideal for the front of a border or for edging. German chamomile is an upright hardy annual, up to 60cm tall, with finely divided leaves and rather similar white daisy flowers. It is more suitable for a wild-flower area.

Varieties The non-flowering variety, *C. nobile* 'Treneague', is popular for chamomile lawns and seats where it can be walked or sat upon to release its fragrance. Double chamomile (*C. nobile* 'Flore Pleno'), has very pretty, long-lasting flowers and is commercially grown for its essential oil. Dyer's chamomile (*Anthemis tinctoria*) is a hardy perennial with larger yellow daisies, grown as an ornamental and dye plant. It cannot be used in the same ways as Roman and German chamomile.

Position Both kinds require a sunny position and well-drained soil.

Propagation Raise each species from seed in spring. Roman chamomile can also be propagated by cuttings or division in spring and summer.

Maintenance Weed regularly, especially if establishing a chamomile lawn.

Pests and diseases There are no significant problems.

Harvesting and storing Gather whole flowers without stalks when fully open. Dry thoroughly and store in an airtight container.

■ Herbal medicine

Matricaria recutita. Part used: flowers. Chamomile has a mild sedative effect on the nervous system. and its relaxing effects can help to ease colic, and alleviate the pain of menstrual cramps. Chamomile's bitter-tasting compounds can help to stimulate the digestion and relieve nausea. Its gentle action makes it suitable for children.

Topically, the soothing and anti-inflammatory effects of chamomile are excellent for treating itchy and inflamed skin conditions; it has also been shown to promote wound healing.

Chamaemelum nobile syn. *Anthemis nobilis*. Part used: flowers. Roman chamomile is used in essential oil form: the dried flowers can be hard to obtain. Some herbalists suggest that the Roman variety has a more pronounced relaxing effect on the gut and uterus, and can be used in a similar way to German.

For the safe use of these herbs, see *Nausea*, page 211. Do not use in greater than culinary quantities if you are pregnant or breastfeeding.

A multipurpose herb

For a relaxing sleep, try combining the essential oils of both chamomile and lavender in an oil burner. Chamomile is also antifungal and antibacterial. Next time you make chamomile tea, brew a second cup that's extra strong and use the liquid to wipe down the kitchen sink and benches, or to wipe out a cupboard to rid it of a musty smell. Also, spray it onto plants and vegetables to deter fungal diseases such as mildew in the garden.

Chervil

Anthriscus cerefolium Apiaceae

Apicius, the renowned gourmet of 1st-century Rome, set his seal of approval on chervil by including a green chervil sauce in his cookbook *De Re Coquinaria*. Today, chervil is indispensable in French cuisine.

OTHER COMMON NAME French parsley
PART USED Leaves

Chervil (*Anthriscus cerefolium*)

 Gardening

Chervil is a hardy biennial, often grown as an annual, with a low-growing rosette of delicate lacy, fern-like leaves which have a subtle anise flavour. The tiny white flowers, borne in umbels on slender stems, are followed by thin black seeds. It prefers cool damp conditions and often does well on the banks of streams or beside a garden pond.

Varieties 'Crispum' has lightly curled leaves which make a pretty garnish. 'Brussels Winter' is tolerant of both heat and cold, forming vigorous, long-lasting mounds of foliage.

Position Chervil requires light but moist soil that is close to neutral, preferably enriched with compost. Grow chervil in a lightly shaded position, as excessive sun exposure will cause the leaves to burn and turn rose pink.

Propagation Chervil does best as an autumn or spring crop, disliking extremes of heat in summer and cold in winter. Sow in rows or scatter seed over the soil in late summer, rake in lightly and water regularly. Seedlings usually emerge in about 10 to 14 days. Chervil has a long taproot and bare-rooted seedlings do not easily transplant.

Maintenance Water the new crop regularly to promote lush growth. The growing season can be further extended with the use of protective cloches as it gets colder.

Pests and diseases There are no significant problems.

Harvesting and storing Plants are ready for harvesting about 8 to 10 weeks after sowing. As with parsley, harvest leaves from the outside, preferably with scissors, as the plant is delicate. Leaves can also be frozen in sealed plastic bags. It does not dry well.

Cooking

Chervil flowers, leaves and roots are all edible, although it is the delicate anise-flavoured leaves that are most frequently used. Add chervil to hot dishes at the last minute, after the dish has been taken off the heat and is ready to serve, as the flavour is destroyed by cooking. Chervil goes well with glazed carrots and in butter sauces and cream-based soups. It is also good in salads and is often included in seed mixes for mesclun (baby salad greens).

Freezing tiny sprigs of chervil into ice cubes adds a refreshing taste to summery fruit drinks. Chervil butter (see *Herb butters*, page 342), makes a delicious spread for savoury biscuits or bread. Also, it can be used as a flavoursome topping for barbecued fish, meat or poultry.

Fines herbes

Chervil is especially popular in French cooking, and essential (along with parsley, chives and tarragon) in the classic herb blend called fines herbes, which is used fresh with poached fish, shellfish and chicken and in green salads and egg dishes such as omelettes.

Grow chervil as a trap crop to lure slugs away from valued vegetable crops.

Chilli

Capsicum sp. Solanaceae

Chillies are the world's most frequently used culinary spice and a key component of African and Asian cooking. They were unknown, except in the New World, until after 1492 when Columbus brought them back from his travels.

PART USED Fruits

Tiny bird peppers (*C. annuum* var. *glabriusculum*)

◼ Gardening

In areas with cool summers, chillies do best in a greenhouse or garden room. They make good container plants and are very ornamental when fruiting. Many exciting varieties are offered in seed catalogues but those bred for the cooler temperatures and lower light levels of northern Europe are likely to give better crops.

Varieties Most chillies and sweet or bell peppers belong to one very variable species, *C. annuum*, differing by a single

Chilli varieties make attractive plants for containers in cool climates.

gene that produces the fiery compound capsaicin. There are hundreds of named varieties of *C. annuum*, and these have been selected worldwide for climate tolerance, colour, size, shape, degree of heat and flavour, which may vary from citrus and prune to smoky, coffee, raisin, almond and tobacco. They are divided into groups by shape: cherry-shaped (Cerasiforme), cone-shaped (Coniodes), clustered longish cones (Fasciculatum), sweet peppers (Grossum) and long hot peppers (Longum).

Some of the most popular varieties of chillies are: 'Fresno' a short, upright plant producing small bullet-shaped, medium-hot chillies that are equally good when green or red; 'Hungarian Hot Wax', a medium hot pepper with waxy yellow skin; 'Jalapeño', a thick-walled variety which is used in salsas or smoked (when it is known as chipotle); 'Poblano', which has large, medium-hot, heart-shaped green fruits, often served stuffed (rellenos), and also known as 'Ancho' in its red-brown dried form; and 'Serrano', an old variety with cylindrical green to red, fairly hot fruits that in Mexico are typically used in salsas, guacamole and

pickle (escabeche). A few chillies have variegated foliage which adds to their ornamental value as container plants. These include 'Purple Tiger', with purple and white variegation and small, red to deep purple, fiery fruits, and 'Fish', an Afro-American heritage variety with white-marbled foliage and pendent, multicoloured, striped fruits. Do not confuse varieties of *C. annuum*, which all have edible fruits, with pot plants sold as winter cherry (*Solanum capicastrum*) which has round, bright orange fruits that may resemble chillies but which are poisonous.

In addition to *C. annuum,* you may come across other species, such as *C. baccatum* from Ecuador and Peru, which includes the yellow Peruvian pepper, 'Aj Amarillo', a slender hot yellow chilli, and the orchid chilli or

'Anaheim' or 'New Mexican', a variety of *C. annuum*, has a mild flavour and is used green or red, depending on the recipe.

'Christmas Bell', which has mild yellow to red fruits shaped like a crumpled bell. The rocoto pepper (*C. pubescens*), from Mexico produces very hot, globose fruits with black seeds. The species *C. chinense* contains some of the hottest chilli varieties, including 'Habañero', 'Scotch Bonnet', and also the surprisingly mild 'Rocatillo'. Tiny bird peppers (*C. annuum* var. *aviculare* syn. *C. a.* var. *glabriusculum*), which can often be found growing wild in Central America and southwestern United States, are commonly known as 'Chiltepjn'. They are ferociously hot. 'Tabasco' is the best-known variety of *C. frutescens*, named after the state of Tabasco in Mexico, from where it was introduced to the United States during the 1840s. This pungent little chilli varies from pale yellow-green to orange and red.

Position All chillies and peppers require good drainage, full sunshine and rich, moist soil. Most importantly, they need ample warmth if fruits are to develop and ripen in cool summers. Even the fastest-maturing varieties require a minimum growing season of 3 months.

Propagation Sow seeds in early spring in a warm sunny place and prick out into individual pots when large enough to handle. Although the flowers are self-pollinating, they also readily cross-pollinate, so seed saved from your own plants may not come true.

Maintenance Keep potting on as pot-bound plants will become starved and unhealthy. Do not be tempted to put plants outside unless night temperatures are reliably above 10°C. You may need to protect your plants from birds when fruits ripen.

Pests and diseases The main problems when plants are grown under glass are aphids, whitefly and red spider mites. Use biological control to minimise these pests, and feed regularly, especially as fruits develop. In low temperatures and poor ventilation, grey mould (*Botrytis*) may be a problem. Remove affected leaves and fruits, and improve growing conditions.

Harvesting and storing You can pick peppers at any time, but remember that they reach the peak of their heat when they turn red.

Too hot to handle!

Most of the capsaicin responsible for the heat in peppers is stored in the seeds and the white membrane within the fruit, so remove these before cooking. Capsaicin is not water-soluble but it is fat-soluble and a glass of milk or yogurt, or the Indian yogurt drink lassi are effectively soothing.

Wear protective gloves when chopping chillies, as they can seriously burn skin, especially if you have a cut or abrasion. Do not touch your face, eyes or mouth. Do not feed pets food with chilli; it may prove fatal.

Chilli heat is measured in Scoville Heat Units (SHU), with 'Habañero' equating to between 200,000 and 300,000 SHU. Until recently, the world's hottest chilli was a variety of *C. chinense*, the 'Red Savina Habañero', which measured 577,000 SHU. 'Tabasco' is a mere 30,000 to 50,000. In 2007, a new record was set by 'Bhut Jolokia', a chilli from Assam in India which reached a very dangerous 1,000,000 SHU.

High pressure liquid chromatography (HPLC) is now used to measure SHU. A relative heat scale, based on a 0 to 10 rating, is also used. Bell peppers rate 0 while 'Habañero' is 10.

Cultivated peppers and chillies belong to five main groups. **1** Cherry-shaped chillies (Cerasiforme) **2** Red and yellow sweet peppers (Grossum) **3** Banana chilli (Grossum) **4** Olive or cone chillies (Conioides) **5** Thai or red cone chillies (Fasciculatum) **6** Long hot peppers (Longum) **7** Bird chillies (*C. frutescens*)

Habañero, a *C. chinense* variety, is among the hottest chillies in common use.

Chilli continued

Cooking

Chillies are green when unripe; when ripe, they may be red, yellow, purple or almost black. Green chillies are always used fresh; red chillies can be used fresh or dried. Dried chillies are fruitier and sweeter than fresh chillies, although still retaining their heat. You can buy dried chillies whole, crushed or powdered. Chillies are also sold in jars, preserved in vinegar or oil; these are a good substitute for fresh varieties when they are unavailable.

The heat level of chillies varies from negligible to positively incendiary (see box on page 37). Generally, the smaller the chilli, the hotter it will be. Heat levels may vary considerably even among chillies of the same variety, so the stated quantity in a recipe should always be adjusted to taste. If you are concerned about the heat level of your chillies, cut the end off one and give it the tiniest, most tentative lick. When adding to taste start off conservatively and add more as you go along.

Dried chillies: **1** Thai chillies **2** Pasilla **3** Guajillo **4** Habañero **5** Chipotle (dried, smoked jalapeño) **6** Pimentos **7** Ancho (dried poblano).

A remedy for chilli burn on the palate is dairy foods, such as cream, milk or yoghurt. To minimise irritation from the fumes when grinding chillies, use a spice grinder rather than a pestle and mortar.

And a note on spelling: 'chilli' (plural 'chillis' or 'chillies') is the usual spelling in the United Kingdom, while the Spanish-originated 'chile' is commonly used in the United States and Mexico. The term 'chili' is reserved for a regional hot and spicy stew, originally from Mexico, which the United States has subsequently made its own.

Chilli and lime sauce

This Caribbean sauce recipe is delicious with barbecued or baked fish or vegetables. Baste the food with it, or serve it separately.
• 2 fresh red chillies
• 1 tablespoon sea salt
• 250ml fresh lime juice
Remove the seeds and white pith from the chillies if you do not want too much heat. Slice chillies finely and pack into a jar. Dissolve the salt in the juice and pour over the chillies. Seal and store in a cool place to let the flavours develop. It is ready for use after 4 days and keeps for up to 4 weeks.

Chilli condiments

There is a range of chilli condiments to choose from.
PAPRIKA is a mildly hot, sweet, bright red chilli powder that is produced by drying and grinding suitable varieties. Spain and Hungary are the world's largest producers. Suitable varieties, which must be intensely red when fully ripened, include 'Hungarian', 'Paprika Supreme' and 'NuMex Conquistador'.
CAYENNE is a spice powder that is derived from dried hot red chillies. 'Cayenne' is a pre-Colombian variety from French Guiana. A number of cayenne-type varieties have been developed from it, including 'Hot Portugal', 'Long Red', 'Ring of Fire' and 'Hades Hot'. Dried chillies and chilli flakes are also used.

Cayenne pepper

TABASCO, the most famous chilli sauce, is made in Louisiana, in the United States, according to a 3-year process invented in 1868 by Edmund McIlhenny.
PERI PERI (or piri piri) is a sauce developed by the Portuguese from the tiny but powerfully hot southern African variety 'Peri Peri'; it also includes lemons, spices and herbs.
MOLE POBLANO compounded of dried chilli (such as pasilla or ancho), chocolate, spices and seeds or peanuts, is a sauce for meat in Mexican cuisine.

Cinnamon

Cinnamomum zeylanicum, C. cassia Lauraceae

Cinnamon and its relatives are rich in aromatic oils, especially in the bark, that have been used since earliest times as flavourings and medicines. Cinnamon was of importance in world trade during medieval times and played a major role in colonial expansion, beginning with the Portuguese conquest of Ceylon (now Sri Lanka).

PARTS USED Wood (camphor), immature fruits ('cassia buds'), bark, leaves, oil

Quills of dried cinnamon bark

Gardening

Cinnamon and cassia need space, warmth and humidity to thrive. Adventurous gardeners may try the hardier camphor tree (*C. camphora*) or Japanese cinnamon (*C. japonicum*), which can briefly survive temperatures close to freezing but prefer a low of 10°C.

Varieties True cinnamon (*C. zeylanicum*) has pale brown, papery bark, and glossy leaves up to 18cm long, with distinctive veins. Mature trees can reach 10m. Cassia or Chinese cinnamon is larger at 12m.

Camphor (*C. camphora*) is an attractive container plant in its early years. Other varieties with culinary and medicinal uses include Japanese cinnamon (*C. japonicum*), Saigon or royal cinnamon (*C. loureirii*), Australian black sassafras or Oliver bark (*C. oliveri*) and Indian cassia or tejpat (*C. tamala*).

Position Cinnamon, cassia and camphor trees need moist, well-drained soil in sun or light shade.

Propagation Sow seed soon after ripening in pots of well-drained, moist seed compost at about 15°C. Semi-ripe cuttings, taken in summer, need constant warmth, humidity and moisture to encourage rooting. Keep in a propagator at 20-25°C.

Maintenance Young container plants thrive in a mixture of peat-free multi-purpose compost or multipurpose and John Innes No3. Cinnamon, cassia and camphor trees tolerate hard pruning. Remove oldest stems from the base in spring, retaining 4 to 6 strong main stems. When new growths reach 2–3m, cut back by a third to encourage side-shoots. Keep well-watered.

Pests and diseases Scale insects and mealy bug may be a problem on plants grown in containers under glass.

Harvesting and storing Stems 1-5cm in diameter are cut as new leaves appear in spring. The bark is then stripped off in 30cm lengths and left in bundles in a warm damp environment overnight to ferment. The next day, the outer layer of corky bark is removed, the rest is dried in the sun or in a low oven at about 65°C. As inner bark strips dry, they curl up and are packed into 'quills' by inserting smaller sections inside larger ones. Bark and leaves, harvested at the same time, are distilled for oil. To obtain camphor, a crystalline compound, both wood and leaves are distilled.

Herbal medicine

Cinnamomum zeylanicum; C. cassia; C. camphora. Parts used: essential oils. Both cinnamon and cassia contain cinnamaldehyde, a compound responsible for most of their therapeutic effects. Cinnamon is warming and stimulating, improving the circulation and digestion, lowering fever and blood pressure, and protecting against infection. Cassia is important in Chinese medicine for colds and chills, low energy and poor appetite. Camphor is blended with peanut oil to make camphorated oil, an ingredient in liniments to ease joint and muscle pain, in inhalants for bronchial congestion and in balms to soothe chapped or sore skin.

Cooking and household

Cinnamon gives a spicy flavour to hot punch or mulled wine and Indian chai tea as well as bakery items. It has an affinity with apples. Cinnamon and cassia oil is added to oral hygiene products, room fragrances, candles and incense. The leaves yield a delicate oil, consisting mainly of eugenol which is used in carnation-type perfumes. Cassia buds are used with Sichuan pepper, star anise, cloves and fennel seeds in Chinese 'five spice'. Camphor is best known as a moth repellent.

Leaves of the cinnamon tree showing their striking vertical veining

Citrus

Citrus spp. Rutaceae

Citruses are native to Asia and were cultivated in China as long ago as 2200 BCE. Today they are grown worldwide, both for their nutritious fruits and as sources of essential oils and other ingredients that are used in a wide range of medicines, food supplements, perfumery and many home and beauty products.

PARTS USED Fruits, flowers, leaves (kaffir lime)

Seville orange (*Citrus aurantium*)

 Gardening

In cool climates, citruses are perfect for growing in containers which can be taken under cover in winter. Most flower in spring and fruits ripen in winter. They are ornamental, with aromatic evergreen leaves and fragrant white flowers which often appear while the plant is still bearing unripe and ripe fruits from the previous year.

Varieties Lime (*C. aurantiifolia*) needs warmer conditions and more humidity than other citruses, with a minimum winter temperature of 13°C. Two popular varieties are the Key lime ('Mexican') with small, thin-skinned yellow-green fruits, originally used in Key lime pie, and the Persian lime ('Tahiti') which has finely flavoured, seedless green fruits.

Bitter orange or Seville orange (*C. aurantium*) is the classic ingredient for marmalade. Its sour but thick-skinned, intensely aromatic fruits have a brief season early in the year. The highly scented flowers are distilled for their essential oil, known as neroli after the Italian Countess of Nerola who promoted its use. Leaves and twigs are also distilled to make petitgrain, a perfumery ingredient.

Bergamot orange (*C. bergamia*) flowers are another source of neroli. Fruits are similar in appearance to lemons but more rounded, with intensely perfumed, thick peel which yields bergamot oil, best known as the flavouring for Earl Grey tea and an ingredient of colognes.

Kaffir lime or makrut (*C. hystrix*) has aromatic leaves with winged stalks and small green fruits with warty skins. The leaves have a wonderful aroma, much used in South-east Asian dishes.

Lemon (*C. limon*) does well in pots, and is fairly hardy, tolerating 5°C with ease. It has relatively large scented flowers and a steady succession of fruits. The hybrid 'Meyer' (syn. *C.* x *meyeri*) blooms and bears golden-yellow fruits all year round. 'Eureka' is very hardy, surviving touches of frost. 'Variegata' has year-round interest with variegated foliage and striped fruits.

Mandarin orange or tangerine (*C. reticulata*) has very fragrant flowers, leaves and fruits but its appearance differs according to variety. 'Clementine' bears seedless fruits which are delicious but lack the typical mandarin scent.

Position Citruses need full sun and well-drained, slightly acid compost which has a high humus content. You can buy citrus compost from specialist nurseries or make your own by mixing John Innes No2 with up to a third ericaceous compost and a little well-

Kumquat and calamondin

If you want a citrus to grow as a pot plant, a good choice is kumquat (*Fortunella japonica*). It is slower growing and hardier than most citruses, with small, narrow leaves, scented flowers and an abundance of miniature fruits. Most have oval fruits but in some, such as 'Marumi', they are round, like tiny oranges. The intensely flavoured fruits are not usually eaten raw but are used in sauces (especially for duck), pickles and preserves. Kumquats have been hybridised with other citruses such as the calamondin orange (x *Citrofortunella microcarpa*), a natural hybrid between the kumquat and

the mandarin which arose in the Philippines where the acid fruits are used to flavour a soy sauce known as toyo mansi. This makes an excellent pot plant too, with very fragrant flowers and small acidic fruits that look like mini satsumas.

rotted manure or garden compost. As citrus trees are often spiny, position containers away from doorways.

Propagation Citruses are propagated commercially but semi-ripe cuttings are worth a try. Take them in summer, dip in hormone rooting powder and insert in pots of sand in warm humid conditions. Citrus plants rarely come true from seed, with the exception of the kaffir lime which has not been hybridised.

Maintenance Citrus plants can be pruned in spring to improve shape, and pinched out during the growing season to keep them bushy. If plants suffer defoliation, cut back hard and keep warm. Repot only when the plant is obviously too large for its container as citruses don't like root disturbance. Instead, top-dress pot plants in spring by replacing the top layer with fresh compost. Add a sprinkle of slow-release fertiliser too. Keep on the dry side in cool conditions but water regularly in summer, allowing compost to become dry to the touch between waterings. A monthly feed and good ventilation are also important to keep plants healthy.

Pests and diseases Scale insects, mealy bugs and red spider mites are often a problem on citruses. Inspect plants carefully and remove using a soft cloth or cotton buds dipped in soft soap solution. Yellowing of leaves is another common problem, either from nutrient deficiency or because the plant is too wet or too dry.

Harvesting and storing Leaves and fruits can be picked at any time. Unripe fruits are sometimes preferred for candying and certain medicinal uses. Dry kaffir lime leaves and citrus peels as store cupboard ingredients. Dry leaves on trays of kitchen paper in a warm place. Peel fruits thinly, avoiding the white layer of pith. Leave pieces whole to retain maximum flavour. When dried, citrus peel is easily crushed or ground.

Herbal medicine

Lemon juice relieves the symptoms of colds and flu, freshly squeezed and

Lime (*Citrus aurantiifolia*)

mixed with honey and hot water. It has anti-inflammatory, anti-bacterial and astringent properties and is rich in vitamin C. In the tropics, lime juice is given as a cure for gastroenteritis. Citrus oils, such as lemon, mandarin, bergamot and neroli, are used in aromatherapy for their refreshing, uplifting effects. In Chinese medicine, both ripe and unripe mandarin peel and pips are used as bitter stimulants for liver, gall bladder and chest complaints.

Cooking

Citrus fruits are vital ingredients in all kinds of foods, from desserts, cakes, biscuits and confectionery to sweet and savoury sauces, marinades, and seafood dishes. The Indian cheese paneer is made by curdling milk with lime juice, and many recipes in Moroccan cuisine use preserved lemons, which are cooked first and then pickled in brine. Sliced lemons and limes, are an indispensable garnish and flavouring for drinks and cocktails. Citrus flowers yield the delicate flavours of orange flower water and orange blossom honey. The pith is rich in pectin which sets jams and jellies. Kaffir lime leaves are essential in South-east Asian curries and soups and in the Indonesian soy sauce known as kecap.

Around the home

Orange and lemon are favourite aromas in soaps, household cleaning products and room fragrances. Some are easy to make at home (see pages 300–301). Lemon juice is a superb cleaner, inhibiting mould, removing stains and deodorising hands and surfaces.

Skin and hair care

Citrus bath and skin cleansing products, shampoos and conditioners can be made at home (see pages 252–270). Lemon juice lightens fair hair. Most perfumes and eau de toilettes have a citrus element too. You can even find citruses in natural deodorants (see page 280).

The versatile bergamot orange

The intensely fragrant waxy white flowers of the bergamot orange (*Citrus bergamia* syn. *C. aurantium* var. *bergamia*), borne in clusters in spring, are the source of the essential oil of neroli, used widely in the perfumery trade, and also orange flower water. The bitter but highly aromatic yellow peel is used to flavour Earl Grey tea, and also yields bergamot essential oil, which is used for aromatherapy purposes.

It can be beneficial for a range of skin conditions, including an oily complexion and acne, but take care when applying skin creams and oils containing the essential oil: one of its compounds, bergapten, has a known photosensitising effect.

The eau de cologne 4711 first made in the 18th century contains bergamot.

Clove pinks

Dianthus spp. Caryophyllaceae

With a rich spicy fragrance, pinks are a garden favourite. Though little used today, they were once important as a clove-like perfume and flavouring. The common name may refer not to the colour but to the serrated petals, as 'to pink' once meant 'to pierce or nick', as in 'pinking shears'.

OTHER COMMON NAME Gillyflower
PARTS USED Petals, whole flowers

■ Gardening

Clove pinks were bred from the grass pink or cottage pink (*D. plumarius*) and the wild carnation (*D. caryophyllus*), which also gave rise to the carnation. They form dense, low, spreading cushions of grass-like foliage, from which emerge many flower stems in early summer. All are hardy perennials, though do deteriorate after a few years and benefit from regular propagation.

Varieties A remarkable number of clove pinks have survived the centuries, including 'sops-in-wine', used in Elizabethan times to flavour wines. 'Bridal Veil', 'Queen of Sheba', 'Ursula le Grove' and 'Pheasant's Eye' date from the 17th century. Eighteenth-century heirlooms include the Paisley Pinks, such as 'Dad's Favourite' and 'Paisley Gem',

Clove pinks (*Dianthus caryophyllus*)

The Greeks and Romans regarded the clove pink as the flower of the gods.

which were bred to resemble intricate Paisley fabric patterning, as well as 'Inchmery' and 'Cockenzie Pink'. Nineteenth-century double-flowered forms include 'Mrs Sinkins', 'Earl of Essex', and 'Rose de Mai'. 'Napoléon III' is a historic variety which involves a cross with sweet william (*D. barbatus*).

Several other species have herbal uses, including the Carthusian pink (*D. carthusianorum*), which was used in medicinal liqueurs by the Carthusian monks. In Chinese medicine, the fringed pink (*D. superbus*) and annual rainbow pink (*D. chinensis*) are used interchangeably to treat urinary tract infections; whole plants, not just the flowers, are combined with roots of red sage or dan shen (*Salvia miltiorhiza*, see pages 119, 186) for this purpose.

Position Pinks require a well-drained, sunny position and thrive at the edges of paths and in wall cavities. They also grow well in terracotta pots, and are drought-tolerant when established. Pinks prefer alkaline soil; if gardening on acid soil, add dolomite or garden lime. Or tuck small pieces of concrete rubble under the plant. These will leach lime into the soil when it rains.

Classic fragrances

Pinks are rich in eugenol, the same volatile oil that is found in cloves (*Syzygium aromaticum*, see opposite). It takes 500kg of flowers to produce 100ml of essential oil, so synthetic eugenol and isoeugenol are often used instead. The absolute (concentrated perfume) of pinks is used in many high-quality perfumes, including Floris's 'Malmaison', Nina Ricci's 'L'Air du Temps', Guerlain's 'Samsara' and 'L'Heure Bleu', Worth's 'Je Reviens', Hermès's 'Bel Ami', Estée Lauder's 'White Linen' and Bvlgari's 'Bvlgari for Men'.

Propagation Only species come true from seed. Named varieties must be propagated by cuttings of non-flowering shoots in summer.

Maintenance Do not let plants become overshadowed by their neighbours or covered by dead leaves.

Pests and diseases Leaves may rot in damp shaded conditions.

Harvesting and storing Harvest flowers as required. Use fresh, removing the bitter white 'heels' of the petals.

■ Cooking

Add petals to fruit salads or crystallise them as decorations for cakes and desserts. Petals were once added to wine which was described as 'sops-in-wine'.

Cloves

Syzygium aromaticum syn. *Eugenia caryophyllata* Myrtaceae

The dried flower buds of the clove tree are known as cloves. They are rich in a volatile oil known as eugenol which gives the typical aroma, and a pain-killing substance called methyl salicylate. During the 16th century, competition between various countries over spices such as cloves resulted in world exploration and colonialisation.

PART USED Flower buds

Immature flower buds on a clove tree.

Gardening

The clove tree is small and bushy, reaching 3-5m tall, with glossy evergreen leaves, 8-13cm long, and pale pink buds, about 2cm long, which drop their petals on opening. The tree is difficult to cultivate outside the tropics, as it needs temperatures around 22°C and high humidity all year round.

Varieties The clove tree has several relatives which are valued for their edible fruits. These include the delicious rose apple (*S. jambos*) from tropical Asia and various kinds of Australian lilli pilly, such as (*S. luehmannii*), with clove-flavoured fruits, and the brush cherry (*S. paniculatum*) that is used for hedging in California. A few of these are in cultivation, making attractive container plants for warm conservatories.

Position Well-drained soil in full sun. Pot plants thrive in John Innes No3.

Propagation Sow seed as soon as possible after fruits ripen and keep at a minimum temperature of 25°C. Take cuttings in summer and keep in a very warm humid propagator.

Maintenance Water regularly and feed monthly during the growing season. Pot on or top-dress in spring.

Pests and diseases Pot plants may be affected by scale insects or mealy bug so check for tell-tale signs, such as sooty mould on the foliage.

Harvesting and storing For commercial uses, cloves are picked and dried in the sun on a daily basis when the buds reach exactly the right size before opening. Dried cloves store well in glass jars but ground cloves deteriorate more quickly and should be used within a year.

Herbal medicine

Syzygium aromaticum. Parts used: dried flower buds, oil. Cloves and clove oil are useful household items for treating minor complaints. A tea made by infusing cloves in boiling water may help to relieve colic and bloating. It is antibacterial, so also useful as a mouthwash after dental extractions or for gum infections. Clove oil is well known as a remedy for toothache. Applied directly using a cotton bud, it has anaesthetic effects which help in the short term.

For the safe and appropriate use of cloves, see *Cold sores, gums and mouth health*, page 225. Do not use cloves in greater than culinary quantities if you are pregnant or breastfeeding except with the advice of a doctor or medical herbalist.

Cooking and flavouring

Cloves are an ingredient of mixed spice, which has endless uses in baking and in preserves such as mincemeat and schutney. Whole cloves are added to the cooking liquid for boiled ham, and hams for roasting are often studded with cloves. They also work well with apple compote and are a vital ingredient in bread sauce for the Christmas turkey, but be sure to remove them before serving as they are unpleasant to chew.

Around the home

Cloves are insect repellent. In Zanzibar, woven circlets of cloves are hung to keep insects pests away, and they are also traditionally used in potpourris (see pages 290-291) and pomanders (see page 295).

Dried cloves (flower buds)

Comfrey

Symphytum officinale Boraginaceae

Comfrey's other common name, knitbone, is a clue to its traditional use in poultices to encourage the healing of broken bones. It contains allantoin, a substance that speeds cell regeneration so effectively that it is now synthesised as an ingredient for healing creams and anti-ageing products.

OTHER COMMON NAME Knitbone
PARTS USED Leaves, roots (high in toxic alkaloids)

Comfrey (*Symphytum officinale*)

■ Gardening

Comfrey is a vigorous hardy perennial, with large bristly leaves and mauve to pink or white, bell-shaped flowers. It reaches about 1m tall and has very deep roots that tap into minerals in the subsoil. The foliage contains very high levels of nitrogen and minerals, making them important in organic gardening as a source of nutrients for the compost heap and as a compost accelerator, or for soaking in tubs of water to make a liquid feed for crops.

Varieties 'Boraston White' has white flowers. Russian comfrey (*S. x uplandicum*) is a vigorous hybrid. Organic gardeners often grow a variety of this hybrid called 'Bocking 14' as livestock

The pretty bell-like flowers of comfrey come in many colour variations, including pink, lavender or white.

feed and for use as a fertiliser and compost accelerator. It has two particularly attractive varieties: 'Variegatum', with cream-edged leaves; and a golden form, 'Axminster Gold'.

Position Rich, moist to wet soil in sun or partial shade. Position carefully as once established it is difficult to remove because the smallest piece of root will grow into a new plant.

Propagation Divide plants in spring or autumn, or take root cuttings in early spring. Space plants 1m apart.

Maintenance Mulch with well-rotted manure in spring. Water regularly in dry conditions.

Pests and diseases Comfrey is generally trouble free. Some strains are prone to rust, usually when the plants are water-stressed.

Harvesting and storing Harvest leaves and stems of mature plants 3 or 4 times a year. Cut with shears and wear protective gloves, as the hairs on the leaves are an irritant. Lift sections of root when the plant is dormant in winter for making healing oil or ointment.

■ Herbal medicine

Symphytum officinale. Parts used: leaves, roots. Traditionally, comfrey has been used as a topical application for bruises, fractures and wounds. It has a remarkable reputation for hastening the repair and renewal of damaged tissue as well as reducing inflammation. While traditionally comfrey was also prescribed

for internal use, this is now discouraged as comfrey contains pyrrolizidine alkaloids that have been shown to have toxic effects.

For the safe and appropriate topical use of comfrey, refer to *Sports injuries*, page 228. Do not use comfrey if you are pregnant or breastfeeding.

Plant food

Comfrey leaves are extremely good for the garden, containing far more nitrogen and potash than farmyard manure. Make your own liquid fertiliser by cutting the bottom from a large fizzy drink bottle and stuffing it tightly with chopped comfrey leaves. Turn it upside down, leaving the cap on the bottle and fill with water. When the leaves have turned into a brown slurry, remove the cap and strain it into a clean bottle, holding your nose as it is smelly stuff. Dilute 1 part to 10 parts of water and use to feed tomatoes, peppers and any other fruiting or flowering plants. It works a treat and costs nothing.

Coriander

Coriandrum sativum Apiaceae

For more than three millennia, coriander has been cultivated for its aromatic foliage, roots and seeds, all of which were found in the tombs of the pharaohs. It appears in the Bible and is one of the bitter herbs traditionally eaten at Passover.

OTHER COMMON NAMES Chinese parsley, cilantro
PARTS USED Leaves, seeds, roots

Coriander (*Coriandrum sativum*)

Gardening

Coriander is a hardy annual, at first glance resembling flat-leaf parsley. Young plants form rosettes of long, slender, stalked leaves which are deep green and dissected into lobed segments. They have a very strong, distinctive aroma which is quite different from the round, pale brown seeds that follow umbels of tiny pink-white flowers. Flowering plants are pretty enough to grow among other herbs and ornamentals. Planting strong-smelling coriander between carrots fools carrot flies that locate carrot plants by their odour. As a leaf crop, coriander can also be grown in rows of mixed baby-leaf salads and in pots.

Varieties 'Spice' is popular for its seeds, while 'Santo' is a variety in which premature flowering is delayed and profuse deep green foliage develops. Three unrelated plants are also grown for their coriander-tasting foliage in hot climates where hardy annuals do not thrive. These are: Vietnamese coriander or rau ram (*Persicaria odorata* syn. *Polygonum odoratum*) and Mexican coriander or culantro (*Eryngium foetidum*), which are both perennial and tolerate tropical conditions; and papalo (*Porophyllum ruderale* subsp. *macrocephalum*), an annual that can cope with dry heat.

Position Moist, well-drained, fertile soil and a sunny position.

Propagation Sow in pots or directly in the garden in spring, and at monthly intervals until late summer for a regular supply of leaves.

Maintenance Thin seedlings, weed regularly and water during dry spells to prevent bolting (premature flowering). For seeds, leave a spring crop to flower and ripen over summer.

Pests and diseases Coriander is generally trouble free.

Harvesting and storing You can pick coriander leaves at any time as soon as the plants are large enough. Either use fresh or freeze in bunches (there is no need to chop as they crumble easily when frozen.) Harvest the seed crop when half the seeds on the plant have turned brown. Tie stems into bunches and hang upside down inside paper bags to trap the falling seed.

Herbal medicine

Coriandrum sativum. Part used: dried ripe fruits (seeds). Seeds have antispasmodic properties and a stimulating effect on the appetite. Traditionally, coriander is often used in conjunction with caraway, fennel, cardamom and anise to ease symptoms of indigestion, including colic, flatulence, and abdominal distension.

For the safe and appropriate medicinal use of coriander, consult your doctor or medical herbalist. Do not use coriander in greater than culinary quantities if you are pregnant or breastfeeding.

Cooking

The pungent leaves and stalks are popular in south-east Asian, Middle Eastern, South American and Mexican cooking, in salads, salsas, guacamole, soups, legume dishes, curries and stir-fries. In India, the leaf is used in fresh chutneys. Long cooking destroys the flavour of the leaves, so add them just before serving.

Roast the seeds to enhance their flavour. Used whole or ground, their mild, slightly sweet taste works well in sweet and savoury dishes and in sauces such as harissa (see recipe page 344). The fibre in ground seeds absorbs liquid and helps to thicken curries and stews. The root has a more intense flavour than leaves. It is used in Thai cooking, especially pounded into curry pastes.

Coriander and figs

Palathai, or fig cakes, date from Roman times. They are popular in Egypt and Turkey. Remove stalks from 400g dried figs (select soft ones). Process figs to a paste in a food processor. Shape into an oval cake with your hands. Combine 1 teaspoon freshly ground coriander seeds and 1 teaspoon flour. Dust cake with mixture. Serve wedges for dessert.

Cumin

Cuminum cyminum Apiaceae

A key ingredient of many spicy cuisines, from Mexico to India and the Far East, cumin's uses date back at least to biblical times. In ancient Greece, cumin was associated with avarice, and mean people were said to have eaten it.

PART USED Fruits

Powdered cumin

Gardening

Cumin is a small, slender, half-hardy annual of the parsley family which is native to North Africa and south-west Asia. It reaches only 15-30cm in height, with shiny, finely divided leaves, and white to pink flowers, borne in small compound umbels. Unless you live somewhere that has guaranteed warm dry summers, growing your own cumin is a challenge. It could be grown in pots under glass but quite a large number of plants are needed to produce a reasonable quantity of seed. A small number of cumin plants will add interest to themed gardens for their importance

Cumin (*Cuminum cyminum*) bears its tiny blooms in frothy flowerheads.

in biblical times and both Asian and Middle Eastern cultures.

Varieties There are no improved varieties of cumin available in Europe. Black cumin or kalonji (*Nigella sativa*) is quite different in appearance and uses. It is closely related to the popular ornamental love-in-a-mist (*N. damascena*), but it is hardier and easy to grow for its black seeds which have a complex peppery-fruity flavour and are much used in Indian and Middle Eastern cuisine, as well as in Ayurvedic medicine (see page 189).

Position Cumin prefers a well-drained, fertile soil in full sun. A sandy soil is the most suitable.

Propagation By seed sown in spring at 13-18°C. In areas with cool climates, start seedlings off under glass in spring and prick out when they are large enough to handle.

Maintenance When the seedlings have hardened off, transplant to a sunny aspect, planting out 8-10cm apart in rows or blocks when night temperatures are reliably above 10°C. Weed regularly. The plants bloom in June and July and seeds are usually ready three to four months after planting.

Pests and diseases Cumin can be subject to aphids, fusarium wilt, powdery mildew and alternaria blight.

Harvesting and storing Cut the plants when the seeds first begin to turn brown and hang in a warm dry place inside paper bags or over sheets of paper to catch the ripe seeds. Store in airtight glass jars for up to a year.

Herbal medicine

Cuminum cyminum Part used: seeds. Cumin is closely related to anise (*Pimpinella anisum*, see page 14) and caraway (*Carum carvi*, see page 30), and like them its main effects are on the digestive system. It can be used internally for indigestion, diarrhoea and colic and to stimulate the appetite. In the West, it is also used mainly in veterinary medicine to prevent the build-up of gas. In India a topical application of cumin ground with onion juice is a remedy for poisonous bites.

Cumin is used in Ayurvedic medicine to promote the assimilation of other herbs and to improve liver function. It is reputed to increase lactation and reduce nausea in pregnancy. For the safe use of cumin, consult your doctor or medical herbalist.

Cooking

Cumin is an essential ingredient of many curries, chutneys, sauces, soups and preserved meats, such as Portuguese sausages. It is often used with lamb in Middle Eastern dishes and works well with legumes, as in the chick pea patties known as falafel. Certain cheeses, especially Dutch Leyden and German Munster depend on cumin for their flavour. Zeera pani is a refreshing Indian drink made from cumin and tamarind water. The seeds should be pan-roasted before using to bring out the aroma. Use sparingly as cumin can easily dominate other flavours. Less than a teaspoon will flavour a meal for four.

Curry plant

Helichrysum italicum syn. H. angustifolium Asteraceae

Curry plants are often planted in herb gardens for their attractive habits, colouring and aroma. The intensely silver, needle-like foliage releases a mouth-watering scent of curry especially after rain. The flowers may be used dried in floral arrangements; the essential oil is used in perfume.

OTHER COMMON NAME Italian everlasting
PARTS USED Leaves, flowers

■ Gardening

The common form of curry plant is *H. italicum* subsp. *italicum*, which is widely sold in the nursery trade as *H. angustifolium*. It is an upright but eventually semi-sprawling shrub to about 60cm, with dense, needle-shaped leaves covered in very fine hairs, which give the plant a silvered appearance. Native to dry sunny places in southern Europe, curry plant makes a good partner in both appearance and cultivation requirements for other shrubby Mediterranean herbs, such as sage (*Salvia officinalis*, see page 119-121)
Varieties Other forms include 'Dartington', which has a more compact habit, and the dwarf curry plant (*H. italicum* subsp. *microphyllum*), which is popular for edging and containers. Among related species is *H. stoechas*. The essential oil of both species is known as 'immortelle' or 'helichrysum' and is used in the perfume industry.
Position Curry plant requires an open sunny position and very well-drained, neutral to alkaline soil. Though fairly hardy, plants may suffer from severe or prolonged frost. In areas where the temperature often drops below −5°C, grow in a sheltered position.
Propagation Take heel or semi-ripe cuttings in summer.

Curry plant
(*Helichrysum italicum*)

Curry tree

Curry plant is sometimes confused with the curry tree (*Murraya koenigii*), which is used in Ayurvedic medicine. This small tree, 3-4m tall, has pinnate leaves which are intensely curry-scented. Bunches of leaves are sold in markets in India and Sri Lanka for making curries. The curry tree makes an attractive container plant for sunny conservatories and garden rooms which are heated in winter to at least 10°C.

Maintenance Curry plants respond well to light shaping but tend to die back if pruned too hard.
Pests and diseases Curry plant dislikes dull wet conditions and crowding by other plants. Damp and poor ventilation encourage fungal disease. To avoid this, give plants plenty of space, keep clear round the base, and mulch with gravel.
Harvesting and storing As a herb it is only used fresh. Pick as required.

Cooking

Though strongly aromatic of curry, curry plant cannot be used to make curries. Adding sprigs to egg, rice and vegetable dishes will impart a hint of curry flavour, but cook only briefly.

The yellow everlasting flowers of curry plants can be dried for floral arrangements and craft work.

Dandelion

Taraxacum officinale Asteraceae

Almost all of the dandelion can be eaten. The flowers make wine, young leaves are used as a vegetable and the roots can be roasted for herbal coffee. Dandelion and burdock is a traditional drink made from fermented roots. Promoted as a temperance beverage in the 19th century, today it is sold as a fizzy soft drink.

PARTS USED Leaves, roots, flowers

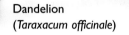

Dandelion
(*Taraxacum officinale*)

■ Gardening

Dandelion is a hardy perennial with a thick, fleshy taproot and a rosette of coarsely toothed leaves. From the leaves emerge many unbranched flower stalks, each terminating in a double golden yellow flower. The flowers are followed by spherical balls of seed, or 'clocks', which are dispersed by the wind. They are worth growing for their many uses, but ensure that they do not seed into your own or neighbouring gardens.

Varieties Improved forms were developed in France in the 19th century. 'Thick Leaved' has tender, broad, thick leaves. 'Improved Full Heart' has profuse foliage that is easily blanched.

Position Moist, fertile, neutral to slightly alkaline soil in a sunny situation.

Propagation Sow the seed directly into the soil in spring. For salads, treat as an annual, mixing a few dandelion seeds with seeds of mesclun (baby salad leaves).

Maintenance Cut off spent flowers to prevent reseeding. Perennials will die down to small rosettes in winter.

Pests and diseases Leaves are prone to mildew, particularly late in the season.

Harvesting and storing Blanch the leaves for culinary purposes by covering them from the light for 2 to 3 weeks before harvesting in late spring and before flowering occurs. When growing for coffee, lift roots at the end of the second season, wash, chop and dry before grinding. Both leaves and roots can be dried for herbal use.

■ Herbal medicine

Taraxacum officinale. Parts used: leaves, roots. Dandelion is well known for its therapeutic effects on both the kidneys and liver. The leaf exerts a powerful diuretic action on the urinary system and may reduce fluid retention and assist the removal of toxins from the body. It also contains high levels of potassium and helps to replenish potassium that would otherwise be lost as a result of increased urination.

The root is used when the digestive system needs stimulus as it promotes bile secretion. It is a valuable remedy for many liver and gallbladder conditions and can be an effective laxative.

What is a weed? A plant whose virtues have not been discovered.

Ralph Waldo Emerson, 1878

For the safe and appropriate use of dandelion, see *Liver support*, page 214. Do not use in more than culinary quantities if pregnant or breastfeeding.

■ Cooking

Dandelion leaves – best blanched to reduce bitterness – can be used fresh in salads, or cooked in stir fries.

Clock flower

Dandelion has acquired a number of names, including *piss en lit* (French for 'wet the bed'), a reference to its diuretic effect. Its common names include fairy clocks and clocks and watches, both of which refer to the children's game of telling time by the number of seeds left after blowing a 'clock'. Another name, *caput monachi*, refers to the tonsure of a medieval monk.

Vivid and spiky, dandelion flowers are rich in pollen and nectar, and are attractive to many beneficial insects including bees.

Dill

Anethum graveolens Apiaceae

Dill looks similar to fennel at first glance, but is different in flavour and uses. All parts have a parsley-caraway aroma prized in Asia and the Middle East for more than 2000 years and in more recent times is associated with Scandinavian cuisine. The word 'dill' comes from the old Norse word 'dilla', meaning 'to soothe' or 'lull', referring to its traditional use as a remedy for indigestion.

OTHER COMMON NAME Dillweed
PARTS USED Leaves, seeds

Dill seed is used in the spice mix, ras el hanout. See the Moroccan lamb recipe on page 368 which incorporates the mix.

■ Gardening

Dill is a hardy annual, reaching 70-80cm, with feathery blue-green foliage and attractive compound umbels of yellow flowers, which are followed by small elliptical flat seeds.

Varieties Dill varieties for harvesting leaves (dillweed) are bred for their vigour and resistance to bolting (premature flowering). They include 'Herkules', 'Tetra' and 'Dukat', which all have fine flavours. For pot culture choose smaller growing, bushy varieties, such as 'Bouquet'. If you are growing for seed, 'Mammoth' bears very large heads on stems up to 1m tall.

Position Dill requires full sun and well-drained, moist soil.

Propagation Sow seeds directly into the soil in early spring and at monthly intervals until late summer for a constant supply of leaves. For seed, sow at any time in spring for summer ripening.

Maintenance Thin plants to about 45cm apart. You may need to stake some tall varieties.

Pests and diseases Dill is usually trouble free but in damp conditions may rot at the roots, causing plants to redden and wilt.

Harvesting and storing Harvest leaves as required. To dry, spread them thinly on paper, then microwave to retain good colour and fragrance. Store in an airtight container in a cool, dry place. Fresh leaves keep well in a plastic bag in the fridge and they also freeze well. Harvest the seeds as they begin to ripen by cutting stems and hanging upside down in paper bags or over sheets of paper to catch the seeds as they fall.

■ Herbal medicine

Anethum graveolens. Part used: dried ripe fruits (seeds). The essential oil found in dill seed is a key ingredient in the preparation of dill or gripe water, a traditional remedy for intestinal colic in infants and children. Dill seed extracts have antispasmodic effects which also relieve gastrointestinal conditions in adults which are characterised by wind, bloating and cramping.

Dill (*Anethum graveolens*)

Another use of dill is to improve the flow of milk in breastfeeding mothers. Used in this way, the herb's medicinal properties are passed on to the baby. For the safe and effective medicinal use of dill, see *Wind, bloating and flatulence*, page 212. Do not use in greater than culinary quantities if pregnant or breastfeeding except with the advice of a doctor or medical herbalist.

■ Cooking

With a taste reminiscent of caraway and parsley, the fresh leaves complement soft cheeses, white sauces, egg dishes, fish, seafood, salads, soups and vegetables dishes, especially potatoes. Dill is famously used to make dill pickles (pickled gherkins or cucumbers) and gravlax, a Scandinavian dish of salmon cured with salt and dill. Add fresh dill to hot dishes just before serving, as cooking diminishes its flavour. Dill seeds are used in pickling spice mixtures, in breads (especially rye bread), and in commercial seasonings for meat.

Echinacea

Echinacea spp. Asteraceae

The name *Echinacea* comes from the Greek 'echinos', or hedgehog and refers to the spiky cone at the heart of the flower. It was used as medicinal herb by native North Americans, but had limited use in Europe until German company Madaus researched its properties in the 1930s.

OTHER COMMON NAME Coneflower
PARTS USED Roots, leaves, flowers, seed

Stratifying seed

To speed germination, stratify your seeds. Mix seed with moist sterile sand or vermiculite and place in a sealed plastic bag in the fridge for 4 weeks before sowing. Alternatively, sow the seeds and leave pots or trays in a cold frame until they germinate the following spring.

Echinacea purpurea in bloom.

▉ Gardening

There are nine species of *Echinacea*, all North American hardy perennials. Three are used medicinally. *E. purpurea* syn. *Rudbeckia purpurea* is the best known and most easily grown species as it has fibrous roots rather than a taproot and tolerates cold, damp growing conditions.
Varieties A number of varieties are valued as ornamentals and as cut flowers while retaining their herbal potency. They include 'Magnus', with huge rose-purple flowers; 'White Swan', a white-flowered form that comes fairly true from seed; and 'Primadonna' Series, available in deep rose and pure white. 'Doubledecker' has a crown-like second tier of petals emerging from the top of the cone. 'Fancy Frills' resembles a fragrant pink sunflower.

The narrow-leaved coneflower (*E. angustifolia*) and pale purple coneflower (*E. pallida*) are more potent medicinally than *E. purpurea*. Yellow coneflower (*E. paradoxa*) is the only yellow-flowered species. It has similar properties to *E. pallida* and has been crossed with *E. purpurea* to give blooms in peach and orange shades, such as 'Sunrise' and 'Sunset' (Big Sky Series).
Position Echinaceas require a well-drained, sunny position. The plants are deep-rooted and, if grown in areas with shallow soil, should be planted into raised beds. They are drought-resistant once established.
Propagation Divide named varieties in autumn and spring. Species and varieties with a range of colours ('Series') are grown from seed which will germinate more readily after stratification (see box).
Maintenance Keep young plants labelled and free from weeds as they may not flower until the second year. Stake tall plants as the flowerheads are heavy.
Pests and diseases Trouble free.
Harvesting and storing Dig up the roots of mature plants in autumn, then clean and dry them. Gather flowers and foliage from mature plants as required.

▉ Herbal medicine

Echinacea angustifolia, E. purpurea, E. pallida. Parts used: roots, aerial parts. Echinacea is widely used as a stimulant for the immune system, and has antiviral, fungicidal, bactericidal, anti-inflammatory and detoxifying properties. Its reputation as an effective treatment for the common cold, flu and acute upper respiratory infections has been the focus of much scientific research. The results of many clinical trials indicate that echinacea can reduce the symptoms and duration of such conditions.

Traditionally, echinacea has also been used as a remedy for the treatment of many contagious illnesses and skin infections. It enhances the immune response, enabling the body to fight off bacteria, viruses and other disease-causing micro-organisms. Individuals with weakened immune systems due to prolonged ill health or drug therapy may also benefit from using echinacea.

For the safe and appropriate use of echinacea, see *Immune system support*, page 208. Do not use echinacea if you are pregnant or breastfeeding.

Elder

Sambucus nigra Caprifoliaceae

The elder has long been endowed with mystical and magical powers. It has been called 'the medicine chest of the people' because of its uses in preventing and curing infections. Garden varieties have handsome foliage with blossoms and fruits that are used for drinks and flavourings.

OTHER COMMON NAMES Black elder, common elder, European elder
PARTS USED Flowers, ripe berries, leaves (insecticidal only)

Elder (*Sambucus nigra*)

 Gardening

The European elder is a very hardy shrub or small, multistemmed tree with brittle branches and deep green foul-smelling compound leaves. Lacy clusters of tiny, creamy white, fragrant flowers are followed by small round black berries. Leaves, stems, green berries and roots are poisonous, and consuming too many raw ripe berries may also cause digestive upsets. Elders are fast growing and tolerant of both wet and dry conditions, and poor alkaline soils.

Varieties Ornamental varieties of elder include: 'Aurea' with golden leaves; 'Eva' syn. 'Black Lace', with finely cut purple-black foliage and pink flowers; 'Madonna' with cream-splashed leaves; and fern-leaved or parsley-leaved elder (f. *laciniata*) which has finely cut foliage.

Position Elder prefers moist but well-drained, humus-rich soil and full sun to partial shade.

Propagation Collect fresh seed in autumn or stratify older seed for 4 weeks (see box opposite). Alternatively, propagate by suckers, by semi-ripe cuttings taken in late summer or by cuttings of ripe wood in late autumn.

Maintenance Ornamental varieties benefit from hard pruning in late winter to encourage vigorous, colourful new foliage. For maximum flowering and fruiting, go easier on pruning, removing a few of the oldest stems and any that are badly placed or crossing.

Pests and diseases Elder is resistant to honey fungus. The leaves have been used to make insecticidal sprays but in spite of its insect repellent effects, elder can suffer from blackfly in poor conditions.

Harvesting and storing Harvest the berries when they are black. They freeze well and can also be made into a syrup to preserve them. Pick flowers early on a dewless morning, spread the heads on clean kitchen paper and leave in a warm, dark, dry place for several days. Using a fork, strip as much stalk as possible from both flowers and berries as the stems have an unpleasant flavour.

 Herbal medicine

Sambucus nigra. Parts used: flowers, berries. Elder flowers and berries are used for alleviating the symptoms of colds and flu, in particular fever and congestion of the nose and sinuses. Elder flowers have also been used to reduce mucus production in hay fever, sinusitis and middle ear infections. Recently, clinical trials found that a commercial elderberry syrup reduced both the symptoms and duration of flu in sufferers. Laboratory studies suggest that constituents in the berries may activate certain immune cells and act directly on viruses to reduce their infectivity.

For the safe and appropriate use of elder, see *Sore throats, colds and flu*, page 206. Do not use elder if you are pregnant or breastfeeding.

Cooking

Use the fresh or dried flowers to make elderflower wine, cordial or herb teas. They can also be added to stewed fruit, jellies and jams, enhancing the flavours of gooseberries and rhubarb. Berries make excellent red wine and are mixed with other fruits in crumbles and pies.

The dark side

In many parts of Europe, elder was used in magic and medicine, acquiring names such as Frau Holle (Hulda) for its association with the goddess of death, transformation and Halloween, and devil's wood and Judas tree for its medieval association with Christ's cross; Judas was said to have been hanged from the bough of an elder.

Evening primrose

Oenothera sp. Onagraceae

At night evening primrose flowers open up to pour forth fragrance to attract pollinating moths. The discovery of evening primrose oil, and its applications in the beauty and health industries, followed scientific research in the 1980s but leaves and stems were a feature of traditional remedies.

OTHER COMMON NAMES Suncups, sundrops
PARTS USED Seeds, roots, leaves

Evening primrose (*Oenothera biennis*)

 Gardening

The principal species cultivated for evening primrose oil extraction is *O. biennis*. This hardy biennial forms a basal rosette of pointed oval leaves from which emerges a central flowering stalk, bearing bowl-shaped, sweetly scented lemon-yellow flowers that open during successive nights. These are followed by slender pods which are filled with tiny seeds.

Varieties Other *Oenothera* species used as sources of evening primrose oil include *O. glazioviana* syn. *O. lamarckiana* and *O. parviflora*.

Position Evening primroses require a sunny position and freely draining soils. They tolerate poorer, sandy soils and are drought-tolerant.

Taming the beast

Theophrastus (371–*c.*287 BCE) wrote two influential botanical volumes, *On the Causes of Plants* and *Enquiry into Plants*; this led to him being regarded by some as the 'father of taxonomy'. He named evening primrose *Oenothera*, possibly from the Greek words *oinos*, meaning 'wine', and *thera*, meaning 'hunt'. It is thought that Theophrastus recommended using evening primrose for taming wild beasts.

Propagation Sow seed in spring to early summer. Extreme heat in summer reduces the gamma-linolenic content of developing seeds. In good conditions, evening primrose self sows freely.

Maintenance Keep free of weeds.

Pests and diseases Where plants are overcrowded, powdery mildew may affect the foliage. Inadequately drained soil may cause root rot.

Harvesting and storing Gather the fresh young leaves as required for using fresh in salads or steaming as a vegetable. Lift parsnip-like roots at the end of the second season and use in soups or stir fries. Harvest seed as capsules start to ripen; if too close to ripening, they will shatter when handled. Crushing the tiny seed to extract oil requires technical know-how and equipment; it is not something you can do at home.

Herbal medicine

Oenothera biennis. Part used: seed oil. Evening primrose oil (EPO) contains significant levels of omega-6 essential fatty acids, especially gamma-linolenic acid (GLA), thought to be involved in many of the oil's therapeutic effects. When taken internally, GLA has notable anti-inflammatory effects and several clinical studies suggest that this effect may help in alleviating the symptoms of rheumatoid arthritis, diabetic neuropathy, eczema and dermatitis.

Further research also indicates that EPO supplementation may help to reduce high blood pressure and improve some of the symptoms of PMS. However, results of some trials have been negative. More recent research suggests that a greater therapeutic effect may be achieved if EPO or GLA supplements are taken in combination with omega-3 essential fatty acids, found in flax seeds and fish.

For the safe and effective use of EPO, consult your doctor or medical herbalist. Do not use EPO if you are pregnant or breastfeeding.

Natural beauty

Evening primrose oil is widely used in cosmetics. To make your own skincare treatment, see *Three roses moisturiser*, page 253.

The most convenient way of taking evening primrose oil is in the form of capsules, which are widely available.

Eyebright

Euphrasia officinalis Scrophulariaceae

Eyebrights occur in heaths and grassy uplands in many parts of the world. Though many different species have been described, they may be variants of a single, very widespread species. The common name refers to their use to treat eye problems including conjunctivitis, styes and inflammation from hay fevers and colds.

PARTS USED Whole plant

■ Gardening

Eyebrights are semi-parasitic on the roots of host plants, namely grasses, plantain (*Plantago* sp.) and clover (*Trifolium* sp.). For this reason, they are extremely difficult to cultivate and have little potential either as ornamentals or as a crop.

Varieties The principal species used herbally as eyebright are *E. officinalis*, *E. brevipila* and *E. rostkoviana*. All are hardy annuals with small, toothed, rounded leaves and yellow-throated white flowers, striped or spotted with purple. The lower flower lip is three-lobed, and each lobe is incised.

Position Eyebright's native habitat is moist subalpine grassland often on alkaline soil and always in a cool climate.

Euphrasia comes from a Greek word meaning 'good cheer'.

Propagation Theoretically, if you have suitable conditions in your garden, you can establish eyebrights by scattering seed around on host grasses during spring – but see above for problems.

Maintenance Ensure that the soil remains moist.

Pests and diseases No problems of significance have been noted.

Harvesting and storing Harvest the whole plant when it is in flower, and dry thoroughly for subsequent use in herbal preparations.

Eyebright (*Euphrasia officinalis*)

Doctrine of Signatures

Eyebright was first recorded as a medicinal herb for 'all evils of the eye' in the 14th century. Faith in its use was strengthened by the Doctrine of Signatures, a philosophy propounded in the 16th century by a Swiss physician who adopted the name Paracelsus. He proposed that, by observation of a plant's colour and form, or the place where it grew, one could determine its purpose in God's plan. Eyebright's purple and yellow spots and stripes were thought to resemble such eye problems as bloodshot eyes. Hence, it could be used to treat such ailments.

■ Herbal medicine

Euphrasia officinalis. Parts used: flowering stems. Eyebright is a traditional remedy for irritated or inflamed conditions of the eye, such as styes and conjunctivitis. The combined astringent and anti-inflammatory effects of eyebright also make it well suited for treating catarrhal conditions. It can also help to clear up postnasal drip, middle ear infections and sinus congestion. Another use is to ease symptoms experienced by hay fever sufferers, including itchy, weeping eyes, watery secretions of the nose and also sinus headaches.

For the safe and appropriate use of eyebright, see *Hay fever and sinusitis*, page 209. Do not use eyebright if you are pregnant or breastfeeding.

■ Natural beauty

The pretty flowers of this plant have a toning, cooling and mildly astringent effect on the eye. Eyebright may be used as a compress or topical lotion to relieve common eye disorders and infections. To make a compress, see *Eyebright compress*, page 262.

Fennel

Foeniculum vulgare Apiaceae

No herb garden should be without this handsome plant. All kinds are useful in cooking and home remedies. In 812 Emperor Charlemagne demanded that fennel be planted on farms and in monastery gardens throughout his empire.

PARTS USED Leaves, flowers, seeds, stems, roots

Fennel (*Foeniculum vulgare*)

■ Gardening

Fennel is essentially a hardy perennial and can reach 1.5m or more, with one to several erect, hollow stems coming from the base, bearing glossy, aromatic thread-like foliage. The tiny yellow flowers are borne in umbels, followed by small, very aromatic seeds.

Varieties Two main kinds of fennel are cultivated: the feathery perennial grown for its aromatic leaves and seeds; and Florence fennel (var. *azoricum* syn. var. *dulce*), which is less hardy and usually grown as an annual for its bulbous leaf bases. Bronze fennel (*F. vulgare* 'Purpureum') and the larger 'Giant Bronze' are striking architectural plants for a focal point or contrast in borders. Two of the best varieties of Florence fennel are 'Romanesco', an autumn cropping variety with good resistance to bolting (premature flowering), and

'Rudy' an F1 hybrid that produces high-quality bulbs in spring and summer.

Position It prefers a light, well-drained, slightly alkaline soil in a sunny position but is adaptable and tolerates cold well.

Propagation Raise all fennel varieties by seed sown in spring at 13-18°C. Follow instructions on seed packet for time to sow varieties of Florence fennel.

Maintenance Cut down and remove old stems of perennials when plants are dormant in winter.

Pests and diseases Trouble free.

Harvesting and storing Harvest foliage and flowers as required. Harvest seeds as they start to turn pale in colour. Place heads in paper bags in a warm place until dry enough for seeds to fall off, then store in airtight containers.

■ Herbal medicine

Foeniculum vulgare. Part used: dried ripe fruits (seeds). Fennel calms the digestive system, relieving flatulence, bloating and abdominal discomfort. Fennel has also been taken by breastfeeding mothers as a remedy for improving breast milk flow; used in this way, the therapeutic effects of fennel can be passed on to babies experiencing colic and griping. Fennel has long been used to treat catarrh and coughing, and is suitable for treating these conditions in adults and children.

For the safe medicinal use of fennel, consult your doctor or medical herbalist. Do not use fennel in greater than culinary doses if you are pregnant or breastfeeding except with the advice of a doctor or medical herbalist.

■ Around the home

Fennel is a natural flea repellent. Crush a handful of fresh fronds and rub them all over your dog or cat. Put handfuls of fennel fronds under your pet's bedding.

■ Cooking

Slice the raw bulb thinly and add to salads and stir-fries, or halve and roast to bring out its sweetness. Use fresh leaves finely chopped in salads, salad dressings and vinegars, with fish, pork and seafood dishes, or as a garnish. The dried seeds are used in cakes and breads, Italian sausages, salads, pickles, and pasta dishes and as a herb tea if lightly crushed.

Field of Marathon

The ancient Greek name for fennel, marathon, was also the name of the battlefield to the north of Athens where, in 490 BCE, a Greek army defeated the invading Persian force. Word of the victory was carried the 42km to Athens from the battlefield by a runner who died on the spot after delivering his message. Today's marathon races are supposedly named after this early example of long-distance running.

The bulbous leaf bases of Florence fennel can be sliced raw in salads or roasted.

Fenugreek

Trigonella foenum-graecum Papilionaceae

Fenugreek is one of the oldest cultivated plants in the world, recorded in Iraq as long ago as 4000 BCE. Valued as a fodder crop, salad and spice throughout the Mediterranean, Middle East and western Asia, it has also been a tonic herb in both Chinese and Ayurvedic medicine since ancient times.

OTHER COMMON NAME Methi
PARTS USED Seeds, leaves

Fenugreek (*Trigonella foenum-graecum*) has lightly perfumed flowers.

Gardening

Fenugreek is a frost-hardy annual with trifoliate grey-green leaves and scented cream flowers, tinged violet at the base, followed by long narrow pods, with up to 20 very hard, yellow-brown, rectangular seeds. Although it is not particularly ornamental, fenugreek is interesting to grow in a wild-flower area with other annuals, such as corn poppies (*Papaver rhoeas*, see page 105) and pot marigolds (*Calendula officinalis*, see page 29). It can also be grown in the vegetable garden where the leaves can be gathered to use fresh as a salad herb or dried as a flavouring. The seeds are good for sprouting too.

Fenugreek (*Trigonella foenum-graecum*)

Position Well-drained, neutral to slightly acidic soil in full sun.
Propagation Sow fenugreek seeds outdoors about 6mm deep in mid to late spring. For sprouting, germinate seeds at 20 to 25°C.
Maintenance Thin and weed seedlings in the vegetable garden, using thinnings in salads.
Pest and diseases Fenugreek can be damaged by frost and is sensitive to cold wet conditions.
Harvest Pick leaves and new shoots to use fresh or for drying throughout summer. Cut sprouted seeds when they develop their first leaves. Collect pods as they change from green to brown and dry before crushing to release seeds.

Herbal medicine

Trigonella foenum-graecum. Part used: seeds. Fenugreek contains trigonelline, an alkaloid which has potential in treating cervical and liver cancer. It is also a source of saponins which are used in the pharmaceutical industry, notably in oral contraceptives. Fenugreek is important in Chinese medicine for kidney-related disorders such as lower back pain and swollen legs. In Ayurvedic medicine it is regarded as a tonic with rejuvenating and aphrodisiac effects, with a wide range of applications, from improving appetite in anorexia and convalescence, to relieving digestive complaints. Topical applications may help to heal leg ulcers, boils and cellulitis. Fenugreek may also have a role in relieving late-onset diabetes, painful menstruation and labour pains. It has hormonal effects and is known to stimulate uterine contractions. The side effects of fenugreek are few, but it may interfere with absorption of prescription drugs. For the safe and appropriate use of fenugreek, consult a doctor or medical herbalist. Do not use fenugreek if you are pregnant or breastfeeding.

The seeds of fenugreek resemble tiny stones. They are roasted before use.

Cooking

Ground fenugreek, made from lightly roasted seeds, is an essential curry spice, especially in vindaloo and fish curries, and in panch phoron, Indian five-spice mixture. Fresh leaves are used as a sag or potherb in vegetable curries, dhal, and chutneys, while dried leaves (*methi*) are a flavouring for root vegetables. Sprouted seeds are a delicious addition to salads and sandwiches.

Feverfew

Tanacetum parthenium syn. *Chrysanthemum parthenium,*
Matricaria parthenium Asteraceae

With a long history in European herbal medicine, the
name feverfew is derived from 'febrifuge', as it was said to
dispel fevers. Its ornamental, long-lasting flowers are as
fresh looking as checked gingham and come in both
tall and more prostrate varieties. Feverfew is used as an
insect repellent and a companion plant.

PART USED Leaves

Daisy-like feverfew has many ornamental
varieties for the garden.

 ## Gardening

Feverfew is a short-lived hardy
perennial, forming a bushy clump of
deeply incised, yellow-green, compound
leaves up to about 50cm tall. Over a
long period in summer, plants bear
clusters of many small, white-petalled,
yellow-centred daisy flowers. Taller
varieties of feverfew are excellent as cut
flowers, while dwarf forms are ideal for
containers and edging borders.

Varieties There are two varieties with
bright yellow foliage: 'Aureum' which
comes true from seed; and 'Golden
Moss', a dwarf form that forms compact
mounds only 10cm tall. 'Rowallane' syn.
'Sissinghurst White' and 'Tetrawhite' are
tall double-flowered forms, 60cm tall,
which are good for cutting. 'Golden

Ball' is dwarf, to 30cm, with button-like
double yellow flowers.

Position It is a very unfussy plant,
although it does best in a sunny
position, good soil, regular watering in
summer and good drainage. The plants
remain evergreen in winter.

Propagation Feverfew self-seeds
readily, but you can also grow it from
seed, by cuttings or by root division
in spring.

Maintenance When flowering is
complete, cut back the flowering stalks.

Pests and diseases In poor conditions
plants may occasionally suffer from
aphids, but otherwise feverfew is
remarkably trouble free.

Harvesting and storing Harvest the
fresh leaves at any time.

(*Caution*: handling plants can cause
dermatitis in some sensitive individuals.)

Herbal medicine

Tanacetum parthenium. Part used: leaves.
Feverfew is used as a valuable remedy
for the treatment and prevention of
migraine headaches. Clinical trials have
shown that the herb can reduce the
severity of symptoms, including visual
disturbances and nausea. Although the
exact nature of its action is not yet fully
understood, laboratory studies suggest
that feverfew's therapeutic effects may be
a result of its anti-inflammatory and
pain-relieving properties as well as
muscle relaxant action.

Fresh leaves of feverfew are
sometimes chewed for medicinal
purposes. However, feverfew is more
likely to cause adverse effects such as
mouth ulcers if taken this way, so the use
of commercially produced feverfew
extracts may be preferable.

For the safe and appropriate use of
feverfew, see *Headaches and migraine,*
page 221. Do not use feverfew if you
are pregnant or breastfeeding.

Around the home

Feverfew is noted for its moth-repellent
qualities. For information on using
moth-repellent herbs, see *Herbs for
your clothes*, page 294, and also *Scented
coathangers*, page 296.

Feverfew (*Tanacetum
parthenium*)

Flax

Linum usitatissimum Linaceae

Beautiful blue-flowered common flax is one of the oldest known crop plants, and has been cultivated for at least six millenia. All of its parts are useful: the stalks produce a fibre that is used to make linen, the seeds are used for food, and the oil is a rich source of linolenic acid (omega-3). The name usitatissimum means 'most useful'.

PARTS USED Seeds, oil

Flax (*Linum usitatissimum*)

■ Gardening

Linum usitatissimum has been developed as two distinct types: the taller forms known generically as long-stalked flax (for fibre); the shorter, more floriferous types known as crown flax (for seed production). The plants are slender, erect, narrow-leafed annuals, about 60cm tall, with multiple stems bearing single, upward-facing, sky-blue flowers, followed by round capsules, about 1cm in diameter, filled with glossy, flattened oval seeds. The seed is milled and extracted for flaxseed oil, also known as linseed oil. Finest-quality cold-extracted oil is used for nutritional supplements. Industrial-grade oil is further processed into a range of products, from printing inks, paints and varnishes to linoleum; the residual linseed cake is used as feed for cattle. Linola is a new crop specifically bred for the production of a cooking oil that is comparable to that of sunflower and corn oil. As a garden plant, treat flax as you would any ornamental annual for borders and gap-filling in planting schemes.

Varieties Seeds of *L. usitatissimum* are sold as ornamentals for dry sunny borders. Though several different varieties are grown commercially, these are only available in bulk for agricultural use.

Position It requires a sunny position and well-drained to dry, sandy soil.

Propagation Sow the seed directly into prepared ground in spring.

Maintenance Keep flax weeded, as it does not compete against weeds.

Pests and diseases A 3 year crop rotation is recommended as flax is prone to fungal problems.

Harvesting and storing Cut plants as seeds start to ripen and hang upside down in bunches to dry, positioning over paper to catch falling seeds. Store seed whole in airtight containers, preferably in the fridge.

■ Herbal medicine

Linum usitatissimum. Parts used: seeds, oil. Taken whole or crushed with a little water, the seeds of flax have a gentle laxative effect and are a popular remedy for constipation. The mucilage content of the seed produces a soothing effect on many irritable and inflamed conditions of the gut.

The seed oil is the most concentrated plant source of the omega-3 essential fatty acid, alpha-linolenic acid (ALA), which is often deficient in the Western diet, especially for vegetarians.

Supplementing the diet with flaxseed oil or ALA may have numerous health benefits. Human studies indicate that ALA has positive effects on cholesterol levels and a potential role in the treatment of other cardiovascular diseases. The anti-inflammatory omega-3 oils can also be useful for treating inflammatory skin conditions such as eczema and psoriasis.

For the safe and appropriate use of flaxseed, see *Eczema and psoriasis*, page 223. Do not use flaxseed if you are pregnant or breastfeeding.

■ Cooking

Flaxseed can be added to homemade breads and muesli or sprouted for salads.

Taking flaxseeds can help digestion.

57

Garlic and onions

Allium spp. Alliaceae

The Sumerians planted onions more than 5000 years ago, while the ancient Egyptians had about 8000 medicinal uses for them, and often placed them in their tombs. In culinary terms, onions are said to be the poor man's truffle but they add extra flavour to almost every recipe and can be delicious raw, fried and roasted as a vegetable.

PARTS USED Leaves, bulbs, bulbils, seed, flowers

Garlic (*Allium sativum*)

■ Gardening

The alliums – approximately 700 species of them – include globe onions, shallots, leeks, garlic and chives, and curious forms, such as walking onions and potato onions. Many long ago made their way into the ornamental garden. Alliums are all bulbous or rhizomatous in habit, characteristically with strap-like or hollow leaves and simple umbels of bell or star-shaped flowers emerging from a papery sheathing bract.

Garlic

Garlic (*A. sativum*) is divided into two groups: 'softnecks' (*A. sativum* var. *sativum*), which are generally shorter, non-flowering plants with leaves that die- back completely, leaving bulbs that store very well; and 'hardnecks' (*A. sativum* var. *ophioscorodon*), which have tough ('hard') flowering stems that remain firmly attached to the centre of the bulb. Hardnecks are hardy and well-flavoured but do not keep as long. They include the rocambole or serpent garlic which produces tall, sinuously looping stems with a head of flowers mixed with bulbils (secondary bulbs that can grow into new plants), while below ground it forms a cluster of 4 to 14 cloves.

Ramsons or bear's garlic (*A. ursinum*) is an intensely garlic-scented species, and both the leaves and bulbils are used.

Sand leek also known as Russian garlic or giant garlic, (*A. scorodoprasum*) develops a large dark purple bulb surrounded by dark red bulblets, and a flowering stem up to 80cm tall, bearing red-purple flowers and bulbils.

Wild garlic or three-cornered leek (*A. triquetrum*) has garlic-flavoured foliage, small garlic-flavoured bulbs and nodding umbels of attractive starry white flowers.

Chives

Four distinct kinds of chives are grown for their foliage: the common garden or onion chives (*A. schoenoprasum*), with umbels of mauve-pink flowers; garlic or Chinese chives (*A. tuberosum*), with white flowers and deliciously garlic-scented, strap-like foliage; Siberian or fragrant Chinese chives (*A. ramosum*) from central Asia, with red-striped white petals; and mauve-flowered, garlic-flavoured society garlic (*Tulbaghia violacea*) which has white-flowered, 'Alba' and variegated forms, 'Silver Lace'.

Onions

Common globe onion (*Allium cepa*) is the best known of this aromatic tribe.

Tree onion or Egyptian onion or walking onion (*A. cepa*, Proliferum Group) forms a basal bulb, while the flowers are replaced by a cluster of small bulbils that weigh the stalk to the ground, allowing the bulbils to take root.

Potato onion (*A. cepa*, Aggregatum Group) forms a large cluster of plump smallish onions at the base.

Shallots (*A. cepa*, Aggregatum Group) form an above-ground cluster of bulbs with a delicate flavour.

Chinese onion or rakkyo (*A. chinensis*) is an Asian species cultivated for its crisp textured bulbs, which are popularly used raw, pickled or cooked.

Nodding onion or lady's leek (*A. cernuum*), a North American perennial, has an intense onion flavour in all parts.

Canada garlic (*A. canadense*) forms crisp strongly flavoured white bulbs and has onion-scented foliage.

Wild garlic (*A. triquetrum*) bears umbels of pretty white flowers.

During the First World War garlic juice was used in field dressings to prevent gangrene.

Leeks

Leeks (*A. porrum*) originate from the Mediterranean. Milder in flavour than onions, they include: hardy heirloom varieties, such as 'Musselburgh' and 'Bleu Solaise' that stand all winter; vigorous, delicate-flavoured 'Carentan'; and 'Jolant', an early variety which is ideal for harvesting as baby leeks.

Garlic leek or Levant garlic (*A. ampeloprasum*) is perennial, with flat, keeled leaves, a large basal bulb and bulblets in the leaf bases.

Welsh onion, which are also known as spring onions, scallions and bunching onions (*A. fistulosum*), forms a perennial clump which are pale at the base but have no bulb as such.

Ramps (*A. tricoccum*), native to damp woodland in North America, forms clumps of slender bulbs which have a pungent onion-and-garlic flavour.

1 Green onions **2** Brown onions
3 Green onions with their tops
4 Red onion **5** Spring onions

Position All the principal *Allium* species require well-tilled and weed-free soil, good drainage and a sunny position.

Propagation Onions can be grown from seeds or 'sets' (first-year bulbs); Raise chives, leeks and their relatives by seed in spring. Propagate garlic by planting cloves vertically, with pointed tip covered by about 2.5cm of soil. It needs a long, cool growing period, so is best planted in autumn or early winter. A few species, such as *A. triquetrum* and *A. tuberosum*, self sow freely and may become invasive in some gardens.

Maintenance Regular weeding is essential, particularly in the earlier stages of growth. Do not overwater.

Pests and diseases The main problems are downy mildew, neck rot and white rot, and rust. Grow resistant varieties, avoid high-nitrogen fertilisers and plant well apart to ensure good air circulation. Do not over water. Clear away and burn all infected parts and do not replant any alliums in the same ground for at least 3 years. Garlic is susceptible to nematode (eelworm) attack. As it is an accumulator, do not use chemicals.

Harvesting and storing If growing species for their aromatic foliage, use fresh. Harvest globe onions at any stage. When they've stopped growing, the tops of both onions and garlic fall over and wither. Choose a sunny day to pull the bulbs of both types, then leave for a few days to dry. Store in a dry, well-ventilated area to prevent fungal rot.

■ Herbal medicine

Allium sativum. Part used: bulbs. Regular consumption of garlic, a potent natural antibiotic, can help to prevent and treat bronchial infections, coughs and colds. Garlic's antimicrobial effects also extend to the gut, and it can be helpful in the prevention and treatment of gastro-

How to peel garlic

Peeling large quantities of garlic is rather tedious. If you're peeling garlic that is to be sliced or chopped, first thump the clove with the flat blade of a large knife. This will distort and crack the skin, making it easier to remove. If you want to use the cloves whole, use a commercially available gadget consisting of a small flexible rubber tube; place the unpeeled cloves in this and roll the tube on a work surface for a few seconds. When you tip out the contents, the cloves should be neatly separated from their husks.

Elephant garlic

Native to the Mediterranean and the Middle East, elephant garlic (*A. ampeloprasum* 'Elephant') has giant cloves with a sweet flavour that is much less pungent than the garlic commonly used in cooking. The plant is actually a member of the leek family (one of its common names is perennial sweet leek). Eat the cloves raw or cook them like onions.

Garlic and onions continued

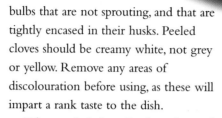

intestinal infections. Furthermore, inclusion of garlic in the diet has also been shown to have a preventative effect against stomach and colorectal cancers. Garlic has a number of beneficial effects on the cardiovascular system, many of which have been confirmed by clinical trials. Garlic supplementation has been shown to lower cholesterol levels, prevent the hardening of arteries and lessen the risk of blood clot formation. It can also help to reduce blood pressure as well as improve general circulation.

For the safe and effective medicinal use of garlic, see *Sore throats, colds and flu,* page 206, and *High blood pressure and cholesterol,* page 234. Do not use garlic in greater than culinary quantities if you are pregnant or breastfeeding.

■ Cooking

Garlic complements almost any savoury dish, and goes well with most culinary herbs and spices. It is an essential ingredient in Asian, Mexican, Mediterranean, Middle Eastern and Caribbean cuisines.

Garlic comes in white, pink and purple-skinned varieties. Choose firm

bulbs that are not sprouting, and that are tightly encased in their husks. Peeled cloves should be creamy white, not grey or yellow. Remove any areas of discolouration before using, as these will impart a rank taste to the dish.

When peeled, then sliced or chopped, the enzymes within a clove of garlic react on exposure to air to produce a lingering, sulphurous aroma. The flavour of garlic gives the impression of heat on the palate. The more finely it is crushed or chopped, the stronger the aroma becomes. When cooked properly, the flavour is mellow and sweet. Bake a whole head in foil, then squeeze out the contents of the cloves. Spread the mellow, creamy paste on bread or meat or stir through mashed vegetables.

Garlic is used raw in aïoli (a French garlic mayonnaise) and tapenade (olive paste). Crushed garlic mashed into butter is a delicious and simple sauce for meats, or it can be spread on a sliced baguette, wrapped in foil and baked in a medium-hot oven for 10 minutes. Bruschetta (Italian garlic bread) uses olive oil instead of butter. To permeate roasts with garlic, make slits in the meat and insert slivers of garlic before roasting, or put a few cloves inside the cavity of a chicken. Processed garlic is available, including crushed pastes and dehydrated flakes, powders and granules. Most produce a less subtle but more permeating odour.

Chives (*allium schoenoprasum*)

Chives

Depending on the variety, chives (*A. schoenoprasum*) have a mild onion or garlic flavour that goes well with sauces, stews, mashed vegetables such as potatoes, fish, poultry and egg dishes (especially scrambled eggs), and cream cheeses and salad dressings. The delicate flavour is easily destroyed by heat, so add chives during the last few minutes of cooking time, or scatter them on a finished dish to garnish.

Snip chives with scissors, rather than chop them with a knife. They are essential (along with chervil, parsley and tarragon) in the French herb blend called fines herbes (see Herb guide, page 334). Snip chives finely and freeze them in ice-cube trays to preserve. The flowers make a pretty garnish.

Chives bear umbels of pale purple bell-shaped flowers in summer.

To remove garlic odour from your hands, rub with lemon and salt and wash in cold water. Keep lemon halves handy for the purpose.

Germander

Teucrium chamaedrys Lamiaceae

The name germander is believed to be a corruption of *chamaedrys*, which comes from the Greek *chamai* meaning ground, and *drus* meaning oak, as its leaves resemble oak leaves. The Holy Roman Emperor Charles V was reputedly cured of gout after taking germander for 60 days.

OTHER COMMON NAME wall germander
PARTS USED Aerial parts

Wood sage (*T. scorodonia*) favours acid soils. It is perfectly hardy in mild areas.

Gardening

Germander is a small shrubby evergreen, native to Europe and south-west Asia, which has a spreading habit and upright to sprawling stems, about 25cm tall, bearing lobed ovate deeply veined leaves. In summer and autumn, small pink to magenta tubular two-lipped flowers appear in the upper leaf axils. As an ornamental, germander is excellent for low edging and for planting on steep banks and in dry stony borders. The leaves turn reddish in autumn and during dry spells.

Varieties Hedge germander (*Teucrium* x *lucidrys*) is a hybrid of *T. chamaedrys* and *T. lucidum*. It is frequently confused with *T. chamaedrys* and often sold under the wrong name. As the name suggests, hedge germander is more upright, with glossier, more leathery, darker green leaves. It is often planted as a dwarf hedge in knot gardens, and is a far better plant for this purpose than wall germander. There is a variegated form which erratically sends up cream-splashed shoots or the occasional leaves with cream markings. It tends to revert to plain green and needs propagating regularly to maintain the variegation.

Two other teucriums with medicinal properties are cat thyme (*T. marum*) which has a similar effect on cats to *Nepeta cataria* (see page 32) and looks rather like thyme, and wood sage (*T. scorodonia*), a British woodland herb with bitter, hop-scented leaves that were once used in brewing.

Position Light, well-drained, neutral to alkaline soil in sun.

Propagation By seed sown when ripe; by softwood or semi-ripe cuttings in summer; by division in spring.

Maintenance Trim plants into shape in spring. Cut back after they have finished flowering to encourage bushy new growth.

Pests and diseases Germander is usually trouble free.

Harvest Cut the leaves and aerial parts of the plant when they are flowering.

Wall germander (*Teucrium chamaedrys*) will thrive on walls and steep slopes.

They should be hung out to dry away from direct sunlight.

Herbal medicine

Teucrium chamaedrys. Parts used: aerial parts. Wall germander has a long history of use in medicine. Dioscorides recommended it for coughs and asthma and Culpeper considered it 'good against diseases of the brain, as continual headache, falling sickness [epilepsy], melancholy, drowsiness and dullness of spirits, convulsions and palsies' (*The English Physician Enlarged*, 1653).

Following several well-publicised cases of hepatitis and liver damage caused by diet formulas containing *T. chamaedrys*, a voluntary ban was initiated by French herbal practitioners and many herbalists no longer prescribe it. Prior to this, it was given in prescriptions to treat digestive disorders, catarrh, rheumatism and gout, and was an ingredient in formulae to encourage weight loss.

Ginger

Zingiber officinale Zingiberaceae

Ginger was highly recommended by none other than the great philosopher Confucius, who is reputed to have flavoured all his food with it. It has many medicinal uses, including the treatment of motion sickness and nausea.

PART USED Rhizomes

Ginger (*Zingiber officinale*)

■ Gardening

Native to tropical Asia, ginger is a tender rhizomatous perennial to about 90cm high, producing many fibrous leaf stalks sheathed in alternating lanceolate leaves. Plump rhizomes, known as 'hands', are pale yellow when freshly dug. The yellow flowers, with purple lips and green bracts, are arranged in dense, reddish, cone-like spikes. The plants have handsome foliage and are good pot plants in conservatories and elsewhere.

Varieties Japanese ginger or mioga (*Z. mioga*) has similar foliage and large cream, orchid-like flowers which appear at ground level in spring, even in pots. It is quite hardy. Variegated 'Dancing Crane' is less hardy but good in a pot.

Position Ginger grows best in rich, moist, well-drained soil.

Propagation Grow rhizome segments with one or two buds, or whole rhizomes to give bigger plants. Place rhizomes just below the surface in pots of rich, fibrous compost at 25–30°C.

Maintenance Lower the temperature when growth is well established but keep above 20°C. Keep the soil moist and feed once a month. Withhold water when leaves start to die down and keep dry when dormant.

Pests and diseases Cool damp conditions cause rhizome rot.

Harvesting and storing For using fresh, dig up rhizomes in late summer or early autumn. Dormant rhizomes are better for drying and grinding.

■ Herbal medicine

Zingiber officinale. Part used: rhizomes. Ginger has been clinically proven as a safe, effective remedy for the prevention and treatment of nausea. It can also benefit other digestive symptoms such as indigestion, colic and flatulence. It is used to relieve 'cold' symptoms as well as period pain, cold hands and feet, arthritis and rheumatism. It may also help to protect the heart and blood vessels by preventing the formation of blood clots and lowering cholesterol levels. For the safe and appropriate use of ginger, consult a doctor or medical herbalist.

■ Cooking

Young ginger is tender and sweet, with a spicy, tangy, warm to hot flavour. Older rhizomes are stronger and hotter. Fresh ginger is essential in Asian, Caribbean and African cuisine, in curries, stews, soups, salads, pickles, chutneys, stir-fries marinades, and meat, fish and vegetable dishes. Crystallised and candied ginger are ingredients in baking, jam and marmalade and eaten as confectionery. Ginger wine is popular on its own or with whisky. Dried ginger is used in baking and commercial spice mixtures. Pickled Japanese ginger, gari, is a condiment for sushi. New shoots and buds are also eaten in Japanese cuisine.

Ginger beer

Ginger beer dates back to the 1800s when 'botanical brewers' began making low alcohol beverages in response to the temperance movement. Recipes vary but basically crushed ginger roots are fermented with sugar, yeast and various flavourings, such as lemon. A ginger beer 'plant' is a yeast culture which is kept alive by feeding daily with a little sugar and ground ginger. It provides the basis for making ginger beer without having to start from scratch each time with separate ingredients.

1 Whole ginger root **2** Pickled ginger **3** Ground dried ginger **4** Sliced dried ginger **5** Crystallised ginger **6** Glacé ginger

Ginkgo

Ginkgo biloba Ginkgoaceae

The ginkgo is ancient, dating back to the Jurassic and Triassic periods, before the evolution of flowering plants. It has no close relatives and is very rare in the wild but following its introduction to Europe, in about 1725, ginkgo is now cultivated worldwide.

OTHER COMMON NAME Maidenhair tree
PARTS USED Fruits, leaves

Ginkgo (*Ginkgo biloba*)

Ginkgo makes a handsome tree in a park but is too large for most gardens.

■ Gardening

Ginkgos are hardy and deciduous, with fan-shaped notched leaves resembling those of the maidenhair fern which turn bright yellow in autumn. It takes about 20 years for ginkgos to mature, with male catkins and female flowers on different plants. Females bear unpleasant smelling plum-like fruits containing edible, almond-sized seeds which are highly prized in China and Japan. Ginkgos are long lived, slow growing and very ornamental. For confined spaces, choose narrow upright (fastigiate) forms or smaller varieties which can also be grown in containers.

Varieties The fastigiate 'Princeton Sentry' and 'Autumn Gold' are excellent male clones. Dwarf forms include 'Chi Chi' and 'Jade Butterflies'. There are also weeping and variegated forms.

Position Ginkgos prefer a sunny position and well-drained, fertile soil. They tolerate pollution and are often planted in city streets.

Propagation Sow seed as soon as it ripens. Named varieties can only be propagated by grafting in winter or semi-ripe cuttings in summer. If you require fruit, plant one male with one or more females.

Maintenance These trees require little pruning but can be trimmed to shape in late winter when still dormant.

Pests and diseases Ginkgo is virtually pest free.

Harvesting and storing Harvest ripe fruits when they fall and extract the seeds. As the leaves have low concentrations of active ingredients and need special processing, making extracts at home is not a realistic proposition.

■ Herbal medicine

Ginkgo biloba. Part used: leaves. Extensive research has identified many pharmacological actions associated with ginkgo leaf, including potent anti-oxidant and anti-inflammatory effects, an ability to enhance blood flow through arteries, veins and capillaries. It may also have a protective effect on many other cells of the body. These properties explain the use of ginkgo for a range of conditions, such as memory impairment and poor concentration in older people, as well as the treatment and prevention of symptoms in certain types of dementia, including those of Alzheimer's disease.

Clinical studies have also shown that ginkgo may be beneficial in treating some circulatory disorders, such as intermittent claudication, where restricted blood flow to the legs results in symptoms of numbness, pain and cramping, and Raynaud's syndrome, where there is poor circulation to the hands and feet. Further clinical trials indicate its use in the treatment of vertigo, tinnitus, asthma and premenstrual syndrome.

For the safe and appropriate use of ginkgo, see *Memory and concentration*, page 219 and *Circulation*, page 232. Do not use gingko if you are pregnant or breastfeeding except with the advice of a doctor or medical herbalist.

Ginseng

Panax spp. and *Eleutherococcus senticosus* Araliaceae

Ginseng has been used in Chinese medicine for at least 5000 years. Today it is widely recognised in Western medicine as an adaptogen, reducing the body's reaction to trauma and stress. The closely related Siberian ginseng and American ginseng have similar uses.

PART USED Roots

◾ Gardening

Korean ginseng (*Panax ginseng*) and American ginseng (*P. quinquefolius*) are long-lived deciduous perennials with branched taproots, from which spring long-stalked, divided leaves.

Siberian ginseng (*Eleutherococcus senticosus*), which is part of the same plant family, is a thorny, deciduous, suckering shrub, reaching 3m or more tall, with thick roots, divided leaves and umbels of black berries. Ginsengs need woodland conditions and are a challenge to grow but well worth the effort.

Position Panax species require warm summers and cold winters, deep shade and slightly acidic soil. Siberian ginseng is more tolerant of different conditions.

Ginseng roots (*Panax ginseng*) gathered for sale in a Chinese market.

All ginsengs require moist, rich, well-drained soil.

Propagation Korean and American ginsengs are grown from seed, which germinates slowly and erratically and is usually stratified (see box, page 50). Propagate Siberian ginseng by seed or suckers in spring, by greenwood cuttings in early summer, and by hardwood or root cuttings in winter.

Maintenance Keep well watered during the growing season.

Pests and diseases Ginseng crops are prone to numerous pests and diseases, especially slugs and snails. Protect with copper bands or animal-friendly slug repellents.

Harvesting and storing Harvest Korean and American ginseng roots in autumn from plants that are 6 years or older. Siberian ginseng can be harvested by removing sections of rhizome, leaving the main plant to regenerate. Use ginseng roots fresh or peeled and dried. Store dried ginseng in airtight containers and use within a year.

◾ Herbal medicine

Korean ginseng (*Panax ginseng*), American ginseng (*P. quinquefolius*), Siberian ginseng (*Eleutherococcus senticosus*). Part used: roots. Modern research has shown that these herbs improve the body's capacity to cope with stress, so they have become popular remedies for enhancing mental and physical function during times of overwork, fatigue, or convalescence.

Ashwagandha, the Indian ginseng

Although not related to the ginsengs, ashwagandha (*Withania somnifera*) is sometimes called Indian ginseng as a result of its ability to improve mood, mental capacity and physical strength during recovery from illness and at times of stress. Ashwagandha also appears to have an adaptogenic-like effect on the body as well as positive effects on immune function. However, in contrast to the ginsengs, ashwagandha has a sedative action and in Ayurvedic medicine is sometimes prescribed for insomnia. It is also a tonic herb, high in iron, and can be a valuable remedy for treating anaemia.

American ginseng has recently been successfully trialled as a treatment for reducing the incidence of upper respiratory infections. A number of studies involving both mice and humans have indicated that ginseng may lower blood sugar and suggest that it may be of benefit in the treatment of diabetes – but a great deal of research still needs to be done to confirm that this is the case.

Although the ginsengs appear to benefit a wide range of chronic illnesses, some clinical trials investigating these herbs have produced mixed results, perhaps due to the large variations in the quality, dose, preparation and duration of the different ginsengs used.

For the safe and appropriate use of Korean ginseng, see *Tension and stress*, page 216. For the safe and appropriate use of Siberian ginseng and ashwagandha, see *Tiredness and fatigue*, page 218.

Do not use these herbs if you are pregnant or breastfeeding except with the advice of a doctor or medical herbalist.

Gotu kola

Centella asiatica syn. Hydrocotyle asiatica Apiaceae

The reputed extraordinary longevity of Professor Li Chung Yon, who is said to have died at the age of 256, was attributed to drinking tea made with this Chinese 'long-life herb', which is also an important Ayurvedic plant.

OTHER COMMON NAMES Arthritis herb, Asiatic pennywort
PARTS USED Whole plant, leaves

Gardening

Gotu kola is closely related to marsh pennywort (*Hydrocotyle vulgaris*) and more remotely to celery and parsley. It is a small, creeping, evergreen perennial that spreads by stolons, in a similar manner to strawberries and violets, forming plantlets that root into the ground and eventually form a dense mat. Individual plants have basal rosettes of kidney-shaped, long-stalked leaves with indented margins. The modest flowers are borne in umbels below the leaves. Its natural habitat is in damp places in the tropics, but in cultivation it has proved to be remarkably resilient, surviving light frosts unharmed. Try growing it in a wide, shallow container or beside a pond or stream.

Position It does best in rich, friable, moist soil in full sun or light shade.

Propagation It can be propagated by seed, but is most easily grown from rooted sections of stolon with at least one plantlet attached.

Maintenance Regularly water and weed gotu kola, and make sure that surrounding plants do not smother it. Leaves tend to die-back in winter, but usually resprout in spring. Pot up a few plantlets in autumn in case you lose your stock plant.

Pests and diseases Aphids attack plants grown under cover.

Harvesting and storing Harvest the leaves and use them fresh as required. Dry the leaves out of direct sunlight, spreading them out in a single layer on sheets of kitchen paper. When dry, store in an airtight container for medicinal use and for tea. You can also juice the leaves and add them sparingly to tonic vegetable juices and smoothies.

Herbal medicine

Centella asiatica. Parts used: whole plant, leaves. Gotu kola has been used

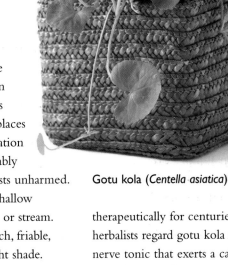
Gotu kola (*Centella asiatica*)

therapeutically for centuries. Ayurvedic herbalists regard gotu kola as an effective nerve tonic that exerts a calming and strengthening effect on nerve and brain cells, helping to improve memory and reduce anxiety.

According to traditional Chinese medicine, gotu kola is believed to slow senility, act as a promoter of longevity and improve rheumatic problems.

Studies investigating the topical and internal use of gotu kola have confirmed an impressive burn and wound-healing capacity, and a strengthening effect on veins, with notable improvement in varicose veins and other vein disorders.

For the safe and appropriate use of gotu kola, consult your doctor or medical herbalist. Do not use gotu kola if you are pregnant or breastfeeding except with the advice of a doctor or medical herbalist.

Gotu kola stimulates collagen production and is used in skin rejuvenation products.

The elixir of youth

According to official records of the Chinese government, Professor Li Chung Yon, a renowned scholar and herbalist, was born in 1677. The story goes that he was a vegetarian who used gotu kola and ginseng and took brisk daily walks while cultivating a calm and serene attitude to life (walking like a pigeon, sitting like a tortoise and sleeping like a dog). When he died in 1933, *The New York Times* reported that he apparently looked like a man in his prime, with his hair and teeth intact. He spent the first 100 years of his life studying and gathering wild herbs, and the latter part lecturing and educating people about herbs and longevity.

Ground ivy

Glechoma hederacea syn. *Nepeta glechoma* Lamiaceae

Ground ivy was important in the brewing of ale until the 16th century when hops became more popular. This gave it the name alehoof, 'hoof' being another word for herb. It was also made into a medicine known as gill tea, from the French *guiller*, to ferment, referring to its use in brewing.

OTHER NAMES Alehoof, gill-go-by-the-hedge, nepeta
PARTS USED Aerial parts

Ground ivy (*Glechoma hederacea*) will thrive in shady areas as well as sun.

■ Gardening

Ground ivy is a hardy evergreen perennial with stoloniferous (creeping) stems that root at the nodes or scramble in hedges. The kidney-shaped leaves have scalloped margins and a minty aroma. In spring and early summer blue-mauve tubular flowers appear in the axils. Ground ivy makes good ground cover under trees and shrubs in semi-wild areas of the garden.

Varieties White-variegated ground ivy ('Variegata') is sold as a trailing plant for containers of summer bedding, although it is perfectly hardy and can be used as an ornamental all year round. It is commercially known as 'nepeta' and is a lovely plant for window boxes and hanging baskets in shaded positions.

Position It prefers well-drained moist conditions in sun or shade.

Propagation The easiest way is by sections of stolon that are starting to root at any time in the growing season. The species can also be raised from seed. Large clumps can be divided in spring.

Variegated ground ivy does not come true from seed but it often produces seedlings with plain green leaves.

Maintenance Ground ivy can be invasive, so it may need controlling.

Pests and diseases None.

Harvesting and storing Harvest plants as they begin to flower and dry on trays in a warm place out of the sun.

■ Herbal medicine

Glechoma hederacea. Parts used: aerial parts. Ground ivy is primarily an anti-catarrhal herb, used mainly to relieve chronic bronchial catarrh, bronchitis and congestive conditions associated with catarrh, such as sinusitis. The volatile oil contains pulegone, which is the main constituent of pennyroyal (*Mentha pulegium* see page 90). This component is known to stimulate uterine muscles and have toxic effects on the liver. Though quantities of this substance are much smaller in ground ivy than in pennyroyal, it indicates that some caution should be exercised when using this herb.

For the safe and appropriate use of ground ivy, consult your doctor or medical herbalist. Do not use ground ivy if you are pregnant, intending to become pregnant, or are breastfeeding.

White variegated ground ivy adds all-year interest to a balcony container.

Heartsease

Viola tricolor Violaceae

This pretty European wild flower, which has acquired an extraordinary number of names, is associated with thought in the language of flowers. Although it may not heal broken hearts, as once reputed, it does have a wide variety of herbal uses.

OTHER COMMON NAMES Herb constancy, herb trinity, Johnny-jump-up, love-in-idleness, wild pansy
PARTS USED Flowers (culinary), aerial parts (medicinally)

Viola tricolor 'Bowles' Black'

■ Gardening

Heartsease is a hardy annual or short-lived perennial with a spreading, low-growing habit and oval, coarsely toothed leaves. It flowers profusely in spring and summer with tiny pansy-like flowers which usually have a purple spur and upper petals, while the remaining three petals are variously coloured purple, white and yellow with characteristic purple 'whiskers'. The flowers are followed by three-valved capsules, which burst open to reveal densely packed, round brown seeds. Heartsease is one of the progenitors of the modern pansy, and the flowers vary considerably in their colour patterns. It makes a delightful subject for containers, borders, gravel areas and the edges of paths, where it will sow itself freely.

Varieties 'Helen Mount' is a heartsease-type with richly coloured flowers of purple, lavender and yellow. In contrast, 'Bowles' Black' has almost black velvety flowers.
Position Heartsease will grow almost anywhere but prefers a moist, cool location in sun or light dappled shade and slightly acidic soil.
Propagation Raise plants from seed in spring or autumn and plant out when large enough. They can also be sown directly into the garden.
Maintenance A gentle clipping over the whole plant in summer will encourage it to bloom through autumn.
Pests and diseases Heartsease encounters few problems.
Harvesting and storing For culinary purposes, harvest the fresh flowers at any time. The aerial parts of the plant are usually harvested for medicinal use when in full flower. To dry the plants, hang them upside down in a well-ventilated place away from direct sunshine.

■ Herbal medicine

Viola tricolor. Parts used: aerial parts. Heartsease may have acquired its name from its reputation as a remedy for heart conditions or from the belief that it acted as a love potion. These days it is regarded as a skin remedy and is used to treat eczema and other weeping skin conditions in both infants and adults. For this purpose it is administered either as an infusion or topically to the area in the form of a compress. When taken internally, the soothing and anti-inflammatory properties of heartsease are also useful for helping to alleviate the symptoms of bronchitis and cystitis. For the safe and appropriate use of heartsease, consult your doctor or herbalist. Do not use if you are pregnant or breastfeeding.

Salad in bloom

Many herbs, including heartsease, have edible flowers, which look very pretty in a salad. (Some flowers are poisonous, so be sure to check before use.) Mix a variety of salad greens with heartsease flowers (the green parts removed) and the flowers of nasturtium, borage, bergamot, fennel, rocket or calendula. Add a light dressing.

Heartsease (*Viola tricolor*)

Hops (*Humulus lupulus*)

Hops

Humulus lupulus Cannabaceae

Malted grains used for brewing beer are very sweet and do not keep well, so bitter herbs, such as ground ivy (*Glechoma hederacea*, see page 66) were traditionally used to improve the flavour and act as preservatives. Hops gradually replaced other herbs in brewing beer and today are one of the most widely grown herbs in the world.

PARTS USED Strobiles (female cones), shoots

■ Gardening

Hop plants are hardy deciduous perennial vines that reach 10m each season. The twining stems are bristly, and leaves are heart-shaped at first, becoming similar to those of a grapevine on mature vines. Only female plants produce strobiles, the small, cone-like inflorescences. Female plants are ornamental and are often planted to climb up arches, pergolas and tripods. **Varieties** 'Aureus' is a popular ornamental form with bright golden leaves. Early maturing 'Fuggle' is one of many varieties grown by home brewers. **Position** Hop plants are very adaptable but prefer an open, sunny position and a moist, humus-rich soil. Choose the position carefully so that the abrasive stems do not catch on passers-by.
Propagation Hop plants can be raised from seed, but as only female plants are required, they are usually propagated by root division in spring or from cuttings.
Maintenance Plants die-back completely in winter. In good conditions, hop plants are invasive, so clumps may need reducing in size when plants are dormant. Clean away all dead material before new shoots appear in spring. Train new growths on a strong support as mature plants are very heavy.
Pests and diseases Downy mildew on leaves and *Verticillium* wilt.
Harvesting and storing Young shoots are harvested in spring for culinary use.

Strobiles are harvested in late summer and dried. Both the pollen and leaves can cause allergic responses.

■ Cooking

Young shoots can be eaten like asparagus, either raw in salads or lightly steamed. Dried hops are an essential ingredient for flavouring beer of all kinds. They can also be added, in very small quantities because of their bitterness, to relaxing herbal tea blends.

■ Herbal medicine

Humulus lupulus. Part used: female flowers (strobiles). Hops are well known for their mild sedative properties and are commonly prescribed with other relaxing herbs for insomnia and difficulty falling asleep. The aromatic essential oil is believed to be responsible for the plant's relaxing effects on the nervous system; the flowers can be used in pillows placed by the bed to induce sleep. Hops' calming effects can also help to reduce anxiety. They also have a gently stimulating effect on sluggish digestion and are a useful remedy for gastrointestinal complaints, particularly those exacerbated by tension and stress. Hops contain oestrogen-like substances and may have potential in alleviating menstrual and menopausal problems.

For the safe and appropriate use of hops, see *Insomnia*, page 220. Do not use if you are pregnant or breastfeeding.

Hopped beer

Brewed in ancient Egypt, hopped beer was mentioned by the Roman writer Pliny, who relished eating the plant's spring growth when it was prepared like asparagus. Hops became widely used in Europe, but in England other bitter herbs were preferred until the 16th century, in part because there was a belief that hops could cause melancholia. Some herbal authorities still advise that patients suffering from depression should avoid hops.

Horseradish and wasabi

Armoracia rusticana Brassicaceae

Horseradish has been used medicinally for a very long time but its popularity as a condiment dates back only to the late 16th century. The pungency of horseradish is caused by mustard oils. Japanese horseradish or wasabi is an oriental relative with an equally strong flavour. It has been cultivated in Japan since the 10th century.

PARTS USED Root and leaves (horseradish); rhizomes (wasabi)

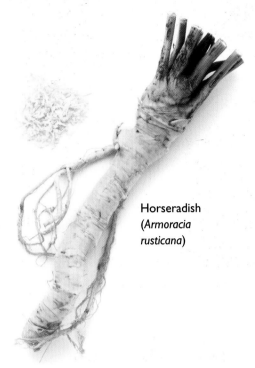

Horseradish (*Armoracia rusticana*)

Gardening

Horseradish is a hardy perennial with a thick, branched taproot and oblong, dock-like leaves up to 20-50cm long. Tiny white flowers appear on tall stems in early summer. Horseradish is very difficult to move or eradicate once established, so think carefully where to plant it. When in doubt, grow in a container. Variegated horseradish ('Variegata') looks very handsome in a large pot. Japanese horseradish or wasabi (*Wasabia japonica*) is a semi-aquatic perennial with heart-shaped leaves about 15cm across, and white cruciform flowers on stems reaching 40cm.

Position Horseradish requires a sunny position and well-dug soil enriched with rotted compost. Wasabi prefers cool shady conditions, between 10°C and 13°C and very clean, slightly alkaline running water.

Propagation In spring, plant pencil-thin sections of lateral horseradish roots horizontally. Cover and firm down. Divide wasabi in spring or autumn.

Maintenance Don't let horseradish dry out, or the roots will become bitter. Keep wasabi shaded, cool and watered.

Pests and diseases Commercially, horseradish is prone to various fungal, virus and rust infections and leaf-eating insects, but garden plants are seldom seriously affected.

Harvesting and storing Pick tender young horseradish and wasabi leaves in spring or whenever new growth is produced. Dig roots and use them fresh at any time in the second and third year; they are at their peak in flavour after the first frost. Store clean roots in sealed plastic bags in the refrigerator for up to 2 months. Lift wasabi roots in spring or autumn of their second year and use fresh or preserve them by drying or freezing. Grind dry roots to a powder and reconstitute as required as the paste does not keep well.

Herbal medicine

Armoracia rusticana. Part used: roots. The hot and pungent nature of these roots is due to the presence of compounds responsible for many of their medicinal properties. Horseradish is antimicrobial and acts as a nasal, sinus and bronchial decongestant, making it a popular remedy for colds and respiratory tract infections. Its antiseptic properties and a diuretic effect have also been used to treat urinary tract infections. Wasabi is believed to have therapeutic effects similar to those of horseradish.

For the safe and appropriate medicinal use of horseradish, see *Hay fever and sinusitis*, page 209. Do not use these herbs in greater than culinary quantities if you are pregnant or breastfeeding.

Cooking

Young horseradish and wasabi leaves can be eaten raw in salads and sandwiches, especially with oily fish or beef. For optimum flavour, peel and grate roots as needed and avoid heating. Alternatively, grate the root (in a well-aired place to avoid the fumes), adding 125ml white wine vinegar and ¼ teaspoon salt to each 250ml of pulp. This will keep for up to two months in the fridge if tightly covered. Use as a condiment for beef or fresh or smoked fish. Wasabi, often in the form of an artificially coloured paste, is served with sushi, sashimi, soba noodles and other Japanese dishes.

Pick the young leaves of horseradish in spring and eat them fresh.

Horsetail

Equisetum arvense, E. hyemale Equisetaceae

The forests where dinosaurs once roamed were full of giant horsetails, some the height of large trees, but the few that remain 350 million years later are small by comparison. An excellent source of silica, they were once used to scrub pots.

OTHER COMMON NAMES Pewterwort, scouring rush
PART USED Sterile stems

Horsetail (*Equisetum hyemale*)

Gardening

Horsetails have slender, hollow, jointed stems with leaves that are reduced to scales. The plants have a deep root system and can spread by rhizomes. Horsetail produces spores in club-like terminal structures, reproducing by cell division of the fallen spores. Long-term grazing on horsetail may cause a condition called equisetosis in livestock.

Horsetails are divided botanically into two major groups: the horsetails, which have whorled branches, and the scouring rushes, which are unbranched.
Varieties The field horsetail, bottle-brush or shave grass (*E. arvense*) grows to 80cm and the sterile stems have whorled branches. The rough horsetail or Dutch rush (*E. hyemale*) produces upright unbranched stems to waist height.
Position Horsetails are primarily located around water sources, but the rhizomes allow them to move into drier

areas. They prefer full sun to part shade and are fully cold-hardy.
Propagation You can grow horsetails in moist soil from small pieces of rhizome or divisions in spring but it can be an invasive weed that is both difficult to control and resistant to herbicides.
Maintenance None required.
Pests and diseases None of note.
Harvesting and storing Harvest the sterile stems in mid to late summer and dry them.

Herbal medicine

Equisetum arvense. Part used: stems. Horsetail has notable astringent and tissue-healing properties due to its exceptionally high silica content. It is particularly helpful for problems of the urinary tract and male reproductive system. With its gentle diuretic action, horsetail is a favoured remedy for mild inflammatory and infectious conditions of the urinary tract, bladder and prostate gland. Perhaps surprisingly considering its diuretic effects, it is also used in the management of incontinence and bedwetting in children.

Horsetail has long been regarded as an excellent herb for removing waste material from the body, and was used for arthritic and skin disorders where the presence of toxins was believed to exacerbate these conditions. Externally, a poultice of horsetail was used to staunch bleeding and promote the repair of slow-healing wounds.

For the safe and appropriate use of horsetail, consult your doctor or medical herbalist. Do not use horsetail if you are pregnant or breastfeeding.

Scouring rush

Rich in silica, horsetails were once every cook's blessing. The hardened longitudinal siliceous ridges on the stems were utilised in ancient Roman times through to the 18th century for scrubbing pots and pans. Horsetail stems were found to be particularly effective for cleaning and polishing pewterware, giving rise to one of the plant's common names – pewterwort. Silica also provided a natural type of non-stick coating for cookware.

Equisetum arvense has whorled branches.

Concentrations of gold have been found in some horsetails — and were seen as a good indicator for gold prospectors.

Houseleek

Sempervivum tectorum Crassulaceae

Houseleeks are the original houseplants, the word *leac* was Anglo-Saxon for 'plant'. In Roman times, houseleeks were grown in urns outside houses. The Holy Roman Emperor Charlemagne decreed that houseleeks should be grown on the roof of every house to protect against lightning.

OTHER COMMON NAMES Common houseleek, hens-and-chicks
PART USED Leaves

Houseleeks (*Sempervivum tectorum*) come in a wide range of leaf colours and forms.

■ Gardening

Houseleeks are hardy mat-forming succulents from mountainous areas of southern Europe. They have rosettes of thick, fleshy, spine-tipped leaves, which are often purple flushed, especially after long dry periods. In summer, mature rosettes produce a solitary, upright stem 20-30cm tall, bearing a cluster of pink star-shaped flowers. After flowering, the rosette dies, having developed several offsets to take its place. Houseleeks are low maintenance plants for pots, troughs and shallow containers, tolerating extended drought and considerable neglect. They also thrive in nooks and crannies where few other plants can be established, such as walls, paving crevices and tiled roofs.

Varieties There are more than 40 species of houseleeks and numerous varieties, but only *S. tectorum* and its varieties should be usedf for medicinal use. They include: 'Nigrum', with maroon-tipped leaves; 'Red Flush', which has reddish green leaves; and 'Sunset', in which the leaves are tinged an orange-red.

Position Well-drained to dry, neutral to alkaline soil in full sun.

Propagation Detach plantlets and pot up separately in spring or summer. Make sure they have a section of stolon (runner) attached to anchor them to the compost or insert into a crevice. Weigh down with a stone or wedge with some moss or mud until established if in a precarious position.

Maintenance Repot containers of houseleeks every 2 to 3 years or when clumps become overcrowded. Do not give houseleeks too much water as they will fail to thrive.

Pests and diseases Overwatering causes rot.

Harvesting and storing Cut leaves as required to use fresh. Houseleeks do not dry successfully.

■ Herbal medicine

Sempervivum tectorum. Part used: Leaves. The fleshy leaves of houseleeks are rich in mucilage and tannins. Mucilage has a cooling, soothing effect, and tannins are astringent, having a tightening effect on tissues, which controls bleeding and helps the healing process. Houseleek is a useful home remedy to have at hand for minor cuts, grazes, stings, scalds, sunburn and burns. A leaf, sliced in half, can be applied directly to the damaged skin, or for larger areas, several leaves can be pulped and applied as a poultice.

Traditionally, houseleek was also used as a remedy for warts and corns, and to soothe the symptoms of conditions that affect the skin, such as shingles and ringworm. Houseleek should not be taken internally.

For the safe and appropriate use of houseleek, consult your doctor or medical herbalist. Do not use houseleek if you are pregnant or breastfeeding except with the advice of a doctor or medical herbalist.

Grow a variety of houseleeks in a pot.

Hyssop

Hyssopus officinalis Lamiaceae

A plant that is grown as much for its beauty and its ability to attract bees and butterflies as for its culinary and medicinal uses, hyssop is an ancient herb that was attributed with cleansing properties in biblical times and for this reason was even used against leprosy.

PARTS USED Flowering spikes, leaves

Hyssop (*Hyssopus officinalis*)

■ Gardening

A hardy, semi-evergreen, perennial sub-shrub that reaches 60cm, hyssop is multistemmed from the base, and has small linear leaves that are borne in whorls up the stems. In summer, the plant bears long slender spikes of lipped, rich blue, nectar-filled flowers borne to one side of the stem only. Hyssop is an attractive, drought-tolerant, easy-going plant that adds colour and interest to borders. It can also be planted as an informal low hedge.

Varieties There is a white-flowered variety, *H. officinalis* f. '*albus*,' and one with pink flowers called 'Rosea'. Rock hyssop (*H. officinalis* subsp. *aristatus*), a dwarf compact form with purple-blue flowers, is good for hedges and edging.

Position Hyssop requires a sunny, well-drained position and will tolerate a poor, stony soil.

Propagation You can easily propagate hyssop by seed sown in spring, or you can grow it from cuttings taken either in spring or autumn. The plants require a minimum spacing of 60cm, or half this distance if you are planting a hedge.

Maintenance To prevent plants from becoming 'leggy', lightly prune after flowering and again in spring.

Pests and diseases Hyssop has few problems. It is often used as a trap plant for cabbage white butterflies around brassicas and planted as a companion plant for grapes.

Harvesting and storing You can harvest the leaves at any time and use them fresh, or dry them out of sunlight before storing in airtight containers. When flowering starts, pick the flower spikes to use fresh, or dry them.

■ Herbal medicine

Hyssopus officinalis. Parts used: aerial parts. Hyssop possesses a remarkable range of medicinal properties. It is particularly suited to relieving conditions of the respiratory tract and is associated with antibacterial and antiviral activity, helping with the removal of catarrh and alleviating fevers. Hyssop is therefore often prescribed for a range of colds, flu, sore throat, feverish conditions, bronchitis and coughs.

Hyssop is also reputed to have a calming effect on the nerves and can assist with reducing anxiety. It has been used to help to bring on delayed menstruation, particularly when the cause has been due to tension and stress. Recent research indicates that hyssop may help to combat herpes infections such as cold sores as a topical agent.

For the safe and appropriate use of hyssop, you should consult your doctor or medical herbalist. Do not use hyssop if you are pregnant or breastfeeding except with the advice of a doctor or medical herbalist.

Rock hyssop (*H. officinalis* subsp. *aristatus*) is a bushy dwarf variety.

The bitter mint-tasting leaves are used to flavour rich foods such as game and pâté.

Iris

Iris spp. Iridaceae

Sculptural and beautiful irises include one important medicinal herb and several that have rhizomes which are dried and ground to make orris root, a powder with a multitude of purposes, from perfumery (as a fixative) and herbal medicine to flavouring gin and chewing gum.

PART USED Rhizomes

Dried orris root can be used in home-made toothpastes (see pages 290–91).

■ Gardening

Two main kinds of iris are grown for commercial orris production: Florentine iris, Iris 'Florentina' (syn. *I.* x *germanica* 'Florentina'), grown near Florence, Italy, for hundreds of years; and the Dalmatian iris (*I. pallida* subsp. *pallida* syn. *I. pallida* var. *dalmatica*, *I. pallida* 'Dalmatica'), which is native to southwestern Croatia. The early flowering 'Florentina' is a tall bearded iris with white, sweetly scented flowers, while those of the Dalmatian iris are a pale lilac with a delicate grape-like scent. Both reach 60-120cm and are excellent hardy perennials for flower borders and herb gardens.

A very different kind of iris, known simply as blue flag (*I. versicolor*), is important in herbal medicine. This is a wetland species from northeastern North American. It is widely grown as an ornamental for garden ponds, reaches 60-90cm tall and has purple or blue-purple flowers with contrasting white veins towards the centre.

Varieties *Iris pallida* has two variegated forms which are very ornamental, even when the plants are not in flower. 'Variegata' has white-striped leaves, and 'Argentea Variegata' has yellow stripes. Blue flag has a form known as 'Kermesina' which bears magenta-plum coloured flowers.

Position Florentine and Dalmatian irises need well-drained soil and full sun. You can grow blue flag in rich, moist to wet soil or shallow water.

Propagation Divide irises in summer after flowering. Each division should have at least one leaf fan attached. Cut back the fans to about 15cm, and plant the rhizomes horizontally so that only the lower half is buried in the soil.

Maintenance Control weeds and remove dead flower stems.

Pests and diseases Rhizome rots can occur in overcrowded or shaded plants. Florentine and Dalmatian iris may be prone to fungal diseases as well as damage by slugs and snails when grown in poorly drained soil.

Harvesting and storing In late summer, dig up the rhizomes, clean them thoroughly and dry them. Cure orris roots for 2 years to intensify the violet fragrance.

The Florentine Iris, *I.* 'Florentina' (syn. *I.* x *germanica* 'Florentina')

■ Herbal medicine

Iris versicolor. Part used: rhizomes. Blue flag has a long history of medicinal use among Native American tribes. Now it is used mainly in the treatment of skin problems such as acne and eczema. In herbal medicine, these conditions are believed to be the result of an accumulation of toxins in the body, and blue flag appears to work by encouraging the liver, bowel and lymphatic system to remove waste material from the body more effectively. Blue flag is often used in combination with other cleansing herbs, such as yellow dock and burdock, for these purposes.

For the safe and appropriate use of blue flag, consult your doctor or medical herbalist. Do not use blue flag if you are pregnant or breastfeeding except with the advice of a doctor or medical herbalist.

■ Around the home

Orris root, a greyish powder with the aroma of violets, is derived from the root of the Florentine and Dalmatian irises. It is used less for its scent than for its fixative ability – it slows the evaporation of essential oils and prolongs the life of perfumes and potpourris. Orris root can be sprinkled around the edges of carpets or under rugs to deter, but not kill, moths and carpet beetles.

Caution: All parts of iris plants, especially the rhizomes, are toxic if consumed. They can also cause skin irritation and allergic reactions in some people.

Jasmine

Jasminum spp. Oleaceae

Many species of jasmine – the delicate floral emblem of Indonesia, Pakistan and the Philippines – are renowned for their superb sensuous scent, and their very valuable essential oil which is produced in several countries for perfumery and aromatherapy.

OTHER COMMON NAME Jessamine
PARTS USED Flowers, roots

Common jasmine (*Jasminum officinale*)

Angel wing jasmine (*Jasminum nitidum*)

▓ Gardening

Common jasmine (*J. officinale*) is a frost-hardy, tall twining climber with compound leaves and five-petalled, intensely fragrant flowers fused into a tube at the base. Brought to Europe in the 16th century, it is now extensively cultivated commercially for its flowers in southern France, Spain, India, Egypt, China, Algeria and Morocco. Jasmines of all kinds are lovely plants for containers, and planted to twine around archways and arbours where their fragrance can be enjoyed to the full. The hardiest species is *J. officinale*. Others need frost-free to tropical conditions but in colder areas make excellent greenhouse plants.

Varieties Colourful forms include 'Argenteovariegatum', with cream variegation, 'Aureum', with gold-splashed leaves, and 'Fiona Sunrise' syn. 'Frojas', which has bright golden foliage. The large-flowered Catalonian jasmine, also known as royal jasmine, poet's jasmine or Spanish jasmine, is variously regarded as a form of *J. officinale* (f. *affine*), or as a separate species, *J. grandiflorum*. Arabian jasmine (*J. sambac*) is used to make a fragrant tisane in China, the blossoms being hand-picked early in the morning and mixed with dried green or Oolong tea. Native to tropical Asia, it forms an arching bush.

Double-flowered forms of *J. sambac*, favoured for garlands and religious ceremonies, include the very double, miniature rose-like 'Grand Duke of Tuscany', known as kudda-mulla, and the semi-double 'Maid of Orléans'. Other fragrant, white-flowered species include angel wing jasmine (*J. laurifolium* f. *nitidum*), the pink-budded *J. polyanthum*, Azores jasmine (*J. azoricum*), and Canary Island jasmine (*J. odoratissimum*), *J. multiflorum* and *J. floribundum*.

Position Jasmine plants prefer rich well-drained soil and full sun.
Propagation Propagate jasmine from semi-ripe cuttings in summer.
Maintenance Trim jasmines immediately after they have flowered, thinning out oldest shoots.
Pests and diseases Jasmine plants grown in the open usually have few problems; however, those grown under glass can be attacked by whitefly, mealy bugs and spider mites.
Harvesting and storing Gather opening flowers in the early morning for adding to tea. You can dry them for herbal use. The roots of *J. sambac* can be lifted in autumn and then dried for medicinal use.

Jasmine essential oil

The delicate, star-shaped flowers of this evergreen vine are distilled to form an essential oil with a rich, warm floral scent that is important in perfumery. It blends well with other 'floral'-style oils, such as rose, and is particularly helpful in preparations for dry, irritated or sensitive skin. The oil is also used in aromatherapy as an antidepressant and relaxant.

The name 'jasmine' comes from the Persian 'yasmin', which means 'gift from God'.

Juniper

Juniperus communis Cupressaceae

Juniper is perhaps best known as the principal flavouring of gin: the word 'gin', a shortened form of the Dutch genever, is derived from the Latin juniperus. In medieval times, juniper was regarded as an antidote to poisons and a protection against snakebite and plague.

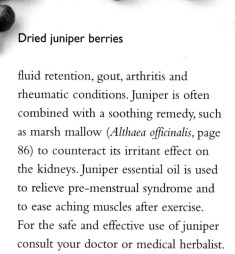

Dried juniper berries

OTHER COMMON NAME Common juniper
PARTS USED Fruits ('berries'), oil

■ Gardening

Juniper is a very hardy small evergreen conifer, rarely more than 6m and very variable, distributed widely throughout the Northern Hemisphere. It has red-brown papery bark and whorls of three linear, sharply pointed, grey-green leaves which have a single white stripe on the inner surface. Tiny oval male cones and rounded female cones form on separate plants, females bearing spherical green fruits that turn black with a grey bloom as they ripen, which takes 2-3 years. Junipers are tough, adaptable plants with a wide range of colours and shapes. Female plants of common juniper are available from specialist herb nurseries.

Varieties Var. *depressa* is a good ground cover, with a prostrate habit and upturned shoot tips. 'Compressa' is small, columnar and slow growing, a perfect accent in alpine troughs or containers for winter interest. 'Hibernica' is larger and more vigorous, reaching 3-5m tall.

Position Juniper thrives in most soils. It also tolerates exposed positions and severe cold.

Propagation The quickest way is by ripewood cuttings in early autumn; seeds may take up to five years to germinate.

Maintenance If branches of columnar bushes are splayed out by snow, tie them back invisibly using black cotton.

Pests and diseases Juniper webber moth, scale and aphids may cause damage to leaves.

Harvest Fruits are gathered by shaking branches over a groundsheet. Dry thoroughly before storing in airtight jars.

■ Herbal medicine

Juniperus communis. Part used: fruits. Juniper contains a complex volatile oil which has diuretic effects, and other compounds with anti-inflammatory, antioxidant, antiseptic and antiviral properties. Used since Roman times to ease rheumatism, digestive and bronchial problems, today it is used for cystitis, fluid retention, gout, arthritis and rheumatic conditions. Juniper is often combined with a soothing remedy, such as marsh mallow (*Althaea officinalis*, page 86) to counteract its irritant effect on the kidneys. Juniper essential oil is used to relieve pre-menstrual syndrome and to ease aching muscles after exercise. For the safe and effective use of juniper consult your doctor or medical herbalist. Do not use juniper for medicinal purposes if you have kidney disease or are pregnant or breastfeeding.

■ Cooking

Juniper berries have a resinous flavour that goes well with rabbit and hare, and in wild boar and venison pâtés. In Germany, juniper flavours hams and sauerkraut and is used in Latwerge, a conserve to accompany cold meats. Adding a few juniper berries when cooking cabbage reduces unpleasant odours. Juniper extracts are also used in perfumery, and as a flavouring in gin, beers, liqueurs and meat products.

Leaves and berries of *Juniperus communis*

Lavender

Lavandula spp. Lamiaceae

Popular around the world, fragrant lavender is becoming one of the most important botanicals with a wide range of medicinal uses, earning it the title of 'the Swiss Army knife of herbal medicine'. Fresh or dried, lavender also has many applications around the home and the essential oil is used in homemade air-fresheners and cleaning products.

PART USED Flowers

English lavender (*Lavandula angustifolia*)

■ Gardening

There are 22 species of lavender, found from the Canary Islands eastward into western India. All are woody sub-shrubs with narrow fragrant foliage, from bright green to silver, and spikes of tiny tubular flowers in every shade of purple, pink and white. They are vital components of herb gardens and cottage gardens and make excellent drought-tolerant container plants and informal dwarf hedges. Several species and numerous varieties are grown worldwide in suitable climates, both as ornamentals for their wonderful scents and colours, and commercially for essential oils and dried flowers. Botanically, lavenders divide into three subgroups and eight sections, but for gardeners, there are four main kinds: true or English lavenders (*L. angustifolia*); lavandin or intermedia hybrid lavenders (*L.* x *intermedia*); butterfly lavenders (*L. stoechas*, *L. pedunculata* and *L. viridis*); and tender lavenders.

English lavender

English or true lavender (*L. angustifolia* syn. *L. vera*, *L. officinalis*) occurs mainly in mountainous areas of southern France and adjoining parts of the Italian Alps at altitudes of 500 to 1500m. It has unbranched flowering stems and reaches 40-80cm, with narrow grey-green leaves and violet-blue flowers.

Both fresh and dried flowers of English lavender are used in cooking (including herb mixtures such as *herbes de Provence*) and craftwork, and its very fragrant camphor-free essential oil, is prized in the perfumery industry, herbal medicine and aromatherapy. Lavender has been grown in the south of France on a large scale for the perfume trade since the 17th century, though some of the finest oil comes from Norfolk. The main variety that is grown in France is 'Maillette', with strongly fragrant flowers and a sprawling, upswept habit, reaching 60-70cm, while in England, 'No. 9' is popular for its prolific flower spikes which are produced early in the season.

Varieties Excellent dwarf varieties include 'Lavenite Petite' (very compact, grey-green with short stubby violet-blue spikes, 50cm) and 'Nana Alba' (white flowers, grey-green leaves, 35-50cm high). Medium-height varieties include 'Hidcote' (grey leaves, long dense spikes of purple, strongly scented flowers, 50-65cm), 'Munstead' (grey-green leaves, violet-blue flowers, 65 x 65cm), and 'Ashdown Forest' (a dense, tidy mound, 60 x 100cm, green leaves, soft lilac flowers). Taller varieties include 'Rosea' syn. 'Jean Davis', 'Munstead Pink' (bright green leaves, soft pink flowers to 75cm),

Propagate varieties of lavender by cuttings taken in summer (see *Stem cuttings*, page 169).

To deter bugs, crumble dried leaves into boxes of documents or drop crushed leaves behind shelved books.

'Melissa' (grey-green foliage, mauve-pink flowers, very sweet scent, 70 x 90cm), and 'Twickel Purple' (75-100cm, long-stemmed, sprawling spikes of fragrant violet flowers).

Lavandin

Lavandin or intermedia hybrid lavender (*L. x intermedia*) is a cross between English lavender (*L. angustifolia*) and spike or broad-leaved lavender (*L. latifolia*). The latter makes a bigger, dome-shaped bush than English lavender, reaching 1m, with branched flower stems and relatively broad silver-grey leaves. It is less hardy and has a wider distribution at lower elevations, occurring in much of Spain, as well as in southwest and central France, northwest Italy and the Balkans.

Spike lavender produces a pungent camphoraceous oil, known as oil of spike or aspic (*oleum spicae*) which has insecticidal effects, widely used in veterinary products. On hillsides where both *L. angustifolia* and *L. latifolia* grow, natural hybrids known as *lavandin* occur, resulting in plants with paired flowering side branches that are stronger-growing than English lavender. Though not quite as hardy, they tolerate humidity better and yield twice the volume of essential oil. Because the oil contains camphor, it is valued at half that of English lavender.

Woolly lavender (*L. dentata*)

Spike lavender is seldom cultivated, but lavandin is a major crop worldwide for its essential oil, which is used for toiletries and household cleaning and laundry products.

Varieties A popular variety for essential oil production is 'Grosso', which gives large yields of a highly camphoraceous oil. It makes a large, splayed bush, up to 1.6m, with long stems that are also good for cutting and drying. 'Super' is another French variety, with low-camphor oil which is much used in soaps. There are many fine landscape and hedging varieties among the intermedias. Some of the best are 'Alba' (vigorous, upright, to 110cm, grey-green leaves, white flowers from midsummer to autumn), 'Hidcote Giant' (a compact dome of green-grey foliage 90 x 185cm, long, blunt-ended spikes of violet flowers), and 'Walvera' syn. 'Walberton's Silver Edge' (shorter plant, cream-edged leaves, violet-blue flowers).

Butterfly lavender

Also referred to as papillon or stoechas lavenders, these have compressed flower spikes shaped rather like a pineapple surmounted by flag-like sterile bracts. They include *L. stoechas*, variously known as French, Italian or Spanish lavender, which grows on dry hillsides and coastal mountain ranges along the Mediterranean basin. It has short flower stems and relatively short sterile bracts, while Spanish or Portuguese lavender (*L. pedunculata* syn. *L. stoechas* subsp. *pedunculata*), which occurs in northeast Portugal and north, south and central Spain, has long stems and longer sterile bracts. The unusual green lavender (*L. viridis*) has bright green, sticky, highly aromatic leaves, tiny white flowers and greenish white sterile bracts. The hardiest of the three is *L. stoechas*, which can take -5°C, though its

Cotton lavender

Cotton lavender (*Santolina chamaecyparissus*) is not related to lavenders but at first glance has similar foliage. The grey, toothed leaves have a chamomile-lavender aroma and are very useful for repelling moths and silverfish. Add the dried leaves to sachets and place with stored blankets and other woollens, or sprinkle under rugs. Cotton lavender has a compact habit that makes it ideal for low hedges or edging paths. Prune hard to remove the yellow button flowers when planted in a knot garden (see page 148).

hardiness depends very much on soil and aspect. All are suited to low-altitude gardens on very free-draining soils, especially those near the sea. They also make excellent drought-resistant subjects for containers and dry sunny borders near walls.

Varieties Good forms include the rather tender 'Kew Red' (compact mounds, 45 x 45cm, deep red-purple flowers, bright pink-red bracts), 'Liberty' (hardier, 40 x 45cm, plump spikes, mauve-violet bracts), and 'Snowman' (small, neat, fairly hardy, white flowers and white, green-veined bracts).

Classic varieties of *L. pedunculata* include 'James Compton', and 'Papillon', which are rather similar, with long purple 'ears'.

Lavender continued

Some of the best butterfly lavenders are recent hybrids between the three different species. They tend to be more compact, fast growing, very flowering and, in optimum conditions, hardy to -5°C. These include 'Fathead' (many stubby spikes, mauve-pink bracts), 'Helmsdale' (vigorous, bushy, to 70cm, distinctive burgundy bracts), and 'Willow Vale' (60 x 50cm, upright habit, almost black flowers, pale purple bracts. Varieties bred in Australia are increasingly popular, including the Madrid Series, which can reach 1m and has long stalks and showy spikes, and the Barcelona Series, with a smaller, more compact habit and short-stalked spikes. Both come in a range of distinctive colours.

Tender lavenders

A number of very beautiful lavenders cannot cope with cold wet winters or severe frosts. They are best grown as container plants or short-lived perennials for summer borders. Canary Islands lavender (*L. canariensis*) has densely hairy, divided leaves, branched flower stems and clusters of narrow dark spikes with pale blue-violet flowers. Fringed or toothed lavender (*L. dentata*) occurs in the Iberian Peninsula, North Africa and southwest Asia. It has linear leaves with neatly scalloped edges and unbranched flower spikes which have conspicuous bracts below each flower. Woolly lavender (*L. lanata*), found in southern Spain, has leaves that are heavily felted with hairs, and three-pronged spikes of deep purple flowers. Cut-leaved or fernleaf lavender (*L. multifida*), a western Mediterranean species, has downy, much-divided leaves and very long, often branched flower stems. This species is very quick and easy from seed, and can be treated as an annual. Pinnate lavender (*L. pinnata*), from Lanzarote and Madeira, has intensely silver-grey foliage, deeply divided leaves and spikes of violet-blue flowers which are often multi-headed.

Hybrids between these species are well worth growing in very sheltered positions or with protection in winter. One of the best is *L.* x *christiana*, a cross between *L. pinnata* and *L. canariensis*,

In Europe lavender is harvested from July to September, often by hand.

which is extremely vigorous and fast-growing from cuttings, reaching 1m, with finely cut grey leaves and branched flower spikes almost all year round. Another is *L.* x *heterophylla* (also known as *L.* x *allardii*), the fairly hardy progeny of *L. dentata* and spike lavender, which makes a large shrub, to 1.2m, with grey-green, slightly toothed leaves and pointed spikes of blue-violet flowers. Also very attractive is *L.* x *ginginsii* 'Goodwin Creek Grey', a cross between *L. dentata* and *L. lanata* has grey-green, slightly toothed leaves and long, often curved, pointed flower spikes. *L.* x *chaytorae*, a fairly hardy cross between English and woolly lavenders, has two good varieties: 'Gorgeous', with outstanding silver foliage, 70 x 70cm; and 'Sawyers' (or 'Quicksilver'), which forms a wide, silver-grey mound, 105 x 150cm. Both have long spikes of intense violet-blue flowers.

Position All lavenders need excellent drainage and full sun. Most prefer calcareous, sandy or stony soils, though *L. stoechas* tolerates dry, slightly acidic conditions. They are better grown fairly hard, with little in the way of watering or feeding. Container-grown lavenders benefit from a slow-release fertiliser when potting, and an annual top-dressing of fresh compost.

Propagation Varieties are propagated by semi-ripe cuttings in summer, but species are grown from seed sown in

These racks of commercially grown lavender will be dried out of direct sunlight in a dry place to retain as much of their natural colour and scent as possible.

Spritz still-damp washing with Lavender linen water (see page 294) and hang it out to dry. Alternatively, you can put the linen water into your steam iron.

spring. All are best propagated every 3 to 5 years as older plants tend to become sparse and untidy.

Maintenance Prune lavenders annually, preferably in early spring. English lavenders and lavandin hybrids can also be shaped during harvesting. Cut back growths by about a half but never into old wood or the plants may die. Deadhead specimen plants regularly.

Pests and diseases Lavenders are generally free of pests as well as diseases.

Harvesting and storing Harvest lavenders in midsummer when spikes are one- to two-thirds open. Tie lavender stems in bunches and hang them upside down to dry before stripping off the flowers. The oil is steam distilled which needs specialist equipment.

■ Herbal medicine

Lavandula angustifolia. Part used: flowers. An age-old remedy for calming and soothing the nerves, improving mood and relaxing muscles, the gorgeous scent of lavender and its essential oil are commonly used for inducing a restful sleep, relieving depression and anxiety and for other disorders relating to a

A history of epic proportions

The ancient Druids threw lavender into bonfires at the midsummer solstice and put it into love spells. It was also burnt during childbirth to cleanse the air, calm the mother and bless the baby. The Romans scented their public baths with it – hence its name, from the Latin word *lavare*, meaning 'to wash'. In the Middle Ages lavender was used in a powdered form as a condiment and food preservative, used to strew earthen floors, and was a favourite in monastery gardens for its many uses in cooking, healing and simple hygiene.

nervous or tense state, including stomach upsets.

Lavender flowers can be taken as an infusion or added to a bath to soothe and aid in relaxation. Apply undiluted essential oil to relieve burns and insect bites or to prevent cuts and grazes becoming infected. You can add essential oil to massage oil to help to relieve muscle tension and headaches.

For the safe and appropriate internal use of lavender, consult your doctor or medical herbalist. For its topical uses, see *Depression and anxiety*, page 217, and *First aid*, page 226.

You should not use lavender if you are pregnant or breastfeeding, except with the advice of a doctor or medical herbalist.

■ Around the home

If you could choose only one herb for household use, lavender would have to be at the top of the list. Apart from its pretty flowers and much-loved scent, lavender is antibacterial, antibiotic, antiviral, antiseptic, deodorising and insect repelling, which means that you can use it in the living room, kitchen, bathroom, laundry, nursery and patio, as

Lavender essential oil is antiseptic and antibacterial, ideal for blemished skin.

well as in your wardrobes and drawers, on your pets and on your skin.

Use the dried flowers and leaves to make moth-repellent sachets and lavender bags (see *Craft*, pages 302–5) – they both contain the aromatic oil that many insects hate.

Infuse distilled white vinegar with the flowers and leaves, fresh or dried, for an inexpensive and very effective spray for cleaning and disinfecting surfaces.

Add drops of lavender essential oil to environmentally friendly unscented kitchen and laundry cleaning products for a fresh, natural scent.

Dampen a cotton-wool ball and add a few drops of lavender essential oil. Drop it into your kitchen bin, or the dust container of the vacuum cleaner, to eliminate stale odours.

■ Cooking

Lavender's culinary applications are limited, although the leaves and flowers are edible. They are used in the Moroccan spice blend *ras-el-hanout* and in the French *herbes de Provence*. Lavender goes well in sweet dishes containing cream, such as ice cream. It can be added to shortbread and icings and used in jams and jellies. Crystallise the flowers as edible cake decorations (see page 386). Make sure that any flowers you use for culinary purposes have not been sprayed with garden chemicals and check the variety for flavour to make sure it is not too camphoraceous.

Lemon balm

Melissa officinalis Lamiaceae

Lemon balm smells like sweet lemon and is used in herbal teas, wines and liqueurs as well as in many eau-de-cologne formulations, including Carmelite water. Handfuls of the leaves, which contain a lemon-scented oil, were once used to polish wooden furniture.

OTHER COMMON NAMES Balm, melissa
PART USED Leaves

Lemon balm (*Melissa officinalis*)

Gardening

Lemon balm is a hardy perennial that bears some resemblance to its close relations, the mints. It is multi-stemmed, growing to about 80cm, with ovate, regularly toothed green leaves. The insignificant lipped flowers, a favourite with bees, are pale yellow, and borne in clusters in the axils of the uppermost leaves. Lemon balm is worth growing for its fragrance alone, and there are some attractive forms that are ornamental too.

Varieties While the common form has a fresh lemon fragrance, varieties with different scents, include 'Lime Balm', with a lime aroma. Two colour variations are available: 'Variegata' is a gold-splashed form, and 'All Gold' has pure golden foliage in spring. The dwarf form, 'Compacta', is good for ground cover, reaching 10-15cm and non-flowering.

Position Lemon balm is happy in either sun or partial shade and well-drained but moist soil. Golden forms tend to scorch in full sun. It also grows well in pots.

Propagation You can raise lemon balm easily from seed, and by cuttings or divisions taken in spring and autumn. Grow named varieties from tip cuttings, which will root easily.

Maintenance If you do not want seedlings, or you desire a new flush of foliage, cut back the whole plant, including the flowering heads. Cut back 'All Gold' regularly to maintain its colour. Remove any plain green shoots from both 'All Gold' and 'Variegata'.

Pests and diseases Lemon balm is prone to powdery mildew, particularly in dry conditions.

Harvesting and storing Harvest the fresh foliage as required. To dry, cut the plant down to about 7.5cm when the dew has dried, secure the stems in small bunches with rubber bands, and hang upside down in a well-ventilated area out of direct sunlight. Strip off the dried leaves and store them in airtight containers in a cool place.

Herbal medicine

Melissa officinalis. Lemon balm's mild sedative and mood-enhancing effects are commonly used to treat sleep disorders, restlessness, anxiety and depression. It is also suited to gastrointestinal problems and can help with flatulence, spasm and nausea, particularly when these are aggravated by periods of stress and tension. Recent scientific studies have shown that lemon balm has antiviral effects, and topical preparations of the herb have been used to relieve the symptoms of cold sores, which are caused by the herpes virus.

For the safe and appropriate use of lemon balm, see *Tension and stress*, page 210. Don't use lemon balm if you are pregnant or breastfeeding, except with the advice of a doctor or medical herbalist.

Cooking

Lemon balm goes with most foods complemented by lemon flavours. Use the leaves in tea, salads, cordials, fruit dishes, wine cups and chilled summer drinks or in stuffings for poultry or fish.

From nymph to bee

Lemon balm's association with bees goes back to ancient times. According to Greek mythology, Melissa was one of the nymphs who hid Zeus from his father Cronus, feeding him milk and honey. Once Zeus was in charge of Olympus, he changed her into a queen bee.

Lemongrass

Cymbopogon citratus Poaceae

Lemongrass, a tall tropical grass with a powerful lemon fragrance, is widely used in the cooking of Thailand, Vietnam and other Southeast Asian countries. It makes a vitamin A rich tea, and the essential oil is used in many commercial toiletries.

PART USED Stems

Harvested lemongrass

Gardening

There are about 55 species of *Cymbopogon*. The best known is West Indian lemongrass (*C. citratus*), one of several species with a citrus aroma. Its narrow, leafy stalks grow in large clumps that reach 1.5m. In cool climates, ideally between 18°C and 38°C, plants can be grown in a large pot and overwintered indoors at a minimum of 10°C.

Varieties East Indian lemongrass or Cochin lemongrass (*C. flexuosus*) is also widely grown for its essential oil. Ceylon citronella (*C. nardus*) and Java citronella (*C. winterianus*) share the lemon scent of citronella. Palmarosa, geranium grass or rosha grass (*C. martinii*) has a smell of rose geranium when crushed. The closely related ginger grass (*C. martinii* var. *sofia*) has a harsher scent.

Lemongrass (*Cymbopogon citratus*)

Position This herb is best suited to a sunny position, well-drained soil, ample warmth and high humidity.

Propagation To propagate, carefully divide the clump. Raise other species, mentioned above, by seed. Feed with seaweed fertiliser.

Maintenance Water plants regularly.

Pests and diseases Crown rot can occur in plants grown in poorly drained or flooded soils.

Harvesting and storing Harvest stems as required. Cut the upper green part into segments and dry out of direct sunlight, store in airtight containers and use it for tea. For cooking, wrap white bulbous lower portion in cling film and store in the fridge for several weeks.

Herbal medicine

Cymbopogon citratus. Part used: stems. Traditionally, lemongrass tea was used to treat digestive upsets, stomach ache, cramping and vomiting. It was also used for coughs, fevers, high blood pressure and exhaustion.

Lemongrass has also traditionally been known for pain relief and used internally as an infusion for nerve and rheumatic pain. As a topical remedy, lemongrass and its essential oil can ease the pain of headaches, abdominal pain, aching joints and muscles, and neuralgia.

For the safe medicinal use of this herb, consult your doctor or medical herbalist. Do not use lemongrass in

Natural protection

A natural insect repellent, lemon grass offers some protection from fleas, ticks, lice and mosquitoes. The essential oil can be used in an oil burner. Alternatively, combine a few drops with equal amounts of eucalyptus oil in a water spray and lightly spritz over outdoor furniture on summer evenings. Or, light a candle made with citronella (below), a close relative of lemongrass.

greater than culinary quantities if you are pregnant or breastfeeding.

Cooking

The subtle citrus flavour of lemongrass goes well in Southeast Asian cooking and is often teamed with chillies and coconut milk. Lemongrass is also an excellent addition to Western cooking, particularly in fish and seafood dishes. Use the lower white part of the fresh stems and slice finely crossways to avoid a fibrous texture in the finished dish. If using a whole stem or large pieces, bruise first to release the flavour and remove before serving.

Lemon verbena

Aloysia citriodora syn. *A. triphylla, Lippia citriodora* Verbenaceae

The delicious lemon fragrance of this herb has long been prized for use in tisanes, liqueurs, cooking, potpourri and perfumery. *Aloysia* is a reference to Maria Luisa, Princess of Parma, wife of King Charles IV of Spain, and the connection gives the herb its Spanish name, *yerba Luisa*.

OTHER COMMON NAMES Herb Louisa, lemon beebrush
PARTS USED Leaves, flowers

Lemon verbena leaves infused in vinegar.

Gardening

A frost-hardy, deciduous shrub, lemon verbena has arching branches and pointed leaves arranged in whorls of three around the stems. In summer it bears terminal panicles of tiny, four-petalled, white or pale lavender flowers.
Position Lemon verbena requires full sun, shelter, and free-draining loam with nearly neutral pH.
Propagation Propagate by softwood cuttings in summer.
Maintenance Lemon verbena is cut back by frost and should be mulched in cold winters. Alternatively, grow it in a pot and give protection during winter dormancy. Trim to shape in spring. Bushes often leaf out very late so don't discard them prematurely.

In mild climates, lemon verbena can grow to 5m, bearing tiny flowers in summer.

Pests and diseases Under greenhouse conditions, lemon verbena is prone to whitefly and spider mites.
Harvesting and storing Leaves can be harvested at any time to use fresh or for air-drying.

Herbal medicine

Aloysia citriodora syn. *Lippia citriodora* syn. *A. triphylla*. Parts used: aerial parts. Lemon verbena is used as a digestive aid for symptoms of flatulence and colic. It is thought to help with insomnia and nervous agitation. Lemon verbena is also prescribed for feverish conditions. For the safe and appropriate use of these herbs, consult your doctor or medical herbalist. Do not use these herbs if you are pregnant or breastfeeding.

Cooking

The leaves are best used fresh and young. Use sparingly, or the flavour can overwhelm the food. Lemon verbena is used in many herbal teas to impart a fragrant flavour, and can be substituted for lemongrass in many Asian recipes.

The leaves give a lemon flavour to fruit salads and other fruit dishes, desserts and drinks. Infuse in custard-based sauces for desserts, or finely chop and add to Asian dishes, poultry and stuffings. Add whole leaves to apple jelly, and chopped young leaves to fruit salads. With its digestive and relaxant properties, lemon verbena tea is ideal for drinking after dinner.

Sweet relation

The herb world has a number of extraordinary sweeter-than-sugar plants, one of which is also a member of the Verbenaceae family. Aztec sweet herb (*Phyla scaberrima* syn. *Lippia dulcis*) is a tender, semi-prostrate perennial with short spikes of white flowers and oval leaves that suffuse red in the sun. It grows wild in various parts of Central America, Mexico and the West Indies. The leaves contain hernandulcin, which is about three times sweeter than sugar, and with a high percentage of camphor. Strains high in camphor taste unpleasant and should be avoided as potentially toxic but there is a Cuban chemotype with only a trace of camphor.

Paraguay sweet herb (*Stevia rebaudiana*) is a tall perennial in the Asteraceae family. It was the *yerbe dulce* of the Guarani Indians, who used it to sweeten yerba maté, a tea made from a species of holly (*Ilex paraguariensis*). Stevia contains stevioside, which is up to 300 times sweeter than sugar.

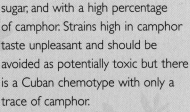

Lime

Tilia spp. Tiliaceae

Known as the 'tree of life' for its many medicinal uses; in the medieval period lime was associated with the Virgin Mary, and was planted for its fragrant healing flowers and to provide shade in monastery gardens.

OTHER COMMON NAMES Linden, tilia
PART USED Flowers

Lime (*Tilia cordata*)

◼ Gardening

Lime trees are grown for their clusters of pale green bracts and fragrant yellow flowers which draw bees to their nectar. Hives placed around flowering trees yield prized lime blossom honey. Small-leafed lime (*T. cordata*) is the main species harvested. It should not be confused with the citrus lime (*Citrus aurantiifolia*). Lime is known as linden in Germany and *tilleul* in France. When planting as landscape trees, avoid overhanging seats and parking areas as foliage can exude sticky honeydew in summer.

Varieties Small-leafed lime (*T. cordata*) is a small to medium deciduous tree (10-25m) with glossy, dark green, heart-shaped leaves. Its varieties include 'Greenspire' with a smaller conical habit. Other species used herbally are common lime (*T. x europaea*) and large-leafed lime (*T. platyphyllos*). Both make much larger specimens, reaching about 30m.

Position Lime trees prefer moist neutral to alkaline soil in a sunny open position.

Propagation The easiest way is by removing suckers in winter and potting up separately. Fresh ripe seed needs stratifying for 3-5 months before sowing in spring (see page 50).

Maintenance Common limes tend to sucker, which spoils the shape of the tree. They should be removed when the tree is dormant.

Pests and diseases Limes are prone to scale insects on branches, and aphids and gall mites on the leaves. They are also susceptible to honey fungus. Ensure good growing conditions to prevent these problems.

Harvesting and storing Collect clusters of flowers as soon as the blossom is open. Do not harvest once the petals have fallen as the developing fruits are narcotic. Spread out the clusters and thoroughly air-dry before storing.

◼ Herbal medicine

Tilia spp. Parts used: flowers (with bracts). Lime flowers are a common ingredient of herbal teas prescribed to help to induce restful sleep, especially in children. The plant has a sedative and calming effect on nerves and muscles, and can help to reduce restlessness, tension and anxiety.

Lime flowers are a specific remedy for certain circulatory disorders. They relax the blood vessel walls, so have been used to treat high blood pressure. The flowers can be helpful as part of the treatment and prevention of atherosclerosis (hardening of the arteries).

Lime flowers are beneficial in feverish conditions such as colds, influenza and other respiratory infections.

For the safe and appropriate use of lime flowers, see *High blood pressure and cholesterol*, page 228. Do not use lime flowers if you are pregnant or breastfeeding except with the advice of a doctor or medical herbalist.

Celebrating lime blossom

Linden trees are popular ornamentals in Europe, where the flowering tips are harvested at their peak and air-dried for use in lime blossom tea, a particularly popular tisane in France.

The centre of production is Buis les Baronnies (below), a medieval town that each July celebrates an annual lime blossom festival, together with their annual harvest sales.

Liquorice

Glycyrrhiza glabra Papilionaceae

In 1305, King Edward I taxed imports of continental liquorice to pay for repairs to London Bridge: domestic crops became concentrated around Pontefract, where it was grown by Dominican monks.

PARTS USED Roots, stolons (runners)

Liquorice (*Glycyrrhiza glabra*)

■ Gardening

Liquorice is a deep-rooted, shrubby, herbaceous perennial to about 1.5m. It spreads underground via extensive stolons. Above ground, it has pinnate leaves with 9-17 leaflets and spikes of tiny purple pea flowers. Native to southern Europe and southwest Asia, liquorice thrives on the rich alluvial plains of Turkey which, with Spain and Greece, is a leading supplier. Liquorice is an interesting focal point or background plant for a herb garden.

Varieties The three recognised botanical varieties are: Spanish or Italian liquorice (*G. glabra* var. *glabra*), Russian liquorice (*G. glabra* var. glandulifera) and *G. glabra* var. violacea. Other species used in a similar way are Chinese or Mongolian liquorice (*G. uralensis*) and Manchurian liquorice (*G. pallidiflora*).

Position Liquorice prefers a rich, deep, sandy loam and a sunny position.

Propagation As liquorice is slow from seed, new crops are usually propagated

Slices of dried liquorice root

using sections of root that are planted out in spring.

Maintenance Restrict spread by selectively harvesting stolons as they spread from the main clump. Cut down dead stems when plants are dormant.

Pests and diseases There are no significant problems.

Harvesting and storing For best-quality root, dig roots in autumn when 3 years old. Clean and dry thoroughly.

■ Herbal medicine

Glycyrrhiza glabra. Part used: roots. Scientific investigations are confirming many of the traditional uses of liquorice root. It is a common ingredient in many respiratory remedies for its soothing effects and ability to expel mucus and

is used to treat coughs, bronchitis and catarrhal lung conditions.

A compound called glycyrrhizin is responsible for the healing effects of liquorice on gastrointestinal ulcers and inflammation of the digestive system. It also acts as a tonic for the adrenal glands, so liquorice is often prescribed as a supportive remedy for stress and exhaustion. As liquorice is a potent herb with serious side effects if taken to excess, for its safe and appropriate use, consult a doctor or medical herbalist. Do not use liquorice if you are, elderly, pregnant, on the Pill, breastfeeding, or have high blood pressure.

■ Natural beauty

This herb is an effective natural lightener for brown age spots. For best results, use for mild discoloration with a natural fruit peel with vitamin C and alpha hydroxy acids to slough off dead skin.

■ Cooking

Liquorice root is one of many herbs used in Chinese master stocks, adding to their intensity and depth of flavour. It is also a mellowing ingredient in some herb teas. Add chopped root sparingly (it can be bitter) when stewing fruit. Liquorice 'sticks' are sections of root which are sucked or chewed like sweets.

Fit for an emperor

Pontefract, or pomfret, cakes became a popular sweet in England in the 16th century. These soft, flat discs made with liquorice, gum arabic and molasses were stamped with a stylised image of Pontefract Castle. They are still made and loved, along with another English favourite, the distinctive multi-coloured liquorice allsorts. It is said that Napoléon Bonaparte always carried liquorice lozenges, which were based on Pontefract cakes.

Lovage

Levisticum officinale Apiaceae

Lovage has an intense celery flavour that's perfect for winter dishes, but it is far easier to grow than celery. Traditionally used in aphrodisiacs and love potions, lovage is sometimes called 'Maggi plant' as its flavour is reminiscent of Maggi bouillon cubes.

OTHER COMMON NAME Love parsley
PARTS USED Leaves, stalks, seeds

Lovage (*Levisticum officinale*)

■ Gardening

Lovage is native to the eastern Mediterranean and is closely related to both angelica and celery. This hardy perennial plant, with large, glossy, celery-like leaves, grows to 2m. The tiny yellow flowers, borne in umbels, are followed by oval seeds (fruits), which can also be used for flavouring. Lovage needs plenty of space and produces large quantities of foliage, so plant a single specimen where it will not crowd smaller herbs. Remember to mark its position as the plant dies down completely in winter.

Varieties Two other close relatives are worth growing for flavouring. Similar in appearance to lovage, alexanders or black lovage (*Smyrnium olusatrum*) is a coastal plant that comes into growth very early in the year when few other herbs are at their best. The black seeds can be ground as a spice. The Scots lovage (*Ligusticum scoticum*) is a smaller plant, 45-90cm, with glossy trifoliate leaves and a strong celery flavour.

Position Lovage requires rich, moist, well-drained soil in sun or light shade.

Propagation It is propagated by seed, which remains viable for 3 years, or by division in spring.

Maintenance Lovage benefits from generous quantities of compost. Remove older leaves as they turn yellow. You can also cut back lovage to about 30cm high in midsummer to encourage fresh new foliage.

Pests and diseases Leaves may be damaged by leaf miners.

Harvesting and storing For cooking, pick the leaves and stems as required. Harvest the seeds when ripe. You can dry all parts of the plant and also freeze the leaves in sealed plastic bags.

■ Cooking

Called *céleri bâtard*, or false celery, by the French, lovage is an ingredient in many commercial bouillons, sauces, stocks and condiments; lovage seed extracts are added to liqueurs and cordials as well as to breads and sweet pastries.

The taste can be overpowering but you can blanch the stems by excluding light in early spring and if you want to eat them raw in salads. You can also candy the stems and eat them as confectionery, or use the leaves and seeds in cooking to provide an intense, celery-like flavouring. Deep-fried lovage leaves are an unusual accompaniment to grilled meats, especially pork and veal.

Love ache

As its common name indicates, lovage, or love ache as it was once called, was traditionally used as an aphrodisiac and an ingredient in love potions and charms. On a more practical note, medieval travellers once lined their boots with lovage leaves to absorb foot odours, while a decoction of lovage root and foliage makes an effective body deodorant. Perhaps lovage was less a love potion than a deodorant, making close physical contact more appealing in a period when people rarely washed.

Mallow and hollyhock

Alcea spp., *Althaea* spp., *Malva* spp. Malvaceae

Hollyhock reportedly reached Europe from China via the Holy Land, a history that gave the plant its original name of holy mallow or holyoke. Musk mallow was once used for magical protection, and common mallow was regarded as a cure-all. Mallows and hollyhocks contain similar mucilaginous compounds.

OTHER COMMON NAME Cheeses (hollyhock)
PARTS USED Roots, leaves, flowers, seeds

Marsh mallow (*Althaea officinalis*)

■ Gardening

Marsh mallow (*Althaea officinalis*) is a hardy herbaceous perennial with velvety, grey-green, toothed leaves; small hibiscus-like pale pink flowers are borne on stems to 1.2m.

Common mallow (*Malva sylvestris*) to 30-90cm, has rounded basal leaves, lobed upper leaves and rose-purple flowers with five notched, dark-striped petals.

Musk mallow (*M. moschata*) is a smaller plant with musk-scented foliage, the lower leaves are kidney-shaped, becoming much divided higher up the stems. Pink flowers with five notched petals, are freely produced all summer.

Hollyhock (*Alcea rosea*) is a biennial or short-lived perennial, with a basal rosette of large, long-stalked, rough-textured leaves, which are rounded and lobed. The tall flowering stems can reach 3m, bearing a succession of pink, purple or white flowers. Hollyhocks and mallows are classic cottage garden plants, often at their best in poor, stony situations. The exception is marsh mallow, a lovely plant for the water garden. All mallows have disc-shaped, nutty-flavoured seeds, known by country folk as 'cheeses'.

Varieties Garden hollyhocks produce large single or double flowers in shades of lemon, apricot, pink, red and purple. 'Majorette' is a dwarf double-flowered strain, 60-75cm. Black hollyhock, *Alcea rosea* 'Nigra', is darkest maroon. Musk mallow has a pure white form (*M. moschata* f. *alba*). Varieties of common mallow are 'Primley Blue', with lilac-blue flowers, and 'Brave Heart', which has bold burgundy-striped flowers.

Position Marsh mallow likes damp to wet conditions but the rest prefer well-drained soil. All need a sunny position.

Propagation Sow seed of all kinds in spring or summer.

Maintenance Stake tall plants in summer; cut down dead stems in winter.

Pests and diseases Hollyhocks and mallows are prone to rust (*Puccinia malvacearum*). Control by removing and burning affected leaves.

Hollyhock (*Alcea rosea*)

Harvesting and storing Gather flowers and leaves as required to use fresh or dried. Dig up and dry marsh mallow roots when they are 2 years old.

■ Herbal medicine

Althaea officinalis. Parts used: leaves, roots. Rich in mucilaginous compounds, the leaves and roots of the marsh mallow are used to treat irritated and inflamed conditions of the respiratory tract, such as coughs, bronchitis and sore throat.

With a higher amount of mucilage, the root is regarded as the more effective remedy for inflammatory conditions of the gut, such as stomach and intestinal ulcers, gastroenteritis and ulcerative colitis. It is also used as a topical agent in mouthwashes for inflammation of the mouth and throat and as an ointment to soothe eczematous skin conditions.

Malva sylvestris. Parts used: leaf, flower. Mallow has been used for similar purposes to marsh mallow, although it is considered less potent. Like marsh mallow, it is used for respiratory and gastrointestinal conditions, with inflammation and irritation, that benefit from the plant's soothing properties.

For the safe and appropriate use of marsh mallow, see *Sore throats, colds and flu*, page 206. Don't use these herbs if you are pregnant or breastfeeding except with the advice of a doctor or medical herbalist.

Marjoram and oregano

Origanum spp. Lamiaceae

The Greeks called these fragrant-leafed herbs 'Brightness of the Mountain', and it is impossible to imagine the cuisines of the Mediterranean and Aegean without their strong, warm aromatic taste.

PARTS USED Leaves, flowers

Marjoram (*Origanum marjorana*)

◼ Gardening

Origanum is a genus of more than 30 species from the Mediterranean and the Middle East. Confusingly, the names marjoram and oregano are often used interchangeably. Commercial dried oregano may include unrelated species, such as Mexican oregano (*Lippia graveolens*). All origanums are aromatic, drought-resistant herbs that are lovely in borders and containers. Choose plants by flavour as well as appearance, and check hardiness; tender and damp-sensitive kinds are best grown in containers which can be protected in winter.

Varieties Sweet or knotted marjoram (*O. majorana* syn. *Majorana hortensis*) is a tender evergreen sub shrub, often grown as an annual, with grey-green leaves and bobble-like heads of tiny white flowers. It has a refined flavour, as does the hardier hybrid, *O.* x *majoricum*, a cross with wild marjoram (*O. vulgare*), known both as Italian oregano and hardy sweet marjoram.

Pot marjoram, Turkish or Greek oregano (*O. onites*) is a frost-hardy species with pale green to grey-green leaves, white flowers, and a robust, peppery flavour. Hybrids and forms of *O. vulgare* are often sold as *O. onites*.

Wild marjoram or oregano (*O. vulgare*) contains six sub species. The most common is *O. vulgare* ssp. *vulgare*, which has pink flowers and burgundy bracts. Though often called oregano, its flavour is mild by comparison. It excels as a hardy garden plant, with colourful forms such as variegated 'Country Cream' and golden 'Aureum' and 'Gold Tip'. There are dwarf forms, 'Compactum' and 'Nanum' as well.

Greek oregano or winter marjoram (*O. vulgare* ssp. *hirtum*) is the next most widely grown sub-species with hairy, pointed leaves, white flowers and green, sometimes purple-tinged bracts. Its pungent flavour has a hint of creosote.

Lebanese oregano, Syrian hyssop or white oregano (*O. syriacum* syn. *O. maru*) is one of the za'atar herbs. It is a tender sub shrub with stiff, hairy stems, highly aromatic grey-green foliage and purple-pink flowers with woolly bracts. A hybrid with *O. vulgare*, sold incorrectly as *O. maru*, has greater cold resistance.

Dittany of Crete (*O. dictamnus*) is a beautiful little plant, often grown as an alpine to protect it from winter wet. It has densely woolly foliage and pendent, reddish, cone-like flower spikes with protruding pink flowers. Dried leaves and flowering tops are used medicinally and for making herb tea.

Position *Origanum* species are found in the wild in sunny, well-drained and often stony places. They thrive in full sun and are more strongly flavoured if grown with tough love.

Propagation Raise the species by division or from seed in spring, and

Za'atar

Za'atar is an Arabic term for a number of aromatic herbs, often varying according to the region and the local flora. While the term often refers to origanums such as *O. syriacum*, za'atar herbs also include conehead thyme (*Thymbra capitata*), za'atar hommar (*T. spicata*), thyme (*Thymus* spp.) and savory species such as za'atar rumi (*Satureja thymbra*). The seasoning mixture called 'za'atar' usually includes sumach (*Rhus coriaria*), toasted sesame seeds and coarse salt, and is used on vegetable and meat dishes and also sprinkled on bread before baking.

Marjoram and oregano continued

Marjoram and sausage pasta

300g rigatoni

250g sausages

2 tablespoons olive oil

1 large red onion, roughly chopped

3 cloves garlic, finely chopped

1 small aubergine, diced

3 small courgettes, diced

500g tomato pasta sauce

1 tablespoon chopped fresh
marjoram or oregano

40g black olives

250g cherry tomatoes

2 tablespoons chopped fresh
parsley

fresh marjoram leaves, for garnish

grated Parmesan, to serve

Cook pasta in boiling water until al dente, about 10 minutes. Drain. Grill sausages until brown. Cool slightly; cut into thick slices. Heat oil in saucepan over moderate heat. Fry onion until starting to colour, about 3 minutes, Add garlic and sausages; cook a few minutes. Increase heat; add aubergine and courgettes; cook, stirring, 5 minutes, until aubergine begins to soften. Add tomato pasta sauce, stir in marjoram and season to taste. Cover and simmer, stirring occasionally, 15 minutes, or until aubergine is tender. Stir in olives and tomatoes. Cover and cook a further 5 minutes. Combine pasta and sauce in a large bowl. Stir in parsley. Sprinkle with marjoram leaves and Parmesan. Serves 4.

ornamental varieties and hybrids by division or basal cuttings.

Maintenance Do not overwater them. Cut back old growth in spring.

Pests and diseases Origanums are very resistant to both.

Harvesting and storing You can harvest the foliage fresh but the flavour is enhanced if you dry it in bunches in a dark, dry, warm, well-ventilated place for several days. When dry and crisp, rub the leaves off the stems and store in an airtight container.

■ Herbal medicine

Origanum vulgare. Parts used: leaves, flowers. An infusion of the herb is a useful remedy for feverish conditions and also for treating coughs, colds and influenza due to its ability to improve the removal of phlegm from the lungs and relax the bronchial muscles. It is also regarded as a herb for the gut; it relieves flatulence and improves digestion as well as treating intestinal infections due to a strong antiseptic effect.

The essential oil of oregano has been shown to possess potent antimicrobial and antioxidant properties, primarily due to the presence of thymol and carvacrol. Some commercial oregano oil products have been used to treat a range of conditions, including respiratory and gastrointestinal infections, although substantial clinical evidence proving its efficacy is lacking.

Origanum majorana syn. *Majorana hortensis.* Parts used: leaves and flowers.

Medicinally, sweet marjoram is used predominantly in the form of its essential oil, which is applied topically to ease headaches, sore muscles and rheumatic pain. As an external remedy it can also relieve catarrhal conditions affecting the lung, digestive colic, flatulence and period pains.

For the safe and appropriate medicinal use of these two herbs, consult a doctor or medical herbalist. Do not use these herbs in greater than culinary quantities or the essential oils of these herbs internally or externally if you are pregnant or breastfeeding.

■ Cooking

Oregano has a more pungent scent than marjoram, with a stronger flavour. The hotter and drier the climate, the more aroma and flavour. Sweet marjoram is a favourite for flavouring, but its aroma is damaged by heat, so use it in uncooked or lightly cooked dishes, or add it at the end. Oregano is more robust and can withstand longer cooking.

Both oregano and marjoram go well with lemon, garlic, wine-based sauces and marinades, meats, oily fish, hearty salads, Greek and Italian dishes, beans, aubergine, peppers and tomato-based dishes and sauces. They are also used in commercial mixed herbs.

Common oregano (*O. vulgare*) in flower

Meadowsweet

Filipendula ulmaria Rosaceae

With its fragrant and beautiful flowers, meadowsweet was one of the most powerful and sacred herbs of the Druids. In medieval times, it was popular as a strewing herb and a favourite of Elizabeth I, who ordered it to be used in her bedchamber.

OTHER COMMON NAMES Queen of the meadow
PART USED Flowers, leaves

Meadowsweet (*Filipendula ulmaria*)

The source of aspirin

In 1838, salicin was isolated from the salicylate compounds in meadowsweet. This was then synthesised to make acetyl salicylic acid (aspirin) by Felix Hoffman in Germany in 1899. His employer, Bayer A G, named the drug aspirin after an old botanical name for meadowsweet, *Spiraea ulmaria*. The herb is considered less irritating to the stomach than the purified drug.

■ Gardening

Meadowsweet is a hardy perennial with a basal clump of pinnate leaves, and tall stems to 1.2m, of frothy, almond-scented, creamy-white flowers in summer. Crushed, the leaves smell like wintergreen. Meadowsweet is widely distributed across Asia and Europe. It occurs in moist meadows and around fresh water, and is the perfect choice for bog gardens and ponds.

Varieties Ornamental but herbally active varieties include the double-flowered 'Flore Pleno'; 'Aurea', with golden foliage; and 'Variegata', with cream-variegated leaves. Dropwort (*F. vulgaris*) is a closely related plant, once employed as a diuretic. It has similar flowers and finely divided leaves. The beautiful North American queen of the prairie, *F. rubra*, is larger, reaching 2.5m, with pink to rose-coloured flowers.

Position Meadowsweet will grow in full sun, provided the soil is very moist. It prefers a well-enriched, alkaline soil.

Propagation Propagate the species by seed in autumn, allowing a period of stratification (see page 50). Both the species and named varieties can be propagated by division in spring.

Maintenance Cut down dead stems in winter. Every 3 or 4 years, lift and divide large clumps in autumn.

Pests and diseases Mildew is the main problem, especially in the double-flowered form. To prevent mildew, keep plants constantly moist.

Harvesting and storing Cut and dry flowers when in full bloom and use fresh for culinary use, or dried for herbal use. Harvest and dry leaves at the same time.

■ Herbal medicine

Filipendula ulmaria. Parts used: flowers, leaves. Meadowsweet is considered to be one of the most important digestive remedies, used for many conditions of the gut, particularly where there is inflammation and excess acidity. It helps to balance stomach acid production as well as a soothing and healing the upper digestive tract. Meadowsweet is commonly prescribed for acid reflux, indigestion, gastritis and stomach ulcers.

Meadowsweet contains aspirin-like compounds that are responsible for its pain-relieving and anti-inflammatory properties. These compounds can also help to bring down fevers, so meadowsweet is often recommended for the treatment of colds and flu. The plant's medicinal effects make it an effective remedy for helping to alleviate joint and muscle pain.

For the safe and appropriate medicinal use of meadowsweet, see *Indigestion*, page 210. Do not use meadowsweet if you are pregnant or breastfeeding, or sensitive to aspirin.

■ Cooking

The flowers are used to flavour jams, stewed fruits and wine as well as mead and the non-alcoholic Norfolk Punch.

Clearly associated with romance, meadowsweet was once used in garlands for brides and strewn at weddings.

Mint

Mentha spp. Lamiaceae

Mints come in an amazing range of flavours and fragrances. While everyone is familiar with spearmint and peppermint, there are many more mouth-watering varieties, including apple, chocolate, lime, grapefruit, lemon and ginger.

PART USED Leaves

Spearmint (*Mentha spicata*)

 Gardening

Mints are indispensable herbs but as garden plants most are very invasive. The answer is to grow them in large pots, or plant them in containers – an old bucket will do - that can be buried in the ground. They will still try to escape, but are much easier to control if confined. Variegated mints are very ornamental and, suitably containerised, can be put to good use as 'gap fillers' in flower borders and as focal points in damp shady corners where little else will grow.

Varieties

Spearmint (*Mentha spicata*) has pointed spikes of lavender flowers but is very variable in terms of its foliage and flavour. Curly spearmint (*M. spicata* var. *crispa*) has fluted foliage with a true spearmint scent. Two of the best for flavour are 'Moroccan' and 'Tashkent'.

Peppermint (*M.* x *piperita*) is a sterile hybrid of water mint (*M. aquatica*) and spearmint (*M. spicata*). It is variable in appearance; the flower spikes can be rounded or pointed. There are two main kinds: black peppermint (var. *piperita*) with dark green, purple-flushed foliage and rounded flower spikes; and white peppermint (var. *officinalis*), with bright green leaves and a spearmint-like inflorescence. 'Mitcham' is the best selection of black peppermint. Bergamot or eau-de-cologne mint (f. *citrata* syn. *M. citrata*) has a lavender-like perfume. Variants of this form, which more closely resembles water mint than spearmint, include 'Basil', 'Chocolate', and 'Grapefruit'.

Water mint (*M. aquatica*) has a strong peppermint-pennyroyal scent, broadly ovate, purplish-green leaves and rounded spikes of lilac flowers. It enjoys wet conditions and thrives beside water.

Red mint or Scotch spearmint (*M.* x *gracilis*) is a cross between corn mint (*M. arvensis*) and spearmint. It has purple-red stems, pointed leaves and whorls of lavender flowers. Clones may have spearmint, peppermint or fruity aromas. Ginger mint (*M.* x *gracilis* 'Variegata') has attractive yellow-marbled leaves and a subtle spicy flavour.

Apple mint (*M. suaveolens*) is a larger plant, to 1m, with downy leaves and tapering spikes of pink to white flowers.

Pineapple mint (*M. suaveolens* 'Variegata' is sweetly fruit-scented, with lax stems, white-variegated leaves and white flowers.

Woolly or Bowles' mint (*M.* x *villosa* var. *alopecuroides*) is a vigorous, tall-growing, sterile hybrid with broadly oval furred leaves and pointed clusters of lavender flowers. Its fine spearmint flavour is prized for making mint sauce.

Pennyroyal (*M. pulegium*) is a creeping mint that forms dense mats. The small smooth leaves are pungently scented and the lavender flowers are in tight whorls.

Above Variegated apple mint (*M. suaveolens* 'Variegata'). *Right* Pennyroyal (*M. pulegium*)

American pennyroyal is *Hedeoma pulegioides*, a bushy annual that looks like a miniature mint.

Corsican mint (*M. requienii*) forms dense, moss-like mats of tiny, powerfully mint-scented leaves which are peppered with minute lavender flowers in summer. It is frost-hardy and best-suited to cultivation in large shallow pots in a damp shady corner.

Horsemint (*M. longifolia*) has tall stems of grey-green, pointed leaves with a spearmint-like aroma and tapering spikes of lilac to white flowers. Ornamental forms include the Buddleia Mint Group, with silver-grey foliage, and 'Variegata', with creamy-yellow markings.

Position The ideal conditions are moist, rich soil and half to full sun.

Propagation Propagate mints from cuttings or by dividing clumps. Pennyroyal, Corsican mint and American pennyroyal are often grown from seed.

Maintenance Mints are rich feeders, so container-grown plants should be lifted in winter and divided. Replant a proportion of the strongest rhizomes in fresh compost, adding some slow-release fertiliser or well-rotted compost.

Pests and diseases Some mints are prone to a rust disease, *Puccinea menthae*. Infected plants should be burnt and the

Peppermint (*Mentha* x *piperita*)

area no longer used for mint. To prevent rust, divide and feed plants regularly.

Harvesting and storing Mints dry well in a warm, airy place away from direct sunlight. Store crumbled leaves in an airtight container. Harvest foliage to use fresh as required.

Herbal medicine

Mentha x *piperita*. Part used: leaves. Peppermint relaxes the gut and can help to relieve indigestion, nausea, wind and cramping. Clinical trials have verified its therapeutic effects on many symptoms of irritable bowel syndrome, including diarrhoea, constipation, bloating and abdominal pain, especially when taken in the form of enteric-coated peppermint oil capsules.

Topically, peppermint essential oil can alleviate joint and muscle pain and headaches. When inhaled, it can also help to reduce feelings of nausea and act as a nasal decongestant.

For the safe and appropriate medicinal use of peppermint, see *Wind, bloating and flatulence*, page 212; *Nausea*, page 211. Do not use peppermint in greater than culinary quantities, and do not use the essential oil if you are pregnant or breastfeeding.

Around the home

Both peppermint and pennyroyal (*M. pulegium*) are insect repellents.

Sprinkle cotton-wool balls with peppermint essential oil and leave them where rodents enter.

Add a few drops of peppermint essential oil to a damp rag and wipe over benches and cupboard interiors to deter ants and cockroaches.

Make a personal insect repellent: mix 1 part lavender, 1 part eucalyptus, 1 part peppermint essential oils with 3 parts unscented moisturiser or sweet almond oil, and rub into the skin.

To deter fleas, put dried pennyroyal under pet bedding or put a spot of oil on its collar. Don't use pennyroyal on cats or pregnant dogs, as it is toxic.

Cooking

Fresh mint can overwhelm other flavours due to its slightly anaesthetic effect on the taste buds. It does not complement other herbs well and is best used with a light hand. Dried mint is less assertive and is favoured in eastern Mediterranean and Arab countries. Spearmint or garden mint, is the most commonly used. It is a classic flavouring with roast lamb, and also goes well with potatoes, peas, salads and yoghurt-based dishes, such as Indian raita and Greek tzatziki. Spearmint is often included in herb tea blends. Peppermint is popular after meals as a digestive tea. Both kinds are used to flavour chewing gum but peppermint is much nicer in ice cream, confectionery and liqueurs.

Mint jelly

- **500g green apples, cored and roughly chopped**
- **15g roughly chopped spearmint leaves**
- **375ml white wine vinegar**
- **500g sugar**
- **15g finely chopped fresh mint leaves, extra**

Place apples, mint and vinegar in medium saucepan; cook, uncovered, until apples are very tender. Purée apples; drain through a sieve (don't push them through or the jelly becomes cloudy). Return liquid to saucepan; add sugar. Return to the

boil, boiling for 10 minutes. Remove from heat, stir through extra mint. Pour into clean container; refrigerate 6 hours, or until set. Makes about 2 cups (600g).

Mustard

Brassica juncea, B. nigra, Sinapis alba Brassicaceae

Mustards are native to Europe and temperate parts of Asia and have been valued as flavourings, leafy vegetables and medicinal plants since ancient times. The Romans were the first to make a condiment with ground mustard.

PARTS USED Leaves, roots

Brown mustard (*B. juncea*) in flower.

◼ Gardening

Mustards are medium to tall, hardy annuals, reaching 80cm to 3m, with branched stems, lobed leaves about 15cm long, and long clusters of small, 4-petalled yellow flowers followed by beaked pods, each containing about 8 perfectly round, golden to brown seeds. Salad mustards are cut before the flowering stem develops. Young leaves may be oval or deeply cut.

Varieties Brown or Indian mustard (*Brassica juncea*) produces pungent seeds that are blended with other mustard seeds in condiments, and used whole in pickles and chutneys, and in curries. It is the main source of commercial 'baby' mustard leaves for salads. Salad varieties are 'Pizzo', 'Red Giant' and 'Red Frills'.

Black mustard (*Brassica nigra*) seeds ground with vinegar give French

Brassica juncea 'Red Giant'

mustard its distinctive flavour. Young leaves are also edible in salads.

White mustard (*Sinapis alba*) has mild-flavoured seeds that are the basis of American mustard and are blended with black mustard seeds and water to make English mustard. Seeds are sprouted with cress (*Lepidium sativum*) in punnets of 'mustard and cress' as a salad garnish.

Position Well-drained in full sun, enriched with compost.

Propagation For salad leaves, sow in early spring and at 28 day intervals until late summer, in large pots or the ground. Seeds can also be mixed with other baby-leaf salad crops, such as lettuce, rocket, spinach and kale. For pods and seeds, sow in early spring. When growing 'mustard and cress', use shallow plastic trays and sow seeds of cress three days earlier than mustard so that they are ready for cutting at the same time.

Maintenance Mustards grown for pods may need support.

Pests and diseases Flea beetles attack leaves during warm dry spells in spring.

Harvesting and storing Harvest salad mustards when young and tender, before flower stems develop. Harvest pods when green in summer for salads and preserving. For ripe seeds, harvest as pods start to turn brown, putting into paper bags to complete ripening.

◼ Herbal medicine

Brassica nigra, Sinapis alba Part used: seeds. Mustards contain sulphur and nitrogen-bearing compounds known as glucosinolates with antibacterial,

antifungal and anti-cancer properties. When seeds are ground and mixed with a liquid, an enzyme is released that turns the glucosinolates into isothiocynates which have similar properties but are also pungent and irritant. The warming, irritant effects have been used to treat rheumatism, arthritis, chilblains, muscular aches, pains in the joints and muscles, and the symptoms of colds. Treatment is given via plasters, poultices or baths which cause reddening of the skin due to increased blood flow.

The process needs careful judgment, as the reddening stimulates circulation and promotes healing, but may cause blistering. For the safe and effective use of mustard consult a medical herbalist.

◼ Cooking

Mustard sprouts, young leaves, flower buds and unripe pods give mild pungency to salads and stir-fries. Use seeds in pickles, chutneys and curries, or grind them with water, fruit juice, ale or vinegar to make a condiment. Make fresh mustard using mustard powder.

Wholegrain and smooth mustards are excellent accompaniments to meats and may be blended with crème fraîche to make a creamy sauce for fish, or added to casseroles and hot sauces just before serving. 'Hot' or 'tartar' mustard contains horseradish and sometimes chilli, which increases pungency.

Nettle

Urtica dioica Urticaceae

The 17th-century herbalist Culpeper noted that nettles 'may be found by feeling, in the darkest night'. Arthritis sufferers once whipped themselves with stinging nettles to relieve pain, a treatment known as 'counter-irritation'.

PARTS USED Leaves, roots

Stinging nettle (*Urtica dioica*)

■ Gardening

The stinging nettle (*Urtica dioica*) is a common weed throughout most of the temperate Northern Hemisphere. It is a hardy herbaceous perennial growing to 1.2m, with coarsely toothed, oval leaves armed with stinging hairs. Tiny green male and female flowers are borne in tassels on separate plants. The spreading roots are yellow.

The young leaves are rich in vitamin C and minerals (particularly potassium, calcium, silicon and iron). Patches of nettles are left undisturbed in wildlife gardens as food plants for the caterpillars of various butterflies and moths. They are also worth leaving to use as a vegetable in spring, and for cutting to make compost.

Varieties The annual nettle (*U. urens*) has similar constituents and uses.

Position Nettles thrive in sun or shade and rich, moist soil high in nitrogen.

Propagation Divide in early spring.

Maintenance Nettles can become invasive but are easily controlled by removing shallow roots.

Pests and diseases So-called pests on nettles are probably the larvae of lovely butterflies.

Harvesting and storing As a vegetable, pick new shoots only in spring when no more than 10cm high, as older plants develop gritty crystals of calcium oxalate. For drying, harvest as flowering begins. Always wear thick gloves to protect your hands. Dig up the roots in autumn and air-dry them away from direct sunlight.

■ Herbal medicine

Urtica dioica. Parts used: Leaves, roots. Nettle leaf is a traditional blood-purifying remedy with a gentle diuretic effect that encourages the removal of toxins from the body. It is used medicinally to treat arthritic conditions and certain skin disorders such as eczema, which some herbalists believe can benefit from a detoxifying action.

The leaf is also associated with anti-allergic properties, and herbalists often prescribe it for symptoms of hay fever and skin rashes.

Modern research has shown that nettle root may inhibit overgrowth of prostate tissue, and clinical trials have provided some compelling evidence that therapeutic use of the root may improve the urinary symptoms associated with disorders of the prostate gland, such as frequent urination and weak flow.

For the safe and appropriate use of nettle, consult a doctor or medical herbalist. Do not use nettle in greater than culinary doses if you are pregnant or breastfeeding.

Relieve the discomfort of nettle stings by rubbing them with ice or the leaves of dock.

■ Cooking

The young leaves were once widely used in the spring diet to revitalise the body after winter. They may be cooked as a vegetable, in similar ways to spinach, or added to soups or to vegetable, egg or meat dishes. A tisane can be made from the leaves; it has a bland taste and can be blended with other herbs or with Indian or green teas. Do not eat nettles raw. Older leaves are high in calcium oxalate and should not be eaten as a vegetable.

Cornish yarg

A handmade semi-hard cheese with a creamy taste, Cornish yarg is wrapped in nettle leaves after pressing and brining. The leaves are carefully arranged by hand to form a pleasing pattern and also to attract natural moulds in various colours that aid in the ripening process, adding a subtle mushroom taste. Remove yarg from the refrigerator about an hour before serving.

Nutmeg and mace

Myristica fragrans Myristicaceae

The 16th-century Portuguese physician García de Orta wrote, 'It is the loveliest sight in the world to see the nutmeg trees laden with their ripe golden fruit, which splits to reveal the red mace within'. The spices probably reached Europe through Arab traders in the 9th century but only when Europeans set out to explore the world and control supplies did anyone see a living plant.

PART USED Seeds

Wild nutmeg surrounded by its 'aril' of red mace. When dried it turns yellow.

Gardening

Nutmeg is a tropical evergreen tree, 10-20m tall, which is native to the Malay Archipelago but is now commercially grown in various parts of the tropics, including the Caribbean island of Grenada. Trees begin fruiting when 4-8 years old and are either predominately male or female, the latter giving better fruits. Each fruit consists of an outer fleshy layer surrounding a single seed (nutmeg) inside a thin woody shell. The shell is enclosed by a leathery red aril (mace) that turns yellow when dried. Nutmeg trees have specific requirements and are not easily grown.

Position Ideal conditions include high light levels, rainfall and humidity, and humus-rich sandy soil in hilly terrain.

Propagation The best trees are grafted or air-layered. Self-sown seedlings are also grown on in order to establish new plantations. Seed viability is very brief – little more than 24 hours – so it is not possible to grow your own plant from a purchased nutmeg.

Maintenance No pruning is needed but plants are kept clear of competition by weeds and scrub.

Pests and diseases Fruits can be damaged by a disease that cause them to open prematurely when they are of no use for flavouring or oil extraction.

Harvesting and storing Fruits are allowed to ripen and fall, giving the best flavour but they must be collected from the ground within 24 hours.

Herbal medicine

Myristica fragrans. Part used: seeds (nutmeg). Nutmeg was historically more important as a medicinal plant before it became popular for flavouring. It is still used in Ayurvedic medicine, mainly for digestive problems. In excess, it is extremely toxic, as it contains several compounds that cause hallucinations and liver damage. You should never use nutmeg medicinally for any purpose.

Cooking

Nutmeg and mace are key ingredients in spice mixes, such as 'ground mixed spice' and the North African *ras-el-hanout*. Grated or ground nutmeg has a very wide range of uses in baking, puddings and spiced drinks. It also works well with a number of kinds of savoury foods, such as pasta fillings, milk- or cream-based sauces (such as béchamel) and spinach.

Mace has a similar but more subtle flavour and a paler colour, which makes it a better choice to use with fish, in clear soups and in soufflés. The flesh of nutmeg fruits can be used to make excellent jellies and syrup.

Dried nutmegs

A little of what you fancy

We don't think twice about the herbs and spices used everyday in the food we eat, but the fact is that these flavoursome plants contain some very potent compounds. Used in the amounts recommended, they do us good. Taken to excess, they can do harm. The earliest known case of nutmeg poisoning was in 1576, when 'a pregnant English lady' with a craving for nutmeg managed to consume about a dozen and became 'deliriously inebriated' and then seriously ill. If only she had followed the recipe!

Olive

Olea europaea Oleaceae

Olea (Greek *elaio*) is the Latin word for both 'olive' and 'oil'. Olive trees have been cultivated since prehistoric times, providing the oil and fruits that are so important in the cuisines and cultures of Mediterranean countries.

PARTS USED Leaves, fruits, oil

■ Gardening

The olive is a frost-hardy evergreen tree, 10-15m tall, with grey fissured bark and grey-green, leathery leaves which have a silvery underside. Tiny fragrant cream flowers, borne in panicles in late spring, are followed by egg-shaped green fruits which ripen black in winter. Trees begin fruiting in their seventh year, reaching their prime at about 35 years, continuing until at least 150 years old, and in some cases living for 1000 years. An olive tree makes a beautiful centrepiece for a herb garden or patio, either in the open ground or in a large container.

Varieties Olives vary in hardiness so choose your tree carefully from a specialist nursery. 'Cipressino' from Puglia, Italy, is upright and compact, ideal for containers. 'Frantoio', a Tuscan variety, is vigorous and early ripening, bearing small oblong fruits that yield excellent oil. 'Picual', from Andalucia in Spain, is resilient and self-fertile, with conspicuous white-backed leaves.

Position Well-drained soil in sun.

Propagation Sow seed at 13-15°C in spring or take semi-ripe cuttings in summer.

Maintenance Cut back the leading shoot when the tree reaches 1.5m. Prune in early spring, removing old branches to encourage new growth as fruits are produced mostly on one-year-old wood.

Pests and diseases Trees may be damaged by scale insects, root-knot eelworm and *Verticillium* wilt.

Harvesting and storing Leaves are picked as needed and used fresh or dried. Fruits are harvested unripe or ripe for eating, and ripe for extraction of oil.

■ Herbal medicine

Olea europaea Parts used: Leaves, oil. Olive leaves are bitter and astringent, with potent antibacterial, antiviral and antioxidant effects. Traditionally made into a tea for feverish illnesses, including malaria, and crushed into a poultice to heal skin inflammations, the leaves are now important in extracts for combating ageing of the skin and cardiovascular system. Olive oil is richly emollient; it is combined with lemon juice to treat gallstones, and is an ingredient in products for dry skin and hair. Regular consumption of olive oil is thought to reduce the risk of circulatory disease and may help to reduce gastric secretions in patients suffering from hyperacidity. For the safe use of olive leaves and oil for medicinal purposes, consult your doctor or medical herbalist.

Grow an olive tree as an appealing container plant

■ Cooking

Olives are a vital component of many Mediterranean dishes, including hors d'oeuvres, salads (such as Niçoise), spreads (such as tapenade), pasta sauces and pizzas. They also give a distinctive flavour to Mediterranean-style meat and fish dishes. Olive oil is important as a cooking oil, also used in salad dressings, mayonnaise, sauces and breads (such as focaccia); also as a dip for bread in Mediterranean regions.

Harvested black olives

Symbol of peace

The story of Noah's Ark tells how the dove returned with an olive branch, showing that the flood waters had abated and the crisis was over, making the olive a symbol of peace to this day.

Parsley

Petroselinum crispum Apiaceae

Once given as fodder for the chariot horses of the Ancient Greeks, parsley is native to the south-eastern Mediterranean, but is now cultivated in temperate climates throughout the world. Parsley has widespread culinary, medicinal and cosmetic uses and is popular for growing in containers.

PARTS USED Leaves, stalks, roots, seeds

Curly parsley
(*Petroselinum crispum*
var. *crispum,* pot)
and flat-leaf parsley
(*Petroselinum crispum*
var. *neapolitanum*)

■ Gardening

Parsley is a biennial, forming a dense rosette of leaves in the first year and flowering in its second summer, when the foliage becomes bitter. It does well in containers, either on a sunny windowsill or outdoors within easy reach of the kitchen. Pots of close-set parsley seedlings bought in a supermarket can be potted on to give large specimens that can be cut for many months.

Varieties There are three distinct types of parsley.

Curly parsley (*P. crispum*) is the most familiar. Excellent varieties include the old favourite 'Champion Moss Curled', 'Lisette' a fast-growing form bred for pot culture, and 'Bravour', a vigorous long-stemmed garden parsley. Plain-leaf types, known as Italian, French or flat-leaf parsley (*P. crispum* var. *neapolitanum*) are rather larger, reaching 60cm. **Hamburg or turnip-rooted parsley** (*P. crispum* var. *tuberosum*) is grown more for its delicately flavoured taproot than its leaves, although they can also be used.

Japanese parsley or mitsuba (*Cryptotaenia japonica*) is in the same family. Its flavour is a mixture of celery, angelica and parsley. There is a handsome dark-leaved form, f. *atropurpurea*.

Position Parsley prefers sun to partial shade, and well-composted, well-drained but moist soil. If the soil is very acidic, incorporate lime before planting.

Propagation This herb is grown only from seed and takes 3 to 8 weeks to germinate. You can speed up this process by soaking the seed in warm water overnight before planting into trays or pots. Alternatively, pour freshly boiled water along seed drills just before planting. Cover seed very lightly with soil. Transplant seedlings into the garden (or thin seedlings sown directly into the garden) to around 25cm apart. Parsley self-seeds under suitable conditions. In cold areas, a cloche will warm the soil and allow for earlier planting of seedlings, or protect a winter crop.

Maintenance Water regularly or parsley will flower ('bolt') in its first season. Cutting out the emerging flowering stalks delays this process to some extent.

Pests and diseases Generally easy to grow, parsley can be attacked by pests of closely related members of the same

Emerald risotto

For a delicious-tasting and attractive emerald green herb risotto, cook a classic risotto recipe using arborio rice, chicken or vegetable stock and white wine, but add a handful of chopped baby spinach leaves when the rice is almost cooked. Once the rice is fully cooked (it should be a creamy, dropping consistency), stir in a generous amount of finely chopped fresh parsley and coriander. Season to taste.

Parsley only does well where the woman wears the trousers.

family – for instance, celery fly and carrot weevil. Septoria leaf spot can also be a problem. In Hamburg parsley, crown rot can occur after periods of prolonged rain.

Harvesting and storing New growth comes from the centre of the stem, so harvest leaves from around the outside of plants. Parsley freezes well but is not a good herb for drying, as it loses much of its flavour. To collect seeds, hang bunches of ripening seed heads upside down inside paper bags. Harvest the roots at the end of the second season and air dry.

◼ Herbal medicine

Petroselinum crispum var. *crispum*. Parts used: leaves, roots, seeds. The leaves are a good source of vitamin C, and both the leaf and root are well known for eliciting considerable diuretic effects in the body. Parsley has been used to treat fluid retention, urinary tract disorders

Hamburg parsley (*P. crispum* var. *tuberosum*) is grown for its roots, not its leaves, has a mild taste. It can be grown in containers as well as in the ground.

and arthritic conditions of the joints, including gout, an inflammatory condition usually affecting a single joint, such as a big toe.

Parsley has a calming effect on the gut, alleviating flatulence and colic, and also a gentle stimulatory action, encouraging appetite and improving digestion. It can also have a notable stimulating effect on the uterus and has been used to encourage menstruation – but should not be used for this purpose if pregnancy is a possibility.

For the safe and appropriate medicinal use of parsley, consult your doctor or medical herbalist. Do not use in greater than culinary quantities if you're pregnant or breastfeeding.

◼ Cooking

Flat-leaf parsley is generally considered to have the best flavour, while curly parsley is more attractive as a garnish. Use either one finely chopped in salads, vegetable and egg dishes and sauces (see *Frankfurt green sauce* recipe, page 344). Add near the end of preparation to retain the flavour. Parsley is essential to

Chimichurri sauce

Parsley is used in many herb and spice mixes around the world (see Chermoula and Persillade recipes, page 358). Try this Argentinian sauce with meat hot off the barbecue.

In a jar, combine 6 cloves garlic, 2 tablespoons fresh oregano leaves and a handful of parsley leaves, all finely chopped. Add 1 tablespoon red onion, chopped, 1 tablespoon finely chopped fresh chilli, 1 teaspoon ground black pepper, 150ml olive oil, 6 tablespoons red wine, ground black pepper and salt, to taste. Seal jar, shake well. Leave 4 hours for flavours to develop.

Rabbit's remedy

According to Greek myth, parsley sprang from the blood of a Greek hero, Archemorus, the forerunner of death, while English folklore has it that parsley seeds go to the Devil and back seven times before they germinate, referring to the fact that they can be slow to sprout. It is also claimed that only the wicked can grow it well. On a more light-hearted note, parsley is traditionally a curative, a fact that Beatrix Potter weaves into *The Tale of Peter Rabbit* when Peter eats too much in Farmer McGregor's vegetable patch: 'First he ate some lettuce and some broad beans, then some radishes, and then, feeling rather sick, he went to look for some parsley.'

many traditional flavouring mixes, particularly in French cooking. Bouquet garni, a small bunch of pungent fresh herbs for slow cooking, usually comprises a bay leaf, sprigs of parsley and sprigs of thyme. Other mixes include persillade (finely chopped parsley and garlic, see recipe, page 358). The edible root of Hamburg parsley (above) is used in soups and stews and can be roasted or boiled in the same way as other root vegetables.

The distictive taste of mitsuba is used in Japanese cooking, in soups, salads, slow-cooked dishes as well as in fried foods. Blanch the leaves briefly to tenderise them and add to food at the last moment in order to preserve their delicate flavour.

'An honest laborious Country-man, with good Bread, Salt and a little Parsley, will make a contented Meal with a roasted Onion.'

John Evelyn, herbalist, 1620–1706

Passionflower (*Passiflora incarnata*)

Passionflower

Passiflora incarnata Passifloraceae

To Spanish missionaries in South America, the passionflower represented the Passion of Christ: the three stigmas symbolised the nails, the corona the crown of thorns, the five stamens the wounds, and the ten petals the Apostles (except Judas Iscariot and Peter).

OTHER COMMON NAMES Maypop, apricot vine, wild passionflower
PARTS USED Dried aerial parts, including flowers (medicine); fruits (culinary uses)

■ Gardening

There are about 400 species of passionflower. Many are ornamental, tendrilled climbers; some produce delicious fruit. Most require warm to tropical conditions, although *P. incarnata* survives occasional light frosts. In cold areas it is deciduous but needs warm summers for good growth and flowers.

A common wild flower in the southern USA, *P. incarnata* was used as a tonic by Native Americans. It was first noted by a European doctor in 1783. It has palmate divided leaves divided into 3 to 5 pointed lobes with finely toothed margins. Fragrant large flowers are pale lavender with a deeper purple, thread-like corona. The fruits, ovoid yellow berries when ripe, are about 5cm long.
Position It prefers light, acidic, sandy soil and a warm, sunny position. In areas with cold winters and cool summer it is better grown as a greenhouse plant.
Propagation Sow passionflower seed in spring at about 20°C, or propagate by semi-ripe cuttings in summer. Mature plants often produce suckers which can be removed and potted up separately.
Maintenance Provide a trellis or other support, and mulch plants well. Shape and prune the vine as necessary in spring.
Pests and diseases Passionflower vines are mainly pest-free when grown outdoors, but when grown under glass can suffer from red spider mite, aphids and mealy bug.
Harvesting and storing Harvest the aerial parts in mid to late summer and air-dry for use in medicinal preparations. For culinary use, the fruits should be picked at the 'dropping' stage.

Passionfruit from the *P. edulis* vine

Passionfruit cordial

Spoon the pulp of 8 passionfruits into a mixing bowl. You need about 180ml pulp. Add 1 teaspoon vanilla extract, 230g caster sugar and 60ml freshly squeezed lemon juice. Stir well. Pour into a clip-lock bottle and refrigerate. Keeps for 1 week. Pour into a jug. Add 1 litre chilled soda water. Serves 8.

■ Herbal medicine

Passiflora incarnata. Part used: leaves. Passionflower can be of great benefit for nervous tension and stress. It has a calming effect on the mind and body, and is often prescribed for insomnia in adults and children, especially when there is difficulty falling asleep.

Results of preliminary human trials have provided supportive evidence for the traditional use of passionflower for treating anxiety disorders. It is also interesting to note that further research has suggested a potential role as a supportive remedy during withdrawal from addiction to narcotic drugs.

The relaxing and antispasmodic effects of passionflower can also be applied in the treatment of digestive complaints, nervous headaches and neuralgic pain that are exacerbated by stress and tension.

For the safe and appropriate medicinal use of passionflower, refer to *Insomnia*, page 214. Do not use passionflower if you are pregnant or breastfeeding.

■ Cooking

The seeds and pulp of ripe fruits have a tangy flavour, and can be eaten raw or used in fruit salads and other desserts, curds, jams, jellies and fruit drinks. The popular cocktail called the Hurricane is made with passionfruit syrup, rum and lime juice.

Peony

Paeonia spp. Paeoniaceae

These beautiful, if rather demanding plants were once the favourite flower of Chinese emperors. Peonies were first mentioned as a medicinal herb in about 500 CE. According to Mrs Grieve, writing in her book, *A Modern Herbal*, in 1931, 'in ancient times, peony was thought to be of divine origin, an emanation from the moon'.

PART USED Roots

■ Gardening

There are 30 or so species of peonies but the three main species used in medicine are among the loveliest. Prized as ornamentals as well as for their roots, they have been bred intensively for hundreds, if not thousands of years to produce innumerable varieties.

Varieties Chinese or white peony (*P. lactiflora* syn. *P. albiflora*) from northwest China, Tibet, Mongolia and Siberia is a herbaceous perennial with erect stems, 50-70cm, lobed leaves and large, scented, single white to pale pink flowers. Good cultivated forms include 'Festiva Maxima', with very large double white, crimson-splashed flowers, and 'Sarah Bernhardt', with fragrant double pink flowers. Both grow to 1m.

Tree peony (*P. suffruticosa* syn. *P. moutan*), found from western China to Bhutan, is a deciduous shrub to 2m with deeply cut leaves. The single white to pink flowers are very large and slightly fragrant. Garden varieties often have oriental names such as the double white 'Renkaku' syn. 'Flight of Cranes'.

Common peony (*P. officinalis*) is native to Europe. A herbaceous perennial to 75cm, it bears leaves divided into nine segments and fragrant crimson flowers. Best-known forms include double white 'Alba Plena', double pink 'Rosea Plena', and 'Rubra Plena' with double deep crimson flowers.

Position Peonies prefer a sunny position and deep, rich, moist soil. Tree peonies need protection from cold drying winds. Early morning sun may damage buds after frost.

Propagation Sow fresh seed in autumn, or stratify older seed and sow in spring. Divide perennials in autumn or early spring, or take root cuttings in winter. Tree peonies are usually grafted in winter but can also be propagated by semi-ripe cuttings in summer.

Maintenance Peonies require heavy feeding, and their roots resent disturbance. Remove dead stems in winter. Stake tall plants as they tend to flop with the weight of flowers.

Pests and diseases Peonies are susceptible to a number of problems: root-knot nematodes (eelworm) and honey fungus. Peony grey mould (peony wilt) causes buds to shrivel.

A sculpture in Wangcheng Park, Luoyang, China, celebrates the beauty of the peony.

Chinese peony (*Paeonia lactiflora*)

■ Herbal medicine

Paeonia lactiflora. Part used: roots. In traditional Chinese medicine, white peony root is considered to nourish the blood and used to treat conditions of the female reproductive system. Laboratory studies have shown that white peony has a moderate effect on hormonal activity. Herbalists prescribe it, often with liquorice, to regulate the menstrual cycle and relieve pain. The combination is used to treat irregular, heavy, delayed or absent bleeding, period pain, premenstrual syndrome, fibroids and polycystic ovarian syndrome.

White peony can also have a relaxing effect on muscles, and it may lower blood pressure due to its ability to dilate blood vessels and improve circulation. Traditionally and in combination with other herbs, white peony has also been used to ease muscle cramps and reduce intestinal griping, enhance memory and concentration, relieve night sweats and treat angina.

For the safe and appropriate use of white peony, consult a doctor or medical herbalist. Do not take white peony if you are pregnant or breastfeeding. The medicinal use of peonies is restricted to qualified practitioners.

Pepper

Piper spp. Piperaceae

From earliest times, pepper was traded thousands of miles from the East to Arabia and overland to Europe. It was the most indispensable of exotic spices and very expensive, and became a major factor in European world exploration, leading to colonisation and the monopolisation of supplies.

Dried peppercorns

PART USED Fruits

■ Gardening

Pepper belongs to a genus of more than 1000 tropical evergreen climbers, shrubs and small trees. It is a multistemmed vine with ovate, clearly veined leaves and minute, petal-less white flowers on pendent spikes which develop green berries that turn yellow then red as they ripen. Unripe fruits yield green and black peppercorns, while ripe fruits are processed into white peppercorns by soaking the berries in water for 7–10 days so that the outer red flesh disintegrates, leaving the pale seed exposed for drying.

A stalk of black pepper (*Piper nigrum*) with fully ripened fruits.

Varieties Many kinds of pepper are grown worldwide and used for flavouring. Those with similar uses to white and black peppercorns include long pepper, pippali or jaborandi (*P. longum*), which has hotter fruits than *P. nigrum*, and cubeb or tailed pepper (*P. cubeba*), the pepper used in the Moroccan spice blend *ras-el-hanout*. An unrelated South America tree, *Schinus molle*, is the source of pink peppercorns.
Position Rich, well-drained, neutral to acid soil in light shade and high humidity, ideally at 26–30°C. In winter, vines can survive 16°C if kept on the dry side and in brighter light.
Propagation By cuttings in summer.
Maintenance Provide a trellis and tie in climbing shoots as they develop.
Pests and diseases Vines are prone to *Phytophthora* and *Fusarium* rots. Increase ventilation and spray with Bordeaux mixture (a copper-sulphur compound).
Harvesting and storing Green peppercorns are picked when the spike has 10 per cent yellow berries or less. For black peppercorns, spikes are picked when fruits are yellow. Ripe fruits, over 75 per cent red, are needed for white peppercorns. All are dried thoroughly before storing whole or grinding.

■ Herbal medicine

Piper nigrum. Fruits, essential oil. Pepper is a warming, antiseptic, antibacterial herb which stimulates and improves digestion. The essential oil is an ingredient of rubbing oils to relieve pain and inflammation in joints. In traditional Chinese medicine pepper is used for digestive upsets and infections, and to treat food poisoning caused by seafoods or fungi. For the safe use of pepper consult a doctor or medical herbalist.

■ Cooking

Ground pepper is as important as salt for seasoning savoury foods. White pepper is hotter but less aromatic, otherwise it is a matter of taste which is used, unless specified in a recipe. Mignonette or 'shot' pepper is a mixture of ground white and black pepper. White peppercorns are more often used in pickling. Green peppercorns are usually used whole in sauces for steak and duck.

A king's ransom

Pepper was so valuable in the past that it was used as currency, hence the term 'a peppercorn rent.' When Atila the Hun laid siege to Rome in 408 CE, he held the city to ransom, demanding 3000 pounds (1360kg) of pepper, which he knew was stockpiled in the Roman treasury. 'They arrive with gold and depart with pepper' wrote a Tamil poet, referring to Roman traders who regularly called at ports in his homeland of southern India.

Perilla

Perilla frutescens syn. P. ocimoides Lamiaceae

Perilla is an indispensable herb in Japanese cuisine. A volatile oil in the leaves contains a compound 2000 times sweeter than sugar, used as an artificial sweetener in Japan.

OTHER COMMON NAMES Beafsteak plant, shiso
PARTS USED Leaves, flower spikes, seed

■ Gardening

Perilla is a slender frost-hardy annual, 60cm-1.2m tall, with aromatic, broadly ovate, serrated leaves, which are green, often with a purple flush. Tiny white flowers are borne in dense spikes 10cm long. Colourful and curly-leafed forms are increasingly popular as ornamental annuals for pots and bedding.

Varieties *P. frutescens* var. *crispa* has crinkled bronze-purple leaves and pink flowers. Some clones have cumin and cinnamon-scented leaves while others are more like ginger. 'Red' or 'Akajiso' has deep red to purple leaves and is used to flavour and colour pickles. Large-leafed 'Kkaennip' or Korean perilla is eaten raw or cooked as a vegetable, or used as a wrap for meat.

Position Perilla flourishes in moist, well-drained, compost-enriched soils. It is happy in sun or partial shade.

Propagation Sow seed in spring at 13-18°C. Prick out when large enough to handle and plant when no risk of frost.

Maintenance Pinch out initial flower spikes to encourage bushy growth.

Pests and diseases If grown indoors, perilla is prone to whitefly.

Harvesting and storing Harvest the leaves in summer. They are usually used fresh. Harvest flower spikes before the flowers develop, and the seed in autumn. Handling the leaves may cause dermatitis in susceptible individuals.

■ Herbal medicine

Perilla frutescens. Parts used: leaves, seeds. Perilla has been used for centuries in traditional Japanese medicine (Kampo), and by Chinese herbalists for similar therapeutic purposes. It is often prescribed with other herbs for colds, flu and coughs, and to ease lack of appetite, nausea and bloating. It is also used successfully to manage hay fever and dermatitis. It is a key ingredient in the Kampo herbal formula Saibokuto, that is used for several allergic conditions.

Laboratory research has confirmed anti-allergic and anti-inflammatory properties in perilla extracts. Clinical trials have shown promising results for oral preparations of perilla for the relief of hay fever symptoms, including watery, itching eyes. Other studies have recorded improvements in allergic dermatitis with the use of a topical perilla cream.

For the safe and appropriate medicinal use of perilla, see *Hay fever and sinusitis*, page 203. Do not use perilla in greater than culinary quantities if you are pregnant or breastfeeding.

■ Cooking

Perilla leaves are used fresh in salads, garnishes and for pickling as a condiment for Japanese dishes. Red shiso contains colour compounds that are commonly used to dye foods pink as well as preserve them. The leaves and seeds have antibacterial properties, which helps to protect against food poisoning from dishes based on seafood and raw fish (sashimi). Immature flower spikes are used in soups and tempura, and the seeds are often sprouted for salads or salted as a condiment.

Japanese cuisine

In Japan perilla leaves are a favourite garnish or wrap for dishes such as sushi. They are also used to colour and flavour pickled plums and Japanese ginger (mioga). Red perilla is more often used for culinary purposes than green, though the latter is preferred for garnishing. Different varieties of perilla are also used in Indonesian, Thai, Vietnamese and Korean cuisine.

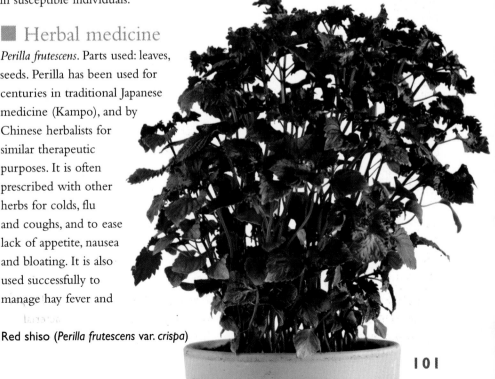

Red shiso (*Perilla frutescens* var. *crispa*)

Pine

Pinus spp. Pinaceae

The bracing aroma of pine has long been associated with health and hygiene and its scent still perfumes modern cleaners. For this reason convalescent homes were traditionally sited in mountain pine forests where it was believed that patients could gain strength simply by inhaling the pine-scented air.

PART USED Oil

Pine nuts

Male flowers of *Pinus sylvestris* borne at the end of the branch.

■ Gardening

Dwarf mountain pine (*Pinus mugo*), from the Central European Alps, and Scots pine (*P. sylvestris*), a widespread species in Europe and Asia, are hardy evergreen conifers with pairs of long, needle-like leaves and ovoid brown cones about 5cm long. As the name suggests, dwarf mountain pine is low growing, seldom reaching more than 3.5m and is often shrubby in habit, whereas Scots pine is a large tree, 15–30m tall. Most pines dislike shade and pollution, but some will tolerate poor soils and coastal sites and make excellent windbreaks.

Varieties There are several varieties of dwarf mountain pine which are small and shrubby, and therefore better suited to confined spaces. These include 'Mops', which is slow growing, dense and rounded, reaching only 1.5m. Scots pine has ornamental, smaller growing varieties too, such as 'Gold Coin', to 2m, with bright golden foliage, and 'Watereri' syn. 'Nana', which is dwarf and upright, to 4m.

Position Well-drained neutral to acid soil in sun.

Propagation Sow seed in spring (species only) or graft named varieties in late winter. Dwarf mountain pine can also be layered if there are low-growing branches.

Maintenance No pruning is required.

Pests and diseases Pines are susceptible to honey fungus. Foliage may be damaged by aphids and insect larvae.

Harvest Leaves and young shoots are collected during the growing season and distilled for oil. Oils are then processed into ointments, gels, inhalants and massage oil.

■ Herbal medicine

Pinus mugo. Part used: oil.
Pinus sylvestris. Part used: oil. Various pines have been used medicinally from earliest times. All are rich in resins and camphoraceous volatile oils, including pinene, which are strongly antiseptic and stimulant. Pine oil extracted from the needles and shoots of *P. mugo* and *P. sylvatica* is widely used in massage oils for muscular stiffness, sciatica and rheumatism and in inhalations and vapour rubs for bronchial congestion. The oil from *P. mugo*, known as pumilio pine oil, is specifically used to treat respiratory tract infections and bronchial congestion. Pine oils may cause allergic reactions in susceptible individuals.

For the safe and appropriate use of pine oils, consult your doctor or medical herbalist. Do not use pine oils if you are pregnant or breastfeeding.

■ Around the house

Pine oils are used in perfumery, bath products, hair lotions, detergents and disinfectants.

Pinus mugo 'Winter Gold' can be grown as a container specimen for the patio.

Plantain

Plantago spp. Plantaginaceae

Common plantain is a weed, but it has long been valued in folk medicine, and continues to find herbal uses. In some parts of the world it is known as 'white man's foot', as it spread by seed caught in trouser turn-ups in colonial times.

PARTS USED Leaves (*P. major*, *P. lanceolata*); seeds, seed husks (*P. psyllium*, *P. ovata*)

Purple-leafed plantain (*P. major* 'Rubrifolia)

■ Gardening

No one would willingly grow common weeds like plantains, but ornamental, less invasive varieties make attractive subjects for containers and borders.

Varieties Common plantain (*P. major*) an evergreen perennial, forms a basal rosette of ovate, deeply veined leaves to 15cm, from which emerge cylindrical spikes of tiny green flowers. Its two excellent forms are the beetroot-coloured 'Rubrifolia', and 'Rosularis', the rose plantain, with leafy flower spikes that resemble green roses.

Ribwort plantain (*P. lanceolata*) is used interchangeably with *P. major* in herbal medicine and looks similar, but with ribbed lanceolate leaves and shorter flower spikes. Variegated and golden forms are 'Streaker' and 'Golden Spears'. Asian plantain (*P. asiatica* syn. *P. major* var.

asiatica) looks like common plantain but with longer flower spikes to 50cm. 'Variegata' has white-marbled leaves.

Psyllium (*P. psyllium*) is an annual to 40cm, with whorls of narrow leaves and clusters of small, rounded inflorescences. Ispaghula or blond psyllium (*P. ovata*) is also widely used, as are black psyllium (*P. indica*) and golden psyllium (*P. arenaria*) to a lesser degree.

Position *P. psyllium* and *P. ovata* prefer full sun and well-drained soil. *P. major* prefers damper, more disturbed ground than *P. lanceolata*, which is happier in grassland.

Propagation Sow seed directly in spring after the soil has warmed.

Maintenance Remove seed heads to prevent excessive self sowing.

Pests and diseases Powdery mildew is a problem for *P. major* in dry weather.

Harvesting and storing Cut leaves as required and dry for herbal use. Collect flower spikes as seed starts to ripen, and dry to release seeds.

■ Herbal medicine

Plantago lanceolata, *P. major*. Part used: leaves. Due to plantain's mucilaginous compounds, it has

reduces inflammation and irritation in the lungs and helps to remove catarrh. Plantain can also help peptic and intestinal ulcers, gastritis and colitis. It can be used as a mouthwash or gargle for inflammation of the mouth and throat, and as an ointment it helps to heal haemorrhoids, cuts and bruises.

Plantago psyllium, *P. ovata*. Parts used: seeds, husks. Psyllium is an excellent bulk laxative. Soluble fibre in the seeds absorbs water, making bowel movements easier and more regular. Clinical trials have confirmed its efficacy in treating constipation and irritable bowel syndrome. It can also be used for anal fissures, recovery from anal/rectal surgery and haemorrhoids. Soluble fibre makes psyllium a valuable part of any cholesterol-lowering programme.

For the safe use of plantain, consult a doctor or medical herbalist. For the use of psyllium, see *Constipation and haemorrhoids*, page 213, and *Detox*, page 215. Do not use if pregnant or breastfeeding, except with the advice of a doctor or medical herbalist.

Constipation and haemorrhoids, page 213, and *Detox*, page 215.

A sacred herb

One of the Nine Sacred Herbs of the Anglo-Saxons, plantain was believed to cure headaches. The *Lacnunga*, a collection of medical texts written in the 11th or 12th century, relates this story of the god Woden: ' ... out of the worm sprang nine poisons. So Woden took his sword and changed it into nine herbs. These herbs did the wise lord create and sent them into the world for rich and poor, a remedy for all...'

Rose plantain (*Plantago major* 'Rosularis')

Pomegranate

Punica granatum Lythraceae

Pomegranates feature in ancient Egyptian tomb paintings and were a symbol of fertility in Classical times. Revered throughout the ages, it is likely that the apple that tempted Eve in the Garden of Eden was in fact a pomegranate. The word pomegranate means 'apple with many seeds'.

PARTS USED Seeds, juice, rind, root bark

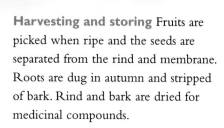

Pomegranate fruit and seeds

Gardening

Pomegranate is a dense, frost-hardy, deciduous shrub or small tree, native to the Middle East but now cultivated worldwide in warm temperate regions. It reaches 6m and has small shiny leaves and funnel-shaped, crinkled orange-red flowers. After pollination, the waxy calyx swells to form the familiar leathery, yellow-red to burgundy fruits, holding pale crunchy seeds surrounded by bright pink pulp and bitter yellowish pith.

Pomegranates flower and fruit freely, and are very ornamental. They make wonderful pot plants for patios and garden rooms, and can even be grown outdoors, perhaps trained against a sunny wall, in mild sheltered areas. Ample warmth and sunshine in summer, and a winter minimum of 10°C is ideal, though plants will tolerate occasional dips to freezing.

Varieties The two most widely grown ornamentals are the dwarf *P. granatum* var. *nana* and the double-flowered *P. granatum* f. *plena*. 'Wonderful', a Californian clone, has tasty fruits and juice, and a high level of antioxidants.
Position Well-drained soil in full sun. Container plants thrive in John Innes No2 Compost with a little well-rotted compost or slow-release fertiliser.
Propagation Sow seed in spring at 20-25°C or take semi-ripe cuttings in summer.
Maintenance Remove awkward shoots in spring to give an open, well-shaped framework. Feed pot-grown plants monthly. Keep on the dry side in low winter temperatures.
Pests and diseases Mealy bug and tortrix moth larvae, which cause leaves to 'web' together, are sometimes a problem for plants grown indoors.

Harvesting and storing Fruits are picked when ripe and the seeds are separated from the rind and membrane. Roots are dug in autumn and stripped of bark. Rind and bark are dried for medicinal compounds.

Herbal medicine

Punica granatum. Parts used: rind, root bark, fruit extracts. Traditional uses of pomegranate focused on the rind and root bark. These parts contain toxic alkaloids that rid the body of intestinal parasites and disrupt the reproductive cycle. Today the emphasis is on the antioxidant and anti-inflammatory compounds in the fruit extracts.

Research has shown that pomegranate extracts stimulate the immune system and have anticancer and antidiabetic activity. Do not use pomegranate rind and root bark for any purpose unless prescribed by a qualified medical herbalist.

Cooking

Pomegranate seeds are eaten fresh, on their own or in fruit salads and other desserts. The juice is delicious, often blended with other juices or made into sorbets and jellies. It is also evaporated to make syrup, known as grenadine, which is used in cocktails, and molasses or *dibs rumman*, a favourite ingredient in Middle Eastern cuisine.

Pick pomegranates that are unblemished, with smooth, thick skin and a heavy feel.

Poppy

Papaver spp. Eschscholzia californica Papaveraceae

Cultivated for 5000 years, poppies were once symbolic both of the earth goddess and of Ceres, the goddess of cereals. Opium poppy is the source of the pain killers, morphine and codeine, but also the addictive drug, heroin.

PARTS USED Aerial parts (*E. californica*); latex (*P. somniferum*); petals (*P. rhoeas*); seeds (*P. somniferum, P. rhoeas*)

▪ Gardening

These poppies are easily grown hardy annuals which are ideal for filling gaps in borders and adding to other annuals to create wild flower meadows.

Varieties Opium poppy (*P. somniferum*) grows to about 1.2m with large, toothed, silvery green foliage and four-petalled mauve to white flowers, followed by globose capsules with an operculum that opens to scatter the ripe seed. The wall of the green capsule oozes bitter white latex when wounded. A number of ornamental forms are widely grown, including the 19th-century red and white 'Danish Flag', and the very old 'Hen and Chickens', which has a ring of tiny flowers encircling each large flower. Most popular of all are peony-flowered varieties (Paeoniiflorum Group), such as 'White Cloud', 'Black Peony' and 'Flemish Antique'.

Corn or field poppy (*P. rhoeas*) has four bright red petals, sometimes with a black blotch in the centre. It was used to breed ornamental Shirley poppies and Mother of Pearl Group.

Californian poppy (*E. californica*) is native to the western United States, with the sub-species *mexicana* extending south into the Sonoran Desert. It is heat and drought-resistant, with blue-green, finely divided leaves and numerous silken, four-petalled flowers in lemon to orange. Ornamental strains include 'Ballerina' with single, semi-double and double fluted flowers in shades of red, pink, orange and yellow.

Position All poppies require well-drained soil and a sunny position.

Propagation Poppies do not transplant successfully, so sow seeds thinly and evenly by mixing them with dry sand. If you sow at 4–6 week intervals from early spring, you will have flowers all summer and autumn.

Maintenance Weed regularly.

Pests and diseases Powdery mildew can be a problem as plants go to seed.

Harvesting and storing Harvest and dry aerial parts and petals when flowers are fully open. Collect seed from ripe capsules and dry them.

▪ Herbal medicine

Eschscholzia californica. Parts used: aerial parts. The aerial parts of Californian poppy were used by Native Americans as a pain killer, and have been incorporated into Western herbal medicine as a valuable pain-relieving and relaxing herb. It is used for treating insomnia, anxiety and over-excitability, and may be a useful remedy for aiding relaxation

Poppy seeds, the source of poppy oil, are harmless flavourings for baked goods.

Opium poppy

Opium derived from the latex of the unripe seed capsules of the opium poppy (*P. somniferum*) was once a traditional herbal medicine as well as a legal recreational drug, but we now know that opiates are addictive and associated with serious adverse effects. In the Western world, opium is a heavily regulated and licensed product used to produce morphine and codeine. Morphine and codeine provide exceptional pain relief as pharmaceutical drugs, but still carry a risk of dependency with overuse.

Californian poppy (*Eschscholzia californica*)

Poppy continued

during times of tension and stress. Californian poppy alleviates many types of pain, including headaches, nervous cramping of the bowel, and rheumatic and nerve pain.

Substances known as alkaloids are responsible for the plant's sedating and pain-killing properties. They are similar to those found in opium poppy, but have a far gentler therapeutic effect and are regarded as non-habit forming.

Papaver rhoeas. Part used: petals. Despite being related to the opium poppy, the corn or field poppy possesses none of its counterpart's potent narcotic effects. Instead, it is used as a reliable traditional remedy for soothing respiratory conditions that are associated with irritable coughing and the presence of catarrh.

Corn poppy is regarded as mildly sedating and can be useful for alleviating poor or disturbed sleep.

For the safe and appropriate use of Californian and corn poppy, consult your doctor or medical herbalist. Do not use these herbs if you are pregnant or breastfeeding.

■ Cooking

Poppy seeds are not narcotic and are enjoyed for their flavour and crunchy texture. They are popular in breads, cakes, pastries, muffins and bagels. In India, the seeds are ground and used to thicken sauces. The seeds also feature in Jewish and German cooking, and make an interesting addition to salad dressings.

Remembrance Day

In the First World War battlefields around Flanders in northern Europe, red or field poppies bloomed everywhere in the ravaged earth. Since then, they have become a symbol of Armistice or Remembrance Day on 11 November each year. John McCrae wrote the poem below in 1915, the day after he witnessed the death of a friend.

On 11 November, Remembrance Day, wreaths of artificial field poppies are placed on war memorials in memory of the fallen.

In Flanders Fields

In Flanders fields the poppies blow
Between the crosses, row on row,
That mark our place; and in the sky
The larks, still bravely singing, fly
Scarce heard amid the guns below.

We are the dead. Short days ago
We lived, felt dawn, saw sunset glow,
Loved, and were loved, and now we lie
In Flanders fields.

Take up our quarrel with the foe
To you from failing hands we throw
The torch; be yours to hold it high.
If ye break faith with us who die
We shall not sleep, though poppies grow
In Flanders fields.

Major John McCrae, 1872–1918

Corn or field poppy (*Papaver rhoeas*) is perfect for enlivening a wild flower garden.

Primrose and cowslip

Primula vulgaris, P. veris Primulaceae

Cowslips were once known as 'cowsloppes', in the belief that they grew in cow droppings, or as the 'keys of St Peter', who supposedly dropped the keys from heaven, causing cowslips to spring up where they fell.

OTHER COMMON NAME Paigle (cowslip)
PARTS USED Leaves, flowers, roots

Primrose (*Primula vulgaris*)

■ Gardening

Primrose (*P. vulgaris*) is a hardy perennial forming a basal rosette of oblong, rugose leaves, from which spring a number of stalked, solitary flowers with a delicate fragrance. The flowers are five-petalled and pale yellow (rarely white), with a central cleft in each petal. The foliage of cowslips closely resembles that of primroses, but the smaller, golden yellow, sweetly scented flowers are borne in clusters at the top of each flowering stem, well above the leaves. According to the English herbalist John Gerard, writing in the 16th century, a tisane made from the flowers was drunk in the month of May to cure the 'frenzie'.

Varieties Primrose varieties that are mentioned in Elizabethan herbals and are still available, include 'Jack in the Green', with a much enlarged persistent ruff-like calyx; 'Hose in Hose', with a second flower emerging from the first; and attractive fully double forms such as the pure white 'Alba Plena', and lavender 'Lilacina Plena'. There is a double cowslip too, 'Katy McSparron'.

Position Primroses require moist, rich soil and light shade, while cowslips prefer a well-drained drier site in full sun or partial shade.

Propagation Propagate cowslips and primroses by seed or by division in spring. Stratify the seed for 10 weeks to break dormancy (see page 50).

Maintenance Mulch the plants. Break up any clumps and replant well-rooted divisions every 2 years.

Pests and diseases Leaf-eating insects can damage plants. Rust may infect leaves, and *Botrytis* can kill plants.

Harvesting and storing Gather leaves and flowers in spring to use fresh, and for use in preserves and wine. Before storing, air-dry flowers, leaves and roots (lifted in autumn). Because of habitat loss and over-harvesting, do not gather them from the wild.

■ Herbal medicine

Primula veris, P. officinalis. Parts used: flowers, roots. Both the flowers and roots of cowslip have been used medicinally for centuries. The flowers have relaxing and sedative properties and are used to treat insomnia and restlessness. They can be a valuable remedy in times of stress and tension. Cowslip is traditionally used to alleviate catarrhal congestion and irritable coughs that occur with respiratory disorders, such as bronchitis.

For the safe and appropriate use of cowslip, consult a doctor or medical herbalist. Do not use cowslip if you are pregnant or breastfeeding.

Traditionally, it was believed that if you nibbled on cowslips you would see fairies.

Strewing herbs

In the Middle Ages, strewing herbs were used often mixed with, rushes or straw as a floor covering. They helped to mask unpleasant odours, deter household pests and, it was believed, protect against disease.

According to Thomas Tusser's *Five Hundred Good Points of Husbandry* (1573), the 21 strewing herbs comprised:' Bassell [basil], Bawlme [lemon balm], Camamel [chamomile], Costemary [costmary], Cowsleps and paggles [cowslips], Daisies of all sorts, Sweet fennel, Germander, Hysop [hyssop], Lavender, Lavender spike, Lavender cotten [santolina], Marjorom, Mawdelin, Peny ryall [pennyroyal], Roses of all sorts, Red myntes, Sage, Tansey, Violets, Winter savery.'

Purslane

Portulaca oleracea Portulacaceae

In centuries past, purslane was taken as a cure for 'blastings by lightning or planets' or for 'anything swollen'. Considered a weed in many parts of the world and yet cultivated for thousands of years in the Mediterranean basin, India and China, this succulent herb is now appreciated once again for its culinary and medicinal uses.

PARTS USED Leaves, stems

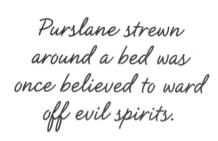

Purslane
(*Portulaca
oleracea*)

■ Gardening

Purslane is a half-hardy annual that grows 20-45cm high, with reddish stems and wedge to spoon-shaped, succulent green leaves. It is variable, sometimes upright and bushy, or low and spreading.

The ephemeral flowers are inconspicuous, five-petalled and yellow, and are followed by capsules containing tiny, spherical black seeds. Cultivated purslane is often referred to as var. *sativa*. The highly nutritious leaves are tender and fleshy, with a slight crunchy texture. Purslane is easily grown at home but is rarely sold commercially as the fleshy leaves do not keep well in pre-packed salad mixes. In light sandy soils, gravel paths and coastal gardens, it will self sow freely.

Varieties There is a golden-leafed variety (var. *aurea*).

Position Well-drained soil in full sun.

Propagation Plant the seeds after the soil warms in spring and again in summer for continuous cropping. Barely press them into the soil, which should be kept moist. Left uncovered, they will germinate rapidly.

Maintenance For a tender, abundant crop, keep the soil moist at all times. An occasional light application of liquid seaweed fertiliser at the recommended rate is also helpful.

Pests and diseases Slugs may be a problem.

Harvesting and storing Leaves and sprigs are best picked before flowering. Wrapped in kitchen paper inside a polythene bag, they keep for up to a week in the fridge.

■ Cooking

Purslane has a slightly sour, salty, lemony spinach flavour and is the highest known plant source of omega-3 fatty acids. Though best used fresh in salads and sandwiches, it can also be cooked like spinach or used in stir-fries. It contains mucilage and when cooked gives the palate a glutinous sensation, serving to thicken soups and sauces, and making a good substitute for okra in Creole dishes such as gumbo. In French cooking, the fleshy leaves are cooked in equal amounts with sorrel to make the classic soup *bonne femme*. They are also a traditional ingredient in fattoush, a Middle Eastern bread salad. Add a few leaves to the version of this dish featured on page 357. Purslane also makes an excellent pickle, using wine or apple cider vinegar spiced with garlic, chilli and whole peppercorns.

Purslane strewn around a bed was once believed to ward off evil spirits.

Purslane soup

250g purslane, chopped
50g butter
1 litre stock
250g potatoes, peeled
   and sliced
3 tablespoons cream
fresh purslane, to garnish

Cook purslane with butter in covered pan. Add stock, cook until potato is tender, then purée in a blender. Stir in cream, then garnish with fresh purslane.

With leaves that are rich in the vitamins A, C and E, purslane is considered to be one of the 'power foods' of the future.

Red clover

Trifolium pratense Papilionaceae

Red clover has been an important agricultural forage and fertility-improving crop since the Middle Ages. The plant contains phytoestrogens and is increasingly important as a medicinal herb, particularly for menopausal symptoms.

OTHER COMMON NAMES Meadow clover, purple clover
PART USED Flowerhead

A commecially grown crop of red clover.

■ Gardening

Red clover is a short-lived hardy perennial with a sprawling habit, producing stems 20-60cm in length, and long-stalked trifoliate leaves, each leaflet marked with a central pale arrowhead. The flowerheads are rounded, composed of many mauve-pink pea flowers, which are rich in nectar, much loved by bees. In common with other clovers and legumes, nitrogen-fixing bacteria in its root nodules assimilate atmospheric nitrogen, thus improving soil fertility. If you are fortunate enough to own some grassland or wild flower meadow, make sure to plant some red clover for the bees – and for herb teas.

Varieties There is an attractive form of red clover with yellow-veined leaves called 'Susan Smith' (also known as 'Dolly North' and 'Goldnet'). It's an unusual and very tolerant plant for containers and hanging baskets. Plugs (mini plants) are sold by wild flower nurseries for planting directly into turf.

Position Red clover prefers light soil, good drainage and full sun.

Propagation Sow seed in spring.

Maintenance Keep young plants clear of competition until well established.

Pests and diseases Powdery mildew can be a problem during dry weather.

Harvesting and storing Harvest flowerheads when fully opened. Use them fresh or dried.

■ Herbal medicine

Trifolium pratense. Parts used: flowerheads, isolated isoflavone compounds. Red clover flowers traditionally have been used, both internally and externally, as a remedy for the treatment of chronic skin conditions such as eczema and psoriasis, particularly in children. Taken as an infusion or syrup of the flowers, red clover also alleviates the coughing associated with some respiratory conditions, such as bronchitis.

These days, the most common application for red clover centres around the use of isolated compounds known as isoflavones that come from the leaves and flowers. These compounds have been shown to possess mild oestrogenic activity, and clinical studies suggest that they can alleviate many of the symptoms associated with menopause.

For the safe and appropriate use of red clover, consult a doctor or medical herbalist. Do not use red clover if you are pregnant or breastfeeding.

The shamrock

In the teachings of St Patrick, the clover's trifoliate leaves (from the Latin tri, meaning 'three', and folium, 'leaf') symbolised the Holy Trinity – the doctrine that God is the Father, Son and Holy Spirit. This is often quoted as being the origin of the shamrock. Although the Celtic harp is the official emblem of Ireland, the shamrock is the national emblem of Northern Ireland.

The rare four-leafed clover is a symbol of good luck.

Red clover (*Trifolium pratense*)

Rocket

Eruca vesicaria subsp. *sativa* Brassicaceae

Native to the Mediterranean basin, eastward to Turkey and Jordan, rocket has been popular since ancient Roman times for its peppery leaves. It is still sometimes known as Roman rocket. Despite its popularity as a salad herb, rocket has only been cultivated commercially since the 1990s.

OTHER COMMON NAMES Arugula, Italian cress, Roman rocket, rucola
PARTS USED Leaves, flowers, seeds

Rocket (*Eruca vesicaria* subsp. *sativa*)

Wild rocket (*Diplotaxis tenuifolia*)

◼ Gardening

Rocket (*Eruca sativa* subsp. *sativa*) is a hardy annual, with usually lobed leaves that are aromatic and peppery, and tall stems of cream, purple-veined, four-petalled flowers. The peppery flavour comes from isothiocyanate compounds similar to those in related horseradish (*Armoracia rusticana*) and wasabi (*Wasabia japonica*); see page 69. The leaves add flavour to other salad greens and have become a salad standard in recent years, while the piquant flowers and buds can also be added to salads. Small round seeds are borne in edible slender pods. Grow your own in pots or shallow containers, or with other fast-growing salad crops in the vegetable garden. In most gardens, rocket self sows freely.

Varieties 'Victoria' is a classic variety, 'Dentellata' has more deeply lobed leaves. Wild rocket (*Diplotaxis tenuifolia*), has a more intense flavour, smaller, more deeply cut leaves and yellow flowers.
Position Moist, rich soil in sun or light shade. Wild rocket also thrives in drier conditions.
Propagation Sow rocket every 4-6 weeks from spring to autumn for a supply of tender young leaves, as it tends to run to seed fairly easily. Rocket is often included in mesclun mixtures, or you can make up your own by mixing one packet each of rocket, lettuce, mustard, radish, coriander, spring onions and chervil (or whichever salad ingredients you like most).
Maintenance Weed and water regularly.
Pests and diseases Flea beetles are the main problem, causing tiny holes in leaves. To prevent them nibbling the leaves, cover crop with fleece or fine mesh to exclude insects.
Harvesting and storing Pick rocket leaves before flowering. Wash and store in the fridge for up to a week wrapped in kitchen paper inside a polythene bag. Harvest flowers and buds as required. Collect seeds when ripe.

◼ Cooking

This herb adds a piquant flavour to salads and can replace basil in pesto.

It can also be rapidly sautéed or steamed in pasta and risotto dishes, stir-fries, soups and sauces. Rocket needs only the briefest cooking. Add a scattering of the fresh herb as a topping for pizzas at the end of baking. The seeds have a mustard-like flavour; they make excellent sprouts and are also pressed for oil.

Roman salad

The Romans considered rocket an aphrodisiac but their recipe for a mixed salad of rocket, chicory, cos lettuce, lavender and tender mallow leaves with cheese and dressing is sufficiently seductive in its own right. A modern take on this salad is rocket simply dressed with good olive oil, balsamic vinegar and some shavings of Parmesan cheese.

Rose

Rosa spp. Rosaceae

Roses have long been associated with health, beauty, and cleansing. Ten tonnes of rosewater are used annually to wash the walls of the holy city of Mecca [Makkah] during the Haj. In 77 CE Pliny the Elder noted that 'rose preparations are of benefit in 32 different human disorders'. Roses symbolise undying love and loyalty too, as witnessed by the enduring popularity of red roses on Valentine's Day, and the pub sign 'Rose and Crown'.

PARTS USED Petals, rosehips

Rosa 'Roseraie de la Hay'

■ Gardening

Old shrub roses, not modern hybrids – are the roses of choice for cooking, fragrance and herbal medicines. With the exception of the native dog rose (*R. canina*), these old varieties originated in the Middle East and eastern Asia, and have been cultivated for so long that their names and exact origins are often obscure. All are hardy and although most flower only once in early summer, they are worth a place in any garden.

Varieties Apothecary's rose or Provins rose (*R. gallica* var. *officinalis*) is very free flowering, with semi-double, deep pink flowers. The oldest of garden roses, grown by ancient Greeks and Romans, it was planted in monastery gardens throughout Europe and cultivated in vast fields around the town of Provins, 50km southeast of Paris, from the 13th to the 19th century for manufacture into conserves, jellies, syrups, cordials, pastilles, perfumes, salves,

Rosehips

Varieties of *Rosa rugosa* are highly productive and tolerant of exposed and coastal locations. They are repeat flowering and bear clusters of cherry-sized hips that are excellent for making syrups and teas. Other hip-bearing roses, such as dog rose (*R. canina*) and sweetbriar (*R. rubiginosa* syn. *R. eglanteria*) are used to produce rosehip oil, also known as rose mosqueta, which has multiple benefits for the skin. It is antioxidant and astringent, and very rich in essential fatty acids, flavonoids and carotenoids.

creams and candles. The petals are tonic and astringent, and were favoured by physicians through the ages. Also known as the red rose of Lancaster (see *The Wars of the Roses*, page 112), the apothecary's rose has a strong fragrance which is retained after drying. The striped form, 'Versicolor' (see *Rosa Mundi,* page 113) is enduringly popular as a garden plant. Other favourite Gallicas for the herb garden include 'Tuscany' or 'Old Velvet', with flat, semi-double, burgundy flowers, and 'Belle de Crécy', an almost thornless rose with richly fragrant pink blooms.

Damask rose (*R.* x *damascena*), named after the city of Damascus, was brought from the Middle East by Crusaders. It is used for the distillation of essential oil, known as attar (otto) of roses, a process invented by the Persian physician Avicenna (Ibn Sina) in the 1st century CE. Historically, attar of roses is produced mainly in Iran, which grows the classic damask rose, a vigorous arching shrub with semi-double pale pink flowers, together with improved damasks, such as 'Gloire de Guilan', with clear pink flowers and 'Ispahan', with a longer period of clear pink blooms. Bulgaria is the other major producer, growing mainly the high-yielding 'Kazanlik' also known as 'Professeur Emile Perrot' or 'Trigintipetala'. The area around Grasse in France still produces attar based on

Rose continued

Rosa gallica 'Tuscany'

the **Provence or old cabbage rose** (*R. centifolia*), with a small amount coming from the Damask 'Quatre Saisons', an ancient repeat-flowering variety with grey-green foliage and deeply fragrant pink flowers. The production of fine-quality organic English rose oil and other rose products was established in the 1990s, using three main varieties: the traditional 'Kazanlik'; the resilient crimson-flowered 'Roseraie de l'Hay' (a variety of *R. rugosa*); and the heavily scented lilac-pink Bourbon 'Louise Odier', which is one of the best for making rose petal jam.

Position Old shrub roses prefer heavier loam and clay soils, enriched with well-rotted manure or compost. Rugosas

During the Second World War wild rosehips were harvested to make a vitamin C supplement for children.

thrive in lighter sandy soils, are salt tolerant and make good hedges. All flower best in full sun.

Propagation Take hardwood cuttings in winter.

Maintenance Prune old shrub roses to shape immediately after flowering as they flower on ripe wood. In winter, take out any unproductive old stems from the base and shorten very long new shoots by about a third. Rugosas flower and fruit into autumn so pruning is a winter job, cutting back shrubs or hedges to a manageable size. Apply mulch after pruning.

Pests and diseases The most likely problems are blackspot on leaves and aphids on buds.

Harvesting and storing Harvest roses when they have just opened, on sunny mornings as soon as the dew has dried. To dry, spread the petals on paper-covered trays out of direct sunlight. Harvest the hips when fully coloured and dry in the same way as the flowers.

■ Herbal medicine

Rosa canina. Part used: Rosehips. The hips of dog rose contain notable levels of vitamin C, and can be taken as a tea or syrup in winter to help fight off colds and flu. Because of their slightly drying nature, rosehips have also been used to reduce symptoms of diarrhoea. Medicinal preparations of rosehip, mainly in powdered form, have been the focus of recent scientific research for the treatment of osteoarthritic conditions. The results of clinical trials suggest that it may help to reduce symptoms of pain and stiffness.

R. gallica var. *officinalis* The petals, either administered as a tea or a syrup, were used to treat the common cold, inflammation of the digestive tract and hysteria. A decoction was used to treat sprains, chapped lips and sore throats.

Rosa x *damascena*, *R.* x *centifolia* Rose otto is used in aromatherapy to treat

Rosa x *damascena* 'Kazanlik', is a sumptuous Damask rose.

The Wars of the Roses

The apothecary's rose, *Rosa gallica* var. *officinalis*, was introduced from the Middle East into England by the Crusaders. It became the symbol of the House of Lancaster in the Wars of the Roses (1455–1487). The opposing House of York adopted the ancient semi-double white rose, *R.* x *alba* 'Alba Semiplena'. At the end of the wars, Henry VII, the father of Henry VIII, combined them into the Tudor Rose, usually depicted as a double rose with white on red, one of the symbols of the House of Tudor.

The frame on this portrait of Edward VI (1537–1553), the son of Henry VIII, shows the Lancaster and York roses combining to form the Tudor rose.

depression and nervous tension, and to balance emotions which are upset by hormonal changes or grief. Rosewater is used in soothing preparations for eye infections, such as conjunctivitis.

For the safe and appropriate medicinal use of rosehips, consult your doctor or medical herbalist, and also see *Pregnancy*, page 236.

Do not use rosehips in greater than culinary quantities if you are pregnant or breastfeeding, except under the supervision of a doctor or qualified medical harbalist.

■ Natural beauty

Both rosehips and petals have many uses in cosmetics. The petals of some varieties yield the fabulously expensive and richly fragrant attar of roses used in perfumery. Rosewater is an inexpensive, fragrant and mildly astringent tonic for the skin; it is especially useful for chapped skin.

The essential oil from both petals and rosehips has anti-ageing effects and may be used in preparations for dry and sensitive skins as well as to reduce the appearance of fine wrinkles. Cold cream, historically known as 'ointment of rosewater', originally contained both rose oil and rosewater.

For instructions on how to make beauty products using rose extracts, see *Three roses moisturiser*, page 253, and *Rose petal bath bags*, page 274.

'Rosa mundi'

The charming *Rosa gallica* 'Versicolor' or *rosa mundi* (rose of the world), is named for Rosamund Clifford, who was the reluctant mistress of Henry II, king of England in the 12th century.

An ancient variety of the apothecary's rose, it bears semi-double deep pink blooms up to 9cm across, with pale pink to white irregular stripes.

Turkish delight

Rosewater, a by-product of the distilling process that makes rose oil from rose petals, is an important flavouring in Middle Eastern cooking. It is used for some Asian and Middle Eastern sweets, including Turkish delight, and the rasgullas and gulab jamuns of Indian cooking. Turkish delight is a sticky, jelly-like but firm sweet, made from starch and sugar. It is traditionally flavoured with rosewater and generously dusted with icing sugar; other flavours include lemon and mint. The sweet was introduced to the West in the 19th century, when a British man, who was fond of it, shipped some home.

Around the home

Place rose and lavender potpourri (see page 290) in bowls around your home.

■ Cooking

The edible petals of old roses make delicious conserves and are used in salads and desserts. The hips (fruits) and petals of some varieties – including *R. canina*, *R.* x *damascena* and *R. gallica* – are edible. The petals can be crystallised and used for decoration, to make rose petal jam, or (with the bitter 'heel' at the base of the petals removed) added to salads. See recipe for *Rose petal jelly*, page 382.

Rosehips are high in vitamin C and can be made into jams, jellies or a syrup that serves as a dietary supplement for babies. Take care to exclude the seeds, which have irritant hairs.

Ras-el-hanout, the Moroccan spice blend (see page 374), has many variations, some of which contain dried rose petals and flower buds.

The beautiful *Rosa canina* is a source of rosehip oil, which has many benefits for the texture and moisture of the skin.

Rose oil was traditionally used to anoint British monarchs during the coronation ceremony.

Rosemary

Rosmarinus officinalis Lamiaceae

Few herbs are as universally grown and loved as rosemary. In many parts of the world it is a symbol of friendship and remembrance, and for this reason the herb is often incorporated into funeral wreaths and wedding bouquets.

PARTS USED Leaves, flowering tops

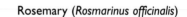

Rosemary (*Rosmarinus officinalis*)

■ Gardening

Rosmarinus means 'dew of the sea', and in the wild the herb is most commonly found growing in coastal areas around the Mediterranean. Despite their different habits and colours, almost all the rosemary varieties that are sold in nurseries belong to one species, *R. officinalis*. All are evergreen with small, dense, narrow, pointed leaves. However, they range from rounded bushes and prostrate varieties to columnar shrubs up to 2m tall. Leaves also vary in size, width and shade of green, and rosemary flowers may be pale to deep blue, purple-blue, pink or white. The majority are well-suited to cooking, although some have a camphoraceous note that is better for medicinal purposes. Rosemary has many garden uses too, from hedging and ground cover to containers and topiary. Some varieties are hardier than others so check before you plant. In cold areas, less hardy varieties are best grown in containers that can be given a protected position in winter.

Varieties Recommended tall, upright rosemary's include: 'Miss Jessop's Upright', syn. 'Fastigiatus' with a narrowly erect habit and pale, speckled flowers; 'Pyramidalis', large-growing and columnar with distinctively broad leaves; 'Herb Cottage', with bright green leaves and vivid blue flowers; and 'Gorizia', which is vigorous, with large leaves and flowers and a very good flavour.

Among the most intensely blue-flowered bush varieties are 'Benenden Blue' syn. 'Collingwood Ingram', 'Tuscan Blue', an old variety from Tuscany, and 'Roman Beauty', which has very dense, narrow leaves. Pink-flowered forms include 'Roseus', with an upright habit, and 'Majorca Pink' which has smaller flowers and is less hardy, while white-flowered forms include var. *albiflorus* syn. 'Albus' with pale blue-white flowers, and 'Lady in White', a smaller growing variety with delicate foliage and pure white flowers.

Semi-prostrate varieties are often less hardy. They are ideal for containers and trailing over walls and rocks. The most common low-growing rosemary goes under the name Prostratus Group and is variable. Named cultivars include: 'Fota Blue', with an arching habit and very dark blue, white-throated flowers; 'Severn Sea', a hardier variety with mid

Rosmarinus 'Miss Jessop's Upright'. Rosemary garlands were worn by ancient scholars in exams to aid concentration.

During the Second World War, rosemary leaves and juniper berries were burned in French hospitals in order to kill germs.

blue flowers; and 'Rampant Boule', a dense, ground-hugging French rosemary which flowers prolifically. Two of the tiniest rosemary varieties are the very fine-leafed 'Mason's Finest', and diminutive 'Baby PJ'. Variegated forms include 'Genges Gold', and the white-margined 'Silver Spires'. 'Joyce de Baggio' syn. 'Golden Rain' is the nearest to a true golden rosemary, and has uniformly yellow-green margined leaves, whereas 'Aureus' has only an occasional yellow marking.

Position This herb requires full sunshine and excellent drainage. Rosemary is tolerant of a range of pH, from moderately acid to moderately alkaline soil, although the latter results in more compact growth and intense fragrance. Being a coastal plant, rosemary tolerates salt-laden winds and poor, stony soil so is excellent for seaside plantings.

Propagation Propagate rosemary by tip cuttings taken in early autumn or spring. Rosemary seed germinates poorly, and plants do not come true to variety.

Maintenance Regular light pruning helps to keep plants in shape and improve air circulation. Rosemary has a vigorous root system so container-grown plants need to be potted on each year and replaced after 3-4 years. Porous clay pots are preferable to plastic ones as they allow better aeration and drainage. In wet areas, mulch rosemary plants with gravel, coarse gritty sand or small pebbles to prevent mud splashing, which can cause rot.

Pests and diseases Overwatered rosemary is very prone to root rot, often first seen as browning of the leaf tips and die-back of branches. Rosemary beetle is an increasingly troublesome pest. Both beetles and larvae feed on the leaves.

Harvesting and storing Harvest rosemary at any time of the year to use fresh, choosing new growths or flowering sprigs. If further supplies are needed, dry on trays lined with kitchen paper, then strip the whole leaves from the stems and store in airtight jars. Pick

Smaller more tender prostrate rosemaries are ideal for hanging baskets.

fresh flowers, minus any green parts, to use as a garnish on salads and desserts.

◼ Herbal medicine

Rosmarinus officinalis. Parts used: leaves, flowering tops. The medicinal properties of rosemary as a tonic and stimulant for the nerves and circulation have made it a popular remedy for combating general fatigue and depression, and for the improvement of poor circulation. While rosemary can be taken as an infusion, the essential oil is commonly used. A few drops can be added to a vapouriser or diluted in a little vegetable oil and applied topically for its beneficial effects. Rosemary also has anti-inflammatory and antioxidant properties, enhancing memory and concentration and possibly helping to prevent dementia.

Used externally, rosemary essential oil can be applied in a diluted form to relieve muscle cramps and arthritic joint pain. It also has a reputation for preventing premature baldness and stimulating hair growth.

Rosemary is regarded as a traditional digestive remedy and, when taken as an infusion, it can help to ease cramping, bloating and gas, and may ease 'liverish' symptoms, such as headaches and poor digestion of fats.

The basic formula uses lavender, rosemary and myrtle, but other herbs can be added.

Rosemary continued

Rosemary stems, stripped of most of their leaves and used as skewers for fish, meat or vegetables cooked on the barbecue, will impart their flavour.

For the safe and appropriate medicinal use of rosemary, consult your doctor or medical herbalist. Also, see *Memory and concentration*, page 219, for advice on external use. Do not use rosemary in greater than culinary quantities if you are pregnant or breastfeeding.

■ Around the home

Rosemary is one of the main ingredients in the famous antiseptic known as Vinegar of the Four Thieves, page 121, and can be used in a number of ways around the home.

Make a rosemary disinfectant by simmering a handful of leaves and small stems in water for 30 minutes. Strain and decant into a spray bottle.

Disinfect and deodorise hairbrushes and combs by soaking them in a solution of 250ml hot water, 1 tablespoon bicarbonate of soda and 5 drops rosemary essential oil.

Rosemary tea makes a fragrant final rinse for darkening brunette hair.

Use dried rosemary in moth-repellent sachets and in potpourri.

Use a rosemary rinse on your dog after washing to deter fleas.

Wash your pet's bedding, then add a few drops of rosemary essential oil to the final rinse. Or, spritz your pets with rosemary disinfectant as they dry themselves in the sun after a bath.

■ Cooking

The bruised leaves of rosemary have a resinous, pine-like scent and a strong taste that can overwhelm other flavours if used too generously. It complements similarly strong flavours such as wine and garlic; starchy foods (bread, scones, potatoes); rich meats such as lamb, pork, duck and game; and vegetables such as aubergines and courgettes. It is also used in sausages, stuffings, soups and stews, or steeped in vinegar or olive oil to flavour them. The leaves have a rather woody texture, so use them finely chopped.

Alternatively, use whole sprigs, or enclose leaves in a square of muslin or tea infuser, and remove just before serving. Dried rosemary has a flavour similar to that of fresh, but its very hard

A herb of goodness

Rosemary has a strong association with the Virgin Mary. It is said that, when the Holy family was fleeing from Herod's soldiers, Mary spread her blue cloak over a white-flowering rosemary bush to dry, but when she removed the cloak, the white flowers had turned blue in her honour. Also associated with ancient magical lore, rosemary was often called 'Elf Leaf', and bunches of it were hung around houses to keep thieves and witches out and to prevent fairies getting in and stealing infant children.

You can crystallise the flowers of rosemary with egg white and caster sugar to make decorations (see page 386).

texture may not soften, even with long cooking. Rosemary is popular in Italian cookery. Make a simple and delicious pizza topping with thinly sliced potatoes, crushed garlic and chopped fresh rosemary leaves.

St John's wort

Hypericum perforatum Clusiaceae

Traditionally, golden-flowered St John's wort was hung over entrances and cast on midsummer fires as a herb of great protection and purification. Today, it is still the symbol of midsummer solstice celebrations in Europe.

OTHER COMMON NAME Perforate St. John's wort
PART USED Flowering tops

◼ Gardening

Hypericum is a large genus comprising about 400 species but only *H. perforatum* is recommended for medicinal use. It is a hardy, woody-based, unpleasant-smelling perennial, forming clumps of upright stems which can reach 1m high. Small, smooth, oval leaves, borne in opposite pairs along the stems, have numerous tiny oil glands. Five-petalled, gland-dotted yellow flowers appear in large cymes in midsummer. The small, ovoid seed capsule contains round black seed. When crushed, flowers ooze a red, blood-like pigment containing hypericin. Do not confuse St John's wort with the ornamental *Hypericums* grown in gardens. It is an attractive wild flower for meadows and woodland margins, but is considered toxic to livestock.

Position Grow in well-drained, moist to dryish soil in full sun to light shade.
Propagation Sow seed as soon as it is ripe in autumn or in the following spring. Germination can take up to 3 months. You can also divide the rhizomes either in autumn or spring.
Maintenance Cut down dead stems when plants are dormant.
Pests and diseases None of note.
Harvesting and storing Harvest the flowering heads in early summer, when buds commence opening, and dry them.

◼ Herbal medicine

Hypericum perforatum. Part used: flowering tops. Traditionally used for treating nerve pain, including neuralgia and sciatica as well as anxiety and depression, St John's wort is still used for these conditions but is now best known for its antidepressant properties.

St John's wort has been proven to be effective against mild to moderate depression in a large number of clinical trials where it was found to be similarly effective to other antidepressant drugs but with fewer side-effects. Two compounds, hypericin and hyperforin, are believed to work in a similar manner to pharmaceutical antidepressants, and many preparations using St John's wort are produced to contain a fixed level of these constituents.

Clinical trials of St John's wort also suggest a beneficial use for treating mood symptoms of menopause and premenstrual syndrome, for obsessive-compulsive disorder and also for seasonal affective disorder.

Laboratory studies have shown that St John's wort possesses anti-inflammatory, pain-relieving and antiviral properties. A tea or extract taken internally as well as external use of the red oil prepared from the flowers can relieve sciatica, shingles, cold sores, genital herpes and rheumatic pain. Topically, the oil is also a valuable wound and burn-healing remedy.
For the safe and appropriate use of St John's wort, see *Depression and anxiety*, page 217. Do not use St John's wort if you are pregnant or breastfeeding.

Midsummer's Eve

Celebrating the summer solstice, the longest day of the year, is a pagan festival that's still observed today. Traditionally, participants would cast St John's wort onto a bonfire and then jump over it to cleanse the body of evil spirits. St John's wort flowers were also placed above religious images to deter evil on the day.

St John's wort (*Hypericum perforatum*)

Saffron

Crocus sativus Iridaceae

Saffron is the world's most expensive spice. It is also unique in being the only herb composed of styles – the red thread-like structure in the centre of each flower. One kilo of the dried herb requires 150,000 flowers and 400 hours of hand picking, a process unchanged for more than 4000 years.

PART USED Styles

Dried saffron

Saffron crocus (*Crocus sativus*)

■ Gardening

The saffron crocus is a hardy perennial with corms, to 5cm in diameter and 1-4 fragrant lilac, purple-veined flowers with purplish filaments, yellow anthers and a red, three-branched style. Flowering takes place in autumn, after which 5-11 erect linear leaves appear, growing through winter and dying down in late spring. Saffron crocuses do not exist in the wild; *C. sativus* is a sterile triploid derived from the Greek *C. cartwrightianus* which was selectively cultivated in Crete during the Late Bronze Age (early 3rd millennium BCE).

Varieties 'Cashmirianus' is a high-yielding Kashmiri strain with large corms and violet-blue flowers with deep orange styles.

Position Well-drained, light, rich, neutral soil in full sun, with hot dry conditions during dormancy.

Propagation Remove offsets from the parent corm in late spring.

Maintenance To encourage flowering, plant corms 15cm deep and 10cm apart. Saffron crocuses often fail to flower in areas with cool cloudy summers. Keep well weeded. Repot container-grown crocuses each year in early autumn.

Pests and diseases Saffron crocuses are prone to fungal diseases. Corms may be eaten by rats and mice.

Harvest Flowers are picked within a day of opening and the styles removed for drying. Store in an airtight jar in a cool dark place and use within a year.

■ Herbal medicine

Crocus sativus. Part used: styles. Saffron is used in Chinese medicine for problems with the circulatory and nervous systems and menstruation. In Indian medicine it has also been used for blood and heart diseases and cancer. Research in the 1990s established that saffron has anti-tumour effects and protects the nervous system from alcohol damage. For the safe and appropriate use of saffron consult a doctor or medical herbalist. Do not use if pregnant or breastfeeding.

■ Cooking

Saffron gives a distinctive flavour and an appetising yellow colour. It is an essential ingredient of rice dishes such as paella (Spain), risotto Milanese (Italy) and biryani (India), and in fish stews, such as zarzuela (Spain) and bouillabaisse (France). It is an important flavouring and colorant for cakes, biscuits, bread, puddings and Eastern sweetmeats.

Red gold

Known as 'red gold' by the Spanish, saffron is literally worth its weight in gold. The high price of saffron through the centuries has given rise to numerous 'tricks of the trade', such as adding dyed fibres from beef and even pomegranates. Punishments were severe; a trader in 15th-century Nuremberg was buried alive with his adulterated product.

Nuremberg (Germany), Valencia (Spain) and Saffron Walden in England were centres of saffron cultivation in the Middle Ages. Today it is grown mainly in Azerbaijan, Spain, Greece, Morocco and the L'Aquila region of central Italy. Priceless Turkish carpets and the robes of Persian emperors were once dyed with saffron, but the so-called saffron robes of Buddhist monks are coloured with much cheaper turmeric.

Sage

Salvia spp. Lamiaceae

A clue to the uses of salvias lies in the name. *Salvia* is derived from Latin words meaning 'safe' and 'well', and these herbs are packed with compounds and aromas that heal and maintain health. Another recommendation for using sages is that they are associated with fertility and longevity.

PARTS USED Leaves, roots, seeds, flowers

■ Gardening

There are more than 900 species of salvias, many of them spectacular when in flower, and a rich source of nectar for bees, butterflies and birds. They vary greatly in habit, from evergreen shrubs to annuals, biennials and perennials. Most have aromatic leaves, often with scents resembling those of rosemary and lavender, but also with scents of pine, eucalyptus, and various kinds of fruit. Many are hardy and others make excellent plants for summer borders and containers.

Varieties

Common or garden sage (*S. officinalis*) is one of the best-known culinary herbs. It has a pleasant pungency and is a potent antioxidant. Native to Mediterranean areas, especially along the Adriatic coast, common sage has grey-green leaves and spikes of purple-blue flowers, though there are variants with pink ('Rosea') and white flowers ('Albiflora'). Several varieties with ornamental foliage make striking small evergreens for tubs and borders. These include: 'Berggarten', with large broad leaves; 'Purpurascens' with purple leaves; the cream and pink-variegated 'Tricolor'; and gold-variegated 'Icterina'.

Greek sage (*S. fruticosa*), closely resembles garden sage except that it is less hardy and most leaves have a pair of lobes or small leaflets at the base. It has an excellent, lavender-like aroma and is a commercial source of dried sage.

Spanish sage (*S. lavandulifolia*), also known as lavender sage, resembles a narrow-leafed garden sage. It has a lavender-and-sage fragrance, and its oil is extracted for toiletries.

Clary sage or muscatel sage (*S. sclarea*), a biennial, is one of the most beautiful sages, forming a large rosette of broadly ovate, hairy, deeply veined leaves and sending up tall dense spikes of pink to white flowers backed by conspicuous

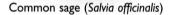

Common sage (*Salvia officinalis*)

mauve-pink bracts. The strong-smelling leaves add a muscatel flavour to various liqueurs, vermouths and wines, while the essential oil is used in perfumery. In water, the seeds become mucilaginous, and were once used to remove specks from the eyes.

White sage (*S. apiana*) is a half-hardy silver-leafed sub-shrub native to deserts in southwestern North America. The leaves are used by Native Americans as a flavouring, to reduce mucus formation and salivation, and as smudge sticks in purification ceremonies.

Chia sages are grown for their nutritious seeds, which can be sprouted, used in baking, or soaked in water as the basis for refreshing drinks. Golden chia (*S. columbariae*), a half-hardy annual, is native to the southwestern North America. Others include *S. polystachya* and *S. hispanica*. The latter was an important staple crop to the Aztecs until colonisation by the Spanish. Its tiny oily seeds are gluten-free, very rich in omega-3 fatty acids (alpha-linolenic acid), and high in anti-oxidants, vitamins, minerals and fibre.

Pineapple sage (*Salvia elegans*)

Sage continued

Fruit-scented sages A number of salvias have delicious aromas that invite comparisons with fruit. Pineapple sage (*S. elegans* 'Scarlet Pineapple' syn. *S. rutilans*) has spikes of slender red flowers and pineapple-scented leaves, while peach sage (*S. dorisiana*), with larger leaves and bright pink flowers, smells like fruit salad. Both can be used to flavour drinks and garnish desserts. Grow them in large containers with a minimum winter temperature of 5°C. The variety of pineapple sage known as 'Tangerine' has a citrus scent and is hardier, able to survive temperatures of -5°C or lower.

Chinese sages Two oriental salvias are important in Chinese medicine and are also ornamental garden plants. They are red sage (*S. miltiorhiza*), which has red roots, dark green, deeply veined, pinnate leaves and purple-blue flowers, and *S. przewalskii*, which has soft, light green leaves and large lilac-blue flowers. Both these sages are hardy herbaceous perennials and are known as dan shen in Chinese medicine.

'The desire of sage is to render man immortal.'

From a medieval manuscript

Position Most salvias, particularly the grey-leafed species, require a sunny, well-drained position. Less hardy species make good container plants providing they have full light. Use a clay pots and John Innes No3 Compost, with some slow-release fertiliser.

Propagation Sages are propagated from seed (species only), and by softwood or semi-ripe cuttings. Perennials can be divided in spring. Most shrubby salvias become woody and 'leggy' with age and are best propagated every 3-4 years.

Maintenance Most shrubby salvias respond well to gentle pruning or pinching back, particularly after flowering. Do not heavily fertilise these plants.

Pests and diseases Sudden wilting indicates poor drainage and root rot.

In France, clary sage (*S. sclarea*) is cultivated and the essential oil extracted for perfumery.

Salvias grown in the greenhouse or garden room may suffer from whitefly, aphids and red spider mite.

Harvesting and storing Harvest fresh leaves and flowers for culinary use at any time. Dry individual leaves and sprigs before flowering; spread them out in a well-aired place, then store in airtight containers.

Potted salvias in flower make a pretty display, but are not really suited to indoor life on a long-term basis.

Sage and thyme stuffing

Gently heat 1 tablespoon olive oil and 25g butter in large frying pan over moderate heat. Add 1 finely chopped onion and 2 finely chopped celery stalks. Cook about 10 minutes, until soft. Remove from heat and tip into a bowl. Stir in 100g fresh white breadcrumbs, 1 tablespoon each chopped fresh sage and fresh thyme and 1 lightly beaten egg. Mix well to bind the mixture; season generously with salt and pepper. Allow stuffing to cool completely. Use it to stuff a turkey or large chicken and cook remaining stuffing in a buttered baking dish, putting it in the oven for the last 30 minutes of cooking time. To avoid the risk of food poisoning, do not stuff poultry until you are ready to cook it. To vary the recipe, try using 1 tablespoon each finely chopped fresh lemongrass and parsley in place of sage and thyme.

Spanish sage (*S. lavandulifolia*)

Herbal medicine

Salvia officinalis. Part used: leaves. Sage is an anti-inflammatory and antimicrobial remedy, and is frequently used as a mouthwash and gargle for sore throats, gum infections, tonsillitis and mouth ulcers. It appears to have a drying effect on excessive sweating and is a useful herb for the treatment of night sweats associated with menopause. Sage also has a beneficial effect on the mind, improving memory, concentration and mood; results of a recent clinical trial suggest that it may have a positive effect on the symptoms of Alzheimer's disease.

Salvia miltiorhiza. Part used: roots. In traditional Chinese medicine, dan shen is described as a remedy that 'moves blood'. Modern research has mostly focused on its beneficial effects on the circulatory system and the heart. The results of some clinical trials indicate that it may have potential uses in the treatment of angina and high blood pressure. Laboratory studies have shown liver-protective effects and may explain dan shen's traditional use for treating liver conditions.

For the safe and appropriate medicinal use of sage, see *Menopause*, page 235. For the safe and appropriate use of dan shen, consult your doctor or medical herbalist. Do not use dan shen if you are pregnant or breastfeeding and do not use sage in greater than culinary quantities if pregnant or breastfeeding.

Around the home

Sage, like so many herbs, is rich in essential oils, antiviral, antibacterial, deodorising and antifungal effects, and this is reflected by its old French name, toute bonne, or 'all is well'. Use the leaves to make *Herb vinegar spray* (see page 298) and insect-repellent sprays (see box, right). Alternatively, simply put a few drops of essential oil on a damp cloth when you're wiping down bathroom and kitchen surfaces.

Sage is also a moth-repellent – use it in the form of either dried herb or essential oil to repel clothes moths and pantry moths. In the garden, plant sage to repel cabbage white butterflies.

Cooking

Common sage (*S. officinalis*) is the type of sage most often used for cooking. The aroma is highly pungent, while the flavour, which intensifies on drying, is savoury, with camphorous overtones. Sage goes with starchy, rich and fatty foods such as duck, with poultry and pork (and stuffings for them), red meats, beans, aubergine, tomato-based sauces, casseroles and soups. It is also used in commercially prepared stuffing mixes and Italian dried mixed herbs. You can also use deep-fried leaves as a garnish.

Best used with a light hand in long-cooked dishes, sage is popular in Italy, less so in France. In the Middle East, it is used in salads. Sage tea is popular in many European countries. In Dalmatia in southeast Europe, where sage is found in the wild, the flowers are used to make honey.

Petrovskia 'Blue Spire' is sometimes known as Russian sage. It has a strong sage scent when the foliage is bruised.

Vinegar of the Four Thieves

This herbal vinegar is a strong insect repellent that can be used on your skin as well as on socks and shoes to discourage ticks and mites. Dilute it 50:50 with water if you are spraying it onto your skin and test it on a small patch of skin before using. In a glass jar, combine 2 litres apple cider vinegar and 2 tablespoons chopped garlic with 2 tablespoons of each of the following herbs: rosemary, rue, sage, lavender, wormwood and peppermint. Steep the mixture in a sunny spot for about 2 weeks, shaking the jar daily. Strain out the herbs, and retain the liquid. Add several cloves of crushed garlic, and seal again. Leave to soak for 3 days. Strain out the garlic fibre and discard. Label the jar and store it in a cool place. Do not use this vinegar if you are pregnant, and do not use it on small children.

He who would live for aye,
Must eat sage in May.

Old English proverb

Salad burnet and greater burnet

Sanguisorba minor and *S. officinalis* Rosaceae

The ferny leaves and rounded flower spikes of burnets are sufficiently pretty to qualify as ornamentals. Sir Francis Bacon, the 16th-century English philosopher, recommended salad burnet for growing along alleys with thyme 'to perfume the air most delightfully'.

OTHER COMMON NAMES Burnet bloodwort, Di Yu, pimpernel (greater burnet)
PARTS USED Leaves, roots

Salad burnet (*Sanguisorba minor*)

Gardening

Salad burnet (*S. minor*), is a dainty, hardy, evergreen perennial to 45cm, which forms clumps of pinnate leaves with many paired, toothed, oval leaflets. In summer, tall slender stalks bear dense bobble-like heads of tiny green, wind-pollinated flowers with deep red anthers.
Greater burnet (*S. officinalis* syn. *Poterium officinalis*), is similar to salad burnet but larger in all respects, with stems to 1m and club-shaped spikes of tiny, burgundy flowers.

Varieties Colour variants of *S. officinalis*, include: 'Arnhem', with cerise flower spikes; 'Pink Tanna' with pink spikes; and 'Shiro-fukurin' with white-edged leaflets.
Position *S. minor* prefers dry alkaline soil and full sun; *S. officinalis* needs moist to wet, neutral to alkaline soil in sun or light shade.
Propagation Sow seed in spring or autumn or divide large clumps in spring. Named varieties will not come true from seed.
Maintenance Cut emerging flower stems for increased leaf production. Remove dead stems before new growth appears in spring.
Pests and diseases None of note.
Harvesting and storing Harvest leaves for medicinal use before flowering. For using fresh as a flavouring, harvest leaves as required. Lift roots in autumn for drying.

Herbal medicine

Sanguisorba officinalis syn. *Poterium officinalis*. Parts used: leaves, roots. Greater burnet has a very long tradition of use in Western and Chinese medicine. The plant is astringent due to the presence of some unusual tanins, together with gums and glycosides. It is used externally in treating minor burns and scalds, sores and skin infections, and to staunch bleeding. In traditional Chinese medicine, the dried root is also used internally for the treatment of bleeding haemorrhoids. For the safe and effective use of greater burnet consult a doctor or medical herbalist.

Cooking

Salad burnet is an ingredient in several sauces, including ravigote, which is used in French cooking and goes well with cold roast chicken or seafood. Add young leaves of salad burnet to salads, chilled summer soups and to soft cheeses. Also use as a garnish or infuse in vinegar. It does not dry well, but the leaves can be frozen in ice-cube trays.

Herb cocktail

The cucumber taste of salad burnet makes it an excellent accompaniment to alcoholic drinks; according to the Elizabethan herbal writer John Gerard, the plants 'make the heart merry and glad'. For a refreshing cocktail, bruise 6 sprays of salad burnet with a rolling pin or with a mortar and pestle, then place in a large jug containing 750ml sweet white wine, 500ml sherry and 1 thinly sliced lemon. Mix well; allow to infuse for at least 2 hours. Sweeten to taste. Add 1 litre of soda water and serve over crushed ice.

Summer flowerheads of greater burnet (*S. officinalis*) showing red anthers.

Savory

Satureja spp. Lamiaceae

Satureja is reputed to have been the source of the mythical satyrs' enormous sexual stamina. Whether or not savories have aphrodisiac effects, they certainly pack a punch in terms of flavourings, used in a wide range of foods.

PART USED Leaves

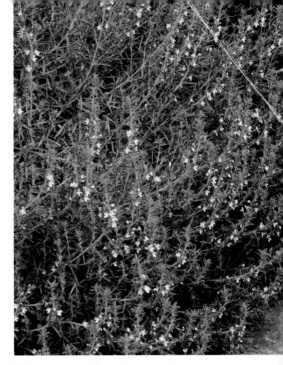

Winter savory (*Satureja montana*)

■ Gardening

Satureja is a genus of about 30 species of mostly annuals and small shrubby perennials. Savories from southern Europe and eastern Asia contain thyme-like oils, whereas species from the Americas have minty aromas. Several species are hardy, attractive little plants that should be in every herb garden; less hardy species suit growing in containers.

Varieties

Summer savory (*S. hortensis*), an annual growing to 45cm, has slender dark green leaves, pink-white flowers.

Winter savory (*S. montana*) is a semi-evergreen sub-shrub with dark green, narrow-leafed foliage and white flowers.

Creeping savory (*S. spicigera* syn. *S. repanda*) is mat-forming; it resembles white heather when in autumn flower.

Thyme-leafed savory, also known as pink savory or za'atar rumi (*S. thymbra*), is a stiffly branched shrublet with whorls of pink flowers and small, bristly greyish leaves. These four main culinary savories have an oregano-thyme aroma. This is especially intense in *S. thymbra*, which is important in the Middle East as a za'atar herb (see page 87).

Indian mint or yerba buena (*S. douglasii*) is a prostrate evergreen perennial from western North America, which has trailing branches of fragrant round leaves.

Costa Rican mint bush or Jamaican peppermint (*S. viminea*) reaches 1.5m, with small, mint-scented, bright green leaves. Both are used locally to relieve digestive problems. An attractive lilac-flowered form of *S. montana* is known as 'Purple Mountain'.

Position Savories thrive in full sun and well-drained neutral to alkaline soil, except for Indian mint and Jamaican peppermint, which prefer moist soil and some shade. In cold areas, Indian mint is best grown in a hanging basket with protection in winter. Jamaican peppermint needs a winter minimum temperature of 10°C.

Propagation All species can be propagated by seed sown shallowly in spring. Perennial species can also be propagated by cuttings in summer.

Maintenance Cut back shrubby plants in early spring to encourage compact new growth.

Pests and diseases None of note

Harvesting and storing You can cut down whole plants of *S. hortensis* before flowering and dry them. Harvest the leaves of other species fresh as required, and dry or freeze in sealed containers.

■ Cooking

Both summer and winter savory have a similar peppery thyme-like aroma although summer savory is stronger. The flavour is better before the plant flowers. Savory retains its flavour when dried and is a key herb in herbes de Provence. Add savory to sauces, pâtés and homemade sausages; it goes well with lentils and peas, slow-cooked soups, stews, meatloaf and egg dishes. Use summer savory in marinades, especially for olives, and in coatings for delicate meats, such as veal, and for fish. In Croatian cooking, a lemon-scented strain of savory is used with fish and seafood.

Summer savory
(*Satureja hortensis*)

Scented geranium

Pelargonium spp. Geraniaceae

Scented geraniums are the great mimics of the plant world. At just the slightest touch they release intense true-to-name fragrances, from lemon sherbet and ripe apples to peppermint and red roses.

PARTS USED Leaves, roots, flowers

Rose geranium (*Pelargonium graveolens*)

Pelargonium hybrid, 'Gooseberry'

■ Gardening

South African in origin, most scented geraniums are half-hardy evergreen shrubs with aromatic leaves. They come in a wide range of colours, shapes and textures, and clusters of small white to pale pink or mauve, five-petalled flowers. The main varieties with herbal uses are described below. Most are not hardy and should be grown as pot plants.

Varieties Rose-scented geraniums include *P. capitatum*, *P.* 'Attar of Roses', *P. graveolens*, *P. radens* and the hybrid 'Graveolens'. Their essential oil with a true rose fragrance is used in perfumery, cosmetics and aromatherapy. It relieves tension, soothes skin irritations, and has antifungal, antibacterial and insect-repellent effects.

Lemon-scented geraniums include: *P. crispum*, cream-edged 'Galway Star' and its variegated form 'Variegatum', all with a stiff upright habit and crinkled leaves: 'Citriodorum', 'Citronella', *P.* x *citronellum*, 'Mabel Grey' and its seedling 'Bitter Lemon'; *P.* 'Limoneum', the finger-bowl geranium and 'Lady Mary'; and 'Rober's Lemon Rose'.

Fruit-scented geraniums coconut-scented *P. grossularoides*; apricot-scented 'Monsieur Ninon'; apple-scented *P. odoratissimum*; fruity 'Sweet Mimosa'; strawberry-scented 'Lady Scarborough'; orange-scented 'Prince of Orange'; and lime-scented *P.* x *nervosum*.

Spice-scented geraniums include 'Old Spice'; the ginger-scented 'Toronto'; and nutmeg geraniums, *P. fragrans*, Fragrans Group, and several variegated cultivars, such as 'Snowy Nutmeg'.

Peppermint-scented geraniums include: *P. tomentosum*, with velvety, heart-shaped, lobed leaves; 'Chocolate Peppermint', with brown-centred leaves; and 'Joy Lucille', a cross between *P. tomentosum* and *P. graveolens*.

All the above can be used for flavouring. They are also useful in potpourri and other fragrant home items.

Position Well-drained soil in full sun. Pelargoniums enjoy dry conditions and do best in clay pots.

Propagation Take 10cm cuttings at any time in the growing season. Propagate regularly as older specimens tend to become straggly and pot-bound.

Maintenance Cut back and repot in spring, and pinch out regularly to encourage compact bushy growth. Lightly fertilise in spring and water only when plants feel dry to the touch. Provide a winter minimum of 2°C.

Pests and diseases Indoor plants may suffer from whitefly, red spider mite and other leaf-damaging pests. Overwatering causes root rot and fungal disease.

Harvesting and storing Harvest and dry leaves at any time for potpourri and for sleep pillows. Pick leaves as required for using fresh in flavouring.

■ Cooking

Infuse fresh scented geranium leaves in warmed cream or milk as the basis for custards, ice cream and dessert sauces, or add them to vinegar and leave for a week before using in summer salad dressings. Fresh leaves can also be used to scent cakes, either by placing at the bottom of the baking tin, or by turning out the cake on a leaf-lined rack to absorb the aroma. Add dried leaves of rose or lemon varieties to the tea caddy.

Pelargonium quercifolium 'Fair Ellen'

Sorrel

Rumex spp. Polygonaceae

Sorrel is easily grown, and its fresh lemony flavour is very versatile in dishes such as salads, soups and frittatas. Water dock, Pliny's *herba brittanica*, may not be a gourmet's delight, but Julius Caesar cured his troops of scurvy with its help.

PARTS USED Leaves (sorrel); roots (yellow dock)

French sorrel (*Rumex scutatus*)

■ Gardening

As sorrel appears early in the year, it is useful for winter salads and flavouring. Three kinds are grown for culinary purposes. All are hardy perennials.
Common sorrel or garden sorrel (*R. acetosa*) forms clumps, with leaves to 15cm. In early summer slender stems, produce spikes of tiny reddish flowers, followed by hard nutlets.
French sorrel or buckler-leaf sorrel (*R. scutatus*) forms low mats, with small ovate to hastate leaves and tiny red-green flowers on stems to about 30cm.
Red-veined sorrel (*R. sanguineus* var. *sanguineus*) has attractive bright green leaves with red midribs and veins. They are more palatable when grown in warm conditions as a baby-leaf salad crop.
Varieties Non-flowering *R. acetosa* 'Profusion' produces fresh new leaves almost all year round. *R. scutatus* 'Silver Shield' has silver-marbled leaves.
Position Sorrel requires rich, moist soil and a sunny to partly shaded position.
Propagation Sow sorrel seed of species in spring. Seeds germinate within 14 days. Divide named varieties in spring.
Maintenance French sorrel can be invasive. Cut back regularly to control spread and keep up a supply of young leaves. Remove flower spikes to stop self seeding and prolong leaf production.
Pests and diseases None of note.
Harvesting and storing Pick sorrel fresh throughout the growing season. It does not dry well but can be frozen.

■ Cooking

This spinach-like leaf is delicious if picked young and tender. Cook briefly to retain flavour. If using raw, select the youngest leaves. A purée of cooked sorrel pairs well with fish, eggs, pork and veal. Sorrel's acidity also acts as a meat tenderiser. Sorrel sauce (page 344), a French classic, goes with poached fish.

Sorrels and docks

Sheep's sorrel (*Rumex acetosella*) and other kinds of sorrel and dock have been found to have a marked diuretic effect, and were often taken as a traditional spring tonic. A juice or infusion of fresh leaves was used to reduce fevers.

Sheep's sorrel is commonly found as an ingredient in a herbal formula called Essiac Tea, said to be based on a traditional Native American remedy. While there is no scientific evidence to confirm its immune-stimulating properties, the tea has been used since the 1920s by cancer patients and more recently by those with HIV and diabetes.

Yellow dock (*Rumex crispus*) is a close relative of the sorrels. It is commonly used for chronic skin conditions and for arthritic complaints. Herbalists believe that many of these conditions are related to a toxin build-up in the body; yellow dock root may alleviate them by enhancing the detoxifying capacity of the liver as well as encouraging more efficient removal of toxins from the bowel as a result of a gentle laxative action.

Sorrel (*Rumex acetosa*)

Sweet cicely

Myrrhis odorata Apiaceae

This delightfully ornamental herb has leaves with a sugary anise scent. It is one of the important ingredients in Chartreuse liqueur, and is also included in Scandinavian aquavit, used as a digestive and an aperitif.

OTHER COMMON NAME Garden myrrh
PARTS USED Young leaves and stalks, young roots

Sweet cicely (*Myrrhis odorata*)

Gardening

Native to cool, moist mountainous areas of Europe, sweet cicely is the lone species in its genus. It is a hardy perennial, forming a clump of aromatic, fern-like, sweet-tasting leaves 1–1.2m tall. Umbels of white flowers are followed by slender, 2.5cm seeds, that are technically fruits with a nutty flavour when eaten raw and green. Mature seeds are a shiny dark brown. Sweet cicely is a useful plant for gardens with damp woodland areas, shady borders and waterside plantings. If you are gathering sweet cicely in the wild, do not mistake it for cow parsley (*Anthriscus sylvestris*) or highly toxic hemlock (*Conium maculatum*), which has dark stems spotted red-purple.
Varieties 'Forncett Chevron' has angular white markings on each leaf.
Position It requires humus-rich moist soil, a cool climate and a shady location.
Propagation Allow the seed to fall

The cooked young roots are considered beneficial for those who are 'dull and without courage'.

around the parent plants, where they will germinate in spring. Alternatively, stratify the seed by placing it in moist, sterile sand or vermiculite inside a sealed plastic bag, and store in the fridge for 8 weeks before sowing in spring (see also page 50). In good conditions, sweet cicely may self sow invasively.
Maintenance Remove excess seedlings before they develop large taproots.
Pests and diseases None of note.
Harvesting and storing Harvest young leaves for fresh use. They retain little fragrance after drying. Pickle the

unripe seeds, and clean and store the young roots in brandy.

Cooking

Both the leaves and green fruits are very high in anethole, which is responsible for their sweet anise flavour. Boil roots as a vegetable; they can also be candied like angelica and used to decorate desserts. The crisp, celery-tasting stems and delicate leaves are good in salads or you can add finely chopped leaves with sharp fruits such as gooseberries and rhubarb, as their natural sweetness will counteract the tartness. They are a safe sweetener for diabetics and the green seeds can be used for the same purpose.

Sweet cicely leaves add a lovely flavour to cream, yoghurt, rice pudding, fruit and wine cups, light soups, and dressings. They can also be used as a substitute for chervil in omelettes. They also make a very pretty garnish.

Sweet cicely in east and west

Sweet cicely's closest relative is the genus *Osmorhiza*, found in rich woodland in Asia and North America and is similarly anise-flavoured. In Japan, yabu-ninjin (*O. aristata*) is eaten cooked or raw. In North America sweet cicely, aniseroot, and sweet myrrh (*O. claytonii, O. longistylis, O. occidentalis*) are used as flavourings and vegetables. The anise-flavoured root was used by Native Americans as a digestive, cough medicine, and antiseptic.

Sweet myrtle

Myrtus communis Myrtaceae

Myrtle was a symbol of peace in the Old Testament and honourable victory in ancient Greece and Rome. It was woven into bay wreaths at early Olympic Games and was sacred to the goddesss Venus who was often worshipped as Myrtilla; fragrant myrtle was grown around her temples. Brides still tuck sprigs of myrtle into their bouquets.

PARTS USED Leaves, buds, flowers, fruits

Gardening

Sweet myrtle is native to the Mediterranean and southwest Europe. It is a borderline hardy, evergreen shrub or small tree with oval, shiny, fragrant leaves. Small scented white flowers with a 'powder puff' of stamens are followed by resinous blue-black berries, 1cm long.

In areas where winters are cold, grow myrtle as a container plant or in a sheltered position against a wall. Choose smaller growing dwarf and variegated forms, which are less hardy and make more ornamental specimens for growing in frost-free garden rooms and on sheltered patios.

Varieties Double-flowered 'Flore Plena' is a choice rarity; box-leafed or dwarf myrtle, (*M. communis* subsp. *tarentina* also known as 'Nana', 'Microphylla' and 'Jenny Reitenbach'), useful for topiary, has small dense leaves and white fruits; 'Variegata' has white-edged leaves.

Position Sweet myrtle requires sunshine, neutral to alkaline soil and good drainage. It is drought-tolerant. Most myrtles survive -10°C but variegated forms need a winter minimum of -5°C.

Propagation Sow seed in autumn or propagate named varieties by semi-ripe cuttings in summer.

Maintenance Prune to shape in spring before new growth begins. Repot or top-dress container-grown plants in spring, and feed monthly. Water when soil feels dry to the touch.

Pests and diseases Plants grown indoors are prone to damage from the larvae of tortrix moths.

Harvesting and storing You can air-dry the buds, flowers, fruits and leaves. Whole branches are distilled to make an essential oil, used in perfumery, aromatherapy and skins products.

Cooking

Sweet myrtle leaves, flower buds and fruits feature in Mediterranean cooking, especially in Corsica and Sardinia, to flavour pork, lamb, pâté and small game

Sweet myrtle (*Myrtus communis*)

Wax myrtles

Bayberry or wax myrtle (*Myrica cerifera*) is an evergreen shrub with catkin-like flower spikes and wax-coated grey fruits that are used to make candles and soap. Fruits are heated in water to melt the wax, which floats on the surface for further processing. Bark extracts are highly astringent and antibacterial, making useful remedies for digestive upsets and upper respiratory tract infections. They are used topically in lotions to stimulate hair growth.

There are several different wax myrtles in North America. Some are planted as ornamentals and hedges for difficult conditions as they tolerate poorly drained sandy soils. Bog myrtle or sweet gale (*Myrica gale*) occurs in wetlands throughout the Northern Hemisphere. Its bitter, resinous leaves are similar to bay (see page 21) in flavour. They make a palatable tea, and an unusual flavouring for soups and stews. In Yorkshire they are traditionally used as a substitute for hops in the brewing of an ale known as gale beer.

birds. They are also used in sauces and some liqueurs. The berries have a mild juniper flavour, and both the dried flowers and fruits are ground into a spice with the same flavour. Infused oil is used in teas, salad dressings, fish and chicken dishes, desserts and bakery items.

Lay sprigs over barbecued or roast meats towards the end of cooking to add a spicy flavour.

Sweet violet

Viola odorata Violaceae

The fragrance of violets is often detected on early spring breezes long before the flowers are seen, the origin of the expression 'shrinking violet'. But violets hold a proud place in history, and have been linked to nobility and emperors.

PARTS USED Leaves, flowers

Napoléon and Josephine

In the 19th century, when violets were very fashionable, entire districts were devoted to their production. The fragrance was captured in many products, from perfumes and toiletries to breath fresheners. Josephine, Napoléon's wife, loved the scent of violets. When he died, a locket was found containing sweet violets and a lock of her hair.

Gardening

Of 500 or so species of *Viola*, only one has uses in flavouring, perfumery, aromatherapy and medicine, the sweet violet (*V. odorata*). Popular since Tudor times, large-scale breeding began in the 19th century when the Russian violet (*V. suavis*) was introduced. At the same time, Parma violets reached England from Europe via North Africa. Sweet violets are hardy and easily grown at the front of borders and beneath deciduous trees and shrubs, while frost-hardy Parma violets are good in containers, raised beds or coldframes. Perfume is extracted from foliage and blooms, as leaf absolute and violet otto respectively.

Varieties Sweet violet has variants with white flowers ('Alba'), double white ('Alba Plena'), and pink flowers (Rosea Group). Historic hybrids, with larger flowers on longer stems include: deep mauve, fragrant 'Princesse de Galles' syn. 'Princess of Wales' (1889); light blue, white-eyed 'John Raddenbury' (1895); dark purple 'The Czar' (1863); cerise 'Perle Rose' (1902); and white 'Comte de Chambord' (1895). Apricot-flowered 'Sulphurea' is scentless. Parma violets have shiny heart-shaped leaves and profuse, large, fragrant flowers. Excellent varieties are: white 'Comte de Brazza' (pre-1878); blue-mauve 'D'Udine (early 20th century); and deep lavender 'Duchesse de Parme' syn. 'Parme Ordinaire' (*c.*1870).

Position Well-composted, moist soil. Full sun in winter encourages flowering.

Propagation Detach runners in autumn and plant separately.

Maintenance Deadhead named varieties to prevent hybrid seedlings.

Pests and diseases Check for red spider mite on plants grown under glass.

Harvesting and storing Gather flowers and leaves fresh when in season.

Herbal medicine

Viola odorata. Parts used: leaves, flowers. The medicinal properties of sweet violet closely resemble those of its relative, heartsease (*V. tricolor*). It is used for skin conditions such as eczema and psoriasis as well as the removal of mucus in respiratory problems. In traditional herbal practice, sweet violet has been used for the treatment of certain cancers, including those of the breast and lung. Recent laboratory studies have identified compounds that may inhibit tumour growth; further investigations are needed before this can be substantiated.

For the safe and appropriate use of sweet violet, consult your doctor or medical herbalist. Do not use sweet violet if pregnant or breastfeeding.

Cooking

Fresh flowers are crystalised or used to flavour syrups, jellies, vinegar, ice cream, and confectionery. Flowers and leaves can also be added to salads, used as garnish, and made into tea.

Sweet violet (*V. odorata*) is a spring highlight in a woodland themed garden.

Tansy

Tanacetum vulgare syn. *Chrysanthemum vulgare* Asteraceae

A very bitter herb with insecticidal effects, tansy had two quite different uses in medieval times. It was eaten in dishes as a penance at Eastertide and used as a strewing herb for floors in the days before carpets were common.

OTHER COMMON NAME Buttons
PART USED Aerial parts

Tansy (*Tanacetum vulgare*)

■ Gardening

A hardy rhizomatous perennial herb, tansy grows to about 1.2m, bearing attractive pinnate leaves, which typically have a strong balsamic scent. There are a number of different chemotypes, with a scent of rosemary, camphor, eucalyptus or chrysanthemum.

Tansy bears flat-topped clusters of long-lasting golden button flowers that dry well. The only drawback of growing tansy is that it tends to take over, so plant it where this rapid and vigorous spread will not be a problem.

Varieties Fern-leafed or curly tansy (*T. vulgare* var. *crispum*) is more compact, with finely cut leaves. 'Isla Gold' is a less vigorous plant and has bright yellow foliage. 'Silver Lace' has pretty white variegation.

Plants that are related to tansy include: pyrethrum (*T. cinerariifolium* syn. *Pyrethrum cinerariifolium*), the source of pyrethrum insecticide, which is a smaller plant with divided leaves and large white daisies; costmary or alecost (*T. balsamita*), which has clusters of white daisy flowers and silvery green, sweetly mint-scented leaves; and the camphor plant (*T. balsamita* subsp. *tomentosum*), which is similar in appearance to alecost but with camphor-scented foliage

Position All *Tanacetum* species listed prefer a well-drained, sunny position.

Propagation Propagate tansy by seed (species only), division or basal cuttings in spring or through semi-ripe cuttings in summer.

Maintenance Tansy can become extremely invasive, so it is important to keep the spread of rhizomes firmly under control.

Pests and diseases There are none of significance.

Harvesting and storing Harvest tansy foliage during flowering for drying or oil extraction.

■ Herbal medicine

Tanacetum vulgare. Parts used: aerial parts. Tansy was once used as a short-term remedy for the treatment of worm infestations of the gut. Today this herb is rarely used medicinally, as we now know that thujone, a component of the essential oil of the plant, can have toxic effects. Thujone also has a strongly stimulating effect on the uterus and can have serious side effects in pregnant women or on those who are attempting to become pregnant.

Do not use tansy or its essential oil, and take extra care with this plant if you are pregnant or breastfeeding.

Bible leaf

Costmary once had the common name of bible leaf, in reference to its use as a Bible bookmark – its mint-like scent was perfect for reviving the faint-hearted during interminable Sunday sermons. The name *Tanacetum* is from *athanasia*, Greek for 'immortality', and in ancient Greece, corpses were packed with tansy leaves to preserve them and ward off insects until burial took place.

■ Around the home

A natural insect repellent, tansy can be grown outside in pots around outdoor entertaining areas to deter flies and mosquitoes. Indoors, use dried tansy to deter ants, clothes moths or fleas in your pet's bedding.

A strong tansy tea can be spritzed over the carpet to keep flea populations under control, but do not spray it directly onto your pet or its bedding. Also, do not use it if you are pregnant or breastfeeding.

■ Cooking

Finely chopped tansy leaves are used to flavour a number of traditional Easter foods. These include tansy cakes, puddings, and a kind of custard known as a tansy.

Tarragon

Artemisia dracunculus Asteraceae

Dracunculus is Latin for 'little dragon', and tarragon was reputed to cure the bites of not only diminutive dragons but also all serpents. Its unique, delicious and piquant flavour is now essential to classic French cuisine.

PART USED Leaves

Following the Doctrine of Signatures (see page 49), tarragon was used against venomous bites.

Gardening

French tarragon (*A. dracunculus*) is a selected form (sometimes designated 'Sativa') with an exceptional flavour that has been cultivated since medieval times. Although it may produce tiny, greenish, ball-shaped inflorescences, it is essentially sterile, with slender linear leaves that have a complex anise-basil fragrance. Plants reach 60-90cm and are hardy and drought-resistant herbaceous perennials.

Varieties Russian tarragon (*A. dracunculoides*) regularly flowers and sets viable seeds but is inferior in flavour, with an earthy balsamic scent.

Mexican tarragon, or Mexican mint marigold or sweet mace (*Tagetes lucida*), is close to French tarragon in flavour. A half-hardy evergreen perennial to 80cm with narrow, finely toothed, deep green leaves, it produces a lavish display of small, bright golden flowers, borne in clusters in late summer. Mexican tarragon thrives in high humidity that would not suit French tarragon.

Position French tarragon enjoys slightly acid, well-drained to dry, stony soil in full sun.

Propagation Take tip cuttings in spring. Plants can also be divided but this runs the risk of spreading root-borne pests and diseases.

Maintenance Cut back dead stems when plants are dormant. In cold wet areas, protect surface rhizomes in winter.

Pests and diseases Tarragon is susceptible to nematodes (eel worms) and fungal diseases, such as rust.

Harvesting and storing Harvest foliage for using fresh until mid autumn. For freezing or drying, pick the best young sprigs in early summer.

Herbal medicine

Artemisia dracunculus. Part used: leaves. These days, tarragon is more likely to be used for culinary than therapeutic purposes. It contains an essential oil that is reputed to have similar properties to that of anise, which is often used to treat digestive symptoms. In some countries, tarragon is traditionally used to treat the symptoms of diabetes; recent scientific research appears to support this. Preliminary studies in diabetic animals found that an alcoholic extract of French tarragon lowered the levels of both insulin and sugar in the blood. For the safe and appropriate medicinal use of tarragon, consult your doctor or medical herbalist. Do not use tarragon in greater than culinary quantities if you are pregnant or breastfeeding.

Cooking

French tarragon's flavour diffuses rapidly through cooked dishes, so use it carefully. Use it fresh with fish and shellfish, eggs dishes, and light meats such as turkey, chicken and veal. Use chopped leaves in salad dressings, fines herbes (see page 362), mustard, ravigote and béchamel sauces, sauce verte and mayonnaise. Tarragon mustard is a favourite in France. In Georgia, where tarragon originated, a cordial known as tarhun is made.

French tarragon
(*Artemisia dracunculus*)

Mexican tarragon (*Tagetes lucida*)

Tea

Camellia sinensis syn. *Thea sinensis* Theaceae

Tea has been the favoured beverage of China for 3000 years. While Western palates favoured the more robust black tea, green tea is richer in antioxidants and is credited with a number of uses in traditional medicine.

PARTS USED Leaf tips, leaves, seeds

Tea (*Camellia sinensis*)

Gardening

Tea (*Camellia sinensis*) is a frost-hardy evergreen shrub. There are more than 350 known varieties. In general, tea bushes have smooth, leathery leaves which are oval and pointed, and small single white flowers with a boss of gold stamens, that appear in early winter. One or two clones are hardy enough to survive English winters, but it is safer to grow a tea bush in a container that can be protected from severe frost.

Position Tea requires full sun to partial shade, and rich, moist, neutral to acid, well-drained soil.

Propagation Tea can be grown from seed, but named varieties are propagated by semi-ripe wood cuttings in summer.

Maintenance Maintain bushes to a height of about 1m.

Pests and diseases None of note.

Harvesting and storing Harvest leaf tips when bushes are 3 years old and dry for making tea.

Herbal medicine

Camellia sinensis. Part used: leaves. Each type of tea has different levels of compounds, known as polyphenols, which are primarily responsible for the plant's medicinal properties. Green tea has the highest levels of polyphenols and is considered to have the greatest therapeutic benefit. Green tea polyphenols have more antioxidants than vitamin C or E, and may help in the prevention and treatment of numerous chronic diseases. Studies of large populations of regular green tea drinkers report lower rates of some cancers and reduced risk of cardio-vascular disease. Further human trials have reported that green tea can protect against sunburn when applied topically, and regular use of chewable green tea tablets has been shown to reduce gum inflammation and plaque formation. As a result of its caffeine content, green tea improves alertness and concentration. It has also been investigated for its use as a potential weight loss agent. New studies also suggest a potential role for green tea in the treatment of diabetes as a result of a blood sugar-lowering effect.

For the safe and appropriate medicinal use of green tea, consult your doctor or medical herbalist. Do not use green tea in greater than culinary quantities if you are pregnant or breastfeeding. Caffeine intake should be monitored during these times.

Cooking

Leaves from the tea plant are processed to produce green, black, white and oolong varieties. Flavour depends on the variety and how the leaves are processed; they are fermented and dried for black tea, but steamed and dried for green tea. In China, leftover tea is used to boil eggs, and the leaves are smoked to flavour meat such as duck. Tea is also a good soaking liquid for dried fruit and hams, giving a distinctive flavour. An essential oil is distilled from the mature leaves, which is used both in perfumery and as a commercial flavouring. The seeds are pressed for a fixed oil that is processed to remove saponins and then used as a cooking oil.

Rooibos tea

The leaves of the rooibos plant (*Aspalathus linearis*) have been brewed in South Africa for centuries. Today, rooibos tea is becoming popular all over the world as a result of its pleasant taste, caffeine-free content and its remarkable antioxidant capacity which has the potential to improve general health and well-being. Rooibos tea cannot be cultivated, growing only in the acid sands of the Cedarberg Mountains.

Tea tree

Melaleuca sp. Myrtaceae

In the 18th century, Aboriginal Australians taught Captain James Cook and his crew how to make poultices of the crushed leaves of tea tree to treat cuts and skin infections. Later, the antimicrobial oil became popular with colonial Australians.

OTHER COMMON NAMES Ti trees
PARTS USED Leaves, branches

Tea tree
(*Melaleuca
alternifolia*)

 Gardening

'Tea tree' is a misnomer, as that term applies to *Leptospermum* species, while *Melaleuca* species are actually paperbarks. This has led to the belief that the tea trialled by the Cook expedition was prepared from Melaleuca, which is not the case. Tea tree (*M. alternifolia*) is plantation-grown in Australia for high-quality essential oil. The species grows to about 7m and occurs naturally on the warm east coast of Australia, where it is often found in swampy conditions. It has whitish, layered, papery bark, pointed linear foliage and white, intensely honey-scented bottlebrush inflorescences which drip nectar. A half-hardy evergreen, tea tree is easily grown in a container for conservatories and warm patios.

Related to tea tree are several other similar-looking, more tender species which are commercially important for their oil. *M. leucadendra* (sometimes spelt leucandendron) is the source of cajeput oil. Both *M. viridiflora* and the broadleaf paperbark (*M. quinquenervia*) are sources of niaouli oil, used in perfumery and as an antiseptic. The latter has become a serious commercial crop in warm parts of the world, such as Florida.

Position Tea tree requires an acid, very moist soil and full sun.

Propagation Sow seed in spring at temperatures of 20-25°C or take semi-ripe cuttings in summer

Maintenance Water regularly in the growing season. Ensure that it is kept frost-free in winter.

Pests and diseases None of note.

Harvesting and storing Trees are cut for foliage, which is water or steam-distilled and cured for 6 weeks.

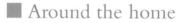 Herbal medicine

Melaleuca alternifolia. Parts used: essential oil from leaves and branches. Scientific research has confirmed that the essential oil of the tea tree plant possesses potent antimicrobial properties against many common bacterial, viral and fungal disease-causing organisms.

These days, tea tree essential oil continues to be used extensively for its topical antiseptic properties. It is used to treat acne, gum infections and fungal infections of the foot, and several clinical trials have shown that its effectiveness

is comparable to a number of conventional treatments.

For the safe and appropriate external use of tea tree oil, see *First aid*, page 226, *Acne*, page 222, and *Athlete's foot*, page 224. Tea tree oil should not be used internally. Do not use tea tree oil if you are pregnant or breastfeeding.

Around the home

Tea-tree oil is powerfully antiseptic, with antimicrobial and antibacterial properties.

Wipe down surfaces with a disinfectant solution – mix tea-tree oil with either water or vinegar.

Disinfect a shower and remove mould by mixing 60g borax, 2 cups very hot water and ¼ teaspoon tea tree oil. Shake in a spray bottle until borax dissolves. Spray on surfaces, leave overnight, then rinse.

Deodorise and disinfect waste bins – wipe them out with a solution of ½ teaspoon tea tree oil and a little detergent in hot water.

Tea tree products

Today, tea tree oil is found in a wide range of commercial products including toothpaste, lip salve, mouthwashes, antiperspirants, antidandruff shampoos, spot creams, skin tonics and face and body oils.

Thyme

Thymus spp. Lamiaceae

There are an astonishing number of aromatic thyme species with many fragrances, flavours and uses, from culinary and medicinal to mystical and magical. No wonder the highest praise in ancient Greece was the expression 'to smell of thyme'.

PARTS USED Leaves, flowering tops

Common thyme
(*Thymus vulgaris*)

■ Gardening

There are some 350 species of thyme, many of which are rich in fragrant essential oils. Cultivated thymes tend to be variable, often complex hybrids and there is much confusion over names. They vary in hardiness but all are sun-loving, evergreen, woody-based perennials and sub shrubs, mostly with a neat creeping or bushy habit.

The majority are small plants, easily grown at the front of borders and in nooks and crannies in paving and pathways. They also thrive in pots, being tidy and drought-resistant. Flowering thymes attract numerous bees and are prized as a source of honey.

Varieties Common or garden thyme (*T. vulgaris*) is the principal culinary thyme. It has tiny, narrow, elliptic, grey-green leaves and whorls of white to mauve flowers.

Selected forms include: 'Silver Posie', with soft green and white variegated foliage and mauve-pink flowers; 'English Winter', a very hardy form; 'Erectus', with strong vertical growth; and 'Fragrantissimus' or orange thyme, a hybrid with fine, erect, citrus-scented grey foliage.

Caraway thyme (*T. herba-barona*) is a wiry carpeting thyme with tiny, almost glossy leaves, a delicious caraway scent and lavender flowers.

Conehead thyme (*T. capitatus* syn. *Coridothymus capitatus*) is an intensely scented, compact sub shrub with tiny rigid, almost fleshy leaves and distinctive conical clusters of deep pink flowers. It has a pungent scent and is the source of Spanish oregano oil. This species dislikes winter wet and is best grown in a pot with protection from damp.

Spanish or mastic thyme (*T. mastichina*) forms a neat grey, upright sub-shrub with a strong oregano-thyme scent that in some chemotypes verges on lavender and eucalyptus. This thyme is frost-hardy and dislikes winter wet, so is best grown in a pot. Its robust aroma is excellent for barbecues.

Lemon thyme (*T.* x *citriodorus*) forms spreading, bushy, fresh green-leafed plants which are redolent of lemon and thyme. They have somewhat sparse heads

T. vulgaris 'Silver Posie' bears pink-purple flowers of in late spring to early summer.

of lilac flowers. The two best-known varieties are the white-variegated 'Silver Queen' and yellow-variegated 'Golden King'. Both are tricky to bring through the winter as garden plants so are best cultivated in pots.

Broad-leafed thyme (*T. pulegioides*) has distinctively broad elliptical leaves, a rather sprawling habit, and whorls of mauve flowers. It is variable in appearance and aroma, some kinds having a good oregano-thyme scent, others more camphoraceous. Varieties include; white-variegated 'Foxley'; low-growing golden 'Bertram Anderson' syn. 'Anderson's Gold'; and lemon-scented 'Archer's Gold', with bright yellow foliage in summer.

Azores thyme (*T. caespititius* syn. *T. azoricus*, *T. micans*) forms a dense, bitter orange-scented, moss-like carpet with white to pink or mauve flowers.

Wild or creeping thyme, mother of thyme (*T. serpyllum*) is native to northern Europe. Creeping thymes may involve two different species, the true *T. serpyllum*, which is strongly aromatic and used in herbal medicine, and the almost scentless *T. praecox* subsp. *arcticus*.

There are many varieties of carpeting thymes with ornamental foliage and a wide range of flower colour, from cerise 'Coccineus' and profuse-flowering 'Pink Chintz' to pure white 'Snowdrift'.

Position Thymes require good drainage and a sunny position.

Thyme continued

Propagation Raise thyme species from seed in spring and propagate named varieties by cuttings in summer. Creeping thymes are more easily propagated by division in spring.
Maintenance Weed regularly. Propagate bushy thymes every 3-4 years as they become woody and less productive. Remove fallen leaves of deciduous plants from thymes in winter to prevent rotting of foliage.
Pests and diseases Excess moisture causes roots and foliage to rot.
Harvesting and storing Pick sprigs of thyme to use fresh at any time. For drying, pick flowering sprigs and dry in bunches or on trays out of direct sunlight. Strip leaves from stems when dried and store in jars. Thyme retains its aroma well when dried.

Herbal medicine

Thymus vulgaris. Parts used: leaves, flowering tops. Thyme has potent anti-microbial properties, which are attributed to the high content of essential oil. It also possesses a muscle-relaxant property and an ability to thin mucus in the lungs, and can be useful in relieving congestion. These combined effects make thyme a formidable remedy when it comes to treating respiratory conditions, such as colds and flu. Thyme can also be used as a gargle for sore throats and tonsillitis. The essential oil, known as thymol, is an ingredient of many oral hygiene products. In addition, thyme alleviates the symptoms of indigestion, such as gas, bloating and cramps, and its antimicrobial properties can also be helpful in the treatment of gastrointestinal infections.

For the safe and appropriate medicinal use of thyme, see *Sore throats, colds and flu*, page 206. Do not use thyme in greater than culinary quantities and do not use the essential oil if you are pregnant or breastfeeding. Thyme oil should not be taken internally.

You can grow thyme in pots or as a border plant in the garden.

■ Around the home

Thyme essential oil is a great addition to cleaning products and disinfectant sprays. For a powerful and fresh-smelling bathroom cleaning spray, mix ¼ teaspoon each of lemon, bergamot, pine, thyme, citronella and tea tree essential oils with 2 teaspoons vinegar, 1 tablespoon ammonia and 1 litre water. Then, to this solution add 2 tablespoons bicarbonate of soda and shake until well combined.

Use thyme essential oil in an oil diffuser in a sick room for its anti-bacterial qualities and soothing aroma.

■ Cooking

Thyme is an essential ingredient in mixed herbs, bouquet garni and herbes de Provence. It is a major culinary herb in Mediterranean cuisines, where it excels in slow-cooked casseroles and dishes containing meat, poultry or game. It can be assertive and dominate other flavours, so robust companions, such as onions, red wine and garlic work well. Use thyme in terrines, pâtés, meat pies, marinades (especially for olives),

Thymus x citriodorus 'Archers Gold'

aubergine and tomato dishes and thick vegetable-based soups. Dried thyme is often used in the jambalayas and gumbos of Creole and Cajun cooking. Various other kinds of thyme are also used for flavouring. Lemon thyme has a delicate flavour that complements fish and chicken dishes.

To see fairies

A recipe for a magical oil, allegedly enabling one to see fairies, was found in a 17th-century manuscript in the Ashmolean Museum in Oxford. The recipe includes a rather oblique instruction for collecting wild thyme: 'The thyme must be garnered near the side of a hill where fairies used to be.'

Turmeric

Curcuma longa Zingiberaceae

The vivid yellow colour of turmeric adds a golden hue to curries and is used as a dye for the robes of Buddhist monks. It has long had medicinal uses, particularly in Ayurvedic medicine, and rhizome constituents, known as curcuminoids, are now exciting scientific interest for their potential in treating a range of diseases.

PART USED Leaves

Turmeric
(*Curcuma longa*)

Turmeric flowers are accompanied by pale green lower bracts and pink to purple upper bracts.

Gardening

Part of the ginger family, turmeric is a tender herbaceous perennial. It forms a dense clump to about 1m of large, elliptic, pointed foliage, spreading by rhizomes that are red-brown with deep yellow flesh. Small yellow flowers are borne in dense, cone-shaped spikes.

Related species include wild turmeric (*C. aromatica*), with mainly medicinal uses, and zedoary (*C. zedoaria*), with citrus-scented leaves and pungently aromatic rhizomes which have both culinary and medicinal uses.

Position Turmeric requires rich, moist soil and a winter minimum of 10°C.

Propagation Divide sections of rhizome in spring.

Maintenance Remove dead foliage in winter. Keep on the dry side when the plant is dormant.

Pests and diseases Cold damp conditions cause rhizomes to rot.

Harvesting and storing Lift rhizomes when plants are dormant and steam or boil before drying and grinding.

Herbal medicine

Curcuma longa. Part used: rhizome. In Ayurvedic and Chinese herbal medicine, turmeric is regarded as a tonic and blood purifier and a remedy for arthritis, skin complaints, such as psoriasis, and digestive and liver disorders.

A compound called curcumin is involved in many of turmeric's medicinal effects. It has antioxidant and anti-inflammatory properties, a protective effect on the liver and increases bile secretion. Turmeric has also been shown to lower cholesterol levels in the blood and limit the development of hardened and blocked arteries. Recent research has shown potential anticancer effects. Clinical trials have shown turmeric to help in reducing symptoms of rheumatoid arthritis and post-operative inflammation. It has also proved effective in treating indigestion, stomach ulcers and bowel conditions, such as Crohn's disease and ulcerative colitis. Studies on large populations have shown that regular consumption of turmeric may cut the risk of developing certain cancers.

For the safe and appropriate medicinal use of turmeric, see *Liver support*, page 214, *High blood pressure and cholesterol*, page 234, and *Psoriasis*, page 223. Do not use turmeric in doses greater than culinary quantities if you are pregnant or breastfeeding.

Cooking

Buy plump, firm, clean rhizomes. They should have a warm, mild aroma and an earthy, musky flavour. Used fresh, or dried and ground, turmeric adds a brilliant yellow colour to foods. It is used in curry powders and pastes, pickles (such as piccalilli), chutneys, vegetable, rice and lentil dishes, and with poultry, fish and shellfish. Turmeric is also an ingredient in the Moroccan spice blend chermoula (see page 358).

Followers of Jainism, a religion founded in India, rub wet turmeric over brides' faces.

Valerian

Valeriana officinalis Valerianaceae

Valerian root is believed to be the attractant used by the Pied Piper in the German town of Hamelin in 1284. It proved to be profitable knowledge for the rat catcher when food supplies were threatened by a plague of rats.

PART USED Root

Valerian (*Valeriana officinalis*) bears clusters of pink-budded white flowers.

■ Gardening

Valerian (*V. officinalis*) is a hardy herbaceous perennial with pinnate, toothed leaves and tall flowering stems to 1.5m bearing clusters of tubular pink-tinged white flowers in summer. The roots contain an essential oil with a strong aroma that in tiny amounts has diverse commercial uses in 'mossy' perfumes and as an ingredient of apple flavours, beer and tobacco.

Valerian is ornamental as well as useful, tolerating damp ground and shade, and providing a good contrast to waterside plants with simple foliage, such as irises.

Note that red valerian (*Centranthus ruber*) is of no value medicinally.

Varieties There is a variegated form, 'Variegata'. Related species include Chinese valerian (*V. coreana*), Indian valerian (*V. jatamansi*) , a much smaller plant which flowers in early spring, and spikenard or jatamansi (*Nardostachys grandiflora*) from the Himalayas, famed as the source of a precious oil that is used in perfumery and ritual. All are used medicinally as relaxants.

Position Native to Western Europe, valerian prefers a cool root run in fertile, moist, well-drained loam, and a sunny to lightly shaded position.

Propagation Sow seeds in spring, gently pressed into the surface, as they require light to germinate. Divide mature plants in autumn or early spring.

Maintenance Recently disturbed plants may need protection from cats until established.

Pests and diseases None of note.

Harvesting and storing Lift the rhizomes from second-year plants when dormant, wash and dry in a cool (100°C) fan oven with the oven door left ajar.

■ Herbal medicine

Valeriana officinalis. Part used: root. Valerian has been used medicinally as a remedy for aiding sleep and relaxation for hundreds of years. Pharmacological studies have confirmed valerian's sedative effects on the nervous system and relaxant action on muscles. A number of clinical trials have assessed the efficacy of valerian on its own or in combination with other relaxing herbs for insomnia and sleep disturbance. The results of these trials suggest that valerian may have positive effects on sleep, particularly if taken consistently for more than 2 weeks. A small number of human trials have also shown the beneficial effect of valerian in alleviating the symptoms of anxiety and mental stress. Valerian's calming effect on nerves and muscles explains its traditional use for gastro-intestinal cramps, period pains and headaches as well, particularly when related to stress.

For the safe and appropriate use of valerian, see *Insomnia*, page 220. Do not use valerian if you are pregnant or breastfeeding. It may be advisable to stop intake prior to surgery as it may increase the sedative effect of an anaesthetic.

Valerian
(*Valeriana officinalis*)

Vanilla

Vanilla planifolia Orchidaceae

The orchid family is the largest family of flowering plants on earth but only a few are commercially important as aromatic or medicinal herbs. Vanilla is the leading herb, being one of the world's favourite flavours, and the most labour intensive, each pod requiring hand-pollination of a single flower.

PART USED Fruits (pods)

Dried vanilla pods

Taste of the divine

Vanilla originated in Mexico where it was used to flavour the Aztec *chocólatl*, a foaming chocolate-based drink spiced with chilli drunk by the nobility. Introduced to Europe by the Spanish, plantations were established in various parts of the tropics during colonial times.

The vines grew well but produced no pods, and it was not until 1841 that the technique of hand pollination was discovered by a 12-year-old slave boy, Edmond Albius on the island of Réunion. Hand pollination is essential because the flower's only pollinator, a Melipona bee, does not live in areas where vanilla is cultivated. It is an intricate procedure, carried out daily on vanilla plantations, mostly by women and children.

When pollinated, each flower develops an elongated, pendent pod which takes 5-6 weeks to mature. After harvesting, it goes through a complex fermentation process for about 6 months. A quicker process (40 days) produces lower-quality pods for making vanilla extract.

Gardening

Vanilla is a robust tropical evergreen orchid with thick, zigzag climbing stems, aerial roots, and fleshy oblong pointed leaves 8-25cm long. Pale green-white scented flowers 5cm across, with a yellow lip, are produced in succession on racemes which appear in the axils.

Varieties Variegated vanilla (*V. planifolia* 'Variegata') has irregular yellow-green stripes on leaves and stems. It makes an attractive climber for a greenhouse wall.

Position Vanilla needs very good drainage, ample moisture, high humidity, partial shade and a minimum winter temperature of 15°C. Special orchid bark is available from orchid nurseries for potting orchids, which do not thrive in loam-based or soilless potting composts.

Propagation Cut sections of stem with one or two nodes and some aerial roots. Place in a tray of perlite or sphagnum moss in a propagator at 25-30°C until new roots have developed.

Maintenance Keep on the dry side in low temperatures. Water freely. Keep warm and humid in growing season.

Pests and diseases Vanilla is prone to root rot, scale insects and mealy bug when grown under glass.

Harvesting and storing Pods are picked when fully developed but still green, and scalded before undergoing fermentation and drying. Keep vanilla pods in a dark, airtight container and use within three months.

Cooking

Vanilla is an indispensable flavouring for custards, ice creams, yogurts, dessert sauces, cream-based desserts, sweets, cakes and biscuits. It can also add an delicious flavour to fish dishes and baked fruits. After splitting open the pod and using the seeds, put the outer pod into a jar of caster sugar to be used in baking. Commercially, vanilla is also used in perfumery, household fragrances, such as candles, and in soft drinks and liqueurs, such as Galliano.

Vanilla (*Vanilla planifolia*)

Vervain

Verbena officinalis Verbenaceae

Despite its plain appearance and lack of scent, vervain was once considered the most magical herb in ancient Celtic, Germanic and Roman cultures. It was used for purifying sacred spaces and in spells and potions for divination, immortality, crop fertility, prosperity and love, and for protection from evil forces and lightning.

OTHER COMMON NAMES Herb of grace, enchanter's herb
PARTS USED Aerial parts

Vervain (*Verbena officinalis*)

■ Gardening

Vervain is native to Europe, Asia and Africa, and is naturalised in North America. A slender erect herbaceous perennial growing to 1.2m, it is found on dry, stony, bare ground such as roadsides. The leaves are coarsely and irregularly toothed, and the slender, branched, terminal flowering spikes bear tiny tubular lavender flowers. Vervain is worth growing as a wild flower but self sows freely and once established, plants are difficult to remove. North American blue vervain (*V. hastata*) has similar uses.
Position Well-drained to dry, neutral to alkaline soil in sun.

Propagation Grow vervain from seed in spring. Germination is erratic and can take 4 weeks.
Maintenance Remove self-sown seedlings regularly before they have had a chance to develop tenacious root systems.
Pests and diseases Knot-like galls caused by insects can form in the stem.
Harvesting and storing Harvest plants just before the flowers open and air-dry. Store under airtight conditions.

■ Herbal medicine

Verbena officinalis. Parts used: aerial parts. Vervain has both calming and restorative effects on the nervous system and an uplifting effect on mood. It can help to relieve nervous exhaustion and depression, and act as a supportive remedy for tension and stress. Vervain is particularly effective as a treatment for those who are feeling miserable and fatigued when they are recovering from feverish illnesses such as flu. The plant's relaxing effects also help to combat muscular tension in the body, and can reduce intestinal cramps and ease the discomfort of period pains.

Vervain is also traditionally prescribed during the early stages of fever. Further, it is regarded as a liver remedy and can be used to treat a number of conditions associated with this organ.

For the safe and appropriate use of vervain, consult your doctor or medical herbalist. Do not use if you are pregnant or breastfeeding except with the advice of a doctor or medical herbalist.

Devil's bane

Derived from the Celtic *ferfaen*, from *fer*, 'to drive away' and faen, 'a stone', from its use as a treatment for kidney stones, vervain has many religious, cultural and magical associations. For instance, the names herb of the cross, holy herb and devil's bane derive from vervain's reputation for staunching Christ's wounds on the cross. It was also used in sacrifice and purification ceremonies by the ancient Romans and Druids. In more recent times, the Iroquois people of North America used a concoction of crushed blue vervain (*Verbena hastata*) leaves to make an obnoxious person go away.

Vervain tea was once believed to protect people from vampires.

Viburnum

Viburnum opulus, V. prunifolium Caprifoliaceae

Viburnums are popular garden shrubs, grown for their outstanding spring displays of usually fragrant flowers, colourful autumn leaves and berries. Two species are also important in herbal medicine, valued for their bark which is used as a muscle relaxant.

OTHER COMMON NAMES Cramp bark, guelder rose (*V. opulus*); black haw, sloe-leaved viburnum, stagbush (*V. prunifolium*)
PARTS USED Stem bark (*V. opulus*); stem and root bark (*V. prunifolium*)

Cramp bark (*Viburnum opulus*)

Gardening

Cramp bark (*Viburnum opulus*) is a hardy deciduous shrub, 2-4m tall, with vine-shaped leaves that turn red in autumn and flat lacy heads of white flowers in late spring, followed by glossy bright red berries. This ornamental, easily grown native shrub is widely planted in gardens and is a popular choice for landscaping for its long period of interest.

Black haw (*V. prunifolium*) forms a spreading deciduous shrub to small tree that reaches 5m. It has ovate leaves and flat-topped lacy heads of reddish buds opening to white flowers in spring, followed by black fruits in autumn.

Another viburnum used is American highbush cranberry (*V. opulus* var. *americanum* syn. *V. trilobum*). All have poisonous berries.

Varieties There are many ornamental varieties of *V. opulus*, including 'Roseum' syn. 'Sterile' (snowball bush), which has globose flowerheads; 'Notcutt's Variety', with excellent autumn foliage and large red fruits; 'Xanthocarpum', with translucent golden berries; and 'Compactum', which is a dense and slow-growing plant.

Position Well-drained soil in sun or partial shade. Autumn colour will be better in drier, sunnier positions.

Propagation The species are easy to grow from seed. Varieties can be propagated by greenwood cuttings in summer.

Maintenance Prune in early spring, removing old or badly placed growths from the base.

Pests and diseases Viburnums are susceptible to honey fungus and leafspot. Leaves may be reduced to a lacework of veins by viburnum beetles.

Harvesting and storing Peel off the outer bark in strips and dry it.

Herbal medicine

Viburnum opulus. Part used: bark. As its name suggests, cramp bark is effective for most types of muscular tension and can help to relax the muscles of the body after strenuous or ongoing physical activity. Cramp bark is also prescribed for tension and cramping in the digestive system, and will ease the symptoms of indigestion and colic. It is particularly useful in treating menstrual and menopausal symptoms. Its muscle relaxant properties help to ease the spasm and discomfort of period pains and, due to a slightly astringent or drying effect, it can also reduce heavy bleeding during menstruation as well as irregular bleeding that can occur during menopause. Black haw (*V. prunifolium*) is used in a similar way.

For the safe and appropriate use of cramp bark, see *Sports injuries*, page 229. Do not use cramp bark if pregnant or breastfeeding, except with the advice of a doctor or medical herbalist.

Black haw (*Viburnum prunifolium*)

The red berries of cramp bark (*Viburnum opulus*) are poisonous.

Walnut

Juglans regia Juglandaceae

Walnut has a reputation as an anticancer remedy and aphrodisiac in folk medicine. The leaves and husks were the main source of brown hair dyes until the early 20th century, and their use in this way was first described by Pliny in the 1st century CE.

Walnut kernels

OTHER COMMON NAMES English walnut, common walnut, Persian walnut
PARTS USED Leaves, kernels, oil

Mature walnut tree

Gardening

The English walnut is not native to the British Isles but has been grown since Roman times for its nuts, oil and timber. It grows wild from southeast Europe to the Himalayas, central Russia and southwest China, and is a spreading tree to 35m, with aromatic leaves, 30cm long, divided into 5-9 ovate leaflets which are bronze when young. Dark yellow male catkins and spikes of female flowers appear in late spring to early summer, followed by dark green, spherical fruits to 5cm, each containing a woody nut. While only suitable for a large garden or orchard, a walnut tree is both ornamental and useful. If you do plant a walnut tree, choose a named self-fertile variety that crops when young.

Varieties 'Broadview' produces large crops of easily cracked nuts. 'Hansen' yields round, thin-shelled nuts at an early age. 'Laciniata' has deeply cut leaflets.
Position Deep fertile but well-drained soil in sun.
Propagation Sow seed when ripe, or in spring after stratifying (species only). Named varieties are propagated by grafting on to seedlings.
Maintenance Remove badly placed and damaged branches in late summer.
Pests and diseases Leaves may be marked by bacterial leaf blotch. Young shoots and flowers may be damaged by frost in cold sites. Squirrels eat the nuts.
Harvesting and storing Leaves are picked during the growing season and used fresh or dried. Fruits are harvested when ripe in autumn and shelled. Store shelled nuts in the freezer or fridge to prevent oxidation and rancidity.

Herbal medicine

Juglans regia. Parts used: leaves, kernels. Walnut has an ancient history of medicinal uses and has been studied intensively for its active compounds. The nuts are rich in serotonin, which may help to prevent heart attack and stroke, and omega-3 fatty acids that have a role in alleviating depression and seasonal affective disorder (SAD) and enhancing brain function. The regular consumption of walnuts has been shown to lower LDL-cholesterol by 10 per cent in a few weeks. Walnut leaf extracts may help to prevent hair loss and heal skin eruptions, such as eczema and herpes. For the safe and appropriate use of walnut products, consult your doctor or medical herbalist.

Cooking

Walnuts add flavour and texture to cakes, biscuits, desserts, ice cream and savoury dishes and sauces including Middle Eastern chicken dishes, Provençal raito (salt cod) and Ligurian walnut sauce (salsa di noci). Walnut oil is used especially with fruit or herb-flavoured vinegars. Leaves are used for wrapping cheeses such as Picadou.

Around the home

Leaves and husks are used to make natural hair colourings and conditioner for dark hair. Added to alum, walnut extracts effectively stain wood and remove scratches on furniture.

Ripe walnut fruit splitting to reveal its nut

Watercress and nasturtium

Nasturtium officinale, Brassicaceae

Nasturtium means 'twisted nose', referring to the effect that its pungent flavour has on the taste buds. Large-scale cultivation of watercress began in the 19th century. Today's watercress beds yield ten crops a year of milder-flavoured varieties.

PARTS USED Leaves, young shoots

Watercress (*Nasturtium officinale*)

◼ Gardening

Watercress is a hardy short-lived perennial found wild in streams passing through chalk soils. It has compound dark green leaves, stems that root along their length to form large clumps, and clusters of tiny white, four-petalled flowers in summer. It is noticeably more bitter when flowering. The cultivated form is preferred, as wild watercress is often a refuge for liver flukes (*Fasciola hepatica*) in areas where sheep graze. Nasturtium or Indian cress (*Tropaeolum majus*) is quite different and unrelated to *N. officinale*, getting its common name because it too has peppery tasting leaves. Watercress can be grown as a marginal in a garden pond, or in pots stood in water; it does not need flowing water.

Position Damp to wet, neutral to alkaline soil in full sun.

Propagation Sow seeds in early spring or plant discarded lower stems from a bundle of watercress.

Maintenance Keep constantly wet.

Pests and diseases None of note.

Harvesting and storing Harvest watercress fresh and only use before flowering. Store at room temperature with its roots in water.

◼ Herbal medicine

Nasturtium officinale. Parts used: aerial parts. Watercress belong to the cabbage family and like its relatives, mustard and horseradish, contains mustard oil glycosides – that are responsible for its major medicinal effects. The pungent compounds have antibacterial and anti-fungal properties that are useful in the treatment of respiratory tract infections. They can help the body to fight off colds, flu and other bronchial complaints. Watercress is high in vitamin C, betacarotene, folic acid, and minerals, including potassium. It has detoxicant effects and was traditionally eaten as a tonic in spring, improving the digestion, stimulating the excretion of waste and clearing the skin.

For the safe and appropriate use of watercress, consult your doctor or medical herbalist. Do not use nasturtium if you are pregnant or breastfeeding.

◼ Cooking

Watercress gives bite to soups, pesto, fish dishes, salads, sandwiches and vegetable juices. The sharp, peppery taste makes it a good salad green. It goes well with a citrus dressing. Use in soups (see recipe, page 352), sandwiches and sauces for fish (see *Frankfurt green sauce*, page 344).

Other cresses

A number of other related species share the hot peppery flavour and have similar culinary uses. Upland or American cress (*Barbarea verna*) and winter or land cress (*B. vulgaris*) are both hardy dry-land cresses, grown for winter crops of watercress-like leaves. The cress sold in trays to be clipped for salads can be either salad rape (*Brassica napus*) or garden cress (*Lepidium sativum*). Traditionally, garden cress was sprouted in punnets with mustard seeds as 'mustard and cress'.

Beds of wild watercress

White horehound

Marrubium vulgare Lamiaceae

Used as a cough medicine since ancient Egyptian times, horehound yields an aromatic bitter juice from which it gets its name – *Marrubium* being from the Hebrew word for bitter juice – *marrob*. This distinctive and not unpleasant smelling liquid is also used as a flavouring for horehound ale and liqueurs.

PARTS USED Leaves, flowering tops

Gardening

White horehound is a hardy perennial with crinkled, downy, grey-white, toothed foliage. The small white flowers, borne in summer, are densely clustered in successive upper leaf axils. A native of North Africa and dry parts of Eurasia, horehound spreads rapidly in low rainfall areas and has become a serious weed in many arid regions. As a herb in British gardens, it poses no threat, and is attractive in white and silver borders.

Another member of the mint family, black horehound (*Ballota nigra*), was once used to adulterate white horehound. It is less effective, so is little used today, but remains popular in herb gardens.

The white-variegated, 'Archer's Variety', is a handsome plant that comes reasonably true from seed. Black horehound grows wild in the British Isles, preferring dry disturbed ground along hedgerows and roadsides.

Position Grow white horehound in a sunny, well-drained to dry position.
Propagation Grow white horehound by seed sown in spring.
Maintenance Avoid overwatering.
Pests and diseases There are none of significance. White horehound has been used as a grasshopper repellent on various crops.
Harvesting and storing Cut down the whole plant just as flowering begins and extract juice or dry for herbal use.

Herbal medicine

Marrubium vulgare. Parts used: leaves, flowering tops. Not to be confused with black horehound, white horehound is best known as a remedy for respiratory conditions such as colds and bronchitis – especially when there is catarrh that is difficult to expel by coughing. White horehound relaxes the bronchial muscles while at the same time encouraging easier removal of mucus from the lungs. As a result of its bitter taste, due to the presence of specific compounds, white horehound has an appreciable and stimulating effect on the digestive system. It can improve appetite and ease symptoms of indigestion, particularly when there is gas and bloating. White horehound also has a positive effect on liver function and increases the secretion of bile, which can aid the digestive process as a whole.

For the safe and appropriate use of white horehound, see *Sore throats, colds and flu*, page 206. Do not use white horehound if you are pregnant or breastfeeding. Do not use with medications containing serotonin.

see *Sore throats, colds and flu*, page 206.

Passover plate

In late March or in April each year, Jews celebrate Passover with a meal that symbolises the flight of the Jews from Egypt. Each of the items on the plate, or *seder*, represents part of the story of their escape: along with romaine lettuce or grated horseradish, white horehound is one of the bitter herbs eaten in the Middle East to symbolise the harshness of living as a slave in Egypt.

White horehound (*Marrubium vulgare*)

White horehound is used to make horehound candy that can ease sore throats and coughs.

Yarrow (*Achillea millefolium*)

Yarrow

Achillea millefolium Asteraceae

Yarrow is one of the world's most long-standing medicinal herbs. In China, stripped and dried yarrow stalks were tossed in order to consult the *I Ching,* the *Book of Changes*, and, in the West, it has been widely used as a herb that possesses a powerful but neutral magic.

OTHER COMMON NAMES Bloodwort, carpenter's weed, milfoil, soldier's woundwort
PARTS USED Leaves, flowers

■ Gardening

Yarrow is a hardy perennial forming clumps of wiry stems and very finely divided feathery leaves with a pungent, refreshing scent that is strangely uplifting to the senses. It multiplies via a series of underground rhizomes. The small white to pink flowers are borne in dense, flat-headed clusters to about 70cm. Many hybrids have been bred from *A. millefolium* to give colourful, long-lasting flowers for borders.

Varieties While hybrids cannot be used for medicinal purposes, there are ornamental forms of the species that can be used. These include: 'Cerise Queen'; 'Cassis'; 'Red Velvet'; and 'Rose Madder' all with names describing their flower colour. Closely related to yarrow are two other attractive herbs that also make good cut flowers: sneezewort (*A. ptarmica*), once used to make snuff; and English or garden mace (*A. ageratum* syn. *A. decolorans*). Also known as maudlin or sweet milfoil, the latter was once used to scent water for washing.

Position Yarrow requires a sunny, well-drained position. When established, it has good drought-resistance.

Propagation Raise the species by seed sown in spring. Propagate named varieties by division, also in spring.

Maintenance Yarrow is quite invasive, so it may be necessary to control spread during the growing season.

Pests and diseases There are no pests or diseases of any consequence.

Harvesting and storing Harvest the flowering stalks just as they fully open, and dry in small bunches hung upside down out of direct sunlight. Harvest leaves at any time.

■ Herbal medicine

Achillea millefolium. Parts used: aerial parts. Yarrow has been used since ancient times for its ability to quickly stop bleeding and reduce inflammation. It is also used to encourage perspiration and reduce body temperature in feverish conditions; for this purpose it is usually taken as an infusion with elderflowers.

Yarrow is a valuable digestive remedy, that helps to alleviate colic and indigestion and improves appetite while also having a stimulatory effect on bile flow and liver function. Traditionally regarded as a herb of benefit to women, yarrow was commonly used to treat heavy and painful menstrual bleeding.

For the safe and appropriate use of yarrow, see *Sore throats, colds and flu,* page 206. Do not use yarrow if pregnant or breastfeeding without the advice of a doctor or medical herbalist.

Caution: Yarrow may cause a reaction if you are sensitive to plants in the Asteraceae or Compositae families.

Achilles the healer

Yarrow was once a useful herb on battlefields, where it gets two of its common names, soldier's woundwort and bloodwort. The herb is named for the ancient Greek hero Achilles who, according to Homer's epic poem *The Iliad,* used it to heal his wounded troops in the Trojan War. Achilles had been taught how to use plants by Cheiron, a learned centaur. At one point, Eurypylus is wounded and begs Patroclus to 'put the right things on it'. 'Patroclus ... crushed a bitter root ... and put it on the wound. The root took away all the pain. The blood stopped and the wound dried.'

Gardening

Thriving herbs are a beautiful sight. Whether you grow them for cooking or for their health and beauty benefits, or simply to enjoy their appearance and aroma, this guide shows you how to grow herbs with great success.

Herb garden styles

Whether you want the herb garden you create to be formal or informal, large or small, simple or complex, the shape, texture and perfume of your plants will all play an integral role in helping to make an inviting outdoor space.

The beauty of herbs

Herbs are such a diverse group of plants, from groundcovers to shrubs and trees, that there are herbs to suit any climate, soil type and position. Even if you live in a flat with a small balcony or have no outdoor space at all, you can still grow culinary herbs in a window box.

And herbs are incredibly versatile. Take the elder, a deciduous shrub or tree that grows to about 6m and produces clusters of tiny, creamy white scented flowers that attract bees in summer, followed by blue-black berries in autumn. Elders make a great hedge, and you can use the flowers and berries to make cordials, wines, jams and jellies. The leaves repel flies and mosquitoes while the flowers are used medicinally to treat coughs, colds, allergies and arthritis, and cosmetically as a skin toner.

Herbs for a knot garden

Traditionally, the most commonly used hedging plant is box, as it is compact, robust and long lived, but you could use other knot garden herbs such as rosemary, lavender, santolina, germander and mugwort (at right). Variegated varieties can also look attractive. Pansies, ground-covering thymes and calendulas are ideal for filling these spaces, but avoid invasive herbs, such as mint, which produces runners.

Your herb garden

Depending on your lifestyle and the space you have, your herb garden can be anything from a showpiece to a personal retreat. Good garden design can seem deceptively simple, and some gardens belie the creativity, skill and hard work involved in their creation, while others leave visitors in no doubt of the years of effort invested in their planning, planting and presentation.

Travel can give great inspiration for ideas and styles. Often, it's not until you explore your own taste that you begin to build a mental catalogue of what you'd like to grow in your own garden.

To help make your 'wish list' a reality, consult the expertise of garden designers and landscape architects – in person, in books or on the internet.

You might prefer a potted herb garden so you can grow your favourite culinary herbs, or perhaps you have the space for an informal cottage garden, where shrubs and trees mingle with annuals, perennials and ground cover.

Or you could design a formal garden that's dedicated to herbs, like the grand knot gardens and parterres that are so characteristic of garden designs of the 16th and 17th centuries.

Formal herb gardens

Traditionally, plants were grown for their uses, not their beauty: herbs were highly valued for their culinary and medicinal qualities, and in medieval monasteries, monks grew a vast range of herbs in apothecary gardens.

Knot gardens

During the reign of Henry VIII, decorative knot gardens became popular. They were often complicated, designed to be viewed from above: low, evergreen hedges were planted in geometric or symmetric interlinking patterns, such as diamonds. The knots or patterns could be intricate scrollworks, such as coats of arms or heraldic symbols. To distinguish the patterns, contrasting foliage textures or colours were planted together.

Originally, there was nothing inside the hedged areas except clipped grass, or gravel and stones, but they were later filled with fragrant herbs, such as rosemary, lavender, sage and hyssop – perfect as drying 'racks' for linen. Imagine sleeping on sheets scented with fresh lavender.

Adjoining the Tudor Old Palace at Hatfield House in Hertfordshire is a excellent example of a knot garden

Repeating shapes, such as spheres, provides continuity and interest, at ground and eye level.

Parterre gardens

In 16th century France, parterre gardens – intricate, complex beds spanning huge areas – developed from the English knot garden. Again, geometry and symmetry were intrinsic elements in these designs. Wide gravel paths separated beds, while flowers were used to balance the green hedging. These fine gardens were also designed to be viewed from above – perhaps from a terrace or upper floor.

Topiaries, a feature of parterres, provided focal points. They were crafted from small-leafed species, such as citrus, yew, bay, box or cypress, and punctuated corners and centrepieces in imaginative designs that ranged from spirals and spheres to cubes, symbols and animals.

While Versailles, outside Paris, showcased extravagant formal gardens fit for royalty, it took an army of workers to build them. You can still visit many examples of these formal gardens, which have been recreated or restored; in the 18th century, many grand European gardens were destroyed and replaced by open, undulating landscapes, designed or greatly influenced by the great landscape architect 'Capability' Brown.

Herbs for a parterre

In more recent times, the range of plants used for topiary in parterres has expanded to include those commonly referred to as 'standards' – plants that can be grown and pruned into a lollipop shape. For their flowers, fragrance or compliant foliage, you could try Swiss willow (*Salix helvetica*), roses, cherry pie (*Heliotropium arborescens*), and lemon verbena (*Aloysia citriodora*).

Some grand restored gardens

Hampton Court Palace gardens are the home of the Privy Garden. Raised walks are lined with rows of yew cones and parterres on either side of a central walk leading to a circular pool and fountain. To the west of the Privy Garden is a small Knot Garden hedged with box.

A little further north is Hatfield House, in Hertfordshire, where Queen Elizabeth I spent part of her childhood. Included within the grounds are splendid examples of herb and scented gardens, kitchen and knot gardens.

A few hours from Paris, in the Loire Valley, is Château de Villandry, one of the most visited gardens in France. Designed to be viewed from above, the replicas of the 17th century beds in the Love Garden have been planted in symbolic designs associated with love – for example, tragic love, represented by the shapes of blades, swords and daggers. Nearby are the Herb Gardens dedicated to about 30 aromatic, cooking and medicinal herbs.

Another fine garden is in the grounds of the Dutch palace Het Loo, near Apeldoorn, in the Netherlands. It features restored parterre gardens, an axial layout, fountains and statues.

Designing a formal garden

You could plant out a simple knot garden in a space of 12 metres square, divided into four sections with low or dwarf hedges. Or design a circular garden by planting out a 'wheel' and 'spokes' with hedging material. Hedges grow best from immature plantings, and gaps will take a few years to close up so be patient. Within the subdivisions, grow herbs for a variety of uses – separating culinary herbs from medicinal ones.

A formal design is often the easiest way to start planning. Mirror images of garden beds are a good way to replicate patterns on either side of a path, lawn area or house. Use the continuity of low green hedges to balance colour and reduce the possibility of overdoing the flower planting, and parallel lines to give a sense of order and calm.

Maintenance

Pruning, clipping and general tidying are the main maintenance tasks for these formal gardens but, in spite of the work involved, there is a satisfying sense of purpose and achievement. The idea is to have no-nonsense clean lines and shapes.

Here, a formal layout, with raised beds and an arch, is softened by informal plantings of herbs.

Plant herbs in decorative clumps at the front of a border such as the catmint, sage and fennel shown here.

Informal gardens

If a softer, wilder cottage garden is more your style, set out beds and paths with sweeping curves, instead of rigid squares and rectangles, and plant herbs in round pots, rather than square ones. But the principles of a formal garden can still be useful in providing structure.

Define planting areas with low hedging but, instead of traditional box, try a softer plant, such as catmint, a billowing flowering herb.

Design informal herbal borders so that shrubs and trees form a high hedge to disguise the fence or an ugly shed, or to provide privacy from the neighbours.

In front of these, grow taller perennial herbs, such as cardoon and angelica (see *Herb Directory*, page 13), which can reach over 2m, then lower-growing herbs, such as salvias (see page 119).

Use trailing, ground-covering plants to blur garden lines and edges, and add self-seeding herbs, such as Californian poppy (see page 105) and pretty heartsease (see page 67), which pop up year after year.

You can even grow a herb lawn with a low-growing plant, such as chamomile (see page 34), or a compact groundcover, such as thyme (see page 135), between paving stones. When walking on these herbs, you will crush them and release their scent.

Themed gardens

Sometimes, it's easier to design your herb garden according to a theme. Here are some suggestions.

SENSORY Appeal to the senses of sight, sound, smell and touch. Grow herbs such as lavender and roses for their fragrant flowers, or others for the oils they release when you crush the stems or leaves – for example, citrus, lemon balm, thyme and aniseed. Contrast the gentle softness of lambs' ears (*Stachys byzantina*) with upright spikes of lavender or the roughness of lemon balm.

CULINARY Choose a flavour theme for cooking. Try experimenting with different combinations of herbs, such as hot chillies, peppery rocket and spicy coriander. Or you could plant traditional French culinary herbs, such as tarragon, chervil and parsley. For information on cooking with herbs, see pages 336-389.

PICKING Create posies with flowers gathered from your garden. Peony, lavender, nasturtiums, scented geraniums, poppies, sage, calendula, feverfew and iris make lovely gifts or display plants. For projects on making herb and flower arrangements, see *Craft*, pages 314-319.

CRAFT Many decorative objects can be made with herbs. Use fragrant herbs in sleep pillows and moth-repelling sachets; press flowers for gift tags and cards; photograph herbs to create a mural; digitally print herbs onto napkins, or plant a hanging herb ball. For projects, see *Craft*, pages 306-331.

HOUSEHOLD USE Harvest roses, spearmint, marjoram and oregano for pot-pourri; make fragrant air fresheners and herbal cleaners; use flea-repellent plants, such as lavender, to protect your dog or cat. For recipes, see *Around the Home*, pages 290-303.

MEDICINAL Many medicines derive their healing properties from herbs. For the safe and appropriate use of herbal treatments you can prepare yourself to treat conditions ranging from sore throats to arthritis, see *Herbal Medicine*, pages 206-245.

COSMETIC With herbal essential oils, fresh herbs and some items from your pantry, you can make natural beauty products to tone your skin, condition your hair, and much more. For easy recipes, see *Natural Beauty*, pages 252-287.

Citrus fruit, such as lemons, are grown for their fragrance and their culinary use.

Knowing your site

Before planting out a herb garden or starting a collection of herbs in pots, take the time to plan a little. By learning about your site and choosing the right herbs for your conditions, you'll create a thriving and productive garden.

Draw a plan

Once you've familiarised yourself with the main characteristics of your property, you can then decide how to utilise them. The easiest way to do this is to document your garden space.

First, measure the dimensions of your property carefully and sketch it out onto a piece of graph paper. A scale of 1:100 or 1:50 is useful. Add the house, garage, drive, shed and other existing structures, paths, paved areas, steps, fences, ponds or pools, power lines, underground services, trees and major shrubs. It doesn't have to be perfect, but a basic plan drawn to scale will help you to design your garden, even if all you are working with is a small courtyard area.

Next, use a compass to determine where north is and mark it on your plan. Now, use coloured pencils to mark in any shady spots, the direction of prevailing winds, parts of the garden that slope or contain gullies, particularly damp or dry areas – in other words, any

peculiarities or characteristics you need to consider before you start planting. Remember to include shade cast by neighbouring trees or buildings: although they aren't part of your property, they will certainly affect what you can grow. As you record all this information, you'll gradually build a picture of the main elements of the garden and which favourite or difficult areas need some special consideration.

Experiment

Once you've created a basic template of your garden, photocopy it several times and use it as a basis for experimenting. You can either draw in existing garden beds or make a fresh start. Mark any areas visible from inside the house that you want to enhance or disguise, and also note potential or existing seating, entertaining areas and play corners.

Planned areas

A garden area should be functional as well as visually stimulating, so the next step is to consider how you plan to use

Measure out new garden beds using a line or rope, then mark the edges clearly using lime or sand.

your outdoor area. Start by asking yourself some questions. Are there areas for entertaining, or just for sitting? Do your children or the family pets need some play space? Do you have enough time, energy and interest to look after a high-maintenance garden, or do you just want a small section to tend?

Are there some elements you'd like to enhance – such as views and wildlife sounds – or aspects you'd prefer to disguise – the utility area, for instance, or traffic noise? Is the space limited or unwieldy? Does the route you take to the washing line or compost heap follow the existing path, or do you traipse across the lawn? If you always take a shortcut to the utility area, think about redirecting the path, rather than wearing out the grass.

Research

Ponder the possibilities and look at the space from every angle. If you're making big changes, get others involved in the planning process: you may be surprised what a difference a new perspective can make. Talk to friends and other garden owners, read gardening magazines and books, watch gardening programs on the television, visit open gardens and shows, pick up colour swatches from paint or fabric stores. In short, explore anything that will give you ideas and inspiration.

A formal herb garden

If you have a sunny, well-drained level area, consider planting a knot garden or parterre (see pages 148–50). Draw your plan to scale on a sheet of graph paper first, then transpose it to the bed itself by using sand, garden lime or landscape-marking paint, which is sold in a spray can.

Use a garden line to ensure straight lines, but for a circular bed, push a stake in the centre of the bed and tie a length of string to another

stake. Then scribe a circle by walking around your central stake at the full length of the string.

Divide a knot garden into sections by planting hedges of low-growing compact herbs, such as rosemary, lavender or cotton lavender, then fill it with more herbs to create a colour or foliage theme.

Finally, add a picket or wrought iron fence to add a touch of whimsy or a sense of discovery.

A design for a formal herb garden

olive
rosemary standard bay in pot
box cone in pot
nepeta
hollyhocks
golden majoram
thyme
parsley
lavender
chives
dill
chives
water lilies
passionfruit on trellis
chillies
lavender
parsley
lemon balm
hollyhocks
rocket
basil
nepeta
artemisia rose
rose artemisia
olive

standard bay in pot rosemary
box cone in pot
nepeta
echinacea
lavender
passionfruit on trellis
lavender
echinacea
nepeta
olive

• This formal herb garden has a classic symmetrical geometric layout, with the height elements provided by an olive tree in each corner and trellises on either side.

• The main colour scheme is lavender and mauve flowers, with grey-green foliage provided by lavender, artemisia, nepeta, olive and rosemary, accented with pink in the roses, hollyhocks and echinacea, and red in the chillies.

• Topiary bay and box draw the eye to the seating area, while the square pond provides the central focal point.

• The central herb garden is planted with culinary herbs, but you could also use the four quadrants to separate culinary from medicinal herbs, for instance. The brick paving radiating out from the pond makes each section easy to access for weeding and harvesting.

• The sandstone flagging and edging help to unify the garden. A peach-coloured gravel, used to fill open areas between the beds, complements the overall colour scheme of the main planting.

• The standard roses on either side of the entrance are reminders of how, in the Middle Ages, monks grew standard roses in their monastic gardens to represent themselves at work.

Aspect

One of the keys to growing successful herbs is plenty of sunlight, so the aspect of your property will determine what you can grow. A southerly aspect is ideal, as many herbs will struggle without daily exposure to the sun.

Remember that the amount of sunlight varies with the seasons: the sun is higher in the sky in summer than in winter, and deciduous trees will provide shade during warmer months but extra light during the cooler months of autumn and winter.

Climatic conditions

Climatic conditions in the British Isles are very variable, with at least two weeks difference in growing season between north and south, and the west being generally wetter and milder than the east. Coastal areas differ yet again, often escaping frosts but suffering instead from salt-laden winds. The milder coastal climate reaches a good 20 miles inland, and on the west coast is further influenced by the Gulf Stream, giving almost sub-tropical conditions.

Generally, planting is carried out in spring or autumn, with the determining factor being the timing of the first and last frosts.

Microclimates

Within each climate zone are natural microclimates that create conditions

A garden with a sunny aspect is ideal for a cottage garden featuring herbs. On the left side of the path, pale pink *Nicotiana tabacum* towers over deep pink dahlias, orange nasturtiums and potted lilies.

outside the general climatic pattern, which affects the growth and suitability of plants. You can also deliberately create microclimates to provide more suitable conditions by planting windbreaks for shelter or building brick walls to retain heat and warmth.

So, if you live in a cold location, and you really want to grow a frost-tender plant, such as olive, you can try creating the protective environment it needs.

If you're unsure whether you're making an appropriate choice, just wander around your neighbourhood and look at what's thriving in other people's gardens and in amenity plantings. Also, seek the advice of a horticulturalist at your local nursery.

Use the vertical planes of your herb garden by installing pots of herbs on trellises.

Design tips

Before you start planting, always prepare new garden beds properly. Clear the area of weeds, rake it flat and improve the soil with organic matter (see pages 156-57).
MAKE paths wide enough for a wheelbarrow or so that two people can comfortably walk side-by-side.
EXPERIMENT with plant placement. Sit rows of pots in position before planting, to ensure that the spacing is correct, the height is accurate and your colour, form and texture choices work well.
INCORPORATE surfaces and structures into the new design – paint fences, trellis, gates or walls to contrast with or complement the garden colour scheme. These features can provide interesting backdrops to garden beds and enhance or tone down flowers and foliage.

The principles of plant selection

What you can grow will be determined by the amount of space and available sunlight you have, soil considerations and, of course, personal preferences.

Think about where your new herbs will be positioned – at the front of a garden bed as a border, as a hedging or screening plant, near the kitchen door for culinary use, as companion plants or as space fillers?

So, make a list of the characteristics your plants need to deliver – for instance, you might need plants that 'prefer full sun, grow to a height of less than 1m, preferably with flowers'. Once you know what you want a plant to do and look like, it's much easier to choose.

And think about specific areas of the garden. If there is a spot that seems to collect water after rainfall or watering, grow thirsty plants there, or improve the drainage. Any area that is hard to access is easily neglected, so plant it with resilient herbs, such as southernwood (*Artemisia abrotanum*) or other survivors.

Planting ideas

Herbs are extremely versatile plants and suitable for a range of garden designs, from formal to cottage gardens.

• Set aside a dedicated area for growing herbs, or intersperse with vegetables, flowering perennials, annuals and shrubs.

• Grow herbs in containers, using them to create focal points or accents. For more impact, choose large containers, rather than small ones (see page 170–71).

• Think about colour combinations throughout the year. For example, tone down summer's heat with soft, soothing blues, mauves and white.

• Plant tall herbs at the back of large beds, or in the centre of circular beds, with other plants graduated in height in front of them.

• Use ground cover or spill-over herbs to disguise borders or path edges.

• Position edible herbs where they're easy to access and can be monitored for growth, health and harvesting.

Choosing aquatic herbs for a pond

An interesting twist on a herb garden is a pond or pool planted with aquatic herbs. Look for a low point in your garden that is consistently boggy or wet, perhaps at the bottom of a small slope where run-off collects. Instead of correcting the drainage problem, consider installing a pond. You can either buy precast ponds, or simply dig a hole and line it with waterproofing membrane. But first consider any boundary or safety issues, and whether you need approval if you live in rented or shared property.

Think about the size and style of your pond. A deeper pool will be less subject to changes in temperature; a small shallow pond may freeze in winter. Make sure the pond is sited where it receives sunlight for about half a day, as too much sun will result in algal blooms.

Some aquatic herbs prefer to grow on the margins of a pond, while others will thrive in the pond itself. When you dig the hole, you'll need to create a level shelf about 25cm below the surface on which to position potted marginals, such as

Water mint (*Mentha aquatica*) can be placed in a pot on a shelf in the pond.

water mint (*Mentha aquatica*) and blue flag (*Iris versicolor*).

In the pond itself, plant such herbs as watercress (*Nasturtium officinale*) and bogbean (*Menyanthes trifoliata*). Both are native British herbs. To help shade the water and prevent algal blooms from developing, plant floating-leafed plants, such as water lily (*Nymphaea* spp.) and fringed water lily (*Nymphoides peltata*). And if you don't have the space for a pond, you can always plant up a large decorative pot full of water.

A number of varieties of iris such as blue flag (*I. versicolor*) thrive in damp conditions, and will provide exquisite sculptural shapes at the edges of a pond.

Soil and organic atter

A good soil gives a plant access to nutrients, water and air, stabilises roots and provides natural resistance to pests and diseases. Poor soils tend to result in weak, stunted plants. Although resilient herbs, such as St John's wort, thrive in these soils, this hardiness can turn such plants into weeds.

Soil types

There are three main types of soil: sandy, loamy or clay. Sandy soil is easy to dig, but it doesn't hold nutrients or moisture, while heavy clay soils tend to become waterlogged, are difficult to dig into smaller clods and set hard when dry.

The ideal soil

Loam, on the other hand, is the ideal garden soil, a good balance of clay and sand. A rich brown colour, it is slightly moist and crumbly, with a good earthy smell. It holds both air and water and releases the nutrients in the soil to the plant roots.

In a loamy soil, clay particles bind the soil together without making it sticky and impenetrable, while sand particles allow moisture penetration without letting the water run away. If a soil has too much clay, it will hold onto nutrients instead of releasing them.

A large component of loam is decomposed organic matter or humus. Soil microbes, such as bacteria, as well as fungi and earthworms help to break down dead plant material – leaves, branches, twigs, sawdust, fruit and vegetable kitchen waste, manure and newspaper – in a process that can occur either naturally or in compost heaps and worm farms.

Improving your soil

Making nutrients available to plant roots is an important aspect of growing healthy plants, so if your soil is too sandy and porous, the best way to improve its structure is to add organic matter in the form of compost or manure.

In addition, to reduce compaction and improve aeration, apply gypsum

Use a kit to test your soil's acidity level

You can buy a simple kit to discover the pH value of your soil – whether it's acid, alkaline or neutral. Try not to touch your soil samples with your bare hands, because the pH value of your skin could affect the final reading. Take a number of soil samples from different areas of your garden for testing to give an overall picture of the soil.

1 Following the kit instructions, all you have to do is crush a sample of soil and add it to the test tube with the chemical supplied. Shake the mixture vigorously and leave it to settle.

2 Then see which colour on the pH test card the liquid most closely matches A greenish shade shows that the soil is alkaline.

3 A yellow colour shows soil at the acid end of neutral.

4 An ochre colour is a neutral soil.

(calcium sulphate), available from landscape suppliers, nurseries and garden centres, at the rate suggested by the manufacturer.

Sweet or sour soil

To determine the levels of acidity ('sourness') or alkalinity ('sweetness') in your garden soils, use a pH soil-testing kit, available from garden centres, mail order and internet businesses. On a scale of 0 to 14, 7 is neutral, while soils above 7 are alkaline and those below are acidic.

To make a comprehensive analysis, select at least five samples of soil from each garden bed or area.

The acceptable range is between 5 and 7, with most plants enjoying a slightly acidic soil of 6.5. There are exceptions, of course – lavenders, for instance, grow naturally in the alkaline, limestone soils of the Mediterranean, while blueberries, rhododendrons and azaleas prefer an acid soil.

Adjusting the pH level

If the pH of the soil is outside the normal range (between 5 and 7), this can mean that the nutrients are either not available to plants or that they are too readily available. Either way, it can make the soil toxic. So, if your plants are showing signs of nutrient deficiency, but you know you have applied the correct amount of fertiliser, be sure to check the pH level of your soil.

If you have space, it's worth constructing more than one compost bin in your garden. You can add to it every time you mow the lawn, deadhead plants or prune a shrub.

If your garden soil is too acidic, lower the pH with an application of agricultural lime (calcium carbonate). This will also have a beneficial effect on the structure of clay soils. If your clay soil is deficient in magnesium, apply dolomite (a combination of magnesium carbonate and calcium carbonate).

Where the soil is too alkaline, and you need to raise the pH level to make it more acidic, add some agricultural sulphur or sulphate of iron. Remember to check the pH again later, as you may need to make annual soil adjustments.

Compost heaps

Sometimes called 'black gold', compost slowly releases nutrients to your soil and conserves moisture.

Successful compost heaps maintain a balance between carbon (dry, brown and woody material, such as dried leaves) and nitrogen (wet, fresh and green material, such as grass clippings). The ideal ratio is 25–30:1, so the rule is: loads of brown material, less green.

The heap should also be moist, not sodden. The moisture helps microbes to break down materials, but if you add too much water, you will create smelly anaerobic conditions – that is, without oxygen - and the pile needs oxygen in order to break down.

Making compost

Include in your compost heap brown and green garden refuse, fruit and vegetable kitchen waste, straw or sawdust bedding from herbivore pets (such as rabbits), and a handful or two of blood and bone, and dig it over at least once a week. You can include cow, horse or chicken manure as well – even natural carpet fibres from a vacuum cleaner. Add a compost activator to build up the heat in the pile and speed up decomposition. Although you can buy powdered activators from nurseries, try adding comfrey, a natural activator (page 44).

Choose from free-standing compost bins or tumblers in a wide variety of shapes and sizes, or build your own frames, about 1m square. Have 2 or 3 compost bins or piles, so you have heaps in various stages of decomposition: by the time the third pile is full, the first will be ready for the garden.

To speed up the decomposition process in your compost heap, add comfrey leaves.

Adding organic matter will improve soil and result in healthier plant growth.

Mulch

Mulch is a layer of material that's laid on top of the soil or potting mix, acting as a natural 'blanket' that has many beneficial functions. This layer can be made up of different types of materials, from bark and straw to pebbles and gravel.

The benefits of mulch

A thick layer of mulch shields the soil and plant roots from temperature fluctuations, keeping them cool and helping to retain moisture in the soil,

As soon as you've finished planting up, add a layer of mulch to protect your new plants, deter weeds and make the whole area look tidier and more complete.

Worm farms

Worms are another good source of fertiliser, as their waste is rich in nutrients and a great way to recycle soft organic waste. You can purchase worm farms from some garden centres, mail order catalogues and specialised internet suppliers.

Worm farms consist of a stack of 3 to 4 trays, each with holes in the bottom. The lowest tray collects the liquid waste that drains from the upper levels; this is then tapped and used as a liquid fertiliser. The next tray initially houses the worms and their bedding material (such as coconut fibre); food scraps are then added to the layer above. The worms seek out food, wriggling their way up to the next layer. As the food is digested, it's turned into waste (worm castings), which can be dug into garden beds.

Only a few species of worms are suitable for this purpose. The most common is the brandling worm (*Eisenia foetida*), and you may need 1000, so it is best to buy them from a supplier. Earthworms are not suitable.

reducing the need to water. This is particularly important for plants that have shallow roots.

Thick layers of mulch help to suppress weeds. Often there isn't enough light for weeds to successfully germinate or, if they do reach the seedling stage, they have to push their way up through thick mulch. This can result in weak, exhausted specimens that are much easier to remove, so mulch also saves you time, effort and energy.

If you use an organic material, such as bark, it will break down, adding organic matter to the soil. This in turn provides the ideal environment for beneficial soil organisms, such as soil microbes, fungi and earthworms.

Aesthetically, mulch adds a 'carpet', which puts the finishing touch to garden beds or container plantings. Choose the appropriate material and colour to blend with your garden type, scale of plantings or the colour scheme of your house and surrounds, and it will make a difference to the overall visual effect. While bright pebbles and mulches look striking in rockeries and Japanese gardens, subtle, natural mulch looks good anywhere.

Sweet violet thrives in a moist, humus-rich soil in sun or partial shade.

Mulch types

There are two types of mulch. Organic mulches – such as various wood or bark products, straw, and mushroom compost – break down, adding organic matter and nutrients to the soil.

Inorganic mulches, such as gravel and pebbles, neither break down and provide soil with extra nutrients nor contribute to the soil structure and its water holding capacity but are effective for a decorative look if the area isn't affected

by fallen leaves and can be tidied easily. It is worth noting that uncomposted bark products set off a chain reaction, stimulating bacterial and fungi activity in the soil, which uses nitrogen from the mulch. This process is known as 'nitrogen drawdown', but you can combat it by applying a fertiliser that is high in nitrogen to the soil before mulching.

Applying mulch

Always apply mulch to a moist garden, preferably after rain; never apply it to dry or frozen soil. Also, make sure the garden beds are weed free, and that you leave a clear space around the trunks of tree and plant stems, otherwise rot can set in as a result of the moisture content.

How thickly you lay the mulch will depend on the type you use, but generally a good layer of 2 to 6cm will be adequate. Finer mulches break down more quickly than the coarser ones and will need to be reapplied more often – perhaps once or twice each year.

Home-made compost is best dug into the garden rather than applied on top as a mulch, especially if it is uneven or unsightly.

Mulches

There are many attractive types of organic and inorganic mulch to choose from.

1 WOODCHIP – inexpensive and durable but not as attractive as fine pine bark.

2 GLASS CHIPS – can be used in architectural gardens and look good in containers.

3 FINE PINE BARK – an aesthetically pleasing, premium product that is slow to break down

4 ORGANIC GARDEN SOIL MIX made up of mushroom compost, sand, soil, ash and chicken manure. Dig it into existing garden beds or use it to create new planting areas.

5 RIVER PEBBLES (20mm) – come in a range of colours, from light grey to dark brown, and look good in native or natural gardens. Quartz pebbles are an alternative.

6 COCOA SHELL – is a good-looking natural mulch that is a by-product of chocolate making.

Cultivation

Choosing healthy plants, preparing the soil to suit their needs and giving them the appropriate care and maintenance will result in a thriving herb garden.

When to plant

The best time to plant depends on your climate and local weather conditions. In general, planting times are divided into two seasons – warm and cool. The warmer months of spring fall between March and April, while the cooler months of autumn fall between October and November. During these months, rainfall is usually reliable and the ground is reasonably moist and warm, enabling hardy plants to make new root growth and establish rapidly.

From year to year, these times may vary slightly, from a couple of weeks to a month, depending on the weather, with the limiting factor being the temperature – or more specifically, frost. Whatever the time of year, do not plant during cold frosty conditions.

Garden plants fall into four groups – hardy (withstanding temperatures down to -15°C), frost hardy (able to survive temperatures down to -5°C), and half hardy (needing temperatures above 0°C), and tender (damaged by temperatures below 5°C, and in some cases below 10°C). Check the hardiness of a plant before planting. Plant half-hardy and frost-tender plants about two weeks

Kick-start a bedding or potted display by buying maturing, flowering herbs in pots.

after the last cold snap in late spring. This applies to seed sowing too. In frost-prone areas, start seeds of half-hardy and tender plants indoors and then transplant the seedlings into the garden when all risk of frost has passed.

Buying herbs at nurseries

At nurseries and garden centres you'll find display benches filled with lush, herbs of all shapes and sizes. You can select from annual or perennial seedlings, or almost ready-to-eat plants in larger pots. It's good to see what's in season and check out other perennial herbs, shrubs and trees, such as salvias, lavender and bay trees – and companion plants.

You may be tempted to select young plants that look like they're maturing well, perhaps even flowering, but if this is the case, they have probably outgrown their pots. In general, smaller, younger specimens will become healthier plants.

Before you buy, check that the herbs have healthy roots and are not pot-bound. Once the roots are tightly compressed, curled around the inside of a container and poking out the bottom, there is no guarantee they will grow well once you plant them in the garden.

And while you're at the garden centre or nursery, ask for advice if you need to. Horticulturalists are employed to share their gardening knowledge with their customers and help them make the best

Check carefully for pests and even growth before buying plants at a nursery.

If you use a mini-hedge as a decorative edging, it will look messy if left untended. Trim it regularly to keep the shape tidy and clean.

choices, so don't hesitate to ask questions. You'll build a friendly, useful relationship with the staff in the process.

As soon as you get your purchases home, give all the plants a good soak in a bucket of water for a couple of hours to ensure the rootball gets a thorough watering before planting.

Ease a herb out of the pot to check that the root system is not pot-bound.

Mail-order plants

Some herbs are hard to find at general nurseries, so you may have to buy them from specialist growers, who usually offer a mail-order and online service.

Once you've placed your order, it's exciting to wait for the arrival of your precious parcel. Plants are packed in various ways, but they will usually be grown beyond seedling stage, but not to maturity, and will be posted in a sturdy cardboard box.

The roots and soil may be encased in cling film or in tube stock pots, and secured with protective material to stop the potting mix from coming loose. Alternatively, you may only receive the roots – as with turmeric and ginger – or the cloves, as with elephant garlic.

Mail-order plants will survive for a day or two in transit, but you need to unpack them soon after arrival and place them in a sheltered area that receives filtered light for several days until they acclimatise to your location.

To minimise transplant shock, water your plants with a weak solution of liquid fertiliser and a seaweed solution.

Preparing garden beds

Before transplanting or buying plants, prepare the areas in which they are going to be grown; these may be existing beds or newly created areas. To achieve the best results, remove any weeds and dig over the soil until it's friable and loose, so the new roots can stretch out and grow unimpeded. It's also a good idea to improve the soil and its water retention and drainage with some organic matter.

Once you've prepared the site, start planting out your herbs. Some herbs benefit from added nutrients in the soil, so give them a good start in their new environment by digging a slow-release fertiliser into your beds. Other herbs – such as anise, sweet basil and the various lavenders – like an application of lime.

For free plants, join a seed-swapping group, or exchange herbs with a friend.

Fertilising

For healthy growth, plants need the right balance of nutrients, applied as fertilisers. These are sold on nursery shelves under a myriad of descriptions, and you will probably find that there is something designed for palms, herbs, roses, citrus trees, indoor plants and many more. You can add fertilisers to the soil so they're absorbed through the plant roots, or you can apply them as a foliar spray to the leaves.

Determine which plants you want to fertilise and find out a little about the chemical make-up of basic fertilisers to make sure you choose the right one.

Balancing the elements

The best fertiliser is one that offers a little of everything. This 'balanced fertiliser', can be used in various ways.
- Add it at the time of planting.
- Sprinkle it around garden beds as a seasonal top-up.
- Apply it as a weak, soluble solution to young seedlings or as a booster throughout the growing seasons.

Nutrient deficiencies

Well-balanced soils play an important role in ensuring that nutrients in the soil are being released and made available to plants. Adding more fertiliser will not necessarily resolve a long-term problem, but improving the soil will.

Nutrient deficiencies can manifest themselves in various ways including: distorted or stunted growth, yellow or mottled leaves, scorched leaf edges, premature maturity of fruit, dieback or poor root growth.

Some deficiencies are common to certain types of plants. For example, fruit trees with yellowing leaves and green veins benefit at times from chelated iron, while the older leaves of gardenias that are yellowing or browning around the outer part usually need the help of an

Keep your herb cuttings out of direct sunlight until the roots have grown more fully, then plant them out.

old garden remedy – a combination of magnesium and Epsom salts (magnesium sulphate) dissolved in water.

Other symptoms might require more investigation. Take a cutting to your local nursery for horticultural advice, join a garden club, read gardening books or search the internet.

Avoid watering when it's windy, as the moisture will soon evaporate.

Types of fertiliser

Some fertilisers are produced from manufactured chemicals (synthetics), others from natural products. The natural products, such as blood and bone, are based on ingredients that include animal by-products and manures, seaweed, rock minerals and fish, which tend to slowly feed plants over a period of several months. Other products combine both chemical and natural ingredients.

Fertilisers sold in a dry granular form are designed to release nutrients slowly. Faster-acting forms are liquid plant foods, which are dissolved in water to give plants a quick lift.

Whether you go synthetic, organic, dry or liquid, the important aspect is the N:P:K ratio (see box left). Always read the label carefully and follow the manufacturer's directions.

Seaweed solutions

Strictly speaking, liquid seaweed-based products are soil conditioners that increase plants' resistance to drought,

---

Chemical elements

Chemical elements – primary, secondary and trace – play a vital role in growing healthy plants. Look at the pack, where you'll find the symbols N:P:K, indicating the ratios of the three major elements – nitrogen, phosphorous and potassium.

Primary elements

NITROGEN (N) – important for vegetative growth (leaves, stems and fruit), making leaves lush. Herbs grown for their foliage, such as mints, need a higher nitrogen value (for example, 12:1:5).

PHOSPHOROUS (P) – for cell formation and chemical reactions involved in growth and reproduction. It promotes root development as well as seed, flower and fruit production.

POTASSIUM (K) – important for fruit-bearing trees and vegetable and flower crops, as it improves the quality of flowers and fruits. It aids plant health, stem and cell thickness and the movement of water within plants, providing resistance to pests, diseases, drought and heat. For a good flush of blooms, flowering plants need a fertiliser containing more potassium (6:14:17).

Secondary elements

CALCIUM (Ca) – needed for healthy cell walls and root growth.

MAGNESIUM (Mg) – a key component in the green colouring of plants (that is, chlorophyll) and therefore vital for photosynthesis, a process whereby plants use the energy of sunlight to produce sugars.

SULPHUR (S) – part of the flavour and odour components (for example, onions and cabbages).

Trace elements

These are iron (Fe), manganese (Mn), boron (B), copper (Cu), zinc (Zn) and molybdenum (Mo), which are only needed in minute quantities.

heat and frost. They also improve their ability to take up nutrients and improve root and stem development as well as the water-holding capacity of the soil. Typically, the ingredients include molasses and humic and fulvic acids, which increase soil micro-organism and earthworm activity, making them a wholesome addition to the watering can. For larger garden-bed areas, use a 'hose-on' application.

Watering

If you give your plants – whether garden plants or pot plants – a good, long soak infrequently, they'll search downwards for water. This in turn encourages strong root growth, so your plants will be better able to cope between waterings. Avoid prolonged watering with a hosepipe or sprinkler as this can leach out nutrients, resulting in poor growth. Raised beds and trays of young plants are especially prone to leaching.

The other extreme is surface watering that wets only a few centimetres. This produces weaker plants that rely on moisture near the soil surface, so they have a hard time coping with drought.

Some potting composts are very difficult to re-wet once they have dried out. You can guard against this by adding special gel or granules that expand when watered and retain the moisture. These moisture-retentive products reduce the amount you need to water, and are a worthwhile investment if you have a large number of containers.

Watering options

How you water your garden depends on its size, the time you have and local water restrictions. You can install a rainwater tank, a grey-water system or an appropriate timer-operated irrigation system. Check with your water supplier, a local gardening group, or a water engineer if you have concerns about the quantity or quality of water you are using in your garden.

If you water by hand, stick to early mornings or late afternoons so the moisture won't evaporate as quickly.

Planting out

Once you've prepared your beds, it's time for planting out. Soak the plant in a bucket of water beforehand, so that it will absorb moisture more easily. The plant here is tarragon, a perennial herb that spreads by rhizomes and needs to be replanted every few years. Plant in a well-drained soil that doesn't retain moisture too long, or the rhizomes may rot.

1 Ensure that your soil has plenty of organic matter, such as good compost or well-rotted manure, then dig a hole that is larger than the root ball.

2 Loosen the potting mix and tease out the roots so that they will seek out nutrients and moisture from the soil around them.

3 Carefully position the plant in the hole, making sure it sits at the same level in the ground as it did in the pot. Don't cover the crown.
4 Backfill and firm down the soil around the plant. Tarragon can also be propagated by root division in spring.
5 Water the plant well, and then water regularly until established. Prune for culinary use and also to discourage woody stems.

Fillers and free plants

While you are waiting for other plants to mature and spread, plant out some annuals as fillers. Although most annual herbs will need to be removed at the end of their life cycle, those that readily self-seed – such as catnip, nasturtiums and borage – will perpetuate themselves.

With larger plants that self-seed, such as fennel, remove any unwanted seedlings, then pot them up and use them elsewhere.

When thinning out plants in the garden, think about giving those excess seedlings to a friend, a novice gardener or school.

Prunings from perennials can also be the start of newly propagated plants. For more information, see *Stem cuttings*, page 169.

Many herbs self-seed in the garden, popping up where you least expect them. Catnip, nasturtiums and borage, above, appear for years, as does heartsease.

Garden maintenance

Routine garden tasks, such as pruning and weeding, will not only keep your garden tidy but will also help prevent pest and disease attack, which often starts within decaying plant debris. If you employ good garden hygiene methods you will have less maintenance to do in the long run.

Pruning

Many herbs benefit from being cut back annually by up to one-third, as this not only makes them look more attractive but also promotes new growth in the following season.

Normally, gardeners are encouraged to prune back spent blooms on annuals and perennials after flowering, but that's not the case with herbs that are grown for their seeds, such as coriander, dill and fennel. Leave them to complete their life cycle. With herbs that are not grown for their flowers, pinch off the blooms to encourage leafy growth.

You only need to prune trees if their branches are rubbing together, which can create open wounds that are prone to disease and insect attack, or if their limbs are congested, reducing light and air circulation. For low branches, use a small handsaw, but for larger ones, call in a professionals. Always protect your eyes from sawdust.

For regular stem pruning, invest in a good-quality pair of secateurs, but for tougher stems and small branches, buy a pair of ergonomic ratchet or anvil pruners. If you regularly clean and oil them, they'll last for years. On the other hand, if you habitually mislay things, buy the cheaper ones.

Eliminating weeds

Weeds compete with other plants for nutrients, light and water, but you can reduce them by following some basic garden practices. If there is little or no bare ground in the garden, weeds can't grow, so plant ground cover, such as

Always keep your herb garden weeded and well mulched, and remove any damaged foliage regularly.

Removing spent flowers will prolong the flowering season.

thyme and Roman chamomile, to fill gaps and stop weeds from taking root.

Hand weeding is the most effective way to remove established weeds, particularly perennials with rhizomatous roots, such as ground elder. Dig up the whole root system, rather than pull off vegetative growth above the soil. Don't put weeds with seed heads in compost, or you will return them to the garden.

Where annual weeds are a major problem, consider covering the area with black weed mat or membrane, which allows air as well as moisture through. You can cut holes in it with a knife or scissors for planting through. When it is in position, add a decorative mulch, such as bark or gravel, and secure the edges, with short lengths of wire. Weed matting is a better option than black polythene, which will foster anaerobic conditions in the soil underneath.

Using herbicides

Use weedkillers, or herbicides, as a last resort or if you're preparing a whole bed, but take care, particularly if you are growing edible herbs or there are valuable or favourite plants nearby. Always read the label and follow the manufacturer's directions carefully. Choose the type of herbicide that's appropriate, effective and safe, and always wear protective clothing, such as a mask, gloves, boots and goggles.

• **Selective herbicides** – kill only specified weeds.

• **Non-selective herbicides** – kill any plant they touch, so use carefully on a still day so the spray drift doesn't land on other plants. The most commonly used non-selective herbicide is glyphosate.

• **Systemic herbicides** – travel through the entire plant, from roots to leaves.

• **Pre-emergent chemicals** – are applied to the soil before seedlings have emerged to eliminate weed seeds.

• **Post-emergent weed killers** – are applied to leaves after the crops have emerged.

Topiary shears are ideal for shaping herbs with compact leaves, such as this variegated thyme.

When weeding, remove the whole root system, not just the foliage.

What is a weed?

A weed is often a plant that's growing in the wrong place – and that includes herbs. Finding the right plant for the right place can be tricky: if you plant tough plants that can cope with drought or survive in difficult conditions or aspects, they are usually the resilient plants that can end up taking over.

CHECK whether a herb has a reputation for being invasive before deciding whether to grow it. The staff at your local nursery should be able to advise you if a particular plant is a problem in your area: a herb that's invasive in one location may not be in another area with different climatic or soil conditions. In addition, not all plants of the same species may be rampant, so look for alternative varieties that may be bred to be sterile (so the seed won't be viable and grow).

PLANT herbs with invasive root systems in pots, either as free-standing pot plants or in pots sunk into the ground, so that their roots

Chicory is a self-seeding herb that can become a weed in the garden.

are restricted. Keep invasives in check by removing flowers before they set seed, which may be spread by wind and birds. Regularly prune those with invasive runners, such as mint, and dispose of the runners responsibly.

IF YOU HAVE concerns about an invasive plant, contact your local Wildlife Trust or horticultural society for advice. If your garden adjoins agricultural land, discuss the matter with the landowner.

Propagation

One of the most satisfying aspects of gardening is growing plants from seeds or cuttings. Some herbs require special treatments, but there are several methods and it's worth experimenting. Annuals are best grown from seed while perennials are propagated by cuttings, layering or division.

To block out the light while seedlings germinate, cover trays with newspaper.

Sowing seed

Obtain your seeds from plants grown in the garden, or buy packets of seed through nurseries, mail-order companies or websites. Collecting seed from the garden is the cheapest way, of course; however, there's no guarantee that plants will come true from seed, as certain herbs may cross-pollinate or simply not represent the parent plant.

For ease of growing, particularly for new gardeners, packet seeds provide good value and instructions that indicate when, how and where to plant. In addition, the plants will be true to type, and available in the right season.

The required depth of planting will vary, depending on seed size. In general, the finer the seed, the shallower it should be sown; sowing at a depth of about twice the diameter of the seed is a good gauge. It is easier to spread fine seeds, such as marjoram, savory and thyme, more evenly if you mix them with a little dry sand.

When to sow

When you plant your seeds will depend on local climatic conditions and the advice given on the seed packet. If your chosen seeds take 6 to 8 weeks to germinate, start them indoors or in a glasshouse about this length of time before the final frosts. Once the good spring weather starts, the seedlings will be ready to transplant. Some annual herbs can be sown successfully in autumn but, to achieve best results, follow the packet instructions.

Sow seeds in cell packs or seed trays, in individual pots or in situ. Herbs that don't transplant well, because disturbing their roots encourages them to 'bolt' (flower prematurely), are best planted either directly in the garden or in biodegradable pots. These include borage, coriander, dill, chervil, fennel and summer savory.

To add interest and colour to paved areas, paths or retaining walls, fill cracks, crevices or nooks with potting mix and sow seeds of compact or trailing plants, such as nasturtium, sweet violet and different varieties of thyme.

Sowing seeds under cover

Some seeds, such as coriander and marigold, need to be in the dark until they've germinated. Block out the light by covering the seed trays with sheets of newspaper and keep in a dry, warm place. Soaking seeds in warm water

Remove seedlings from cell-packs by gently squeezing the bottom of each cell.

Seed-raising mix

The growing medium plays a critical role in plant propagation. The tiny roots of new plants need to be able to grow in a lightweight material that provides support, aeration, moisture and good drainage.

Potting mixes are developed especially for propagation and are usually sold as seed-raising mix or propagation mix. The ingredients may include:

SAND Coarse river sand, not builder's sand, is best for good drainage.

VERMICULITE This lightweight silicate material has been heated so that it expands, soaks up water and attracts nutrients.

PERLITE Derived from volcanic rock that has also been mined and heated, it is used to aerate soil and improve drainage.

COCONUT FIBRE, coco-peat or coir. This is a natural waste product with excellent water-holding capacities. It is used in gardening products instead of peat moss, which is a non-renewable natural resource.

Heat

Warmth is also an important factor for germination. Depending on location and the type of seed, you can provide extra heat in a number of ways. Propagators come in various sizes and specifications, the simplest warmed by ambient temperature, and the most sophisticated being both electric and thermostatic.

In a greenhouse, you can also heat trays from the base with purpose-built heat mats or soil warming cables. On a larger scale, you can purchase portable greenhouses through garden centres and mail-order suppliers. These are compact, lightweight and easy to assemble, and come in various sizes so you can position them against an outdoor wall or even on a balcony.

Alternatively, place seed trays by a sunny window, in a warm kitchen or outdoors in a warm, frost-free location.

Possible problems

At this stage, you may experience a couple of problems.

1 Damping off is a fungal disease that thrives in cool or cold, damp or overcast conditions. The best way to prevent this is to keep seed trays in a location with good air circulation, light and warmth, although you could also try watering the seedlings with chamomile tea, an old herbal remedy. If seedlings collapse or a white mould appears, discard the mix and start again, transplanting any surviving seedlings into new sterilised containers.

2 Seedlings become leggy when there is not enough light or the conditions are overcrowded. Simply move the tray to a brighter spot and thin out the seedlings by cutting the unwanted seedlings at the base. If you pull them out, you run the risk of disturbing the roots of the others.

Using the Latin name to identify plants is the professional way to go. It ensures that, should you wish to grow the same plant again, you will purchase exactly the right one.

overnight before planting will help basil and parsley to germinate, while other seeds need to be stratified. For details on this process, see *Echinacea*, page 50.

Once seedlings appear, prick them out. See *Pricking out*, page 168.

Raising seeds

Keep seeds and seedlings moist but don't overwater. Seeds, in particular, need to be kept damp but must not be soggy. Once seeds dry out, their germination will be stunted, or even stop.

It is important to water the seed tray gently. Either lightly mist the mix with a spray bottle, or damp it before planting. Alternatively, you can water the tray from the bottom so the moisture can be drawn up into the mix.

Fertilising

Once seedlings are growing strongly, give them just a half-strength solution of an 'all-purpose' soluble fertiliser. Later, after transplanting them, increase the dosage, but remember: more is not better; plants can only absorb so much.

Seed sowing

YOU WILL NEED

- seed tray
- bag of propagating or seed-raising mix
- various seed packets or collected seed
- piece of dowel or pencil
- plant tag
- spray bottle
- plastic wrap (optional)

1 Fill the seed tray with good quality seed-raising or propagating mix. (For best results, use clean sterilised trays and tools that have been washed in a weak solution of bleach.) Gently smooth the surface with a piece of dowel or a small block of wood, but do not compact the mix.

Using a pencil or a piece of dowel, create a shallow channel. Gently shake the seeds evenly over the mix or, if they are large enough to handle, drop them one at a time, spacing them according to the packet instructions.

2 Smooth the mix so seeds are just covered, or use a sieve to add a light covering. Very fine seeds may not need any covering. Select the fine spray setting on the spray bottle and water the tray thoroughly, or stand in water until the compost is damp.

3 Place in a warm, dry location with natural indirect light (each plant type has different light requirements). To retain moisture and humidity, cover trays with cling film, newspaper or a sheet of glass. Label with plant name and date of sowing. Remove cover when the seeds begin to germinate.

Pricking out

Once the first true leaves have emerged, move seedlings so they get maximum light. When they have several leaves and are becoming crowded, 'prick out' into larger containers or single pots. Use a small wooden skewer to gently ease the delicate roots out, then carefully handle the seedlings by the leaves.

Minimising transplant shock

Here are some tips for easing your plants into the garden.

- **Gradually 'harden off'** (acclimatise to outdoor temperatures) by moving plants into cooler conditions and stronger light before transplanting into the garden.
- **If the plants don't like** their roots being disturbed, grow them in small pots

or individual cells so you won't need to thin them out from other seedlings.

- **Don't transplant** – simply grow plants directly in the garden bed.
- **When watering**, add a seaweed-based solution to increase the plants' resistance to drought, heat and frost. Seaweed-based liquid products improve the seedlings' ability to take up nutrients, and they also improve root and stem development as well as improve the water-holding capacity of the soil. The ingredients include molasses and humic and fulvic acids, which boost earthworm activity and the number of soil micro-organisms.
- **Apply an anti-transpirant foliar spray** to protect against frost and reduce the effects of transplant shock, sudden climatic changes, drying winds, water loss and heat. These products are biodegradable, and the effects last for several months.

Runners

Strawberries, sweet violet, mint and ground ivy all send out runners that will take root wherever they touch the soil. Carefully detach and lift satellite plants that have developed roots and plant them in a new position. Herbs that spread excessively are best planted in a pot to keep them contained.

Layering

With this propagation method, the herb is still attached to the parent plant, but the stem is encouraged to take root before it is separated. Use this technique with perennial herbs, such as rosemary and sage, in late spring or early summer.

Bend a soft, flexible stem so that it touches the soil, remove the leaves surrounding the bend, and using a sharp knife, nick the underside of the stem. Secure the stem to the ground or pot surface using hairpins or several pieces of soft wire; cover with soil or potting mix.

Water and keep the soil moist until the roots develop in 4 to 8 weeks. You can then separate the new plant and plant it elsewhere.

Division

Another way to multiply plants is by dividing them. This method will work best with perennials, such as yarrow, bergamot, tarragon and chives, when they are dormant, or just before new growth appears in early spring. It is a good way of revitalising an established plant that has become too large or if you want to use it elsewhere in the garden.

Dig up the plant clump with a sharp spade. You may need to loosen the soil around the plant first, then cut away old stems and leaves in order to determine where the new shoots are appearing. Either use the back of two forks to separate the clump into two pieces, or a spade or sharp knife, depending on the density of the roots and stems.

Ensure that there is new growth in each half. If the pieces are a reasonable size, divide the two new plants in half again. Some plants are easy to pull apart by hand, and can be divided into many new plants. Replant the new plants into the garden or in pots, watering well until fully established.

Some seed heads may shatter as they dry. Hang stems upside down in a paper bag to capture the seeds as they dessicate and fall off.

Cuttings

You can take soft-wood stem-tip cuttings from the new growth of herbs such as lemon balm and mint, in spring and early summer, and semi-ripe cuttings from firmer shoots of woodier herbs, such as rosemary, from midsummer to mid-autumn.

USING HORMONE POWDER Cut a piece of soft-stemmed plant 4 to 6cm long and remove the lower leaves. Dip the stem into a hormone powder (or gel), which will stimulate new root growth. Plant the stem in a small planting hole in a container filled with propagating mix. Using a spray bottle, water thoroughly, then place the cutting in a protected position with natural indirect light. Make a mini cloche from a plastic soft-drink bottle cut in half and inverted over cuttings.

Dip the stems in hormone powder before planting in propagating mix.

Recycled plastic bottles are ideal mini cloches for protecting your plants.

USING A GLASS OF WATER Another method is to place stem cuttings in a glass of water in a position with indirect light, then wait for roots to form within 1 to 2 weeks. Change the water every few days and then transplant the cuttings into individual containers or into the garden. Herbs suitable for this treatment include mint and basil.

Container gardening

With more people choosing urban life, homes and gardens are getting smaller. But no matter where you live, you can plant a selection of herbs, whether on a balcony, deck or verandah, or in a courtyard – any garden space where they can thrive in hanging baskets, pots and other containers.

A potted herb garden

Herbs love growing in pots, and some herbs, such as mint and sweet woodruff, spread easily and take over garden beds, so even if you have a huge garden, it's best to contain them. Put containers in the right position, use good-quality potting mix and give your herbs the care they need and they will flourish.

The best position

Many herbs, such as marjoram, fennel and thyme, prefer to grow in full sun. Few herbs actually need the shade, but some, such as mint, lemon balm, chervil and feverfew, are happiest in partial shade. So, determine how much sun your balcony, courtyard or window box will receive throughout the year, and choose your plants accordingly. Alternatively, choose the plants you want to grow and then find the most suitable spot in which to grow them.

In very warm dry positions, such as south-facing balconies, it's best to give plants some shade protection, as the heat can be too intense, even if they enjoy full sun in cooler locations. Another important factor is good air circulation; humid conditions can create fungal problems. In positions open to strong winds, take care that containers are secure; a barrier such as trellis, can diffuse the breeze.

The right pot for the job

Before you buy pots or containers, think about their different shapes, sizes and materials, as these will play an important part in the success of your herbs and the design of your display.

Herbs such as parsley, peppermint and thyme enjoy being contained, and look attractive spilling exuberantly over pot rims, so consider the shape and form of what you're growing and select containers that suit their 'personality'.

Don't use lots of little pots in different styles and colours, as they make small spaces look cluttered. You can still grow a variety, but keep it simple: select a single colour to pull one area together. Choose containers that complement the location and its surroundings, pick textures and colours to match the area's paintwork, paving or surface, and go for the biggest container that's practical.

A collection of herbs in pots, including sage, chives and mints, highlights their different shapes, textures and colours.

Stagger the heights of pots or containers and underplant tall herbs with trailing plants that will spill over the edge of the pot.

Shapes and sizes

Round, square or rectangular, squat or tall, with straight or tapered sides: any of these container types is perfect for growing herbs, as they all allow for good root growth and the display of foliage and flowers. Varying sizes of the same design will give an area a uniform look.

Although they look attractive, urns and 'oil jars' have narrow necks, making it extremely hard to remove plants without damaging them. Another disadvantage is that they often have narrow bases and become unstable in windy conditions.

Troughs are generally long and narrow, like window boxes, and are perfect for formal or narrow areas.

Team them with a square pot of similar material to create a right angle, then add a round pot to create a point of difference. Troughs and square pots are also much more stable than pots that narrow to a round base.

Materials

The type of pot material will also affect both the look and the portability of your herb garden. Terracotta pots are popular with gardeners because they are practical, affordable and look attractive in most situations, although check that they are frost resistant if you get cold winters. Limestone and concrete pots, with their lovely pale colourings, are also popular, while alternative materials, such as plastics, are worth exploring.

In fact, the new generation of 'plastic' materials offers a range of good-looking, practical choices. Polyethylene and fibreglass (including marine grade) are most commonly used, as they're long-lasting, lightweight, waterproof and available in a wide range of colours. They can also be frost-, UV- and scratch-resistant. And, because these materials are not porous, they will hold moisture for longer than concrete or terracotta so may need less watering.

Experiment with unusual containers, such as old colanders and wicker baskets. If your chosen pot doesn't have drainage holes (many pots are designed for indoor use and don't have them), just drill a few into the base.

Potting mix

One of the most important elements in growing herbs successfully is the right soil or planting mix. Potting mix is better than garden soil, as it's specially designed for container conditions and will provide just the right balance between holding water and providing good drainage. At your local nursery, you'll find various organic mixes that are tailored for different situations, such as hanging baskets.

The best products contain extra ingredients, such as a wetting agent to stop the compost drying out too fast, vermiculite to keep the mix lightweight, and a slow-release fertiliser that will gradually feed the roots. The old adage 'you get what you pay for' is true here: it is worth investing in a good quality mix as, over time, you'll have healthier, happier plants.

Feeding tips

There are many fertilisers on the market. A good all-rounder that will suit most herbs is a 'balanced' or 'all-purpose' one: it will contain all the necessary nutrients to promote strong, healthy roots, flowers and leaves as well as help herbs grow into vigorous, sturdy plants. A soluble fertiliser is ideal for container-grown herbs and also for seedlings, which need to be fertilised regularly so that they will flourish. Always follow the directions on the packet.

If you notice that white 'salt' deposits (fertiliser residues) are appearing on the outside of terracotta pots, you can easily wash them off.

Add a liquid seaweed product to your watering regimen, as this is an excellent tonic. Apply it when you are first planting up pots and containers to help minimise transplant shock (see page 168).

Watering

While most herbs like to be kept moist, they also need to be allowed to dry out in between waterings so they're not left standing with constantly damp roots.

A good potting mix provides good drainage, while holes in the base of the pots allow the excess moisture to escape. Buy a colourful watering can that's easy to find, fill and carry. Keep it out of direct sun so that it lasts longer.

Hanging gardens

You can also grow herbs in hanging baskets (see *Hanging herb ball*, page 312). Those that have a trailing habit, such as heartsease, thyme, ground ivy and pelargonium, are ideal for hanging at eye level where you can easily see your plants maturing and enjoy their fragrance. If you hang baskets higher than eye

Vibrant petunias add a splash of colour to thyme, lovage, chamomile and erigeron.

level, you will tend to forget about them and won't see them properly.

Baskets are commonly made of plastic or wire. Wire baskets can be lined with sphagnum moss, which is a spongy fibrous material that will hold the potting mix and retain moisture, or use a ready-made basket liner made from coconut fibre. Hanging baskets are prone to drying out in winds, so keep an eye on their moisture levels – another reason to hang them at the right height.

Re-potting

About every 12 months or so, give your potted herb garden a boost by re-potting or replenishing it.

Discard annual herbs and start again. Remove perennial herbs carefully, re-use the old potting mix in the garden, and re-fill the base of the pot with fresh mix. Then trim the roots of the plants if they look congested, and cut off any old stems to give the plant a tidier shape and to promote new growth. Replant them in the container and backfill with fresh mix, gently firming it as you go. Finally, water the herbs thoroughly.

Planting ideas

DECIDE what exactly what you want to use your herbs for – for example, cooking – and plant containers accordingly.

CHOOSE a theme when growing culinary herbs. Select hot and spicy herbs such as chillies and coriander for Mexican or Asian dishes; and dill, lemon balm, chervil and fennel for fish dishes.

PLANT contrasting colours in the same pot. Try 'Purple Ruffles', the dark-leafed basil, on one side and fine-stemmed chives with mauve flowers on the other.

TRY bay trees to create a focal point against a wall or flanking a doorway. Standard bays have a lollipop shape that makes them perfect pot specimens.

USE wooden barrels for a rustic look. For a classical style, use decorated terracotta.

POT up culinary herbs, such as chives, rocket, parsley or basil, in a spot near the barbecue, and let your guests snip off their own herbs.

Planting a strawberry pot

It's fun to plant up a strawberry pot with your favourite herbs and flowers. Buy a few more herbs than you will actually need. Experiment with positions and combinations of herbs to get a look you like. Then get planting. Always open bags of potting mix in a well-ventilated area. Avoid breathing in the dusty particles, and consider wearing a protective face mask.

YOU WILL NEED
• large terracotta strawberry pot
• selection of trailing herbs (we used variegated and common oregano, several kinds of marjoram and strawberry) and an upright plant (we used fan flower).
• bag of quality potting mix
• potting scoop or trowel
• small bag of coconut fibre (optional)

1 Fill the pot with potting mix until it comes to just beneath the level of the first hole.

2 Carefully remove the first herb from its container; tease the roots out so that the surrounding potting mix is loosened. Gently ease the roots into the lowest hole in the pot. Fill pot with more potting mix, gently firming the inside with your hand to ensure that the roots are covered. Add mix until you reach the level of the next hole.

Plant until all holes are filled. To stop potting mix falling out the sides of the pot, tuck a small amount of coconut fibre around the edges of each hole.

3 Finish by creating an attractive centrepiece, tucking potting mix around its roots. This final plant doesn't have to be a herb. For a dash of colour, you could use a flowering annual or perennial. We selected a fan flower (*Scaevola aemula*), but any plant with an upright habit will balance the composition of the pot. Place the pot in a sunny spot and water well.

Companion planting

Farmers, gardeners and herbalists have long believed in a symbiotic, often beneficial relationship between certain plants that grow near each other. By growing some herbs together for protection, and others to attract beneficial insects, you can grow healthy herbs without chemicals.

Types of companions

Farmers and gardeners have practised companion planting for thousands of years, and there are several different types of companion plants. There are 'nurse' plants, such as climbers, which shelter tender herbs from the wind or sun; 'trap' plants, which lure pests away from your favourite plants; and 'barrier' crops, which exude a chemical or oil that deters pests. So, when you are choosing which herbs to grow, always consider which ones enjoy each other's company or provide your garden with a particular benefit.

For instance, you can confuse the pests so they can't find the plants they're seeking. Carrot flies locate carrots by smell, so planting onions and carrots close together makes it difficult for them

to find the carrots. You need four times as many onions as carrots for this to work. Planting a companion, such as the poached egg flower, *Limnanthes douglasii*, that attracts beneficial insects while they feed on the target pest is another worthwhile strategy. It can also look lovely to grow colourful annuals among the vegetables and herbs.

Place plants with similar sunlight or watering requirements together, and grow heavy feeder crops, such as cabbages, which need high levels of calcium, with others that don't, such as sage or thyme.

Nitrogen 'fixers'

Leguminous plants – including peas, beans, sweet peas and fenugreek – play an important role in the garden. Known

Plant cabbages with dill, as it attracts beneficial insects (see opposite), or with sage and thyme.

as nitrogen-fixing plants, they can absorb nitrogen gas from the air and convert it into a nutrient form through their roots.

Once they've matured, dig legumes and garden compost into the soil to replenish nitrogen sources. This is particularly beneficial before or after planting root crops or heavy feeders of nitrogen, such as basil and parsley. In other words, rejuvenate the soil by rotating seasonal crops that have a variety of different needs.

These leguminous plants are all useful nitrogen-fixers. From left: lupins, mange tout peas and sweet peas.

Nematode repellers

There is some evidence that if you plant Mexican marigolds (*Tagetes minuta*), a chemical exuded from their roots will prevent nematodes in the soil.

Some practices may be folklore, others based on scientific fact, and what works in one location may not work elsewhere, so experiment with various combinations.

Insect types

Insects are important in the garden's natural ecosystem. As plant pollinators, they both bring life and sustain it, and may also defend your garden against unwanted predators and parasites.

For example, most ladybirds feed on aphids, but some prey on scale insects, mealy bugs and spider mites. Larvae of common lacewings eat caterpillars, aphids and other soft-bodied insects, while flower bugs inject lethal saliva into prey before sucking out the insides.

Parasites often lay their eggs on or in the bodies of their prey where, once hatched, they will feed off their host, eating them from the inside; tachinid fly larvae are parasites of caterpillars.

Natural herbal insect repellents

Many herbs have aromatic oils containing chemical compounds that repel pests, but you need to brush against them before they release their scents, which are usually pleasantly aromatic. These herbs are good to grow in traffic areas, such as alongside pathways. Here are some planting suggestions.

WORMWOOD repels mosquitoes.

TANSY banishes flies or ants.

BASIL wards off both flies and mosquitoes.

FENNEL and pennyroyal both repel fleas.

RUE deters cats.

So if you spray your susceptible herbs with insecticide, you're likely to kill all the beneficial insects as well. If you grow your herbs organically, essentially you're letting your garden – a balanced ecosystem – regulate itself.

Trap crops or lures

Using natural decoys not only draws unwanted insects away from your plants but also makes pest control easier: once they've congregated on the decoy plant, you can destroy the lure (and the pests). Find out when the peak pest times occur and decide whether one well-timed growing period is all that's required, or whether you need to plant trap crops successively throughout the season to keep the pests under control. It's also important to know the life cycle of various insects so you can successfully break their breeding cycle.

Nasturtiums, for instance, are ideal trap crops to grow near brassicas (cabbage family) and roses, as cabbage white caterpillars and aphids love them (aphids are often attracted to yellow flowers). Planting borage, dill or French marigolds close to your tomato plants may repel pests such as whiteflies and tomato moths.

Beneficial insects

Find out which insects you actually need to deter or destroy. Though some caterpillars may eat a few leaves, unless they're rampant, consider leaving them alone; they may turn into beautiful butterflies and adorn your garden. Establish which ones are doing the damage and must be stopped, and those which you can ignore.

Bees pollinate edible food crops and ornamental flowers. Both bees and butterflies are attracted by colourful, nectar-rich flowers. In the herb garden, these include hyssop, lavender, garlic chives, and marjoram, along with echinacea, bergamot and the yellow daisy-like flowers of marigold and tansy. Other choices include borage, coriander, anise hyssop, lemon balm, lovage, sage, nasturtium, poppies, rosemary, rue, pinks and thyme. Many of these repel pests;

Grow butterfly-attracting plants to draw insects, such as this small tortoiseshell butterfly, to your garden.

tansy wards off aphids, fruit fly, cabbage moth and cabbage white butterfly.

Welcome other beneficial insects, such as lacewings and hoverflies, to your garden by planting pollen-rich flowering herbs of the celery family, *Apiaceae*, such as dill, coriander and fennel.

If spraying your garden with pesticides, take great care not to kill beneficial pollinating insects.

Pests and diseases

If you find a problem plant, note the symptoms before you pull it out, or use an insecticide or fungicide. It could be caused by a pest, bacterial disease or virus, or simply by poor conditions, and each requires a different solution.

Leafhoppers (top) are minute sapsuckers that damage plants and also spread plant pathogens. Remove caterpillars (second top) by hand or plant 'trap' crops to keep them under control (see page 175). Female mealybugs (second bottom) are sapsuckers and protect themselves with an unsightly powdery wax. To treat powdery mildew (bottom), remove any affected foliage and use a fungicidal spray.

Causes of pests and diseases

Pests and diseases are usually the symptoms of an underlying problem. Generally, healthy plants are insect- and disease-free, so look at the basics first.

• **Does the herb have enough light?** If not, you have three options: thin out the surrounding plants, move the herb or plant something more suitable. Herbs that are leggy and straggly are often reaching for more light.

• **Is it being overwatered?** Many herbs like to dry out between waterings.

• **Is underwatering the problem?** Watering can require a fine balancing act. Stick a finger a few centimetres into the soil or potting mix to check on its moisture content.

• **Is the herb being neglected?** Move it to a more accessible position, remove it or write yourself reminder notes.

• **How often is fertiliser applied?** Giving plants access to the right nutrients will produce growth and vigour when and where it's needed. Check to see if the herbs need an all-purpose feed or one that is specifically for leaf or flower and fruit production and apply accordingly. Remember that over-fertilising won't produce faster growing or healthier plants. Always remember to follow the manufacturer's recommendations.

Insecticides and fungicides

Basically, there are two major problems you can treat with chemicals – insect pests and fungal diseases. If you have any herbs that are affected by a virus, you'll have to destroy them.

Common problems

Familiarise yourself with the plant's condition, or take a sample cutting to a garden centre or horticultural society and ask for help with identifying the problem for you. There are some excellent books about pests and diseases.

Problem	Possible cause
Irregular holes, chewed leaves; black droppings	Caterpillars
Meandering silver lines across distorted leaves	Leafminers
Discoloured or distorted leaves	Thrips; lack of nutrients
Speckled dots on leaves and 'cobwebbing'	Spider mite
Flowers dropping off before blooming; brownish marks on petals	Petal blight (fungus)
Stunted, wilted plant	Soil-borne fungus
Stunted plants; yellow, mottled leaves	Mosaic virus
Orange/brown powdery pustules underneath leaves	Rust, a fungal disease
Sticky leaves, black 'soot' and ants	Sooty mould (a fungus) growing on honeydew, a secretion produced by aphids, scale insects or mealybugs. The insects are the problem, the fungus and the ants a by-product.
Buds not opening; leaves twisted and distorted	Aphids

Natural remedies

Of course, it's much healthier to use natural remedies, particularly if you're growing edible herbs.

TREAT mites, mealybugs, scale, whitefly and aphids with horticultural 'soft soap' that coats the insect, which dies of suffocation and dehydration.

TACKLE leaf-eating caterpillars of moths and butterflies with the bacteria *Bacillus thuringiensis*.

PICK off by hand large caterpillars, lily beetles, vine weevils, slugs and snails.

CONTROL various pests and diseases with products based on neem oil (*Azadirachta indica*).

TRY plant-based oils (rather than petroleum-based) to smother insects such as mites, aphids, mealybugs, whiteflies and scale insects.

USING a cotton bud or small cosmetic brush, apply powdered cinnamon from your spice rack to control fungal disease and stem rot in greenhouse and indoor plants.

A beer trap will attract slugs and snails. You can also recycle a plastic food container.

AVOID spreading pests and diseases by burning infected plant material or enclosing the plant in a plastic bag and sealing round the base before pulling out or cutting off at soil level.

CHECK regularly in the gardening press or on websites for the latest information on permitted chemicals. Many traditional insecticides and fungicides, both synthetic and natural, are now banned by EU legislation.

Fungicides

These are supplied as sprays, or as concentrates or powders to add to water. They are used to treat a variety of air- or soil-borne fungal diseases. Check the type of plant on which the product can be used. Some are preventive and some systemic. Fungicides may be toxic to livestock, bees, and aquatic life. They can also harm skin and eyes. Sulphur-based fungicides may also taint edible crops.

Integrated pest management

An environmentally friendly alternative to pesticides is biological control or integrated pest management (IPM), which is available by mail order. Packages of tiny predatory insects are mailed with full instructions on how to release them on the affected plants. These beneficial insects are mostly so small that they are unnoticeable, and they do no harm to other insects or plants, or to the environment.

Phytoseiulus persimilis is a predatory mite that is used to control red spider mites. These mites suck the sap from indoor and greenhouse plants, causing them to become mottled, yellow and finally die. Aphids are also susceptible to biological control in the form of either a midge or parasitic wasp. *Encarsia formosa* is a minute parasitic wasp that preys on whiteflies. Vine weevils can be controlled by watering infested garden plants and containers with a solution containing beneficial nematodes that infect the vine weevil grubs with a fatal disease.

It could be that insects such as aphids are carrying the virus, so perhaps you need to deal with the problem by using appropriate pest control. It's also a good idea to go back to basics and check the plant's environment.

Insecticides

Formulated to kill only insects, insecticides fall into two broad categories: contact insecticides, which kill the pest on direct contact with the chemical, and systemic insecticides where the insect ingests the chemical by chewing or sucking the plant, poisoning its nervous system.

However, the disadvantage of using insecticides is that they are very likely to kill beneficial insects (see page 175) and harm the environment, as well as destroying the pests. Fortunately, over recent years, many changes have been made to the active ingredients used in insecticides, and most of the more toxic

chemicals have been removed from the marketplace.

At your local garden centre you'll find low toxicity sprays that are less harmful to waterways, bees and other beneficial insects. Check with the garden centre so you can make an informed choice before tackling your specific problem. Finally, take extra care when applying sprays to edible plants. Follow the manufacturer's instructions.

A bug with benefits

Ladybirds devour aphids, but ladybird larvae (juveniles), like all youngsters, have an even bigger appetite than their parents. The larvae look like tiny grey crocodiles and they feed voraciously on aphids. Learn to recognise these creatures and leave them alone as they do nothing but good in your garden.

Harvesting, preserving and storing

Harvesting the flowers, leaves, seeds, roots and bark of the herbs you've nurtured is one of gardening's delights, and it's just as special to gather them in the wild. To make the most of your harvest, follow our tips for collecting, preserving and storing herbs as well as using them safely.

Safety

At best, mistaking the identity of a plant or using the wrong part of a herb could mean that your herbal remedy is ineffective, but at worst you could make yourself or someone else very ill.

Identification

From a safety standpoint, there's nothing more important than ensuring that you only harvest a herb if you are confident you know what it is. This should be reasonably straightforward in your own garden, but can get tricky in other situations. Bear in mind that the same common name may apply to several different plants, and that herbs as different as comfrey and foxglove may be difficult to tell apart at the non-flowering stage.

Once plants are dried, it becomes even more difficult to tell them apart, so harvest and dry only one herb at a time to prevent different batches of plants getting mixed up, and always tag or label them immediately, so they are easy to identify.

Use the correct part

The chemical characteristics of different parts of each plant vary, and as a result will have different effects on the body. For example, just as coriander leaves and seeds each bring different flavours to a recipe, so too do the leaves and roots of the dandelion have different medicinal actions.

Before harvesting a plant for culinary or medicinal purposes, double-check which part of the plant you need to use.

Once again, making a mistake could have dire consequences – bark from the shrub called cramp bark (*Viburnum opulus*) is a very useful medicine, but the berries from the same plant are toxic and should not be consumed.

Harvesting and drying herbs

Freshly cut herbs add extra zing to your cooking and boost the refreshing flavour of herbal teas (see *Infusions*, page 196). But most of the time, you'll want to dry your herbal harvest so it's on hand to use when needed – regardless of the season. Stored in labelled glass jars, in a cool dark place, most dried herbs will keep for about a year.

For more information on the best time and way to harvest specific herbs, consult the *Herb Directory*, pages 12–145. Most of the equipment you'll need for harvesting herbs are everyday household items.

SHARP SCISSORS, SECATEURS OR GARDEN KNIFE Prevent damage to the plant by always using a sharp blade.

GLOVES Protect your hands from thorns, bristles and allergic reactions by wearing good-quality gardening gloves.

BASKET Gather herbs in a tray or in a shallow basket, so you can spread out the samples, rather than pile them up. Don't bags or sacks that limit airflow or allow separate bunches of herbs to mingle.

GARDENING FORK When digging up roots, use a gardening fork, not a spade or shovel, as it is less likely to damage the plant.

STRING Tie bunches of herbs together with string.

LABELS The sooner you label your cut or dried herbs, the less likely you are to forget what they are.

PAPER BAGS Use paper bags to collect seeds, and remember to label their contents as you go.

RACK OR TRAY Herbs dry best when there is good air flow around them, so a cake rack is perfect. You could also stretch mesh or netting over a frame.

Dried leaves should be brittle and easily snap in your fingers. Store them in an airtight glass jar.

A cake rack is perfect for drying leaves, or you could stretch some mesh over a wooden frame.

GLASS JARS Glass is airtight and moisture-proof, so it's perfect for storing dried herbs. If you notice condensation building up in the jar, the herbs may not be completely dry – remove them and allow them to dry further before storing.

Leaves

The best time to collect leaves is on a dry, sunny morning before flowering has started. Wait until the dew has fully evaporated, but before the sun gets too hot and starts causing the essential oils in the plant to evaporate.

Use gardening scissors or secateurs to snip sprigs or stems of young, healthy leaves, or gently pluck individual leaves from the plant by hand. Remove any dirt by gently brushing the leaves, but don't wash them in water. Discard any leaves that look diseased or damaged.

If you've collected sprigs of leaves, strip the lower leaves from each stem, tie the stems together and hang the bunches upside-down. Spread individual leaves out to dry – a cake rack covered with kitchen paper is ideal.

Keep the leaves in a warm, airy place away from sunlight, and check them every day or so until they have completely dried.

Flowers

Collect flowers shortly after the buds have opened and well before they start losing their petals. Flowers that grow in clusters – for example, elder flowers, angelica and meadowsweet – and those with long stalks, such as lavender and roses, can be picked on the stem, but it is preferable to collect individual flower heads of others, such as calendula blooms.

To dry flowers, follow the instructions for leaves (see opposite) and hang bunches of flowers or spread individual flower heads in a place where there is plenty of warm air circulating over a

Hang bunches of flower stems upside down and with their stems straight in a place where warm air can circulate freely around them to encourage drying.

period of a few weeks. Flowers contain high levels of moisture, so to prevent mould from forming, make sure the petals aren't overlapping on the tray.

Once the flowers are completely dried, they should feel papery, not limp. Calendula heads take a particularly long time to dry thoroughly.

Store petals or dried flower heads in a dark glass jar, or use in a pot-pourri (see *Around the Home*, page 290).

To ensure the best flavour in the dried product, begin the drying process as soon after harvesting as possible.

Collecting wild herbs

Wandering through fields and forests and alsong footpaths as you collect wild herbs sounds rather romantic, but there are several important issues to be aware of before you start: identification, pollution, legal issues and ecology.

IDENTIFICATION Identifying plants is a difficult skill, and even trained experts can make mistakes. Always carry a plant guide as a reference, and check both the photographs and the written description against each herb. If you are doubtful of a plant's identity, don't pick it. Prevent different plants from becoming jumbled or difficult to identify later by tying the samples into bundles and labelling them as you harvest. Make sure you collect the correct medicinal part of the plant, too.

POLLUTION Many plants that seem to be growing in the clean, green countryside are actually exposed to large quantities of pollution, which can accumulate in their tissues and be passed on to those who consume them. Be aware that, in farming districts, agricultural chemicals are often sprayed on crops, and may drift to adjacent areas. Plants growing by the side of busy roads are constantly exposed to exhaust fumes. Even a patch of healthy-looking herbs that you discover in a country lane may have been sprayed with weedkiller just moments before you arrived. Whenever possible, ask locally about any chemicals used in the area before you start collecting herbs, and always wash them thoroughly before using.

LEGALITIES In some countries, including the United Kingdom, it is illegal to collect plants without first seeking permission from the landowner. It is also illegal to pick, uproot or damage plants that are rare or endangered, or in national parks and nature reserves.

ECOLOGY Over-harvesting of some medicinal herbs has resulted in them becoming endangered. An example is the North American goldenseal which has a deserved reputation as a potent antimicrobial remedy. Goldenseal is in great demand but is slow growing and difficult to cultivate. Over the years, this has led to an extremely lucrative market for wild-harvested (or 'wildcrafted') goldenseal root, and consequently the plant is now rare or endangered throughout most of its range and trade is strictly controlled. You can play your part in protecting our herbal heritage by finding out which plants are scarce or endangered in your own area, and leaving them alone. Even when plants appear to be plentiful, it's good practice to err on the side of caution. Harvest only what you really need and always leave at least a third of each plant, especially flowers and fruits, so that they are able to regenerate.

Harvest sweet-smelling elder flowers in spring, just as the flowers have opened fully.

Seeds

Timing is vital when collecting seeds. Harvest them in late summer in the short period between the ripening of the seed pod or seed head and when it opens or shatters to disperse the seeds.

Keep a close eye on the plant, and when you judge that the seed pod is starting to ripen (its colour will start changing from green to brown), cut the seed pods from the plant, taking plenty of the stem at the same time.

Gather the stems in a loose bunch, place the ends with the seed pods on them inside a paper bag, and use string to tie the opening of the bag around the stems. Hang the bag containing the herb in a warm, airy spot (see page 169). As the seed pods ripen over the next week or two, seeds will be released into the bag for you to collect. When the stems are dry, rub off any seeds still attached to the seed pods into the paper bag.

If you're going to use the seeds for planting, you can keep them in the same bag, as long as you tape it shut and clearly label the bag with the plant name and the date on which it was harvested. If you're using seeds for culinary or medicinal purposes, they will have a stronger flavour if you store them in glass jars, but again, make sure that you label each one accurately. Avoid storing seeds in plastic containers, as they allow moisture to build up and can cause mould to develop.

Roots and rhizomes

Harvesting roots and rhizomes in autumn or winter maximises their flavour and beneficial ingredients. Choose a time when the parts of the plant above the ground are starting to die back as this makes it easier to locate and identify them.

Using a gardening fork, dig out the whole plant and its roots. Carefully separate the portion of the root that you want to use, and re-plant the rest straight away.

Gently brush as much dirt as possible from the root. To clean more substantial roots and rhizomes, such as ginger and

Freeze whole mint leaves or borage flowers in ice cubes and use them in fruit juices and cocktails.

An Omani man taps a Boswellia tree for its resin, better known as frankincense.

horseradish, scrub with a vegetable brush; however, gently rinse finer and more delicate samples, such as valerian, under running water. Don't soak them, or they'll take up water and lose flavour, and take much longer to dry.

Once the roots are clean, cut them into small pieces and dry them in the oven at a very low heat (50° to 60°C). You may need to keep the oven door ajar to prevent the temperature rising too much. Turn the root pieces regularly to ensure they dry out evenly; you will know that they are ready when they become brittle.

Allow the roots to cool before storing them in a dark glass jar.

Bark

It's easy to kill or injure a tree when collecting its bark, so in many cases it's better to use commercially harvested varieties of these herbs. If you do decide to collect bark yourself, choose a damp day, and use clean, sharp tools to remove it from the tree in vertical strips at least a metre above the ground. You should never take a horizontal band of bark from trees or collect bark from saplings, or they will die.

Clean the bark to remove any dirt, and then flatten it out as much as you can before leaving it in a warm, airy place to dry for a few weeks.

Freezing herbs

Freezing herbs is a great way to retain their colour and flavour. Although it isn't suitable for herbs you're going to use medicinally, it is ideal for culinary herbs with very fine leaves or a high moisture content, and for those that lose their taste when dried. Good candidates are fennel and dill, tarragon, coriander, chives, parsley, chervil and basil.

For herbs you intend to use in small quantities or add at the last moment to dishes such as soups and casseroles, freeze herbs into ice cubes. Rinse fresh herbs under cold running water before chopping finely. Place a tablespoonful of the chopped herb into each segment of an ice-cube tray, add a little water, and then place the tray in the freezer. When the cubes are frozen, transfer them into a labelled plastic bag or container, and they'll keep for months.

Freeze whole bunches of herbs to use in larger quantities or in recipes that won't benefit from the extra water of the melted ice. After rinsing the herbs, pat them dry with a paper towel and tie them loosely together. Place the whole bunch inside a sealed and labelled plastic bag and store it in the freezer. Frozen herbs will become quite brittle, so before use, just scrunch the bag with your hand to break up the leaves.

Buying dried herbs

A wider variety of herbs than you could ever hope to dry or harvest yourself is available at your local healthfood store. The more popular herbs are available as teabags, but while convenient, these sometimes contain a lower grade of herbal material, and tend to be more expensive by weight than loose herbs. Look for dried herbs that retain the colour and texture of the plant and have a clean, characteristic scent. Reject those that are faded, powdery or have little smell. See pages 334–35 for more information.

Another way to store chopped herbs is to freeze a large quantity in a small plastic container. Label carefully.

An ice-cube tray is ideal for freezing small quantities of herbs that you tend to use sparingly in cooking.

Herbal medicine

Treating common ailments and conditions safely and effectively with herbs is an area of growing interest as well as the focus of research around the world. Find out which herbs have healing properties and learn the best ways to use them.

A herbal **tradition**

Humankind has been accumulating and utilising knowledge about the medicinal uses of herbs for at least 60,000 years.

The ancients

Ancient Egypt, though itself a centre of advanced medical practice, drew additional knowledge from the Middle East and imported dried spices, herbs and fragrant oils from Mesopotamia. Its first recorded healer of importance was Imhotep, who was physician to the Pharaoh Zoser in about 2600 BCE. So great was Imhotep's reputation that he became part of Egyptian mythology.

As Ancient Greece rose to power, its knowledge of medicine was, in turn, built on that inherited from the Middle East and Egypt. A number of schools of medicine evolved around its greatest healers. The earliest recorded Greek physician, Asclepius, was credited with performing miracles of healing; the rod of Asclepius, consisting of a snake wound around a staff, became the symbol of

Egyptian healers employed rhizomatists to supply their herbal needs from the wild.

medicine that is still widely used today.

Perhaps the greatest of all the Greek physicians was Hippocrates of Kos (b. 460 BCE), who deserves to be remembered as much for his sensible advice on lifestyle as for his remarkable insights into healing. Hippocrates developed a systematic approach to diagnosis and his rational attitude to healing was based on a profound knowledge of both herbs and human psychology.

While Hippocrates did not, as far as is known, write a herbal; Theophrastus of Eresus (b. c. 379 BCE), who was a pupil of Aristotle, wrote two excellent herbals that encapsulated Greek herbal knowledge of the time. The Greek herbals also included Aristotle's writings on botany, *Historia Plantarum* and *De Causis Plantarum*.

The Alexandrian School

The most influential of all the medical schools was founded in Alexandria, on Egypt's Mediterranean coast, a great centre of culture where Oriental and Greek influences met. The hybridisation of the great medical traditions under the Alexandrian School saw herbal medicine make many advances.

Much of the knowledge contained within the Alexandrian School was encapsulated in the very influential herbal *De Materia Medica*, produced by Dioscorides, a 1st century CE Greek physician. His herbal, containing some 600 precisely described medicinal plants, became the cornerstone of medicine for approximately 1400 years, as first the great Roman Empire contracted and then European learning stagnated.

In medieval monastery gardens, medicinal herbs and edible plants were usually grown separately from one another.

Monastic gardens

During the medieval period, much of Europe's knowledge was held in religious institutions. Monasteries and nunneries, became medical centres not just for the religious but for surrounding villages, travellers and pilgrims.

The gardens of the religious orders were usually constructed on a cross, created by intersecting paths. A number of specialised gardens were created within that layout, including cloister gardens; a physic garden of healing herbs; productive gardens where each bed was dedicated to a particular vegetable or herb; a picking garden to supply the church with flowers; and an orchard, where members of the religious order were often laid to rest.

> *'Women with child that eat quinces will bear wise children.'*
>
> Rembert Dodoens, 1517–1585

A surviving 820 CE plan for the model monastery, intended for St Gall in Switzerland, reveals gardens arranged like this, together with plantings laid out according to a list that had been decreed by the Carolingian king, Charlemagne the Great.

Compiling herbal knowledge

The 10th century *Glastonbury Herbal* revealed an extensive knowledge of herbs, while the *Leechdom*, produced in the same century, is an outstanding compilation of medical and veterinary herbal knowledge of the time. (Leechdom was a word for a medical formula or remedy and doctors were sometimes known as leeches.) An extensive herbal was also produced by the pre-eminent medical school in Europe during this period, the Welsh Physicians of Myddfai.

The Norman invasion of England saw a refinement in the gardens of pleasure attached to castles and manor houses. Filled with fragrant herbs as well as flowers, they might include such plants as the legendary *Rosa gallica* 'Officinalis', that had found their way back to Europe from the Crusades.

The 16th and 17th centuries saw the publication in Britain and Europe of several books that took a more scientific approach to the study of herbs. They included works by William Turner and John Gerard (see box). Important later works included John Parkinson's *Theatrum Botanicum* (1640), *A Curious Herbal* by Elizabeth Blackwell (published 1737) which contained detailed illustrations of medicinal plants and their medical uses; and *Medical Botany* by William Woodville (published 1790-95) and illustrated by James Sowerby, which was the standard work on the pharmacological uses of British plants until the last quarter of the 19th century.

Modern herbal medicine

The modern practice of herbal medicine, coupled with an interest in culinary and fragrance herbs, has seen a resurgence in herb usage and herb culture worldwide. At the same time, the complex interaction between body, mind and spirit is again being acknowledged in the field of holistic medicine. We are now in an era of complementary medicine where herbal medicine is accorded respect in its own right.

The great herbals

The greatest of the English herbals emerged from the 16th century onwards. William Turner's *New Herball*, in three volumes published in 1551, 1162 and 1568 included no fewer than 238 British plants. It was the first systematic study of British plants and included detailed descriptions of the plants and woodcut illustrations. It was the first English herbal with pretensions to scientific status.

John Gerard, a physician, apothecary and gardener, published his *Herball or General History of Plants* in 1597 (below), probably based on work by the Flemish botanist Rembertus Dodoens. While studying in London, Gerard started a garden near his home in Holborn. In 1596 he compiled a list of the plants he had cultivated, the first complete catalogue of a single garden ever published. While Gerard wrote about plants primarily for their medicinal properties, the book catalogued common English and Latin botanical names, habitats, physical descriptions, growth times and flowerings, other uses of plants such as for food as well as a great deal of herbal folklore.

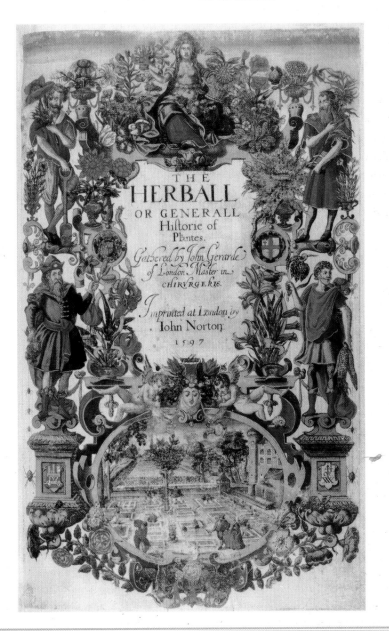

Western herbal philosophy

The style of herbal medicine currently practised in the Western world has its roots in the traditions of Europe and North America, but it has also adopted remedies from Africa and South America as well as from the practice of Chinese and Ayurvedic medicine.

Returning the body to balance

At its heart, Western herbal medicine retains some of the philosophies espoused by the Greek physician Hippocrates and his contemporaries more than 2000 years ago. These teachings included the crucial theory that a patient's diet, environment and mental state all contributed to his or her total wellbeing.

Today's Western herbalists take a similar holistic approach to healthcare, prescribing dietary and other lifestyle changes as well as herbal remedies, based on the principle that the factors that contribute to ill health need to be removed in order for healing to occur.

This is an extension of their view that the body often repairs itself when provided with the optimal conditions in which to do so – another concept associated with the Hippocratic tradition, which taught the *vis medicatrix naturae*, or innate, self-healing capacity of the human body.

> *'Cure sometimes, treat often, comfort always.'*
>
> Hippocrates, c 460–370 BCE

In many ways, this goal of returning the body to a state of balance is central to every decision a herbalist makes in treatment. Whereas the medical approach largely focuses on fighting disease and pathology, the Western herbalist mainly works towards optimising the function of the organs and body systems so that the body can heal itself.

In most serious conditions, medical intervention is entirely appropriate. The specific, targeted, disease-fighting approach is exactly what's required when dealing with dangerously high blood pressure, a life-threatening infection, a burst appendix or an anaphylactic allergic reaction – all of which require drastic and fast-acting treatment. But herbal medicine can help many acute conditions. Consult a medical herbalist for further advice and to discover if a herbalis may be able to help you.

Treating chronic health problems

On the other hand, herbs are often appropriate for chronic disease states, which develop over a longer period, and where the symptoms may be less well-defined. These conditions are commonly linked with unhealthy dietary and lifestyle habits, and they often respond well to slower-acting, gentler herbal remedies – especially if healthier habits are adopted at the same time. By addressing these chronic states of ill-health, herbs may help prevent some conditions developing into more serious diseases that require acute intervention; disease prevention is often an important goal of herbal treatment.

How herbs can help

To restore the body to a state of balance, the Western herbalist will consider each of the body's major organs and systems. The digestive system and the excretory organs are of key importance in overall health: optimising their ability to assimilate nutrients and process the bodily wastes is a major focus of many treatments. The herbalist may also prescribe remedies to:

• help patients to cope better cope with stress by either building up or calming downthe nervous system;
• increase resistance to infection or allergy by supporting the patient's immune system;

Native American herbalism

It is said that when the Pilgrims arrived in North America, fewer than 90 diseases were known among Native American people, whose fitness and vitality was noticed by European doctors.

Native American healers were highly respected and played a valuable role in the physical and spiritual wellbeing of their society. They also had a rich herbal tradition on which to draw when treating illness or injury, and for midwifery and contraceptive purposes.

Today many of the remedies found in the Western herbalist's dispensary – including the very popular herbs echinacea, golden seal (below) and black cohosh – were first introduced to settlers by the Native Americans.

• restore hormonal balance, relieving the symptoms of the menopause or premenstrual syndrome and getting the body ready for conception;
• relieve pain and inflammation; and
• support the heart and blood vessels.

Individualised care

Before determining an appropriate treatment, the herbalist considers each patient's individual circumstances and constitution. For example, in formulating a prescription for supporting weight loss, the herbalist may take into account factors such as the patient's bowel habits, energy levels, hormonal status and ability to cope with stress. This individualised approach to treatment – 'treating the person, not the disease' – is the opposite of the 'one size fits all' approach that can be characteristic of the medical or pharmaceutical model.

Science and tradition

Modern Western herbal medicine, which is mainly based on the traditional practices of Europe and North America, has also adopted key remedies from Africa and South America and Chinese and Ayurvedic medicine.

Clinical trials

Unlike Chinese and Ayurvedic herbalism (or the Hippocratic approach to medicine – see box), modern Western herbalism does not incorporate a humoral or 'elemental' approach to disease and the herbal remedies borrowed from other traditions are rarely used in their original context. The Western herbalist prescribing dan shen (*Salvia miltiorrhiza*) is likely to be thinking of its clinically proven actions on angina and heart problems, not its Chinese attributes as a cooling herb.

Western herbalists are increasingly finding that scientific evidence confirms their traditional knowledge. But the scientific study of herbal medicines and herbal practice has to overcome a unique set of challenges. Given that relatively few herbs have been subjected

The humours of Hippocrates

The Hippocratic school of medicine theorised that the world and everything in it – including the human body – was influenced by the four elements of fire, water, earth and air. In humans, the elements ruled four fluids referred to as the humours, and these, in turn, influenced each individual's constitution and personality. Sickness was also blamed on an imbalance of the humours, and the particular imbalance involved helped to dictate the appropriate remedies to be used in treatment.

Element	Fire	Water	Earth	Air
Humour	Yellow bile	Phlegm	Black bile	Blood
Personality	Choleric (quick to anger)	Phlegmatic (lazy, slow-thinking and slow-moving)	Melancholic (prone to depression and sorrow)	Sanguine (relaxed and cheerful)
Health issues	Hot, dry conditions, eg. liver problems	Cold, damp conditions, eg. respiratory infection and other catarrhal conditions	Cold, dry conditions, eg. constipation	Hot, damp conditions, eg. diarrhoea and other conditions associated with over-indulgence

to any scientific scrutiny, a prescription from your Western medical herbalist is likely to combine remedies that have been clinically proven with others whose use is based on traditional experience. In many cases, five or six different herbs – or more – are blended toghether in one prescription.

Synergy

The prescription of combinations of remedies demonstrates the herbalists' belief in synergy – the concept that different botanical medicines work together to produce an effect that is greater than any of the individual remedies acting alone.

Synergy also applies to the compounds within a plant, with most Western herbalists believing that the whole remedy provides a safer, more effective medicine than its individual active constituents.

For example, aspirin, a salicylic acid compound originally derived from meadowsweet, sometimes causes gastric bleeding as a side effect, whereas the herb in its entirety does not, and even seems to offer some protection from the gastric irritation caused by salicylates.

Eastern herbal philosophy

The ancient practices of traditional Chinese and Ayurvedic – from southeast Asia – herbal medicine, are both holistic approaches to healing. They are based on the principle of humours or elements and focus on creating internal harmony or balance in the body.

An ancient tradition with spiritual roots

Chinese herbalism has a history that can be traced back thousands of years. The most famous of the Chinese herb books, *The Yellow Emperor's Inner Classic (or Huang Di Nei Jing)*, may have been written in about 100 BCE, but its origins are even older: the emperor for whom it was named ruled from 2698 to 2596 BCE.

Since then, Chinese scholars have continued to document this complex method of healing, and traditional Chinese medicine continues to thrive today in mainland China, in other Chinese communities throughout Asia, and increasingly in the Western world.

The philosophy of traditional Chinese medicine (TCM) has its basis in the spiritual practice of Taoism, which teaches that human beings should strive to live in accordance with the rules of nature and emphasise the importance of balance and harmony. In keeping with the Tao teachings, the goal of all healing in TCM is to restore internal harmony.

1 Boxthorn (*Lycium barbarum*)
2 Ginkgo (*Ginkgo biloba*) **3** Chinese haw (*Crataegus pinnatifida*) **4** Ginseng (*Panax ginseng*) **5** Schisandra (*Schisandra chinensis*)
6 Dan shen (*Salvia miltiorrhiza*)
7 Bitter orange (*Citrus aurantium*)
8 Dong quai (*Angelica polymorpha* var. *sinensis*) **9** Qing hao (*Artemesia annua*)
10 Chinese date (*Ziziphus jujuba*)

'He who takes medicine and neglects to diet wastes the skill of his doctors.'

Chinese proverb

This philosophy of returning the body to a state of balance in order to bring about healing is not unique to TCM – in fact, it is also central to the philosophies of Western herbalism and Ayurveda. But the methods used to achieve this aim in TCM are unique, and the concepts and practices involved may be unfamiliar to many not versed in the traditions, especially as they encompass not only herbal medicine, but also acupuncture, massage, diet therapy and healing exercises, such as qi gong.

The life force

The Chinese use the word *qi* (sometimes westernised as *chi* or *ki*) to refer to the life force that inhabits not only the human body, but also all aspects of the environment and everything in it. *Qi* is a moving energy, sometimes defined as 'breath' or 'air', which also has many characteristics of fluids.

In the human body, *qi* is believed to flow along channels called meridians. These are not physical anatomical structures like the blood vessels, but nevertheless TCM practitioners can identify their locations with pinpoint accuracy so they can insert acupuncture needles into any one of over 500 individual points, and affect the flow of *qi* through the body.

Yin and yang

Another important concept in TCM is that of yin and yang, two opposite but complementary qualities that can be attributed to all things. The familiar circular symbol of black and white tear-drop shapes, each containing a small piece of the opposing colour, is called the *taijitu*. It shows the dichotomy of yin and yang by illustrating that any two opposites are dependent on each other, and cannot exist in isolation – each needs the other to make up the whole.

Yin is represented by the black segments of the *taijitu*. It is characterised as feminine, passive, dark, cooling and associated with night. Yang is depicted in white in the *taijitu*, and has active, masculine qualities associated with heat, lightness and daytime.

When yin and yang are balanced, the body will be in a state of harmony, but a relative excess of one quality (and the consequent deficiency of the other) causes an imbalance that can lead to illness and disease. Herbs and foods are

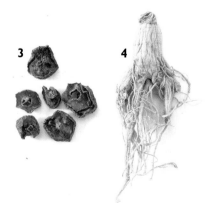

classified according to how yin or yang they are, and the effects they have on the body; these qualities are an important consideration in helping to restore harmony and health.

The five elements

Like several other ancient systems of medicine, TCM is based on a theory of elements or humours. Each of TCM's five elements or 'phases' has different qualities, governs different bodily functions and can be influenced by different medicines and foods, with the taste of each medicine giving insight into which element or elements it affects. Each of the elements – fire, earth, metal, water and wood – interacts with and influences the others in many ways.

Visiting a TCM practitioner

A TCM practitioner will use a tongue, facial and pulse diagnosis, as well as your description of your symptoms, to determine whether there is an imbalance in the five elements, in the yin and yang of the body, or the flow of *qi*. The terms used can be bewildering – patients may hear the practitioner make a diagnosis of spleen *qi* deficiency when they had come in for a consultation about their persistent headaches!

Depending on individual needs, a practitioner is likely to prescribe herbs and sometimes a course of acupuncture. Chinese herbal formulas often contain numerous herbs, which are boiled together for up to an hour to make a traditional decoction that concentrates the herbs' flavours and medicinal actions. The full course of your treatment may be dispensed to you in a series of paper packets, each containing your daily dose.

Ayurvedic medicine

Ayurveda, a traditional healing system from India, is an ancient holistic health practice with many similarities to traditional Chinese medicine (TCM). As with TCM, the aim of Ayurvedic and western medicine is to bring the body into balance. This is achieved through dietary change, the prescription of herbal medicines and also through meditation and yoga. 'Ayurveda' is a Sanskrit word that literally means 'the science of living', reflecting the principle that an individual's health is their own responsibility and that a physician can only guide his patients.

Again, like TCM, Ayurveda is based on a humoral philosophy, but there are three elements, called *doshas*, rather than five. You have all three of them in different proportions, and your constitution partly determines the ratio of each, but they are also affected by diet, climate and other lifestyle factors. Your *doshas* dictate your personality, the nature of the illnesses you experience and the types of food, herbal medicine and exercise that are best suited to you.

As with TCM, each of the *doshas* can be influenced by the tastes of the food and medicines you consume.

1 Fenugreek (*Trigonella foenum-graecum*) **2** Gymnema sylvestre **3** Nigella (*Nigella sativa*) **4** Winter cherry (*Withania somnifera*) **5** Ginger (*Zingiber officinale*) **6** Brahmi (*Bacopa monnieri*) **7** Gotu kola (*Centella asiatica*) **8** Tamarind (*Tamarindus indica*) **9** Long pepper (*Piper nigrum*)

VATA governs movement of the body and mind, and the functioning of the circulation, nerves, muscles and bones. It is associated with dryness, cold and wind. When vata is low, it can be stimulated by bitter, astringent and pungent tastes,; sour, sweet and salty tastes help bring it into balance.
PITTA governs the power of transformation, such as the conversion of food into energy, and has moist, hot qualities. Associated with focus and concentration, it is stimulated by salty, sour, pungent tastes; sweet, bitter, astringent tastes reduce excess pitta.
KAPHA is binding, provides structure to the body and governs lubrication – for example, in keeping the joints from getting stiff. Its qualities are earthy, watery and cold. Kapha will be stimulated by sweet, salty and sour tastes, and is suppressed by pungent, bitter and astringent flavours.

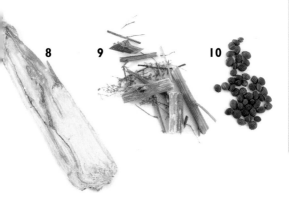

8　**9**　**10**

The **science** of herbal **medicine**

Herbal medicine is both an art and a science, combining centuries of tradition with modern research methods and analytical techniques. Once self-taught, or apprenticed to an experienced practitioner, many modern herbalists are university trained, studying a range of scientific disciplines.

The study of chemicals in plants

Although still regarded as unproven and old-fashioned in some sections of conventional medicine, the modern practice of herbal medicine is increasingly underpinned by scientific rigour and academic research, and gaining credibility as a result. Herbalists now study elements of botany, chemistry, biochemistry, pharmacology, toxicology and medicine.

Much of what we know about herbal medicine has been handed down through the ages. But plants are highly complex chemical entities, and the herbalists of centuries past could only observe their effects; they lacked the tools to work out why a certain herb works the way it does, or how it achieves its actions.

Today, the science of phytochemistry, the study of the chemicals in plants, reveals a much deeper level of information, which helps us understand how medicinal plants work.

> *'The art of healing comes from nature and not from the physicians.'*
>
> Paracelsus, 1493–1541

Synergistic effects

It's quite likely that the combinations of active constituents in many herbs work together to create synergistic effects that are more powerful than any of the individual components acting alone. Even so, understanding the actions of the individual compounds helps researchers to make herbal medicine safer, more effective and more reliable.

In some cases, this type of research has identified new uses for existing remedies as well as potential adverse interactions between herbal medicines and pharmaceutical drugs.

Standardised herbal preparations

The compounds in herbal medicines are subject to natural variation. Weather and soil conditions, the age of the plant and even the time of day the herbal remedy is harvested can all affect the levels of active constituents in a batch of herbal medicine.

In clinical trials, to guarantee that each patient receives a medicine of the same potency, many are now performed using herbal remedies that have been standardised to contain consistent levels of one or two key marker constituents. Herbal tablets, capsules and liquid extracts made for commercial sale are made in the same way. In many cases, but not always, the marker used is one of the compounds that plays an important role in the plant's medicinal actions.

Herbs in close-up – a series of scanning electron micrographs showing: caffeine (top); the oil glands on the surface of the corolla petal of a peppermint plant (*Mentha x piperita*) (centre) and morphine crystals, another alkaloid (bottom).

A problem with this approach is that it assumes that it is possible to identify active constituents and also that it is only the active constituent that is important, rather than the herb itself, used unadulterated. Herbalists, instead of using these kind of commercial extracts, tend to use the whole herb, taking into account an array of constituents that work synergistically.

Major classes of phytochemicals

Thousands of different chemicals with physiological activity have been identified in plants, and no doubt there are many more still to be discovered. Interestingly, many of the plants that have traditionally been prescribed for similar indications also share similar groups of active constituents. Some of the most important classes of phytochemicals are summarised below.

ALKALOIDS are potent compounds with very strong physiological effects, so herbs that contain them tend to be used in low doses or not at all. Alkaloids tend to affect the central nervous system, and some well-known examples include morphine and codeine from the opium poppy, which are central nervous system depressants, and caffeine from coffee, a nervous system stimulant.

ANTHRAQUINONES are a group of compounds with potent laxative action. Found in herbs such as senna and Chinese rhubarb, they stimulate peristaltic movements in the colon and trigger a bowel movement some hours later. These effects are magnified if the herbs are taken in overdose, and excessive use may cause diarrhoea and the loss of important electrolytes. Excessive or long-term use of any kind of laxative may render the bowel unable to function normally. Like conventional laxatives, anthraquinone-containing herbs should therefore only be used occasionally and at recommended doses.

BITTER PRINCIPLES are substances that stimulate the bitter taste receptors at the back of the tongue. This is believed to trigger a reflex response in the vagus nerve, which in turn stimulates the production of various gastric secretions. Herbs that taste bitter have had a long history of use in stimulating digestive function in this way, and in many traditional systems of medicine they are taken as tonics for the stomach, liver, gall bladder and pancreas. With its extremely bitter taste, gentian is one of the most potent bitter tonics, but even herbs with a milder bitter flavour – such as dandelion root – can act as digestive stimulants.

ESSENTIAL OILS, largely responsible for the aroma of herbs such as lavender, peppermint and basil, are often retained as one of many constituents of a herbal medicine. They can also be extracted from plants by processes that concentrate the essential oil, making it more potent, and enabling it to be used in aromatherapy, perfumes and food. They commonly have anti-spasmodic and antimicrobial actions, and a number of mental and emotional effects have also been documented with their use.

FLAVONOIDS, an extensive class of compounds found in many plant foods as well as in herbs, are responsible for a large number of beneficial effects. They have anti-oxidant properties and also a strong affinity with the blood vessels. Among their many actions, key flavonoids strengthen and maintain the integrity of the capillaries, stimulate circulation to the peripheral areas of the body and protect cholesterol molecules from harmful oxidative processes. Specific groups of flavonoids are responsible for the medicinal effects of ginkgo, hawthorn and horse chestnut, among other herbs.

GLUCOSINOLATES are sulphur compounds that are converted in the body into substances called isothiocyanates. The glucosinolates in horseradish and nasturtium are responsible for the anti-infective and mucus-liquefying properties of these herbs; those in cabbage, broccoli and brussels sprouts are credited with helping to prevent cancer.

MUCILAGE is a type of fibre that binds with water to form an indigestible gel. Mucilage-rich plants such as psyllium have numerous benefits for the digestive system, including the ability to enhance bowel function and promote the removal of cholesterol from the body. Other mucilage-containing herbs, such as marsh mallow and slippery elm, are predominantly used for their soothing topical effect on inflamed mucous membranes.

PHYTOESTROGENS are plant compounds with oestrogen-like activity. The two main classes are the isoflavones found in red clover and soy, and the lignans found in flaxseed, some grains and other foods. Phytoestrogen-containing plants have been used in many herbal traditions for the treatment of female reproductive problems. And the dietary intake of phytoestrogens has been associated with a number of health-protecting effects, including a possible reduction in the risk of breast cancer. On the other hand, consumption in excessive doses (above those normally consumed in the diet) is considered controversial by some authorities.

TANNINS interact with proteins with which they come into contact, making the tissue tougher and less permeable. They are used to turn animal hides into leather in a process known as tanning. These astringent effects are utilised in herbal medicine to tighten mucous membranes and make them less easily penetrated by infective organisms, and also to reduce diarrhoea, bleeding and other excessive secretions. Tea is the most widely used tannin-containing plant in the world, and its astringent nature can easily be felt by drinking a cup of tea that's been allowed to steep for too long and noting its drying, tightening effects on the mouth, gums and tongue.

Herbs in the future

In the future, science, technology and economics will have more and more influence on how herbal medicine is practised. Research is continually revealing new applications of herbal medicines, which could lead to ground-breaking improvements in health worldwide.

Morphine, an addictive drug, is derived from the white latex that weeps from the opium poppy's capsule when it is wounded (see also page 105).

Unlocking nature's treasure chest

The plant kingdom has long been recognised as a rich and bountiful source of potential medicines. Increasingly, researchers are reviewing the chemistry of herbs in an attempt to reveal their therapeutic secrets. In some cases, laboratory studies will identify new compounds that have potential benefits for human health, and further work will be undertaken to either isolate and purify the compound, or replicate it in a synthetic form to be used as a pharmaceutical drug.

This kind of research may appear speculative, but many drugs already used are produced in this way: aspirin is a synthetic compound that was based on the salicylic acids found in meadowsweet and other herbs (although today it is synthesised from coal tar).

And there are exciting discoveries to be made: stevioside, found in a sweet herb called *Stevia rebaudiana*, is 300 times sweeter than sugar, minus the fattening or glucose-altering effects (see page 82).

Endorsing local traditions

Approaching the same goal from a different but equally rigorous angle, ethnobotanists explore the role that herbs and other plants play in different societies and cultures. The World Health Organization (WHO) recognises that many people around the world rely on local traditional remedies for their healthcare, and that – particularly in developing countries – these are often more affordable than pharmaceuticals. In the future, ethnobotany will continue to play an important role in documenting these traditional practices so that their safety and efficacy can be evaluated and, where appropriate, endorsed by local healthcare providers.

Validating herbal medicines

The double-blind, placebo-controlled clinical trial is regarded in some circles as a gold standard for medicinal research, attempting to provide unbiased statistical analysis of the safety and efficacy of medicines. As more herbs are subjected to clinical trials and proven to have therapeutic benefit, their credibility in conventioal medicine increases, and doctors become more open to the idea of prescribing them for their patients. Where clinical trials produce negative results, the use of particular remedies

Appetite suppressant of the future

A medicine that successfully treats or prevents weight-related problems has enormous potential. Researchers have been excited by the possibilities of the succulent plant hoodia (*Hoodia gordonii*), which has been long used by the San people of the Kalahari Desert, to help stave off hunger during long hunting trips. After preliminary research indicated that hoodia has significant appetite-reducing effects, scientific study into the plant and its safety is ongoing. It will be some years before hoodia's potential is fully understood, but if it does turn out to be the wonder weight-loss drug of the future, the San people will benefit through a ground-

breaking royalty agreement with the developers of the drug. In the meantime, the herb is in danger of extinction due to overharvesting, and some of the products that are on sale in the United States and Europe are alleged to be counterfeit, containing little or no hoodia.

Each year, more than 500 million people become seriously ill with malaria; every 30 seconds, a child dies of it.

into question – but also the way the trial itself has been conducted.

Using clinical trials to verify herbal therapeutics can provide researchers and clinicians with a great deal of valuable information, but there are unique challenges involved in testing herbal medicines in this way.

The first potential problem is that all patients in the study should take exactly the same medicine; but as they are natural substances, herbs can contain chemical variations from batch to batch.

So the herbal products used in many studies are standardised, and we possess a significant body of evidence supporting the use of standardised herbal products (commonly single herbs dispensed as tablets or capsules). But there is far less evidence about the effectiveness of more traditional preparations, such as homemade infusions and decoctions and compound medicines made up of several herbs or of the efficacy of the traditional herbalist and how they prescribe and treat, as opposed to just the herbs or herbal consituents.

The processes involved in creating standardised herbal products provide companies with a level of ownership of the research results, giving them more leeway to recoup their investment funds by claiming that their specific product has been clinically proven, while other non-standardised products have not.

These issues have major implications for the way herbal medicine is practised, and may have already influenced the prescribing habits of doctors who prefer to focus on prescribing remedies that have been clinically trialled.

Qing hao – changing the future of malaria

The story of qing hao (*Artemisia annua*), or Chinese wormwood, provides a snapshot of the way medicines derived from herbs may have a dramatic impact on the future of healthcare. In the 1970s, Chinese researchers seeking herbal remedies for malaria rediscovered qing hao's potential. Subsequent research revealed that the active constituent artemesinin is extremely effective against the malaria parasite, which is spread from person to person by mosquitoes, and kills millions every year.

Today, malaria treatment has been revolutionised by artemesinin-based combination therapy (ACT), which pairs artemesinin derivatives with pharmaceutical agents into a single drug. As ACT safely treats malaria in just three days, WHO has endorsed it as the preferred approach for malaria treatment; to date, it has saved millions of lives around the world. However, it is expensive, costing as much as 15 times more than the previous generation of anti-malarial drugs.

But economically, artemesinin has also proved revolutionary. In 2003, the medical charity Médecins Sans Frontières teamed up with research institutes from Africa, Asia, Europe and South America to form the Drugs for Neglected Diseases Initiative, known as DNDi.

To date, this collaboration has developed two forms of ACT that are now in use in Asia, Africa and South and Central America, where, as the world's first patent-free medicines, they are changing not only the health outlook of many communities badly affected by malaria, but also their economic prognosis.

A Chinese farmer with stalks of qing hao containing the constituent artemisinin.

It is also worth pointing out that the economics of scientific research are such that the herbs most likely to be investigated and 'proven' to be effective are those for which there is the largest potential market. We therefore have a good understanding of the way that some herbs work, and the roles that herbs can play in extremely common conditions, such as arthritis and heart disease. However, this focus on financially lucrative remedies may mean that our knowledge of the whole range of herbs (including those less well known and researched) and the methods employed by herbalists for treating a great array of health problems over centuries could languish in the future.

Using herbs safely

It's easy to fall into the trap of thinking that as herbs are natural they're also safe. Consult a professional if you have a serious illness or severe symptoms, or are pregnant or breastfeeding. If picking herbs yourself, be sure to identify the plant correctly. Finally, choose a reputable herbalist.

Take the correct dose

The active constituents in herbs have the power to affect the physiological functioning of your body – some have a gentle impact while others are extremely potent medicines. As a rule of thumb, the stronger the action of the herb, the lower the dose required to cause a physical effect: some herbs are so potent they are prescribed only in small doses, because higher intakes may cause serious adverse effects.

Our understanding of an appropriate dose for each herb is largely based on

traditional and historical knowledge accumulated over hundreds of years and supplemented over recent times with a growing body of scientific study.

Always follow the dosage instructions, and do not exceed recommended doses or take a particular herb if there is a caution against its use in your circumstances. Seek professional advice before taking any herb over an extended period of time. In the majority of cases it is wise to seek professional advice before treating children or babies with herbs, as different doses may be required, depending on the child's age or condition. All medicines, inclding herbal medicines should be kept out of the reach of chilren.

Identify the plant correctly

Identifying the correct herb to take as a medicine is not always easy, especially if harvesting plants yourself rather than buying commercial remedies. But correct identification is absolutely essential as plants that look alike sometimes have very different chemical make-ups. Some plants from the same family have vastly different medicinal effect – and some can even kill – wild carrots and hemlock, a deadly poison, are members of the same family.

There are also many instances where the same common name is applied to several different species – for example, at least five different plants are referred to by the common name of balm of Gilead, making it very confusing, as well as potentially dangerous, for the amateur herbalist.

Like pharmaceutical medicines, herbal medicines should always be kept out of children's reach.

Seek professional help

Self-treatment with herbs is appropriate for minor conditions and for providing symptomatic relief from some diseases. However, any condition that is serious, life-threatening, long-term, has severe symptoms or minor symptoms that do not resolve should be treated by a trained medical herbalist who understands of disease processes and suitable treatments. Professional treatment is also recommended if you are pregnant or breastfeeding, as many herbs are not safe or appropriate to use at this time.

Herbalists overcome these problems by referring to plants by their botanical (Latin) names. This system of naming was developed by Linnaeus, the 18th century Swedish botanist. The first word of a plant's botanical name refers to its genus – for example, all mint plants fall into the Mentha genus. The second word of the name refers to the plant's species, so the plant we commonly refer to as spearmint is named *Mentha spicata*.

Don't harvest or consume a plant if you have any doubt at all about its identity. Check which part of the plant to use before you harvest it, too – there is absolutely no point in collecting the leaves of a particular herb if the medicinal constituents are only present in the roots!

Avoid any adverse effects

Even when they're taken at appropriate doses, both herbal and pharmaceutical medicines can sometimes cause adverse effects, which generally fall into one of three categories.

• **Side-effects** are symptoms or physiological changes that can be predicted to occur in a percentage of all users of a particular medicine. For

'Shrieks like mandrakes torn out of the earth.'

William Shakespeare,
Romeo and Juliet, Act IV, Scene III

example, herbalists can anticipate that a small number of patients who take valerian will report having vivid dreams, and similarly that some patients who take liquorice will experience an increase in blood pressure. (Important side-effects are listed on the relevant pages of this book.)

• **Drug interactions** may occur when a patient is taking two or more medicines simultaneously. For example, St John's wort is metabolised in the body in the same pathway as certain drugs and may interfere with how they work. Conversely, there may be positive reactions between herbs and certain drugs and some herbs may even reduce the dose or even the need for a drug. Not all of these types of effects are predictable, while others are well-documented. The *Conditions* section of this book, pages 206–245, details major potential drug interactions where appropriate, but should not be considered an exhaustive reference on this important issue. If you are taking pharmaceutical medications, talk to your doctor or medical herbalist before adding herbs to your treatment regimen, even if you are using them to treat a different condition.

• **Allergies** occur when the immune system over-reacts to a substance that is otherwise innocuous, and can range from minor inconveniences to severe, life-threatening problems. Some herbs are more likely to cause allergies than others; however, the real reason that allergies are unpredictable is that the underlying issue is in the patient's immune system, rather than the plant itself. If you are an allergic person, take care with herbal medicines just as you

Deadly herbs

Hemlock (*Conium maculatum*) can be misidentified – be very careful.

HEMLOCK The Greek philosopher Socrates (c. 469–399 BCE) was found guilty of corrupting the youth of Athens and sentenced to death, so, according to Athenian law, he drank a cup of the poison hemlock. His student Plato recorded the effects of the poison, which started as a heavy sensation in Socrates's legs, gradually turning into a paralysis that crept up his body until his heart stopped beating.

MANDRAKE The root of the hallucinogenic poisonous plant mandrake (*Mandragora officinarum*) is shaped like a crude impression of a person, and has been associated with magical qualities since biblical times. Legend has it that, when the root is unearthed, it emits such an ear-piercing shriek that anyone hearing it will die instantly.

BELLADONNA In spite of its attractive, glossy berries, belladonna is both poisonous and hallucinogenic. Also known as deadly nightshade, its common name (*bella donna*, or 'beautiful woman' in Italian) derives from its former cosmetic use, dilating women's pupils to make them more attractive; however, prolonged use led to blindness. It was also believed to have been used by witches in the preparation of 'flying ointments'.

Belladonna (*Atropa belladonna*)

would with other substances, and always carefully patch test topical remedies before using them.

If you develop any symptoms that could be due to a herb you are taking, stop using it immediately and, if necessary, seek medical treatment.

Choose a trained herbalist

Make sure you consult a herbalist who is appropriately trained. Do not be afraid to ask about their qualifications, whether they are a member of any professional associations, how long they've been practising, or about the type of public liability insurance they carry. The answers to these questions may depend on the legal status of herbal medicine in your country, but should give you an indication of the professionalism and experience of the practitioner.

It is also important to have a good rapport with your herbalist, just as you have with your doctor so assess whether you feel comfortable and confident with them. For this reason, many people prefer to seek a referral to a herbalist. Consult the National Institute of Medical Herbalists (www.nimh.org.uk) for recommended practitioners.

Medicinal preparations

It's rewarding – and surprisingly simple – to make your
own herbal medicines. Follow these step-by-step
instructions to ensure you achieve the best results.

Infusions, decoctions, tinctures and
syrups can all be prepared for internal
use, while infused oils, compresses or
poultices are more suitable for external
applications. Some active constituents
in herbs are readily soluble in water,
while others require a more vigorous
extraction process that involves alcohol.

Infusions

The word 'infusion' refers to a herbal
tea or tisane that is made by
pouring boiling water over fresh or
dried herbs. When you make tea with a
tea bag, you are making an infusion.

An infusion is an effective preparation
method for delicate or fine plant parts,
such as petals, leaves and other aerial
parts. It is ideally suited to extracting
water-soluble components from the
plant and is often used for aromatic
herbs that contain essential oils (such as
peppermint, fennel and chamomile).

1 Place the recommended quantity of
loose dried herb (dried chamomile is
used here) or finely chopped fresh herb
into a pre-warmed glass or china teapot
or coffee plunger.

2 Pour about 200ml freshly boiled
water over the herb and stir. Place the
lid on the teapot to trap the steam and
stop the essential oil evaporating. Allow
it to steep for 10 to 15 minutes.

3 Stir again before pouring through a
strainer into your teacup.

Usage Drink one cup of tea three times
a day over several weeks for chronic
(long-standing) problems, or up to
six cups a day in the shorter term for
acute problems.

Storage Infusions do not store well,
so it's always best to prepare a fresh pot
of tea for each cup.

Decoctions

A decoction is a herbal tea made by boiling a herb in water. This method is most suitable for the woodier parts of a plant – such as the bark, roots, twigs and seeds – and is used to extract as many of the water-soluble active constituents as possible.

1 Grind the required quantity of dried herb (dried dandelion root is used here) into a coarse powder.

2 In a saucepan, cover the powder with about 500ml cold (not hot) water; stir. Bring water slowly to the boil. Reduce heat to low and, with the lid still on, simmer for 10 to 15 minutes. (If your stove top doesn't have a sufficiently low heat setting, use a double boiler.)

3 Stir again before pouring through a strainer into a teacup.

Usage Drink one cup three times a day over several weeks for chronic (long-standing) problems, or up to 6 cups a day in the shorter term for acute ones.

Storage Decoctions keep for a maximum of 3 days in the refrigerator. If you have the time, it's preferable to make a fresh decoction for each dose.

Chinese decoctions

Decoctions are revered by Chinese herbalists for their therapeutic effects and their versatility. They enable the herbalist to tailor remedies to the patient's needs, and allow the treatment to be amended as the patient's condition changes in response to the medicine.

The Chinese herbalist or pharmacist consults with the patient and determines the appropriate remedies to include in the prescription – the number of herbal ingredients (and their doses) is often larger than those used by Western herbalists.

Each daily dose of herbs is dispensed into a separate bag for the patient to prepare at home. The amount of water required, the boiling time and the quantity and frequency of medicine to be consumed may all vary.

Traditionally, ceramic clay pots with lids are used for Chinese decoctions, as chemical interactions can occur when herbs are exposed to metals such as iron, aluminium or copper.

Tinctures

Many of the active constituents in herbal medicines are readily soluble in alcohol, which is also an effective preservative. Professional herbalists use alcohol-based liquid herbal medicines to prescribe and dispense individualised herbal medicines.

For professional use, liquid extracts of herbs are made using a high concentration of pharmaceutical-grade alcohol (ethanol). Typically, 1 part of the herb is extracted in either 1 or 2 parts of alcohol.

Less concentrated preparations called tinctures are used for herbs that have a stronger taste (such as ginger or cayenne), and for those that are safest in very low doses (such as wormwood).

The recipes featured here use vodka in place of ethanol and a standard ratio of 1 part herb to 4 parts vodka. Note that while homemade remedies are often not as potent as the professional-strength remedies dispensed by a herbalist, they are still strong medicines and contain alcohol. Always store tinctures in a safe place, out of the reach of children, and always carefully observe the dosage guidelines, taking care that they are not consumed in situations where alcohol intake is ill-advised.

Herbal tinctures can be made from nearly every plant and every plant part, with the exception of mucilage-containing herbs (such as marsh mallow root and slippery elm bark), which are better extracted in cold water.

Two different methods are used to make tinctures from dried or woody herbs, and from the more delicate fresh herbs.

Fresh plant tincture

Use a kitchen scale to measure out 40g fresh herb (thyme is used here), then wash it carefully to remove any dirt. Chop the herb into small pieces, then blend to a pulp using a stick blender (add some water to aid the blending, if necessary). If you don't have a stick blender, chop the herb very finely.

1 Add 160ml vodka to the pulped herb, and then blend again before pouring the mixture into a glass jar with a screw-top lid. Seal the bottle tightly and shake vigorously.

2 Store the bottle in a cool, dark place for 10 to 14 days, shaking it once or twice a day. Strain the mixture through a piece of fine muslin.

3 Squeeze as much moisture as possible from the remaining pulp. Pour into a dark glass bottle, seal and label with the name of the herb and the date on which you prepared the tincture. Makes about 200ml.

Usage Using a dropper, dispense the required dose into 60ml water before drinking (this is usually taken three times daily).

Storage Refrigerate and store for 6 to 12 months. Make sure it is stored safely out of reach of children.

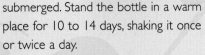

Dried herb tincture

1 Weigh 40g dried herb. Chop or grind into a coarse powder to create a larger surface area; this allows for greater penetration of the liquid. (Cinnamon quills, used here, have a large surface area so do not need chopping.) Place the herb in a large glass jar with a secure lid and pour 160ml vodka over it, ensuring that the herb is completely

submerged. Stand the bottle in a warm place for 10 to 14 days, shaking it once or twice a day.

2 Strain the mixture through a piece of fine muslin. Squeeze as much moisture as possible from the remaining pulp.

3 Pour the tincture into a dark glass bottle. Seal and label with the name of the herb and the date that you

prepared the tincture. The recipe makes about 200ml.

Usage Using a dropper, dispense the required dose into 60ml water before drinking (usually three times every day).

Storage Refrigerate the tincture and store for 6–12 months. Make sure the tincture is always stored safely out of reach of children.

Herbal creams

Herbal creams help to relieve itchy skin, soothe burns and irritations, relax tense muscles, aid wound healing and treat infection.

To make your own medicated herbal creams, start with an unscented non-greasy cream base, such as vitamin E cream. Add some herbal tincture, using a ratio of 1 part tincture to 10 parts cream, or essential oil at 1 to 2 per cent of the weight of your base cream. Stir until your cream has an even consistency. (Some essential oils are not suitable for topical use. Seek advice if you are not sure.)

Homemade herbal creams have a short life span, so make a small quantity as you need it and use it quickly. To help extend the shelf-life of your cream, add a few drops of lavender essential oil or the contents of some vitamin E capsules.

Syrups

Syrups are mostly used to ease coughs and sore throats, as the thick, sweet liquid has a very soothing effect. Commonly used herbs include marsh mallow, licorice, thyme and white horehound. Although syrups can also be made using an infusion or decoction, this recipe uses a tincture, so the result is a syrup with a stronger medicinal action.

Cough syrup from tincture

1 Stir together 100g sugar (or honey) and 50ml water in a small saucepan over a low heat until the sugar is dissolved and the mixture is thick but still runny. Remove from the heat and leave to cool. Add 50ml of the appropriate tincture; stir.

2 Pour the cough syrup into a dark glass jar and seal with a cork. Makes about 200ml.

Usage Take the correct dose directly from the spoon without diluting it.

Storage Refrigerate the syrup for up to 3 months. The sugar may crystallise as a result of the refrigeration, but the syrup will easily become liquid again if the bottle is allowed to stand in a bowl of hot water for a few minutes.

CAUTION

Occasionally, when syrups are stored, fermentation occurs, so it's best to make a small quantity at a time and to use it quickly. Syrups are traditionally stored in bottles with a cork stopper so that the bottle will not explode if fermentation does take place.

Compresses

A compress is a cloth that has been soaked in an infusion (or a diluted tincture) and applied to the skin. Compresses are used to relieve headaches and pain, disinfect wounds and soothe tired eyes. Make a fresh one each time.

Make a strong infusion of dried herb (lavender flowers are used here), using 2 to 3 teaspoons of dried herb per 250ml water.

Cover and steep for 10 to 15 minutes. Remove the cover and leave the infusion to cool to a temperature that is comfortable to the skin. Soak a facecloth or flannel in the infusion and wring out the excess water.

Usage Apply to the affected part. As the compress dries out, it can be re-soaked and reapplied.

Poultices

A poultice is a topical application of a fresh herb. It is most commonly used to encourage healing of injured muscles and bones (strains, sprains and fractures), or to draw matter out of the skin (for example, to help remove a splinter or bring a boil to a head).

1 Chop sufficient fresh herb (comfrey leaves are used here) to cover the affected body part. Place in a container and blend using a stick blender, adding a little water to aid the blending, if necessary. The finished mixture should be of a mushy consistency.

2 Place the mixture on a piece of folded muslin. Use a spatula or the back of a spoon to spread the mixture thinly so that the surface area will cover the whole area of the affected body part.

3 Rub a little body oil onto the affected body part to prevent the poultice sticking to the skin. Apply the poultice, covering the muslin with cling film to keep it in place. To make it more secure, if necessary, wrap a bandage around the poultice.

Usage Change the poultice about every couple of hours, or, if possible, leave it in place overnight.

Infused oils

Oil-soluble components can be extracted by infusing a herb in oil over an extended period of hours or days. The pure infused oil is then used for topical applications or added to a cream or ointment. Medicated infused oils are similar to (although much stronger than) culinary infused oils. They are quite different to the essential oils used in aromatherapy, which are commonly extracted from plants by distillation.

Cold infused oils

A cold infusion process (shown below) is used for fragile or delicate plant parts such as flowers, petals and leaves. Among the most popular cold infusions are calendula flowers (for eczema and other skin complaints), St John's wort flowers (for the relief of nerve pain) and lavender flowers and rosemary leaves (both to help relieve muscle soreness).

1 Pack a wide-necked, clear glass jar with fresh or dried herb (fresh calendula flowers are used here), leaving about 1cm space at the top of the jar. Pour vegetable oil (such as olive oil) over the herb until it is covered to a depth of about 5mm. Stir gently.

2 Fold some fine muslin and place on top of the oil. Seal the lid tightly and give the bottle a good shake. Store in a warm, sunny place for 3 to 10 days. Shake the bottle several times a day.

Filter the oil through fine muslin into a clean jug. Squeeze as much oil as possible through the remaining pulp. If any sediment remains in the oil, cover the jug and leave the oil to stand for a day or two until the sediment settles to the bottom.

3 Gently pour the oil into a dark glass bottle, taking care to leave the sediment layer behind. Seal; label with the name of the herb and the date on which you prepared the oil.

Usage Apply topically as is or add it to a cream or ointment.

Storage Store in a cool, dark place for up to 6 months, but discard at the first sign of rancidity or fermentation.

Hot infused oils

Hot infused oils are used for woodier, denser plant parts, and for plants with 'heating' characteristics. Popular examples are hot infused oils of cayenne (chilli pepper), black pepper and ginger, all of which are used to warm stiff, painful muscles and joints. For dried herbs, use a ratio of 1 part herb to 3 parts oil. For fresh herbs, the ratio is 1 part herb to 1.5 parts oil.

1 Coarsely chop or grind the herb (fresh birds-eye chillies are used here). Add to a saucepan or glass bowl and stir in the required quantity of oil. Place the covered saucepan in a frying pan half-filled with water (or use a double boiler). Simmer over very low heat for 2 to 3 hours. Do not allow oil to boil.

2 Allow to cool before straining through fine muslin into a clean jug. Squeeze as much oil as possible through the remaining pulp. Gently pour the oil into a dark glass bottle. Seal; label with the name of the herb and the date you prepared the oil.

Usage Apply topically or add to a cream or ointment. Do not use oils from hot-flavoured plants on inflamed or sensitive skin. Do not get them in your eyes.

Storage Store in a cool, dark place for up to 6 months, but discard at the first sign of rancidity or fermentation.

Flower essences

The healing powers of flowers are harnessed in a large range of flower essences, subtle remedies that can gently help to resolve emotional problems.

Bach Flower Essences

Dr Edward Bach was an eminent researcher in the fledgling science of immunology. But in 1930 he gave up medicine to find a way to treat both mind and body together. Bach thought that most illness was caused by mental and emotional issues, and he used this as the basis for his research, devoting his life to identifying a series of gentle natural remedies that were intended to bring both the heart and the mind back to a state of balance. He aimed to 'treat the patient, not his disease'.

Bach spent much of his time in the English countryside, where he explored the healing properties of flowers – sometimes by noting the reaction he got when he passed his hand over specific plants. Here he developed a system of preparing his remedies – or flower essences – that is still in use today.

Bach believed the subtle energetic qualities of the plant could be captured by floating freshly picked flowers in bowls of pure spring water, which were then allowed to sit in a sunny place for several hours before he used brandy to preserve and stabilise the essence.

This concentrated flower essence, called the 'stock' remedy, can be further diluted with spring water and brandy for dispensing to patients, animals or plants. The stock is also sometimes added to creams and ointments.

Dr Bach identified 38 flower essences that are still used throughout the world, as well as developing the popular Rescue Remedy (see box). Each remedy can be used either alone or in conjunction with other remedies.

Building on Bach's original work in Britain, over the years, researchers have developed ranges of essences from flowering plants that are found in other parts of the world, including Australia, New Zealand, South Africa, Hawaii and even such faraway places such as Alaska, the Himalayan mountains and the Amazon jungle.

Introducing the remedies

Here's a list of the main situations that Bach remedies are used for.
Agrimony helps cheerful people who are secretly troubled to deal with their underlying problems.
Aspen supports people who are anxious or worried, but have been unable to

Clematis (*Clematis vitalba*) may also encourage great creativity and make you more alert.

identify exactly what it is that is frightening them.
Beech fosters a spirit of compassion in those who are intolerant of people who are different to them.
Centaury helps people who over-extend themselves helping others to learn to say 'no' so they don't wear themselves out.
Cerato boosts self-confidence, teaching you to listen to your own counsel instead of others' opinions.
Cherry plum is for people who fear for their sanity, who feel they are heading for a nervous breakdown, or who are frightened they will harm themselves or others.
Chestnut bud teaches you to learn from your experiences, so you don't repeat the same mistakes again.
Chicory is for people who risk stifling their relationships by clinging too tightly to their loved ones.
Clematis brings those who are always dreaming about the future back down to earth to focus on the present.
Crab apple helps you to heal yourself of any feelings of unworthiness and uncleanliness.
Elm helps people who are overwhelmed by responsibilities to feel able to cope .
Gentian provides energy and enthusiasm for people who have suffered discouraging setbacks.

Star of Bethlehem (*Ornithogalum umbellatum*) is a perennial bulbous plant with a delicate flower.

Gorse renews optimism in those who feel hopeless, and enables them to see the positive steps they can take.

Heather helps self-centred people who constantly seek attention from others to become less needy.

Holly helps release anger, aggression, jealousy and hatred, and encourages a more positive, open outlook on life.

Honeysuckle is for people who are stuck in the past, re-living either their past mistakes or past happiness.

Hornbeam supports people who procrastinate because they are so overwhelmed by tasks before them that they feel exhausted before they begin.

Impatiens is for critical, irritable or impulsive people who are easily frustrated by the slowness of others.

Larch builds self-confidence in those people who consider themselves inferior to others, and helps overcome an expectation of failure.

Mimulus helps heal fears and phobias, ranging from anxiety about public speaking to fear of illness or death.

Mustard brings clarity and light during times of despair and despondency.

Oak helps determined, driven people to realise when to sit back and take a rest, or to realise that their goal is neither achievable nor worth striving for.

Olive brings renewed energy to those who are exhausted by struggle and ready to give up.

Pine helps those who feel guilty about past failing to put it behind them.

Sprigs of cherry plum (*Prunus cerasifera*) in blossom.

Rescue Remedy

Rescue Remedy, the most popular of Dr Bach's creations can be used in a number of stressful situations to create a greater feeling of calmness and control. The remedy is a combination of 5 flower essences, each with its own benefits: cherry plum (to stop irrational thoughts and lack of self control), clematis (to focus attention and counteract faintness), impatiens (reduces irritation and impatience), rock rose (relieves terror and panic) and star of Bethlehem (reduces shock). It is mostly taken by mouth, but can also be added to a bath, applied to the wrists or forehead, or applied as a cream.

Rescue Remedy is still made using the method developed by Dr Bach over 70 years ago. So-called 'vitalised water' is obtained from flowers, plants or shrubs using heat from either the sun or through boiling. The water is mixed with spring water and brandy to produce the 'mother tincture'. This is diluted with 27 per cent grape alcohol to produce the final product and the Rescue Remedy is then bottled.

Red chestnut releases excessive anxiety or fear for the wellbeing of others.

Rock rose brings calm during times of terror, panic or extreme fear.

Rock water is for those who deny themselves pleasure in favour of some higher goal and feel a failure when they cannot maintain their own impossibly high standards.

Scleranthus helps people who dither when making decisions to feel confidence in their convictions.

Star of Bethlehem heals feelings of shock, regardless of whether the unpleasant event occurred recently or in the distant past.

Sweet chestnut strengthens those who feel they are in a hopeless situation and cannot go on.

Vervain brings flexibility and detachment to people who zealously try to convert others to their own beliefs, and who can become quite worked up by their own efforts.

Vine eases the need to dominate and control, and is for those who are prone to aggression and the abuse of power.

Walnut helps you confidently stand your ground when those around you have different opinions, and eases you through times of change.

Water violet helps isolated or aloof people to re-connect with others.

White chestnut calms an overly busy mind, helping to settle circular or repetitive thoughts and allowing concentration and focus to return.

Wild oat helps those who can't decide on a direction in life to be able to identify their path.

Wild rose rekindles motivation in people who no longer strive for change because they have become resigned to their particular lot in life.

Willow helps people who feel overly sorry for themselves and resent the success and happiness of others to return to a more positive outlook.

Medicinal herbs

Modern botanical medicine has become truly international and herbalists now have access to the most effective herbs from all corners of the globe.

Albizia

Albizia lebbeck

Part used Stem bark

The traditional Ayurvedic applications for albizia include a range of inflammatory and allergic skin and respiratory conditions. Laboratory research indicates that it does indeed have anti-allergenic properties with particular benefits for mast cells, which play a major role in allergic reactions. For this reason so it may help some people become less sensitive to substances to which they have allergies.

Andrographis

Andrographis paniculata

Parts used Leaves, aerial parts

Andrographis features in the traditional medicine of China, Thailand, India and Korea. An extremely bitter herb, it is used as a digestive tonic in Ayurvedic medicine. In traditional Chinese medicine, its cooling properties mean that it is used for dispelling heat and treating infections and toxins. Andrographis also has immune-stimulating properties, and is used to treat colds and flu and their symptoms.

Astragalus

Astragalus membranaceus

Part used Roots

One of the most important *qi* tonics in traditional Chinese medicine, astragalus or milk vetch is taken to enhance vitality and increase energy. It has potent immune-boosting properties, so it may be prescribed to build resistance against infections as well as for helping the body's defences cope with aggressive anti-cancer treatments such as chemo- and radiotherapy. Herbalists also prescribe astragalus for a wide range of other conditions, including liver and kidney dysfunction, heart problems and to aid recovery from blood loss (especially after childbirth).

Buchu

Agathosma betulina

Part used Leaves

The South African herb buchu is mainly regarded as a remedy for the urinary tract, although traditionally it was also used to treat digestion and joint problems. Its volatile essential oil has antiseptic properties and is considered to be responsible for the herb's benefits in treating infections of the kidneys, bladder, urethra and prostate. Buchu also has diuretic actions, so it is indicated for fluid retention.

Cat's claw

Uncaria tomentosa, U. guaianensis

Part used Vine bark

Cat's claw grows in tropical South and Central America and takes its name from the shape of the long thorns that help it to climb over other plants in the jungle. It has been used for hundreds of years by Peruvians to treat inflammatory conditions, such as arthritis, asthma and skin problems, and is also a traditional remedy for infections, fatigue and cancer. Laboratory studies attribute it with a number of immune-stimulating and anti-inflammatory properties, which may be behind many traditional applications but little research has been conducted in humans.

Dang shen is known in English as bonnet bellflower. It should not be confused with Dan shen which is a kind of sage.

Dang shen

Codonopsis pilosula

Part used Roots

Chinese herbalists regard dang shen as a gentler version of the more famous stress and energy tonic, Korean ginseng. This distinction means that it can be prescribed for patients who are frail or debilitated, for whom ginseng is considered to be too stimulating. Dang shen is also traditionally used for treating digestive, respiratory and cardiac problems (especially when caused by stress) and as a nourishing blood tonic for nursing mothers and other patients who may be suffering from anaemia.

Cat's claw has hook-like thorns, which enable it to scramble over other plants.

Devil's claw
Harpagophytum procumbens
Part used Tubers

Devil's claw grows in the grasslands of southern Africa and has been used there as a topical treatment for ulcers and wounds, and taken internally for fevers, allergies, digestive problems and as a pain reliever. Numerous scientific studies confirm its benefits, most notably as an effective analgesic and anti-inflammatory for arthritis pain and backache. Some studies have shown devil's claw to be as effective as pharmaceutical pain killers and anti-inflammatory drugs.

Goldenseal
Hydrastis canadensis
Part used Rhizomes

Goldenseal is named for its rhizome's characteristic yellow colour, and it was used as both a dye and a medicine by Native Americans. It is still beloved by herbalists today, who regard it as a bitter digestive stimulant, an astringent tonic for the mucous membranes and a potent broad-spectrum antimicrobial remedy. Some of its most medically important alkaloids are also present in other plants (such as barberry and Indian barberry), and these are now largely used in its place, as golden seal has become endangered by over-harvesting.

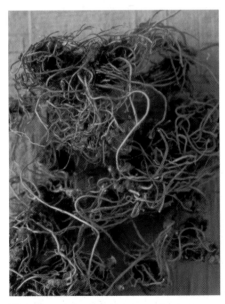

The Cherokees used to pound together rhizomes of goldenseal with bear fat to make an insect repellent.

Each seed in the milk thistle bears a tuft of white hairs that help it to become airborne.

Milk thistle
Silybum marianum
Part used Seeds

Milk thistle has such a remarkable ability to prevent and repair liver damage that certain constituents are sometimes used intravenously to treat poisoning caused by the death cap mushroom. It is also employed against more frequently encountered toxins, such as alcohol and environmental pollutants, and can help digestive and cholesterol problems, thanks to its effects as a liver and gall bladder tonic. The constituent silymarin is considered to be responsible for many of the herb's medicinal benefits.

Pau d'arco
Tabebuia impetiginosa
Part used Inner bark

In the 1960s, pau d'arco developed an international reputation as a cancer cure, but it had been used as a traditional medicine in Brazil for hundreds of years before that. Some of the herb's constituents have been shown in a laboratory setting to inhibit the growth and activity of tumour cells. An immuno-stimulant action that may further help the body fight cancer (as well as fungal diseases and other infections) has also been documented. However, further extensive research will be required before its potential can be fully understood.

Senna
Senna alexandrina syn.
Cassia angustifolia
Part used Leaves, pods

Senna's purgative action is due to its content of anthraquinone glycosides, which stimulate intestinal peristalsis, triggering a bowel movement some 12 hours later. Probably the most popular laxative herb, senna has an effect that is strong and reliable, if a little drastic. Habitual use may lead to 'lazy bowel syndrome', in which the colon becomes unable to function without the laxative.

You can use dried senna pods, available at health food stores, to make an infusion.

Uva-ursi (Bearberry)
Arctostaphylos uva-ursi
Part used Leaves

Uva-ursi's antimicrobial properties are specifically indicated for urinary tract infections, and seem to be more effective when the urine is alkaline. Since many urinary tract infections cause the urine the become more acidic, the herb is sometimes prescribed with an alkalising substance (such as bicarbonate of soda) to maximise its effects. The compounds responsible for the antibiotic action are not present in uva-ursi itself, but are formed from its content of phenolic glycosides after the herb is ingested.
CAUTION
• Do not take the herbs on these pages if you are pregnant or breastfeeding, except with the advice of a qualified medical herbalist.

Sore throats, colds and flu

The choice of an appropriate remedy to relieve a cold or a bout of flu is determined by the symptoms that you are experiencing. The sniffles, sore throat and blocked nose of a typical head cold demand a different solution to the more serious debilitation and aching limbs that you will get with a severe dose of flu.

Sage
Salvia officinalis

Sore throat soother Certain compounds in sage have been documented as having antimicrobial properties, which may help to explain the herb's traditional use as a gargle for sore throats and tonsillitis.

Dosage Make a strong infusion of dried sage; use as a gargle several times per day, as required.

Yarrow
Achillea millefolium

Fever remedy Native Americans traditionally used yarrow to treat feverish conditions, and modern herbalists still follow their lead. It is often called for in the early stages of cold or flu, and is commonly combined with elder flower, which is also considered helpful in lowering high temperatures.

Dosage Infuse 1 teaspoon (4g) dried yarrow (flowers, seeds and leaves) in boiling water; drink 3 cups a day.

Elder
Sambucus nigra

Fever and flu relief Elder flowers are used to treat upper respiratory infections with fevers or sinus congestion. The berries have long been used to make cordials and wines, but more recent research in Israel has established that a commercial preparation of elderberries, standardised for its content of anthocyanins – the purple compounds that give the berries their colour – helps relieve the symptoms of flu and shorten the duration of the infection. The researchers in Israel hypothesise that

Elder flowers and berries have many applications in natural beauty preparations and in cooking.

the extract works by altering the surface of the virus, preventing it from taking hold in the body.

Dosage Infuse 1 to 2 teaspoons (2 to 5g) dried elder flowers in boiling water; drink 3 cups per day. Alternatively, look for a commercial preparation made from elderberries and follow the manufacturer's instructions.

Andrographis
Andrographis paniculata

Clinically proven to reduce symptoms of respiratory infection Used in many parts of Asia for the treatment of infectious and feverish conditions, andrographis has been investigated in several clinical trials. These studies document improvements in symptoms of cold, flu and pharyngo-tonsillitis, such as fatigue, sore throat, muscle aches, shivering, excessive nasal secretions, sinusitis and headache, and suggest that andrographis may also reduce the amount of sick leave that patients need in order to recover. Like echinacea, astragalus and garlic, andrographis also appears to have some preventative qualities and may help to reduce the incidence of colds.

Dosage For the best results, take andrographis as soon as possible after the onset of cold or flu symptoms. Look for commercial preparations standardised for their content of andrographolides, which are considered responsible for much of the herb's activity, and follow the manufacturers' instructions. Doses of up to 6g dried herb per day are normally used to treat infection.

Garlic

Allium sativum

Broad-spectrum infection fighter
In vitro research has shown that garlic and several of its constituents have broad-spectrum activity against a wide variety of disease-causing organisms, including strains of the virus that causes flu. Garlic also helps fight colds and flu by enhancing the activity of immune cells and, when taken prophylactically – that is, as a preventative medicine – may help protect you from catching a cold.

🍃 **Dosage** To treat infection, take up to 2 cloves fresh garlic per day. Chop them and leave them to sit for 5 to 10 minutes before cooking with them. This will allow the medicinally active component allicin to form. For prevention, aim for a dose of up to 3 cloves per week, or buy a commercial preparation that provides a standardised quantity of either alliin or allicin, and follow the manufacturer's instructions.

Thyme

Thymus vulgaris

Antimicrobial and antispasmodic
The essential oil of thyme is regarded as one of nature's most potent antimicrobial substances, so herbalists commonly prescribe the plant to help

resolve respiratory tract infections, such as colds, flu, tonsillitis and laryngitis. It also has antispasmodic properties, so it can be used to help reduce coughing.

🍃 **Dosage** Infuse up to 1 teaspoon (4g) dried thyme leaves or 2 teaspoons fresh leaves in boiling water; drink 3 cups per day.

White horehound

Marrubium vulgare

Loosens the mucus in unproductive coughs White horehound has expectorant properties, helping to break up thickened phlegm and encouraging you to cough to remove it from the respiratory tract. It is particularly favoured by herbalists when treating coughs that are dry, hacking and unproductive.

🍃 **Dosage** Infuse up to 1 teaspoon (2g) dried flowering tops of horehound in boiling water; drink 3 cups per day.

Marsh mallow

Althaea officinalis

Soothing expectorant for irritated airways Both the roots and leaves of the marsh mallow plant can be used to treat coughs. However, herbalists prefer the root as it has a higher mucilage content, which is responsible for the herb's soothing actions on the respiratory mucous membranes. Marsh mallow is traditionally used as a remedy for the relief of irritated and inflamed throats and airways, and to help expel mucus when lungs are congested.

🍃 **Dosage** Infuse 2 to 5g dried marsh mallow root in cold (not hot) water, and steep for 8 hours to release mucilage; drink up to 3 cups per day

CAUTIONS

• Exceeding the recommended doses of yarrow, andrographis or white horehound may cause side-effects and should be avoided.

• If you are taking blood-thinning or blood pressure medications, don't take garlic, andrographis or yarrow. Stop taking any of these herbs at least 2 weeks before undergoing surgery.

• Marsh mallow may interfere with the absorption of other medicines, so separate doses by 2 hours.

• Marsh mallow and andrographis may affect blood sugar levels, so should not be taken by people with diabetes, except under professional supervision.

• Don't use yarrow if you are allergic to members of the Asteraceae family of plants (for example, chicory, daisies, echinacea and chrysanthemums).

• Do not eat isolated essential oil of thyme. Use only the fresh or dried herb.

• Uncooked fresh elderberries may cause diarrhoea and vomiting. Use only the dried or cooked berries.

• Andrographis may exacerbate pre-existing cases of heartburn and gastric ulcer. Garlic may cause minor gastric upset in some people, but these symptoms are less likely when the herb has been cooked.

• Yarrow may very occasionally increase sensitivity to sunlight. If you develop this symptom, stop using it immediately and seek medical advice.

• Do not use large doses of elder flower over long periods of time.

• Black horehound (*Ballota nigra*) should not be used as a substitute for white horehound (*Marrubium vulgare*).

• With the exception of normal culinary quantities of sage, garlic and thyme, do not take the herbs on these pages if you are pregnant or breastfeeding, except with professional advice.

The main active constituent of garlic is allicin, which is released when you crush fresh cloves.

Immune support

It is increasingly clear that we can improve our immune system with diet. Protect yourself against disease-causing bacteria and viruses with immune-stimulating herbs.

Echinacea
Echinacea sp.
Strengthens resistance to infection
Laboratory studies into several different echinacea species and constituents isolated from the plant have identified a variety of immunological effects, and seem to validate the use of the herb to support immunity. The results of human clinical trials have not always demonstrated the anticipated effects, however, causing the popular use of echinacea for the prevention of colds and flu to become controversial.

But a meta-analysis published in 2007 may go some way to clarifying the situation. In this study, researchers pooled the results of 14 clinical studies. They estimated that taking echinacea decreased the likelihood of developing a cold by 58 per cent and, that when a cold did occur, its duration was shortened by about 30 hours.

Dosage The most appropriate dose of echinacea depends on both the plant part and the species used, but it is important to start taking the herb as soon as possible after symptoms develop. Preparations made from the root of *Echinacea angustifolia* or *E. pallida* are generally taken at doses of about 1g taken 3 times daily to treat colds or, in lower doses, as a preventative. For *E. purpurea*, either the whole plant (including roots) or the aerial parts may be used. The dose is up to 2g taken 3 times daily as an infusion of dried herb, or 3ml juice made from the fresh plant and taken 3 times daily.

To make the juice, liquefy fresh aerial parts of *E. purpurea* with a little water using a home juicer or stick blender. The juice doesn't store well, so make only as much as you need to use immediately.

Astragalus
Astragalus membranaceus
Improves immunity in chronic conditions In traditional Chinese medicine, the herb astragalus is attributed with warming properties and is regarded as a lung tonic. It is used for patients with longstanding illnesses and for those who are susceptible to recurrent infection, and appears to improve the functioning of the immune system so that the body can better defend itself against pathogens – especially viruses. Astragalus is a good herb to try if you're run-down and tired and repeatedly catch colds or flu since, in addition to its immune-boosting properties, it is also traditionally used to raise overall vitality and energy.

Dosage Boil 3 to 10g dried astragalus root in 180ml water for 10 minutes before straining; drink the decoction in 2 doses during the day. Alternatively, take tablets or capsules according to the manufacturer's instructions, up to a maximum dose of 7.5g dried root per day.

CAUTIONS
• Do not use echinacea if you are allergic to members of the Asteraceae family of plants (for example, daisies, chrysanthemums, chicory and chamomile); people with pollen allergies should also take care, as some preparations may contain pollen. Cases of contact dermatitis have also occasionally been reported.
• Talk to your doctor before taking echinacea if you have an autoimmune condition, such as lupus, or a progressive disease, such as multiple sclerosis or HIV/AIDS. Echinacea should also not be used by patients who are taking immunosuppressive medications.
• Note that astragalus is recommended for chronic (longstanding) rather than acute infections; discontinue use if you develop an infection while taking it.
• The resistance-boosting effects of astragalus may help reduce the side-effects of some immunosuppressive cancer treatments, such as radio- and chemotherapy, but it should only be used in this way in consultation with your doctor.
• Do not use the herbs on this page if you are pregnant or breastfeeding, except under the advice of a medical herbalist.

Three species of echinacea are cultivated for medicinal purposes: *Echinacea angustifolia*, *E. pallida* and *E. purpurea* (shown above). Their vivid, drooping flowerheads also make very attractive additions to the flower garden.

Hay fever and sinusitis

A number of herbs including horseradish and eyebright can provide relief from, and may even prevent, the debilitating pain of sinusitis and the symptoms of hay fever.

Horseradish
Armoracia rusticana
Relieves congested sinuses If you've ever tasted horseradish (or its Japanese cousin wasabi), you'll know that it is an effective decongestant, clearing the sinuses and easing breathing almost immediately after ingestion. This effect is due to the ability of compounds called glucosinolates to liquefy thickened mucus, making it easier to clear and relieving the pressure and head pain associated with sinus congestion. These are the same compounds that give horseradish its spicy taste. They also have antimicrobial properties, so horseradish helps fight sinus infections, too. In clinical trials in Europe, researchers found that a combination of horseradish and nasturtium (which also contains glucosinolates) was just as effective in treating sinus infection as antibiotics but produced fewer side-effects.

Dosage Use horseradish paste or wasabi as a condiment. Alternatively, take commercially prepared tablets or capsules (with or without nasturtium) at a dose of up to 3 g per day.

Eyebright
Euphrasia officinalis
Traditional remedy for catarrh
Eyebright is traditionally used for respiratory conditions with watery discharges, so it's an ideal herb to take when you are suffering from hay fever symptoms, such as constant sneezing, a runny nose and watery or irritated eyes. It can also be used for colds and flu with similar symptoms.

Dosage Infuse up to 1 teaspoon (1 to 4g) dried aerial parts of eyebright in boiling water; drink 3 cups per day.

Albizia
Albizia lebbeck
Ayurvedic anti-allergy herb
Albizia lebbeck has a long history of use in Ayurvedic medicine, where it is prescribed for allergies and inflammatory conditions, including hay fever, asthma, hives and allergic conjunctivitis. Studies suggest that albizia works by stabilising the cells that release histamine and other allergic mediators, thereby relieving allergic tendencies and helping to manage the symptoms of allergies.

Dosage Look for commercial preparations providing the equivalent of 3 to 6g per day of the dried stem bark, and take it according to the manufacturer's instructions.

Perilla
Perilla frutescens syn. P. ocimoides
May prevent hay fever symptoms
Also known as shiso or beefsteak plant, perilla is a common ingredient in the traditional diet of Japan. Scientists there have also carried our crucial work to identify its potential for the prevention of hay fever symptoms. Both the leaf and the seed of perilla contain compounds that help reduce allergy symptoms, such as sneezing, itchiness of the nose and scratchy, watery eyes. Preliminary research suggests that the herb (and particularly the constituent rosmarinic acid) may help seasonal allergy sufferers experience fewer hay fever symptoms during periods of high-pollen exposure.

Dosage Take up to 9g of dried leaf per day in tablet or capsule form. If you suffer from hay fever on a seasonal basis, it may help to start taking a dose of perilla about a month before the hay fever season begins.

Horseradish root is rich in vitamin C. It was once eaten by sailors on long ocean voyages to prevent scurvy.

CAUTIONS
• Horseradish may irritate the digestive tract in some people and should be avoided by those with gastric ulcers. It may also cause irritation and burning if it comes into contact with the skin or eyes.

• If you suffer from thyroid disease or are taking blood-thinning medications, do not take horseradish at doses higher than normal culinary intake, except under professional supervision.

• Albizia and perilla should not be taken at the same time as pharmaceutical anti-allergy medications (such as antihistamines) except under professional supervision, as the effects of the drugs may be enhanced.

• Except for normal culinary quantities of horseradish, do not use the herbs on this page if you are pregnant or breastfeeding, except with the advice of a medical herbalist.

Indigestion

The burning pain and discomfort of indigestion or dyspepsia can spoil the enjoyment of the most delicious meal, but several effective herbal tonics can help to ease it.

Slippery elm
Ulmus rubra

Soothing and healing The mucilage in slippery elm bark forms a gel that lines the gastrointestinal tract, acting as an anti-inflammatory and encouraging healing. Slippery elm is an ideal herb for indigestion sufferers, because the gel helps protect the stomach lining from the effects of excess acid.

Dosage Stir 1 teaspoon powdered slippery elm bark into water and drink 15 to 30 minutes before meals. (As slippery elm trees are becoming increasingly rare, it is preferable to buy bark in powdered form rather than collect it yourself.)

Meadowsweet
Filipendula ulmaria

Acid balance Meadowsweet relieves indigestion, reflux and other problems caused by over-acidity. Taken over a period of several weeks, it helps to normalise stomach acid production while soothing inflamed gastric tissues and promoting healing.

Dosage Infuse 4 to 6g dried leaves and flowering tops of meadowsweet in boiling water; drink 3 cups per day.

Gentian
Gentiana lutea

Stimulates digestion Bitter-flavoured gentian improves digestion by stimulating the bitter taste receptors on the tongue, triggering the release of saliva, gastric acid and other digestive fluids. Gentian helps with many of the symptoms that can occur due to poor digestion, including heartburn, flatulence, nausea and poor appetite. It is best taken before meals over several weeks, but a single dose after a heavy meal can also be beneficial.

Dosage Take 2 to 5 drops gentian root tincture in water, or infuse 1g dried root and rhizome in boiling water. Take gentian 3 times per day, preferably 15 to 30 minutes before meals.

Anise
Pimpinella anisum

Relieves fullness and bloating Anise helps to relieve the discomfort and pain of indigestion, and is particularly beneficial when wind or bloating are also present. Other aromatic herbs – such as caraway, fennel and dill – can be used in the same way.

Dosage Grind up to 1 teaspoon (2g) ripe anise seeds to release the essential oil before infusing in boiling water. Drink up to 3 cups per day.

CAUTIONS

• See a doctor if you have indigestion or heartburn or if vomiting occurs.

In the Middle Ages, the flowers of meadowsweet were a popular flavouring for both wine and beer.

Herbal aperitifs

Many popular aperitifs are based on traditionally used bitter herbal medicines, such as wormwood, which not only stimulate stomach secretions but also act as tonics for the liver and gall bladder. Many other aperitifs, including ouzo from Greece and pastis from France, are dominated by the liquorice-like aroma of anise or star anise. Taking a dose of one of the bitter or aromatic herbs before your meal can have the same benefits; try peppermint, fennel, ginger or globe artichoke.

• A heart attack can sometimes mimic the symptoms of indigestion. You should call for an ambulance immediately if the 'indigestion' symptoms are accompanied by a sharp pain that radiates down the arm or up the neck, or by severe dizziness, weakness or shortness of breath.

• Slippery elm may interfere with the absorption of other medicines, so separate doses by 2 hours.

• Do not take meadowsweet if you are taking blood-thinning or anticoagulant medications (including aspirin), or if you are allergic to salicylates.

• Do not confuse anise and star anise.

• Do not take gentian if you suffer from peptic or duodenal ulcer.

• With the exception of normal culinary quantities of anise, do not use the herbs on this page if you are pregnant or breastfeeding, except with the advice of a doctor or medical herbalist.

Nausea

Whether it's caused by a 24-hour tummy bug, a migraine, a case of food poisoning or a bout of seasickness, nausea can make you feel miserable. These herbs can ease it.

Ginger
Zingiber officinale

Settles the stomach If you're feeling queasy, try ginger first. Several clinical trials support its traditional reputation as an effective treatment and preventative for nausea from a variety of sources, including morning sickness, motion sickness and post-operative vomiting and nausea. For more information on ginger and morning sickness, see *Pregnancy*, pages 242-43.

Dosage Add 20 to 30 drops ginger tincture to water, or infuse ½ teaspoon powdered ginger or 1 to 2 teaspoons grated fresh ginger root in boiling water; take 3 times per day. For children over 4 years old, add 10 to 15 drops of ginger tincture to lemonade or ginger beer.

To prevent seasickness and travel sickness, take 1g dried ginger 30 minutes before the trip starts and every few hours during the journey. The same dose can be taken before surgery to reduce post-operative nausea (but discuss this with the surgeon first – see *Cautions*).

Peppermint
Mentha × piperita

Antispasmodic Peppermint is particularly helpful when nausea is accompanied by churning sensations in the stomach or gripping pains in the bowel. Its antispasmodic actions in the gastrointestinal tract are due to its content of a menthol-rich essential oil.

Dosage Add 10 to 15 drops peppermint tincture to water, or infuse 1 teaspoon fresh or dried aerial parts in boiling water; take 3 to 4 times per day. *Caution* Children over 4 years should take a third to a half of the adult dose.

German chamomile
Matricaria recutita

Eases anxiety The essential oil that gives chamomile its characteristic smell also imparts antispasmodic and anti-inflammatory properties, while its bitter principles help stimulate the secretion of gastric juices. This combination of actions, along with the herb's renowned calming effects, make chamomile an especially useful herb for the treatment of nausea, especially when it is due to, or accompanied by, anxiety and emotional upset.

Dosage Infuse 1 to 2 teaspoons dried chamomile flowers in boiling water; drink 3 to 4 cups per day. Children over the age of 4 years can take a third to a half of the adult dose.

CAUTIONS

• In some cases, nausea and vomiting may be symptomatic of underlying disease. See your doctor if symptoms are severe, prolonged or occur frequently.
• Medical attention should also be sought if nausea is accompanied by severe abdominal pain, confusion, headache or a stiff neck, or is triggered by a head injury.
• Dehydration can occur as a consequence of vomiting. Watch out for symptoms such as dry lips and mouth, decreased urination and rapid pulse, especially in children. Rehydrate using an electrolyte replacement supplement (available from pharmacies), and seek medical advice immediately.
• Ginger should not be taken for 2 weeks prior to undergoing surgery. In consultation with your physician, a single dose can be taken just prior to surgery to reduce post-operative nausea.

German chamomile grows wild throughout Europe where it has long been used medicinally.

• Don't use peppermint if you suffer from gastro-oesophageal reflux disease (GORD) or hiatus hernia, as its antispasmodic effect may worsen your symptoms by relaxing the oesophageal sphincter and allowing reflux to occur more readily. Ginger is also inappropriate in cases of reflux and should not be used medicinally if you suffer from either a gastric ulcer or gallstones.
• Don't use chamomile if you have an allergy to members of the Asteraceae family of plants (for example daisies, chicory, chrysanthemums and echinacea).
• With the exception of normal culinary quantities of peppermint and German chamomile, do not use any of the herbs on this page if you are pregnant or breastfeeding, except with the advice of a doctor or medical herbalist.

Wind, bloating and flatulence

We all produce a certain amount of wind every day, but it can be uncomfortable and embarrassing if it occurs to excess. Peppermint, dill and caraway can all offer relief.

Peppermint
Mentha x piperita

Irritable bowel relief Long known to relieve wind and gastro-intestinal spasm, peppermint is an ideal remedy for people with irritable bowel syndrome (IBS), a condition characterised by abdominal pain, bloating and excessive flatulence. Several clinical trials support the use of peppermint to relieve the symptoms of IBS, especially when taken as enteric-coated peppermint oil capsules that break down in the bowel, where their antispasmodic effects are most needed.

Dosage Add 10 to 15 drops peppermint tincture to water, or infuse 1 teaspoon fresh or dried aerial parts in boiling water; take 3 to 4 times per day. Alternatively, use commercial peppermint oil capsules and follow the manufacturer's instructions.

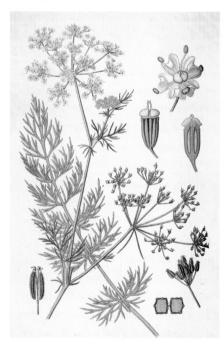

Caraway is used with fennel and dill to make an infusion for intestinal problems.

Caraway
Carum carvi

Aromatic antispasmodic Caraway is another herbal medicine that has been traditionally used to relieve wind, bloating and flatulence. Like peppermint, it helps to decrease spasm in the muscles of the digestive tract, and the essential oils of the two herbs are sometimes combined in commercial products.

Dosage Grind up to 1 teaspoon (2g) caraway seeds to release the essential oil before infusing them in boiling water. Drink up to 3 cups per day. Alternatively, use commercial caraway oil capsules (often combined with peppermint) and follow the manufacturer's instructions.

Dill
Anethum graveolens

Soothes colic Of the many herbs with calming actions on the digestive system, dill is the preferred remedy for the treatment of colic in babies and is equally beneficial for adults suffering from uncomfortable wind pain. As with other digestive remedies, it is the herb's essential oil that is responsible for its actions as a gastrointestinal antispasmodic, and has the effect of releasing wind and reducing pain and discomfort.

Dosage Grind up to 2 teaspoons (4g) dill seeds to release the essential oil before infusing them in boiling water. Drink up to 3 cups per day to relieve bloating and flatulence in yourself or colic in a baby who is breastfeeding. When using with babies over the age of 3 months, allow the infusion to cool and give 1 to 3 teaspoons at a time up to 4 times a day.

Star anise and colic

Chinese star anise (*Illicium verum*) has long been used in Spain, Latin America and the Caribbean as a treatment for colic, but following a number of serious adverse reactions in infants and young children, this practice should now be avoided. Some of the cases have been attributed to contamination by the related Japanese star anise (*Illicium anisatum*), which is toxic. Chinese star anise is also considered responsible for at least some of the reactions and even in low doses may cause severe reactions in young children.

CAUTIONS
• Products containing the essential oils of peppermint and/or caraway are not recommended for infants, children, pregnant or breastfeeding women, or for people with gall bladder, kidney or gastro-oesophageal disease. Do not exceed the recommended dose.
• If you take prescribed medicines, talk to a doctor before taking peppermint oil, as it may interact with some drugs.
• Caraway can cause an allergic reaction. Stop using it if you experience adverse effects, such as diarrhoea or runny nose.
• Do not use the herbs on this page in greater than culinary quantities if you are pregnant or breastfeeding, except with the advice of a medical herbalist.

Constipation and haemorrhoids

Ongoing problems with constipation can lead to haemorrhoids and an increased risk of more serious illness including diverticular disease and bowel cancer.

Witch hazel is native to North America, where it was used medicinally by Native American tribes.

Psyllium

Plantago ovata, P. psyllium

Soluble fibre supplement Mucilage-rich psyllium husks are a valuable source of soluble fibre, often lacking in the Western diet. In fact, psyllium is one of the few types of fibre supplement that have been proven to aid in the management of chronic problems with constipation.

Dosage Psyllium husks are available in tablets, capsules and soluble powders, and should be taken according to the manufacturer's instructions. A teaspoon of the powdered husks can also be sprinkled on fruit or breakfast cereal once a day. Every dose of psyllium should be taken with a large glass of water.

Chinese rhubarb

Rheum palmatum

Strong laxative Chinese rhubarb root is a strong laxative with a potent content of anthraquinone glycosides. In traditional Chinese medicine it is prescribed for constipation and is considered to promote bile secretion, improve appetite and act as a liver and gall bladder tonic.

Dosage Boil 20g dried or 40g fresh Chinese rhubarb rhizome in 750ml water. Simmer until reduced to 500ml. Take 50 to 100ml of the decoction with your evening meal.

Yellow dock

Rumex crispus

Gentle cleanser Yellow dock is a gentle digestive stimulant that is excellent for sluggish liver or bowel function. Though it does contain anthraquinone glycosides (see box), its laxative action is less marked than that of Chinese rhubarb or other herbal laxatives such as senna and cascara.

Dosage Boil 1 to 4g dried yellow dock root in a cup of water for 10 minutes; drink the decoction up to 3 times daily.

Witch hazel

Hamamelis virginiana

Haemorrhoid healer In several clinical trials, topical applications of witch hazel have been shown to be as effective as other medications (including corticosteroids) for the relief of the pain, itching and bleeding of haemorrhoids. The herb is also traditionally taken internally for the treatment of haemorrhoids, but its astringent nature makes it unsuitable for people who have a tendency to be constipated.

Dosage Rub witch hazel gel, ointment or tincture into the affected area once a day. A medical herbalist can determine whether internal use of witch hazel is appropriate for your condition.

A natural trigger

Laxative herbs tend to contain varying quantities of compounds called anthraquinone glycosides, which travel through the digestive system to the intestine, where they stimulate peristalsis and trigger a bowel movement. Since this effect usually occurs about 8 hours after the herbs are consumed, they are traditionally taken in the evening, with the objective of developing a regular bowel habit in the mornings.

CAUTIONS

- Anthraquinone-containing herbs should not be taken in excessive doses, or for more than 10 days at a time.
- Do not use herbs to treat constipation in children, or if you are pregnant, breast-feeding, have undiagnosed abdominal pain or an intestinal or gall bladder blockage.
- If you suffer from arthritis or kidney or urinary tract disease consult a medical herbalist before using Chinese rhubarb.
- People with an intestinal illness should only use herbal medicines on the advice of a medical herbalist.
- Psyllium may interfere with the absorption of other medicines, so separate doses by 2 hours.
- Drink lots of water when using psyllium, as choking has been reported in people who have taken psyllium powders without adequate fluids.
- Rhubarb leaves are toxic.
- Topical applications of witch hazel may cause contact allergy. Stop using it immediately if you are concerned.
- Except for topical applications of witch hazel, do not use these herbs if you are pregnant or breast-feeding, except with the advice of a medical herbalist.

Liver and gall bladder support

Your liver and gall bladder are vital parts of your digestive system and for the removal of toxic substances from the body. Look after them, so they can look after you.

Milk thistle

Silybum marianum syn.
Carduus marianus

Liver protection and repair Seeds of milk thistle (or St Mary's thistle) contain a group of anti-oxidant compounds referred to collectively as silymarin.

Studies show that silymarin helps protect liver cells from damage and aids the repair or replacement of injured cells. Under professional supervision, milk thistle and silymarin can aid the management of a wide range of serious liver problems, including non-alcoholic and alcoholic liver disease and some forms of hepatitis.

Milk thistle can also be used to prevent or treat the effects of overindulgence in alcohol and fatty foods, to prevent liver damage from exposure to toxins, and for headaches and skin problems that are associated with poor liver function.

Dosage Put ½ teaspoon of the seed and leaves in 1 cup of boiling water. Infuse for 15 minutes. Take ½ cup up to 3 times a day.

Schisandra

Schisandra chinensis

Liver support Although there is less scientific evidence to support its use, schisandra may have similar liver-protecting properties to milk thistle. Several laboratory studies have demonstrated a number of anti-oxidant effects in schisanndra and suggest that it, too, has the ability to prevent cell damage by harmful substances and to reduce some of the symptoms that are associated with liver disease.

The white veins on the leaves of milk thistle were said to be milk from the Virgin's breast.

Dosage Take the equivalent of 500 to 1500mg of the dried fruit 3 times per day, in either tablet or tincture form.

Dandelion root

Taraxacum officinale

Traditional hepatic tonic As a bitter herb, dandelion root stimulates gastrointestinal function and is traditionally used for minor digestive ailments, especially sluggish liver and gall bladder function, indigestion and mild cases of constipation. An infusion of the roasted root is a popular caffeine-free alternative to coffee and a pleasant way to stimulate digestion before or after a heavy meal.

Dosage Infuse ½ to 2 teaspoons (2 to 8g) dried or roasted dandelion root in boiling water; drink 3 cups per day. If using the roasted root, add milk or soy milk to taste, but avoid sweeteners, as they may diminish the herb's effectiveness. Tablets, capsules and a tincture are also available.

Turmeric

Curcuma longa

Stimulates gall bladder function
Among many other medicinal actions, turmeric helps to stimulate bile secretion and may offer some protection against the development of gall stones. Its effects on the liver and gall bladder may also be responsible for the herb's ability to help lower blood cholesterol levels.

Dosage Mix ½ teaspoon powdered turmeric with cold water and drink 2 to 3 times per day for up to 4 weeks at a time. Or, take turmeric capsules, standardised for their content of curcumin.

CAUTIONS

• If you suffer from liver or gall bladder disease (including gall stones), do not attempt to treat yourself using these or any other herbal medicines. Instead, seek the care of a trained medical herbalist or doctor.

• Minor gastrointestinal symptoms, such as nausea, diarrhoea and flatulence are sometimes experienced when these remedies are taken. If you experience any discomfort, discontinue use.

• Don't use milk thistle or dandelion root if you are allergic to members of the Asteraceae family of plants (daisies, chrysanthemums and echinacea).

• If you have a gastric or duodenal ulcer, or take blood-thinning medications, do not take turmeric at doses higher than normal culinary intake.

• In traditional Chinese medicine, schisandra is contraindicated in the early stages of coughs and colds.

• With the exception of normal culinary quantities of turmeric, do not use the herbs on this page if you are pregnant or breastfeeding, except with the advice of a medical herbalist.

Detoxing

If you are feeling tired, sluggish and run-down, it could be worth taking time out for a detox, especially if you've been overindulging or neglecting your diet.

Dandelion leaf
Taraxacum officinale

Herbal diuretic Dandelion leaves have a powerful diuretic effect: they promote the production and excretion of urine. The leaves also stimulate the liver and gall bladder (although, traditionally, these actions are considered to be milder than the actions of the dandelion root).

Dosage Infuse 1 to 2 teaspoons (4 to 10g) dried dandelion leaves in boiling water; drink 3 cups per day.

Cleavers
Galium aparine

Lymphatic cleanser Cleavers is traditionally regarded as a gentle yet effective tonic for the lymphatic system, which collects wastes and foreign material from the body and returns them to the blood stream for disposal. It is specifically used when the lymph glands are chronically enlarged or congested, and when skin problems, such as acne or eczema, are present.

Dosage Infuse 1 teaspoon (4g) dried aerial parts of cleavers in boiling water; drink 3 cups per day. Alternatively, juice the fresh herb and drink 5 to 15 ml 3 times daily.

Psyllium
Plantago ovata, P. psyllium

Facilitates excretion of toxins Soluble fibre of the type found in psyllium husks is especially beneficial when you're detoxing because it forms a gel-like substance in the intestines, trapping toxic compounds so they can be excreted.

Dosage Psyllium husks are available in tablets, capsules and soluble powders, and should be taken according to the manufacturer's instructions. A teaspoon of powdered husks can also be sprinkled on fruit or breakfast cereal once a day. Take every dose of psyllium with a large glass of water.

CAUTIONS

• Most people can safely undergo a gentle detox program by adopting a diet of fresh fruit and vegetables, drinking plenty of water, and avoiding caffeine, cigarettes, alcohol and processed foods for a few days. However, transient side-effects do sometimes occur during a detox. These include gastrointestinal disturbances, headaches, joint and muscle pain, fatigue and skin rashes.

• The following people should not undergo detox regimens or take the herbs listed on this page except under the supervision of an appropriately qualified healthcare professional or medical herbalist: children, teenagers, pregnant and breastfeeding women; people with chronic illness, diabetes, diagnosed intestine, kidney, liver or gall bladder disease; cancer patients; people taking prescribed medications; people with a history of eating disorders or alcohol or drug abuse; people who have had a higher than normal exposure to toxins (for example, through occupational exposure).

• Don't use dandelion leaf if you are allergic to members of the Asteraceae family of plants (for example, daisies, echinacea and chrysanthemums) or are taking potassium-sparing diuretics or ACE inhibitors.

• Psyllium may interfere with the absorption of other medicines, so separate doses by 2 hours.

• Always drink lots of water when using psyllium, as cases of choking have occasionally been reported in people taking psyllium powders without adequate fluids.

• Do not use any of these herbs if you are pregnant or breastfeeding, except with the advice of a medical herbalist.

The roots of dandelion are dried and roasted to make a caffeine-free substitute for coffee.

Eliminating toxins

Herbalists believe that it's difficult for the body to function at its best if the organs of elimination are overloaded. In the philosophies of many traditional healing systems, the resulting build-up of toxins can lead to symptoms as varied as headaches, fatigue and skin problems. The liver and gall bladder play a major role in the formation and excretion of the faeces, so remedies such as the ones detailed on this page tend to be central to any detox prescription, often with the support of other herbs for the urinary and lymphatic systems.

Tension and stress

We are all under more pressure these days, but if you are suffering real stress from the feeling of too much to do in too little time, these herbs may help you to cope.

Korean ginseng
Panax ginseng
Improves performance under stress The most highly valued of all Chinese herbs, Korean ginseng has a long-held reputation for helping the body and mind cope with stress. It has been the subject of numerous clinical trials, which have documented (among other effects) improvements in alertness, relaxation, mood and performance on various tests. Not all clinical trials have supported Korean ginseng's traditional reputation.

✒ **Dosage** Take commercially prepared Korean ginseng tablets according to the manufacturer's instructions (up to a maximum of 1000mg of dried root per day). Look for products standardised for their content of ginsenosides. Note that Korean ginseng is traditionally taken for 8 to 12 weeks at a time, followed by a break of several weeks. It is also not appropriate for frail or anxious patients.

Oats
Avena sativa
Traditional restorative for the nervous system The leaves, stems and other green parts (sometimes called 'oat straw') of the oat plant are used to help restore a depleted or debilitated nervous system and aid with coping in times of stress or nervous exhaustion. Herbalists consider this herb a gentle and reliable nervous system tonic, that is capable of calming or energising as required. Even the very frail or anxious patient can take it safely.

✒ **Dosage** Infuse 1 to 1½ teaspoons (3g) dried oats greens in boiling water; drink 3 cups per day. Children over

4 years of age can take up to half the adult dose.

Lemon balm
Melissa officinalis
Calming and relaxing Lemon balm is traditionally used during times of tension, restlessness and anxiety, and is ideal when you are feeling uptight, agitated or overwrought. In clinical trials, people affected by stress have reported feeling increased levels of calmness and improved mood after just a single dose of lemon balm, but it can also be taken over a longer period when stress is ongoing.

✒ **Dosage** Infuse 1 to 2 teaspoons of fresh aerial parts of lemon balm in boiling water and drink 1 cup 2 to 3 times per day. The herb has a mild sedative action, so if you are suffering from fatigue, take it only in the evening.

CAUTIONS
• Do not take Korean ginseng if you have diabetes, cardiovascular disease (including high and low blood pressure), depression, anxiety, hyperactivity, mental illness (including bipolar disorder and similar conditions), asthma, insomnia, blood clots or bleeding disorders.
• Korean ginseng is suspected to interact with many pharmaceutical medications – including antidepressants, antipsychotic medications, anticoagulants, insulin and hormonal therapy – so consult with your doctor or medical herbalist before taking it. Do not take it at the same time as stimulants such as caffeine.
• Korean ginseng is traditionally contra-indicated during acute infections.
• Side-effects are occasionally reported with the use of Korean ginseng. These

An infusion of oats seed is used topically to soothe itchy skin.

may include headache, disturbed sleep and skin problems. If this occurs, stop taking the herb.
• Do not use oats if you have coeliac disease or gluten-intolerance.
• Lemon balm may interact with some pharmaceutical drugs, including certain sedatives, thyroid medications and a group of medicines referred to as cholinergic (or parasympa-thomimetic) drugs, which are prescribed for Alzheimer's disease and a range of other conditions – if you are taking prescribed drugs, talk to a medical herbalist before using lemon balm.
• Do not take any of these herbs if you are pregnant or breastfeeding, except with the advice of a medical herbalist.

Depression and anxiety

Used appropriately, there are a number of herbs that can help lift your mood or calm your nerves when you find aspects of life more difficult to deal with than usual.

St John's wort
Hypericum perforatum

Herbal antidepressant Clinical research has proven the anti-depressant effects of St John's wort, with some studies demonstrating a level of efficacy in mild to moderate depression that is similar to that of important pharmaceutical anti-depressants, but with fewer serious side effects. Interestingly, the way that the herb works in the body is also similar to the action of some of these pharmaceutical medicines.

Dosage Look for supplements that are standardised for their contents of hypericin and hyperforin (considered to be the main active constituents) and with a daily dose of 900mg per day of the concentrated (6:1) extract, equivalent to 5.4g of dried herb.

Lavender
Lavandula angustifolia

Aromatherapy to relieve anxiety The scent of lavender has long been attributed with promoting relaxation, and there is a growing body of evidence to support this traditional practice. Studies indicate that inhaling lavender essential oil helps ease anxiety and improves feelings of calmness and well-being in a range of stressful situations, including dental waiting rooms and intensive-care units. Research also shows that lavender inhalation has the effect of reducing the body's production of the stress hormone cortisol.

Dosage To enjoy the anti-anxiety effects of lavender, use a ratio of 4 drops of lavender essential oil for every 10ml carrier oil and massage into the shoulders and temples. Or, inhale the steam from 4 drops essential oil diluted in 20ml hot water (for example, in an oil burner). You can also drink an infusion made from ½ teaspoon (1 to 1.5g) of the dried flowers twice a day, and again at bedtime.

CAUTIONS
• St John's wort is known or suspected to interact with many pharmaceutical drugs (including antidepressants, cardiovascular medicines and contraceptives), so consult a doctor or medical herbalist before taking it.

• Depression is a serious condition and is not suitable for self-treatment. Do not stop taking prescribed antidepressants except with the advice and supervision of your doctor. A 2-week wash-out period is advised if you are switching from pharmaceutical antidepressants to St John's wort.

• Research into the use of St John's wort in severe depression has not yet demonstrated safety or efficacy and so should be avoided unless medically prescribed. It should not be used by people with bipolar disorder.

• The effects of St John's wort take 2 to 4 weeks to develop. If there is no noticeable improvement after 6 weeks, this herb may not be suitable for you; consult your doctor or medical herbalist.

• St John's wort occasionally causes minor side-effects (for example, gastrointestinal upset, headache). The most common of these is photosensitivity, a condition in which the skin becomes more prone to sunburn. Avoid sunbathing or prolonged sun exposure while taking St John's wort and consult your doctor if you develop this symptom.

• Stop taking St John's wort at least 2 weeks prior to undergoing surgery.

• Unless advised to do so by your doctor or medical herbalist, do not take St John's wort if you are pregnant or breastfeeding. Do not give to children.

• Do not ingest lavender essential oil and do not use it during pregnancy or breast-feeding, except with the advice of a medical herbalist

Soothing and aromatic, lavender flowers are cultivated commercially. For instructions on how to make a herb pillow that will help you to relax and sleep, see page 306.

Tiredness and fatigue

When your energy levels are flagging, a stimulating herbal pick-me-up may be all that you need to fight against fatigue and restore your body and mind.

Siberian ginseng
Eleutherococcus senticosus

Extra energy during stressful times Herbalists recommend Siberian ginseng as a stimulating herb for people who are tired and run-down, especially those affected by stress. It is traditionally used to help rebuild energy levels during the recovery period following an illness, and may be beneficial for some sufferers of chronic fatigue syndrome when professionally prescribed.

Dosage Take commercially prepared Siberian ginseng tablets according to the manufacturer's instructions (up to a maximum of 500mg per day) for a period of up to 6 weeks, followed by a 2 week break.

Withania
Withania somnifera

Blood-building herb In Ayurvedic medicine, withania (also known as ashwagandha or Indian ginseng) is used to enhance energy and stamina and to help the body cope with stress, so it's considered especially beneficial for patients who are physically or emotionally exhausted. Withania contains iron, so it can also be helpful for fatigue that has been caused by anaemia or low iron levels. A small number of studies have indicated that it helps to promote the formation of blood

Native to Mongolia and parts of China, astragalus is also called milk vetch.

cells and raise the level of haemoglobin in the blood.

Dosage Take commercial withania tablets according to the manufacturer's instructions. Look for a product providing the equivalent of 3 to 6g of the dried root per day.

Astragalus
Astragalus membranaceus

Energy tonic with immune support Astragalus is one of the most important energy tonics in traditional Chinese medicine. It is used to help increase the vitality of patients who are debilitated, and is specifically indicated for cases of fatigue accompanied by poor appetite. Astragalus is particularly useful if you are constantly feeling run-down as well as tired, since it also supports the immune system, helping the body to fight off infections, such as colds and flu.

Dosage Boil 3 to 10g dried astragalus root in 60ml of water for 10 minutes before straining; drink the decoction in 2 doses during the day. Alternatively, take tablets or capsules according to the manufacturer's instructions, up to a maximum dose equivalent to 7.5g dried root per day.

CAUTIONS
• Do not exceed the recommended dose of Siberian ginseng.
• Siberian ginseng is unsuitable for people with hyperactivity disorders, bipolar disorder or similar. If you have cardiovascular disease (including high and low blood pressure), or if you are taking anticoagulant medication, only use it under professional supervision.
• Siberian ginseng and astragalus are contraindicated during acute infections.

Why am I so tired?
Fatigue is your body's way of telling you that it's time to rest. However, if your energy levels seem to be much lower than usual, or you are too tired to participate in normal everyday activities, then it's time to see a medical herbalist, who can help determine the underlying issue behind your fatigue. Although most causes of fatigue are related to lifestyle factors, such as the amount of sleep, exercise and healthy food you are getting each day, tiredness can also present as a symptom of an underlying health problem, such as anaemia, under-active thyroid conditions or glandular fever. As well as the herbs detailed on this page, the remedies for Tension and stress (see page 216) and Insomnia (see page 220) may also be useful.

• Stop using Siberian ginseng at least 2 weeks before undergoing surgery.
• If you are diabetic, only use Siberian ginseng, with the supervision of a doctor or medical herbalist.
• If you take tranquillisers, sedatives, antidepressants, thyroid medication, chemotherapy or immunosuppressant medication, do not take withania, except under professional supervision.
• Resistance-boosting astragalus may help reduce the side-effects of some immuno-suppressive cancer treatments, but should only be used in this way in consultation with your doctor. Siberian ginseng may also interact with chemotherapy.
• Do not take withania if you are sensitive to plants belonging to the Solanaceae family (for example, potato, tomato, aubergine).
• Do not use these herbs if you are pregnant or breastfeeding, except with the advice of a medical herbalist.

Memory and concentration

If you keep forgetting people's names or where you have left the car keys or your glasses, it could be time to mix yourself up a herbal memory tonic.

Ginkgo
Ginkgo biloba

May delay the progression of dementia Ginkgo is the world's most popular memory tonic, and is believed to work in a number of ways, including improving blood flow to the brain, acting as an anti-oxidant and helping to prevent injury to blood vessels. It may help delay the progression of Alzheimer's disease and other forms of dementia, so can improve quality of life for sufferers of these debilitating conditions. Ginkgo can also be taken for more minor memory problems or as a supportive tonic during study periods. However, there is little scientific evidence available to help us understand whether the herb is also beneficial in healthy people.

Dosage Look for supplements standardised for their content of the important active constituents ginkgo flavone glycosides, ginkgolides and bilobalides, with a daily dose of 120mg of a concentrated (50:1) extract, providing the equivalent of 6g of the dried herb. Ginkgo takes a month or two to reach its maximum effect, so use it for 6 to 12 weeks before assessing whether or not it is helping you.

Brahmi
Bacopa monnieri

Aid for learning Brahmi appears to enhance the way the brain processes new information, which makes it a perfect herbal tonic for students. It also helps relieve anxiety, so it can be of real benefit at exam time – but it does take up to 3 months to start working, so don't leave it too late!

Dosage Infuse 1 to 2g dried brahmi in boiling water; drink 3 cups each day. Alternatively, take commercial preparations, up to a maximum of 6g per day, according to the manufacturer's instructions.

Rosemary
Rosmarinus officinalis

Traditional memory tonic Rosemary has had a reputation as a memory tonic since the time of the ancient Greeks, and it can help increase alertness, reduce anxiety and encourage a calm state of mind.

Dosage Add a few drops of rosemary essential oil to an oil burner in the room or area where you are studying or working.

CAUTIONS

• If your memory problems worsen or become serious, it is essential to discuss your concerns with a doctor.

• If you have been diagnosed with Alzheimer's disease or any other form of dementia, do not take ginkgo or brahmi without first talking to your doctor.

• Ginkgo is known or suspected to interact with many pharmaceutical medications (including antipsychotic medications, anticonvulsants, anticoagulants and anticholinergic medications), so consult your doctor or pharmacist before taking it. Stop taking ginkgo at least 2 weeks before undergoing surgery.

• Always use prepared ginkgo products from a reputable company. Do not eat unprocessed ginkgo leaves, as they can cause an adverse reaction. Do not eat

Ginkgo trees, which date back to the Jurassic period, can live for more than a thousand years.

large amounts of the seeds or allow children to do so.

• Ginkgo sometimes causes mild adverse reactions, which may include dizziness, gastrointestinal upset, headache and allergic skin reactions. More severe reactions have occasionally been recorded, including bleeding problems and seizures. If symptoms occur, stop taking the herb and seek medical advice.

• Brahmi occasionally causes gastrointestinal irritation (for example, reflux). It should not be taken with anticholinergic medications.

• Do not take ginkgo if you suffer from a bleeding disorder.

• Do not take brahmi if you suffer from coeliac disease, malabsorption syndromes, gall bladder blockage or gastric reflux problems except with the advice of a medical herbalist.

• Both brahmi (*Bacopa monnieri*) and gotu kola (*Centella asiatica*) are both sometimes called 'brahmi' in Ayurvedic herbal texts, so make sure you don't confuse the two.

• Don't take ginkgo or brahmi, or apply rosemary essential oil to the skin, if you are pregnant or breastfeeding, except with the advice of a medical herbalist.

Insomnia

Missing out on a good night's sleep can be enough to ruin your whole day. The right herb – such as valerian or hops – may prevent that from happening.

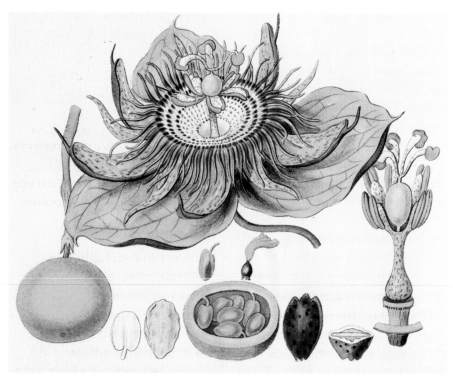

The aerial parts of passionflower are collected at the end of summer and then dried.

Valerian
Valeriana officinalis
Clinically proven herbal sedative
A number of clinical studies support valerian's traditional reputation as a sedative herb. It helps insomnia sufferers to fall asleep more quickly, wake less often during the night and generally experience a better night's sleep. In contrast to some pharmaceutical sedatives, it is very rarely associated with side-effects, and doesn't tend to cause sleepiness and difficulty waking up in the morning.

Dosage Infuse 3g dried valerian rhizome in boiling water and drink 1 cup an hour before bedtime. Alternatively, take commercial preparations according to the manufacturer's instructions.

Hops
Humulus lupulus
Traditional sleep-inducer Although more famous as an ingredient in beer, hops has a long history of being used to help treat insomnia and sleep disorders. This herb is also traditionally regarded as helpful in treating anxiety and restlessness, although there is conflicting evidence about its effects on depression. In many cases, hops is taken in combination with other sedative herbs, such as valerian and passionflower.

Dosage Infuse up to 1g dried hops in boiling water and drink 1 cup an hour before bedtime. Dried hops can also be used to make pillows to aid restful sleep in the same way that lavender is sometimes used. To make a herbal sleep pillow, see page 306.

Passionflower
Passiflora incarnata
Sleep problems with anxiety
Passionflower is traditionally taken to aid insomnia – especially when sleep troubles are accompanied by nervousness or anxiety – so it is ideally suited to those whose insomnia has an emotional basis. Although there hasn't been much scientific research into passionflower's actions, there is some preliminary data to support its traditional applications. Herbalists commonly prescribe passionflower in combination with other relaxing herbs, such as valerian.

Dosage To treat insomnia, infuse 2g dried passionflower leaves in boiling water and drink 1 cup an hour before bedtime. For anxiety, take the same dose twice more during the day. Passionflower may take several weeks to achieve optimal effect.

CAUTIONS
• Do not exceed the recommended dose of the herbs listed here.
• If you are taking pharmaceutical tranquillisers, sedatives or antidepressants, do not take the herbs listed here, except under professional supervision. If you are taking anticoagulant medication, do not use passionflower except with the advice of a medical herbalist.
• If valerian worsens your insomnia and/or causes exceptionally vivid dreams, discontinue it and try an alternative herb.
• If you suffer from depression, do not use hops, except on professional advice.
• Allergic symptoms sometimes occur from contact with hops, and may include dermatitis and respiratory symptoms.
• Do not use hops if you have a history of hormone-sensitive tumours or are taking anti-oestrogenic medication.
• Do not use these herbs if you are pregnant or breastfeeding, except with the advice of a medical herbalist.

Headache and migraine

Headaches can be utterly debilitating. Whether you suffer from headache or migraine frequently or occasionally, a herbal alternative may bring welcome relief.

White willow bark is harvested from young branches in late winter and spring.

Feverfew
Tanacetum parthenium
Reduces migraine frequency and symptoms Feverfew is the most famous herb for treating headache, and particularly good for migraines. If taken over several months, it lowers the frequency of migraines and reduces symptoms, such as headache, nausea and vomiting, as well as decreases the duration of the attacks.

Dosage Take feverfew either by eating 1-2 large or 3-4 small fresh leaves every day (with or after food) or by using commercial preparations according to the manufacturer's instructions. It may take from 1 to 4 months before the effects become evident – perhaps even longer if you are taking the fresh leaves.

White willow bark
Salix alba
Herbal aspirin White willow bark contains compounds called salicylates, similar to the active ingredient in aspirin. It has traditionally been used to relieve headaches of all types, especially those accompanied by fever. In one small-scale study, white willow bark was combined with feverfew to prevent migraine, producing significant improvements in the frequency, intensity and duration of the attacks.

Dosage Boil 1 to 3g dried white willow bark in a cup of water for 5 to 10 minutes; drink the decoction up to 3 times daily. Or, take commercially prepared products according to the manufacturer's instructions.

Peppermint oil
Mentha × piperita
Rapid relief for tension headaches
Applying peppermint essential oil to the forehead and temples has been scientifically proven to be as effective as paracetamol (acetaminophen) for the relief of tension headaches. This effect occurs very quickly – a significant reduction in the headache's intensity may be noted as quickly as 15 minutes after the oil has been applied.

Dosage Apply a solution containing 1 part peppermint oil diluted in 9 parts alcohol (or water if alcohol is not available) to the forehead and temples every 15 to 30 minutes after the onset of symptoms. Take care not to allow the solution to come into contact with the eyes. Using both peppermint oil and paracetamol simultaneously may enhance the effects of both treatments.

CAUTIONS
• Severe or frequent headaches may require medical investigation – always consult your doctor.
• Feverfew sometimes causes allergic side-effects, most commonly mouth symptoms, such as mouth ulcers and soreness of the tongue. These symptoms are more likely to occur in people chewing fresh leaves (as opposed to taking tablets or capsules).
• Do not take feverfew if you develop a rash after coming into contact with the plant or if you are allergic to Asteraceae plants (chicory, daisies, chrysanthemums, sunflower and echinacea).
• Do not take white willow bark if you are allergic to salicylates (such as aspirin).
• Do not take feverfew or white willow bark with antiplatelet or anticoagulant medication, or if you suffer from a blood disorder except with the advice of a doctor or medical herbalist.
• Peppermint oil should always be diluted before application. Do not on or near the face of children and babies.
• Do not take feverfew or white willow bark, or apply peppermint oil to the skin, if you are pregnant or breastfeeding, except with the advice of a medical herbalist.

Is it really a migraine?

Although we often use the word 'migraine' to describe a particularly severe headache, in medical terms a migraine is a specific type of debilitating headache that may be accompanied by other symptoms, such as nausea and vomiting, blurred vision or other visual disturbances, and tingling or numbness of the limbs. Sufferers may also be particularly sensitive to noise or light during an attack, and may retreat into a dark, quiet room until the episode has passed.

Acne

Skin eruptions can be a painful as well as disfiguring affliction and can cause sufferers great social anxiety. Try these herbal solutions for treating problem skin.

Tea-tree oil
Melaleuca alternifolia
Nature's powerful pimple healer

With a combination of broad-spectrum antimicrobial properties and anti-inflammatory activity, tea-tree oil is an ideal topical treatment for acne. In a recent study, people with mild-to-moderate acne experienced reductions of more than 40 per cent in both the number of acne lesions and the severity of their acne when they used a tea-tree oil gel over a 6-week period. A previous study had already shown that tea-tree gel had a similar level of efficacy to benzoyl peroxide (also used topically for the treatment of acne), but with a much lower incidence of side-effects.

 **Dosage** In these scientific studies, a gel containing 5 per cent tea-tree essential oil was used – a more concentrated preparation may have yielded even more impressive results, but may also have increased the risk of side-effects (see *Cautions*). To replicate the study conditions at home, apply tea-tree gel to the affected area twice a day, washing it off thoroughly with water after 20 minutes.

Chaste tree
Vitex agnus-castus
Herbal hormone balancer

Hormonal imbalance can be an important factor in the development of acne – not just in teenagers, but also for many adults. To restore hormonal balance and help resolve problem skin, herbalists often prescribe chaste tree. This herb, *Vitex agnus-castus*, is more widely known for its role in the treatment of premenstrual syndrome (PMS) and female reproductive issues, but can also be taken by both males and females for treating acne. It is especially useful for premenstrual acne flare-ups.

Dosage Take tablets, capsules or tincture according to the manufacturer's instructions. Look for products that are standardised for their content of the compounds casticin and/or agnuside. Results may take up to 12 weeks or longer to become noticeable.

Cleavers
Galium aparine
Skin and lymphatic detoxifier

In the Western herbal tradition, skin problems, such as acne, are considered an indication that toxins in the blood stream are being excreted via the skin. Cleavers is one of a wide range of blood-cleansing herbs that are used to detoxify the blood and lymph and support the body's organs of elimination, thus improving skin health.

Dosage Infuse 4g (1 teaspoon) of dried aerial parts of cleavers in boiling water; drink 3 cups per day. Alternatively, juice the fresh herb (excluding the root) using a stick blender, and drink 5 to 15ml 3 times daily.

CAUTIONS
• Tea-tree oil sometimes causes reactions, such as contact dermatitis, itching, burning or scaling of the skin, especially if used in high concentrations or on inflamed or eczematous skin. Use diluted preparations to reduce the likelihood of these reactions occurring, and patch test on an unaffected area of skin 24 hours before applying to any infected or inflamed area.
• Do not ingest tea-tree oil.
• Chaste tree occasionally causes mild, reversible side-effects, such as headache, nausea and gastrointestinal upset. Stop taking it if you experience these symptoms.
• Do not take chaste tree at the same time as the oral contraceptive pill, hormone-replacement therapy (HRT) or drugs containing progesterone, except under professional advice. People with a history of hormone-sensitive tumours should not take chaste tree, as safety in people with these conditions has not been established.
• Do not take chaste tree or cleavers, or apply undiluted tea-tree oil to the skin, if you are pregnant or breastfeeding, except with the advice of a medical herbalist.

The chaste tree is also called monks' pepper because it was once used to suppress libido.

Eczema and psoriasis

Herbalists use a combination of internal and topical treatments to relieve the pain and aggravation of itchy, inflammatory skin conditions.

Chickweed
Stellaria media
Soothing relief from the garden
You probably have some chickweed growing in your garden – it's one of the most common weeds in the world. Chickweed is traditionally used to relieve itchy and inflamed skin conditions, including eczema, dermatitis and psoriasis. It's gentle enough to use on the most delicate and inflamed skin, and is even suitable for use on babies (see *Cautions* before using).

🖊 **Dosage** Juice the fresh aerial parts of the chickweed plant, then mix into a cream or ointment base using a ratio of 1 part chickweed to 5 parts base cream. Apply to the affected area as required. Alternatively, use a commercially prepared cream in the same way.

Flaxseed oil
Linum usitatissimum
Herbal source of omega-3 fatty acids Without fats and oils in your diet, your skin can become dry, flaky, scaly and itchy, so the quality and type of fats you eat is very important. The omega-6 group of fatty acids (found in safflower, sunflower, corn and grapeseed oils) can exacerbate inflammation. On the other hand, omega-3 fatty acids, such as those found in flaxseed (as well as other seeds, nuts and seafood), enhance the body's production of anti-inflammatory compounds, and can be beneficial in the treatment of psoriasis, eczema and other inflammatory skin conditions.

🖊 **Dosage** Take flaxseed oil in either capsules or liquid form, according to the manufacturer's instructions. Alternatively, grind fresh whole seeds and serve them with breakfast cereal, smoothies or yogurt. Note that the oil is more unstable than other culinary oils, so keep it refrigerated to ensure its freshness.

Turmeric
Curcuma longa
Ayurvedic anti-inflammatory In Ayurvedic medicine, turmeric has been used for centuries as a topical treatment for psoriasis and other inflammatory skin disorders. Modern Western herbalists sometimes also prescribe it internally for the well-documented antioxidant, anti-inflammatory and immune-stimulating properties of both turmeric and a yellow pigment it contains, called curcumin. As the herb is also a liver and gall bladder tonic, this use reflects the traditional view that cleansing the body of toxins can help to resolve chronic skin problems.

🖊 **Dosage** Mix ½ teaspoon powdered turmeric with cold water and drink it 2 to 3 times per day for up to 4 weeks at a time. For topical use, mix 50g turmeric powder with 1 teaspoon bicarbonate of soda and some hot water and apply as a poultice. For more detailed instructions, see page 200.

CAUTIONS
• Chickweed and turmeric occasionally cause allergic skin reactions. Patch test on an unaffected area of skin 24 hours before applying to inflamed skin or before using either herb on infants or children.
• Although they are made from the same plant, flaxseed oil is a different preparation from the refined oil sold as 'linseed oil' and used for industrial purposes (for example, in paints), which should never be consumed.

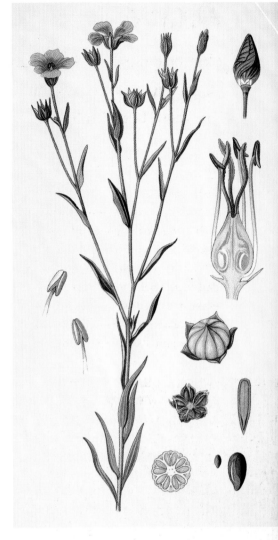

The stalks of the flax plant are used to make linen, while its seed oil is used in several ways in herbal medicine.

• If you are taking anticoagulant or blood-thinning medications, talk to your doctor or medical herbalist before taking high dosages of flaxseed oil or other omega-3 fatty acids.
• Turmeric is a safe herb, although high doses can cause minor gastrointestinal symptoms. Do not use it at higher than culinary doses if you have liver and gall-bladder disease (including gallstones), gastric or duodenal ulcer, or take blood-thinning medication, except with the advice of a doctor or medical herbalist.
• Do not use flaxseed oil or turmeric in greater than culinary quantities if you are pregnant or breastfeeding, except with the advice of a doctor or a medical herbalist.

Athlete's foot and fungal infections

Once a fungal infection takes hold, it can be hard to get rid of. When trying out these herbal options, be prepared to wait a little while to get results.

Tea-tree oil
Melaleuca alternifolia

Proven tinea treatment Tea-tree oil is effective against a vast number of disease-causing fungi. Clinical trials also support its use, especially in foot conditions, such as tinea pedis (athlete's foot) and onchomycosis, a fungal infection of the toenail that is very difficult to treat and can lead to destruction of the nail.

To be effective, the tea-tree oil needs to be used at just the right concentration – in one study, a solution containing 50 per cent tea-tree oil killed the fungal infection in 64 per cent of tinea sufferers after 4 weeks. But in another study that used tea-tree at a concentration of just 10 per cent, the symptoms improved but the infection remained present.

With fungal nail infections, applying 100 per cent tea-tree oil for a minimum of 3 months has been shown to achieve similar results to pharmaceutical topical agents, with about half of all people experiencing improvements in symptoms and the appearance of the affected nails.

Dosage To treat athlete's foot (tinea), make a solution containing 25 to 50 per cent tea-tree oil in water, and apply to the affected area twice daily for several weeks. Alternatively, add 15 drops of pure tea-tree oil and some salt to an electronic foot bath (the heat and salt may enhance the antifungal activity of the essential oil), and use for 20 minutes twice a day. For onchomycosis, apply 100 per cent tea-tree oil to the affected area twice daily for at least 3 months.

Specially formulated tea-tree oil products can also be useful for some other types of fungal infections – talk to your medical herbalist.

Pau d'arco
Tabebuia impetiginosa

Anti-fungal remedy from the Amazon The wood of the South American tree pau d'arco is famously resistant to fungi. In the traditional medicine of Brazil, a poultice or decoction made from the tree's inner bark is applied to the skin to treat fungal infections as well as conditions such as eczema, psoriasis and skin cancer. Laboratory studies support a number of pau d'arco's traditional uses, including fungicidal activity.

Dosage Add 10g inner bark of pau d'arco to 600ml water and simmer gently for 15 minutes. Cool it to a comfortable temperature and then use the decoction as a compress or poultice on the affected area twice daily. For more detailed instructions, see page 200.

CAUTIONS

• Tea-tree oil may cause reactions, such as contact dermatitis, itching, burning or scaling of the skin in as many as 1 in 25 people with tinea, especially if used at high concentration or on inflamed or eczematous skin. Use more dilute preparations to reduce the likelihood of these reactions occurring, and patch test on an unaffected area of skin 24 hours before applying to any infection or inflammation.

• Pau d'arco can be taken internally to support the immune system during systemic fungal infection. However, such conditions are not suited to self-treatment, especially as certain components of pau d'arco may be toxic if taken in excessive amounts. Always consult a trained medical herbalist for more information before using.

• Do not use any of the herbs listed on this page if you are pregnant or breastfeeding, except with the advice of a medical herbalist.

A native of mountainous regions of South America, pau d'arco will thrive most readily in a tropical to subtropical climate.

Cold sores, gums and **mouth health**

Whether you're suffering from the pain of cold sores, toothache or bleeding gums, herbs are an excellent way of helping to keep your mouth healthy.

Lemon balm
Melissa officinalis

Cold-sore treatment Clinical studies show that lemon balm is an effective topical remedy for cold sores, helping to decrease healing time, prevent lesions from spreading and relieve symptoms. Symptomatic relief is particularly impressive on the second day of the outbreak, which is usually the time when symptoms are at their most acute. These effects aren't surprising, since laboratory tests show that the herb, and particularly its fragrant essential oil, has the ability to quickly kill the herpes simplex viruses 1 and 2.

🌿 **Dosage** The lemon balm cream used in the clinical studies mentioned was extremely concentrated (containing the equivalent of 700mg of lemon balm extract per gram). Look for commercial preparations of the same strength, or ask a medical herbalist to make some for you. Or make a strong infusion of lemon balm and use the liquid in a compress.

Clove oil
Syzygium aromaticum
syn. *Eugenia caryophyllata*

Rapid toothache relief Clove oil is a remarkably effective pain-killer and anaesthetic. When applied to toothache or inflamed gums, it reduces pain within minutes – although only for a relatively short time. It works by decreasing the affected tissue's perception of pain, and also has anti-inflammatory and antibacterial properties.

🌿 **Dosage** Dab a small quantity of clove essential oil directly onto the site of pain. If essential oil is not available, gently rub powdered cloves or clove buds on the affected area, but take note that they may not be as effective as the essential oil, which is rich in eugenol, the most important active constituent.

Myrrh
Commiphora myrrha syn. *molmol*

Traditional antiseptic for gums The gum (or resin) of the myrrh tree is used for the treatment of mouth and gum problems in many traditional healing systems. It's a useful, fast-acting treatment for mouth ulcers, gingivitis, periodontitis and bleeding gums because it is an effective antiseptic, helps reduce swelling and inflammation, has a local anaesthetic action and encourages wound healing.

🌿 **Dosage** Myrrh is normally used as a tincture, which is available from a herbalist. It can be painted onto mouth ulcers and infections without being diluted, or added to water (30 to 60 drops at a time) as a mouthwash or gargle for more general gum problems.

CAUTIONS

• Only apply clove oil as a topical treatment to teeth and gums. Do not take it internally.

• Clove oil sometimes causes contact dermatitis or worsens irritation of the gums and mucous membranes. If this occurs, stop using it and rinse your mouth thoroughly with water.

• Use clove oil only as an emergency or short-term remedy until you are able to access professional dental care. Avoid using it repeatedly or for long periods of time, as it may damage gum tissue.

• Do not confuse myrrh (*Commiphora myrrha*) with *Myrrhis odorata* (sweet cicely).

• Do not use any of the herbs listed on this page if you are pregnant or breastfeeding, except with the advice of a medical herbalist.

A biblical herb

Myrrh has long been a valuable trading commodity, and was used in ancient times in both incense and cosmetics. It was often worth more than its weight in gold, hence its status as a suitable gift for the infant Jesus. According to the Bible, myrrh was also used to anoint Jesus's body after the Crucifixion. Uses throughout the ages include: mummification; the preservation of wine; as a treatment for snake bite, intestinal worms and scurvy; and as an aphrodisiac. It is known to kill various pests that carry human parasites, including mosquitoes and ticks; pellets of myrrh were burned in ancient Egyptian homes to help rid them of fleas.

If you brush past lemon balm, the leaves release a delicious lemon and mint scent.

First aid

Stock your herb garden and medicine cabinet with the right remedies and you'll be ready to handle all life's minor mishaps, from itches, to grazes, scrapes and burns.

Aloe vera
Aloe vera syn. *A. barbadensis, A. ferox*
Speedy burn repair Keep an aloe vera plant (*Aloe* spp., including *Aloe vera* and *A. ferox*) on your kitchen windowsill so that it's handy if you accidentally burn yourself while cooking. Not only does the cooling aloe vera gel soothe the pain of burns, it also reduces inflammation. And if the skin is broken, aloe vera helps protect the burn site from infection as well as encourages the skin's collagen to repair itself. The result is that burns (and other kinds of wounds) heal more rapidly when aloe vera is used; in fact, researchers estimate that using aloe vera gel speeds up burn healing time by more than 8 days.

🌿 **Dosage** Apply the mucilaginous gel from the centre of the aloe vera leaf to the affected area 3 times per day, or use a commercially prepared gel that contains a high per centage of aloe vera. Avoid using small, young leaves, as the active constituents are most prevalent at about 3 years old. When shopping for commercial products, choose those certified by the International Aloe Science Council (IASC), which ensures the product is of high quality.

Arnica
Arnica montana
Bumps and bruises Arnica has a long history of use as a topical treatment for bruises and for helping them to heal quickly. Users often report that their bruises change colour more quickly and consider this an indication that the healing process is enhanced. It is also traditionally indicated for the treatment of swollen or sprained tissue. Homoeopathic preparations of arnica can be taken internally for the same conditions.

🌿 **Dosage** Apply arnica cream, ointment or infused oil to the affected area 3 times per day. Choose a product that contains 10 to 20 per cent arnica tincture or oil.

Calendula
Calendula officinalis
Skin healer A traditional remedy for burns, wounds, grazes and rashes, calendula has been documented as encouraging skin healing in a range of circumstances, and may also be useful in helping to stop bleeding.

🌿 **Dosage** For broken skin, first cleanse the wound with an antiseptic solution to ensure that it is completely clean, then apply calendula tincture to the affected area 3 times per day. For closed wounds, grazes, rashes and burns, apply calendula cream, ointment or infused oil to the affected area 3 times per day.

Chickweed
Stellaria media
Soothes itches and relieves rashes Cooling chickweed is a traditional remedy for all manner of itchy skin conditions, so it's useful to have on hand to relieve rashes and bites. It may also be effective in soothing the irritation and itch of urticaria or hives.

The gel found in the aloe vera plant is reputed to have been used by the Egyptian queen, Cleopatra as a beauty preparation.

Dosage Juice the fresh aerial parts of the chickweed plant, and mix into a cream or ointment base using a ratio of 1 part chickweed to 5 parts base cream. Apply to the affected area as required. Alternatively, use a commercially prepared cream in the same way.

Lavender oil
Lavandula angustifolia

Takes the sting out of insect bites Lavender essential oil can quickly relieve inflammation and swelling when applied to insect bites and stings. It also has antimicrobial activity to help prevent wounds becoming infected. Its use in burns is reputed to have started when the French scientist Gattefosse (one of the pioneers of aromatherapy) put his hand in a nearby bowl of lavender oil after burning himself in his laboratory, and was intrigued by how quickly his skin healed.

Dosage Dab undiluted lavender oil onto insect bites or stings as quickly as possible after they occur. For wounds and burns, first cleanse the wound with an antiseptic solution to ensure that it's clean, then apply undiluted lavender oil to the affected area 3 times a day.

Slippery elm
Ulmus rubra syn. U. fulva

Drawing agent for splinters and boils In the same way that slippery elm is used internally to reduce inflammation in the gastrointestinal tract, its soothing properties can also be applied to irritated and inflamed skin. When mixed with water, it forms a gel-like layer that protects the wound and allows it to heal. Slippery elm poultices can also be used to draw splinters and other foreign bodies from the skin, and to encourage boils and abscesses to come to a head.

Dosage Mix slippery elm bark powder with hot water until it has a paste-like consistency, and use it as a poultice on wounds, to draw foreign bodies out of the skin or to hasten the resolution of boils and abscesses. For more detailed instructions, see page 200.

Tea-tree oil
Melaleuca alternifolia

Nature's potent antiseptic Tea-tree oil is one of nature's most important antiseptics, and its activity against an extensive variety of bacteria, viruses and fungi is well documented. Since it also has anti-inflammatory properties, it is very useful for cuts, grazes and deeper wounds, and can help prevent them from becoming infected.

Dosage Tea-tree oil can be used undiluted to help cleanse wounds at risk of infection or on tougher skin surfaces (for example, the soles of the feet), but will often make an open wound sting and smart, so in most cases a solution containing 15 per cent tea-tree oil is more appropriate. Creams and lotions containing tea-tree oil are also available.

New Zealand tea tree and manuka honey

The essential oil of the New Zealand tea tree or manuka (*Leptospermum scoparium*) is strongly antimicrobial and can be diluted and used to disinfect wounds. A particularly important remedy is honey from bees that graze on manuka. Manuka honey contains a compound called Unique Manuka Factor (UMF), which super-charges its ability to heal infections. Extensive research at the University of Waikato in New Zealand has demonstrated that high-UMF honey disinfects wounds and also encourages them to heal, making it an ideal dressing for leg ulcers and other slow-healing skin infections. High-UMF honey is labelled as 'active manuka' honey. Other manuka honeys without the 'active' label (or a UMF rating of at least 10) are not likely to be as potent.

CAUTIONS

• Do not consume essential oils of tea-tree or lavender.

• Do not consume aloe vera gel unless in a commercial form that is specifically intended for internal use.

• Do not take arnica internally, except in its very dilute homoeopathic form. Do not apply it to broken skin or near the eyes or mouth. Do not use topical applications of arnica for more than 10 days at a time.

• Topical applications of any herb can sometimes cause reactions, such as dermatitis, or itching and burning sensations, so perform a patch test at least 24 hours before use. Discontinue use if a reaction develops. Take particular care with arnica and calendula if you are allergic to the Asteraceae family (for example, daisies, chrysanthemum and echinacea) and with arnica if you are allergic to the Lauraceae family (for example, sassafras, avocado, camphor laurel). Take note that topical use of essential oils may also irritate the skin, especially if it is already inflamed.

• With the exception of topical applications of calendula and aloe vera, do not use the herbs listed on these pages if you are pregnant or breastfeeding, except with the advice of a medical herbalist.

Sports injuries, sprains and strains

If you've taken a painful knock or strained a muscle, these herbs can help you get up and about and back in the gym, on the playing field or running track more quickly.

Arnica
Arnica montana
Reduces bruising and repairs swollen or injured tissue Topical applications of arnica have traditionally been used to reduce bruising and stimulate the healing of muscles and other soft tissues after trauma. As long as the skin is not broken, arnica can be rubbed into sprains, strains, swollen joints, fractures and dislocations. It is also used internally in extremely dilute homoeopathic preparations, and although this use is controversial in the medical world, several clinical trials have been published that suggest arnica may have a beneficial effect. For example, marathon runners have been documented to experience less incidence of muscle soreness when they take homoeopathic arnica pills in the days before and after a race.

 Dosage Apply arnica cream, ointment or infused oil to the affected area 3 times per day. For internal use, take commercially prepared homoeopathic arnica pills or liquid in the strength 30x (sometimes labelled 30D) according to the manufacturer's instructions.

Comfrey
Symphytum officinale
Traditionally used to heal strains, sprains and fractures Comfrey was once widely used internally as well as externally to encourage broken bones to heal, and was so highly regarded for this use that it was also known by the names 'knitbone' and 'boneset'. However, following the revelation that in some

The hairy foliage of the comfrey plant may cause skin irritation in some people.

varieties of comfrey, some of its compounds (known as pyrrolizidine alkaloids) are potentially toxic, these days its use is restricted to topical applications. As well as being used for fractures, comfrey helps soothe and take the swelling out of strains and sprains.

 Dosage Juice the fresh aerial parts of the comfrey plant, and mix into a cream or ointment base using a ratio of 1 part comfrey to 5 parts base cream. Apply to the affected area as required. Alternatively, blend a few fresh leaves from a comfrey plant into a pulp and make a poultice from them. For detailed instructions, see page 200. If you don't have access to a comfrey plant, commercial cream and ointments are also available.

Cramp bark
Viburnum opulus
Muscle relaxant and anti-spasmodic If you're prone to tension or spasms in your muscles, cramp bark may be just the herb you're looking for. Native Americans used it to relieve cramps and other types of muscle pain, and herbalists still prescribe it today. With an ability to reduce both long- and short-term muscle tension, it is considered particularly effective for overuse injuries and backache.

 Dosage Take commercially prepared cramp bark tablets or tincture, up to a maximum dose of 1g, 3 times per day or 5ml, 3 times a day.

Devil's claw
Harpagophytum procumbens
Highly effective anti-inflammatory This African herb has a long history of use to reduce pain and inflammation in muscles and joints, and is traditionally prescribed for joint, back and tendon pain caused by injury and overuse. These traditional applications are supported by scientific studies in which devil's claw reduced muscle stiffness when taken for 4 weeks, and reduced back pain and increased mobility in 4 to 8 weeks.

 Dosage The most important active constituent of devil's claw is a compound called harpagoside, and according to researchers, preparations standardised for their content of harpagoside are more effective than non-standardised preparations. Look for commercial tablets or capsules providing at least 50mg harpagoside per day, and take according to the manufacturer's instructions. Take between meals to reduce damage to its active constituents by stomach acids.

St John's wort
Hypericum perforatum
Topical treatment for nerve pain Topical applications of St John's wort have historically been used to treat nerve pain of various kinds, but it has been especially effective in treating the pain of

sciatica. This traditional use is supported by laboratory tests that have demonstrated both anti-inflammatory and painkilling properties.

🖝 **Dosage** Rub the infused oil of St John's wort flowers into the affected part, 2 to 3 times per day. For instructions on how to make infused oils, see page 201. Alternatively, buy a commercial product.

White willow bark
Salix alba

Aspirin-like pain relief Studies have shown that white willow bark preparations, standardised for their content of salicin, provide effective relief of lower back pain, with up to 40 per cent of volunteers becoming pain-free after taking the herb for 4 weeks. These results are not surprising, since salicin (which has aspirin-like properties), has well-documented anti-inflammatory and analgesic effects.

🖝 **Dosage** Take commercially prepared white willow bark tablets or capsules (standardised to contain 15 per cent salicin per day). Take 1-2 tablets 3 times a day.

With the help of a witch hazel wand, a witch performs a curative spell on a man's swollen foot. The word 'witch' in witch hazel comes from the Old English *wice*, meaning 'bendable'.

Witch hazel
Hamamelis virginiana

Stems bleeding and reduces swelling With its high concentration of tannins, witch hazel is highly regarded as an astringent remedy with the ability to stop bleeding and reduce inflammation – especially the localised swelling caused by sprains and other injuries. It is also used to encourage the healing of bruises.

🖝 **Dosage** Apply commercially prepared witch hazel cream or ointment to strains, sprains, grazes or bruises 2 to 3 times per day. Alternatively, prepare a decoction using 1 to 2 teaspoons of the dried leaves or bark, and use the liquid to make a compress for the affected part. For detailed instructions, see page 201.

CAUTIONS

• Arnica and comfrey should not be taken internally (except in their very dilute homoeopathic forms), and should not be applied to broken skin or near the eyes. Avoid using comfrey for more than 10 days at a time.

• Topical applications of any herb can sometimes cause reactions, such as dermatitis or itching and burning sensations, and ideally a patch test should be performed at least 24 hours prior to use; discontinue if a reaction develops. Take particular care with arnica if you are allergic to the Asteraceae (for example, daisies, chrysanthemum, echinacea) or Lauraceae families of plants (for example, sassafras, avocado, camphor laurel).

• Cramp bark berries are poisonous and should not be ingested.

• Do not take white willow bark if you are allergic to salicylates (including aspirin). If you are taking antiplatelet or anti-coagulant medication, or if you suffer from a blood disorder, only take it under the advice of a medical herbalist.

• Devil's claw may occasionally cause digestive problems, such as diarrhoea, and should not be used by people with pre-existing gastrointestinal complaints, such as ulcers, gall stones or diarrhoea, except under professional advice.

• Do not take devil's claw if you are taking warfarin or antiarrhythmic drugs, except under professional advice. Stop taking devil's claw at least 2 weeks before undergoing surgery.

• Devil's claw does not appear to be effective for back pain that radiates down the legs, a symptom that may indicate nerve involvement. It should be investigated by a medical herbalist.

• With the exception of topical applications of St John's wort and witch hazel, do not use any of these herbs if you are pregnant or breastfeeding, except with the advice of a medical herbalist.

Take action

The actions you take immediately after a soft tissue injury have a direct influence on how quickly the problem heals.

• Reduce blood flow and slow both swelling and bleeding by resting the injured part as quickly as you can.

• Apply an ice pack to the injured area to reduce inflammation, pain and tissue damage, but always make sure you protect your skin from ice burn by placing a wet towel or cloth beneath the ice and your skin.

• Apply a firm, wide bandage, known as a compression bandage, over the injured area to help reduce bleeding and swelling.

• Raise the injured part so it is higher than the heart, further reducing blood flow to the area.

• Consult a physiotherapist or doctor as soon as possible, as many soft tissue injuries require professional treatment.

Arthritis and gout

Don't let the stiffness, debilitating pain and inflammation of arthritis cramp your style. A range of effective herbal remedies are available to relieve the symptoms.

Boswellia
Boswellia serrata

Relief from rheumatoid and osteoarthritis The resin from the boswellia (Indian frankincense) tree has been used in Ayurvedic medicine for the treatment of inflammatory and rheumatic conditions for centuries. With a combination of anti-inflammatory, analgesic and immune system-modifying effects, it is particularly relevant for rheumatoid arthritis, an auto-immune form of arthritis that is both debilitating and difficult to treat.

In a review collating the results from 12 rheumatoid arthritis studies, researchers concluded that boswellia was just as effective as some medicinal treatments (for example, gold therapy), and could be particularly useful for sufferers whose arthritis responds poorly to more conventional medication, for those who have had the disease for a long time, and for children with juvenile chronic arthritis. Boswellia also offers improvements in osteoarthritis, and is documented to help decrease pain and swelling, improve range of motion and increase walking distance in people with osteoarthritis of the knee.

Dosage Look for commercial preparations standardised for their content of the active constituents boswellic acids, and take according to manufacturer's instructions or as professionally prescribed. The research into osteoarthritis used the equivalent of 1000mg of boswellia resin (sometimes referred to as oleo-gum or gum resin) per day, standardised to contain 40 per cent (400mg) boswellic acids. Research indicates that it may take up to 2 months for significant effects to be felt,

but that they persist for some time after the herb is stopped. Rheumatoid arthritis is a complex condition that is not well suited to self-treatment – ask your medical herbalist to assess whether boswellia is an appropriate treatment for you, and only take it according to the prescribed dosage.

Celery seed
Apium graveolens

Handy gout remedy Celery seed is a traditional remedy for all kinds of arthritis, but it is considered particularly effective for the treatment of gout. This extremely painful form of arthritis classically affects a single joint, such as the big toe, which rapidly becomes hot, swollen and inflamed.

Dosage Boil 0.5 to 2g dried celery seed in a cup of water for 10 minutes; drink the decoction up to 3 times daily. Alternatively, you can take a commercially prepared tincture, tablet or capsule according to the manufacturer's instructions.

Devil's claw
Harpagophytum procumbens

Clinically proven for arthritis pain
Devil's claw has anti-inflammatory and analgesic properties, and is a proven treatment for osteoarthritis, with several studies demonstrating its benefits – particularly for osteoarthritis of the knee and/or hip. In some of these studies, devil's claw was compared to pharmaceutical analgesics, with researchers concluding that the herb was just as effective as the drug, but with a lower incidence of side-effects. Laboratory tests suggest that devil's claw may provide more than just symptomatic relief – it also appears to inhibit some of the processes that both damage cartilage and trigger the joint changes characteristic of osteoarthritis. Clinical trials indicate that pain and other symptoms of osteoarthritis start to abate after about 2 months of taking the herb.

Dosage The most important active constituent of devil's claw is a compound called harpagoside, and according to researchers, preparations that have been standardised for their content of harpagoside are more effective than non-standardised preparations. Look for commercially prepared tablets or capsules that provide at least 50mg harpagoside per day, and take them according to the manufacturer's instructions.

Devil's claw, a creeping perennial, gets its name from the hooks on its strange-looking fruits.

The rhizomes of the leafy ginger plant are harvested at least a year after planting.

Ginger

Zingiber officinale

The spicy anti-inflammatory

The humble spice ginger is also a potent medicine with impressive anti-inflammatory capabilities. Laboratory tests show that ginger inhibits a number of the compounds that promote inflammation in the body – including several of the enzymes that are targeted by pharmaceutical anti-arthritis medications. As a result, it provides relief from arthritis pain, and some studies have even found it to be as effective as the non-steroidal anti-inflammatory drug ibuprofen.

Dosage Add 20 to 30 drops of ginger tincture to water, or infuse ½ teaspoon powdered ginger or 1 to 2 teaspoons of grated fresh ginger root in boiling water; take 3 times per day. Concentrated ginger tablets may also be useful.

White willow bark

Salix alba

Herbal pain reliever The bark of the white willow tree is believed to have been used as a herbal painkiller since at least the time of Hippocrates. Laboratory tests have demonstrated the anti-inflammatory and analgesic properties of its aspirin-like substances. Most (but not all) clinical trials also support its role in relieving the pain of osteoarthritis, but there has not been enough research to confirm its effectiveness in the treatment of rheumatoid arthritis.

Dosage Take commercial white willow tablets or capsules standardised to contain 240mg of salicin per day according to the manufacturer's instructions.

CAUTIONS

• Boswellia occasionally causes mild adverse effects, such as diarrhoea or hives. If this happens, discontinue its use. Little is known about potential interactions between boswellia and other medications, so if you are taking prescription drugs, talk to your doctor or medical herbalist before using it.

• Devil's claw may occasionally cause digestive problems such as diarrhoea, so should not be used by people with pre-existing gastrointestinal complaints, such as ulcers, gall stones or diarrhoea, except with the advice of a medical herbalist.

• Do not take devil's claw if you are taking warfarin or anti-arrhythmic drugs, except under professional advice. Stop taking devil's claw at least 2 weeks before undergoing surgery.

• Do not take white willow bark if you are allergic to salicylates, including aspirin. If you are taking antiplatelet or anticoagulant medication, or suffer from a blood disorder, take it only under professional supervision.

• Ginger should not be taken in medicinal doses by people suffering from gastric ulcer or gall stones, or those taking warfarin or antiplatelet medication, except under professional advice. Stop taking it at least 2 weeks prior to undergoing surgery.

• Celery seed may interact with medications, including warfarin and thyroxine. It may also increase the risk of side-effects associated with some forms of ultra-violet light therapy. Consult your doctor before use.

• Do not use celery seed if you have a kidney disorder, or if you have low blood pressure.

• Celery occasionally causes allergic reactions. Do not take the seed if you are allergic to the plant or vegetable, and exercise caution if you are allergic to dandelion or wild carrot.

• With the exception of ginger, do not take these herbs if you are pregnant or breastfeeding, except with the advice of a medical herbalist.

White willow has been known as a painkiller since ancient times. It thrives near ponds and streams.

Circulation problems and **varicose veins**

Inadequate circulation – particularly in the legs – can become a persistent and debilitating problem as you age. Several herbs can reduce pain and swelling.

Horse chestnut
Aesculus hippocastanum
Relieves symptoms of chronic venous insufficiency

The term 'chronic venous insufficiency' is used to describe leg veins that are having trouble pumping blood back up to the heart. In time, the legs become heavy and swollen, and can feel itchy, tense and painful. Varicose veins may also develop. At least 17 clinical trials have examined the effects of horse chestnut seed extract (HCSE), standardised for its content of escin, on the symptoms of chronic venous insufficiency. This research demonstrates that HCSE can help to relieve the pain, swelling and itchiness associated with chronic venous insufficiency. It appears to do this by helping to maintain the integrity of the blood vessel walls.

🌿 **Dosage** Take commercial tablets or capsules of HCSE that are standardised for their content of escin (sometimes spelt aescin). Look for a product that provides 100 to 200mg of escin per day, and always take it with food.

Grapeseed
Vitis vinifera
Anti-oxidant support for blood vessels Grapeseed extract is rich in a potent group of antioxidants referred to as oligomeric proanthocyanidins (OPCs). OPCs help to maintain the integrity of the blood vessels and stabilise the capillary walls, so may be beneficial for a wide range of circulatory problems. In people with chronic venous insufficiency, grapeseed extract has been shown to relieve symptoms such as

Vine leaves and bunches of grapes were a favourite motif of the Victorian designer William Morris as here on a wallpaper.

itchiness and leg pain in as little as 10 days, and it's likely to have even more benefits for the circulatory system when taken over a longer period of time.

🌿 **Dosage** Look for commercial grapeseed tablets, or capsules that are standardised to provide 150 to 300mg OPCs per day, and take them according to the manufacturer's instructions.

Ginkgo
Ginkgo biloba
Tonic for peripheral circulation

Ginkgo helps relieve symptoms of both Raynaud's syndrome and intermittent claudication – two conditions associated with peripheral circulation issues. Raynaud's syndrome is characterised by cold extremities and severe cramping pain in the legs that is triggered or exacerbated by walking.

🌿 **Dosage** Look for supplements standardised for their content of the active constituents ginkgo flavone glycosides, ginkgolides and bilobalides, with a daily dose of 120mg of a concentrated (50:1) extract, providing the equivalent of 6g of the dried herb. Higher doses may be needed for intermittent claudication – for more information, talk to a medical herbalist.

CAUTIONS

• Horse chestnut, ginkgo and grapeseed are known or suspected to interact with some prescription medications, so consult your doctor or pharmacist before taking them. Stop taking ginkgo and grapeseed at least 2 weeks before undergoing surgery.

• HCSE occasionally causes side-effects including gastrointestinal symptoms, nausea, headaches and itchy or irritated skin. If this occurs, stop taking the herb and seek medical advice.

• Do not take homemade horse chestnut or ginkgo preparations, as they may contain toxic compounds and/or cause adverse reactions.

• Do not use horse chestnut if you are allergic to latex.

• Do not take HCSE if you have diabetes, liver or kidney problems, or coeliac or other intestinal diseases, or if you are taking anti-platelet or anticoagulant medication, except under professional supervision.

• Grapeseed may reduce iron absorption, so separate doses by 2 hours.

• Ginkgo may cause mild adverse reactions, including dizziness, gastrointestinal upset, headache and allergic skin reactions. More severe reactions, including bleeding problems and seizures, have occasionally been recorded. If symptoms occur, stop taking the herb and seek advice from a doctor or medical herbalist.

• Do not take ginkgo if you have any kind of bleeding disorder.

• Do not use any of these herbs if you are pregnant or breast-feeding, except with the advice of a medical herbalist.

Leg ulcers

A leg ulcer is painful and messy – and can often be difficult to treat. Use herbs, including horse chestnut and calendula, to speed up the healing process.

Horse chestnut
Aesculus hippocastanum
Helps heal ulcers from the inside
According to a small clinical trial, a standardised extract of horse chestnut seed (HCSE) has been demonstrated to enhance the standard medical treatment of leg ulcers. Australian researchers found that compared to those taking a placebo, the wound dressings on the legs of people taking HCSE could be changed less frequently, resulting in a significantly lower cost of treatment. These effects are probably an extension of the actions of horse chestnut on peripheral circulation (see opposite), as about half of all leg ulcers occur as a result of chronic venous insufficiency.

Dosage Take commercial tablets or capsules of HCSE that are standardised for their content of escin. Look for a product that provides 100 to 200mg of escin per day, and always take it with food.

Gotu kola
Centella asiatica
syn. *Hydrocotyle asiatica*
Nature's tissue healer Gotu kola contains compounds that encourage wounds, ulcers and scars to heal, and can be used both internally and externally for this purpose. Taken internally, it can also aid symptoms of chronic venous insufficiency so, like horse chestnut, it may encourage the healing of ulcers.

Dosage Take commercially prepared tablets or capsules of gotu kola extract according to the manufacturer's instructions. For topical use, add gotu kola tincture to a cream or ointment base (see page 199), and apply to the affected area 2 to 3 times per day.

Calendula
Calendula officinalis
Accelerates ulcer healing Calendula ointment was recently the subject of a small-scale clinical trial that suggests it may play a valuable role in helping to heal leg ulcers. In this study, ulcers were treated with either calendula ointment or saline solution dressings for 3 weeks.

At the end of the trial, the ulcers treated with calendula ointment had shrunk in size by more than 40 per cent, while those treated with saline had only decreased by about 15 per cent.

Dosage Apply calendula ointment to the affected area 2 to 3 times per day, or soak dressings with calendula tincture and then apply to the affected area. You can also use fresh calendula flowers to make a poultice (see page 200). If the skin is broken, disinfect the wound by washing it with an antiseptic before using calendula.

CAUTIONS
• Ulcers are not well-suited to self-treatment, as they may be symptomatic of underlying vascular problems. Always seek medical advice before commencing any self-prescribed treatment, including topical applications.
• HCSE occasionally causes side-effects, including gastrointestinal symptoms, nausea, headaches and itchy or irritated skin. It should not be taken by people with a latex allergy.
• Do not consume homemade horse chestnut preparations, as they may contain toxic compounds.
• Do not take HCSE if you have diabetes, liver or kidney problems, or coeliac or other intestinal diseases, or if you are taking anti-platelet or anticoagulant medication, except under the supervision of a healthcare professional.
• The skin around leg ulcers is particularly prone to dermatitis and rashes. Ideally, a patch test should be performed at least 24 hours before any topical application. If a reaction develops, discontinue use and seek medical advice. Take particular care with calendula if you are allergic to the Asteraceae family of plants (for example, daisies, chrysanthemum and echinacea).
• With the exception of topical applications of calendula, do not use any of the herbs listed on this page if you are pregnant or breastfeeding, except with the advice of a medical herbalist.

Horse chestnut is also known as buckeye, because the seeds are said to resemble the eyes of deer.

High blood pressure and high cholesterol

Your blood pressure and cholesterol levels can be important indicators as to the health of your heart and therefore your potential risk of cardiovascular disease.

Hawthorn

Crataegus laevigata, C. monogyna, C. pinnatifida

Classic heart tonic Herbalists regard hawthorn as the most important of all cardiovascular remedies, with a protective action on the heart and its function. It is prescribed for a range of cardiovascular problems, including high blood pressure, high cholesterol, angina, irregular heartbeat and heart failure. Numerous clinical trials support the use of hawthorn as an adjunctive treatment for heart failure, and in this context it is documented to help reduce blood pressure as well as improve other symptoms, such as tiredness and shortness of breath. Some of hawthorn's active constituents have potent anti-oxidant activity, and these compounds may be responsible for the herb's cholesterol-lowering effects, helping to prevent the oxidation of LDL-cholesterol (so-called 'bad' cholesterol), and decreasing both the production and absorption of cholesterol.

Dosage Ask your doctor or medical herbalist to assess whether hawthorn is an appropriate treatment for you, and take it according to the dosage prescribed. To ensure you receive a guaranteed dose of the herb's key active constituents, your practitioner may stipulate a standardised hawthorn preparation. Take it for at least 2 months before assessing whether it is working effectively. Western herbalists have long used *Crataegus laevigata* and *C. monogyna* to treat cardiovascular problems. In traditional Chinese medicine, *C. pinnatifida* has an extensive history of use as a digestive tonic, but its application has now been extended to heart complaints, in line with the promising results that have been attributed to the European species.

Garlic

Allium sativum

Protects the heart and blood vessels There is good evidence to suggest that the more garlic you include in your diet, the less likely you are to suffer from cardiovascular disease. And when taken as a herbal medicine, it has been shown to lower blood pressure, reduce total cholesterol levels and the development of plaque in the arteries, and inhibit the formation of blood clots. Some of these actions in the body are only mild, temporary or applicable to certain groups of people, but because it works via several pathways, the collective effect is a degree of protection for overall cardiovascular health.

Dosage The scientific research into garlic's potential as a treatment for high blood pressure and cholesterol is controversial – not least because different commercial garlic preparations have different chemical characteristics, and some may not retain the medicinally effective compounds, which can degrade quickly after the garlic bulb is cut or crushed. If you decide to take garlic tablets or capsules, opt for those that are enteric-coated and labelled with a guaranteed yield of the compound allicin, or standardised for their content of alliin. Other high-quality supplements may be standardised for their content of S-allyl-L-cysteine (SAC). Follow the dosage recommendations of the manufacturer. If you prefer to consume garlic as a food, aim to eat at least 3 cloves per week, or even more if you are at particular risk of cardiovascular disease. Chop or mince the cloves, then leave them to stand at room temperature for 5 to 10 minutes, so that enzymatic reaction allows the biologically active compounds to develop.

With its bushy habit and white flowers followed by red berries, the hawthorn makes a pretty hedge and its medicinal benefits are many and varied.

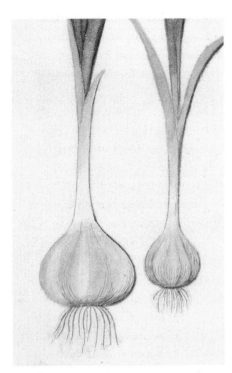

Each garlic bulb comprises 10 to 15 cloves, which form the plant's underground storage system.

Turmeric

Curcuma longa

Cholesterol-clearing spice

Turmeric is another culinary spice that supports heart and blood vessel health. It contains a yellow-coloured pigment called curcumin – the compound that is credited with most of the herb's medicinal activity. For example, curcumin has been shown to lower levels of total cholesterol, increase levels of HDL-cholesterol ('good' cholesterol), and protect both HDL- and LDL-cholesterol from the damaging effects of free radical activity. In laboratory and animal studies, it has also been shown to help lower blood pressure and reduce the ability of cholesterol to form plaque on artery walls.

Dosage Add up to 3g of grated or powdered turmeric root to your cooking each day. Alternatively, look for a commercial preparation that has been standardised to contain 95 per cent curcumin, and take it according to the manufacturer's instructions, up to a maximum of 300mg per day.

Psyllium

Plantago ovata, P. psyllium

Lowers cholesterol levels Psyllium is an important source of water-soluble fibre, which forms an absorbent gel in the bowel, trapping cholesterol and facilitating its excretion from the body. Combining psyllium with a low-fat diet for as little as 8 weeks has been shown to reduce LDL-cholesterol without adversely affecting HDL-cholesterol levels. Under professional supervision, psyllium may be particularly beneficial for patients with type 2 diabetes, because it can also help control their blood glucose and insulin responses after meals.

Dosage Psyllium husks are available in tablet, capsule and soluble powder form, and should be taken according to the manufacturer's instructions (note that the dose of psyllium used in cholesterol research is generally about 10g per day). Every dose of psyllium should be taken with a large glass of water.

Lime flowers

Tilia cordata, T. platyphyllos, T. × europaea

Calming blood pressure remedy

Lime flowers are a traditional European medicine for high blood pressure, especially when it is accompanied by heart palpitations or hardening of the arteries. They are also indicated as a gently calming remedy for anxiety and restlessness, so are particularly useful when high blood pressure is caused or worsened by worry.

Dosage Infuse 1 teaspoon of dried lime flowers in boiling water and drink up to 3 cups per day.

CAUTIONS

• Heart disease and other cardiovascular conditions are potentially serious issues, and should not be self-treated. Always follow the advice of your doctor, and if you experience any symptoms that may indicate a heart attack, such as chest pain (which may radiate to the jaw, back or arms), shortness of breath, or a general feeling of discomfort in the upper body, call for an ambulance without delay.

• Hawthorn, garlic and turmeric are known or suspected to interact with many prescription medications (including heart, blood pressure, cholesterol and blood-thinning drugs), and may alter the dosage requirements of your existing medication, so consult your doctor or medical herbalist before taking these particular herbal remedies.

• Occasionally, some adverse effects from hawthorn have been reported in clinical trials, but they tend to be mild and transient. The symptoms may include digestive problems, headache, dizziness, sleepiness and palpitations. If you experience any of these symptoms, consult your medical herbalist.

• Garlic sometimes causes side-effects, including gastrointestinal discomfort, nausea, indigestion, bad breath and body odour. Some of these can be reduced by eating cooked, rather than raw garlic.

• Turmeric can cause gastrointestinal upset when taken in large doses. Except with professional advice, do not use at higher than culinary doses if you have liver and gall bladder disease (including gallstones), gastric or duodenal ulcer, or people taking blood-thinning medicine.

• People who have diagnosed intestinal illness should only use psyllium on medical advice.

• Psyllium may interfere with the absorption of other medicines, so separate doses by at least 2 hours.

• Always drink plenty of water when using psyllium, as occasionally cases of choking have been reported when psyllium powders have been taken without adequate fluids.

• Lime flowers may reduce iron absorption, so separate doses by 2 hours.

• Contact allergies to lime flowers have occasionally been reported.

• If you are pregnant or breastfeeding, do not take hawthorn, lime flowers or psyllium, except under professional supervision. Do not take garlic or turmeric in greater than culinary quantities.

Premenstrual syndrome

If you're someone who is at the mercy of your hormones, there is gentle herbal help available to treat hormonal imbalances, period pain, mood swings and cravings.

The fruits of the chaste tree are used as a pepper substitute and in Middle Eastern spice mixes.

Chaste tree
Vitex agnus-castus
Clinically proven to reduce PMS symptoms In clinical trials, chaste tree extracts have shown a remarkable ability to relieve many of the symptoms of premenstrual syndrome (PMS), including depression, anger and irritability, mood swings, food cravings, bowel problems, and headaches. It achieves these effects by helping to normalise the complex hormonal fluctuations that govern the

female menstrual cycle, and can help set up a regular pattern of menstruation. In clinical practice, herbalists also prescribe chaste tree (often in combination with other herbs) for women who are experiencing difficulties conceiving.

Dosage To relieve the symptoms of premenstrual syndrome, take tablets, capsules or tincture throughout the month, according to the manufacturer's instructions. Look for products that are standardised for their content of the

compounds casticin and/or agnuside. Results may take 12 weeks or longer to become noticeable. If you are experiencing difficulty in conceiving, consult a medical herbalist who has been professionally trained and who can help to determine whether chaste tree is appropriate for you.

White peony
Paeonia lactiflora syn. *P. albiflora*
Hormone balancer In the traditional medicine of China and Japan, white peony root is combined with other herbs to treat period pain, heavy bleeding, uterine fibroids and other issues that, in Chinese medical philosophy, are associated with pelvic congestion. It is commonly prescribed with liquorice for conditions such as polycystic ovarian syndrome (PCOS) and endometriosis and, like chaste tree, is thought to exert its effects via a balancing influence on hormone levels.

Dosage Talk to a professionally trained herbalist, who can help to determine whether white peony is appropriate for your individual needs.

Dong quai
Angelica polymorpha var. *sinensis*
Chinese tonic for female problems Dong quai is another herb that is prescribed in traditional Chinese medicine for female reproductive disorders. Among other indications, and generally in combination with other herbs, it is prescribed for a range of gynaecological conditions, including painful, irregular, scanty or absent periods.

Dosage Boil 1 to 3g dried dong quai root in a cup of water for 10 minutes; drink the decoction 3 times daily. Alternatively, you can take commercial tablets or capsules that contain dong quai, according to the manufacturer's instructions.

Revered in traditional Chinese medicine, the peony is an inspiration to many Chinese artists.

St John's wort
Hypericum perforatum
Proven antidepressant PMS causes many women to experience depression, increased anxiety as well as difficulty in relating to family and friends. Since its efficacy for the treatment of depression from other causes is well established, it is likely that St John's wort is also an effective treatment for these PMS symptoms. In a small pilot study published in 2000, women taking St John's wort reported that the severity of their mental and emotional PMS symptoms had improved by more than 50 per cent after just two menstrual cycles. Further investigation is required to determine whether longer-term use has additional health benefits.

🌿 **Dosage** Look for supplements that are standardised for their content of hypericin and hyperforin, which are considered the main active constituents, and with a daily dose of 900mg per day of the concentrated (6:1) extract, which is equivalent to 5.4g of the dried herb. Take the supplements throughout the month.

Cramp bark
Viburnum opulus
Pain relief for cramps and spasms
Women who experience period pain of any kind will find cramp bark invaluable because, as its name suggests, it has a long history of use for the relief of cramps. It is traditionally used for any type of spasmodic or cramping pain, including the uterine, ovarian, abdominal, back and leg pains that occur during the premenstrual phase of the monthly cycle.

🌿 **Dosage** Take commercially prepared cramp bark tablets or tincture, up to a maximum dose of 1g, 3 times daily, as required for symptomatic relief.

Clary sage
Salvia sclarea
For period pain and emotional upsets The essential oil of clary sage is one of the most popular aromatherapy treatments for PMS, especially as it is also considered to have antidepressant, anti-fatigue and stress-relieving properties. Laboratory research supports the oil's use by demonstrating an antispasmodic action on uterine tissue, but the efficacy of this treatment has only recently been tested in human studies. In 2006, researchers conducted a clinical trial in which college students who suffered from period pain and menstrual cramps used either aromatherapy massage oil containing clary sage, lavender and rose essential oils; massage without aromatherapy; or no treatment at all. The symptoms of the women who received the aromatherapy massage were significantly less severe during the first 2 days of their period than the women in either of the other treatment groups.

🌿 **Dosage** To relieve period pain, make a massage oil using 1 drop of clary sage, 1 drop of rose and 2 drops of lavender essential oil per 5ml of almond oil, and rub into the abdomen or lower back as required. For premenstrual mood swings or emotional problems, clary sage can also be added to an oil vaporiser.

CAUTIONS
• The herbs featured on this page have known or suspected hormonal activity and should not be taken at the same time as the oral contraceptive pill, hormone replacement therapy or other medications that affect hormonal balance, except under professional supervision. Women who have a history of hormone-sensitive tumours should only take these herbs under professional advice and supervision.

• Chaste tree occasionally causes mild, reversible side-effects, such as headache, nausea and gastrointestinal upset. If you experience any of these symptoms, stop taking it.

• Do not take white peony or dong quai if you are taking warfarin or other blood-thinning or anticoagulant medicines.

• Dong quai is traditionally contraindicated in women with bleeding disorders, heavy periods or a history of recurrent miscarriage. It should not be used during bouts of diarrhoea or acute viral infection.

• Cramp bark berries are poisonous and should not be ingested.

• Clary sage essential oil is very potent and should always be diluted and used sparingly. It may cause headaches or sedation in some people, and may also cause contact dermatitis or skin irritation. Do not apply it to inflamed skin or open wounds, and do not use it topically if you are prone to dermatitis.

• For the safe and appropriate use of St John's wort, see *Depression and anxiety*, page 217.

• Do not use any of the herbs listed on this page if you are pregnant or breastfeeding, except with the advice of a medical herbalist.

Fluid retention and cystitis

All of these herbs are useful for keeping your bladder and kidneys in good order and for preventing inflammation and infections such as cystitis.

The fruit of the cranberry appear after the bell-shaped pink flowers.

Cranberry
Vaccinium macrocarpon

Prevents cystitis Cranberry is famous for its ability to help prevent cystitis, a bladder infection that causes burning pain on urination. It works by preventing the bacteria *E. coli* (which causes the vast majority of cystitis cases) from taking hold on the bladder wall and setting up an infection. This herb is particularly useful for women who have recurrent urinary tract infections (UTIs), as clinical trials indicate that, over a 12-month period, the frequency of UTIs in women taking cranberry is significantly reduced. Other people who are prone to recurrent UTIs – such as the elderly and people with spinal cord injuries – may also benefit from taking cranberry as a prophylactic against cystitis, but there less scientific data to confirm its efficacy in these groups.

Dosage Cranberry can be taken in juice, tablet or capsule form. Many people prefer to take the tablets or capsules, as up to 300ml per day of pure juice may be required in order to reach therapeutic levels. Few commercial juice products contain 100 per cent cranberry juice, so if you do decide to take the juice for medicinal purposes, you will need to calculate how many glasses of juice you require, depending on the percentage of cranberry that's present in the product. Alternatively, cranberry tablets and capsules are made from concentrated juice, and are generally taken at doses of approximately 30g (30,000mg) per day, in divided doses.

Marsh mallow
Althaea officinalis

Soothes inflamed mucous membranes With its rich content of mucilage, marsh mallow can provide soothing relief to irritated mucous membranes in the urinary tract. Herbalists often prescribe it to ease the pain and discomfort caused by infections or inflammation of the bladder and kidneys.

Dosage Infuse 2 to 5g of dried marsh mallow root in cold (but not hot) water, and steep for 8 hours to release the mucilage; drink up to 3 cups per day.

Self-help for cystitis

Cranberry is an effective preventative medicine for cystitis, but once an infection takes hold, you may need to take stronger medicine. Your doctor may prescribe antibiotics, or your professionally trained medical herbalist may treat you with urinary antiseptics, such as the herb uva-ursi. Meanwhile, these steps can help.

ACT QUICKLY While cystitis is generally a relatively mild and self-limiting condition, if it is left untreated, the infection can spread to the kidneys – with far more serious consequences.

INCREASE YOUR FLUID INTAKE Although the intense pain during urination may discourage you from drinking more, it's vital that you do. At the first sign of symptoms, increase your fluids to about a litre per hour, if possible. This helps to flush bacteria from the bladder, and can help prevent infections from becoming more serious. Choose water or soothing herbal teas (such as marsh mallow), and avoid alcohol, caffeine and fizzy soft drinks, which may aggravate the problem.

MAKE SURE YOUR BLADDER IS COMPLETELY EMPTY every time you go to the toilet. Wait a few moments after urinating, and then try again to expel the last few millilitres of urine from the bladder. Afterwards, women should wipe from front to back to ensure that bacteria from the anus aren't accidentally transferred to the urinary tract.

ALKALISE YOUR URINE Reducing urinary acidity may help to relieve burning symptoms, and can also make it more difficult for bacteria to survive. Avoid acid-producing foods, such as citrus and tomatoes, and consider taking a commercial urinary alkaliser (available from pharmacies). A home remedy of a teaspoon of bicarbonate of soda in water is also an effective urinary alkaliser.

Dandelion leaf
Taraxacum officinale

Nature's diuretic with plenty of potassium Dandelion leaf is traditionally regarded as one of the most important herbal remedies for the elimination of excess fluid. Although there is little data available to confirm its efficacy in humans, a small number of animal studies suggest that it may be as effective as some commonly prescribed pharmaceutical diuretic drugs. Dandelion leaf is a natural source of potassium; therefore, it doesn't tend to cause the adverse effects associated with potassium depletion that are sometimes observed with the use of pharmaceutical diuretics.

Dosage Infuse 1 to 2 teaspoons of dried dandelion leaf in boiling water; drink 3 cups per day.

Grapeseed
Vitis vinifera

Relieves premenstrual fluid retention Hormonal fluctuations during the menstrual cycle can cause troublesome fluid retention in some women. Although predominantly considered a remedy for the blood vessels, grapeseed extract has also been documented to effectively reduce premenstrual fluid retention and associated symptoms, including weight gain and abdominal pain and swelling.

Dosage Look for grapeseed tablets or capsules that are standardised to provide 150 to 300mg oligomeric proanthocyanidins (OPCs) per day, and take them during the second half of the menstrual cycle. You may need to take them for several months before experiencing the full benefits.

CAUTIONS

• UTIs are potentially serious – consult your doctor at the first sign of symptoms or if your symptoms worsen during treatment. Always investigate UTIs in children immediately.

• Fluid retention is sometimes a symptom of heart problems or other serious health conditions, in which case medical treatment is required. Always talk to your doctor before commencing self-treatment.

• High doses of cranberry juice may cause diarrhoea and other gastrointestinal symptoms – if this occurs, discontinue use immediately.

• If you are taking warfarin or have a history of kidney stones, do not take medicinal quantities of cranberry except under professional supervision.

• If you have diabetes, avoid drinking high quantities of sugar-sweetened cranberry juice and do not take marsh mallow except under professional supervision, as it may affect your blood sugar levels.

• Marsh mallow may interfere with the absorption of other medication, and grapeseed may reduce iron absorption, so separate doses by at least 2 hours.

• Don't use dandelion leaf if you are allergic to members of the Asteraceae family of plants (for example, daisies, echinacea).

• Grapeseed and dandelion leaf (and, particularly, the potassium found in dandelion) may interact with some medications, so check with your doctor or medical herbalist before taking them.

• Do not use dandelion if you suffer from liver or gall bladder disease (including gall stones).

• Stop taking grapeseed at least 2 weeks before undergoing surgery.

• Excepting culinary quantities of cranberry, do not take these herbs if you are pregnant or breastfeeding, except with the advice of a medical herbalist.

There are hundreds of cultivars of the grape vine, grown for fruit (fresh and dried) as well as wine.

Menopause

The onset of menopause can be a trying time, but there are several herbal remedies that can support your body through the demands of this mid-life change

Black cohosh

Cimifuga racemosa

Proven treatment for hot flushes

An extract of the North American herb black cohosh has been used as a treatment for the relief of symptoms of menopause for more than 50 years. As the subject of numerous clinical trials, black cohosh extract has demonstrated significant improvements in symptoms such as hot flushes, night sweats, insomnia, depression and anxiety. Of these, it is probably most effective against hot flushes, which many women consider to be the most troublesome aspect of menopause. Some research indicates that hot flushes may be reduced by more than 50 per cent after just 4 weeks of therapy with standardised black cohosh extract. When taken under medical supervision, this extract may

also be beneficial for some women who, for medical reasons, are unable to use menopause treatments that are oestrogen-based, or who prefer to use natural alternatives.

Dosage Take black cohosh tablets standardised for their content of triterpene glycosides according to the manufacturer's instructions, or as prescribed by your doctor. You may need to take black cohosh for up to 3 months before your symptoms start to improve.

St John's wort

Hypericum perforatum

Relieves anxiety and depression

While black cohosh is very effective for the treatment of hot flushes, night sweats and insomnia, its effects against the anxiety and depression that sometimes come with menopause are less marked. Consequently, herbalists often prescribe black cohosh alongside St John's wort for women whose menopausal symptoms include emotional upset. When the two herbs were taken together during a 2006 study, significant improvements were noted in both the psychological and physical symptoms. In other research, St John's wort alone demonstrated a significant ability to reduce menopausal symptoms in women whose primary concerns were related to their mood.

Dosage Buy supplements that are standardised for their content of hypericin and hyperforin, which are considered to be the main active constituents, and with a daily dose of 900mg per day of the concentrated (6:1) extract, equivalent to 5.4g of the dried herb. Take supplements throughout the month.

Many sages produced flowers for long periods and make an ornamental addition to the herb garden.

Menopause and soy products

Soy foods, especially in fermented forms, are a major dietary source of phytoestrogens, plant compounds that have mild oestrogen-like effects in the body. Soy phytoestrogens can help to reduce menopausal symptoms and appear to have protective effects against some of its associated health problems.

Soybeans, soy flour, miso, tofu and tempeh can all help to top up the small quantities of phytoestrogens you obtain from other dietary sources.

Alternatively, supplements that contain concentrated phyto-estrogens (or isoflavones) are now widely available, and most (but not all) research indicates that they can reduce hot flushes and night sweats.

Consuming soy phytoestrogens at levels higher than normal culinary intake may cause problems for women with some health conditions or who are taking certain types of drugs, so always talk to your doctor or medical herbalist before taking a soy supplement.

Red clover

Trifolium pratense

Herbal phytoestrogens Red clover is an interesting example of a herb whose modern application is largely different to its historical uses. While the flower heads have long been regarded as a detoxifying remedy for skin problems, the relatively recent discovery that the leaves contain phytoestrogens similar to those found in soybeans means that red clover is now predominantly thought of as a treatment for menopause. Clinical trials investigating the effects of phyto-estrogens from red clover have yielded ambiguous results, so more research is needed to clarify their effects, but there are some indications that they may help to prevent the decline in cardiovascular and bone health that many women experience after menopause.

🌿 **Dosage** Take commercially prepared red clover isoflavones in doses of 40 to 86mg per day, or as prescribed by your doctor or medical herbalist.

Sage
Salvia officinalis
Traditionally used to reduce hot flushes Sage is not only a popular culinary herb, but also a widely used traditional remedy for the relief of hot flushes. The plantis rich in tannins, giving it astringent properties and supporting its use to reduce excessive bodily secretions.In addition to hot flushes, these drying properties may benefit other menopausal symptoms such as night sweats and heavy periods. Laboratory studies have demonstrated that some compounds in sage possess oestrogenic effects, which may further help to explain its traditional use in menopause.

🌿 **Dosage** Infuse 1 to 4g of dried sage in boiling water; drink 3 cups a day.

Lemon balm
Melissa officinalis
Helps anxiety, insomnia and concentration A traditional remedy for restlessness and anxiety, lemon balm is ideal for women worry or are more sensitive to stress during and after menopause. Its relaxing properties can also help with sleep disturbances. Lemon balm helps promote feelings of calm and can be beneficial as a mood lifter when you're feeling emotionally flat. It has also been used to promote mental function, and preliminary research indicates that it may help memory and concentration.

🌿 **Dosage** Infuse 1 to 2 teaspoons of fresh aerial parts of lemon balm in boiling water; drink 1 cup 2 to 3 times per day, with the last cup 30 to 60 minutes before bed.

The old French name for sage was toute bonne, meaning 'all is well'.

CAUTIONS

• Do not take any of the herbs listed on these pages if you have a history of hormone-sensitive tumours, endometriosis or uterine fibroids, except under the supervision of a doctor.
• Do not take black cohosh if you are taking any prescription medication, except under medical supervision.
• Do not take black cohosh except under medical supervision if you have a history of liver disease, as some authorities believe that black cohosh may occasionally cause severe liver damage. These instances are extremely rare, but potentially very serious. If you experience minor side-effects, such as mild, reversible stomach upset and skin problems, stop using the herb and seek medical advice.
• Do not confuse black cohosh with blue cohosh (*Caulophyllum thalictroides*), which you should only take under medical supervision.
• Black cohosh may cause side-efects which include headeaches and mild gastrointestinal discomfort. If this occurs, stop taking the herb and consult your medical herbalist.
• Do not take red clover isoflavones if you are taking warfarin or anticoagulant medication, except under medical supervision.
• Due to its astringent nature, sage tea has sometimes been reported to cause dryness and irritation of the mouth. If this occurs, try reducing the dose of sage

relative to the amount of water used, and make sure you drink plenty of water throughout the day.
• Sage may reduce the absorption of minerals such as calcium and iron, so separate doses by at least 2 hours.
• Lemon balm may interact with some medications, so consult your doctor or pharmacist before taking it.
• For the safe use of St John's wort, see *Depression and anxiety*, page 217.
• Do not use the herbs on this page if you are pregnant or breastfeeding, except with the advice of a medical herbalist.

Lemon balm was called the 'elixir of life' by the medieval Swiss botanist, physician and alchemist, Paracelsus.

Pregnancy

Only the safest and most gentle of herbal medicines –
mainly fruit and flower-based – are recommended for
women to use when they are pregnant and breastfeeding.

Ginger
Zingiber officinale
Reduces morning sickness Many
women are understandably reluctant to
take drugs to help deal with the nausea
and vomiting of morning sickness, so it
is reassuring to know that ginger, which
has been used medicinally for thousands
of years, is both safe and effective to
use. Ginger has been compared to other
drugs and placebos in a number of
clinical trials, with overwhelmingly
positive results. It does occasionally cause
minor, self-limiting side-effects in some
women, but the results of these scientific
studies indicate that ginger doesn't have
any negative effects on the baby's health.
    Dosage Clinical trials for morning
sickness have generally used doses of
1 to 2g of ginger in tablet or capsule
form, in divided doses throughout the
day. Ginger tea made from freshly
chopped or powdered ginger may also
be effective, but different preparations
of ginger have different chemical
characteristics, so if your homemade
ginger remedy doesn't work, try a
commercial preparation.

Witch hazel
Hamamelis virginiana
**Relieves haemorrhoids and
varicose veins** Bowel habits can
become less regular during pregnancy –
yet another effect of the hormonal
changes your body is going through.
Aside from being uncomfortable,
constipation sometimes leads to
haemorrhoids, or piles, which are
actually varicose veins in the blood
vessels supplying the anus and rectum.
Swollen, itchy and painful varicose veins
can also appear in the legs or around the
genitals. Topical applications of witch
hazel may help relieve the pain and
itchiness of both varicose veins and
haemorrhoids, and can also stop
haemorrhoids from bleeding.
    Dosage Rub witch hazel gel,
ointment or tincture into the affected
area once a day. It may take up to
3 weeks before you notice any
improvements.

Calendula
Calendula officinalis
Great all-round healer Calendula has
many uses during pregnancy. If your
gums bleed, try a strong infusion of the
flowers as an antiseptic mouthwash.
Calendula cream, ointment or infused
oil are rubbed into aching or itchy
haemorrhoids and varicose veins, and
bring relief to cracked nipples. Herbalists
and midwives may even use the tincture
to encourage the healing of vaginal tears
or caesarean section scars after delivery.
    Dosage For haemorrhoids, varicose
veins and cracked nipples, apply
calendula cream, ointment or infused oil
to the affected area 3 times a day; the
infused oil is preferred for use on the
nipples if you are breastfeeding, as it is
safe for your baby to consume in small
quantities. For bleeding gums, prepare a
strong infusion of dried calendula, and
use it as a mouthwash after brushing
your teeth. Don't use calendula tincture
on surgical wounds or vaginal tears
without talking to your doctor or
midwife first, as it's vital to ensure that
the wound is clean and free of infection
before you start. Tissue treated with
calendula heals remarkably quickly, so, it
is important to check that no infection
remains beneath the treated wound.

Gather calendula flowers from early
summer onwards, then dry them in a
cool, dark place.

Rosehip oil
Rosa canina
May help prevent stretch marks
Rosehip oil is growing in popularity as a
remedy for the prevention of stretch
marks – including those of pregnancy.
The herb has a rich content of anti-
inflammatory compounds, including
vitamins A and C and essential fatty
acids, all of which are important for skin
health. So, although its efficacy hasn't yet
been scientifically confirmed, there may
be some substance to its reputation.
    Dosage Massage commercially
prepared rosehip oil into the abdomen
twice daily.

Raspberry leaf
Rubus idaeus
Prepares the uterus for childbirth
The traditional use of raspberry leaf
to help the body prepare for labour is
supported by laboratory studies
indicating that the herb has a range of
effects on the pregnant uterus. Although
very little clinical research has been
conducted, in one small study, Australian
researchers concluded that raspberry leaf
may help to shorten labour time and
decrease the likelihood of babies being
born either prematurely or after their
due date. This study also suggested that
taking raspberry leaf may help to reduce
the risk of forceps or vacuum delivery,
or caesarean section. In a second study,
192 women with low-risk pregnancies

took either raspberry leaf or a placebo from the 32nd week of pregnancy. In this trial, the second stage of labour was about 10 minutes shorter in those women who took raspberry leaf, and fewer forceps deliveries were required. At 1.2g of raspberry leaf twice daily, the dose used in this study is only 10 per cent of that recommended by herbal authorities.

Dosage Infuse 4 to 8g dried raspberry leaf in boiling water; drink 3 cups per day from the 32nd week of pregnancy. Alternatively, take raspberry leaf tablets or capsules according to the manufacturer's instructions, at a dose equivalent to 4 to 8g of dried herb, 3 times daily.

CAUTIONS

• Self-treatment with herbal medicine is only appropriate for women whose pregnancies have been assessed as low-risk. Use of any herbal medicine during pregnancy and breastfeeding, including those on this page, is best carried out under professional supervision. Seek immediate professional care for any but the most minor problems during pregnancy, or if you are concerned about the health or wellbeing of your baby. Always inform your doctor or midwife of any herbal medicines you are taking.
• Ginger occasionally causes minor, self-limiting symptoms, such as heartburn

Breech babies and Chinese medicine

Towards the end of pregnancy, most babies position themselves so that they exit the birth canal head first. The term 'breech' is used to describe those babies not in this position, and who are at greater risk of complications during labour. If a baby is breech, your doctor will probably suggest that he or she manually adjust the baby into a more suitable position – a procedure that's both very safe and highly effective.

Alternatively, you could consider traditional Chinese medicine, which has a good success record for turning breech babies. Your acupuncturist will use an acupuncture needle on a specific point on your little toe and simultaneously burn the herb

mugwort (*Artemisia vulgaris*) near the skin in the same place. While this process, called moxibustion, may seem peculiar if you haven't experienced acupuncture before, research in both Asia and Europe suggests that it is quite effective at encouraging breech babies to turn. In one trial conducted in Japan, 92.5 per cent of babies whose mothers had acupuncture and moxibustion subsequently rotated into the head-first position, compared to only 73.7 per cent of those whose mothers did not. Other researchers have monitored unborn babies' reactions to this procedure and reported that it does not appear to cause any foetal distress.

and gastrointestinal discomfort. If this occurs, stop taking the herb, or try taking it in a different form.
• Ginger has documented blood-thinning effects, and should not be taken concurrently with anticoagulant or anti-platelet medication, except under professional supervision. Women at risk of haemorrhage should not take ginger in greater than culinary quantities.
• Ginger should not be taken for 2

weeks prior to surgery. However, in consultation with your physician, a single dose can be taken just prior to surgery to reduce post-operative nausea.
• Topical applications of any herb can some-times cause reactions, such as dermatitis or itching and burning sensations, and ideally a patch test should be performed at least 24 hours before use. Discontinue use if a reaction develops. Take care with calendula if you are allergic to Asteraceae plants (for example, daisies and echinacea).
• Like ginger, raspberry leaf has traditionally been used as a treatment for morning sickness. However, do not use it during the first trimester of pregnancy, without the advice of a medical herbalist or doctor.
• Raspberry leaf may reduce the absorption of minerals, such as calcium and iron, so separate doses by at least 2 hours.
• Do not use raspberry leaf if you are suffering from constipation, peptic ulcer, or any inflammatory disease of the digestive system except with the advice of a medical herbalist.

An 1890s American advertisement extols the virtues of the raspberry.

Sexual and prostate health

The traditional use of herbs to support male reproductive health, including libido and prostate problems, is being increasingly backed up by medical science.

The berries of the saw palmetto were used by both Native Americans and European settlers.

Saw palmetto

Serenoa repens syn. *S. serrulata*

Clinically proven for prostate problems With prostate problems affecting about half of all men aged 50 and over, saw palmetto is one of the world's most popular herbs for male health. It's been the subject of numerous clinical studies, the majority of which show it to be an effective treatment for mild cases of benign prostatic hyperplasia (BPH), and specifically for symptoms such as reduced or hesitant urinary flow and the need to urinate during the night. It has been compared with several of the key pharmaceutical treatments for the same condition and shown to have a similar level of efficacy, but with fewer side-effects. Research also suggests that, unlike some pharmaceutical medications, saw palmetto does not interfere with the measurement of a marker called prostate-specific antigen (PSA), the levels of which are used to predict the presence of prostate cancer.

Dosage Most research has used a special extract from saw palmetto berries that is standardised for its content of free fatty acids and other oily compounds, referred to as a liposterolic extract. Take 160mg of the concentrated liposterolic extract in capsule form, twice daily with meals. You may need to take saw palmetto for 1 to 2 months before your symptoms improve.

Nettle root

Urtica dioica

Support for mild prostate conditions Like saw palmetto, nettle root has been clinically trialled for the relief of mild BPH, and the two herbs are often taken in combination. Nettle is documented to improve a range of BPH symptoms, including night-time urination, frequent urination and incomplete emptying of the bladder. In a study of over 2000 patients taking a formula containing nettle root and saw palmetto, improvements were noted in both symptoms and pathological changes – an indication that the herbal combination helps treat the disease, rather than simply suppresses the symptoms.

Dosage Look for tablets or capsules that provide the equivalent of up to 6g of dried nettle root per day, and take them according to the manufacturer's instructions.

Korean ginseng

Panax ginseng

Potent male tonic In traditional Chinese medicine, Korean ginseng is regarded as the most important herbal medicine for men, and ginseng roots with a shape resembling a man's body are highly prized. Its traditional indications include replenishing vital energy (referred to in Chinese as *qi*), helping the body and mind to cope with stress, and as a tonic to promote general health and longevity. Ginseng is also widely used to enhance men's sexual

Tomatoes for a healthy prostate

Tomatoes – along with other red- and pink-coloured fruit and vegetables, such as guava, watermelon and pink grapefruit – contain a pigment called lycopene, which has important benefits for men's health. Population studies suggest that men whose diets are highest in tomatoes have up to 40 per cent less chance of developing prostate cancer than those men whose tomato consumption is low. As a potent anti-oxidant, lycopene also supports the heart and blood vessels and may help to reduce the risk of cardiovascular disease. For optimal absorption, lycopene needs to be consumed with a little oil, so tomato-based products such as pasta sauces and tomato paste are all valuable inclusions in your diet.

performance, and has been shown in a few clinical trials to have a beneficial effect on erectile dysfunction. Results of these trials, as well as animal studies, suggest that the effects on sexual performance cannot be attributed to a purely hormonal effect, but may be caused at least in part by the herb's impact on the central nervous system and on the blood supply to the penis.

Dosage Take Korean ginseng tablets up to a maximum of 1000mg of the dried root per day, according to the manufacturer's instructions. (Higher doses may sometimes be appropriate under professional supervision.) Look for products that are standardised for their content of ginsenosides. Traditionally, Korean ginseng is taken for 8 to 12 weeks, followed by a break of several weeks. This herb is not appropriate for frail or anxious people.

Ginkgo
Ginkgo biloba

Stimulates circulation With its documented ability to improve circulation, ginkgo can be a useful remedy for male sexual dysfunction that is known or suspected to be due to reduced blood flow to the penis.

Problems with both libido and sexual performance are fairly common side-effects of some groups of pharmaceutical medicines, and there is a small amount of evidence that treatment with ginkgo can help to resolve these issues in some patients when taken under the supervision of a professional.

Dosage Look for supplements standardised for their content of the important active constituents ginkgo flavone glycosides, ginkgolides and bilobalides, with a daily dose of 120mg of a concentrated (50:1) extract, providing the equivalent of 6g of the dried herb.

Ginkgo takes a month or two to reach its maximum effect, so use it for 6 to 12 weeks before assessing whether or not it has helped you. If you suspect you are experiencing any adverse effects of

your prescribed medication, talk to your doctor or medical herbalist before taking ginkgo, and refer also to the *Cautions* section that follows.

CAUTIONS
• The symptoms of BPH and prostate cancer can be very similar, so it's important to see your doctor for a diagnosis before commencing self-treatment. Only mild cases of BPH are suitable for self-treatment. All men over 50 years of age should consider regular screening for prostate cancer, which can easily go undetected without testing.
• Do not take saw palmetto or nettle root if you are taking pharmaceutical medication for BPH or prostate cancer, except on professional advice.
• Saw palmetto occasionally causes mild adverse effects, such as digestive upsets and headaches. Nettle root infrequently causes mild adverse effects; if this occurs, stop taking the herb and consult a medical herbalist.
• Nettle plants cause urticaria, or hives, if they touch the skin, so if you choose to harvest nettle root, take appropriate precautions. Do not take nettle root if you have had an allergic reaction to the nettle plant.
• Do not take Korean ginseng if you have diabetes, cardiovascular disease (including high and low blood pressure), depression, anxiety, hyperactivity, mental illness (including bipolar disorder and similar conditions), insomnia, blood clots or bleeding disorders, except with the advice of a medical herbalist.
• Korean ginseng and ginkgo are known or suspected to interact with many pharmaceutical medications (including antidepressants, antipsychotics, digoxin, blood-thinning drugs (anticoagulants), anticonvulsants, insulin and hormonal therapy), so consult your doctor or medical herbalist before taking.
• Do not take Korean ginseng at the same time as stimulants such as caffeine.
• Korean ginseng is traditionally contraindicated in people suffering from acute infections.

In the First World War, German soldiers wore uniforms woven from nettle fabric, made from the plant's stalks.

• If you have been diagnosed with Alzheimer's disease or any other form of dementia, do not take ginkgo without first talking to your doctor.
• Stop taking ginkgo at least 2 weeks before undergoing surgery, and do not take it if you have a bleeding disorder.
• It is best to use commercially prepared ginkgo products from a reputable company. Do not consume unprocessed ginkgo leaves as they may cause adverse reactions. Do not eat large quantities of the seeds or allow children to do so.
• Ginkgo sometimes causes mild adverse reactions, which may include dizziness, gastrointestinal upset, head-ache and allergic skin reactions. Occasional severe reactions recorded have included bleeding problems and seizures. If symptoms occur, stop taking the herb and seek medical advice.

Natural beauty

Using aromatic herbs and essential oils to make your own natural body-care and beauty treatments brings many rewards. These easy and inexpensive recipes will cleanse, detoxify, soothe and energise.

Herbs for beauty and wellbeing

Nourish your whole body with natural homemade herbal preparations that can be used to exfoliate, cleanse, tone, condition, heal and soothe.

We drink herbal tea, add fresh herbs to recipes for extra flavour and take medicinal herbs to ward off colds and other common ailments. So it makes sense to use herbs in skin and hair-care products. Effective for fighting the signs of ageing, such as wrinkles and dark spots, herbs also cleanse, tone, moisturise and exfoliate your skin and add condition and colour to your hair.

Herbs contain thousands of active biochemicals and, thanks to the principle of synergy, they provide various benefits: your skin and hair recognise these substances as biocompatible and absorb them more readily than mineral oils or petrochemicals. Herbs can help to heal an array of skin and hair problems, ranging from facial lines to dandruff.

These healing botanicals, which contain minerals that calm and fatty acids that soothe, are among the most effective of cosmetic and personal care ingredients. Herbs also enhance each other. The right combination – such as antiseptic pine and cooling sage – makes a homemade recipe even more effective.

Make your own products

Making your own herbal skin and hair-care products is easy and rewarding. It's also a very practical way of avoiding exposure to undesirable and potentially harmful solvents, surfactants, silicone, artificial fragrances and other synthetic additives that are found in conventional products. And it's a means of contributing to a healthier environment and saving some money at the same time.

On the following pages, there are dozens of simple, effective step-by-step recipes for herbal moisturising lotions and creams, toners and astringents, powders, oils, scrubs, soaps and masks, plus special treatments to solve specific problems such as acne. Some recipes have been inspired by centuries-old texts from Western herbalism and Ayurveda, India's traditional medical system. Others are tried-and-tested remedies handed down by generations of 'herb-wyfes' who knew the healing secrets of wild plants. The rest are recommendations from natural health practitioners who continue to use herbs as a primary healing method.

Nutrients for skin

What you eat affects not only how you look day to day but also in the longer term how well your skin ages. That's why it's a good idea to try and eat a diet of foods that are known to protect against the effects of inflammation. Such foods include whole grains; fruits and vegetables of different hues; omega-3 fatty acids from cold-water fish; walnuts; extra-virgin olive oil and flaxseed; and anti-oxidant-rich herbs and spices, such as green tea, ginger and cumin. To keep skin hydrated, it's also

Super skin supplements

A good multi-vitamin and mineral supplement will help to provide your complexion with all the nutrients it needs. Extra amounts of certain vitamins may be recommended in particular conditions notably:
• vitamin A (which rebuilds tissue and balances sebum production),
• vitamin C (which your body uses to produce collagen, the connective tissue that keeps skin firm) and
• vitamin E (which reduces wrinkle formation, protects skin cells and prevents UV-light damage).
The following five supplements combat the ageing process because they are anti-oxidants or natural anti-inflammatory agents.

ALPHA LIPOIC ACID is a powerful anti-oxidant that defends against damage caused by free radicals that accelerate ageing.
COENZYME Q10 is an anti-oxidant with anti-inflammatory properties. It is helpful for gum health.
FISH OIL contains essential fatty acids docosahexaenoic acid (DHA) and eicosapentaenoic acid (EPA), which plump skin, keeping it supple.
GRAPESEED contains anti-oxidant oligomeric proanthocyanins (OPCs) that strengthen blood vessels and slow signs of ageing.
ZINC balances oil-gland production, encourages wound healing and regenerates skin cells.

worth making sure you get enough water – a sensible average is eight glasses of water a day.

It's important, too, to avoid partially hydrogenated oils, trans fats and polyunsaturated vegetable oils, which are all pro-inflammatory. Steer clear of foods that can cause a rapid rise in blood sugar and insulin – such as sugary or starchy processed foods – and trigger inflammation. This occurs in a process called glycation: sugar binds to collagen fibres in the skin, which makes it stiff and inflexible and can lead to the formation of wrinkles. Other causes of premature ageing of the skin are sun damage, too much stress, pollution and lack of exercise, so be sure to avoid these factors, too, where possible.

Essential oils starter kit

These five essential oils will form a excellent foundation to begin your collection.

GERANIUM Astringent and refreshing, this oil has a balancing effect on the skin, making it a great choice for homemade massage oils and footbaths. Invaluable for female reproductive health, it is particularly useful in helping to overcome irritability and bloating caused by premenstrual syndrome (PMS).

LAVENDER Helpful for cramps, headaches, nervous disorders and insomnia. Healing and antiseptic, this oil helps heal burns and other skin disorders, and prevents scarring. It's also a great insect repellent.

PEPPERMINT Stimulating, digestive and anti-inflammatory. Use in an inhalation to relieve nausea and respiratory problems, or in a bath to soothe muscle aches.

ROSEMARY For mental fatigue, headaches, colds and flu.

TEA-TREE Renowned as an antifungal and antiseptic, this oil can be used for clearing yeast infections, athlete's foot and acne, and also as first aid for minor wounds.

Tools of the trade

The basic tools for making your own herbal skin and hair-care products are very simple. It is a good idea to keep them separate from the ones you use for everyday cooking, though – plastic and wood absorb flavours and smells; metallic bowls and spoons can oxidise (react) with fruit and vegetable juices; and substances such as vegetable wax and beeswax are difficult to clean thoroughly from surfaces. Here's what you need.

- measuring cups and spoons
- kitchen scales
- non-aluminium saucepans, including a double boiler (bain-marie)
- heat-resistant, non-metallic mixing bowls, such as Pyrex
- non-metallic strainers – for example, cheesecloth or muslin squares and coffee-filter papers
- funnels, in different sizes
- glass dropper
- wooden spoons
- spatulas, in different sizes
- chopping boards
- airtight glass jars and bottles with non-metallic caps; pump, squeeze and spray bottles
- food processor
- hand-held mixer
- kitchen thermometers
- electric coffee grinder or mortar and pestle

Aromatherapy

Essential oils are very versatile and add a wide variety of benefits to homemade skin and hair-care products. They offer potent protection against a range of common ailments and help improve skin and hair health. Their small molecule size means that they can penetrate deep into the dermis to provide a profound healing effect and their wonderful scents also help you to relax and de-stress.

Depending on the essential oil you select, you can add antiseptic, rejuvenating, tonic or relaxing properties to a cleanser, moisturiser, ointment or body splash. Different oils can help prevent or clear skin problems; stimulate the generation of new cells; improve muscle tone; encourage circulation of blood and lymph; eliminate waste; counter inflammation; balance sebum (oil) production; and reduce stress.

Hydrotherapy at home

Considered to be a source of life in almost every culture, water is included in all manner of spiritual and religious ceremonies to cleanse the skin and replenish the mind.

Spa-goers can embrace the benefits of hydrotherapy: a dip in a hot jacuzzi, followed by a dunk in a cool pool, a hot sauna and then a cold shower all get your systems flowing and working in harmony, and your body works more efficiently afterwards. You can easily replicate this effect with some herbal hydrotherapy treatments at home.

Herbal hydrotherapy

Massage your body with a homemade scrub, such as Orange body polish (see page 285). Take a hot shower for about 5 minutes, then turn the water temperature down as low as your body can tolerate for 1 to 2 minutes. Repeat 2 to 3 times. When you step out of the shower and pat yourself dry, follow with an all-over spritz of Citrus zinger (see page 285). This will give your skin an instant refresh.

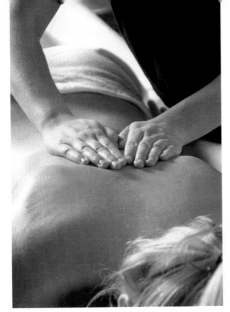

The essential oils used in aromatherapy massage have profound healing effects.

Body brushing

Skin is the body's largest detoxification organ. Sluggish elimination via the skin places a greater load on other organs, especially the liver. To boost circulation and stimulate the lymphatic system to release toxins, naturopaths and herbalists recommend dry body brushing with either a soft body brush or a loofah.

Body brushing also improves muscle tone and reduces puffiness and cellulite. It sloughs off the dead skin cells that clog pores and encourages cellular renewal, giving your skin a youthful glow. Here's what you need to do.
• Buy a natural (not synthetic) brush with a firm bristle. Soft bristles won't do the job. Make sure it has a long handle, so you can get at hard-to-reach spots.
• Do your dry brushing on alternate days, first thing in the morning before showering.
• Always brush towards your heart, using gentle, circular movements. Start with the soles of your feet and work your way up your legs, then hands and arms. Reach over and brush your back from the buttocks up the back and around to the stomach. Brush your stomach in an anti-clockwise direction. Avoid tender areas, such as the nipples, or wherever your skin is thin, irritated or damaged.
• Wash your brush regularly in warm water and mild soap. Rinse and leave to air-dry.

Before you start...

You will find the majority of the ingredients used in these recipes at your local pharmacy, supermarket or health food store, even in your kitchen cupboard. Others, such as cosmetic clays and soap moulds, are available from specialist suppliers or craft shops and websites. When a recipe calls for fruit, vegetables, fresh herbs or eggs, opt wherever possible for organic to avoid exposure to pesticides.

If a vegetable oil is required (for example, olive, almond or avocado), make sure that you choose an unrefined, cold-pressed variety that has not undergone heat or chemical extraction. In between uses, store these oils in the refrigerator. Use filtered or distilled water wherever water is listed as an ingredient; failing this, cooled, boiled water is acceptable.

Make allowances

Homemade herbal skin and hair-care products are free from the emulsifiers, thickeners and colourings found in conventional ones. As a result, they may not look like the creams and lotions you're used to buying in the shops. You will also need to make allowances for differences in the texture and quality of some raw materials – for example, oatmeal, oils, waxes and the herbs themselves. Feel free to adjust the quantities.

Storage and keeping properties

Adding a small amount of vitamin E oil, citrus seed extract or benzoin (from pharmacies) to your products will extend their life and reduce the risk of rancidity. As a general rule, the herbal creams, oils and balms described here will last up to 12 weeks in the refrigerator; dry scrubs and powder mixes will last up to 6 months in the refrigerator; infusions made with fresh herbs and masks or pastes made with fruit should be refrigerated and used within 2 days.

Hygiene

Adopting a commonsense approach to hygiene when preparing herbal skin and hair-care products will keep them as safe and pure as possible. Before commencing, tie your hair back, wear an apron and wash your hands thoroughly.

Sterilise glass or plastic bottles and jars for storing your products by placing them in boiling water for 15 minutes, then allowing them to air-dry, upside-down, on a rack. Ensure all utensils are clean and dry when you finish.

Patch testing

Finally, always patch-test products and ingredients first, especially if you have sensitive skin or a history of allergies. Natural products are less likely to cause an allergic reaction, but it can happen.

To test, place a small amount of one of the ingredients – for example, 2 drops of essential oil diluted in ½ teaspoon of vegetable oil – on a cotton-wool ball and tape it to the inside of your elbow; leave it for 24 hours. If the area becomes red or sore, do not use this ingredient in your beauty products.

Transform your bathroom into a haven where you can experience your own salon-style treatments.

251

Normal skin

Normal skin is soft and even-textured with medium pores and is not too oily or dry. Wash with a gentle cleanser then a toner enhanced with balancing herbs like elderflower or chamomile. Moisturise with a lightweight face serum or a cream moisturiser made with vitamins and plant oils.

Cinnamon scrub

A gentle scrub that leaves your skin exceptionally smooth and soft, this will brighten and refine all skin types. Almond meal soothes the skin while sugar buffs away dead skin cells. The cinnamon has a mildly antibacterial effect.

2 tablespoons fine-ground almond meal
1 tablespoon rice flour
2 teaspoons caster sugar
½ teaspoon ground cinnamon
plain yoghurt

1 Combine almond meal, rice flour, sugar and cinnamon in a bowl. Add enough yoghurt to form a gritty paste.

2 To use, gently massage the scrub into dampened skin, then rinse off.

Green tea toner

This herbal blend is healing and mildly astringent. Vinegar restores the skin's pH balance, the anti-oxidant-rich green tea is calming and hydrating, and the fennel adds a light liquorice-like scent. Elderflower is mild enough to suit the most sensitive skin and helps to reduce redness and inflammation.

1 tablespoon green tea
1 teaspoon crushed fennel seeds
1 teaspoon dried elderflower
125ml boiling water
2 tablespoons apple cider vinegar
1 teaspoon vegetable glycerine

1 Place herbs in a bowl and cover with the boiling water. Cover bowl and leave herbs to steep until water cools. Strain. Combine herbal water, vinegar and glycerine in a bottle.

2 To use, shake well. Saturate a cotton-wool ball with the liquid and wipe over skin after cleansing. Store toner in the refrigerator. Use within 10 days.

Floral milk

Milk, nature's own skin softener, contains lactic acid. This mild exfoliant gently lifts dead cells and tones your skin. Milk's fat content acts as a moisturiser and soothes any irritation.

2 tablespoons dried rose petals
1 tablespoon dried lavender
1 tablespoon dried chamomile
90ml full-fat fresh milk
1 tablespoon vegetable glycerine

1 Place herbs in a glass jar. Add milk and glycerine and seal. Chill overnight in the fridge. Strain and pour into an airtight bottle.

2 To use, shake bottle well and upend onto a cotton-wool ball. Wipe gently over skin 2 to 3 times, then rinse. Store floral milk in the refrigerator. Use within 1 week.

Three roses moisturiser

Rosehip oil is used for its anti-inflammatory and anti-allergenic properties; rose geranium oil is used to tone while rose oil is helps to soothe, heal and slow down the ageing process.

2 tablespoons jojoba oil
2 tablespoons rosehip oil
1 tablespoon grated beeswax
1000mg evening primrose
  oil capsule
250IU vitamin E capsule
1 tablespoon Rescue Remedy
  (from health food stores)
2 tablespoons rosewater
5 drops rose geranium essential oil
5 drops rose essential oil

1 Place jojoba oil, rosehip oil, beeswax and the contents of both capsules in the top of a double boiler, set over simmering water. Stir until melted. Warm Rescue Remedy and rosewater together in a separate saucepan.

2 Remove oil mixture from heat and add warmed Rescue Remedy mixture, beating vigorously with a small whisk or electric mixer set on low speed until cream thickens. Add essential oils and mix again. Allow to cool slightly before spooning into a shallow tub or jar. To use, massage a small amount into skin. Store in a cool place.

Get steamy

A herbal steam is simple and inexpensive. It gives a healthy glow naturally by improving micro-circulation to the surface of the skin and flushing out the toxins and debris. A steam also helps to open pores, making it easier for your skin to absorb the essential oils and aromatic herbs in the water.

Special care

When faced with stress, allergens and other environmental factors, even normal skin can change temporarily. Help your skin to stay in good condition with these strategies.

MASSAGE your face fortnightly to improve circulation and create a glow.

TO CALM overstimulated adrenal glands, take 200mg Panax ginseng daily. To ease tension, add 10 to 20 drops of an essential oil – such as lavender, lemon verbena or clary sage – to a bath.

TAKE a skin-clearing herb such as nettle (right) in tincture form. Drink 2 cups of green tea daily to scavenge free radicals and keep skin looking vibrant.

USE a humidifier in your bedroom to help your skin stay hydrated at night. Clean the filter regularly; add essential oils such as jasmine to help you relax.

Cucumber and chamomile steam

Cucumber has a cooling, mildly astringent effect, while chamomile softens skin.

2 chamomile tea bags
boiling water
2 or 3 drops chamomile essential oil
1 small cucumber, thinly sliced
almond or apricot kernel oil,
  or moisturiser

1 Place tea bags in a sink or bowl and cover with boiling water. Add essential oil and cucumber.

2 Drape a towel over your head and shoulders to create a tent and lean over the steaming bowl, keeping your face about 10cm above the water. Close your eyes and stay leaning over the bowl for 5 to 10 minutes.

3 Splash your face and neck with cool water; pat dry. Using a small amount of the nut oil or another moisturiser, finish with a soothing massage.

Pawpaw mask

This mask exfoliates and stimulates micro-circulation to the skin's surface, resulting in a warm, rosy glow. Pawpaw contains papain, an enzyme that helps dissolve dead skin cells. Honey helps skin to retain moisture. Yoghurt is a source of lactic acid, which helps to dissolve dead skin cells, while the mild bleaching effect of lemon juice evens out skin tone.

90g ripe pawpaw, diced
1 tablespoon plain
2 teaspoons honey
2 drops orange essential oil
1 teaspoon lemon juice
rice flour

1 Mash pawpaw in a bowl. Add yoghurt, honey, oil and juice; mix until smooth. Add sufficient rice flour to form a paste. Cover; chill in the refrigerator for 30 minutes.

2 Lightly remix and apply a thick layer to clean, dry skin, covering face and neck but avoiding the eye area. Lie still for 15 minutes. Rinse and pat dry. Apply light moisturiser.

Dry skin

Dry skin can feel rough, tight and itchy and may look dull. Untreated, dry skin can lead to severe chapping and cracking. The solution is to avoid harsh detergent-based skin-care products and to use herbal hydrating agents such as marsh mallow, which lubricate and moisturise the skin.

Softening rice bran scrub

Finely ground oats and powdered rice bran are gentle exfoliants that are suitable to use on dry skin, as they provide moisture as well as safely sloughing off any dead skin cells. Green tea provides additional anti-oxidant protection while helping to gently tighten up the pores.

1 tablespoon green tea
1 tablespoon dried calendula
1 tablespoon dried rose petals
35g finely ground oats
35g powdered rice bran
25g almond meal
cream or almond oil

1 Grind green tea, calendula and rose petals to a fine powder.

2 Combine the powder with oats, rice bran and almond meal, and mix thoroughly. Store the mixture in an airtight jar.

3 To use, mix 1 to 2 tablespoons of scrub with sufficient cream or almond oil to make a paste.

4 Let it thicken for 1 to 2 minutes, then massage it into damp skin with your fingertips; rinse off.

Avocado-cream mask

Nourish dry skin and protect it from the effects of the sun, wind and central heating with this rehydrating mask. The recipe contains cooling cream, to restore skin's moisture levels, and a swirl of soothing and healing honey.

half a ripe avocado, peeled
and stoned
1 tablespoon thick fresh cream
1 tablespoon honey
1000mg evening primrose
oil capsule
5 drops sandalwood essential oil
rice flour, sufficient to form
a paste

1 Mash avocado in a bowl. Add cream, honey, the contents of the capsule and the essential oil. Mix until smooth.

2 Add enough rice flour to form a paste. Cover and refrigerate for 30 minutes.

3 Lightly remix and apply a thick layer to clean, dry skin over face and neck, avoiding eye area. Lie still for 15 minutes. Rinse skin with lukewarm water and pat dry. Apply a light moisturiser.

Marsh mallow cleanser

Marsh mallow and soapwort grow in swampy, watery areas, where their roots soak up moisture to create a slippery sap that can both cleanse and relieve dry skin. The glycerine in this soothing formula binds water to thirsty skin.

1 tablespoon chopped dried marsh
mallow
1 tablespoon chopped dried
soapwort
60ml water
60ml rosewater
60ml vegetable glycerine
1 tablespoon sunflower seed oil
1 tablespoon aloe vera gel
5 drops chamomile essential oil

1 Place herbs and water in a small saucepan; bring to boil. Reduce heat, cover and simmer 15 minutes. Cool and strain, pressing down on herbs to extract as much liquid as possible.

2 Combine herbal liquid with rosewater, glycerine, sunflower seed oil and aloe vera gel in a bottle. Add chamomile oil.

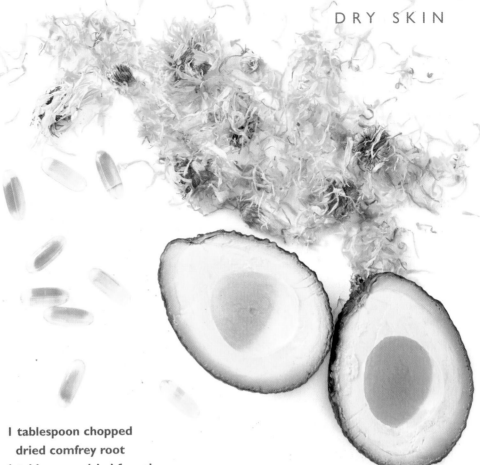

Dos and don'ts

DO drink at least eight 250ml glasses of water a day to provide your skin with the moisture it needs from within.

DO use lukewarm water. It's less likely to strip skin of moisture.

DO use regular massage and dry-skin brushing (see page 251) to stimulate sebum (oil) production and circulation. Use light, gentle pressure to avoid irritation.

DON'T use soap on your skin.

3 To use, dampen skin with warm water and massage a little cleanser into skin; rinse off. Store in the refrigerator but use it within 10 days. Follow with a mild toner, such as Flower balm (see below), then moisturise.

Flower balm

This ultra-mild herbal blend of comfrey, elderflower, fennel and rosewater helps keep moisture close to the pores of dry skin. Elderflower eases irritation, fennel restores skin pH levels, while comfrey produces soothing mucilage which has excellent hydrating properties.

1 tablespoon chopped dried comfrey root
1 tablespoon dried fennel
1 tablespoon dried elderflower
180ml rosewater
60ml witch hazel
1 teaspoon vegetable glycerine
5 drops rose essential oil

1 Place herbs in a dark glass jar with a tight-fitting cap. Add rosewater and witch hazel. Steep mixture in a dark place for 2 weeks, gently shaking once a day. Strain well.

2 Add glycerine and rose oil to herbal mixture. Pour into a pump-spray bottle.

3 To use, mist onto clean skin before applying moisturiser. Store in the refrigerator. Use within 10 days.

Rich repair elixir

This hydrating serum is especially designed for the needs of dry or sensitive skin. Sandalwood and calendula essential oils are anti-inflammatory and regenerative, while the rosehip and macadamia nut oils are rich in essential fatty acids that are good for the skin.

2 tablespoons jojoba oil
2 tablespoons rosehip oil
1 tablespoon apricot kernel oil
1 teaspoon macadamia nut oil
1 teaspoon carrot seed oil
4 drops palmarosa essential oil
3 drops calendula essential oil
3 drops sandalwood essential oil

1 Combine the first five oils in a small dark-coloured glass bottle. Add essential oils.

2 To use, shake well and massage a few drops of elixir into damp skin.

Mother Nature's moisturiser

Honey is a time-honoured treat for dry skin. Its unique texture holds the key to its many benefits. The high sugar content makes it a natural humectant, meaning it pulls moisture from the air into the skin, helping to keep it hydrated and plump, and because it's so thick, it's occlusive, which means it locks moisture in. In addition, its anti-oxidant properties fight free radicals from the sun and pollution that age skin. Its low pH makes it acidic and provides a mild antibacterial effect.

Oily skin

Oily skin may have clogged pores, a tendency to develop pimples and blackheads and an unwelcome shine. Make it look its best by using a toning cleanser; a hard-working scrub; an oil-absorbing mask with soothing minerals; and a light lotion with aromatherapy oils and herbal essences.

Lemony whip cleanser

This quick and easy cleanser removes make-up and grime, and helps to balance the skin. The yoghurt tones skin, honey is naturally antiseptic, while lemon juice controls oiliness and tightens up the pores.

2 tablespoons plain low-fat yoghurt
1 teaspoon manuka honey, warmed
juice of half a lemon
2 drops lemon essential oil

1 Place yoghurt, honey and juice in a bowl and mix well. Add the lemon essential oil and mix again.

2 To use, massage mixture into face and throat, avoiding eye area. Rinse off.

Mint astringent

Barley water is a good source of zinc and sulphur, two minerals that help balance oil production. Peppermint is a refreshing, stimulating and cooling herb, which also calms inflammation.

1 tablespoon fresh peppermint leaves
1 tablespoon fresh lemon balm leaves
1 tablespoon fresh rosemary leaves
125ml witch hazel
1 tablespoon vodka
1 tablespoon pearl barley
125ml water
5 drops peppermint essential oil

1 Crush herbs with a mortar and pestle. Transfer to a jar with a tight-fitting lid.

2 Add witch hazel and vodka and steep for 10 days. Strain.

3 Place barley in a saucepan with water. Bring to the boil then simmer, covered, for 15 minutes. Cool, then strain.

4 Combine barley water and herbal liquid in a bottle. Add oil.

5 Shake well before use. Store in the refrigerator, but make sure you use it within 2 weeks.

Fruity scrub

This scrub is great for problem areas on the shoulders, chest and back. Papain, an enzyme found in pawpaw, dissolves dead cells; the oats and almonds buff skin; white willow bark is anti-inflammatory; and the clay absorbs excess oil. Lemon essential oil adds a fresh, zingy fragrance and also helps to tone and refine the skin.

25g almond meal
35g coarse-ground oats
1 tablespoon white cosmetic clay
1 white willow bark tablet, crushed
2 drops lemon essential oil

1 Peel, seed and chop pawpaw. Mash to form approximately ½ cup pulp.
2 Add almond meal, ground oats, clay, white willow powder and oil. Mix well.
3 Apply to clean skin using firm, circular movements. Rinse off.

Aromatherapy skin spritz

Use this instant refresher to remove cleanser residue and excess perspiration and oil, especially during hot weather. Grapefruit and lemon have gentle astringent and bleaching properties, while apple cider vinegar balances the skin's pH.

125ml carbonated mineral water
125ml witch hazel
1 tablespoon apple cider vinegar
5 drops lavender essential oil
5 drops grapefruit essential oil
3 drops lemon essential oil

1 Place water, witch hazel and vinegar in a pump-spray bottle with a fine mist head. Add oils.

2 To use, shake and lightly spritz over face and neck, avoiding eyes. Store in the refrigerator for up to 1 month.

Brewer's yeast mask

Brewer's yeast absorbs excess oil from the skin's surface and stimulates a sluggish complexion. Egg white shrinks pores, while spirulina is an aquatic herb that is full of skin-supportive nutrients such as vitamin A and trace minerals.

1 tablespoon powdered
** brewer's yeast**
1 teaspoon powdered spirulina
1 tablespoon plain yoghurt
1 egg white
cornflour

1 Place yeast, spirulina and yoghurt in a bowl. Mix well.

2 In a separate bowl, beat egg white with a whisk until foamy. Add to yeast mixture and stir to combine. Add a little cornflour to make a workable paste.

3 To use, apply to clean, slightly damp

Eat herbs from the sea

If your skin produces excess oil, especially in the face's T-zone (forehead, nose and chin), these delicious seaweeds can make a difference by working from within.
KELP (*Laminaria* sp.) This source of vitamins C and A is a blood purifier, while its natural iodine content normalises the lymph system.
KOMBU (*L. setchelli*) Also known as horsetail kelp, kombu is a staple ingredient in Japanese cooking that is rich in skin-balancing minerals such as silica and zinc as well as the healing trace element germanium.

skin, avoiding eyes and lips. Leave for 15 minutes, then rinse off. Follow with a light moisturiser.

Herbal serum

Even oily skin needs a light moisturiser to put a barrier between your skin and environmental pollutants. Jojoba oil is compatible with skin and leaves little residue; the cinnamon and essential oils counteract the bacteria and toxins on the skin's surface.

ARAME (*Eisenia bycyclis*) High in protein and iodine, arame contains compounds that help to detoxify the body, improve metabolism and tone the skin.

1 small cinnamon stick
3 tablespoons jojoba oil
2 drops tea-tree essential oil
2 drops cypress essential oil
2 drops grapefruit essential oil

1 Lightly crush cinnamon and place in a small container with a lid. Add jojoba oil and steep for 10 days. Strain. Add essential oils.

2 Pour serum into a small bottle with a dropper opening. To use, warm a few drops between your fingertips and lightly massage into clean, slightly damp skin.

Sensitive skin

Sensitive skin can be irritated by artificial ingredients and even hot water. To soothe it, use gentle skincare products formulated with calming herbal extracts and essential oils.

Aromatherapy face wash

Use this light cleanser whenever your skin feels tight and dry. The glycerine draws moisture from the air to the skin.

125ml rosewater
60ml vegetable glycerine
10 drops rose essential oil
5 drops chamomile essential oil

1 Combine all the ingredients in a bottle.

2 To use, shake well. Massage a small amount into damp skin, then rinse. Store in a cool, dry place away from direct sunlight.

Toning mist

Chamomile and elderflower eliminate redness and blotchiness, marsh mallow and aloe vera are hydrating, and the vinegar restores the skin's pH balance.

1 teaspoon dried chamomile
1 teaspoon dried elderflowers
1 teaspoon dried marsh mallow root, chopped
60ml water
60ml rosewater
1 teaspoon aloe vera gel
1 teaspoon apple cider vinegar

1 Place herbs and water in a saucepan. Bring to the boil, remove from heat, cover and steep for 15 minutes. Strain.

2 Pour liquid into a pump-spray bottle. Add rosewater, aloe vera and vinegar. To use, shake well and mist face before applying moisturiser.

Calendula cream

Calendula is excellent for irritated skin, and it is included in many baby products for just this reason. This moisturiser soothes sensitive skin and helps to protect it from environmental stress.

4 tablespoons jojoba oil
4 teaspoons rosehip oil
3 teaspoons grated beeswax
4 tablespoons rosewater
250IU vitamin E capsule
1000mg evening primrose oil capsule
7 drops calendula essential oil
3 drops chamomile essential oil

1 Place jojoba oil, rosehip oil and beeswax in a double boiler. Place over a low heat and allow to melt. Warm rosewater in another saucepan.

2 Remove pans from heat. When the contents of both are lukewarm, whisk rosewater into oil mixture. Using an electric mixer set on low, beat for 2 to 3 minutes.

3 Add contents of capsules and the essential oils; whisk until cool. Spoon mixture into a small, wide-mouthed jar. To use, warm a little cream in your palms, then massage into skin.

Pear hydrating mask

A luscious treat for sensitive or reactive skin, the pear in this mask is cooling and emollient, while the cream is rich with fats that help to nourish the skin.

1 tablespoon peeled and grated pear
1 tablespoon fresh double cream
5 drops rose essential oil
2 drops sandalwood essential oil
rice flour

1 Combine pear, cream and oils in a bowl. Mix in sufficient rice flour to thicken into a paste.

2 Smooth mask over face and neck, and leave for 10 minutes. Rinse off.

Mature skin

As you get older, regular use of a natural peel will keep skin cell turnover high and help your skin glow. Boost it further with moisturising treatments and essential oils.

Strawberry skin peel

Strawberries have high levels of skin-brightening alpha-hydroxy acids, while white willow bark contains salicylic acid to remove dead surface cells and clean pores.

4 large fresh strawberries
I white willow bark tablet
I egg yolk
I teaspoon honey
2 drops frankincense essential oil
cornflour

1 Mash strawberries in a bowl. Grind tablet to a powder and add to bowl. Add egg yolk, honey and oil and mix to combine. Mix in sufficient cornflour to thicken.

2 Smooth mask onto damp skin and leave for 10 minutes. Rinse off.

Green tea skin polish

Refine the skin's surface and boost its radiance with regular exfoliation. As a bonus, sloughing off dead cells primes skin for a rich moisturising treatment.

I tablespoon ground adzuki beans
I teaspoon white cosmetic clay
I tablespoon almond meal
I teaspoon green tea
I teaspoon lemon juice
I teaspoon honey
about 2 tablespoons mashed
  fresh pineapple

1 Combine ground beans, clay, almond meal and tea in a bowl. Add juice, honey and enough pineapple to make a gritty paste.

2 To use, massage mixture into damp skin. Rinse off.

Immortelle nourishing oil

The immortelle (everlasting) flower has impressive anti-ageing properties, while carrot seed and rosehip oils plump up the epidermis, so skin looks more youthful.

I ½ tablespoons jojoba oil
I teaspoon carrot seed oil
I teaspoon rosehip oil
500IU vitamin E capsule
10 drops immortelle essential oil
5 drops rose essential oil
3 drops frankincense essential oil
2 drops palmarosa essential oil

1 Place all the ingredients in a bottle. To use, massage a small amount into face and neck.

Age spot lightener

Liquorice blocks tyrosine, an enzyme that controls melanin production. Here, it's paired with fruit acid from apples and vitamin C, a mild bleach.

I tablespoon dried liquorice root
60ml boiling water
1000mg vitamin C tablet
I tablespoon apple pulp
5 drops lemon essential oil
rice flour

1 Place dried liquorice root in a bowl with boiling water. Cover bowl and leave to steep for 15 minutes. Strain into a clean bowl.

2 Grind tablet to a powder. Add powder, pulp and oil to herbal liquid; thicken with sufficient flour to make a paste.

3 To use, paint paste over spots and leave to dry. Rinse off. Store remaining paste, covered, in the refrigerator. Repeat daily for 2 weeks.

Rosehip oil softens dry skin, fades scarring and eases sun damage.

Blemished skin

If you suffer from a surfeit of spots, use natural topical treatments to treat acne and pimples, and cleansing herbal tonics to detoxify your system from within.

Lemon grass skin saver

In an Indian study, researchers found lemon grass essential oil was effective in discouraging 22 types of bacteria that can cause skin infections. It is also high in tannins, natural vaso-constrictors (constrictors of blood vessels), which reduce inflammation. Add a couple of drops to a homemade toner, or sprinkle 5 drops in boiling water for a clarifying steam treatment.

Citrus steam

Steam opens the pores while adding herbs and essential oils enhances the detoxifying effect: lemon tones skin; lemon grass is healing; and rosemary stimulates circulation.

1 lemon, sliced
6 fresh rosemary sprigs
5 drops lemon grass essential oil

1 Fill a bowl with boiling water. Add lemon, rosemary and oil.

2 Drape a towel over your head and shoulders to create a tent and lean over bowl, keeping your face about 10cm above the water. Steam your face for 10 minutes. Splash with water; pat dry.

Healing green mask

This deep-cleansing mask helps remove impurities and heal blemishes. The clay absorbs excess oil, tea tree is antibacterial and parsley is a skin-clarifying herb. Oat flour helps bind the mixture and softens the skin.

1 tablespoon green cosmetic clay
1 tablespoon chopped fresh parsley
1 teaspoon oat flour
2 tablespoons aloe vera gel
5 drops tea-tree essential oil

1 Mix clay, parsley, flour and gel in a bowl. Add oil to make a paste.

2 Spread paste over face, avoiding eye and lip areas. Leave for 10 minutes. Rinse off.

Herbal antiseptic lotion

Thyme is antibacterial and antimicrobial while witch hazel is a natural astringent. Yarrow and comfrey are both superb skin healers.

2 teaspoons dried thyme
1 teaspoon dried yarrow
1 teaspoon dried comfrey
100ml boiling water
60ml witch hazel

1 Put herbs in a bowl and cover with boiling water. Cover bowl and steep for 15 minutes. Strain.

2 Pour liquid into a bottle. Add the witch hazel.

3 To use, shake bottle well and upend onto a cotton-wool ball. Wipe gently over skin. Store in the refrigerator. Use within 10 days.

Detox tea

The humble dandelion is a powerful detoxification agent, helping rid the body of waste. Red clover and alfalfa are traditional digestive and kidney tonics.

2 teaspoons dried dandelion
1 teaspoon dried red clover
1 teaspoon dried alfalfa
1 teaspoon lemon zest
500ml boiling water

1 Place herbs in a teapot and pour on boiling water. Cover pot and steep for 15 minutes. Strain. Drink 2 to 3 cups daily.

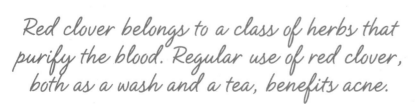

Red clover belongs to a class of herbs that purify the blood. Regular use of red clover, both as a wash and a tea, benefits acne.

Sunburn and sun damage

While a degree of sun exposure is healthy, helping to strengthen bones and balance hormones, too much damages skin. Always apply sunscreen and wear protective clothing in strong sun. If you do get sunburn, these herbal remedies will ease the pain and speed healing.

Aloe vera wrap

Slice open a fresh aloe leaf as shown (see also page 264) and wrap it around the problem area like a bandage, so the gel sits against your skin. Leave it for 10 minutes, or until skin feels better, then rinse off. Aloe vera has a long history as a first aid treatment.

Cooling calendula bath

Rice bran is an effective remedy for heat rash and sunburn. Antiseptic calendula is an all-round healer, while milk soothes.

35g dried calendula flowers
35g rice bran
25cm square piece of muslin; string

1 Pile all the ingredients in the middle of the muslin square.

Native Americans called aloe vera 'the wand of heaven' and used it to heal desert sunburns and treat scorpion bites.

Gather up sides and tie securely with string to make a bag.

2 Toss into the bath as it is filling. To use, squeeze herbal liquid over skin and use bag as a compress on sore spots.

Green tea body spray

Green tea contains powerful polyphenols that protect skin and slow inflammation triggered by sun exposure. Feverfew reduces redness and lavender is healing.

4 teaspoons green tea
2 teaspoons dried feverfew
125ml boiling water
60ml rosewater
10 drops lavender essential oil

1 Place tea and feverfew in a pot and pour on boiling water. Cover the pot and steep for 15 minutes, then strain and refrigerate.

2 Stir in rosewater and oil. Pour into a spray bottle.

3 To use, shake and lightly mist over skin. Store in the refrigerator. Use the spray within 10 days.

Kitchen sunburn cures

DAB with cold, wet tea bags.
SNIP open 2 to 3 vitamin E 500IU capsules and massage the oil into skin.
SWIRL 200ml apple cider vinegar or bicarbonate of soda into lukewarm bath water and soak.
TAKING anti-oxidant nutrients may offer some limited protection against sun damage. A study at Munich University found that people who took a dose of 1000IU vitamin E and 2000mg vitamin C daily demonstrated a 34 per cent greater resistance to sunburn.

Eyes and lips

The skin around the eyes is the first part of your face to show stress and tiredness. Lips dry out because they are just a thin layer of skin that is always exposed to the elements.

Gift of the Magi

Frankincense is an aromatic gum resin obtained from trees of the genus *Boswellia*, primarily *B. sacra*. The bark of the tree is incised and a milky resinous liquid oozes out, hardening to droplets, or 'tears'. Used since ancient times by various cultures, including the Greeks, Romans, Egyptians, Assyrians and Babylonians, frankincense is familiar to many Westerners through the Christian story of the Magi, who brought gifts of gold, frankincense and myrrh to the baby Jesus. The name comes from the Old French franc encens, or 'pure incense'; that was, and remains, one of its principle uses. In China, *fanhunxiang*, as it is known, is categorised as a herb for vitalising the blood, and is used to treat painful swellings and other ailments. Steam distillation of the dry resin produces an essential oil

The three Magi presented the baby Jesus with gifts of gold, frankincense and myrrh.

valued in modern aromatherapy to treat wounds, scars, acne and bacterial and fungal infections. Frankincense oil is also an ingredient in cosmetics, soaps and perfumes.

Chamomile-milk soother

Chamomile contains anti-inflammatory azulene, which reduces redness, while milk fats calm irritated skin. Using very cold milk constricts the blood vessels, reducing puffiness.

2 chamomile tea bags
60ml ice-cold milk

1 Soak tea bags in milk for 5 minutes. Squeeze out excess liquid.

2 Place tea bags over eyes. Rest for 10 minutes.

Eyebright compress

This recipe refreshes eyes that are tired and irritated by dust, allergies or computer use. Tannins in the herbs tighten tissue and stimulate lymphatic drainage.

1 tablespoon dried eyebright
1 teaspoon crushed fennel seeds
1 teaspoon dried elderflower
250ml boiling water

1 Place herbs in a bowl and cover with boiling water. Cover and refrigerate until cold.

2 Strain through muslin or a coffee filter.

3 Dip a clean cloth into the liquid and place over eyes. Rest for 10 minutes.

Herbal eye oil

This fine-textured eye oil uses vitamin E to moisturise lashes and jojoba to reduce the appearance of fine lines. As a bonus, vitamin E also helps to slow down ageing.

1½ tablespoons jojoba oil
3 drops rose essential oil
2 drops frankincense essential oil
500IU vitamin E capsule

1 Combine oil, essential oils and the contents of the capsule in a dark glass bottle.

2 To use, upend bottle onto your ring finger. Pat a small amount of the oil around your eyes.

Honey lip balm

Conventional lip balms may contain petrolatum derivatives, fake fragrances and potential carcinogens. Try this plant-derived balm as a natural alternative.

1 tablespoon grated beeswax
2 tablespoons almond oil
2 tablespoons castor oil
1 tablespoon cocoa butter
1 teaspoon honey
500IU vitamin E capsule
10 drops rose essential oil

1 Place beeswax, almond and castor oils, butter and honey in the top of a double boiler. Melt over low heat, whisking constantly.

2 Remove from heat. Add contents of the capsule and rose oil. Place pan in a shallow ice-water bath and whisk until mixture becomes creamy.

3 Spoon mixture into small jars. Store in a cool spot for 6 months.

Teeth and gums

Using herbal toothpastes and mouthwashes heals gums, freshens breath and even whitens teeth, and they are far less drying and damaging than conventional pastes.

Cinnamon tooth powder

This inexpensive recipe polishes and whitens teeth, leaving your mouth feeling super-clean. Cinnamon has antibacterial properties, while clove is both antiseptic and healing.

2 tablespoons bicarbonate of soda
I teaspoon fine sea salt
½ teaspoon powdered cinnamon
5 drops clove essential oil
3 drops peppermint essential oil

1 Sift soda, salt and cinnamon together to remove lumps. Add essential oils, then sift again. Store powder in an airtight container.

2 To use, dampen your toothbrush and then dip it in the powder.

Double-mint mouthwash

Cooling peppermint and spearmint are effective in banishing odour and making your mouth smell sweet and fresh. Tea-tree essential oil fights gum disease and aloe vera soothes oral tissue.

Herbal breath fresheners

Try these natural alternatives to artificially coloured and flavoured breath mints.
CHEW ½ teaspoon fennel seeds or aniseed, which will leave your breath smelling of liquorice.
NIBBLE on fresh parsley. It fights bacteria and plaque.
GARGLE a solution of liquid chlorophyll and water to fight odour-causing bacteria. Dilute I teaspoon chlorophyll in a small glass of water.

I tablespoon dried spearmint
I tablespoon dried peppermint
I80ml boiling water
I tablespoon aloe vera juice
5 drops tea-tree essential oil
3 drops peppermint essential oil

1 Place herbs in a bowl and cover with boiling water. Cover bowl and steep for 30 minutes. Strain.

2 Add aloe vera and essential oils. Mix well. Store in a dark glass container.

3 Shake well, then swish 1 to 2 tablespoons around your mouth. Do not swallow. Store in a cool place. Use within 1 week.

Mouthwash for bleeding gums

Black tea and witch hazel are rich in tannins, which have a tightening effect. Green tea is an anti-oxidant, and goldenseal is a natural antibiotic. Myrrh has antiseptic and astringent properties.

I tablespoon black tea
I tablespoon green tea
I80ml boiling water
I tablespoon witch hazel
½ teaspoon powdered goldenseal (from capsules)
5 drops myrrh tincture
3 drops lemon essential oil

1 Place black and green teas in a bowl and cover with boiling water. Cover bowl and steep for 30 minutes. Strain.

2 Add other ingredients. Mix well. Store in a dark glass bottle.

3 To use, shake well and swish 1 to 2 tablespoons around mouth. Do not swallow. Store in a cool place. Use within 1 week.

Strawberry tooth whitener

For a brilliant polish that will give your teeth a silky feel, mash a ripe strawberry and dip a toothbrush in it to clean your teeth. Rinse thoroughly, as strawberries are very acidic. Use every 1 to 2 months.

Hands and nails

Hands reveal our health and character and, more than any other feature, betray our age. They contain only a few oil-producing glands, so are prone to dryness. A weekly manicure will prevent problems such as split nails and chapped skin.

Peppermint hand gel

This scented formula has a restorative effect on dry, work-roughened hands.

1 teaspoon honey
2 tablespoons glycerine
2 tablespoons powdered arrowroot
60ml cooled, strained
  peppermint tea
5 drops peppermint essential oil
5 drops frankincense essential oil

1 Place honey and glycerine in a small saucepan over low heat and slowly warm through, stirring constantly. Add arrowroot powder and whisk together. Remove from heat and stir in tea and oils.

2 Let mixture cool slightly, then pour into a clean glass jar with a non-aluminium lid. To apply, massage a small amount into your hands.

Anti-ageing hand mask

Masks aren't just for your face. This softening and moisturising recipe also helps to even out skin tone and fade age spots.

1 tablespoon honey
3 tablespoons aloe vera gel
  (see below)
1 teaspoon lemon juice
10 drops lemon essential oil
almond meal, sufficient to
  make a paste

1 Melt honey over low heat. In a small bowl, combine the aloe vera gel with the honey and lemon juice. Add the essential oil and mix thoroughly.

2 Add sufficient almond meal to make a soft, workable paste; it should not be too sloppy. Smooth mask over clean hands, paying particular attention to the backs of hands and knuckles. Leave for 20 minutes. Rinse off with warm water and apply moisturiser.

Harvesting aloe vera gel

At their centre, aloe vera leaves contain a thick, colourless gel. This soothing gel is useful for treating burns and dry skin conditions. Use it fresh, as soon as you have harvested it, because it is unstable and quickly loses its consistency. Do not use any gel that has a green tinge. The gel is available from health food stores.

1 Cut off a healthy large leaf close to its base.

2 Slice carefully along the centre of the leaf, along its entire length. Gently peel back the two cut edges. Use a blunt-edged knife to scrape the clear gel from the centre of the leaf, then place it in a bowl.

Aromatherapy cuticle oil

The essential oils in this fine-textured blend help to counter cracked and ragged cuticles. Calendula and myrrh essential oils both have antiseptic properties to help prevent common nail infections, while lavender is anti-inflammatory and healing.

1 tablespoon jojoba oil
1 tablespoon avocado oil
5 drops myrrh essential oil
5 drops lavender essential oil
10 drops calendula essential oil

1 Pour the jojoba and avocado oils into a small, dark-coloured glass bottle, which will help preserve the oil.

2 Add essential oils, screw on cap and shake to combine.

3 Before using the cuticle oil, shake the bottle well, then massage a few drops into your nails and cuticles daily to soften your cuticles and prevent them from splitting.

Healthy nails

MAXIMISE nail health with herbal products. Tea-tree oil, for instance, can clear up fungal infections of the nails, while a daily application of vitamin A-rich cod liver oil rubbed into nails and cuticles helps strengthen them.

EAT a healthy, varied diet rich in whole foods and essential fatty acids (EFAs), and make sure you get adequate hydration – a much better insurance policy for nail health than using commercial nail potions that promise to increase nail growth and strength.

WEAR rubber gloves to protect your hands whenever you are washing the dishes or using cleaning products.

Honey and almond balm

To moisturise your nails, rub a little rosehip essential oil into them, using small, circular movements. Then massage your hands with this balm, which is will soothe rough hands and is a good all-purpose skin salve for minor cuts and abrasions.

2 x 1000mg lecithin capsules
1 tablespoon rosewater
1 teaspoon honey
90ml almond oil
1 tablespoon cocoa butter
2 teaspoons beeswax granules
10 drops lavender essential oil
10 drops rose essential oil

1 Pierce lecithin capsules and combine contents with rosewater. Set aside. Combine almond oil, cocoa butter and beeswax granules in the top of a double boiler over simmering water.

2 Heat, stirring with a small whisk until the beeswax has melted. Whisk in lecithin and rosewater mixture and remove from heat. Stir in essential oils.

3 Let mixture cool slightly before pouring into a clean glass jar with a non-aluminium lid. To use, massage a small amount into your nails and cuticles every night before bed. Store in a cool, dry place away from direct sunlight for up to 6 months.

If you do not have a double boiler, use a pan that sits in the top of another saucepan. The base of the upper pan should be well clear of the simmering water in the base of the lower pan.

Years ago, Japanese women who splashed their faces with the water used for rinsing rice were called 'rice bran beauties'.

Foot care

Give yourself a regular pedicure and care for your feet with soothing natural products. Let your feet breathe and exercise naturally by walking barefoot whenever you can. Being vigilant about foot care helps prevent problems such as corns and keeps your feet feeling smooth and soft.

Keep feet sweet

Your feet have more sweat glands than any other part of your body, but they're usually trapped inside shoes for most of the day. Here are several ways to keep them odour-free.

• Wash feet daily with Tea-tree antiseptic soap (see page 279). Tea-tree oil is excellent for inhibiting bacterial growth and odour. Dry feet thoroughly.

• Apply an astringent herbal foot spray. Make strong sage tea by steeping 2 tablespoons dried sage in 100ml boiling water; allow to cool. Add 50ml witch hazel and 10 drops lavender essential oil. Pour into a pump bottle. Refrigerate. Shake well before use. Use within 10 days.

• Wear cotton socks, which absorb moisture better than synthetic ones, and rotate your shoes. Dust the inside of shoes with bicarbonate of soda.

Peppermint foot scrub

Peppermint cools and deodorises the skin and sugar buffs away dead skin cells. Your feet will feel soft and refreshed with this easy and effective scrub.

1 tablespoon coarse-ground oatmeal
1 tablespoon polenta (cornmeal)
1 tablespoon sugar
2 teaspoons dried peppermint leaves
1 tablespoon natural yoghurt
juice of 1 lemon
5 drops peppermint essential oil

1 Combine oatmeal, polenta, sugar and peppermint in a bowl.

2 Add yoghurt, lemon juice and oil; mix to form a gritty paste.

3 To use, sit on the edge of the bath tub and massage mixture into feet, paying particular attention to heels and soles. Rinse and dry thoroughly and follow with a rich moisturiser, such as Rose geranium foot balm (see below).

Rose geranium foot balm

This fragrant balm is perfect for softening leathery or dry, calloused feet. To get the best results, leave it on overnight, wearing socks. This will help to seal in moisture and protect the sheets.

2 tablespoons cocoa butter
2 tablespoons apricot kernel oil
1 tablespoon beeswax granules
1 tablespoon vegetable glycerine
1 teaspoon honey
10 drops rose geranium essential oil
10 drops lemon essential oil

Try flower power

Bunions are painful, bony bumps that protrude from the side of the big or little toe joint, usually as a result of wearing high-heeled or ill-fitting shoes. Custom-made orthotics can strengthen the arch and surgically shaving the bone will realign the toe, but it would be better to avoid such drastic methods. Why not try marigolds? A study in *The Journal of Pharmacy and Pharmacology* found that applying a paste of alcohol and crushed marigolds (*Tagetes* sp.), then covering it with a pad can reduce the size and pain of a bunion. The researchers concluded that flavonoids in the marigold reduce inflammation in the joint.

1 Put the cocoa butter, apricot kernel oil and beeswax in the top of a double boiler over low heat, and stir until melted together.

2 Remove from heat and whisk in glycerine and honey. Add essential oils and stir.

3 Pour into a glass jar and cool before sealing. The finished formula has a waxy consistency that softens when applied to skin.

Fragrant foot soak

The herbs and essential oils in this aromatic blend are astringent and antibacterial, helping to reduce sweatiness, fight odour and leave feet fresh and clean. Both rosemary and ginger are warming herbs and stimulate circulation of blood; their uplifting scents raise the spirits.

2 tablespoons fresh rosemary
2 tablespoons fresh sage
1 tablespoon fresh ginger root,
  finely grated
1 litre water
1 tablespoon bicarbonate of soda
1 tablespoon Epsom salts
10 drops eucalyptus oil
10 drops lavender essential oil
extra water
small ice cubes or crushed ice

1 Place rosemary, sage and ginger root in a large saucepan with water. (If you have no fresh herbs to hand, use 1 tablespoon of each herb in dried form instead.) Bring to the boil. Remove from heat, cover bowl and steep for 10 minutes. Strain.

2 Add bicarbonate of soda, Epsom salts and essential oils. Mix well. Pour into a foot spa or shallow dish big enough for both feet. Top up with extra water and add ice.

Treat your feet

This therapeutic and relaxing home pedicure avoids the toxic polishes and potentially dangerous fungal infections associated with nail salons.

1 Use an acetone-free product to remove old nail polish. Remove stains by rubbing nails with a few drops of lemon essential oil. Buff with a fine emery board. Fill a large flat-bottomed bowl with warm water and add 250ml apple cider vinegar and 250ml strong lavender tea (steep 4 teaspoons dried lavender in 250ml boiling water for 10 minutes; strain). The acetic acid in the vinegar softens the skin, while lavender heals any minor infections.

2 While skin is still damp, massage with Peppermint foot scrub (opposite) or make a simple foot scrub with equal parts sea salt and Castile soap (available from health food stores). Buff heels and soles with a pumice stone or loofah. Rinse off residue and pat dry.

3 Soak feet for 15 minutes; pat dry. Finish with a light dusting of Orange-blossom powder (see page 280).

Super-soft powder

Cornflour and arrowroot add a silken texture to the powder, while the clay will absorb more than 200 times its weight in moisture. In addition, the essential oils will eliminate bacteria that cause unpleasant odours. To boost this powder's ability to stop sweatiness, try adding 1 tablespoon zinc oxide powder (available from your chemist).

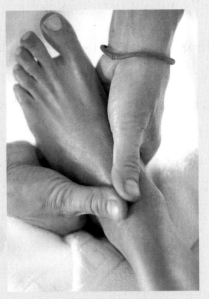

Cut nails straight across with nail clippers. Smooth with an emery board, remembering to always file in one direction. Gently push back cuticles with a cuticle stick. Never cut cuticles, as they protect nails from bacteria.

3 Massage your feet with Rose geranium foot balm (opposite). Wipe over nails with acetone-free remover, then paint with a toluene-free polish.

60g bicarbonate of soda
60g cornflour
2 tablespoons powdered arrowroot
2 tablespoons white cosmetic clay
15 drops lemon essential oil
15 drops neroli essential oil
10 drops lemon grass essential oil

1 Sift bicarbonate of soda, cornflour and arrowroot to remove lumps. Add clay and mix well. Add the oils and sift again.

2 Store the finished powder in an airtight, lidded container in a cool, dark place.

3 To use, dip a powder puff into the mixture and apply after bathing, or decant mixture into a small shaker.

Horsetail tablets contain keratin-producing silica, which strengthens nails.

Normal hair

Too much styling takes a toll on your hair. as does a poor diet and lifestyle factors, such as hormonal fluctuations, stress, alcohol, smoking and inadequate exercise or sleep. Be kind to hair with a nutrient-rich diet and products based on herbs and essential oils specific to your hair type.

Keep the balance

If your hair is normal, you'll want to keep it that way. Use a gentle SLS (sodium lauryl sulphate)-free shampoo. SLS is the detergent ingredient in most shampoos and washing-up liquids and it can irritate the scalp. Reduce static with a fragrant herbal rinse and keep hair manageable and smooth with Aromatherapy detangling spray (below).

Nutrients for healthy hair

Boost your intake of the following and start seeing results in weeks.

Protein fortifies hair and promotes growth. Food sources: beans, dairy products, eggs, fish, meat and poultry.

Iron oxygenates blood and boosts circulation in the scalp. Food sources: dried fruit, egg yolks, legumes, meat, leafy greens and whole grains.

Omega-3s (essential fatty acids) prevent dryness and add moisture. Food sources: flax seeds, sardines, soybeans, walnuts and wild salmon.

Silica strengthens the hair cuticle, boosting strands' elasticity. Food sources: cabbage, celery and oats.

Vitamin A supports the health of the scalp. Food sources: leafy greens, pumpkins, carrots, peppers and sweet potatoes.

Biotin (vitamin B_7) maintains hair growth and may be beneficial for hair loss. Food sources: eggs, liver, kidneys, dried fruit and molasses.

Zinc is essential for skin and hair health and for balancing hormones. Food sources: meat, eggs, poultry, crab, oysters, brazil nuts and soybeans.

Steps to success

• Wash hair gently with a mild shampoo. Vigorous scrubbing can damage hair and cause the sebaceous glands to produce too much oil.

• Unless you use a lot of hairspray, one wash with a small amount of shampoo should be sufficient; too much strips the scalp's naturally protective sebum (oil).

• To stimulate your circulation and enhance shine, rinse out shampoo and conditioner with cool water.

• If you use a hairdryer, turn down the heat setting. Ideally, let your hair air-dry naturally.

• Wear a hat to protect hair from drying and colour-fading sunlight (especially if you have colour-treated hair). Always remember to wear a cap when you swim in chlorinated pools.

• Stress and depressed spirits can cause dull, lifeless hair and, sometimes, hair loss. Learn to meditate, or take up yoga or another calming pursuit.

Lavender shampoo

This mild, lightly fragranced shampoo is suitable for all hair types. Lavender calms and tones the scalp and rosemary boosts shine.

2 tablespoons dried lavender
I tablespoon dried rosemary
I teaspoon orange zest
250ml water
125ml Castile shampoo
20 drops lavender essential oil
10 drops orange essential oil

1 Place dried herbs, zest and water in a saucepan. Bring to the boil, then reduce heat and simmer until liquid is reduced to 60ml. Strain.

2 Combine herbal liquid and shampoo. Add essential oils. Store in a plastic squeeze-bottle.

3 To use, shake well and massage a tablespoonful into the scalp. Leave for 2 to 3 minutes before rinsing.

Aromatherapy detangling spray

This detangling spray keeps hair shiny and manageable during cold, dry weather or high humidity. The oils stimulate circulation to the scalp and balance sebum production.

10 drops rosemary essential oil
10 drops chamomile essential oil
10 drops ylang ylang essential oil

I teaspoon jojoba oil
125ml water

1 Add oils to water and pour into a pump-spray bottle. Store in a cool, dark place.

2 To use, shake well and mist hair 2 to 3 times, then use a comb or fingers to style.

Fragrant hair rinse

Nettle is restorative, horsetail is a rich natural source of silica, and sandalwood and clary sage add a lingering fragrance. Apple cider vinegar restores the scalp's natural pH balance.

I tablespoon dried burdock
I tablespoon dried nettle
I tablespoon dried horsetail
10 drops sandalwood essential oil
5 drops clary sage essential oil
375ml boiling water
125ml apple cider vinegar

1 Place herbs, oils and water in a bowl. Cover and steep till cool. Strain. Stir in vinegar.

2 To use, pour through hair as a final rinse after shampooing.

Colour boost

Herbal hair rinses accentuate your hair's natural colour and make any highlights appear brighter. If your

Do-it-yourself scalp massage

A regular scalp massage encourages fresh blood supplies to flow to the scalp and feed the hair follicles. Tip your head forward and, using small, circular movements, massage your scalp gently with your fingertips for 3 to 5 minutes. Pay particular attention to the crown and hair line. If hair is very dry, rub a few drops of Rosemary hot oil intensive (see page 271) onto your fingers first.

hair is permed, chemically coloured or very dry, patch-test a small amount of hair first.

FOR BLONDE HAIR
250ml water
4 tablespoons dried chamomile
I tablespoon lemon zest
2 tablespoons lemon juice

FOR RED HAIR
250ml water
3 tablespoons dried calendula
I tablespoon dried hibiscus
2 tablespoons red wine

FOR DARK HAIR
250ml water
3 tablespoons dried sage
I tablespoon dried rosemary
2 tablespoons apple cider vinegar

1 Place water and dried herbs of your choice in a saucepan. Bring to the boil; remove from heat. Cover and steep for 1 hour. Strain. Add juice, wine or vinegar. Pour into a plastic spray bottle.

2 To use, spray through hair after shampooing. Comb through, squeeze out excess, but do not rinse.

Save the whale

Jojoba is a shrub that's native to parts of California, Arizona and Mexico. After the banning of the importation of whale oil into the United States in the 1970s, jojoba oil (a liquid wax from the seeds of the plant) was discovered as a replacement. With its very fine texture and skin nutrients, its application in skin and hair-care products was soon considered superior to that of whale oil.

Oily hair

Clean oily hair with a refreshing, herbal-scented shampoo and use essential oils to encourage blood flow to the scalp. Vinegar rinses and astringent herbs will reduce oiliness.

Bee business

Melissa, the botanical name for lemon balm, comes from the Greek word for honey bee. Lemon balm was once planted around hives to help guide bees back home: '…when they are strayed away, they do find their way home by it', observed Pliny, a Roman writer on natural history.

Cleansing clay shampoo

Clay is useful for deep-cleansing the scalp, absorbing excess oil and removing dead skin. Peppermint produces a tingling effect, while the citrus oils and zest counter oiliness and stimulate circulation.

1 tablespoon dried lemon balm
1 tablespoon dried peppermint
1 teaspoon lemon zest
250ml water
125ml Castile shampoo
3 teaspoons green cosmetic clay
10 drops lemon essential oil
10 drops orange essential oil
10 drops peppermint essential oil

1 Place herbs, zest and water in a saucepan. Bring to the boil, then reduce heat and simmer until liquid has reduced to 60ml. Strain.

2 Combine herbal liquid and shampoo. Add clay and oils. Store in a squeeze-bottle in the fridge.

3 To use, shake well and massage a tablespoonful into the scalp. Leave for 2 to 3 minutes before rinsing.

Aromatherapy dry shampoo

Banish that greasy look in just a few seconds. Neem and sandalwood have a tonic effect on hair follicles, and orris root absorbs oil and impurities and also leaves behind a light floral scent.

1½ tablespoons powdered orris root
1 tablespoon semolina
10 drops lavender essential oil
10 drops sandalwood essential oil
5 drops neem oil

1 Place orris root and semolina in a bowl and mix well; sift to remove lumps. Add oils and mix well.

2 To use, hang head upside-down and lightly massage small pinches of the mixture into scalp and hair, moving forwards from the neck. Throw head back and brush hair lightly to distribute mixture.

Scarborough Fair rinse

This refreshing rinse tones an oily scalp and stimulates hair growth. The four herbs in the classic folk song 'Scarborough Fair' are perfect for correcting the pH balance of the hair and scalp, and boost shine.

1 tablespoon fresh parsley
1 tablespoon fresh sage
1 tablespoon fresh rosemary
1 tablespoon fresh thyme
375ml boiling water
juice of 1 lemon

1 Place herbs in a bowl and pour boiling water over. Cover and steep until cool. Strain. Stir in the lemon juice.

2 To use, pour through hair as a final rinse after shampooing.

Give hair lustre and help reduce oiliness by adding a few drops of rosemary essential oil to your hairbrush before brushing.

Dry hair

Sun, chlorine, over-zealous styling and even central heating conspire to damage the hair shaft and turn hair dull and dry. To repair hair and restore sheen, try these recipes.

Rosemary hot oil intensive

The molecular structure of apricot kernel oil is small enough to penetrate the hair shaft, where it nourishes, strengthens, protects and repairs, and also brings a sheen to dull or damaged hair.

125ml apricot kernel oil
20 drops rosemary essential oil

1 Combine oils and mix well. Drape a towel around your shoulders.

2 Massage oil into hair and scalp, starting at the ends and working towards your scalp. Continue until all your hair is coated in oil. Cover with a shower cap. Warm another towel, then wrap it around and over the cap. Leave until cool.

3 Wash out, using a small amount of shampoo. Finish by adding

125ml apple cider vinegar to a sink of tepid water and dunking your hair into it. Let hair dry naturally.

Leave-in conditioner

This treatment coats and protects hair even after blow-drying and styling. It also helps to seal the hair cuticle, which causes light to reflect off the hair's surface. This conditioner makes an excellent styling wax, especially for curly or unruly hair.

1 tablespoon beeswax
2 tablespoons cocoa butter
1 tablespoon almond oil
1 tablespoon wheatgerm oil
1 teaspoon honey
2 tablespoons rosewater
10 drops lime essential oil
10 drops lavender essential oil

1 Combine beeswax, cocoa butter, almond and wheatgerm oils with honey in the top of a double boiler over low heat, until melted. Remove from heat.

2 Gently heat rosewater. When both oil mixture and rosewater are lukewarm, whisk together. Using a mixer set on low speed, add the essential oils and continue to beat until creamy. Spoon into a wide-mouthed jar and store in a cool, dark place.

3 To use, take a small pinch of the conditioner and warm between palms, then work it thoroughly through dry or freshly washed hair.

Too much sun?

Unlike the skin, which undergoes continuous renewal, UV-damaged hair cannot spontaneously repair itself. Too much UV exposure weakens the hair's keratin (protein) and also causes discolouration, known as melanin oxidation, resulting in brassiness as well as dryness. Use a sun hat or a nourishing hair pomade such as the Leave-in conditioner (see left) to protect your hair.

Tropical hair mask

Eggs have a high protein content that helps improve hair's resilience and lustre. Banana is hydrating and moisturising, and avocado is a rich source of natural oils that help soften and condition dry hair.

1 egg yolk
1 small banana
1 large avocado, peeled and stoned
1 tablespoon mayonnaise
1 tablespoon rum

1 Combine all ingredients in a bowl; mash to form a creamy paste.

2 Massage the mixture through dry hair and wrap hair in a hot, moist towel. Leave for 10 minutes. Rinse out mixture, then shampoo as usual.

Dandruff

A scurfy scalp can be triggered by alkaline hair products, poor diet, stress and fungal infection. Herbal shampoos and aromatherapy treatments can relieve itchiness and flakiness.

Natural medicine chest

CLEAN up your diet by limiting sugar and refined carbohydrates. Avoid deep-fried foods, excess alcohol, red meat and chocolate. Eat more fresh fruit and vegetables. Drink plenty of water daily.

ELIMINATE allergens if you suspect you're sensitive to dairy or wheat. Try cutting them out for a month to see if your dandruff clears.

TAKE out nutritional insurance. The B-group vitamins, vitamin A, zinc and selenium are all important for hair and scalp health.

CATCH some rays. While too much sunshine damages hair, some exposure is beneficial for scaly skin conditions. Spend 30 minutes outdoors every day.

Anti-dandruff shampoo

Unlike conventional shampoos, Castile soap is free from the potentially irritating ingredient sodium lauryl sulphate. It will keep hair clean and soft and as a bonus it is also completely biodegradable. Tea-tree essential oil is a powerful antifungal and antiseptic which will protect and soothe the scalp.

180ml liquid Castile soap
25 drops tea-tree essential oil
20 drops rosemary essential oil
15 drops cedarwood essential oil

1 Place all the ingredients in a bowl and stir to combine. Pour into a plastic squeeze-bottle.

2 To use, massage shampoo into wet hair, then rinse several times, finishing with the Herbal vinegar rinse (see below).

Herbal vinegar rinse

Apple cider vinegar normalises the scalp's delicate pH balance and aids in toning the scalp. It also successfully removes oil and shampoo residue from the hair. Nettle is a traditional hair tonic, used for its stimulating effect on the scalp. It also has anti-allergenic properties, making it useful for itchy scalp conditions.

4 tablespoons dried nettle
1 tablespoon dried rosemary
1 tablespoon dried sage
250ml boiling water
60ml apple cider vinegar
5 drops eucalyptus oil

1 Place herbs in a saucepan with water and vinegar, and bring to a simmer. Remove from heat, cover bowl and steep overnight.

2 Strain liquid and add oil; stir. To use, pour through freshly washed hair; do not rinse out.

Warm oil treatment

With its slightly medicinal scent, this treatment eases a flaky, dry, irritated scalp. It also gives hair lustre and body. Warming the oil increases absorption and promotes circulation to the scalp.

4 tablespoons jojoba oil
10 drops rosemary essential oil
10 drops birch essential oil
5 drops cedarwood essential oil
5 drops tea-tree essential oil

1 Place ingredients in a saucepan and warm gently over a low heat.

2 Massage mixture into clean, damp hair, paying particular attention to scalp and hair roots. Cover with an old shower cap, then wrap head in a warm towel. Leave for 1 hour.

3 Rinse, then shampoo. Finish with Herbal vinegar rinse (see left).

Reach for birch

Used since Roman times to treat hair and scalp disorders, birch leaves are a rich source of salicylate, which is used in many conventional dandruff treatments to lift and break down dead skin cells, encourage new ones and keep hair follicles healthy.

Hair loss

Hair loss that is not linked to hereditary conditions can be due to hormonal imbalance, the contraceptive pill and other drugs, stress, illness and nutrient deficiencies.

Stimulating scalp oil

Rosemary oil increases peripheral circulation and brings nutrients and oxygen to the tiny blood vessels where hair follicles are located.

1½ tablespoons sesame oil
15 drops rosemary essential oil
10 drops cedarwood essential oil
5 drops clary sage essential oil

1 Combine all ingredients in a small bottle. Store in a cool, dark place.

2 To use, pour a teaspoonful into your palm and rub hands together briskly before massaging into the scalp, using small circular movements. This treatment is best applied just before bedtime, because most hair growth occurs while you are asleep. Shampoo in the morning.

Aromatherapy hair tonic

Neem oil has long been used in Ayurveda, India's centuries-old healing tradition, to treat hair thinning and scalp problems. Aloe vera relieves dryness and has a mildly antifungal effect. It is also useful for any scalp conditions that require soothing and astringency.

60ml witch hazel
1 tablespoon aloe vera gel
1 tablespoon vodka

Herbs prevent hair loss in women by balancing hormones.

Hang your head in hope

An easy way to increase the flow of blood to the scalp – which is known to help hair growth – is to lie across a bed and hang your head over the side each day for 10 minutes. Certain yoga poses, notably headstands, are also thought useful for hair health.

1 tablespoon orange flower water
30 drops neem oil
15 drops rosemary essential oil
15 drops lemon grass essential oil

1 Combine all ingredients together in a small bottle. Store in a cool, dark place.

2 To use, massage a small amount of the tonic vigorously into scalp once a day.

Hair scare

Thinning hair is likely to make you panic, but you should stay calm and help minimise the loss.

FEED your follicles. Hair that breaks easily or looks dull may need nutrients. For example, insufficient vitamin A leaves hair dry; B vitamins strengthen the hair shaft and help your body handle stress, which can cause or worsen hair loss. Zinc is needed for strong hair and normal growth; iron deficiency causes hair loss. Hair also requires good-quality protein to grow. Good sources include cold-water fish, free-range and organic eggs and chicken, and soy foods such as tofu.

ADD flaxseed oil, which provides alpha linolenic acid, an omega-3 fat that makes hair shiny and strong. Take 1 tablespoon daily.

EAT sushi. If an iodine deficiency is causing hair loss, eat sea vegetables such as kelp and dulse, which are naturally high in iodine.

GET herbal help. Grapeseed extract contains powerful anti-oxidants that stimulate hair growth. Horsetail, alfalfa and oats are all rich in silica, which helps thinning hair and hair that splits easily and is slow to grow. Ginkgo, cayenne (from chillies) and ginger help micro-circulation.

Herbal and aromatherapy baths

Enjoy your own spa-style soak at home with a bath using essential oils or herbs. It can soothe your nerves, ease aching limbs, help you sleep or stimulate you into action.

Cooling green tea bath bags

Oats ease itchy skin while the fat in whole-milk powder moisturises as its lactic acid gently exfoliates. Green tea soothes skin, while spearmint and peppermint add a refreshing scent and tingly sensation.

70g fine-ground oats

50g whole-milk powder

6 teaspoons dried green tea

6 teaspoons dried spearmint

20 drops peppermint essential oil

6 x 15cm square pieces of muslin or fine cotton

Turn your shower into a spa

This treatment will strengthen the immune and lymphatic systems.
SPRINKLE a few drops of lavender and rosemary essential oils onto the bristles of a long-handled body brush. Starting with the soles of your feet and working upwards, briskly brush your body, using firm, circular movements.
ADD a few extra drops of each oil onto the shower floor and run the water as hot as you can tolerate it for 2 minutes.
TURN off the hot water and stand under the cold water for a few seconds. It will close your pores, stimulate the circulation and smooth hair follicles, leaving skin glowing and hair shiny.

1 Place oats, milk powder and dried herbs in a bowl; mix well. Add essential oil, several drops at a time, mix well after each addition.

2 Place 1 to 2 spoonfuls of oat mixture in the centre of a muslin square, then gather up the sides and secure with ribbon or twine. Store bath bags in an airtight container until ready to use.

3 To use, run a bath and drop a bath bag in the water. Allow to steep for 5 to 10 minutes before getting into the tub. Use the wet bath bag as a soothing compress for skin, squeezing it to release the milky oat essence. Soak for 15 minutes.

Invogorating ginger bath bags

Ginger is the perfect pick-me-up. The warming, spicy blend in this bath bag helps relieve lethargy, settle the nerves and ease muscle aches and soreness.

60g sunflower seeds

70g Epsom salts

6 teaspoons dried rosemary

6 teaspoons dried orange rind

1 tablespoon powdered dried ginger

10 drops sandalwood essential oil

10 drops orange essential oil

6 x 15cm square pieces of muslin or fine cotton

1 Grind sunflower seeds in a food processor to a fine meal. Place Epsom salts, sunflower meal, rosemary, orange rind and powdered ginger in a bowl; mix well. Add essential oils, several drops at a time, mixing well after each addition.

2 Place 1 to 2 spoonfuls of mixture in the centre of a muslin square, then gather up the sides and secure with ribbon or string. Store bath bags in an airtight container until ready to use. Use as for Rose petal bath bags (see below).

Rose petal bath bags

This sensuous blend transforms an ordinary bath into an indulgence. Marsh mallow root and chamomile both soften the skin, while the delicate fragrances of lavender and rose balance the emotions and soothe the psyche.

150g fine-ground oats

4 teaspoons dried chamomile

4 teaspoons dried rose petals

4 teaspoons dried lavender

1 tablespoon powdered dried marsh mallow root

10 drops rose essential oil

5 drops frankincense essential oil

5 drops ylang ylang essential oil

6 x 15cm square pieces of muslin or fine cotton

1 Place oats, dried herbs and powdered marsh mallow root in a bowl; mix well. Add essential oils, several drops at a time, mixing well after each addition.

2 Place 1 to 2 spoonfuls of mixture in the centre of a muslin square, then gather up the sides and secure with ribbon or twine. Store bath bags in an airtight container until ready to use.

3 To use, hang bag from the hot water tap so the water runs through it as you fill the bath. Then untie the bag and let it float in the water. Soak for 15 minutes.

Herb-filled bath bags

For a bath bag that's a little more special than herbs wrapped in muslin, embroider a ready-made organza bag.

WHAT YOU NEED

The finished bag is 15cm high.

☐ purchased ready-made 15cm high organza drawstring gift bags (from craft stores)

☐ fine lead pencil

☐ Anchor Stranded Embroidery Cotton.
Rosemary: 855 Ultra V. Light Tan, 858 V. Light Fern Green, 861 Dark Avocado Green, 939 Baby Blue. Lavender: 101 Very Dark Violet, 1030 Dark Blue-Violet, 860 Fern Green. Chamomile: 291 Dark Lemon, White

☐ crewel embroidery needle

☐ 4 small yellow buttons (for Chamomile bag)

☐ herbs and spices for filling (the Lavender bag is filled with a mixture of lavender, rolled oats, dried orange peel and bay leaves; the Chamomile bag is filled with a mixture of dried chamomile, bay leaves and rose petals; the Rosemary bag is filled with a mixture of dried rosemary, lavender, sage and bay leaves)

1 Draw the motif of your choice (see the Rosemary motif at right). For both the Rosemary and Lavender, you only need to draw the stalk positions.

2 Slip the traced motif inside the organza bag and very lightly trace over the stalks, using a fine lead pencil.

3 To embroider Rosemary, using 1 strand of each of 855, 858 and 861 in the needle (3 strands in all), embroider the stalks by working several long straight stitches along the traced line for each stalk, taking a tiny back stitch to anchor each straight stitch. To work the leaves, thread the needle with 2 strands of 858 and 4 strands of 861 (6 strands in total) and work a series of straight stitches on an angle down each side of each stalk. Work neatly and do not drag the thread for any great distance, as the work on the back is visible on the front. Using 2 strands of 939, work random small flowers among the leaves, working 3 straight stitches per flower.

4 To embroider Lavender, using 2 strands of 860, embroider the stalks by working 2 or 3 long straight stitches along the traced line for each stalk, taking a tiny back stitch to anchor each straight stitch. Thread the needle with 2 strands of each colour (6 strands in total) and work the flowers in small straight stitches on each side of the stalks, using your diagram as a guide.

5 To embroider the Chamomile bag, place the buttons on the front of the bag in a pleasing arrangement and mark their positions lightly with a pencilled cross. Using 2 strands of White, work lazy daisies around the pencilled crosses, leaving room for the button centres.

6 Stitch a button to the centre of each flower, using 2 or 3 strands of 291.

7 Loosely fill the bag with the herb combination of your choice and pull the drawstring.

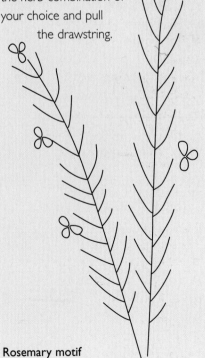

Rosemary motif

Bath salts and oils

Adding salts, oils and active ingredients such as milk, vinegar or seaweed to a bath will restore the skin's pH balance, improve circulation and aid a range of ailments.

Lavender bath salts

Epsom salts are rich in magnesium, which eases muscle aches and tension. Borax and bicarbonate of soda leave skin silky smooth, while lavender's relaxing aroma will lull you to sleep.

140g Epsom salts

30g bicarbonate of soda

30g borax

20 drops lavender essential oil

10 drops clary sage essential oil

10 drops chamomile essential oil

1 Place dry ingredients in a bowl; mix well. Add essential oils, several drops at a time, mixing well after each addition.

2 Store mixture in an airtight jar in a cool, dark place.

3 To use, sprinkle 2 to 3 tablespoons of mixture into warm bath water. Swish water with your hands to disperse evenly. Soak for 10 to 15 minutes.

Mermaid bath

Sea salt and seaweed help ease irritating skin disorders such as psoriasis, while iodine-rich kelp is a natural antiseptic and tonic. Calendula oil is an excellent calming remedy for red or inflamed skin. Do not use this if skin is broken or very inflamed.

130g sea salt

60g bicarbonate of soda

20 drops calendula essential oil

10 drops pine essential oil

1 tablespoon kelp powder

2 to 3 strips wakame (dried culinary seaweed)

1 Place sea salt and bicarbonate of soda in a bowl; mix well. Add essential oils, several drops at a time, mixing well after each addition.

2 Store mixture in an airtight jar in a cool, dark place.

3 To use, sprinkle 2 to 3 tablespoons of the mixture and 1 tablespoon of kelp powder (available from health food stores) into warm bath water; swish with your hands to disperse evenly. Drop the wakame strips (available from health food stores or Asian supermarkets) into the water, and swish again. Soak for 15 minutes.

Rich vanilla bath oil

This bath oil is a luxurious blend with a warm, sensual aroma that lingers on the skin; it is also ideal for massage. The cold-pressed nut and seed oils are rich in essential fatty acids that nourish and moisturise your skin. Take care when stepping in and out of the tub, as the oils will make the bath slippery.

4 vanilla beans

1 tablespoon jojoba oil

125ml almond oil

60ml macadamia oil

60ml avocado oil

15 drops rose essential oil

5 drops ylang ylang essential oil

Do-it-yourself home beauty treatments are inexpensive and easy to make.

5 drops sandalwood essential oil

2 x 500IU natural vitamin E capsules

1 Slit beans lengthwise and scrape out seed paste. Snip pods into short lengths. Place paste and pods in a glass jar or bottle and add oils, essential oils and contents of capsules. Seal securely; set aside in a cool, dark place for 1 month.

2 Strain oil through a fine-mesh sieve; strain again through a coffee filter to remove residue. Pour into a glass bottle.

3 To use, add 1 to 2 tablespoons to bath water; swish to disperse evenly. Soak for 10 to 15 minutes.

Chamomile essential oil contains strong anti- spasmodic ingredients that reduce muscle aches and pains.

Herbal vinegar bath

If your skin's natural pH balance has been disrupted, perhaps through the use of harsh deodorant soaps, you may have dry, itchy skin. The apple cider vinegar helps restore the correct acid/alkaline ratio; it also relieves sunburn.

500ml apple cider vinegar
50g dried chamomile flowers
30g dried comfrey root powder
60ml aloe vera juice

1 Place apple cider vinegar and chamomile in a non-aluminium saucepan over medium heat. When mixture comes to a simmer, remove from heat. Cover; let stand 3 hours, or overnight.

2 Strain off herbs. Add powder and juice to vinegar Stir well. Pour into a glass bottle with a plastic cap. Store in a cool, dark place.

3 To use, shake well and add 125ml to bath under a running tap. Soak for 10 to 15 minutes.

What works, and why

Each mineral salt possesses specific health properties. These useful tools can be harnessed in many natural beauty treatments.
SULPHUR stimulates the mucous membranes and helps relieve the symptoms of colds and other respiratory problems; it may also be of benefit to acne and eczema.
CALCIUM and potassium may improve the symptoms of arthritis as well as some disorders of the central nervous system.
MAGNESIUM is essential for strong bones and a healthy heart and aids the proper functioning of the nerves and muscles.

Citrus bath bombs

These bath bombs have a zingy, uplifting scent that refreshes the senses and clears the mind. Neroli and lemon create an energising and stimulating atmosphere, while grapefruit has a detoxifying effect. To prevent the scent fading too fast, store the bath bombs in an airtight container in a dry, dark place; they will keep for 3 to 6 months.

125g bicarbonate of soda
60g citric acid
60g cornflour
2 tablespoons almond oil
1 tablespoon water
10 drops neroli essential oil
10 drops lemon essential oil
10 drops grapefruit essential oil
1 teaspoon borax
spray bottle filled with witch hazel

1 Place bicarbonate of soda, citric acid and cornflour in a bowl; mix well. In another bowl, combine almond oil, water, essential oils and borax. Drizzle wet ingredients into dry ingredients, pouring with one hand and squishing mixture together with the other.
2 Pack firmly into soap moulds or flexible silicone muffin pans; leave overnight.
3 To remove, flip over and tap out onto baking paper. Lightly mist the bombs with witch hazel; this forms a crust to reduce cracking.

After bathing, almond oil leaves a fine film on the skin, helping to 'lock in' moisture.

Aromatherapy soaps and **gels**

Adding herbal extracts and essential oils to soap will leave skin feeling silkier. As even the mildest soap is strongly alkaline, which means that it disrupts the skin's delicate pH balance and natural oils, prevent dryness and irritation by using soap sparingly and rinsing with warm water.

The soap herb

The ancient Egyptians were the first to make soap, using soapwort. This herb is distinguished by its unusual ability to foam in water. Soapwort is still used as the basis of some of the more expensive vegetable soaps.

Peppermint shower soap

An aromatic, pick-me-up cleanser for the entire body, this contains calendula essential oil to soothe the skin, peppermint to provide a cooling, refreshing effect and comfrey to heal skin problems. Glycerine is an excellent moisturiser often recommended for delicate skin.

about 60ml boiling water
2 tablespoons chopped dried comfrey root
125ml liquid Castile soap
1 tablespoon vegetable glycerine
15 drops peppermint essential oil
10 drops calendula essential oil
10 drops lemon balm essential oil

1 Pour boiling water over comfrey root. Steep for 15 minutes. Strain off through muslin.

2 Measure 60ml comfrey mixture and add to soap. Add glycerine and essential oils. Stir thoroughly to combine.

3 Pour into a plastic pump dispenser. To use, apply 1 to 2 teaspoons and work into a gentle lather. Rinse off. Pat skin dry with a soft towel and apply a body lotion or oil.

Grapefruit and white clay soap

Perfect for washing oily skin, this soap uses white clay and orange zest to exfoliate and extract surface

The science of suds

All soaps are derived from two basic ingredients: a fat (animal or vegetable) and an alkali (usually lye or sodium hydroxide). Soap is made by combining the two in a process called saponification, which creates a molecule that attracts both water and the dirt or oils on the surface of your skin. Some conventional soaps are made with tallow (animal fat), while others are made primarily from glycerine, a by-product of soap production that helps moisturise.

dirt from pores. Pink grapefruit essential oil is refreshing, while orange essential oil is toning and invigorating. The finely milled oatmeal increases the soap's scrubbing power and also helps to smooth and soften your skin.

150g vegetable glycerine soap
1 tablespoon fine-ground oats
1 teaspoon white cosmetic clay
1 tablespoon almond oil
1 teaspoon finely grated orange zest
10 drops pink grapefruit essential oil
10 drops orange essential oil

1 Lightly grease soap moulds, as for Rosehip soap balls (see opposite). Chop or grate soap and

Widely valued for its antiseptic properties, tea-tree oil is a useful remedy for minor skin infections, bites and stings.

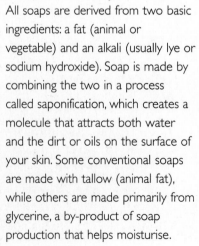

place in the top of a double boiler over simmering water. Stir until it has melted.

2 Remove the liquefied soap from the heat and add oats, clay (available in pharmacies, or online), almond oil, zest and essential oils. Stir the mixture to thoroughly combine.

3 Pour soap mixture into greased moulds and leave in a cool, dark place to harden for 1 week.

4 To remove soaps from moulds, run the tip of a sharp knife around the edge. Wrap soaps carefully in tissue paper.

Castile soap facts

CASTILE soap is thought to have originated in the Castile region of Spain. Originally made from olive oil, it is now made with olive, hemp, coconut and palm oils.

UNLIKE conventional soap, which is made from tallow (from beef fat) or glycerine (a by-product of soap production) and a small amount of coconut or palm kernel oil, Castile is less likely to strip the skin of its natural oils.

TO MEET government standards, organic Castile soap must support sustainable farming methods, farm worker health and ecological processing methods.

CASTILE is the only soap that camping authorities approve for use in the wilderness, because it has no impact on the environment.

Tea-tree antiseptic soap

This invigorating body wash for oily skin is also an effective antibacterial hand soap.

125ml unscented liquid Castile soap
I teaspoon jojoba oil
10 drops tea-tree essential oil
10 drops lavender essential oil
10 drops sage essential oil

Rosehip soap balls

Olive oil soap's rich lather helps calm irritated skin, while the natural rosehip oil imparts a sweet but subtle scent. Aloe vera and honey are added to maximise moisture, while sandalwood and vitamin E both have anti-ageing properties. Buy olive oil soap and aloe vera gel at health food stores or online.

150g soft olive oil soap
I tablespoon aloe vera gel
I tablespoon honey
I teaspoon rosehip oil
10 drops sandalwood essential oil
10 drops patchouli essential oil
I x 500IU vitamin E capsule

I Lightly grease small silicone soap moulds with sunflower or peanut oil. Chop or grate soap and place in a double boiler over simmering water. Stir until melted.

1 Place all ingredients in a bowl and stir well to combine.

2 Pour into a plastic or glass pump dispenser. To use, apply about 1 to 2 teaspoons and work into a gentle lather. Rinse off.

2 Remove liquefied soap from heat and stir through aloe vera gel, honey, rosehip oil and essential oils, and the contents of vitamin E capsule. Mix thoroughly. Pour soap mixture into moulds. (Decorative soap moulds are available from craft suppliers. Alternatively, use silicone mini muffin tins. Do not use metal, as it's too difficult to pop out the soap.)

3 Leave in a cool, dark place to harden for 1 week.

4 To remove soaps from moulds, run the tip of a sharp knife around the edge. Wrap soaps in tissue paper. Note that this type of soap will remain slightly soft.

Deodorants

Natural deodorants with herbs and essential oils will keep you feeling dry and smelling fresh by controlling surface bacterial growth – the main trigger for underarm odour.

Aromatherapy body powder

Absorbent bicarbonate of soda, cornflour and arrowroot protect against wetness, while sage and thyme fight the bacteria that cause body odour. Lavender is strongly antiseptic and also provides a fresh scent.

60g cornflour
2 tablespoons bicarbonate of soda
2 tablespoons arrowroot
1 tablespoon powdered thyme
1 tablespoon powdered sage
20 drops lavender essential oil
10 drops rosemary essential oil
10 drops patchouli essential oil

1 Sift dry ingredients into a bowl to remove any lumps and grit.
2 Stir in essential oils. Sift again.
3 Store in an airtight jar or tin. Apply with a powder puff, or sprinkle on with your fingers.

Orange blossom powder

This silky, fine powder is gentle enough to use on the most delicate parts of the body. The three citrus-derived essential oils (neroli comes from orange blossoms, petit grain from the leaves and sweet orange from the peel) are uplifting.

3 tablespoons white cosmetic clay
30g bicarbonate of soda
30g cornflour
20 drops neroli essential oil
10 drops petit grain essential oil
10 drops sweet orange essential oil

1 Sift dry ingredients to remove lumps. Place in a bowl. Add essential oils and stir. Sift again.
2 Store in an airtight tin or jar. Apply with a powder puff or fingers.

Lavender fresh deodorant

This lightly scented deodorant spray uses lavender, patchouli and clary sage to control odour, and antibacterial citrus seed extract and aloe vera to soothe skin that may be irritated by shaving.

180ml witch hazel
1 tablespoon vodka
2 teaspoons aloe vera juice
15 drops patchouli essential oil
15 drops citrus seed extract
10 drops lavender essential oil
10 drops clary sage essential oil
5 drops bergamot essential oil

1 Place ingredients in a glass spray bottle. Store in a cool, dry place.
2 Shake well before using.

Rosemary and thyme deodorant

Coriander and hempseed essential oils both neutralise odour-causing bacteria, while sage, rosemary and thyme essential oils are high in chlorophyll and have strong, clean fragrances that effectively mask odours.

2 tablespoons dried rosemary
2 tablespoons dried thyme
2 tablespoons dried sage
180ml witch hazel
60ml apple cider vinegar
1 tablespoon hempseed essential oil
15 drops coriander essential oil
15 drops citrus seed extract
10 drops lavender essential oil

1 Place dried herbs in a glass jar; add witch hazel and vinegar. Seal securely. Store in a cool, dark place for 2 weeks, shaking daily.
2 Strain liquid and pour into a glass spray bottle. Add oils. Shake well before using.

Unlike conventional antiperspirants, natural deodorants don't block sweat — they simply absorb it.

Men's grooming

The average man will shave 21,900 times in his life, so a soothing shaving cream and calming aftershave balm is a must. Herbs and natural oils are a soothing solution.

Dream shaving cream

This super-shave solution softens bristles and keeps your skin smooth and nick-free. Olive, jojoba and grapeseed oils are all emollient and replenish moisture; glycerine facilitates blade glide over your skin; witch hazel is useful for inflamed and tender skin; and comforting aloe vera moisturises and heals. Avoid conventional aftershaves based on alcohol: they burn and dry out skin and can also stimulate oil production and upset the skin's acid balance.

6 tablespoons coconut oil
2 tablespoons witch hazel
1 tablespoon olive oil
1 tablespoon jojoba oil
1 tablespoon grapeseed oil
2 tablespoons aloe vera juice
10 drops sandalwood essential oil
10 drops lavender essential oil

1 Place coconut oil in a double boiler over low heat and liquefy.

2 Remove from heat and stir in witch hazel and also the olive, jojoba and grapeseed oils.

3 Add aloe vera juice and the essential oils. Using an electric mixer, beat on low speed for 2 to 3 minutes. Spoon into a wide-mouthed jar.

4 To use, scoop up about 1 tablespoon of the shaving cream, warm it between your palms, then smooth it over your face and neck. After shaving, remove any traces of shaving cream with a warm, damp face flannel.

Herbal balm

Comfrey is a natural soother that helps to regenerate the thin layer of skin that has just been removed with shaving. Chamomile contains azulene, a powerful anti-inflammatory, while vitamin E softens and heals.

2 tablespoons dried comfrey
2 tablespoons dried chamomile
2 tablespoons dried calendula
180ml witch hazel
1 tablespoon vegetable glycerine
1000IU vitamin E capsule

1 Place dried herbs in a jar; add witch hazel. Seal securely. Store in a cool, dry place for 2 weeks, shaking daily.

2 Strain liquid; pour into a bottle. Add glycerine and contents of capsule. To use, shake well and pat onto skin after shaving.

Sandalwood aftershave

Sandalwood is antiseptic and also provides a calming, earthy, masculine scent. Tea tree fights inflammation, spearmint is cooling and rosemary stimulates circulation.

180ml witch hazel
1 tablespoon apple cider vinegar
10 drops sandalwood essential oil
5 drops spearmint essential oil
3 drops rosemary essential oil
2 drops tea-tree essential oil

Place all ingredients in a bottle. To use, shake well and pat onto skin after shaving.

Body lotions and moisturisers

Body creams and lotions help to improve the skin's barrier function by locking in moisture. For best results, apply a moisturiser when skin is still slightly damp from bathing; this will help to seal in the moisture. Using long strokes to work in the product, gently massage your arms and legs.

Spicy body oil

This is a silky, exotically scented oil that provides luxurious, long-lasting moisture. Vitamin E revives your skin and fights free radicals, while manuka honey helps to heal any minor skin abrasions. The fragrance of sandalwood and orange calms the senses.

100ml grapeseed oil
1 tablespoon manuka honey
60ml jojoba oil
2 x 500IU vitamin E capsules
10 drops sandalwood essential oil
10 drops sweet orange essential oil
10 drops frankincense essential oil

1 Place grapeseed oil and honey in a small saucepan over low heat. Warm gently until honey has liquefied. Remove from heat.

2 Stir in jojoba oil and the contents of the vitamin E capsules. Add essential oils, several drops at a time, mixing well after each addition. Pour into a dark-coloured glass bottle. To use, massage a small amount into the skin and rub in thoroughly.

Rich body butter

For winter-worn cracked, scaly skin, this luscious body butter delivers peerless relief. Rose, calendula and chamomile are all naturally soothing, while the plant fats in avocado oil and shea butter sink in quickly to keep skin soft and elastic.

60g grated shea butter
1 tablespoon grated beeswax
125ml avocado oil
2 tablespoons coconut oil
3 tablespoons vegetable glycerine
10 drops rose essential oil
10 drops calendula essential oil
10 drops chamomile essential oil

Rose essential oil

The rose is the mystical symbol of love and romance and its essential oil, made from the petals of damask roses, is thought to be an aphrodisiac. Often included in beauty preparations for its refreshing and mild tonic effect, rose essential oil is particularly recommended for sensitive skin.

Sandalwood, the rescuer

• Sandalwood (*Santalum album*) grows in India, and the best quality is found in the province of Mysore. The dried bark and essential oil have been used for centuries, both in traditional Ayurvedic herbal medicine and as a perfume and incense.
• Soothing, relaxing and toning, sandalwood essential oil is renowned for its rejuvenating effects, especially for dry, mature or weather-beaten skin. It is used to soften wrinkles, replenish moisture, help reduce puffiness, and stimulate the body's lymphatic system to speed the removal of toxins.
• Its sultry, sensuous aroma is soothing and harmonising, helping to promote restful sleep.

1 Place shea butter, beeswax and avocado and coconut oils in the top of a double boiler over simmering water. Heat gently until beeswax and shea butter have liquefied. Remove from heat and cool slightly.

2 Whisk in vegetable glycerine, then add essential oils, several drops at a time, whisking after each addition. Pour into an airtight, wide-mouthed glass jar, and store in a cool, dark place.

Rosemary and mint body lotion

A lighter-textured blend than the two moisturisers described above, this is a highly effective moisturiser that helps to both heal and nourish dry skin. It is appealingly scented with a refreshing mixture of rosemary and peppermint essential oils.

1 tablespoon grated beeswax
60ml almond oil
60ml grapeseed oil
60ml rosewater
60ml vegetable glycerine
 teaspoon borax
10 drops rosemary essential oil
10 drops peppermint essential oil
10 drops lavender essential oil

1 Place beeswax, almond oil and grapeseed oil in the top of a double boiler over simmering water. Heat gently until beeswax has liquefied. Remove from heat.

2 Meanwhile, place rosewater, glycerine and borax in another small saucepan and heat gently until borax has dissolved. When both liquids are lukewarm, stir rosewater mixture into oil mixture; whisk to combine.

3 Add essential oils, several drops at a time, and whisk again until cool, using either a small wire whisk or a blender set on low. Pour into an airtight jar or bottle. Shake well before using.

Orange flower body cream

Use this cream on rough spots such as elbows, knees and heels. It is particularly effective on mature skin. The cocoa butter and carrot seed oil are both ultra-hydrating, while the neroli provides a light, citrus fragrance.

2 tablespoons cocoa butter
60ml apricot kernel oil
60ml soybean oil
1 tablespoon vegetable glycerine
1 teaspoon carrot seed oil
10 drops neroli essential oil
10 drops lemon essential oil
10 drops jasmine essential oil

1 Place cocoa butter and apricot kernel and soybean oils in the top of a double boiler over simmering water. Heat gently until cocoa butter has melted. Remove from heat.

2 Add vegetable glycerine and carrot seed oil; mix well. Add essential oils, several drops at a time; mix well after each addition. Pour into an airtight, wide-mouthed jar.

Spotlight on shea

Shea nut butter is made from the fruit of the shea (or karite) tree (*Butyrospermum parkii*), which is indigenous to West Central Africa. It is rich in anti-oxidants such as vitamins A and E, plus countless nutrients that combine to provide your skin with deeply hydrating effects. A versatile product, it has been used for centuries for culinary, medicinal and cosmetic purposes. Traditionally, it has been regarded as sacred to women. In Africa, only village women may harvest the nuts and extract the butter, and profits from the enterprise are returned to them. Shea trees are an important resource for West Africa, where they are grown wild, without the use of chemical pesticides.

The world is a rose. Smell it and pass it to your friends.
Persian proverb

Body scrubs and **splashes**

Body scrubs and polishes work wonders on rough, dehydrated skin. Scrubbing whisks dead, dull cells away, resulting in brighter, more radiant skin. It also improves the skin's absorption of other products, such as moisturisers and oils, so that they can produce more noticeable results.

Smooth and glow

Every day the epidermis (the outermost layer of the skin) sheds millions of dead cells. The rate at which your body renews its skin slows as you get older, however, so exfoliation (scrubbing) becomes increasingly important for maintaining healthy, youthful skin. Scrubbing also helps loosen ingrown hairs, stimulate circulation and lift away dirt and sebum without the use of potentially drying soaps. Get the most benefit out of your homemade herbal body scrub or polish by following these steps.

• Cleanse your body as usual before scrubbing, but hold off on shaving until another time, as scrubs may aggravate newly shaved skin.

• Linger in the bath or shower to soften your skin before attacking tough spots

The pelargonium produces an essential oil that helps balance the amount of oil that is produced by the skin.

with your scrub. Use more scrub on your knees, heels and elbows.

• Massage scrub into damp skin with circular motions, working your way up

Splish, splash!

Body splashes are lightly scented toners that help hydrate the skin, balance the pH level and remove excess perspiration and oil. Depending on the essential oils and herbs you use, body splashes have the power to heal skin and to energise you or calm you down. To use, spray all over body after bathing; let skin air-dry. Store in the refrigerator between uses.

from your feet to your heart; avoid your genitals and nipples.

• These scrub recipes contain essential oils, each with a different purpose and scent: chamomile, for instance, calms sensitive skin. Leave scrub on your skin for 2 to 3 minutes to let oils penetrate.

• If you have delicate or acne-prone skin, use scrubs with caution, as scrubbing can actually spread breakouts and irritate sensitive skin. Start with gentle pressure, avoid scrubbing if you experience any discomfort, and exfoliate just once a week.

• These recipes contain oil, so they can make the floor of the shower slippery, so always stand on a rubber mat.

Spicy body scrub

This skin-softening blend combines coffee, known for its toning and stimulating properties, with the sweet, uplifting scent of cinnamon. The coffee grounds exfoliate skin, while the oil from the peanut butter moisturises it.

1 tablespoon used coffee grounds
3 tablespoons crunchy peanut butter
1 teaspoon wheatgerm oil
½ teaspoon powdered cinnamon
¼ teaspoon powdered nutmeg
¼ teaspoon powdered ginger
5 drops cedarwood essential oil

1 Place all ingredients in a bowl; mix to form a gritty paste.

2 To use, stand in the shower and massage handfuls of paste into wet skin. Rinse off and pat dry.

Orange body polish

The fruit acids in the orange juice and the lactic acid in the yogurt remove dead cells. These acids gradually stimulate growth of collagen and possibly elastin (proteins and fibres in the skin that tend to break down over time). Sea salt is healing to the skin when used with care, but it can sting and irritate sensitive, fair, mature or sunburned skin. If you have any concerns, substitute raw sugar for the sea salt.

1 orange
2 tablespoons fine sea salt
3 tablespoons plain yogurt
1 teaspoon almond oil
5 drops lemon essential oil
rice flour, sufficient to make a paste

1 Cut the orange in half; juice one half, and set the other aside.

2 Combine orange juice, salt, yogurt, oil and essential oil; mix well. Add a little rice flour to thicken the mixure and form into a workable paste.

Swathed in patchouli

Patchouli essential oil is distilled from the dried branches of the bushy patchouli tree, a member of the lavender family. In Victorian England, there was a craze for wearing Bengali cashmere shawls that were packed in chests with patchouli leaves to deter moths. The patchouli-scented shawls eventually created a demand for the perfume itself.

3 To apply treatment, first rub the exposed side of the cut half of the orange over knees, elbows, heels and other rough spots. Then massage in the salt mixture to remove dead skin. Rinse off and pat dry.

Gentle walnut scrub

Rich in skin-softening essential fatty acids, walnut is a particularly gentle exfoliant, while oats contain beta-glucan, a soluble fibre that creates a moisture-retaining film on the skin's surface.

60g shelled walnut pieces
2 tablespoons rolled oats
1 small avocado, stoned, peeled and chopped
1 teaspoon avocado oil
2 tablespoons honey
5 drops geranium essential oil
5 drops chamomile essential oil

1 Place walnuts and oats in the bowl of a food processor; blend at slow speed to create a fine-textured powder.

2 Add avocado, avocado oil and honey; process again briefly to form a workable paste. Add the essential oils, and mix well.

3 To use, stand in the shower and gently massage the mixture into skin. Rinse off and pat dry.

Citrus zinger

A refreshing, clean blend that is wonderful to use chilled in the warmer months.

juice of lemon, strained
125ml witch hazel
125ml distilled water
10 drops neroli essential oil
5 drops lemon essential oil
5 drops grapefruit essential oil

Combine all ingredients in glass spray bottle. Shake well before use.

Softly, softly splash

The soothing, relaxing aroma and the softening properties of aloe vera and marsh mallow are perfect for skin that tends to be dry.

1 tablespoon dried marsh mallow root
60ml apple cider vinegar
125ml distilled water
2 tablespoons aloe vera juice
1 tablespoon vegetable glycerine
10 drops rose essential oil
5 drops sandalwood essential oil
5 drops patchouli essential oil

1 Chop marsh mallow root and place in a glass jar with vinegar; seal securely. Steep for 10 days.

2 Strain liquid through muslin into a glass spritzer bottle

3 Add water, aloe vera juice, glycerine and the essential oils. Shake well before use.

Massage oils

Massage relaxes tight muscles, stimulates blood and lymph flow, and speeds the elimination of toxins. It also calms the nervous system, reduces stress hormones, alleviates depression, boosts immunity and diminishes pain.

Creamy massage blend

An exceptionally nourishing oil, with the richness of shea butter and macadamia nut oil, this is an excellent restorative for dry, mature, sensitive, inflamed or weather-beaten skin. Use to soothe period pain or ease cramps.

1 tablespoon shea butter
125ml macadamia nut oil
1 tablespoon soybean oil
2 x 500IU vitamin E capsules
10 drops geranium essential oil
10 drops sweet orange essential oil
10 drops chamomile essential oil
5 drops rose essential oil
5 drops clary sage essential oil

1 Place shea butter, macadamia nut oil and soybean oil in a small saucepan over low heat; stir until melted and well combined.

2 Remove from heat and stir through contents of vitamin E capsules and essential oils. Pour into a wide-mouthed, dark-coloured glass jar and seal securely.

3 This blend will thicken in cool weather. To liquefy, simply place the jar in a pan of hot water for 5 to 10 minutes.

Floral massage oil

With its fine, silky texture and sensuous, luscious vanilla aroma, this is the perfect choice for a loving and relaxing partner massage. Jojoba oil is chemically quite similar to human sebum, so that it is more readily absorbed than other oils.

4 vanilla pods
125ml jojoba oil
2 tablespoons grapeseed oil
10 drops ylang ylang essential oil
10 drops rose essential oil
10 drops lavender essential oil
5 drops geranium essential oil
5 drops jasmine essential oil

1 Split pods in half lengthwise; scrape out the seeds. Chop pods into small pieces and place in a glass jar with seeds, jojoba oil and grapeseed oil. Seal securely.

2 Store in a dark place for 1 month. Strain off oil, then strain again through muslin to remove fine vanilla particles.

Instant energiser

Whether typing, cleaning, lifting or driving, your arms, shoulders and hands work hard. Look after them by taking regular breaks from repetitive work and trying this self-massage sequence, using the Stimulating massage oil (see right).

SUPPORT your left elbow with your right hand. Make a loose fist of your left hand and gently pound across your right shoulder. Using your thumb and fingertips, make small circular movements to work muscles, moving from the back of your neck down your right shoulder. Repeat, using your right hand on the left-hand side of your body.

STRAIGHTEN your right arm, open your palm and tap down the inside from the shoulder to the open hand with your left hand. Turn your arm over and tap up the back of your arm, from the hand to the shoulders. Repeat this sequence 5 times, then do the same again on your left arm.

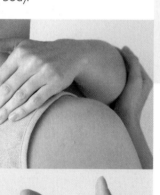

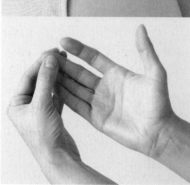

USE your left thumb to work your right hand, gently massaging the palm, then the mound at the base of the thumb, pressing deep with your knuckles to release tension. Search out sore spots and press with the thumb, holding for a count of 5. Squeeze and massage the joints of each finger, using your index finger and thumb. Pull out the fingers and briskly rub your fingertips to release stress and tension in your hands. Repeat on the left hand.

3 Pour oil into a dark-coloured glass bottle. Add essential oils and seal securely. Shake before use.

Warming massage oil

Mustard is the secret ingredient in this recipe. Its pronounced warming and reviving effect helps to relax tight, cramped muscles. Ginger is also a highly effective ingredient because it stimulates circulation, helping blood flow to the skin's surface, making this recipe ideal for people with arthritis.

125ml olive oil

2 tablespoons avocado oil

10 drops wintergreen essential oil

10 drops rosemary essential oil

10 drops ginger essential oil

5 drops sandalwood essential oil

5 drops frankincense essential oil

good pinch of dry mustard

1 Combine all ingredients in a dark-coloured glass bottle; seal securely.

2 Store in a cool place away from direct sunlight. Shake the bottle well before using.

Stimulating massage oil

This invigorating, skin-conditioning oil blend is an effective pick-me-up for when your energy levels are sagging. Eucalyptus and peppermint have a warming, head- clearing effect, making this recipe ideal for anyone with respiratory congestion.

125ml almond oil

2 tablespoons grapeseed oil

10 drops eucalyptus oil

10 drops peppermint essential oil

10 drops rosemary essential oil

5 drops lemon essential oil

5 drops basil essential oil

1 Combine all ingredients in a dark-coloured glass bottle and seal securely.

Different strokes

There are several different types of massage movements, and each is designed to have a specific effect on the body.

GLIDING This involves the use of the whole hand in long, slow, smooth, broad movements. The first and last strokes of a massage usually consist of gliding strokes.

CIRCLING With circling, the hands move over large areas in a circular motion, typically along or across the length of muscle fibres in the back, shoulders, legs or arms. This helps to release tension before deeper strokes are used.

KNEADING After the recipient has been relaxed by the steady gliding movements, kneading (or petrissage) helps to loosen any cramped muscles and knots. These movements involve a firm, squeezing action to encourage the elimination of waste matter and to allow the free flow of fresh, oxygenated blood.

PRESSURE Deeper massage involves using your thumbs, knuckles or the flat heel of your hand to apply strong, focused pressure on a particular trouble spot.

PERCUSSION Also known as tapotement, these percussive strokes are performed quickly to stimulate the circulation under the skin and to tone the associated muscles. An example is hacking, whereby the sides of the fingers are used to tap rhythmically up and down.

2 Store in a cool place away from direct sunlight. Shake well before using.

Around the home

For a healthier home the natural way, use air fresheners, cleaning agents, pest repellents and pet-care items made from herbs, essential oils and other non-toxic products. They're kind to you and your family and all your belongings.

Air fresheners

Don't reach for a commercial air freshener when you want to sweeten your surroundings. Homemade herbal solutions are much cheaper than their artificial counterparts, smell beautiful, do not rely on an arsenal of chemicals and neutralise unpleasant odours rather than masking them.

Pot-pourri

As far back as the 12th century, sweetly perfumed herbs and flowers were salted and left to ferment or rot into potently perfumed mixtures, which were then used to disguise household odours and, it was believed, help prevent the spread of disease. The dry pot-pourri mixtures on these pages still have a heavenly scent but they are somewhat easier to prepare. They also have the advantage of looking much more attractive than their mediaeval counter-parts. Display your pot pourri mixtures in decorative bowls and stir them gently once in a while to release their scent anew.

Rose and lavender pot-pourri

This is a classic pot-pourri recipe – fragrant, delightfully spiced and pretty to look at.

10g dried rosebuds and/or petals
30g dried lavender flowers
10g dried rose geranium leaves
peel of 1 orange, cut into thin strips before drying
2 tablespoons whole cloves, lightly crushed
1 tablespoon whole allspice, lightly crushed
5 cinnamon sticks, broken into pieces
2 tablespoons orris root powder
6 to 10 drops lavender essential oil
½ teaspoon rose geranium essential oil

1 Combine all the ingredients and mix well. Put the pot pourri into a sealed container and leave for a few weeks to mature.

2 To use, transfer to open bowls and stir gently to release the scent.

Lemon-scented pot-pourri

If you like a citrus scent, you'll love the fresh perfume of this colourful mixture. If you have other lemon-scented leaves, such as lemon-scented geranium, lemon-scented tea-tree or lemon-scented gum, feel free to add them.

15g dried calendula flowers
20g dried chamomile flowers
10g dried lemon balm
10g dried lemon verbena
15g dried lemon thyme
10g dried basil
80g finely diced dried lemon peel
2 tablespoons orris root powder
½ teaspoon lemon verbena essential oil
6 drops chamomile essential oil

Mix and use as for Rose and lavender pot-pourri. This mixture makes a lovely, scented filler for placing inside cushions on chairs and sofas.

Smell busters

Mix a few drops of antibacterial essential oil (such as lavender, tea-tree, rosemary or peppermint) into some bicarbonate of soda. Pack the mixture into a sock or stocking, and stuff it into your sneakers. Leave in overnight to deodorise them. When re-using the mixture, add extra oil.

Rosemary pot-pourri

This combination of fresh peppermint and aromatic rosemary is a good mix for bathrooms or sick rooms.

100g dried rosemary leaves
5g dried peppermint leaves
30g whole cloves, lightly crushed
20g crumbled cinnamon sticks
60g orris root powder
¼ teaspoon rosemary essential oil

Mix the ingredients together and use in the same way as the Rose and lavender pot-pourri described opposite.

Simmering or steaming pot-pourri deodoriser

As its name suggests, a simmering pot-pourri is simmered gently on the stove in order to release a sweet fragrance that will pervade the whole house. Vary the spices to suit your individual taste. Simply keep topping up the water until the fragrance has disappeared, or allow the spices to dry out on a tray between uses.

40g dried or fresh lemon peel
80g dried or fresh orange peel
120g whole cloves, lightly crushed
100g whole allspice
75g coriander seeds, crushed
handful of dried or fresh bay leaves, roughly crushed (optional)
5 cinnamon sticks, roughly broken
250ml boiling water

1 Mix all the ingredients together in a bowl and store in an airtight container until needed.

2 Simmer the spices in a small saucepan of water on the stove, topping up the water as needed.

Alternatively, place 2 tablespoons of the pot-pourri mixture in a heatproof container, cover with boiling water and leave in the room that needs deodorising until the spicy fragrance released by the steaming pot-pourri replaces the unpleasant smell.

Air freshener spray

Lightly mist this delicious-smelling air freshener around the room whenever you feel the need to sweeten your surroundings.

50ml vodka
¼ teaspoon bergamot essential oil
8 drops clove essential oil
5 drops lemon essential oil
200ml distilled water

1 Put the vodka and oils into a spray bottle and shake well to disperse the oils. Add the distilled water and shake again to thoroughly combine.

2 Leave for a few days to allow the mixture to mature. Spray briefly to refresh a room.

Room fresheners

HANG sachets of aromatic pot-pourri from door handles or sunny windows.

PUSH herb or spice sachets down the sides and backs of lounge cushions or inside cushion covers.

PLACE a container of pot-pourri in a sitting room or bedroom. Whenever you spend time in this room, remove the lid and stir the pot-pourri.

KEEP a small porous pottery bottle filled with a favourite essential oil near a sunny window so that the heat will cause the oils to evaporate.

DAB a little essential oil onto a light bulb before you turn it on.

PUT a couple of drops of spicy essential oil on a cotton-wool ball; wipe this over your heater in winter for a comforting fragrance.

Caring for clothing

Forget the marketing hype and get right back to some basic principles with your laundry. Soap and water are the time-honoured enemies of dirt and nothing beats the delicious fresh scent and non-toxic disinfectant qualities of simple herbs such as lavender and lemon.

Herbal pre-wash stain remover

Ammonia is a strong cleaning agent with fumes that can irritate, but it quickly breaks down in the environment and is safer than many commercial products.

125ml water
125ml phosphate-free washing powder or washing-up liquid
125ml ammonia
10 drops lavender or lemon essential oil or eucalyptus oil

1 Combine all the liquids in a spray bottle, then shake.

2 Spray onto stains before washing, then wash immediately. (Do not leave clothes that have been sprayed with this solution unwashed because it can have a bleaching effect.) Do not use it with chlorine bleach.

A stain buster from down under

Eucalyptus oil is one of the most powerful natural antiseptic oils, but is also invaluable for removing stains – particularly grease and perspiration – from clothing and other fabric. Moisten a clean rag with a little oil and dab the stain from the edge to the middle, then launder as usual.

Lemon laundry soap powder

Borax is a mildly toxic disinfectant, stain remover, deodoriser and water softener that is considered environmentally safe. Both borax and washing soda can irritate sensitive skin, so wear rubber gloves whenever you use this powder to hand wash garments.

125g washing soda
200g finely grated pure soap
120g salt
120g borax
125g bicarbonate of soda
¼ teaspoon or more lemon, lavender or peppermint essential oil or eucalyptus oil

1 Put the washing soda crystals in a clean plastic bag and crush them finely with a rolling pin.

2 Mix the crushed washing soda with the rest of the dry ingredients.

3 Add the essential oil and, wearing rubber gloves, distribute it through the powder. Store in an airtight box or jar.

4 Use 1 tablespoon for a small load, 1½ tablespoons for a medium load and 2 tablespoons for a large load. Dissolve powder in a small amount of hot water and add to the dispenser drawer in your washing machine.

Lavender liquid laundry soap

This simple liquid soap is gentle on your laundry and on the environment. Far cheaper than a commercial washing powder, it will

To whiten sheets, add 3 tablespoons of lemon juice to the washing cycle, then dry them in the sun.

leave both clothes and bedlinens smelling wonderful and feeling ultra soft.

125ml liquid Castile soap
125g washing soda
120g borax
2 to 3 teaspoons lavender or lemon verbena essential oil
7 litres hot water

1 Mix all the ingredients in a large bucket and stir well until soda crystals and borax are dissolved.

2 Decant into clean plastic detergent containers (recycle your old ones).

3 Shake the mixture before using. Use about 60ml per load.

Rose geranium fabric softener

This simple treatment will leave fabrics soft and fluffy without the cloying scent of artificial perfumes.

250ml white distilled vinegar
250g bicarbonate of soda
500ml water
10 drops rose geranium, lavender or lemon essential oil or eucalyptus oil (or a combination of your favourite oils)

1 Combine ingredients slowly and carefully over the sink, because the mixture will fizz. Pour into a plastic bottle and replace the lid.

2 Add 60ml to the final rinse or place it in the fabric softener dispenser of your washing machine.

Easy being green

Add your favourite scent to perfume-free, environmentally friendly laundry powder (from organic or health food shops). Just add a few drops of herbal essential oil to the powder as you put it into the machine.

Eucalyptus wool wash

This recipe is particularly good as a wash for woollen garments, but it's ideal for blankets, quilts and pillows, too. The eucalyptus helps to keep the wool soft and acts as a moth repellent. There is no need to rinse it out unless you are washing white items, in which case a thorough rinsing will prevent them from yellowing

500ml water
200g pure soap flakes
125ml methylated spirits
2½ teaspoons eucalyptus oil

1 Bring the water to the boil and stir in the soap flakes. Remove the pan from the heat and continue to stir until the soap has dissolved and the mixture is smooth.

2 Add the methylated spirits and the eucalyptus oil and mix well.

3 Spoon the mixture into a wide-mouthed jar, where it will set to a fairly solid consistency.

4 To use the wool wash, dissolve 1 to 2 tablespoons in a bucket of warm water. Keep the unused mixture tightly sealed.

Moth-repellent herbs

When you need to repel moths, choose from any or all of the following herbs.

- Lavender
- Cotton lavender
- Rosemary
- Wormwood
- Sweet woodruff
- Feverfew (right)
- Tansy
- Patchouli

Queen Victoria had all the rooms of her residences perfumed with lavender.

Lavender linen water

Known in France as *eau de linge*, this spray imparts a beautiful fresh lavender scent when used to dampen clothes and linen before ironing. It can also be used directly in some steam irons, if the manufacturer says it is safe to do so.

¼ teaspoon lavender essential oil
40ml vodka
500ml filtered water

1 Combine the lavender essential oil and vodka in a clean, dry glass bottle. Replace the lid and leave for 24 hours.

2 Add the water, shake to combine and cap tightly. Transfer to a spray bottle when ironing and use as required.

Herbs for your clothes

When you've washed, ironed and folded your clothes and household linen, you want them to remain pristine after you put them away. It's so disappointing to pull out a favourite jumper or sheet set to discover that it's full of tiny moth holes. Banish clothes moths and keep your wardrobe smelling fresh and sweet with the following easy

Fragrant clothes drying

Put several drops of your favourite essential oil – a combination of lavender, rosemary, lemon and pine is lovely – on a damp face washer and throw it into the tumble dryer with a load of damp clothes.

herb projects. Few everyday pleasures are more delightful than sleeping in herb-scented sheets.

Moth-repellent sachets

Take advantage of the natural moth-repellent qualities of many common herbs and spices and tuck these sachets into drawers or hang them from coat-hangers in your wardrobe. To make moth-repellent sachets, see page 308.

Quick moth repellent

Combine equal amounts of lavender, rosemary, clove and lemon essential oils in a small bottle. Take everything out of your cupboards and wipe the interior and shelves with a damp cloth that's been sprinkled with a few drops of the oil blend. You can also sprinkle it onto cotton-wool balls, then place them in the wardrobe when you replace the clothing.

Pomanders

Pomanders are small balls of perfumes and fragrant spices which, from the 14th to the 17th centuries, were used to mask unpleasant odours and ward off disease in times of pestilence. They could be hung in rooms or worn on chains, rings or girdles. The name comes from the French pomme d'ambre, or 'apple of amber', and refers to both the round shape and ambergris, one of the ingredients. The term also refers to the small filigree metal, ivory or china container that housed the ball. In the late Middle Ages, these were often lavishly embellished with gems and enamels and carried as fashion accessories.

WHAT YOU NEED

☐ **1 medium to large thin-skinned orange**

☐ **25 to 30g whole cloves**

☐ **1 teaspoon orris root powder (from health food shops and craft stores)**

☐ **1 teaspoon each ground cinnamon, nutmeg and cloves**

☐ **enough ribbon to tie twice around the orange, and to make a hanging loop, if desired**

☐ **tape of the same diameter as the ribbon**

☐ **pins**

☐ **toothpicks or cocktail sticks**

1 Use the tape to mark the orange into quarters. (Once the pomander has dried, the tape will be replaced with ribbon.)

2 Insert the cloves at intervals of 3 to 6mm. If you have difficulty pushing them in, use a cocktail stick, toothpick or darning needle to make a small hole before you insert each clove. You can place the cloves randomly or in a pattern. As the pomander dries, it will shrink to fill up the spaces between the cloves.

3 Carefully remove the tape when all the segments are covered in cloves.

4 Combine the orris root and spices in a small bowl or paper bag. Roll the orange in the spice mixture, thoroughly coating it. (Complete each pomander to this stage within 24 hours to prevent mould from forming.)

5 Leave the pomander in the spice bath in a warm, dry place for 2 to 4 weeks, until it is dry and hard.

6 Turn the pomander daily and make sure it is evenly coated with spices. The pomander will be ready when it feels light in weight and sounds hollow when tapped.

7 When cured, shake or brush off any spice powder. Wrap ribbon around the pomander in the tape tracks. Finish with a hanging loop.

Drawer liners

These drawer liners, lightly filled with lavender or a mixture of moth-repellent herbs, can also be placed between layers of bed or table linen. Unryushi paper is a strong and fibrous, but porous, Japanese paper, available from paper specialists and gift stores.

WHAT YOU NEED
☐ sheets of unryushi paper
☐ sewing thread
☐ dried herbs and spices for filling

1 Cut 2 sheets of unryushi paper a bit smaller than the size of the drawer bottom, or just cut 30cm squares, a good workable size. Machine stitch the 2 pieces together about 1cm from the edge, leaving an opening for the filling.

2 Fill the liner with dried herbs and spices and stitch the opening closed.

Scented coathangers

Padded coathangers keep delicate clothes and knitted garments in better shape than the wire variety, and these ones have the added advantage of both smelling sweet and keeping moths at bay.

WHAT YOU NEED
☐ wooden coathanger with screw-in hook
☐ herbal essential oil of your choice, such as lavender
☐ bias binding or ribbon, for covering hook (optional)
☐ quilt wadding
☐ craft glue
☐ two 45 x 16cm rectangles fabric
☐ sewing thread
☐ dried lavender (or other herbs/spices)
☐ 50cm decorative braid (optional)

1 Use a small cloth or cotton-wool ball to rub a little essential oil over the wooden hanger. To cover the hook, make a narrow bias tube,

Lavender wands

Place these charming 'wands' among your clothes and linen. When the scent begins to fade, add a few drops of lavender essential oil to refresh them.

WHAT YOU NEED
☐ 7 or 9 long stems of young lavender (it must be an odd number and the stems must be as pliable as possible)
☐ sewing thread
☐ 5mm wide ribbon

I Remove all the leaves and arrange the stems around a 50 to 60cm length of ribbon so that the end of the ribbon extends about 15cm above the flowers and the rest of the ribbon hangs down with the stems. Wind a piece of cotton around the stems

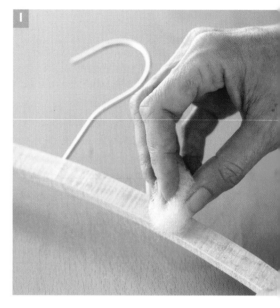

or wind ribbon or bias binding tightly around it. Secure the end by taking a stitch or two around the hanger to hold it in place.

2 Cut 5cm wide strips of quilt wadding and glue them end to end, to make one long strip. (The length depends on how tightly padded you like your hanger.) Glue a couple of small pieces of wadding

just below the flower heads and tie off securely.

2 Gently bend the stems back over the flower heads to enclose them in a sort of cage, evenly distributing them around the heads.

3 Take the longer length of ribbon (which is now at the top, extending beyond the flower heads) and weave it alternately over and under the stems, working around the flower heads.

over the ends of the hanger, then wind the long strip around the hanger from end to end until it is evenly padded. Secure the ends in place with a dab of glue or a stitch.

3 Centre the hanger on the wrong side of the fabric rectangles and trace around the top to give you the curved outline. Also mark the centre point of the hook.

4 Stitch around the sides and top of the cover, leaving a tiny opening in the centre top edge for the hook. Trim the seam allowance, clip the curves and turn the cover right side out. Press under the raw edges on the lower edge. Fit the cover over the hook and onto the padded hanger. Topstitch the pressed edges together, leaving an opening for the filling.

5 Fill with a couple of handfuls of dried herb, then stitch the opening closed. Stitch a piece of decorative braid along the bottom edge, if desired.

Continue weaving in this manner, pushing each row of ribbon up close to the previous row. When you get to the bottom of the flower heads, having enclosed them completely in a woven cage, you will meet the piece of ribbon that you left extended at the beginning. Wrap the weaving end firmly around the stems a couple of times, then tie the two ends of ribbon into a neat bow and trim.

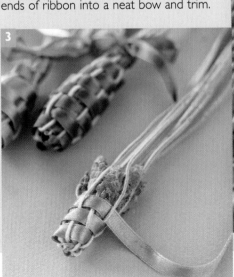

297

Cleaning with herbs

Whether you're committed to a greener way of cleaning or want to simplify and save money, herbal cleaning makes sense. Herbal cleaning products are mainly composed of one main substance – the cleaning agent. And fresh herbs or essential oils almost invariably leave a fresh, clean smell.

All-purpose herb vinegar spray

This all-purpose, environmentally friendly, non-toxic spray is great to have on hand for wiping, cleaning and deodorising almost every surface (except marble). If you don't have any fresh herbs, add drops of essential oil instead.

fresh or dried herbs (you can also use herbal tea bags)
distilled white vinegar

1 Roughly chop 1 to 2 large handfuls of fresh or dried herbs (such as lemon verbena, peppermint, rosemary, lemon balm or lavender), or place 5 to 10 tea bags in the bottom of a wide-mouthed glass jar.

2 Add vinegar to fill the jar. Replace the lid, leave for a few days to infuse, then strain out the herbs. (If you are using tea bags, you can gently warm the vinegar before pouring to ensure maximum diffusion.)

3 Decant into a plastic spray bottle. This spray is perfectly safe and very effective to use at full-strength, but it can also be diluted half-and-half with water for lighter jobs.

How to use herb vinegar spray

KEEP your dishwasher clean and fresh: add 125ml Herb vinegar to the rinse cycle.

CUT grease and make glasses sparkle: add 3 tablespoons Herb vinegar to the sink with the dishwashing detergent.

DISSOLVE mineral build-up on clogged shower heads: soak overnight in diluted Herb vinegar.

CLEAN soap scum from a glass shower screen: mix 2 parts salt with 1 part Herb vinegar. rub onto the screen with a cloth or fine steel wool. Rinse and dry.

STOP mould: mix 2 teaspoons borax and 250ml Herb vinegar. apply with a cloth, leave for 30 minutes then wipe off.

CLEAN the refrigerator: wipe out the fridge with Herb vinegar, then rub over with a sponge dipped in vanilla essence.

REMOVE mould from refrigerator door seals: scrub the mould from the folds with an old toothbrush dipped in Herb vinegar.

KEEP kitchen cloths fresh: soak overnight in a solution of boiling water with a good dash of Herb vinegar and a few drops of eucalyptus oil. Rinse well.

STEAM-CLEAN the microwave: place 250ml water and 60ml Herb vinegar in a bowl in the microwave and zap on High for 5 minutes. When it cools a little, use it to wipe the walls of the oven with a damp cloth.

Many herbs are antibacterial, making them natural disinfectants.

All-purpose non-vinegar herbal cleanser

If you don't want to use vinegar in your herbal cleanser – perhaps because you have marble worktops that may be damaged by the strong acid in vinegar – you can still make an all-purpose cleaning spray with water and get a little extra boost from borax.

fresh or dried herbs (or herbal tea bags)
2 tablespoons borax
herbal essential oil (optional)

1 Prepare the herbs as for the All-purpose herb vinegar spray (opposite).

2 Pour over hot water to cover and allow to steep for a few days. Strain, then add the borax and a few drops of essential oil, if using.

3 Shake to mix well and decant into spray bottles.

Lemon-grapefruit dishwashing liquid

When washing dishes use a tablespoonful of this citrussy washing-up liquid dissolved in hot water. You could also use lavender or rosemary essential oil instead of the lemon and grapefruit: both are good at cutting grease. As this is a soap, it does not produce as many suds as detergent, but it is still very effective as a cleaner.

3 tablespoons liquid Castile soap
500ml warm water
2 teaspoons vegetable glycerine
2 tablespoons distilled white vinegar
10 drops lemon essential oil
10 drops grapefruit essential oil

Mix all ingredients in a jar, cover and shake well to blend. Store in a plastic squeeze bottle.

Rosemary handwash

This delicious smelling foamy gel is ideal for keeping your hands clean while you are cooking, and the rosemary essential oil is a natural antibacterial agent.

50 to 100g pure soap flakes
500ml very hot water
60ml glycerine
½ teaspoon rosemary essential oil (or the herbal essential oil of your choice)

1 Put the soap flakes and the water in a bowl and whisk vigorously until the flakes have dissolved and you have a foam that is rather like whipped egg white. Cool to lukewarm.

2 Stir in the glycerine and the essential oil, whisk again and leave to cool. As the mixture cools, it becomes more solid, but if you have whisked enough, it should

remain foamy. If it is too thick for a pump bottle, beat in more water.

3 To use, squirt a little into the palms of your hands, lather and rinse off.

Your green cleaning kit

BICARBONATE OF SODA Gentle, moderately alkaline, non-toxic abrasive; cuts through grease and oil; absorbs odours.

BORAX Disinfecting, stain-removing, deodorising, mould-inhibiting, strongly alkaline salt that breaks down easily in the environment; softens water and kills ants and cockroaches.

DISTILLED white vinegar Moderately strong acid that is grease-cutting, mould-inhibiting, deodorising and a disinfectant.

HERBAL ESSENTIAL OILS Many oils are disinfectant, antibacterial and anti-fungal as well as sweet-smelling; use 100 per cent pure essential oils.

LEMON JUICE Mould-inhibitor, deodoriser, stain-remover and mild bleach.

PURE SOAP FLAKES or liquid Castile soap 100 per cent bio-degradable, low-toxic, phosphate-

free. Castile soap is available from health food or organic stores. For more information about this product, see Castile soap facts, page 279.

SALT Mild abrasive and disinfectant.

VEGETABLE GLYCERINE Non-toxic, useful cleaning product that helps mix oil with water and dissolves many forms of dirt.

WASHING SODA Moderately alkaline crystals; softens water, cuts grease and removes stains.

Pure and simple washing-up liquid

If you don't want to make your own washing-up liquid from scratch, buy an unscented, undyed, phosphate-free detergent from your local health food or organic store. Add your own essential oil plus a couple of sprigs of matching herb, decant into a pretty bottle and enjoy your washing up!

Citrus and tea-tree disinfectant

Spray this disinfectant in the kitchen or bathroom, or to deodorise a smelly rubbish bin. Increase its cleaning properties by adding 1 teaspoon liquid Castile soap to the solution. For extra disinfectant power, choose vinegar rather than water.

50ml vodka or methylated spirits
¼ teaspoon tea-tree oil
¼ teaspoon lemon essential oil
¼ teaspoon grapefruit essential oil
250ml water or white distilled vinegar

1 Pour the vodka or methylated spirits and essential oils into a spray bottle and shake to combine.

2 Add the water or vinegar and shake for several minutes.

White goods cleaner

Regular wiping with this cleaner will remove grubby fingermarks and leave the surfaces of freezers, refrigerators and washing machines looking like new without scratching them.

2 tablespoons phosphate-free dishwashing liquid
1 tablespoon cornflour
250ml water
250ml distilled white vinegar
a few drops of herbal essential oil of your choice

1 Put the ingredients in a plastic spray bottle and shake gently to combine.

2 Spray a fine film of the mixture over the grubby surface and wipe clean with a soft cloth.

Disinfectant scouring powder

Use this simple cleaner as you would a commercial powdered cleanser. To use it in a toilet, sprinkle the powder into the bowl, then spritz with All-purpose herb vinegar spray (see page 298) and allow it to fizz before brushing the toilet bowl and flushing.

250g bicarbonate of soda
10 drops each of grapefruit, cinnamon, thyme and rosemary essential oil

1 Blend the ingredients well and store in a sealed glass jar. Leave for a couple of days before using.

2 Apply the powder with a damp cloth and rinse well.

Lemon creme cleanser

This slightly abrasive cleaner is great for cleaning baths, basins and stainless steel appliances, sinks and benchtops, but do not use it on fibreglass bathroom fixtures. You can substitute a different essential oil if you prefer.

125g bicarbonate of soda
5 to 6 teaspoons liquid Castile soap or phosphate-free liquid detergent
½ teaspoon lemon essential oil
1 teaspoon glycerine

1 Combine all the ingredients and mix well. Store in a sealed glass jar.

2 To use, scoop the mixture onto a cloth or sponge, rub over the surface, then wipe off with a rinsed cloth.

Tea-tree anti-mould spray

Tea-tree, cloves and borax are powerful mould inhibitors. Keep this spray in the bathroom to use on the shower recess or for wiping the shower curtain.

2 teaspoons borax
250ml warm water
10 drops clove essential oil
1 tablespoon tea-tree oil

1 In a spray bottle, dissolve the borax in the warm water.

2 Add the clove and tea-tree oils and shake well.

3 To use, spray onto areas susceptible to mould and mildew, then leave to dry.

Peppermint–lemon glass cleaner

This fresh-smelling cleaner leaves glass sparkling clean. When used on windows, it will also help to deter flies from settling.

juice of 1 lemon
500ml soda water
½ teaspoon peppermint essential oil
1 teaspoon cornflour

1 Combine all ingredients in a bowl and stir until blended.

2 Pour into a plastic spray bottle. Shake well before using.

Spicy carpet deodoriser

Banish pet smells and other stale odours from your carpet with this sweet-smelling mixture. Before measuring the dried herbs, you need to grind them very finely in a spice or coffee grinder.

500g bicarbonate of soda
4 tablespoons borax
4 teaspoons ground cloves
4 teaspoons ground cinnamon
4 tablespoons each of finely ground dried mint, rosemary, lavender and thyme

1 Combine all the ingredients in a bowl and mix thoroughly.

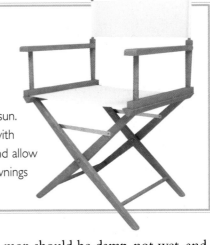

To clean mould from canvas

Scrub the canvas with very salty water (1kg salt in a bucket of water) and allow the solution to dry on the canvas in the sun. Brush away any salt crystals, then spray with Tea-tree anti-mould spray (see below) and allow to dry. This method is good for canvas awnings and director's chairs.

2 To use, sprinkle the powder over the carpet and leave for an hour or more (even overnight) before vacuuming the carpet thoroughly.

Eucalyptus stain foam

Use this fresh-smelling foam as a stain remover for both carpets and upholstery. For extra-tough stains, add 60g washing soda to the hot water and Eucalyptus wool wash, and whisk until the crystals have completely dissolved.

3 tablespoons Eucalyptus wool wash (see page 293)
1 litre hot water

1 Vigorously whisk the Eucalyptus wool wash in the hot water until suds form.

2 Rub just the foam over the carpet stain and leave for 10 minutes.

3 Wipe the foam away with a damp sponge dipped in distilled white vinegar (this neutralises the alkalinity left by the foam).

4 Blot well with a clean pad.

Eucalyptus floor wash

This simple solution can be used on both wood and lino floors. When washing a timber floor, remember not to saturate it. Your mop should be damp, not wet, and the floor should be well-swept or vacuumed before mopping.

1 teaspoon eucalyptus oil
2 tablespoons methylated spirits
5 litres hot water (about half a bucket)

1 Combine all the ingredients in a bucket.

2 Wring out a mop in the solution and use it to damp mop the floor. Leave to dry; you don't need to rinse.

Peppermint floor wash

This is a great fresh-smelling rinse for tiled floors. If you use it on tiled areas outdoors, it will help to keep flies away in hot weather.

250ml distilled white vinegar
250ml methylated spirits
250ml strong peppermint tea (from tea bags or leaves)
5 to 10 drops peppermint essential oil
5 drops dishwashing liquid

1 Combine all the ingredients in a large plastic bottle, shake thoroughly and then decant into a spray bottle.

2 Spray onto the floor and apply with a damp mop.

Use eucalyptus oil to remove scuff marks and sticky spills from all types of hard floor.

Rosemary beeswax furniture polish

This is a thick liquid polish. If you like more of a paste, increase the amount of beeswax and decrease the turpentine to about half-and-half. Gum turpentine is highly flammable, so take care when making up the polish.

60g pure beeswax pellets
  (or grated beeswax)
250ml pure gum turpentine
1½ teaspoons rosemary essential oil

1 Put the beeswax and turpentine into a heatproof bowl.
2 Carefully sit the bowl over a saucepan of barely simmering water

and stir until the beeswax melts and the solution is smooth. Take great care not to spill the liquid as you stir. Alternatively, to avoid exposing the mixture to a naked flame, sit the bowl in an electric frying pan on a low heat.

3 Remove from the heat and allow to cool before adding the rosemary oil. Store in a glass bottle with a screw top lid.

4 To use, pour a little onto a soft cloth and apply to wooden surfaces. Polish off with a second cloth until the surface shines.

Quick lavender furniture polish

Make up this polish in small quantities, as you need it. The vinegar cleans, the oil nourishes and the lavender disinfects, leaving that incomparable scent.

125ml distilled white vinegar (or
  better still, Herb vinegar on page
  298 made with lavender)
2 teaspoons olive oil
5 to 10 drops lavender essential oil

1 Combine all the ingredients in a jar or bottle.

2 To use, pour a little onto a soft cloth and rub the surface until you achieve a soft shine.

Lavender dusting cloth

Keep this lightly scented cloth for general dusting. Being slightly oily, it works much better than a plain cloth and will hold the dust as you pick it up.

250ml hot water
2 tablespoons olive oil
10 drops lavender essential oil

1 Whisk ingredients in a bowl.

2 Dip clean soft rags into the solution, wring them out and hang them to dry. Store them in a sealed container and use them for dusting as required.

3 When the cloth is grubby, simply wash and re-dip it.

Quick vacuum deodoriser

For a clean fresh scent as you vacuum, sprinkle a few drops of a disinfectant essential oil, such as rosemary, or a mix of your favourites, onto a cotton-wool ball and drop it into the dust bag or canister of your vacuum cleaner.

Herbal pet care

You can use herbs effectively for minor ailments that may sometimes trouble your cat or dog. But remember, if any symptoms persist, you must seek veterinary help.

Scald, sunburn or hotspot salve

Aloe vera gel takes the sting out of scalds and sunburn and soothes an itch with its moisturising properties. Cut an aloe vera leaf and apply the gel directly onto scalds, sunburn or hotspots caused by excessive scratching. Make sure you always break off the more mature leaves from the aloe vera plant.

Arthritis infusion

The pain and debilitating effects of arthritis can affect elderly cats or dogs as well as particular breeds. Try these two herbal remedies.
• Add a little chopped fresh parsley or grated ginger to your pet's diet.
• Pour 250ml boiling water over 1 teaspoon fresh rosemary leaves. Stir and cover for 15 minutes. Strain and store in the refrigerator for up to 3 days. Over several weeks, mix a little into your pet's food.

Fight-the-fleas spray

Fleas can drive cats and dogs quite crazy, and the incessant scratching can make owners pretty edgy, too. To keep fleas at bay, spray this mixture onto your pet's bedding and directly onto your pet.

250ml water
4 to 6 drops tea-tree oil
4 to 6 drops lavender essential oil

1 Mix ingredients together and pour into a spray bottle.

2 Keep spray by the door and spritz your dog or cat each time it goes outside, taking care to avoid the eyes.

Sunburn soother

Relieve the discomfort and sting of sunburn by spraying the affected area with cool water mixed with witch hazel. It has a numbing effect. Be sure to keep it away from your pet's eyes.

Winter paw moisturiser

In cold weather, your dog's paws can become dry, particularly if they spend a lot of time out in the snow. Rub a daily smear of calendula ointment over the affected areas.

Peppermint kennel cleaner

Keep your dog's sleeping quarters flea-free and smelling fresh with this easy herbal spray.

500ml boiling water
2 to 3 peppermint (or spearmint) tea bags
¼ teaspoon clove essential oil

1 Make a strong tea with the water and tea bags.

2 Allow to cool and add the essential oil. Transfer the cleaner into a spray bottle.

3 To use, spray onto the inside surfaces of the kennel and wipe clean. Spray again and allow to dry on the walls without rinsing. Wash the bedding regularly, too.

To deter fleas, scatter dried wormwood beneath bedding.

Craft

Embroidery, flower pressing and arranging, photography, woodworking – whatever your favourite craft or hobby, herbs have a part to play. Choose from these easy, stylish projects that feature both fresh and dried herbs.

Herbal sleep pillows

Rest your head on a pillow filled with aromatic herbs and you'll quickly find yourself relaxing and drifting into an untroubled sleep. It's a good way of using up scraps of attractive fabrics and short lengths of trim that are too small for conventional cushions.

Fill your sleep pillow with a single herb or with a combination of herbs. Take care to choose ones that will help to ease your mental and physical fatigue and also complement each other. Herbs known for their calming properties include lavender and roses. Avoid herbs such as eucalyptus and cinnamon, as their more insistent aromas tend to energise rather than relax.

To make your pillow

WHAT YOU NEED
The pillows vary in size from about 25 cm square to 32 x 24cm. These instructions are for a 25cm square.
☐ 30 x 50cm cotton print
☐ 30 x 30cm contrast cotton print
☐ 1.3 m ric-rac or bobble braid
☐ matching sewing thread
☐ 30 x 60cm calico, or other fine material
☐ dried herbs of your choice, for filling (for example, lavender, chamomile, rose petals, myrtle, lemon verbena)

1 For pillow Front, cut one 27cm square (finished measurement + 1cm seam allowance on all sides). From the same fabric, cut one rectangle, 27 x 15cm, for the Flap (same height as Front x 12cm Flap + 1cm seam allowance + 2cm hem). From the contrast fabric, cut one Back, 27 x 30cm (same height as Front x finished width + 1cm seam allowance + 4cm hem).

2 Starting and finishing in the centre of one side and with right sides together, baste the ric-rac to the edge of the pillow Front,

remembering to allow for ease around the corners.

3 Press under and stitch a 1cm double hem (2m in all) on one long edge of the Flap.

4 With right sides together and allowing a 1cm seam, stitch Flap to one side of the pillow along the 27cm edge. Press seam open.

5 Press under 1cm on one side of Back. Press under another 3cm. Stitch hem in place. (Back now measures 26 x 27cm.)

6 Place pillow Front, right side up, on your work surface, with the Flap extended. Place the Back on top, right side down, so that raw edges match the Front and the hemmed edge of the Back aligns with the seam line of the Flap. Fold the Flap back over the Back, so that the right side of the Flap is against the wrong side of the Back.

7 Allowing 1cm seams, stitch around the three edges, through all layers. (If you have used a very bulky braid, you might need to use a zip foot.) Trim corners, fold Flap back over and turn the cover right side out.

8 From calico, cut and stitch an inner pillow the same finished size as the finished cover measurements (in this case, 25cm square). You will need to leave an opening for filling and turning.

9 Turn the calico pillow to the right side out, and use a cone of greaseproof paper to loosely fill it with the herb of your choice. Stitch opening closed, then insert the pillow into the cover, using the Flap to hold it in place.

Moth-repellent sachets

Protect your clothes with pretty sachets filled with herbs that deter fabric-munching insects. Choose fine or loose-weave fabrics so that the aroma comes through strongly.

Wormwood, whole cloves, bay leaves, eucalyptus, lavender, chamomile, crushed cinnamon sticks, peppermint and feverfew will all repel moths and other insects that can damage fabrics such as wool, mohair and other animal fibres. These herbs also help purify stale air, while rue is useful for keeping flies at bay. For the best effect, give the sachets an occasional quick squeeze or shake to release more scent.

felt flower template

To make your sachet

WHAT YOU NEED
Each finished sachet measures 13cm approximately in diameter.
- ☐ **2 x 15cm squares plain or embroidered organza, lawn or pretty brocade**
- ☐ **sharp pencil**
- ☐ **machine thread**
- ☐ **dried moth-repellent herbs and spices (use a mixture of any, or all, of the herbs mentioned above)**
- ☐ **pinking shears**
- ☐ **length of ribbon, for the hanging loop**
- ☐ **small or decorative button (optional)**
- ☐ **scraps of felt in two toning colours (optional)**
- ☐ **stranded embroidery cotton (optional)**

1 Using an appropriately sized cup or saucer, lightly trace a 10cm diameter circle in the centre of one square. If using embroidered organza or brocade, try to centre motif or embroidery in the circle.

2 Place second square beneath the first, wrong sides together. Carefully machine-stitch around

traced line, leaving an opening of about 4cm for the filling. Tie off threads neatly on the back (remember you're working on the right side of the fabric).

3 Trim around edge of circle with pinking shears, cutting about 1.5cm from stitched line.

4 Carefully fill the sachet with moth-repellent herbs, using a funnel or cone of paper. Don't fill too tightly.

5 Stitch opening closed, trying to be as accurate as possible. If you want to add a hanging loop, insert the ends of the ribbon into the opening and secure them in the seam. Tie off thread ends.

Use several sachets. The stronger the fragrance, the greater the protection against destructive insects.

6 To add a felt flower, use the templates (see opposite) to trace and cut a Small flower and a Large flower from two different-coloured scraps of felt.

7 Place the Small flower on top of the Large one and centre a button on top. Place the flower unit in the centre of the sachet and stitch it in place through all the layers with two or three strands of embroidery cotton in a complementary colour. Tie off the thread securely at the back of the sachet.

Lavender heart sachets

Every thime you rearrange a shelf or drawer, tuck one of these sachets under a pile of linen or clothing, and the gentle, aromatic fragrance will permeate the fabric, giving a delightful fresh smell when you put sheets on the bed or pull on your clothes.

Lavender has a fresh scent associated with cleanliness, which isn't surprising when you consider that the name is derived from the Latin word for 'to wash'. The sachets work best in small, enclosed areas and their fragrance should last for about three months. After this time, they can be reopened and refilled with some newly dried lavender.

Alternatively, you could try a filling of cotton lavender. A moth-deterrent, it also has a fresh, aromatic scent.

Use this heart-shaped template to trace the sachet outline.

You can easily make other simple shapes by drawing your own cardboard templates.

To make your sachet

WHAT YOU NEED
Finished sachets are approximately 12 x 12cm.
- [ ] **thin cardboard or template plastic**
- [ ] **2 x 20cm squares cotton print (or 1 square print and 1 square embroidery linen)**
- [ ] **fine lead pencil**
- [ ] **matching machine thread**
- [ ] **narrow ribbon, for hanging (optional)**
- [ ] **dried lavender**
- [ ] **small button (optional)**
- [ ] **Anchor Stranded Cotton: 101 Very Dark Violet; 1030 Dark Blue-Violet; 860 Fern Green (optional)**
- [ ] **crewel embroidery needle (optional)**

1 Trace heart outline onto thin cardboard or template plastic and cut out. (Using template plastic makes it easier to centre the embroidered design and the centre back seam on the fabric.)

2 To make the cotton print sachet, cut one fabric square in half, then

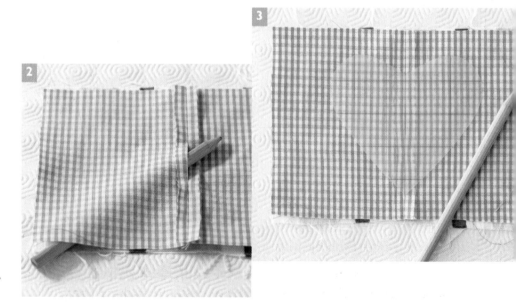

around the traced outline, taking care not to catch the ribbon loop in the seam. Trim away excess fabric about 6mm outside the stitching. Trim the point, clip the curves and finally turn the sachet right side out through the centre back seam.

5 Using a paper funnel (greaseproof works well), loosely fill the sachet with lavender and slipstitch the opening closed.

6 Stitch a small button to the centre of the heart, through all layers, using a double strand of machine thread or embroidery cotton. Tie it off securely at the back of the heart.

7 To make the embroidered sachet, construct the back from a cotton print fabric, as described above. For the embroidered front, trace the stalk positions on the diagram very lightly onto the centre of the embroidery linen. (You don't need to trace on the flowers.)

8 Using two strands of 860, embroider the stalks by working two or three long straight stitches along the traced line for each stalk, making a tiny back stitch to anchor each straight stitch. Thread the needle with two strands of each colour (to make six strands in total) and work the flowers in small straight stitches on either side of the stalks, using the diagram as a positional guide.

9 Making sure the embroidered motif is centred on the heart shape, trace around the template on the wrong side.

10 Join the back and front together, stitching around the traced outline and making sure the back seam is centred. Finish as for the cotton print sachet, above (step 6), but omit the button.

stitch the halves back together again, allowing a 6mm seam and leaving a small opening in the centre of the seam for turning and filling. (This will be the centre back seam.) Press seam open.

3 Making sure the back seam is centred, trace around the heart

template onto the wrong side of the joined fabric square, but do not cut it out yet.

4 Place the two fabric squares right sides together. If you are using a hanging loop, insert the ends into the seam at the dip in the top of the heart shape. Stitch

Hanging herb ball

Form and function go hand in hand in this mini hanging garden. Change the contents to reflect each new season and pop in a few flowering varieties for added colour.

When you choose your herbs, think about their leaf shapes, colours and growing habit. We selected wild creeping thyme as a groundcover and oregano to cascade over the sides, then contrasted the broad-leafed herb comfrey with the feathery foliage of the curry plant. Then we selected lime-scented geranium for its delicious fragrance, yellow-flowered marigolds for a colour burst, and finally basil, parsley, chives and mint for their versatile culinary value.

To care for your ball

• Select a secure position to hang the finished herb ball, as it is heavy when watered. Choose hooks and brackets that are designed to withstand the weight and make sure they are firmly fixed. Never attach brackets to crumbling brickwork or rotting wood.

• Until the roots are established, hang the ball in a position that receives only morning sun for one to two weeks. Herbs love the sun, so move it to a sunny spot, away from drying winds.

• Feed the ball fortnightly with water-soluble fertiliser.

• Water daily through the holes on top of the ball.

• Use a spray bottle to water the foliage so the herb ball gets a good drink. Don't allow it to dry out as the plants will yellow.

Wear garden gloves of closely woven material to protect your fingers from the sharp edges of cut wire.

To make your herb ball

WHAT YOU NEED
- ☐ **2 metal hanging baskets**
- ☐ **2 coconut fibre basket liners (or bark liner or sphagnum moss)**
- ☐ **small bag of perlite and vermiculite mix**
- ☐ **good-quality potting mix containing both a slow-release fertiliser and a wetting agent**
- ☐ **cling film**
- ☐ **wire**
- ☐ **corrugated cardboard**
- ☐ **selection of herbs (see opposite)**
- ☐ **wire-cutting pliers**
- ☐ **scissors**
- ☐ **garden gloves**
- ☐ **florist's watering can**
- ☐ **spray bottle**
- ☐ **water-soluble fertiliser (see To care for your ball)**

1 Support one of the wire baskets on a suitable stand (we used a small rubbish bin) with the basket liner in place. Decide which basket is to be the upper one. Thoroughly wet the liner so it expands, making it easier to create insertion points.

Create a series of holes in the liner so you can plant the herbs (we used a cutting/piercing tool and forced the fibre outwards with your fingers). Protect individual herbs with cling film. Carefully push them into holes in prepared liner. Repeat for second basket.

2 For a lightweight growing medium, blend potting mix with perlite and vermiculite mix and partially fill baskets. Gently press potting mix into place to ensure all the air pockets are filled around the roots, planting comfrey through the bottom of the upper basket. Once you have put the ball together, the comfrey will be growing out of the top of the upper basket.

3 Cut out a circle of corrugated cardboard to cover the top of the upper basket. Pierce with holes to allow water to drain through. Wire into place.

4 Align the baskets to create the ball. Wire together (we used wire fencing clips, but twisted wire will do the same job). For maximum security, attach the hanging chains on the wire baskets to the rim of both baskets.

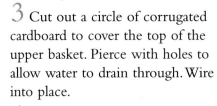

If you like Indian and southeast Asian dishes, plant a range of strongly flavoured herbs, such as coriander, perilla, Thai basil and chillies. Or, if you're fond of Mediterranean recipes, plant oregano, sage, thyme and savory, which thrive in the region.

Herb and flower wreath

Use wreaths to decorate your home, just as you would pot plants or flowers. Quick and easy to make, they make a delightful welcome at any time of year.

A wreath can be rich in meaning. The circular shape is a symbol of infinity, without beginning or end. It represents unity, perfection and the cycles of both nature and time. A laurel wreath was used as a symbol of excellence by the ancient Greeks, who awarded it to great scholars, artists, soldiers and athletes. The ancient Romans also crowned their successful military commanders with wreaths.

Today, a wreath can be either purely decorative or significant in some way. You can choose flowers and herbs that symbolise a religious festival or a personal event, such as a birthday or wedding. Or you can simply make wreaths that feature what's in season in your garden – for example, in autumn, berries and rose hips can look stunning.

Obviously, a herb and flower wreath is not designed to last, but most frames can be reused many times and each one is simple to make. Once one wreath begins to fade, start planning the next one.

Leafy wreaths can be just as attractive as floral ones. Try a mixture of leaf shapes and colours. Bay and olive are lovely alone or can be enhanced with violets.

Frames

You can buy ready-made frames made of raffia, styrofoam, wire, dried grasses or some form of pliable timber. You can also make a timber frame from wisteria twigs or olive branches (you will need to strip them of leaves). The important thing to remember is that whatever you use, the material must bend smoothly into a circle but be sufficiently sturdy to hold the flowers and foliage without pulling out of shape. Finally, it should be easy to attach foliage and flowers to your frame.

Decorating the frame

How you decorate your frame is a matter of individual taste. You can keep things simple, as we have here, or build up more layers with some supplementary flowers and herbs. Try using a combination of fresh and dried herbs and flowers, bearing in mind that, once cut, some will have a shorter lifespan than others. With the flowers, experiment with a single colour, several tones of one colour or several contrasting colours.

Plant meanings

Olive branches Peace, fruitfulness, purification, strength, victory and reward.
Bay leaves Victory and excellence. Bay is an aromatic, broad-leafed evergreen.
Evergreens Eternal life and resurrection.
Violets Faithfulness.

To make your wreath

If you are using a ribbon, tie this onto the base first, as it is difficult to add it later without squashing or hiding the foliage. Attach a length of florist wire to make a loop for hanging. At the end of each step, place the wreath in an upright position to check the coverage and

balance. It is hard to judge if something is lopsided or overworked when it is lying flat on a bench.

WHAT YOU NEED
- ☐ **wreath frame (the one used here is 30cm in diameter and made of wisteria), from florist supply shops and craft shops**
- ☐ **green florist's wire (18 or 22 gauge), cut into short lengths**
- ☐ **secateurs**
- ☐ **ribbon for hanging or for decoration (optional)**
- ☐ **olive branches**
- ☐ **bay sprigs**
- ☐ **violets**

1 Lay the frame on a work surface. Using the wire, attach short lengths of olive branch to the whole circle, allowing them to overlap each other.

2 Add short lengths of bay sprigs, tying them on securely with the wire. Keep them small; the result should not be too bushy.

3 Add small bunches of violets or other flowers, such as lavender, roses (trimmed of thorns), clove pinks or jasmine. If your chosen flower has particularly attractive leaves that are worth featuring, include them, too. Here, the broad leaves of the violets contrast with the narrow olive and bay leaves.

Don't over-engineer your wreath by making it too neat and tidy. A relaxed, natural look is far more appealing.

Table centrepiece

An arrangement of fresh herbs will brighten any table. Balance the colours, shapes and textures of your chosen flowers and herbs to give your centrepiece a unique look.

Pieris, sweet peas, flat-leaf parsley, sea holly and hellebores.

Exploit the natural characteristics of each plant: floppier, softer plants look good gently overhanging the sides of a container, while stiffer, bolder ones act as focal points and accents as well as provide support for the softer plants. Also work out how the flowers are best viewed. For example, the hellebore flowers that we used do not look their best if seen from above; ensure that such flowers are cupped by other foliage so that their faces can be seen. Sweet peas, in contrast, have stiff stems and a ruffled profile, so feature them in the centre of the arrangement. Choose plants with a gentle perfume and make your centrepiece a reasonable height so that guests can easily see one another across the table.

Suggested plants

Pieris *Pieris japonica, P. formosa* and *P. floribunda* Pieris is also known as lily of the valley shrub, andromeda or pearl bush. The small bell-like flowers form elegant sprays, and range in colour from ivory white to a deep pinky red. The leathery, oval leaves grow in attractive spiral whorls. Young spring leaves are sometimes bright pink or red.

Sweet peas *Lathyrus odoratus* These old-fashioned, sweetly scented flowers come in many colours, from white to pink, mauve and red through to velvety purple-black. The seeds are poisonous (they contain a neurotoxin) and should not be eaten.

Flat-leaf parsley *Petroselinum crispum* The bright green, serrated leaves of this herb act as both a filler and a background for showier flowers. Parsley is the least hardy of all the plants used here, so replace it with fresh cuttings as needed during the life of the centrepiece, or experiment with other sturdier herbs, such as rosemary and lavender.

Sea holly *Eryngium planum, E. alpinum* and *E. maritimum* These plants bear thistle-like flowers in various shades of blue or green, and have a metallic sheen. They are surrounded by spiky white, silver, blue, green or violet bracts. The flowers dry well and are attractive in dried arrangements. In the 17th and 18th centuries, the candied roots were considered an aphrodisiac.

Hellebores *Helleborus niger, H. orientalis* If you pick these beautiful cup-shaped flowers when they're mature, they will last for weeks as they slowly fade and change colour. They are lovely in float bowls. All parts of the plant are toxic. Use gloves when using this plant, as bruised foliage can cause skin irritation.

To make your centrepiece

WHAT YOU NEED
- container (we used a low, rectangular metallic container)
- secateurs
- florist's foam (optional)
- large pebbles or glass marbles, to anchor the flowers
- flowers and herbs of your choice

1 Trim the flowers and herbs to an appropriate height and remove spent blooms or yellowing leaves.

2 Before you start making the centrepiece, soak the stems in water for at least an hour.

3 If you are using florist's foam, cut it to the shape of the container, making sure it sits about 2cm below the top, otherwise it will be visible once the arrangement is finished.

4 Soak the foam in a bucket of water, allowing it to sink naturally. The foam should be completely sodden before you use it. Place it in the container. If you are not

using foam, half-fill the container with pebbles or marbles, then add some water.

5 Starting from the outside in, poke the stems of the flowers or herbs into the foam, pebbles or marbles to hold them in place.

6 Turn the container around as you work, checking for visual balance and filling in any sparse patches. Where necessary, intertwine some pieces of foliage to provide more support. Finish with a light misting of water from a spray bottle to refresh the flowers and give them a dewy look.

Tussie-mussies

You really can say it with flowers – in a delighfully nostalgic way. These pretty little bouquets combine flowers and herbs with a personalised message.

Tussie-mussies are small posies of flowers and aromatic herbs. They were used in medieval and Elizabethan times to mask unpleasant odours and their scent was believed to protect the holder from diseases, such as the plague. This use led to their other name, 'nosegays'. They were also credited with refreshing the mind and sharpening the memory.

Tussie-mussies reached a peak of popularity with floriography, the art of sending messages by flowers, in the Victorian era. Various plants were believed to represent qualities or emotions. Some meanings were adapted from classical mythology, others from ancient lore and religious symbolism.

Young ladies and their suitors were well-versed in the meanings of various flowers and herbs. At the start of a courtship, a man might express his feelings with a 'word-posy'. There were risks attached to this method: a slight mistake in shade or pattern could alter the intended meaning. And some flowers have ambiguous or contradictory meanings: hydrangeas can signify both 'thank you for understanding' and 'heartlessness'.

Among the most common meanings were those relating to love and fidelity and they were often used for wedding bouquets. Suitable plants include bluebell (constancy), chervil (sincerity), forget-me-not (true love), holly (domestic happiness), honeysuckle or violet (fidelity), ivy or lime blossom (wedded love)

To make your tussie-mussie

WHAT YOU NEED
- ☐ **prominent flower(s) for the centre (traditional tussie-mussies had a single central flower, generally a rose, but ours uses several roses)**
- ☐ **1 or 2 types of smaller complementary flowers**
- ☐ **a variety of herbs and leaves**
- ☐ **wax florist's tape**
- ☐ **about five large, broad leaves to frame the bouquet (optional)**
- ☐ **ribbon or strips of leftover wedding-dress fabric**
- ☐ **pearl pins**
- ☐ **gift card**

1 Soak the stems in water for at least an hour, or overnight if possible.

2 Remove from the water and wipe the stems dry.

3 Cut the stems on the diagonal to about 12cm.

4 Strip any thorns and all the lower leaves from the stems.

5 If using one central flower, hold it in one hand and use the other to surround it with the first ring of smaller flowers and herbs. If replicating the pictured tussie-mussie, start with a small handful of greenery and build a circle of roses and filler flowers around this. Rotate the posy as you go to ensure a balanced shape. Tightly wrap the stems of each layer with florist's tape, pressing so the tape will adhere to itself (the ribbon will disguise any untidiness).

6 Continue adding concentric layers until all the flowers and herbs are used. Lastly, frame the bouquet with large leaves.

7 Wrap the stems tightly from top to bottom with florist's tape.

8 Wrap the stems with ribbon or fabric, securing it with pearl pins inserted into the stems (at the top) and up the stems (at the bottom).

9 Tie matching or contrasting ribbon near the top of the stems, leaving the ends to trail decoratively.

10 If your tussie-mussie is a gift, include a small card on which you have written the names of the plants and their meanings.

Use a thorn remover (from florist suppliers) to strip thorns from stems.

Tussie-mussies for other occasions

• The posy pictured uses white roses (innocence and purity), sweet peas (tender memory), lily of the valley (purity of heart, sweetness), rosemary (remembrance) and parsley (festivity).

• For a bouquet of condolence, you could choose from red poppies (consolation), rosemary (remembrance), wormwood (grief), weeping willow (sorrow), lemon balm (sympathy), fennel (strength) and borage (courage).

• To wish someone luck for an exam or job interview, consider basil (good wishes), four-leaf clover (happiness), juniper (protection), buttercup (promise of riches), hawthorn or snowdrop (hope), lavender (luck), sage (wisdom) or dandelion (wishes come true).

• It's not only traditional occasions that can be enhanced by a little floriography. For a racier message, try your luck with gardenia (ecstasy), tuberose (dangerous pleasure or voluptuousness), coriander (lust), forsythia (anticipation), chickweed (rendezvous) or red camellia (you're a flame in my heart)!

Herb pot trio

Customised pots are a pretty and practical way of displaying and labelling your herbs. Choose from blackboard paint, stencils and felt.

Stencilled herb pot

This simple and bold treatment uses a stencil of the herb's initial letter. It can be applied to a plain galvanised metal pot, or one that has been painted a contrast colour first. This style of pot is useful if you always have a crop of the same herb on the go.

We used a laser printer to create the stencil, but you can use hand lettering if you prefer. Whichever method you choose, pick a style of lettering that is not too complicated and that does not have very thin areas, as these will weaken the stencil and are less likely to transfer well. Plain, rather blocky lettering will give the most reliable results. Use spray paint in a well-ventilated area, preferably outdoors.

WHAT YOU NEED

- ☐ galvanised metal flower pot
- ☐ vinegar or methylated spirits (denatured alcohol)
- ☐ commercial stencil (optional)
- ☐ thin cardboard or stencil film (from craft stores)
- ☐ fine craft knife and cutting mat
- ☐ spray adhesive
- ☐ spray paint (or paint of your choice and a stencil brush)
- ☐ cotton buds
- ☐ white spirit
- ☐ newspaper or other waste paper

1 Wash the pot in warm soapy water, then rinse. Wipe over with vinegar or methylated spirits and allow to dry.

2 Trace your chosen letter onto thin cardboard or stencil film, and carefully cut out the stencil using a fine craft knife.

3 Lay down some newspaper to protect the work surface. Use spray adhesive to stick the stencil to the surface of your flower pot.

4 Spray the newspaper until the spray is fine and even, then spray lightly over the cut-out area of the stencil. To avoid seepage and drips, spray two or three thin coats rather than one thick one. Allow the paint to become touch-dry between coats, then peel off the stencil.

5 Remove any oversprays or seepages with a cotton bud dipped in white spirit.

6 Allow to dry completely, painted side up, to prevent the paint from running. Plant with herbs.

Pot with blackboard paint

If you change your herb plantings frequently, try this great option. When one herb is finished, you can wipe off its name with a damp cloth, wait for it to dry, then write the new name on with chalk.

WHAT YOU NEED

- ☐ terracotta pots
- ☐ small can of blackboard paint
- ☐ straight-edged paintbrush
- ☐ chalk

1 Clean the surface of the pot as directed on the paint can (the paint will not adhere properly to a greasy or dusty surface). Allow the pot to dry thoroughly.

2 Carefully paint the rim of the pot with the blackboard paint. Allow it to dry thoroughly then plant up with herbs.

3 Use chalk to write the name of the herb on the pot. For fun, use both the common and Latin or botanical names; if you bought the herbs at a nursery, both names should be given on the label.

Felt pot

This unusual pot stands about 13cm high. Fill it with herbs and either leave it above ground or plant it in the garden – the herbs' roots will eventually grow right through the fabric.

WHAT YOU NEED

- ☐ 30 x 40cm industrial felt, 3 to 4mm thick
- ☐ sewing thread and needle
- ☐ stranded embroidery cotton
- ☐ terracotta, galvanised iron or plastic flower pot to use as a template
- ☐ brown paper or newspaper
- ☐ 2 pins or toothpicks
- ☐ sticky tape
- ☐ pencil
- ☐ paper scissors

1 To make the template, tape a pin or toothpick to the top and bottom edges of the pot, aligning them, and letting them protrude a little beyond the edge; these will act as markers for the start and finish point of the template.

2 Lay the pot on the paper, pins down. Mark this point, which will be the left edge of the template. Starting at the pins, slowly roll the pot across the paper, tracing along both top and bottom edges as you go. Stop when you reach the pins again.

3 Remove the pot, then draw vertical lines at each end of the template to join the two curved lines. This forms the template for the body of the pot.

4 Draw around the base of the pot to make the base template.

5 Cut out the paper pieces along the marked lines. Note that you do not need a seam allowance. When you have finished, you should have one pot piece and one base piece.

6 Pin the paper pieces to the felt and cut carefully around them.

7 Butt the straight edges of the pot and oversew them together with a sewing thread in a matching colour. With stranded embroidery cotton, work a line of cross stitch along the seam, from side to side. This decorative stitch strengthens the join. Using sewing thread, oversew the circular base into the bottom of the pot.

Digital print transfers

The digital camera and print shop put a contemporary spin on craft, so being creative has never been easier. Use this method to beautify plain items around the home.

This is the simplest of projects, requiring no more than a photograph or other image, a handtowel or napkin to apply it to, and a trip to the nearest digital print shop. Many craft projects require weeks of work, but if patience isn't your strong point, this is the project for you. Whether you make it for your home, or as a gift for someone else, the results are impressive.

Choosing an image

You'll get the best results from an image that has a simple shape and not too many complicated areas, such as the lavender flowers used on the handtowel here (see opposite). Avoid using dark images, as they tend to become darker during the transfer process. Images with a good contrast between light and dark will work best.

If photographing your own image, place your chosen herb on a white background and shoot from straight overhead. If using a digital camera, set it to the highest resolution you can. This will ensure a crisp, clear image.

Remember that white does not print; the fabric will show through any parts of the design that are white, so you will not, for example, be able to print white flowers onto a coloured fabric. Images will show up best on white, cream or pastel fabrics; very dark colours and busy prints, on the other hand, are both unsuitable.

Because the image will be printed face down, it will be a mirror image of the original photo. This means that you may need to ask the print shop to flip the image if you want it to be facing a particular way.

Preparing the fabric

Choose the article you want the print to go onto. We used handtowels, but other options are T-shirts, teatowels, napkins or tablecloths. For the clearest print, choose a smooth, closely woven fabric in a natural fibre, such as cotton or linen. Fine-knit fabrics work well, too, but textured fabrics, such as towelling or waffle weave, will result in an unclear image, while synthetic fibres may melt under the high heat that is needed for the transfer process. If you are transferring the image to an item of clothing, put a piece of brown paper inside the garment so that the transfer does not go through to both the front and the back.

Next, wash the fabric to eliminate the possibility of shrinkage, which can cause the transferred image to crack, then iron the fabric smooth.

If you want the image centred but don't trust yourself to do this by eye, mark a crease by folding the fabric item in half in both directions. Using cotton thread and long stitches, baste along this crease. The point at which the stitches intersect is the centre. On the back of the transfer, draw horizontal and vertical lines through the centre of the design, then match these with the basting stitches. Once the image has been transferred and allowed to cool, remove the basting stitches.

Creating the transfer

Take the photograph or an image on disk to a digital print shop. If your image needs touching up or cropping, the print shop will be able to do this for you. They can also digitally manipulate your image and, if it is small enough, repeat it so that you get some spare images on the transfer sheet, thus saving money (transfer paper is expensive).

WHAT YOU NEED
- a good-quality image
- fabric item such as a handtowel to which to transfer the image
- small, sharp scissors
- masking tape

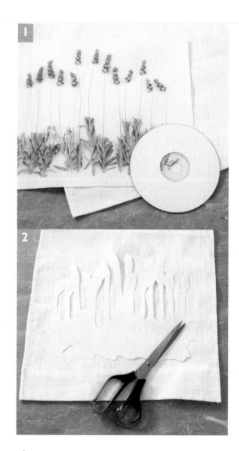

1 Ask for the image to be photocopied onto transfer paper at a size that fits your chosen item. Avoid handling the transfer paper while the ink is drying.

2 Carefully cut out the image around the outline (do this at home in an unhurried manner, then bring the project back to the print shop for the next step). Using masking tape, position the transfer print onto the fabric, face down, ensuring it is in exactly the position you want. Then get the print shop to transfer the image onto the fabric (they will use a high-pressure heat press). Allow the item to cool for a few minutes, then remove the backing from the transfer paper. You can further embellish the item with ribbon, beads or embroidery, if desired.

Laundering

Using mild detergent, wash and dry the finished item on a cool setting only. Do not use bleach.

Don't iron the image, as this can cause the transfer to move.

A note on copyright

If you take your own photograph, you own the copyright to it and can use it as you wish. However, if you use someone else's image, you may risk infringing their copyright; you cannot copy such an image for articles that you will sell.

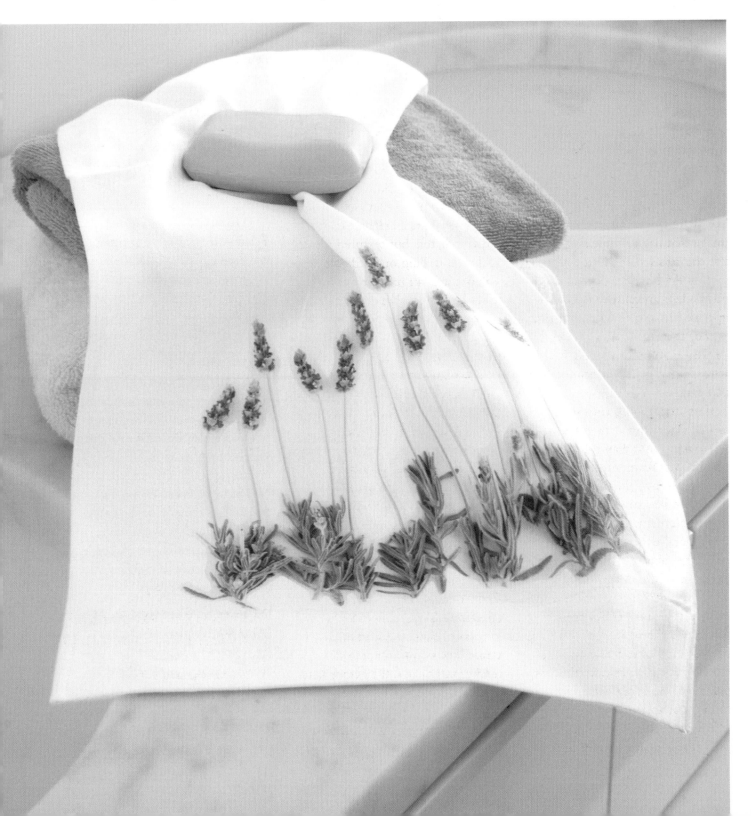

Kitchen print triptych

Take a series of your favourite herb photographs from camera to canvas and you can decorate your walls with beautiful images that bring the garden into the house.

Making your own masterpiece has never been easier. Many homeware stores, photographic shops and on-line digital photography companies now offer a service that enables you to transfer your photographs onto canvas, to a size and format that suits your setting.

To make your triptych

WHAT YOU NEED
- ☐ **3 good-quality images of herbs (we used flowering rosemary, heartsease and flowering sage)**
- ☐ **dimensions of finished print (ideally, discuss this first with your chosen supplier; see step 1)**

1 Check out suppliers of photographic prints on canvas, and find out what sizes are available and how best to supply your image.

2 Think about where you want to hang your prints. Bear in mind that prints are made with pigment ink, which is fade-resistant. But they should not be exposed to direct sunlight for long periods of time.

3 Consider whether to have your print laminated. Unlaminated prints can be cleaned by dusting them lightly with a soft cloth, while laminated prints can be wiped down very gently with a damp cloth. Remember, the image is water-resistant, not waterproof.

4 Take your photographs. Today, many of even the most basic digital cameras do much of the hard technical work for you. What you need to concentrate on is creating a good composition. To do this, think about your viewpoint and the angle at which you are photographing the plant, taking time to mentally arrange the shot before you take it.

5 Decide if you want to have the whole image in focus or whether you want to concentrate on just one particular area. Experiment with scale. A small flower such as heartsease looks dramatic if it occupies the entire frame. Placing the subject directly in the centre of the frame may works, but zooming in or shifting the angle can turn an ordinary image into something dynamic.

Digital photography gives you immediate control over what you are doing in a way that conventional photography does not. If you don't like the preview image, delete it and shoot another. Experiment until you get the picture you want to live with.

Herb candle holders

Candlelight generates a special aura that's both romantic and flattering. This project adds a natural touch to simple high-ball glasses to create glamorous candle holders.

Creating a relaxed atmosphere is easy with candles, particularly if they are scented with herbs, such as roses, lemon verbena or lavender. With a few herbs, some vellum paper and a photocopier, you can customise your candles to suit your décor, setting and the fragrance of your candles. Vellum paper (from the French vélin for calfskin) was originally used for scrolls and handwritten manuscripts bound into books. Today's vellum is made from cotton, comes in a wide range of colours and is suitable for many papercrafts. It is available from specialist stationery suppliers.

To make your candle holder

WHAT YOU NEED
These can be made to fit a glass of any size.
- [ ] **fresh herb leaves or sprigs, such as bay, fennel or rosemary**
- [ ] **colour photocopier**
- [ ] **pale green translucent vellum paper**
- [ ] **straight-sided high-ball glass**
- [ ] **double-sided tape**
- [ ] **tea light or small herb-scented candle**

1 Work out the size of vellum you will need to wrap around your glass, remembering to add a small overlap. Cut out as many pieces as you need.

2 Lay a few appropriately sized herb sprigs or leaves on the paper to get an idea of the arrangement you like best. Try spiky leaves (rosemary); simple, bold leaves (bay); or feathery foliage (fennel).

Arrange the herbs on the copy plate of a photocopier and print an image onto ordinary paper until you are happy with the arrangement. Then insert the vellum into the paper tray and print your design onto it.

3 Wrap the printed vellum around the outside of the glass, then fix the edges together with double-sided tape. Place a candle in each glass.

Experiment with sprigs and leaves to get the effect you want.

Orange blossom wedding card,
Scented Valentine card in front
(instructions overleaf), Lavender card
and Pressed flower wreath card.

Herb cards and tags

A personalised handmade card gives its recipient something unique to treasure, and pressed and dried flowers and herbs are a perfect natural way to decorate them.

If you want the cards to last a long time, use acid-free paper, and card. A vast range of papers and cardstocks available, many of them handmade. Handmade unryushi paper is semi-transparent with short and long fibres. Mulberry paper comes in a range of textures and thicknesses. It is torn, not cut, producing a pretty frayed edge. We have given finished measurements but you can adapt them to any size.

Lavender card

WHAT YOU NEED
This card measures 15 x 11cm.
- ☐ **22 x 15cm purple cardstock**
- ☐ **9.5 x 13.5cm purple spot scrapbook paper**
- ☐ **8 x 12cm textured mauve decorative paper**
- ☐ **purple sewing thread**
- ☐ **sewing machine**
- ☐ **dried lavender sprigs and leaves**
- ☐ **tacky craft glue**

1 Score the purple cardstock in half crosswise, then fold it in half to forma single-fold card.

2 Secure the mauve decorative paper to the centre of the scrapbook paper using just a tiny dab of glue.

3 Using purple machine thread, work a line of zigzag stiches around the edges of the decorative paper to hold it in place. (It's always a good idea to test your stitch width and tension on scraps of paper before you start.)

4 Glue the stitched unit to the centre of the cardstock card.

5 Carefully glue lavender sprigs and leaves in place on the front.

Pressed flower wreath card

WHAT YOU NEED
This card measures 12cm square.
- ☐ **12 x 24cm pale green cardstock**
- ☐ **12cm square pale green unryushi or mulberry paper**
- ☐ **spray adhesive**
- ☐ **pinking shears**
- ☐ **dried herbs and flowers (we used chervil, heartsease and chamomile)**
- ☐ **PVA glue**

1 Score the pale green cardstock in half crosswise and fold it in half to make a single-fold card.

2 Using pinking shears, trim the square of unryushi paper to 11cm.

3 Use spray adhesive to glue the unryushi square to the centre of the card.

4 Arrange dried herbs and flowers into a wreath shape and carefully glue each piece in place.

Microwave it!

The traditional method of pressing flowers is to place them between layers of absorbent materials in a book or flower press. While this is an enjoyable way to go about things, it is quite time-consuming. You can now buy flower presses that enable you to press and dry flowers in the microwave in a process that takes only a few minutes or less. Presses are available from craft shops and via the internet.

For best results, pick flowers and leaves in the morning when they are fresh but free of moisture. Give thought to how they'll look once flattened: heartsease will flatten much better than a rose, for instance.

Scented Valentine card

WHAT YOU NEED
This card measures 10.5 x 14cm.
- ☐ purchased tri-fold card with heart cut-out (or make your own)
- ☐ gingham-patterned scrapbook paper
- ☐ fine craft knife and cutting mat
- ☐ spray adhesive
- ☐ small amount organza or other sheer fabric
- ☐ tacky craft glue
- ☐ dried rose petals and lavender

1 Cut a rectangle of scrapbook paper 5mm smaller all round than the size of the card front.

2 Using the card as a template, trace the heart outline onto the wrong side of the paper rectangle. Now add 3 to 5mm all round the traced outline and cut out carefully with a craft knife.

3 Using spray adhesive, glue the paper rectangle to the front of the card, taking care to position it accurately.

4 Glue a small piece of organza behind the heart-shaped opening by running a thin line of glue around the edge of the heart. Don't stretch the fabric too tightly across the opening – it needs some give to contain the herbs.

5 Place a small amount of dried lavender and rose petals on the organza, and use tacky craft glue to secure the card flap, enclosing the herbs.

Orange blossom wedding card

WHAT YOU NEED
This card measures 13.5cm square.
- ☐ 13.5 x 27cm cream cardstock
- ☐ 9cm square firm cardboard
- ☐ 11cm square pale green silk dupion
- ☐ spray adhesive
- ☐ tacky craft glue
- ☐ 10cm square olive green cardstock
- ☐ small amount white cardstock
- ☐ daisy punch (from craft and scrapbooking stores)
- ☐ yellow stranded embroidery cotton
- ☐ large embroidery needle
- ☐ small pressed leaf sprays
- ☐ craft glue
- ☐ orange essential oil (optional)
- ☐ cotton bud (optional)

1 Score the cream cardstock in half crosswise and fold in half to make a single-fold card.

2 Lightly spray the front of the 9cm cardboard square with spray adhesive and place it face down in the centre of the wrong side of the silk dupion square. Fold the edges of the silk to the back, folding the corners neatly, and secure in place with tacky craft glue.

3 Glue the silk-covered square to the centre of the olive green cardstock square. Glue this unit to the front of the cream card.

4 To make the orange blossoms, punch as many as you desire from the white cardstock with a small daisy punch. Lightly score each petal from the edge of the centre to the tip. (This technique will make the petals curve slightly, giving them a more realistic three-dimensional appearance.)

5 Using all six strands of yellow embroidery thread in a large needle, push the needle through the centre of a daisy from the front. Bring the needle back to the front, close to the original entry point (as though you were sewing on a button), leaving a tail of thread on the front (above). Insert it again into the first hole, then back to the front again. Unthread the needle and trim the loops and ends of thread to about 1cm long, creating a set of stamens. (They will be held in place when you glue the blossom to the background.)

6 Fold up the edges of the petals around the centre and along the score lines.

7 Arrange and glue the dried leaf sprays on the silk background in the desired pattern. (This can be quite fiddly – you might find it easier to use spray adhesive.) Add the orange blossoms and glue in place with craft glue to hold them securely.

8 If you wish to add fragrance, dab the centre and stamens of each blossom with a cotton bud dipped in orange essential oil or one of your choice.

Herb tags

WHAT YOU NEED
This card measures 9cm square.
- ☐ **5.5 x 7cm fine corrugated board**
- ☐ **9cm square cardstock**
- ☐ **6 x 7cm plain calico**
- ☐ **tacky craft glue**
- ☐ **herb sprigs (we used chervil, rosemary, parsley and sage)**
- ☐ **hole punch**
- ☐ **natural string**

Bay in myth

In Greek mythology, the bay tree was considered sacred to Apollo, the sun god, and later to his son Aesculapius, the god of medicine. Apollo became infatuated with a lovely nymph called Daphne. She spurned him and begged the gods to rescue her. Their solution was to turn her into a bay tree.

While victors at the first Olympic games were crowned with olive leaves, later they were replaced with bay and dedicated to Apollo. The tradition is still retained in terms such as 'poet laureate' and the important French secondary school examination, the 'baccalaureate'.

1 Glue the corrugated board to the cardboard square on an angle.

2 Fray the edges of the calico; glue to the centre of the board, off-setting it again.

3 Glue a sprig of dried herb to the calico background.

4 Punch a hole in one corner and add a string tie.

329

Herb pot window box

Create a garden on your windowsill, outdoors or in, and enjoy the fragrance, taste and colour of herbs through the seasons. Only basic carpentry skills are required.

A window box is a miniature portable garden. Whether you sit it on a windowsill or attach it to brackets to cheer up an outside wall, this simple container is both decorative and practical. The design neatly accommodates three pots of herbs. Trailing herbs, such as evening primrose or nasturtiums look good when contrasted with upright ones, such as chives or dill. Try grouping herbs with different textures – for example, position velvety, furry sage alongside smooth-leaved basil and tightly curled parsley. Customise your window box to suit your culinary requirements, teaming the freshness of mint with citrus-flavoured lemon balm and pungent, peppery thyme. Colour can play a part, too. Purplish-red perilla, cream-and-green variegated apple mint and bright red chillies all make a visually striking splash.

If you position your window box outdoors, it will be constantly exposed to the vagaries of the weather, so make sure you choose quality materials. If you decide to hang it on brackets, check that they are strong enough to support the weight of the pots and that

the surface on which you place them and the box is not cracked or crumbling.

As for your chosen herbs, keep an eye on the moisture content of the soil in the pots. Wind and sun can quickly dry it out.

To make your window box

WHAT YOU NEED
Finished box is 488 x 228 x 170mm.
☐ **40 x 2.65mm galvanised nails**
☐ **drill and 2mm bit**
☐ **900 x 190 x 19mm pine**
☐ **2100 x 42 x 19mm pine**
☐ **external undercoat paint**
☐ **external gloss acrylic paint for top coat**
☐ **sandpaper, handsaw**
☐ **pencil, tape/square measure**
☐ **small paintbrush**
☐ **hammer, putty**

1 Cut a piece of 190 x 19mm pine into a 1 x 450mm length for the base and 2 x 170mm lengths for the ends. Cut the 42 x 19mm pine into 4 x 488mm lengths. Sand all edges and corners.

2 Drill 3 holes in each of the end pieces 30mm up from the bottom: two holes 10mm in from each side and one in the centre. Nail the ends to the base, one end at a time.

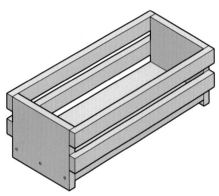

3 Position a 488mm length on each side of the box, level with the tops of the ends. Drill 2 holes at each end of these lengths. Hammer in nails. Repeat on the other side. Position remaining 2 x 488mm lengths 30mm below the top rung and repeat drilling and hammering.

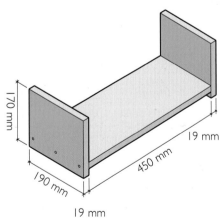

4 Sand timber all over. Punch nail heads and putty over them. Seal with one coat of undercoat. Sand again. Apply two top coats of your chosen colour. Allow each coat to dry before sanding. Sanding the final coat will give the box a rustic, distressed look.

Other ideas

• Try colour theming your window box with flowering herbs. A mauve and purple theme could include herbs that enjoy a sunny position, such as sage, hyssop and lavender.
• Or plant a variety of the same herb. Try common mint, peppermint and spearmint, or different kinds of basil such as sweet basil and Thai basil.
• Choose a colour theme that will complement your house's exterior paint scheme. For example, white-flowering herbs such as valerian and Roman chamomile look fresh with a blue colour scheme.

To create an interesting paint finish, use a sponge to stipple on a contrasting colour of gloss acrylic.

Cooking

Cuisines around the world derive much of their distinctive character from the addition of herbs and spices. Go globetrotting with this collection of recipes, from pasta and pickles to meat and fish, from oils and breads to cakes and drinks.

A world of herbs and spices

An extraordinary range of herbs and spices is available to us today, and it is expanding all the time, with frequent introductions of new varieties and forms of preserving.

Bouquet garni is a mix of herbs used in classic French cuisine. Held in a muslin bag it includes parsley, bay and thyme.

A multitude of flavours

Can you imagine pasta sauces with no basil, Japanese food without wasabi, Indian food without cumin and coriander or Mexican food minus the chillies? Creating authentic dishes from around the world has never been easier.

Herbs used in Indian and southeast Asian cooking have enjoyed a huge surge in popularity in recent years, and Thai basil, coriander, perilla, kaffir lime leaves, lemon grass and turmeric are becoming easier to source – many are now freely available in a number of supermarkets as well as specialist markets and food shops. In addition, the seasonings used in Africa, the Middle East, the Caribbean and Latin America are more readily available as well.

And it's not just the leaves that are used in recipes: flowers, seeds, stems and roots are also often included as well as powdered forms of the herb.

Balancing act

The recipes in this book give measures for the amount of herbs and spices to use, but you can vary them to suit your taste. One of the great bonuses of using herbs is that you'll find you can cut back on the amount of salt you add to your food. The herbs will be flavour enough!

One golden rule is to avoid allowing one flavour to dominate the others. Herb and spice mixes such as garam masala and ras el hanout are a delicate exercise in balancing a wide range of flavours. Even if you like a bit of heat, too much fresh chilli can overwhelm the more subtle herbs and spices accompanying it. Similarly, very pungent herbs, such as fresh coriander, are not to everyone's taste, so a light hand is recommended.

You can always add more fresh herbs at the table. In Iranian and Vietnamese cooking, a bowl of fresh herbs is a standard appetiser or accompaniment. Similarly, the Lebanese offer a platter of fresh herbs and vegetables as part of a mezze table.

As a general rule, when cooking with herbs, the soft-leafed ones, such as coriander, are best added late in the cooking process to preserve their flavour. The coarser ones, such as rosemary, are ideal for dishes that require long, slow cooking. Dried herbs are usually more concentrated in flavour than fresh ones, so you will need less of them.

Fresh herbs

• Select vibrant, aromatic leaves with no signs of wilting or yellowing.

• Buy fresh herbs as and when you need them. However well you store them, they quickly deteriorate in flavour and appearance, particularly the soft-leafed varieties such as flat-leaf parsley, lovage and coriander. The coarser herbs, such as thyme and rosemary, are a little hardier.

• Store fresh herbs for no more than 3 or 4 days. Loosely wrap unwashed bunches in damp paper towels and store in an airtight container or sealed plastic bag in a cool place.

• Alternatively, stand the stems in a jug with a little water and loosely cover the leaves with a plastic bag. Store in the refrigerator, changing the water daily.

• Or store herbs in plastic bags and place them in the crisper in your fridge.

Get chopping!

Chop herbs with a mezzaluna (half-moon-shaped blade), a sharp knife or scissors. You can use a food processor for large bunches, but don't over-process them. Fine-leafed herbs can also be shredded by hand, but coarse herbs, such as rosemary, need fine chopping unless whole sprigs are appropriate for the recipe. Herbs such as basil, coriander and sage discolour if they are chopped too early before use.

• Buy herbs sold in plastic boxes or cellophane bags – they keep well if stored in the refrigerator.

• Preserve chopped fresh herbs by freezing them in a little water in ice-cube trays.

• For more detailed information, see *Harvesting, preserving and storing*, pages 178–81. Delicate herbs such as basil do not dry well, but more robust herbs such as thyme and rosemary retain their flavour well and are a convenient alternative to fresh.

• When you are ready to use them, wash herbs in a bowl of cold water rather than running water, which can bruise them. Pat them dry with paper towels.

The must-haves

This selection of herbs and spices that you can grow yourself or buy is a useful culinary starting point. (If you enjoy making herbal teas, add chamomile, dandelion and lemon verbena.)

Basil, bay, chillies, chives, coriander, dill, garlic, ginger, lemon grass, lemon tree (it's a herb, too), lovage, marjoram or oregano, mint, parsley, rosemary, sage, tarragon, thyme and mint are all superb culinary herbs.

Dried herbs and spices

While you may prefer the taste of herbs picked fresh from the garden, there is always a place for dried or frozen ones as well as for dried spices. In Greek cooking, for example, dried oregano (rigani) is used extensively in preference to fresh, while paprika, rather than fresh chillies, is an important ingredient in Hungarian food.

• Buy dried herbs and spices in small quantities to avoid waste, and store in airtight containers in a cool, dark place.

• Ignore the use-by date on commercial products, as the dried herb or spice may deteriorate long before the given date. The best way to check for freshness is by smell, taste and appearance – for example, colour fading is a good indicator of flavour loss.

• Whole spices, such as coriander and cumin seeds, retain their flavour and aroma longer than ground. Grind them in a spice grinder, or in a coffee-grinder kept specifically for the purpose, or use a mortar and pestle.

• Spices add colour as well as flavour. Paprika adds a glorious red colour, while saffron and turmeric transform a dish into a golden yellow.

'Garlic is as good as 10 mothers.'

Traditional proverb

Herb oils

Quality ingredients make great-tasting oils that enhance dips, marinades, sauces and dressings and you can change herbs with the season. Below are three oils made with classic culinary herbs that can be used with a wide variety of vegetables, fish and meats.

Basil oil

3 tablespoons fresh basil leaves
250ml boiling water
500ml olive oil

MAKES 500ML
Preparation 15 minutes plus
2 to 3 days for infusing

1 Place basil leaves in medium bowl and cover with boiling water. Stand 2 minutes. Drain; pat leaves dry. Process basil and oil in food processor until combined. Alternatively, finely chop basil leaves, add 2 tablespoons oil and mash basil into oil with a fork. Add remaining oil.

2 Leave 2 to 3 days to allow flavours to develop. Strain oil through muslin; pour into clean 500ml bottle. Store in a cool, dark place. Use with tomatoes and salad greens.

Rosemary oil

2 or 3 large sprigs fresh rosemary
3 cloves garlic
3 fresh bay leaves
500ml olive oil

MAKES 500ML
Preparation 15 minutes plus
2 to 3 days for infusing

1 Lightly bruise rosemary, garlic and bay leaves by hitting them with the flat of a knife. Place herbs in clean 500ml bottle; pour in olive oil.

2 Leave for 2 to 3 days to allow flavours to develop. Store in a cool, dark place. Use with pork and lamb.

Lemon grass oil

2 to 3 fresh lime leaves
1 stalk fresh lemon grass
2 cloves garlic
3 x 5mm slices fresh ginger
500ml peanut oil

MAKES 500ML
Preparation 10 minutes plus
3 to 4 days for infusing

1 Lightly bruise lime leaves, lemon grass, garlic and ginger by hitting them with the flat of a knife. Place herbs in clean 500ml bottle; pour in peanut oil.

2 Leave 3 to 4 days to allow flavours to develop. Store in a cool, dark place. Use with fish and seafood.

Herb guide

The more robust the herb, the better the finished oil. Experiment with marjoram or oregano, chillies, garlic, chervil, coriander, chives or mint. Clean the leaves very carefully to remove all traces of dirt or pesticides.

Tools of the trade

Muslin is a type of very finely woven cotton fabric. It is used in the same way as a sieve, allowing liquid to pass through while retaining any unwanted sediment. Look for it in kitchen supply or fabric shops.

Cook's tip

To sterilise jars, wash jars and lids thoroughly in warm, soapy water, using a bottle brush. Rinse well in cold water to remove all traces of soap. Stand jars on baking tray and place in oven. Heat oven to 100°C. Leave oven on for 45 minutes; turn off. Remove jars when cool enough to handle. Or, wash jars and lids in dishwasher on the hottest cycle. Cool before handling.

Rosemary oil,
Lemon grass oil and Basil oil

Herb vinegars

As with oils, wine vinegars vary greatly in price and quality, so buy the best you can afford. Wine vinegars have been used as the base here but experiment with different types of vinegar and herbs to see which flavour combinations you prefer.

Tarragon and red wine vinegar

15 fresh tarragon leaves
10 juniper berries
500ml red wine vinegar

MAKES 500ML
Preparation 10 minutes plus
3 to 4 days for infusing

1 Lightly bruise leaves and berries by hitting them with the flat of a knife. Place bruised leaves and berries in clean 500ml bottle; pour in vinegar.

2 Leave 3 to 4 days to allow flavours to develop.

Rice vinegar with coriander

3 fresh lime leaves
4 x 5mm slices galangal
2 cloves garlic
15 to 20 fresh coriander leaves
250ml rice wine vinegar

MAKES 250ML
Preparation 10 minutes plus
3 to 4 days for infusing 250ml
Preparation 10 minutes plus
3 to 4 days for infusing

1 Lightly bruise lime leaves, galangal and garlic by hitting them with the flat of a knife. Place herbs, including coriander leaves, in clean 250ml bottle; pour in vinegar.

2 Leave 3 to 4 days to allow flavours to develop.

Fennel and saffron vinegar

4 sprigs fresh fennel leaves
2 to 3 whole dried chillies
2 cloves garlic
¼ teaspoon fennel seeds
pinch of saffron
500ml white wine vinegar

MAKES 500ML
Preparation 10 minutes plus
3 to 4 days for infusing

1 Place fennel leaves, chillies, garlic, fennel seeds and saffron in a clean 500ml bottle; pour in the vinegar.

2 Leave 3 to 4 days to allow flavours to develop.

Try these, too...

RED CHILLI VINEGAR
Cut 1 long red chilli in half lengthwise and place in clean 750ml bottle with 2 whole long red chillies. Pour in 750ml white wine vinegar. Seal and store.

BERRY VINEGAR
Combine 500g berries (such as a mixture of raspberries, strawberries and blueberries) and 750ml white wine vinegar in a large ceramic or glass bowl and stir well to lightly bruise fruit. Cover mixture and leave in a cool place for a few days to infuse. Pour mixture into saucepan, bring to the boil and remove from heat. Allow to cool. Strain mixture through a double layer of muslin into clean jars. Seal and store. Makes 750ml.

Cook's tip

The seeds of herbs, such as dill, fennel, celery and coriander, can be used to make seed vinegars. Prepare in the same way as herb vinegars. To retain their flavour, store herb vinegars and oils in a cool, dark place.

Rice vinegar with coriander,
Tarragon and red wine vinegar,
and Fennel and saffron vinegar

Herb and spice pickles

Many pickles rely on spices for their assertive – and distinctive flavours. When using in pickling, you'll find that the fresher the spice, the better the result you get, so it's a good idea to buy them frequently and in small quantities so that they don't get stale.

Chilli jam

250g char-grilled peppers, seeded
  and skin removed
2 long red chillies, roughly chopped
1 small red chilli, roughly chopped
60ml olive oil
1 small brown onion, finely chopped
2 cloves garlic, finely chopped
1 tablespoon palm sugar
1 tablespoon fish sauce
2 teaspoons tamarind paste
1 tablespoon finely chopped fresh
  coriander leaves
1 tablespoon finely chopped fresh
  mint leaves

MAKES approx. 250ML
Preparation 5 minutes
Cooking 15 minutes

1 Process peppers and chillies in food processor until smooth.

2 Heat oil in small saucepan over medium heat. Cook onion 1 to 2 minutes, until softened. Add garlic; cook 30 seconds.

3 Add pepper mixture, sugar, fish sauce and tamarind; cook 10 minutes on low heat, stirring occasionally. Stir through herbs; bottle until needed. Serve with barbecued food.

Spicy aubergine relish

2 tablespoons vegetable oil
1 large red chilli, finely chopped
1 clove garlic, finely chopped
1 tablespoon finely grated
  fresh ginger
1 teaspoon turmeric powder
1 teaspoon mustard seeds
1 medium aubergine, cut into
  1cm cubes
1 teaspoon salt
60ml white wine vinegar
1 tablespoon sugar
125ml water
3 tablespoons roughly chopped
  fresh coriander leaves

MAKES approx. 500ML
Preparation 5 minutes
Cooking 12 minutes

1 Heat oil in medium saucepan over medium heat. Add chilli, garlic, ginger, turmeric and mustard seeds; cook, stirring, 1 minute.

2 Add aubergine, salt, vinegar, sugar and water. Cook 10 to 12 minutes over low heat, adding extra tablespoons of water if mixture gets dry.

3 Remove from heat, stir through coriander. Refrigerate until required. Serve with eggs, chicken or fish.

Date, lime and mint chutney

1 tablespoon vegetable oil
2 teaspoons finely grated
  fresh ginger
¼ teaspoon ground cloves
½ teaspoon ground cinnamon
½ teaspoon ground cumin
½ teaspoon chilli flakes
350g roughly chopped stoned dates
125g raisins
1 tablespoon sugar
60ml white wine vinegar
125ml fresh lime juice
zest of 1 lime
250ml water
2 tablespoons finely chopped
  fresh mint leaves

MAKES approx. 500ML
Preparation 5 minutes
Cooking 12 minutes

1 Heat oil in small saucepan over medium heat. Add ginger, cloves, cinnamon, cumin and chilli flakes; cook, stirring, 1 minute.

2 Add dates, raisins, sugar, vinegar, lime juice, zest and water; cook over low heat, stirring regularly, until fruit is soft.

3 Remove from heat, stir through mint. Refrigerate until required. Serve with meat or cheese.

Date, lime and mint chutney,
Chilli jam and Spicy aubergine relish

Herb butters

We're all familiar with the garlic butter used on bread to accompany pizza – but you can use all kinds of other herbs to make wonderful flavour-packed butters. Spread them on crusty bread, or use them to dress up cooked vegetables and barbecued meat.

Sage butter

250g butter, softened
I tablespoon finely chopped fresh
   sage leaves
3 tablespoons finely chopped fresh
   flat-leaf parsley leaves
10 pitted medium green olives
30g, roughly chopped
2 anchovy fillets, finely chopped

MAKES 250G
Preparation 10 minutes

1 Place softened butter in medium bowl. Add remaining ingredients; mix until well combined.

2 Place butter mixture on a piece of cling film about 20cm long. Roll mixture into a log about 5cm in diameter; wrap tightly. Chill until required.

Coriander and chilli butter

40g macadamia nuts, roughly
   chopped
250g butter, softened
3 tablespoons roughly chopped fresh
   coriander leaves
2 fresh lime leaves, finely chopped
I large red chilli, finely diced
I tablespoon lime juice

MAKES 250G
Preparation 10 minutes
Cooking 2 minutes

1 Toast chopped macadamia nuts in dry frying pan on medium heat, tossing until smallest pieces are just golden. Transfer to small bowl; cool before use.

2 Place softened butter in medium bowl. Add toasted nuts and remaining ingredients; mix until well combined.

3 Place mixture on a piece of cling film about 20cm long. Roll mixture into a log about 5cm in diameter; wrap tightly. Chill until required.

Try these, too...

PARSLEY AND LEMON BUTTER
Combine 250g softened butter, 3 tablespoons finely chopped fresh parsley, 2 teaspoons grated lemon zest, 3 teaspoons lemon juice, and salt and freshly ground black pepper.

BLUE CHEESE AND HERB BUTTER
Combine 250g softened butter and 125g blue vein cheese, chopped. Add I tablespoon each chopped fresh chives, mint and dill. Add I tablespoon white wine.

HORSERADISH AND MUSTARD BUTTER
Combine 250g softened butter, 2 tablespoons horseradish cream, I tablespoon Dijon mustard and 2 tablespoons finely chopped fresh parsley.

GINGER AND SPICE BUTTER
Combine 25g softened butter, 2 teaspoons finely grated fresh ginger, I teaspoon mild chilli powder and I tablespoon Worcestershire sauce.

Cook's tip

All herb butters are prepared in the same way and are very versatile. Fresh or dried herbs, ground spices, sun-dried tomatoes, chopped nuts, mustards, wine, lemon or lime juice and many other ingredients can be incorporated. Formed into a log and wrapped in cling film, butters will keep for up to I month in the freezer and up to 5 days in the refrigerator. Allow to soften slightly at room temperature before slicing into rounds. You can halve the quantities given here, if preferred.

Coriander and chilli butter
and Sage butter

Herb and spice sauces

Featured in many cuisines, these delicious sauces can be used as dips, served on the side or incorporated into a wide variety of cooked dishes including stews and curries. The ones below are inspired by the cooking of France, Germany, North Africa and Vietnam.

Harissa

8 dried chillies
2 cloves garlic, peeled
½ teaspoon salt
2 tablespoons olive oil
1 teaspoon ground caraway seeds
1 teaspoon ground coriander
½ teaspoon ground cumin

1 Soak dried chillies in very hot water 30 minutes. Drain. Remove stems and seeds. Place chillies, garlic, salt and olive oil in a food processor; blend to a paste.

2 Add the remaining spices and blend. Pack into an airtight container and top with a thin layer of olive oil. Keeps for a month in the refrigerator. Thin with a little oil and lemon juice or hot stock before use. Use as a condiment with eggs and couscous-based dishes.

This fiercely fiery, chilli-based sauce is a feature of North African cooking. If using fresh chillies, omit the soaking step.

Sorrel sauce

200g sorrel leaves, chopped
310ml fish or chicken stock
20g unsalted butter
1 tablespoon plain flour
4 tablespoons cream
salt and freshly ground black pepper

1 Simmer leaves in stock 5 minutes. Allow to cool slightly. Purée in blender or food processor.

2 Melt butter in saucepan, add flour and stir over gentle heat until blended. Add purée to the pan; simmer about 4 minutes, stirring.

3 Add cream and season to taste. Serve with poached white fish or salmon. It also goes well with pasta.

A classic in French cuisine, fresh sorrel gives this sauce a sharp, lemony taste. When preparing sorrel, cut out the central stalk, which can be rather tough.

Frankfurt green sauce

15g each fresh borage, salad burnet, parsley and sorrel
20g each fresh chives and cress or watercress
10g each fresh tarragon and chervil
125g mayonnaise
1 teaspoon German mustard
2 hard-boiled eggs, chopped
1 small pickled gherkin, with dill, chopped
1 small onion or shallot, chopped
1 clove garlic, chopped
salt and pepper
grated rind and juice of 1 lemon
2 tablespoons sour cream or yoghurt (optional)
1 egg yolk

1 Chop all the herbs finely.

2 Add ingredients in given order, seasoning to taste and beating in egg yolk last of all. Serves 4.

You can vary the herbs used in this German sauce, but be sure to always use 7 or 8 different ones. Serve with fried or poached fish or cold fish with hard-boiled eggs, with cold meat, or use as a sandwich filler.

Nuoc cham

2 (or more, to taste) small red chillies, seeds removed
2 cloves garlic
1 teaspoon sugar
2 limes, peeled and chopped
1 tablespoon hot water
1 tablespoon vinegar
5 tablespoons fish sauce

1 Pound chillies and garlic to a fine paste. Add sugar and limes; pound to a pulp.

2 Add water, vinegar and fish sauce.

An indispensable seasoning in Vietnamese cooking, this spicy mixture can be served with mixed salad greens and herbs or used as a dipping sauce or marinade.

Béarnaise sauce

60ml white wine vinegar
6 black peppercorns
I fresh bay leaf
I spring onion, roughly chopped
I tablespoon each finely chopped
    fresh tarragon and chervil leaves
2 egg yolks
pinch each salt and white pepper
I10g unsalted butter, softened
I teaspoon each finely chopped
    fresh tarragon and chervil
    leaves, extra

1 Combine vinegar, peppercorns,
bay leaf, spring onion, tarragon and
chervil in small saucepan.

2 Bring to the boil, then leave to
boil, uncovered, until liquid is
reduced to about 1 tablespoon.
Remove from heat; set aside.

3 Place egg yolks in medium
heatproof bowl; add salt, pepper
and 20g softened butter. Strain
reduced vinegar mixture into
same bowl.

4 Place bowl over saucepan of
simmering water, ensuring water
doesn't touch bowl. Keep stirring
until the butter has melted.

5 Repeat with remaining butter,
adding small amounts at a time; stir
after each addition until melted.

6 Remove sauce from heat, stir
through extra herbs and serve.

Tarragon is synonymous with this
French classic, a relation of
hollandaise sauce, which uses a
reduction of lemon juice. One of
the most versatile of sauces, it goes
well with meat, chicken or fish.

Herb and yoghurt sauce

4 tablespoons fresh chopped mixed
    herbs such as chives, coriander, dill,
    lemon balm or parsley
I clove garlic, crushed
2 tablespoons lemon juice
250g yoghurt
salt and freshly ground black pepper
pinch of paprika

1 Combine herbs, garlic, lemon
juice and yoghurt.

2 Season to taste with salt, pepper
and paprika.

A light alternative to egg-based or
creamy sauces, this recipe can be
varied according to what herbs you
have to hand, but use at least three
types. Serve with salads, curries or
as a dip.

Herb and yoghurt sauce, lemon, dill,
chives, garlic, pepper and paprika.

Pesto bread

The utterly distinctive taste of pesto is a showcase for fresh basil. Pistou, the French variation of this Italian sauce, is made without pine nuts. In this sumptuous bread, pesto is cooked in with the dough, then more is added as a topping when the bread is served.

310g plain flour
3 teaspoons baking powder
1 large egg
375ml buttermilk
5 tablespoons basil pesto
4 tablespoons sun-dried tomato pesto
40g chopped sun-dried tomatoes packed in oil
30g freshly grated parmesan
extra basil pesto, to serve

MAKES 1 LOAF
Preparation 15 minutes
Cooking 45 minutes

1 Preheat oven to 200°C. Sift flour and baking powder into a large bowl.

2 Add egg, buttermilk and basil pesto; mix until well combined.

3 Line a 10.5cm x 21cm loaf tin with baking paper. Spoon loaf mixture into tin. Swirl tomato pesto through top of loaf; sprinkle with sun-dried tomatoes and parmesan.

4 Bake 40 to 45 minutes, or until cooked. Turn out onto a rack to cool. Serve warm, spread with extra basil pesto.

> *Try this, too...*
> Sweet basil has a spicy aroma with a mild aniseed flavour. Basil is synonymous with pesto, but other soft-leaf herbs such as fresh coriander or rocket can also be used. For another variation, try a mixture of equal quantities of a strong-tasting herb such as purple (opal) basil or lemon basil and a milder one, such as flat-leaf parsley or mint.

Making pesto

1 Use 2 fat cloves garlic, peeled, 30g pine nuts, 30g freshly grated parmesan or pecorino cheese, 4 heaped tablespoons fresh basil leaves (tough stalks removed) and 3 tablespoons good-quality olive oil.

2 Process dry ingredients roughly. Add oil in a steady stream; mixture should be slightly grainy. Add more oil, if needed. Pack in a jar; top with a film of olive oil. Seal; refrigerate. Use within 2 weeks.

Rosemary focaccia

The dough for this Italian flatbread is enriched with olive oil. Brush the top with the oil and press in sprigs of fresh rosemary and salt before baking. The same recipe can be varied with different herbs or chopped olives used as a topping instead.

7g dried yeast
pinch of sugar
150ml lukewarm water
185g plain flour
½ teaspoon salt
3 tablespoons olive oil
1 tablespoon finely chopped fresh
   rosemary leaves
1 tablespoon olive oil, extra
1 tablespoon finely chopped fresh
   rosemary leaves, extra
1 teaspoon sea salt

MAKES 1 LOAF
Preparation 15 minutes
plus 55 minutes standing
Cooking 30 minutes

1 Mix yeast and sugar with 2 tablespoons lukewarm water. Stir in remaining water; stand 10 minutes.

2 In large bowl, mix flour, salt, olive oil, rosemary and yeast until well combined.

3 Turn out dough onto lightly floured surface; knead lightly, about 5 minutes.

4 Replace dough into lightly greased bowl. Cover with clean tea towel and leave to rise in warm place about 45 minutes, or until doubled in size.

5 Preheat oven to 200°C. Turn out dough onto lightly floured surface; knead lightly a further 2 minutes. Shape dough into a ball; lightly press down to make disc about 2cm thick.

6 Place disc on oven tray; brush with extra oil and sprinkle with extra rosemary and sea salt. Bake about 20 minutes, or until well risen and golden.

Try this, too…

Eat focaccia just as it is, or split it and toast or grill it for sandwiches. For a quick pizza, pan-fry on the cut side, then top with hot roasted or barbecued vegetables and grated cheddar or parmesan, or thin slices of mozzarella. Sprinkle with fresh basil.

Sage and prosciutto damper

Traditionally, this basic bread was cooked in the hot ashes of an open fire in outback Australia. Our modern version has a number of special gourmet touches; a little prosciutto, feta cheese and sage leaves for extra taste and interest.

50g prosciutto, roughly chopped
250g self-raising flour
2 teaspoons baking powder
I teaspoon salt
50g feta, crumbled
I tablespoon finely chopped
  fresh sage leaves
250ml milk
I tablespoon milk, extra

MAKES I LOAF
Preparation 15 minutes
Cooking 30 minutes

1 Preheat oven to 220°C. Cook prosciutto in dry frying pan on medium heat, stirring until browned and slightly crisp. Drain on paper towel; cool.

2 Sift flour, baking powder and salt into large bowl. Add cooked prosciutto and rest of ingredients; mix together until well combined.

3 Turn out dough onto lightly floured surface; knead lightly about 1 minute. Shape dough into ball and flatten slightly. Using sharp knife, cut a cross on surface of dough, about 2cm deep.

4 Place dough on oven tray; brush with extra milk. Bake 25 to 30 minutes, or until golden.

Ingredient guide

Prosciutto is a type of Italian ham that has been seasoned, salt-cured and air-dried. You can buy it thinly sliced from delicatessens and supermarkets. As an alternative, use thinly sliced pancetta, ham or bacon.

349

Scones and muffins

Chive and cheesy bacon muffins

150g bacon, finely chopped
215g plain flour
2 teaspoons baking powder
½ teaspoon salt
2 tablespoons chopped
   fresh chives
2 tablespoons freshly
   grated parmesan
1 large egg
185ml buttermilk
60g butter, melted

MAKES 10
Preparation 10 minutes
Cooking 15 minutes

1 Preheat oven to 180°C. Cook bacon in dry frying pan on medium heat, stirring until crisp. Drain on paper towel; cool.

2 Sift flour, baking powder and salt into large bowl. Add bacon and remaining ingredients; mix until well combined.

3 Spoon into lightly oiled muffin pan. Bake 12 to 15 minutes, or until cooked. Turn out onto wire rack to cool.

Tarragon and pumpkin scones

250g self-raising flour
½ teaspoon salt
40g chilled butter
250g mashed cooked pumpkin, cold
2 tablespoons finely chopped fresh
   tarragon leaves
60g freshly grated parmesan
1 large egg
2 tablespoons milk

MAKES 12
Preparation 15 minutes

1 Preheat oven to 200°C. Sift flour and salt into medium bowl; using fingertips, rub butter into flour until mixture resembles breadcrumbs.

2 Using a plastic spatula or wooden spoon, fold in remaining ingredients until combined. Turn out dough onto lightly floured surface; knead lightly until smooth.

3 Press or roll out dough evenly to about 2cm thickness. Cut out scones, using 5cm round cutter.

4 Place scones on tray lined with baking paper. Bake 18 to 20 minutes, or until scones look evenly browned and sound hollow when tapped. Turn scones onto wire rack to cool.

Thyme and goat's cheese muffins

250g plain flour
1½ teaspoons baking powder
1 tablespoon sugar
½ teaspoon bicarbonate of soda
1 tablespoon finely chopped fresh
   thyme leaves
3 tablespoons finely chopped fresh
   flat-leaf parsley leaves

100g goat's cheese, crumbled
1 large egg
310ml buttermilk
50g butter, melted

MAKES 12
Preparation 10 minutes
Cooking 18 minutes

1 Preheat oven to 200°C. Sift flour, baking powder, sugar and bicarbonate of soda into large bowl. Add remaining ingredients; mix until well combined.

2 Spoon mixture into lightly oiled muffin pan. Bake 15 to 18 minutes, or until muffins are cooked. Turn out onto wire rack to cool.

Watercress soup

Rich in anti-oxidants, peppery watercress is one of the most nutritious of salad greens. Combined with potatoes, crème fraîche and horseradish, it makes a warming, healthy soup. Cook the watercress only briefly to preserve its vitamins.

SERVES 6
Preparation 10 minutes
Cooking 30 minutes

1 Heat oil in large saucepan; sauté spring onions until softened. Add potatoes and stock. Bring to the boil. Reduce heat; simmer 15 to 20 minutes, or until potatoes are tender.

2 Add watercress and horseradish sauce. Add crème fraîche, reserving a little. Stir until watercress wilts. Do not overcook.

3 Using food processor or hand-held blender, process soup until smooth. Divide among 6 serving bowls, add a swirl of the remaining crème fraîche and sprinkle with chives.

1 tablespoon olive oil
6 spring onions, thinly sliced
700g washed potatoes, peeled and diced
1½ litres chicken stock
2 bunches fresh watercress (about 200g in total), tough stalks removed
2 teaspoons horseradish sauce
125g crème fraîche or sour cream
2 tablespoons fresh chives, cut into 2cm lengths

Try these, too…

SPICY-STYLE WATERCRESS SOUP

In place of horseradish sauce, stir in 2 teaspoons very finely chopped fresh ginger. Omit crème fraîche. Sprinkle with chopped fresh Thai basil and coriander leaves. Serve with lime wedges.

SUMMER CHILLED SOUP

Use a mixture of half potatoes and half leeks. Season cooked soup with salt to taste. Refrigerate 3 to 4 hours before serving. Sprinkle with chopped fresh dill.

Seafood coconut soup

Tangy kaffir lime leaves are a traditional flavouring in Thai cooking and here they are accompanied by white fish, large prawns and noodles for a soup that will serve as a light meal or a substantial starter. Shred the leaves needle-thin for this recipe.

100g flat rice noodles or
  noodles of your choice
1 tablespoon peanut oil
3 stalks fresh lemon grass,
  inner white part finely sliced
  (about 3 tablespoons)
5cm piece galangal, cut into
  thin slices
1 tablespoon chilli paste
1 litre chicken stock
500ml coconut milk
2 tablespoons shredded fresh
  kaffir lime leaves
1 tablespoon palm sugar,
  finely chopped
60ml fish sauce
400g firm white fish fillets,
  cut into 2cm cubes
8 large prawns, shelled and
  deveined, leaving tails intact
2 tablespoons fresh lime juice
1 tablespoon roughly chopped fresh
  coriander leaves, to serve
1 tablespoon roughly chopped
  fresh Thai basil leaves, to serve
lime wedges, to serve

SERVES 6
Preparation 20 minutes
Cooking 12 minutes

1 Place noodles in heatproof mediumbowl and cover with boiling water. Stand 10 to 15 minutes, or until soft; drain and set aside.

2 Heat oil in large saucepan. Add lemon grass, galangal and chilli paste; cook, stirring, 1 minute. Add stock and coconut milk. Bring to the boil. Reduce heat; simmer 5 minutes.

3 Add kaffir lime leaves, palm sugar, fish sauce and noodles; simmer a further 3 minutes. Add fish; cook 2 minutes. Add prawns; cook 1 minute, or until prawns turn pink.

4 Remove from heat. Stir through lime juice, coriander and basil. Place noodles in serving bowl. Add soup and serve with lime wedges.

353

Soup with herb dumplings

Herb dumplings flavoured with parmesan, parsley and chives turn a soup of beef, tomatoes and onions into a hearty meal. To give the dumplings a stronger celery flavour, use leaves of fresh lovage in place of the parsley.

1kg tomatoes, halved
4 cloves garlic, unpeeled
1 red onion, peeled and quartered
1 teaspoon sea salt
2 tablespoons olive oil
500g beef chuck steak,
   cut into 2cm cubes
1 litre vegetable stock

HERB DUMPLINGS
190g self-raising flour
60g butter, chilled and cut
   into cubes
2 tablespoons grated parmesan
1 tablespoon finely chopped
   fresh chives
1 tablespoon finely chopped
   fresh parsley
125 ml milk

SERVES 6
Preparation 20 minutes
Cooking 1 hour 30 minutes

1 Preheat oven to 180°C. Place tomatoes (cut-side up), garlic and onion on baking tray, sprinkle with salt and drizzle with 1 tablespoon oil.

2 Roast vegetables 30 minutes. Remove from oven, cool slightly; roughly peel tomatoes and peel garlic.

3 Using food processor or hand-held blender, process vegetables in medium bowl until smooth.

4 Heat remaining 1 tablespoon oil in large saucepan; brown meat in batches. Return meat to saucepan with tomato mixture and stock; simmer for 45 minutes before adding dumplings.

5 To make dumplings, place flour in medium bowl. Using fingertips, rub butter into flour until mixture resembles breadcrumbs. Using a wooden spoon or plastic spatula, fold in parmesan and herbs. Add milk, using flat-bladed knife; mix until just combined. Knead briefly.

6 Using a teaspoon, scoop dough roughly into balls. Shape with floured hands. Drop balls into soup, and simmer, covered, 15 minutes. Divide soup among serving bowls.

Herb guide

In France, lovage is called *céleri bâtard*, or false celery. It has a much stronger flavour than parsley when used raw but its pungency diminishes in cooking. Try the leaves and stems in salads.

Assembling the dumplings

1 Rub butter and flour together until mixture resembles breadcrumbs.

2 Use a wooden spoon to fold in parmesan and herbs. Add milk to form dough.

3 Scoop mixture roughly into balls. Shape quickly with floured hands to stop them sticking.

Potato and horseradish salad

This crunchy salad goes well with barbecued meats – especially lamb and beef. It is also a good accompaniment to cold cuts including salt beef and ox tongue. Fresh horseradish roots can be grated and frozen; grating releases their pungent volatile oil.

1kg small salad potatoes, halved
2 small heads of chicory
20g chopped fresh flat-leaf
   parsley leaves
2 tablespoons roughly chopped fresh
   tarragon leaves
60g roughly chopped walnuts
juice of 1 lemon
1 tablespoon grated fresh
   horseradish root
200g crème fraîche or sour cream
pinch of sea salt

SERVES 6
Preparation 15 minutes
Cooking 10 minutes

1 Cook potatoes in large saucepan of boiling water until tender. Drain; cool briefly.

2 Place potatoes in large bowl. Add chicory leaves, parsley, tarragon and walnuts; toss to combine.

3 Combine lemon juice, horseradish and crème fraîche in a small bowl; season with sea salt. Pour dressingover potatoes; toss to combine.

Cook's tip

Potatoes are used warm in this salad because they absorb the flavours of the dressing more easily. A dressing added to cold potatoes tends to coat them rather than soak in.

Fattoush

Sumac is a dark purplish-red ground spice that has a slightly sour, lemon taste. Found throughout the Middle East, it is used with rice in Turkey and Iran and as a dry seasoning in place of lemon juice on salads such as this Lebanese bread salad.

4 pitta breads
1 tablespoon olive oil
1 tablespoon sumac
500g cherry tomatoes, halved
1 cucumber, quartered and cut into
  2cm lengths
1 red onion, halved and finely sliced
5 tablespoons finely chopped fresh
  coriander leaves
5 tablespoons finely chopped fresh
  mint leaves
5 tablespoons finely chopped fresh
  flat-leaf parsley leaves
12 Little Gem lettuce leaves,
  torn in half
150g feta, crumbled
7g kalamata olives

SUMAC DRESSING
1 clove garlic, crushed
60ml lemon juice
125ml olive oil
¼ teaspoon sumac
pinch of sea salt

SERVES 4 to 6
Preparation 15 minutes
Cooking 15 minutes

1 Preheat oven to 180°C. Cut each pitta into quarters; lightly brush with oil and sprinkle with sumac. Place pitta on oven tray; bake 10 to 15 minutes, or until golden and crisp.

2 Combine remaining salad ingredients in large bowl. Tear pitta quarters into small pieces; add to salad.

3 To make dressing, whisk all ingredients in small bowl. Pour over salad; toss gently and serve.

Try this, too…

Instead of baking, try frying pitta bread in a little olive oil until crisp. This salad is one of many such frugal peasant dishes around the world that use bread (often stale bread) to add bulk and texture.

Tabbouleh beef wraps

Parsley is a key ingredient finely-chopped in tabbouleh, a traditional Middle Eastern salad. An irresistable combination of tomatoes, cucumber and herbs with the nuttiness of bulghur wheat, tabbouleh is a fresh-tasting foil to roast beef and Swiss cheese.

4 large pitta breads, halved
8 thin slices rare roast beef
4 slices (90g) Swiss-style
  cheese, halved
8 cherry tomatoes, quartered
1 medium avocado, peeled
  and sliced
2 tablespoons hummus

TABBOULEH
200g bulghur or cracked wheat
2 medium tomatoes, peeled,
  seeded and finely chopped
1 Lebanese or small cucumber,
  finely diced
5 tablespoons finely chopped
  fresh mint leaves
30g finely chopped fresh flat leaf
  parsley leaves
2 spring onions, finely chopped
2 tablespoons olive oil
juice of 1 lemon

SERVES 4
Preparation 10 minutes
plus 15 minutes soaking

1 To make tabbouleh, soak bulghur in hot water 15 minutes. Drain; squeeze out excess water. Combine with remaining ingredients in medium bowl, and season to taste.

2 Fill pitta bread halves with tabbouleh, beef, cheese, tomato, avocado and hummus.

Try these, too...

PERSILLADE
This combination of chopped fresh parsley and garlic gives a great flavour boost to a dish if it is added at the very end of the cooking process. It can also be used as a garnish. Vary it with the addition of lemon zest or anchovies. Tarragon or thyme can be used in place of parsley. Use 20g parsley to 2 cloves garlic.

CHERMOULA
A Moroccan herb and spice mixture, chermoula is used as a marinade for meat, poultry and fish. It can also be applied as a paste, which forms a crust during cooking. Chermoula traditionally includes a mixture of fresh coriander and parsley but the combination of spices can vary. For this version, combine 20g each finely chopped fresh coriander and parsley with 1 small finely chopped red onion, 2 cloves crushed garlic, 1 teaspoon each ground cumin, paprika, turmeric and chilli powder, 125ml olive oil and 2 tablespoons lemon juice.

Herb guide

When eaten in portions of at least 30g, fresh parsley contains useful amounts of vitamin C, iron and calcium.

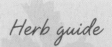

Chermoula (above), Tabbouleh (right) and Persillade (top right).

Vegetarian spring rolls

With rice paper wrappers instead of traditional batter, and a filling of finely sliced raw vegetables and salad herbs, these are a light, healthy alternative to deep-fried spring rolls. For variety you could add prawns or chicken to this basic version.

50g vermicelli
12 medium round rice paper
   wrappers
2 small cucumbers, seeded and
   cut into thin strips
4 spring onions
1 red pepper, cut into strips
12 mange touts, cut into strips
1 carrot, cut into strips
12 fresh mint leaves
12 fresh coriander leaves
12 fresh basil leaves

DIPPING SAUCE
2 tablespoons lime juice
1 tablespoon fish sauce
1 teaspoon sugar
1 small red chilli, seeded and
   finely sliced

SERVES 4
Preparation 30 minutes

1 Place vermicelli in heatproof medium bowl and cover with boiling water. Stand 10 to 15 minutes, or until soft; drain and set aside.

2 Place rice paper rounds in medium bowl of warm water until just softened (about 30 seconds). Carefully lay out each one flat on work surface or cutting board and gently pat dry with paper towel.

3 Divide vermicelli, vegetables and herbs among rounds, placing them in the centre of each one. Fold in one edge of the round to partly enclose vegetables, then fold in the two opposing sides. Fold in remaining side, then roll into cigar shape to completely enclose filling.

4 To make dipping sauce, combine all ingredients in medium bowl; stir to dissolve sugar. Serve in a small bowl with rolls.

Folding the rolls

1 Place vegetable mixture in centre of rice paper wrapper.

2 Fold in one side of the round and then two opposing sides.

3 Roll into a compact cigar shape to enclose filling.

Chervil, pea and feta quiche

The sharpness of feta and chervil give a twist to a conventional quiche recipe. For a touch of extra heat, try adding a little finely chopped red chilli to the filling. Use a combination of half cream and half milk, for a lighter mixture if preferred.

4 large eggs
300ml cream
½ teaspoon salt
3 tablespoons roughly chopped
  fresh chervil
I tablespoon finely chopped
  fresh chives
I to 2 sheets ready-made
  shortcrust pastry
155g fresh shelled peas
120g soft feta, crumbled
60g grated cheddar

SERVES 4
Preparation 20 minutes
Cooking 35 minutes

1 Preheat oven to 180°C. In medium bowl, whisk together eggs and cream; season with salt and stir through herbs.

2 Lightly oil 35cm x 12cm rectangular or 23cm round tin. Gently place pastry into tin, using 2 sheets if required; mould pastry into sides and trim any excess.

3 Sprinkle top of pastry with peas and fetta. Pour over egg and herb mixture; sprinkle with cheddar.

4 Place quiche on bottom shelf in oven; cook 30 to 35 minutes, or until quiche is set. Serve with salad.

Herb guide

Chervil belongs to the parsley family, but is much more aromatic than parsley. One of the staples of classic French cooking, it is used with tarragon, chives and parsley in the seasoning blend fines herbes.

Lovage and fennel omelettes

An omelette is flexible fast food at its best and herbs give a tasty boost to a classic recipe. Accompany with a salad of fresh leaves, cucumber and tomato. For variation, use spicy perilla or Thai basil in place of the celery-flavoured lovage.

8 large eggs
80ml milk
1 teaspoon salt
25g roughly chopped fresh chives, sliced into 2cm lengths
3 tablespoons roughly chopped fresh lovage
2 tablespoons roughly chopped fresh fennel leaves
1 tablespoon butter
60g grated full-flavoured cheese such as gruyère

SERVES 4
Preparation 10 minutes
Cooking 10 minutes

1 Whisk eggs and milk in a large bowl. Season with salt; stir in herbs.

2 Melt butter in small non-stick frying pan over high heat. Pour one quarter of egg mixture into pan. Cook about 1 minute, stirring gently. Egg will begin to set around edge of pan almost immediately. Using fork or wooden spoon, gently pull back cooked egg from edge of pan, allowing any uncooked egg mixture to run underneath.

3 Cook a further 45 seconds to 1 minute, or until egg is just set. Sprinkle over cheese. Fold over one half of omelette and slide onto serving plate. Cover with aluminium foil to keep warm. Continue with remaining mixture. Serve at once accompanied by a crisp mixed salad.

Cook's tip

Work quickly when making omelettes and do not overcook them. Remove from the pan when just set or the omelette will continue cooking. Sprinkle on all the herbs at the end of cooking, if preferred, rather than adding them to the eggs and milk.

Thyme and oregano soufflés

Individual soufflés never fail to impress as a smart starter or light meal and they are surprisingly easy to make. The fruit chutney base is a surprise extra that complements the savoury flavours of the herb mixture, cheddar and cayennne pepper.

60g butter
2 tablespoons plain flour
330ml milk
100g grated mature cheddar
¼ teaspoon cayenne pepper
4 large eggs, separated
2 teaspoons finely chopped fresh
  thyme leaves
2 teaspoons finely chopped fresh
  oregano leaves
2 tablespoons finely chopped fresh
  parsley leaves
2 tablespoons fruit chutney

SERVES 4
Preparation 30 minutes
Cooking 20 minutes

1 Preheat oven to 200°C. Lightly oil 4 x 250ml ramekins. Melt butter in small saucepan over low heat. Using wooden spoon, fold in flour; stir mixture continuously, about 1 minute. Remove from heat.

2 Gradually add milk to mixture, stirring until smooth. Return pan to medium heat, stirring until mixture thickens and thickly coats back of spoon. Fold in cheese and cayenne pepper. Transfer mixture to large bowl, cover with plastic wrap; cool. When mixture is cool, stir through egg yolks and herbs.

3 In clean, small bowl, beat egg whites until soft peaks form. Lightly fold egg white into soufflé mixture, just until white streaks are not visible. Do not overmix.

4 Place ½ tablespoon chutney in each ramekin. Divide soufflé mixture among ramekins, taking care not to mix in chutney. Run small spatula around rim to shape the top of soufflés. Place ramekins on oven tray.

5 Bake soufflés 20 minutes, or until risen and golden. Serve at once.

Making the soufflés

3 Run spatula around rim of ramekin to shape top of soufflés.

1 Carefully fold egg whites into soufflé mixture. Do not overmix.

2 Place fruit chutney in the bottom of each ramekin.

Pumpkin pancakes with sage

The sweetness of pumpkin is here teamed with the warm, musky, spicy taste of sage, plus parmesan and ricotta with a dash of chilli and mustard in this pancake stack. Bruise the sage leaves lightly with a rolling pin to maximise their flavour.

310g plain flour
pinch each of salt and pepper
2 large eggs
2 teaspoons olive oil
500ml chilled water
2kg pumpkin, peeled, seeded and
    coarsely chopped
2 tablespoons olive oil, extra
200g fresh ricotta
180g grated parmesan
half a small red chilli,
    finely chopped
1 teaspoon dijon mustard
1 tablespoon finely chopped
    fresh chives
1 tablespoon finely chopped
    fresh parsley leaves
1 clove garlic, finely chopped
60g grated parmesan, extra

BURNT BUTTER AND SAGE SAUCE
250g salted butter
20 fresh sage leaves

SERVES 6
Preparation 40 minutes
Cooking 40 minutes

1 Combine flour, salt and pepper, eggs, oil and water in large bowl. Whisk until smooth; mixture should be consistency of single cream. Stand 30 minutes before cooking.

2 Heat lightly oiled non-stick frying pan; pour a tablespoon of batter into pan, tilting pan to coat base with batter. Cook 1 minute, or until underside is golden. Using plastic spatula, loosen pancake; turn and cook other side for a further 30 seconds. Repeat with remaining batter to make 6 pancakes.

3 Meanwhile, preheat oven to 180°C. Toss pumpkin and extra oil in roasting dish; bake 30 minutes, or until pumpkin is cooked and golden.

4 Combine cooked pumpkin, ricotta, parmesan, chilli, mustard, chives, parsley and garlic in large bowl; mash mixture with fork, then cool.

5 Preheat oven to 180°C. Lightly oil 20-cm springform tin. Place one pancake flat on bottom of tin, then top with some pumpkin mixture; repeat layers, finishing with pancake. Press down lightly and sprinkle with extra parmesan. Bake 15 minutes, or until golden.

6 To make sauce, melt butter in small saucepan over medium heat until butter foams and turns dark golden brown. Remove from heat; add sage leaves.

7 Carefully remove pancake stack from tin onto cutting board; cut into wedges. Serve drizzled with burnt butter.

Cook's tip

The term 'burnt butter' or 'beurre noir' is misleading. The butter should be heated until it is a rich golden brown, not black. It will taste nutty and sweet with a hint of richness. Keep a watchful eye on it while it is cooking.

Chive and ricotta gnocchi

Make your own gnocchi extra special with a mix of two cheeses and chives then top them with a rich blue cheese dressing – or try the buttery, nutty taste of fontina cheese instead. A few chopped fresh basil or sage leaves can be added to the chives.

750g fresh ricotta
185g grated parmesan
2 small eggs
115g plain flour
60g finely chopped fresh chives
1 tablespoon butter, melted
250ml cream
100g blue cheese, crumbled
6 slices prosciutto (about 60g),
  torn into strips
3 tablespoons chopped fresh chives

SERVES 6
Preparation 30 minutes
Cooking 30 minutes

1 Preheat oven to 180°C. Place ricotta, parmesan, eggs, flour and chives in medium bowl; season to taste. Using wooden spoon, mix until well combined.

2 Bring large saucepan of water to the boil then reduce heat to simmer. Using two dessertspoons, shape spoonfuls of mixture into ovals and drop into simmering water; cook 4 to 5 minutes, or until gnocchi float to surface. Remove gnocchi; place on absorbent paper. Repeat with remaining mixture, in batches, avoiding overfilling saucepan.

3 Lightly grease shallow ovenproof dish with melted butter; place gnocchi in dish.

4 Combine cream, blue cheese and prosciutto in medium bowl. Pour over gnocchi, then bake 10 to 12 minutes, or until gnocchi are lightly browned. Serve the gnocchi warm, with green salad.

Making gnocchi

1 Shape the gnocchi mixture between two dessertspoons.

2 Scoop gnocchi from pan with a slotted spoon; drain on paper towels.

3 Combine cream, blue cheese and prosciutto and pour over gnocchi.

Rubs and marinades

Homemade rubs and marinades enrich the flavour, texture and aroma of meat, chicken, fish or vegetables, particularly when barbecuing or roasting. Rubs are good for when you want to add flavour quickly; allow more time for a marinade to work its magic.

Jamaican jerk seasoning

50g ground allspice berries
155g brown sugar
6 cloves garlic
4 Scotch bonnet chillies (a variety of habañero and very hot)
1 tablespoon dried thyme or 2 tablespoons fresh thyme leaves
8 spring onions, chopped
1 teaspoon cinnamon
½ teaspoon ground nutmeg
salt and pepper, to taste
2 tablespoons soy sauce

Place all the ingredients in a food processor and blend to a paste. Store in an airtight container in the refrigerator up to 1 month.

Ingredient guide

'Jerk' is the term given to the process of spicing and grilling meats. It is also used as a noun to describe the dry or wet seasoning mix used to jerk particular foods. In Caribbean cooking, pork and chicken are the most popular. Road-side jerk shacks are part of the local fast-food industry in Jamaica.

Spicy barbecue rub

2 tablespoons salt
2 tablespoons brown sugar
2 tablespoons ground cumin
2 tablespoons chilli powder
2 tablespoons freshly ground black pepper
1 tablespoon cayenne pepper
3 tablespoons paprika

Combine all ingredients. Use on a large piece of beef, chicken, lamb or pork when barbecuing or spit-roasting. Store in an airtight container in the refrigerator up to 1 month.

Mediterranean rub

1 tablespoon dried oregano
1 tablespoon dried marjoram
1 tablespoon dried parsley
1 tablespoon dried basil
1 teaspoon sea salt
½ teaspoon black peppercorns
2 cloves garlic, roughly chopped
1 tablespoon lemon zest

Using a pestle, pound all the ingredients in a mortar until fine and well combined. Store in an airtight container in the refrigerator up to 1 month.

Lemon and marjoram baste

1 tablespoon freshly squeezed lemon juice
1 teaspoon finely chopped fresh marjoram
2 teaspoons olive oil

Combine all the ingredients. Use as a baste for barbecued chicken kebabs in the last few minutes of cooking.

Madras curry blend

2 dried chillies
4 tablespoons coriander seeds
2 tablespoons cumin seeds
1 teaspoon mustard seeds
1 tablespoon black peppercorns
6 curry leaves
1 teaspoon ground ginger
1 teaspoon turmeric

Dry roast chillies, coriander, cumin, mustard and pepper in a frying pan until aromatic. Leave to cool. Dry curry leaves briefly in pan and add to spices. Grind to a powder, sieve and stir in ginger and turmeric. Store in airtight container in the refrigerator for up to 2 months.

Cajun rub

2 tablespoons paprika
1 tablespoon chilli flakes
1 tablespoon celery salt
1 teaspoon allspice
2 cloves garlic
2 tablespoons dried onion flakes
2 tablespoons dried oregano
2 tablespoons dried thyme
1 teaspoon peppercorns

Using a pestle, pound the ingredients in a mortar until fine and well combined. Store in an airtight container in the refrigerator for up to 1 month.

Classic herb marinade

125ml balsamic vinegar
125ml olive oil
3 tablespoons chopped fresh
   parsley or fresh coriander
1 tablespoon sugar (optional)
2 tablespoons finely chopped
   fresh dill
½ teaspoon salt
pinch of freshly ground
   black pepper

Place all ingredients in screw-top jar and shake well to combine. Use to marinate raw or briefly blanched vegetables such as yellow squash or courgettes and carrot. Serve as a side salad. Make the marinade on the day you want to use it.

Moroccan rub

1 teaspoon saffron
1 teaspoon harissa (see page 346)
1 teaspoon ground cardamom
4 cloves
1 teaspoon cumin seeds
2 cloves garlic
3 tablespoons fresh mint leaves
3 tablespoons fresh coriander leaves

Pound ingredients in a mortar until fine and well combined. Store in airtight container in refrigerator up to 1 month.

Lamb with herb and garlic rub

The rich, tender sweetness of lamb is complemented by herbs that pack a punch, as this trio of thyme, rosemary and parsley does. It is combined with garlic to make a herby crust. Or try the sharper, fresher combination of oregano, thyme and mint or coriander.

2kg leg of lamb
1 lemon, halved and seeded

HERB AND GARLIC RUB
3 tablespoons finely chopped
   fresh thyme
2 tablespoons finely chopped
   fresh rosemary
2 tablespoons finely chopped
   fresh parsley
8 cloves garlic, finely chopped
1 tablespoon sea salt flakes
½ teaspoon ground black pepper
60ml olive oil

SERVES 6
Preparation 20 minutes plus
1 hour marinating
Cooking 2 hours

1 To make rub, mix herbs, garlic, salt and pepper in medium bowl. Pour in the oil and mix until well combined.

Cook's tip

It's important to rest a joint of meat for at least 10 minutes before carving and serving. When rested, the internal and external temperatures even out and the juices are redistributed, making the meat more succulent and easier to carve.

2 Using a sharp knife, make several slits about 5mm long all over lamb. Rub herb mixture all over meat, pushing it into slits; leave lamb 1 hour at room temperature to marinate.

3 Preheat oven to 180°C. Place lamb on baking tray, fat side up, and cook about 2 hours 30 minutes per 500g). Cover with aluminium foil after 1 hour.

4 Transfer lamb to cutting board. Squeeze lemon juice over lamb; rest 10 to 15 minutes before cutting and serving. Serve with roasted vegetables.

Using the rub

3 When the lamb has cooked through, the flavours of the herb rub will have fully permeated the meat.

1 Combine herbs, garlic and seasoning. Pour in olive oil and mix all the ingredients well.

2 Make slits in the meat. Rub mixture all over it, pushing it into the slits to flavour the whole joint.

Moroccan lamb with couscous

Ras el hanout is a Moroccan mixture of 20 or more spices and herbs that typically includes cinnamon, cloves, lavender, orris root, cloves and turmeric. It pairs marvellously with lightly grilled lamb on a bed of couscous, chickpeas and red peppers.

40g almond slivers
40g butter
2 cloves garlic, finely chopped
500ml chicken stock
pinch of saffron threads
370g quick-cook couscous
2 tablespoons ras el hanout
1 tablespoon olive oil

1kg lamb fillet
2 red peppers, cut into strips
3 courgettes, cut into long ribbons
400g can chickpeas, drained
4 tablespoons roughly chopped
  fresh mint leaves
4 tablespoons fresh
  coriander leaves

SERVES 6
Preparation 20 minutes
Cooking 30 minutes

1 Toast almond slivers in dry frying pan on medium heat, tossing until just golden. Transfer to small bowl; cool before use.

2 Melt butter in large saucepan; sauté garlic until softened. Add stock and saffron; bring to the boil.

3 Stir couscous through boiling stock. Remove saucepan from heat; cover and stand 5 minutes, or until couscous has absorbed stock. Using a fork, separate couscous grains.

4 Meanwhile, preheat grill to medium. Rub seasoning and oil into lamb; grill 3 to 4 minutes each side, or to your liking. Remove lamb from grill; set aside to rest, keeping meat warm until required.

5 Cook pepper and courgettes on grill 2 to 3 minutes each side.

6 Toss pepper, courgettes, chickpeas and herbs through warm couscous; top with sliced lamb and sprinkle with almonds.

Ingredient guide

A traditional ingredient in North African cooking, couscous is coarse-ground wheat made into tiny balls and pre-cooked. Preparing traditional couscous is time-consuming, but good-quality, quick-cook (or instant) varieties produce an excellent result.

Tandoori chicken pizza

A traditional thin-crust pizza base takes on an oriental topping with tender pieces of tandoori chicken and cashew nuts. The lemon-and-ginger flavour of fresh coriander is a good partner for spicy tandoori paste; fresh oregano can be used as an alternative.

7g dried yeast
pinch of sugar
150ml lukewarm water
220g plain flour
½ teaspoon salt
60ml olive oil
2 x 250g skinless chicken breasts,
    sliced into 2cm slices
3 tablespoons tandoori paste
2 tablespoons plain yoghurt
75g roughly chopped cashew nuts
250ml Italian tomato sauce
4 spring onions, thinly sliced
2 tablespoons finely chopped
    fresh coriander
125g plain yoghurt, extra
2 tablespoons finely chopped
    fresh mint leaves
lime wedges, to serve

SERVES 4
Preparation 30 minutes plus
1 to 2 hours for marinating
Cooking 20 minutes

1 Mix yeast and sugar with 2 tablespoons lukewarm water. Stir in remaining water; stand for 10 minutes.

2 Mix flour, salt, oil and yeast mixture in a large bowl until well combined.

3 Turn out dough onto lightly floured surface; knead lightly, about 5 minutes.

4 Return dough to lightly greased bowl. Cover with clean tea towel and leave to rise in warm place for about 45 minutes, or until dough has doubled in size.

5 Turn dough onto lightly floured surface; knead lightly 2 minutes. Divide dough in half; shape into two balls. Roll out each ball into

circle 25cm in diameter. Place on pizza tray; set aside until required.

6 Combine chicken, tandoori paste and yoghurt in large bowl; refrigerate 1 to 2 hours to allow flavours to develop.

7 Preheat oven to 230°C. Toast cashew nuts in dry frying pan on medium heat, tossing until just golden. Transfer to small bowl; cool before use.

8 Spread tomato sauce evenly on each pizza; top with chicken slices, spring onions, coriander and cashews, spreading all evenly. Bake for 5 minutes near bottom of oven.

Reduce heat to 200°C; cook further 15 minutes.

9 Combine extra yoghurt and mint in small bowl. Drizzle over each pizza. Serve with lime wedges.

Cook's tip

Lightly grease your hands before mixing or kneading dough so that the dough doesn't stick to them. Pizza bases require cooking at a high heat, so use heavy-gauge tins and baking trays to avoid warping

Mexican chicken with green rice

Give chicken a Latin American slant with a spicy baste of herbs and wine. Lay it on a bed of arroz verde (green rice) that's packed with spinach, parsley and coriander. A garnish of sliced avocado complements the robust flavours of the dish.

4 cloves garlic, finely chopped
2 teaspoons finely chopped fresh
   oregano leaves
½ teaspoon ground cinnamon
½ small red chilli, finely diced
I teaspoon ground cumin
½ teaspoon ground coriander
½ teaspoon ground allspice
125ml red wine
4 x 250g skinless chicken breasts

GREEN RICE
400g long-grain rice
150g spinach
5 tablespoons roughly chopped
   fresh flat leaf parsley
5 tablespoons roughly chopped
   fresh coriander
2 spring onions, roughly chopped

I clove garlic, finely chopped
125ml water
60ml peanut or safflower oil
750ml chicken stock
¼ teaspoon salt
2 long green chillies, finely sliced

SERVES 4
Preparation 10 minutes plus
30 minutes refrigeration

1 Using a food processor or hand-held blender, process garlic, oregano, cinnamon, chilli, cumin, coriander, allspice and wine. Coat chicken breasts with mixture; refrigerate 30 minutes.

2 Preheat oiled grill plate or frying pan to medium heat. Cook chicken 10 minutes, turning once, or until cooked through.

3 Pour boiling water over rice in heatproof medium bowl. Soak 10 minutes; drain.

4 Rinse spinach. Cook undrained, in small saucepan uncovered on medium heat, 1 to 2 minutes or until just wilted.

5 Process spinach, parsley, coriander, spring onions, garlic and water until smooth.

6 Heat oil in large saucepan. Add rice, stir uncovered on medium heat, until golden.

7 Add stock and spinach purée; cook, stirring occasionally, until rice is tender (about 15 minutes). Stir through chilli. Serve chicken on a bed of green rice.

Cook's tip

Keep fresh garlic in a dry, dark, cool place. It will last longer and retain its flavour. Store it in a terracotta pot made especially for the purpose, or in something as simple as a brown paper bag. Never store garlic in the refrigerator as it is likely to sprout and become bitter.

Tarragon chicken

Pan-fried chicken breasts cooked in a white wine, onion and tarragon butter sauce are a time-saving version of a French dish that traditionally uses a whole chicken. In that version the tarragon butter is inserted under the skin rather than poured on top.

Herb guide

A bouquet garni comprising fresh tarragon, parsley, bay and bruised lemon grass adds a beautiful flavour to slow-cooked poultry dishes. The slightly aniseed, spicy taste of tarragon can overwhelm the flavour of other herbs, so use it with a light hand.

60g unsalted butter
1 tablespoon olive oil
4 x 250g skinless chicken breasts
2 spring onions, finely chopped
1 clove garlic, finely chopped
60ml dry white wine
125ml cream
1 tablespoon roughly chopped fresh tarragon

SERVES 4
Preparation 10 minutes
Cooking 15 minutes

1 Melt butter and oil in large frying pan on medium heat. Add chicken; cook, turning occasionally, until browned and cooked through.

2 Add spring onion and garlic; cook until garlic softens. Add wine, cream and tarragon; cook a further 2 minutes, stirring to coat chicken.

3 Serve chicken with steamed vegetables of your choice.

BBQ swordfish kebabs

Substantial and meaty, swordfish is perfect for the barbecue, and cooking it on bay and rosemary skewers infuses the meat with a delicious flavour. Serve in a tortilla wrap with salad and a little baba ganoush – aubergine dip with lemon juice, garlic and tahini paste.

3 swordfish steaks (about 600g in total), cut into 3cm pieces
2 tablespoons lemon juice
1 tablespoon finely chopped fresh oregano
2 bay leaves (preferably fresh), shredded
1 clove garlic
2 tablespoons olive oil
4 fresh rosemary sprigs
4 large fresh bay sprigs
4 large flour tortillas
100g baby spinach leaves
2 small tomatoes, halved and thinly sliced
1 cucumber, thinly sliced diagonally
4 tablespoons baba ganoush (aubergine dip)

SERVES 4
Preparation 10 minutes plus 30 minutes marinating
Cooking 4 minutes

1 Strip all but the top leaves from rosemary and bay sprigs to make skewers.

2 Combine swordfish in large bowl with lemon juice, oregano, shredded bay leaves, garlic and oil; marinate 30 minutes.

3 Preheat barbecue grill on medium. Thread swordfish pieces onto skewers.

4 Cook skewers 2 minutes each side, or until cooked to your liking.

5 Place tortillas on a work surface or cutting board; top with baby spinach, tomato, cucumber and skewers. Remove fish from skewers. Roll up tortillas; cut crosswise to serve. Serve baba ganoush on the side.

Try this, too…

Use any type of pliable, soft flatbread to make these wraps. Flatbreads such as mountain bread, lavosh and focaccia are available at supermarkets. Alternatively, split open small pitta breads and use them as pockets for the fish and salad.

Pad Thai

The Thai word 'pad' is used to describe stir-fried food. This version combines peanuts with large, juicy prawns, crunchy bean sprouts and rice noodles. To counteract the nuttiness, tamarind paste gives the dish a fruity, sweet-and-sour flavour.

180g dried flat Thai rice noodles
80ml peanut oil
2 spring onions, finely chopped
2 cloves garlic, finely chopped
2 large eggs, beaten
2 tablespoons fish sauce
2 tablespoons tamarind paste
2 teaspoons sugar
2 tablespoons fresh lime juice
2 tablespoons tomato sauce
16 large prawns, shelled and
   deveined, leaving tails intact
40g roughly chopped roasted
   peanuts
100g bean sprouts
3 tablespoons fresh
   coriander leaves
3 tablespoons fresh
   Thai basil leaves
lime wedges, to serve

SERVES 4
Preparation 15 minutes
Cooking 10 minutes

1 Place noodles in heatproof medium bowl and cover with boiling water. Stand 10 to 15 minutes, or until soft; drain.

2 Heat peanut oil in wok or large frying pan. Cook spring onion 1 minute until softened. Add garlic; cook 30 seconds. Add eggs, stirring, until lightly cooked. Add fish sauce, tamarind paste, sugar, lime juice and tomato sauce; mix until well combined.

3 Toss drained noodles through sauce. Add prawns; cook 2 to 3 minutes, or until prawns turn pink. Remove from heat; add peanuts, sprouts, coriander and basil. Serve with lime wedges.

Ingredient guide

Rice noodles are available dried, frozen and fresh. They vary in width from the very finest vermicelli to sheets of dough. Rice noodles are a common ingredient in east and southeast Asian cooking. They are transparent and have a gelatinous, chewy texture.

Coriander salmon parcels

Cooking delicately flavoured fish such as salmon in aluminium foil or baking paper is an ideal way to retain its taste, texture and nutrients. A combination of herby leaves, chillies, limes and nuts is piled around the fish to infuse it with sensational flavours.

150g baby spinach leaves
4 x 200g salmon fillets
2 limes, cut into 1cm rounds
4 fresh kaffir lime leaves,
  cut into slivers
1 large red chilli, finely sliced
  (optional)
5 tablespoons fresh
  coriander leaves
5 tablespoons fresh
  Thai basil leaves
2 spring onions, finely sliced
100ml coconut milk
1 tablespoon fish sauce
1 teaspoon sesame oil
70g roughly chopped
  cashew nuts, toasted

SERVES 4
Preparation 20 minutes
Cooking 12 minutes

1 Preheat oven to 180°C. Lay 4 x 30cm squares of foil on a work surface. Divide spinach among foil squares. Place salmon fillet in centre of each; top each fillet with lime rounds, lime leaves, chilli, coriander, basil and spring onion.

2 Combine coconut milk, fish sauce and oil in a small bowl.

Herb guide

Thai basil has a warm, peppery taste and a lingering aniseed flavour. Fennel fronds have an aniseed taste and can be used instead.

3 Fold in two opposite sides of foil square, forming seam down middle. Fold over bottom end several times to secure. At open end of each parcel, pour in 2 tablespoons coconut milk mixture; fold and secure top ends.

4 Place fish parcels on oven tray. Cook in oven about 12 minutes (for medium-rare salmon), or until cooked to your liking. Serve fish in the parcels, with steamed vegetables and rice. Garnish with cashew nuts, if desired.

Assembling the parcels

3 Completely seal the parcel, ready for cooking in the oven.

1 Layer spinach, fish, lime and herbs and spices on a square of aluminium foil.

2 Wrap and seal the fish at one end. Pour in coconut milk mixture.

Rose petal jelly

For a special celebration, this pretty dessert is a winner with its delicate colour and sweet scent. Choose an attractively shaped mould to make it look its best. Other edible flower petals that could be used include borage and scented geraniums.

4 gelatine leaves (or 2 heaped
   teaspoons gelatine crystals)
500ml sparkling wine
145g caster sugar
I tablespoon rosewater
18 small rose petals,
   carefully washed
raspberries and cream, to serve

SERVES 2
Preparation 20 minutes
Cooking 5 minutes

1 Soak gelatine leaves in cold water to soften (about 2 to 3 minutes).

2 Heat 125ml sparkling wine and sugar in large saucepan over medium heat, stirring until sugar dissolves.

3 Add gelatine leaves to sugar mixture, stirring to melt gelatine. Remove from heat to cool. Stir through remaining sparkling wine, rosewater and rose petals.

4 Pour mixture into individual glasses or lightly oiled mould; refrigerate at least 8 hours, or until set. Serve jelly with raspberries and cream.

Herb guide

There are many varieties of scented geranium, ranging in aroma from apple to nutmeg and mint to pine. Rose- and lemon-scented plants are the best for cooking.

Basil sorbet and minted lemon

Sorbet and herbs make a refreshing dessert – proving that basil is not just a good accompaniment for savoury dishes. For a variation, you could try mango or a mixture of raspberries and alpine strawberries instead of the honeydew melon.

375ml water
170g sugar
125ml fresh lime juice
20 fresh basil leaves,
  roughly chopped
1 honeydew melon
2 tablespoons roughly chopped
  fresh mint leaves
2 tablespoons lime juice, extra
1 tablespoon sugar, extra

SERVES 6
Preparation 20 minutes plus
6 hours freezing
Cooking 7 minutes

1 Combine water and sugar in medium saucepan, stirring until sugar is dissolved. Bring to the boil then reduce heat; simmer a further 5 minutes. Remove from heat to cool.

2 Using food processor or hand-held blender, process sugar syrup, lime juice and basil leaves until well combined.

3 Pour mixture into shallow dish. Freeze for at least 3 hours, or until firm. Process mixture again; return to dish and freeze several hours.

4 Meanwhile, peel melon and remove seeds. Slice thickly. Combine mint leaves, extra lime juice and extra sugar in small bowl. Pour over prepared melon. Chill until required. Serve chilled melon topped with sorbet.

Try this, too…
MIXED HERB SORBET
Bring 115g caster sugar and 250ml water to the boil, stirring until sugar dissolves. Add 4 tablespoons finely chopped mixed fresh herbs, such as a combination of apple mint leaves, lemon balm and scented geranium or rosemary. Cover; remove from heat; let mixture infuse about 20 to 30 minutes. Test for flavour; add more herbs, if preferred. Strain; add juice of 1 lemon. Pour mixture into shallow dish and freeze at least 3 hours, or until firm. Process in food processor or use hand-held blender. Freeze again for several hours.

Bay-scented panna cotta

Panna cotta is a softly textured Italian dessert. Its name translates as 'cooked cream' and it is a perfect accompaniment for all kinds of fresh fruits – here a profusion of forest berries. Flavour with a little ground cinnamon or cardamom, in place of the vanilla.

10g gelatine leaves
500ml full-cream milk
1 vanilla bean, split lengthwise, seeds scraped out
70g caster sugar
2 fresh bay leaves
350ml crème fraîche
400g fresh berries
1 teaspoon sugar
2 teaspoons chopped fresh mint leaves
juice of half a lime

MAKES 8
Preparation 20 minutes
Chilling 4 hours

1 Soak gelatine leaves in cold water to soften (about 2 to 3 minutes).

2 Heat milk, vanilla, sugar and bruised bay leaves in large saucepan, stirring until sugar dissolves. Add gelatine leaves, stirring to melt gelatine; remove from heat to cool slightly. Add crème fraîche, stirring until well combined.

3 Remove bay leaves and vanilla. Pour mixture into 4 lightly oiled 150ml moulds; refrigerate at least 4 hours, or until set.

4 In medium bowl, toss berries with sugar, mint and lime juice; stand 5 minutes.

5 To remove panna cotta from moulds, carefully slide thin knife around the circumference and invert onto serving plates. Serve with berries.

Cook's tip

Turning desserts out of moulds can often be somewhat traumatic. For a successful result, you should always lightly coat the moulds with an oil, such as peanut or almond oil. Instead of running a knife around the edge, dip the mould very briefly into a bowl of hot water and it should turn out cleanly.

Chocolate mint cake

A sumptuous, moist cake of the darkest chocolate is enhanced with the freshness of mint and the sweetness of ground almonds. This cake will sink slightly in the centre during cooling; the resultant dip provides a perfect space for the topping of soft fruit.

125g unsalted butter
150g dark chocolate
  (at least 70 per cent cocoa),
  broken into pieces
handful finely chopped fresh mint
  or chocolate mint leaves
  (or 1 teaspoon peppermint
  extract)
6 large eggs, separated
pinch of salt
80g caster sugar
150g ground almonds
450g soft berries
  (strawberries, blackberries,
  blueberries or raspberries)
icing sugar, for dusting
whipped cream, to serve

SERVES 8
Preparation 25 minutes
Cooking 35 minutes

1 Preheat oven to 170°C. Grease 20cm springform cake tin; line base with baking paper.

2 Melt butter and chocolate in heatproof medium bowl over saucepan of just simmering water, stirring occasionally. Remove from heat; cool slightly. Stir through mint leaves.

3 In medium bowl, whisk egg white swith pinch of salt until soft peaks form. Gradually add sugar, whisking well after each addition until just dissolved.

4 Beat egg yolks in large bowl, and stir through ground almonds. Pour in cooled chocolate mixture; mix well. Using metal spoon, fold in 2 large spoonfuls of egg white to lighten mixture, then carefully and quickly fold in the remainder. Do not overwork.

5 Pour mixture into prepared tin. Bake 35 to 40 minutes until cake is well risen and just firm to the touch. Cool in tin 15 minutes before turning out onto wire rack. It will sink slightly in the centre.

6 Decorate cooled cake with fresh berries; dust with sifted icing sugar. Serve with whipped cream.

Herb guide

Chocolate mint has the taste and aroma of an after-dinner chocolate mint. Use in chocolate desserts such as mousse and ice cream. With its dark green to purple leaves, it also makes an attractive garnish

Cupcakes with crystallised flowers

Gorgeously decorated cupcakes are the height of culinary fashion – and they are so easy to make. Crystallised flowers are available from shops that sell cake-decorating supplies – or for extra satisfaction, make your own sugar dipped edible flowers.

Cupcakes

225g butter, softened
230g caster sugar
1 teaspoon vanilla extract
4 large eggs
235g self-raising flour
1 tablespoon milk
12 to 24 crystallised flowers
   (see below)

ICING
125g butter, softened
230g icing sugar
2 tablespoons milk
food colouring

MAKES 12
Preparation 30 minutes plus 1 to 3 days for flowers (if making your own)
Cooking 15 minutes

1 Preheat oven to 180°C. In a large bowl and using an electric mixer, beat butter and sugar until thoroughly combined and light and creamy.

2 Add vanilla and eggs, one at a time, mixing after each addition until well combined.

3 Sift flour into mixture. Using a plastic spatula or wooden spoon, fold in flour and milk until combined.

4 Divide mixture among 12 cupcake cases until two-thirds full; bake 15 minutes, or until golden. Turn out onto a wire rack to cool.

5 To make icing, mix butter and icing sugar until creamy (about 2 minutes), using electric mixer. Add milk and food colouring, mixing until combined.

6 Ice cooled cakes and decorate with crystallised flowers.

Crystallised flowers

12 to 24 rose or violet petals,
   or other edible flower petals
1 egg white, at room temperature
few drops of water
230g caster sugar

1 Combine egg white with water; using a fork, beat lightly until white just shows bubbles. Place sugar in shallow dish.

2 Hold flower or petal in one hand; with other hand, dip a small paintbrush into egg white and gently paint flower or petal, covering flower or petal completely but not excessively. Gently sprinkle sugar over flower or petal.

3 Place flower or petal on wire rack covered with baking paper to dry. Repeat with remaining flowers or petals.

4 Allow flowers or petals to dry completely before use (about 12 to 36 hours, depending on humidity). Store crystallised flowers or petals in airtight container until required.

Drinks with herbs

Forget buying fizzy drinks – they are just a quick fix and won't quench your thirst for long. Instead, take the heat out of long, hot summers with these sublimely refreshing drinks made simply and easily with a variety of fresh herbs and fruit.

Coriander and lime juice

4 tablespoons fresh coriander leaves
2 stalks celery
1 lime, peeled
2 medium green apples, cored and quartered
250ml cranberry juice
ice cubes

MAKES APPROX. 750ml
Preparation 5 minutes

1 Put coriander, celery, lime and apples through juicer. Pour juice into large jug; add cranberry juice and ice. Serve chilled.

Lemonade with mint

230g sugar
250ml water
250ml lemon juice
1 litre soda or mineral water
50g fresh mint leaves
lemon slices, to serve

MAKES APPROX. 1.5 litres
Preparation 15 minutes

1 Place sugar and water in small saucepan. Bring to the boil over a high heat, stirring until sugar is dissolved; cool.

2 Mix sugar syrup with lemon juice, soda or mineral water and mint leaves. Serve with lemon slices and ice.

Frozen petals

Heartsease flowers are edible and can be scattered through salads or crystallised for cake decoration. Freeze them in water in ice-cube trays and then pop a few cubes into a jug of lemonade.

Try these, too…

LASSI

For a traditional Indian drink, place 125ml plain yoghurt, 310ml cold water, ½ teaspoon dry-roasted cumin seeds, ¼ teaspoon salt and 1 teaspoon chopped fresh mint leaves in a blender. Process to combine. Serve chilled, garnished with mint sprigs.

MULLED WINE

To beat the winter chills, place 750ml dry red wine, 225g white sugar, 125ml brandy, 125ml water, 2 thinly sliced oranges and 1 thinly sliced lemon, 2 small lightly crushed cinnamon sticks, 9 whole cloves and a pinch of grated nutmeg in a large saucepan over low heat. Bring to simmering point. Simmer, stirring occasionally, 5 to 10 minutes, or until sugar has dissolved and mixture is aromatic. Remove from heat. Strain into a large jug. Serve while still warm.

Index

Bold page numbers refer to photographs; *italic* page numbers refer to recipes and craft projects.

INDEX

Photography credits

Cover *T* iStockphoto.com/Rebecca Paul, *L* iStockphoto.com/Oscar Gutierrez, *CL* iStockphoto.com/Valeria Titova, *C* iStockphoto.com/Tatiana Pavlova, *CR* iStockphoto.com/Valeria Titova, *R* iStockphoto.com/Vera Bogaerts **1** © Reader's Digest **6-7** Gap Photos Ltd/Clive Nicols/Design: del Buono Gazerwitz, Spencer Fung Achitects **10** *TL* © Reader's Digest, TC © Reader's Digest, *TR* iStockphoto.com/Heidi Steinbach, *CL* © Reader's Digest, *C* The Garden Collection/Torie Chugg, *CR* © Reader's Digest, *BL* © Reader's Digest, *BC* © Reader's Digest, *BR* © Reader's Digest **12** *TR* © Reader's Digest, *BL* © 2009 Photolibrary.com **13** © Reader's Digest, *T* The Garden Collection/Derek St Romaine **14** *L* ShutterStock, Inc, *R* © Reader's Digest **15** *L* Gap Photos Ltd/Richard Bloom, *R* © Reader's Digest 16 *TR* Deni Bown, *BL* © Reader's Digest **17** *T* Still Pictures/© Biosphotos/Matt Alexander, *B* © Reader's Digest **18** *TR* © Reader's Digest, *BL* © Reader's Digest **19** *TL* © Reader's Digest, *TR* © Reader's Digest, *B* © Reader's Digest **20** *T* The Picture Desk/Biblioteca Nazionale Marciana Venice, *CR* Maddie Thornhill/Gap Photos Ltd, *BL* © Reader's Digest **21** *L* © Reader's Digest, *R* Corbis/National Gallery Collection **22** *TR* © Reader's Digest, *BL* © Reader's Digest, *BR* The Bridgeman Art Library **23** The Garden Collection/Nicola Stocken-Tomkins **24** Corbis/Mike Grandmaison, *TR* iStockphoto.com/Alasdair Thomson **25** *TR* © Reader's Digest, *BL* © Reader's Digest **26** *TR* © Reader's Digest, *BL* Deni Bown **27** © Reader's Digest, *TR* Keith A McLeod **28** *TR* © Reader's Digest, *BL* The Garden Collection/Andrew Lawson **29** *TR* Keith A McLeod, *B* © Reader's Digest **30** *TR* © Reader's Digest, *B* © Reader's Digest **31** © 2009 Photolibrary.com/Tim Hill **32** *TR* © Reader's Digest, *BL* © Reader's Digest **33** *TR* © Reader's Digest, *BR* © Reader's Digest **34** *TR* © Reader's Digest, *B* © Reader's Digest **35** *TR* © Reader's Digest, *BR* © Reader's Digest **36** *TR* © Reader's Digest, *BL* © Reader's Digest **37** BL © Reader's Digest, *BR* © Reader's Digest **38** TL © Reader's Digest, *BL* © Reader's Digest **39** *TR* © Reader's Digest/Danny Smythe, *BL* Still Pictures/R.Koenig **40** *T* iStockphoto.com/Stefano Tiraboschi, *B* The Garden Collection/Derek Harris **41** *T* The Garden Collection/Torie Chugg, *BR* Corbis/Anna Watson **42** *R* © Reader's Digest, *BL* Keith A McLeod **43** *TR* Corbis/Owen Franken, *B* iStockphoto.com **44** *TR* Gap Photos Ltd/Howard Rice, *BL* ShutterStock, Inc/Florin C **45** iStockphoto.com/Sandra Caldwell **46** *T* iStockphoto.com, *BL* © 2009 Photolibrary.com/Botanica/Photo Dinodia **47** *R* © Reader's Digest, *BL* © Reader's Digest **48** *TR* © Reader's Digest, *BL* iStockphoto.com/ Gianluca Padovani **49** *TR* © Reader's Digest, *B* iStockphoto.com/Sandra Caldwell **50** L Frank Lane Picture Agency/Jurgen & Christine Sohns, *TR* © Reader's Digest **51** *T* © Reader's Digest, *B* © 2009 Photolibrary.com **52** *T* iStockphoto.com/Sergey Chushkin, *B* © Reader's Digest **53** © 2009 Photolibrary.com/Irene Windridge **54** *TR* © Reader's Digest, *BL* © Reader's Digest **55** *TR* © Reader's Digest, *CR* Deni Bown, *BL* Deni Bown **56** *TR* © Reader's Digest, *B* © Reader's Digest **57** *TR* Corbis/Dave Reede, *BL* iStockphoto.com/Eric Naud **58** © Reader's Digest, *TR* The Garden Collection/Lisa Shalet **60** *TR* iStockphoto.com/Sandra Caldwell, *BL* © Reader's Digest **61** *TR* © Reader's Digest, *BL* © Reader's Digest **62** *T* Inga Spence/Visuals Unlimited/Getty Images, *B* © Reader's Digest **63** L iStockphoto.com/Sining Zhang, *R* iStockphoto.com/Andreas Kaspar **64** iStockphoto.com/Juergen Sack **65** © Reader's Digest **66** *TR* © Reader's Digest, *BL* Gap Photos Ltd/Friedrich Strauss **67** *T* © Reader's Digest, *B* © Reader's Digest **68** TL iStockphoto.com/Heidi Steinbach, *B* Corbis **69** *TR* Getty Images/Dave King/Dorling Kindersley, *BL* Gap Photos Ltd/Howard Rice **70** *TR* Garden World Images/Gerald Majumdar, *BL* Keith A McLeod **71** *TR* iStockphoto.com, *CR* iStockphoto.com/Linda Steward, *BL* © 2009 Photolibrary.com **72** *TR* Garden World Images/Steffen Hauser, *BL* © 2009 Photolibrary.com/Brian Carter **73** *TR* © Reader's Digest, *BL* © 2009 Photolibrary.com **74** L © Reader's Digest, *R* Keith A McLeod **75** *TR* iStockphoto.com/Linda & Colin McKie, *BL* © Reader's Digest **76** *TR* Frank Lane Picture Agency/Imagebroker, *BL* © Reader's Digest **77** L © Reader's Digest, *R* © Reader's Digest **78** *TR* © Reader's Digest, *B* Keith A McLeod **79** © Reader's Digest **80** *TR* iStockphoto.com/Hazel Proudlove, *B* © Reader's Digest **81** *TR* © Reader's Digest, *CR* © Reader's Digest, *BL* © Reader's Digest **82** L Gap Photos Ltd/Janet Johnson, *TR* iStockphoto.com/Hazel Proudlove **83** *T* Corbis/Clay Perry, *B* © 2009 Photolibrary.com **84** TL © Reader's Digest, *TR* Alamy Images, *B* © Reader's Digest **85** *TR* Gap Photos Ltd/Juliette Wade, *B* © Reader's Digest **86** *T* © Reader's Digest, *B* Keith A McLeod **87** *TR* Gap Photos Ltd/Visions, *B* © Reader's Digest **88** *T* © Reader's Digest, *B* Keith A McLeod **89** *T* © Reader's Digest, *B* Mary Evans Picture Library **90** *T* © Reader's Digest, *BL* © Reader's Digest, *BR* Frank Lane Picture Agency/Bob Gibbons **91** *T* © 2009 Photolibrary.com/Gilbert S Grant, *B* © Reader's Digest **92** *T* Frank Lane Picture Agency/Nigel Cattlin, *B* Garden World Images/Gilles Delacroix **93** *TR* Garden World Images/Sandra O'Connor, *B* Lynher Dairies Cheese Company **94** *T* naturepl.com/Willem Kolvoort, *B* iStockphoto.com/Elena Schweitzer **95** *TR* Garden World Images/Floramedia, *BL* iStockphoto.com/Sabrina Dei Nobili, *BR* iStockphoto.com/Maceofoto **96** *T* © Reader's Digest, *B* © Reader's Digest **97** Getty Images/StockFood **98** *T* Corbis/Tony Arruza, *B* © Reader's Digest **99** *TR* Garden World Images/Rita Coates, *B* Corbis/Demetrio Carrasco **100** *T* iStockphoto.com/Norman Chan, *BL* Frank Lane Picture Agency/Parameswaran Pillai Karunakaran **101** L © Reader's Digest, *BR* © Reader's Digest **102** *TR* iStockphoto.com/Rudi Tapper, *CL* © Reader's Digest, *BR* Gap Photos Ltd/Visions **103** *T* © Reader's Digest, *B* © Reader's Digest **104** *T* iStockphoto.com/Mehmet Can, *B* iStockphoto.com **105** *TR* iStockphoto.com/Brent Melton, *B* Corbis/Stefano Bianchetti, **106** *R* iStockphoto.com/Carole Gomez, *BL* © Reader's Digest **107** *TR* Science Photo Library/Maria & Bruno Petriglia, *BL* © Reader's Digest **108** *T* iStockphoto.com/dirkr, *B* © 2009 Photolibrary.com/Howard Rice **109** *TR* Garden World Images/Trevor Sims, *BL* Photoshot/Imagebroker.net, *BR* iStockphoto.com/esemelwe **110** L © Reader's Digest, *TR* iStockphoto.com, *BR* © Reader's Digest **111** *TR* Garden World Images, *BL* © Reader's Digest **112** Keith A McLeod, *TL* Keith A McLeod, *TR* Corbis/Stapleton Collection **113** *T* © Reader's Digest, *B* © 2009 Photolibrary.com/Janet Seaton **114** *T* © Reader's Digest, *BL* Gap Photos Ltd/Neil Holmes **115** © Reader's Digest, *T* © Reader's Digest **116** TL © Reader's Digest, *TR* © Reader's Digest, *B* © 2009 Photolibrary.com/Howard Rice **117** Keith A McLeod **118** L Gap Photos Ltd/J S Sira, *R* iStockphoto.com, **119** *TR* © Reader's Digest, *BL* Garden World Images/Gilles Delacroix **120** *T* Keith A McLeod, *BL* © Reader's Digest, *BR* © Reader's Digest **121** Photoshot, L Photoshot/© Photo Horticultural **122** *T* © Reader's Digest, *B* © 2009 Photolibrary.com/Jo Whitworth **123** *T* Gap Photos Ltd/Juliette Wade, *B* The Garden Collection/Jonathan Buckley **124** TL Keith A McLeod, *TR* © Reader's Digest, *BR* Keith A McLeod **125** L Deni Bown, *R* © Reader's Digest **126** *T* The Garden Collection/Andrew Lawson, *B* Getty Images/Bridgeman Art Library **127** Keith A McLeod **128** L The Garden Collection/Andrew Lawson, *TR* Corbis/The Gallery Collection **129** *TR* © Reader's Digest, *B* Deni Bown **130** *TR* © 2009 Photolibrary.com/Ingram Publishing/Superstock, *B* © Reader's Digest **131** © Reader's Digest, *TR* Keith A McLeod **132** *TR* © Reader's Digest, *BL* Corbis/Dave G. Houser, *BR* © Reader's Digest **133** *T* Getty Images/De Agostini Picture Library, *B* Garden World Images/Deni Bown **134** © Reader's Digest **135** *TR* © Reader's Digest, *B* Gap Photos Ltd/Neil Holmes **136** *TR* © Reader's Digest, © Reader's Digest **137** © Reader's Digest, *TR* © 2009 Photolibrary.com/Photo Dinodia/Botanica, *BR* Corbis/EPA **138** *T* © Reader's Digest, *B* © Reader's Digest **139** *T* © Reader's Digest/Wolfgang Amri, *B* Still Pictures/R.Koenig **140** *T* © Reader's Digest, *B* Corbis/Adam Woolfitt **141** *TR* Alamy Images/Pat Tuson, *BL* Garden World Images/Derek Fall, *BR* Keith A McLeod **142** *TR* iStockphoto.com/Andrzej Burak, *CL* © Reader's Digest, *BR* Frank Lane Picture Agency/ ImageBroker **143** *T* © Reader's Digest, *B* Garden World Images/Francoise Davis **144** L © Reader's Digest, *R* © Reader's Digest **145** *T* iStockphoto.com/dirkr, *B* Mary Evans Picture Library **148** *TR* © Reader's Digest, *TR* Keran Barrett **149** Corbis/Clay Perry **150** © Reader's Digest **151** *T* © Reader's Digest, *BR* ShutterStock, Inc **152** © Reader's Digest **155** Gap Photos Ltd **159** Gap Photos Ltd/Clive Nichols, The Garden Collection/Liz Eddison **161** The Garden Collection/Derek St Romaine **174** © Reader's Digest, © Reader's Digest, © Reader's Digest, © Reader's Digest **175** *T* Frank Lane Picture Agency/Peter Entwistle, *B* © Reader's Digest **176** © Reader's Digest, © Reader's Digest, *T* © Reader's Digest, TC © Reader's Digest **177** Garden World Images/Nicholas Appleby, © Reader's Digest **178** L © Reader's Digest, *R* © Reader's Digest **179** © Reader's Digest **180** © Reader's Digest **181** *T* © Reader's Digest, *BL* © Reader's Digest, *BR* © Reader's Digest **184** *T* © 2009 Photolibrary.com, *B* Corbis/Gianni Dagli Orti **185** The Picture Desk **186** © Reader's Digest **187** © Reader's Digest **188-189** B © Reader's Digest **189** *TR* © Reader's Digest **190** © 2009 Photolibrary.com/Science Photo Library **191** © Reader's Digest, © iStockphoto.com/Jowita Stachowiak **192** *T* © Reader's Digest, *BR* © Reader's Digest **193** © Reader's Digest **194** © Reader's Digest **195** Corbis/Klaus Honal, *TL* © Reader's Digest, *TR* © 2009 Photolibrary.com **196** Science Photo Library/Cordelia Molloy, © Reader's Digest **202** TC iStockphoto.com, *BL* © Reader's Digest **203** *T* Science Photo Library/Mauro Fermariello, *B* Getty Images/ DeAgostini **204** *T* © 2009 Photolibrary.com/Botanica, *B* © 2009 Photolibrary.com **205** Getty Images/Ken Lucas, *T* © Reader's Digest, *BL* Getty Images/James Worrell/Time & Life Pictures, © Reader's Digest **206** © Reader's Digest **207** © Reader's Digest, © Reader's Digest **208** © Reader's Digest, © Reader's Digest, Corbis/Elizabeth Blackwell/Stapleton Collection **209** © Reader's Digest **210** © Reader's Digest, © Reader's Digest **211** © Reader's Digest **212** © Reader's Digest **213** © Reader's Digest **214** © Reader's Digest **215** © Reader's Digest **216** © Reader's Digest **217** © Reader's Digest **218** © Reader's Digest **219** © Reader's Digest **220** Corbis/Michael Maslan **221** © Reader's Digest **222** © Reader's Digest **223** © Reader's Digest **224** © Reader's Digest **225** © Reader's Digest **226** Corbis/Philip de Bay/Historical Picture Archive **228** © Reader's Digest **229** Getty Images/Time Life Pictures **230** Corbis/Martin Harvey/Gallo Images **231** *T* © Reader's Digest, *B* naturepl.com **232** Corbis/Stapleton Collection **233** © Reader's Digest **234** © 2009 Photolibrary.com/Michael P Gadomski, © Reader's Digest **235** © 2009 Photolibrary.com/The Bridgeman Art Library **236** © Reader's Digest **237** Corbis/Artkey **239** © Reader's Digest **240** © 2009 Photolibrary.com/The Bridgeman Art Library **241** *T* © Reader's Digest, *B* © Reader's Digest **242** Keith A McLeod **243** Corbis/Cynthia Hart **244** *T* © Reader's Digest, *B* © Reader's Digest **245** © 2009 Photolibrary.com/The Bridgeman Art Library **249** © Reader's Digest **250** © Reader's Digest **251** *T* © Reader's Digest, *B* © Reader's Digest **252** © Reader's Digest **253** © Reader's Digest **254** © Reader's Digest **255** *T* © Reader's Digest, *B* © Reader's Digest **256** © Reader's Digest **257** *T* © Reader's Digest, *B* © Reader's Digest **258** *T* © Reader's Digest **258-259** © Reader's Digest **260** *T* © Reader's Digest **260-261** © Reader's Digest **261** *T* © Reader's Digest **262** © Reader's Digest **263** © Reader's Digest **264** *T* © Reader's Digest, *B* © Reader's Digest **265** © Reader's Digest **266** © Reader's Digest **268** *T* © Reader's Digest, *B* © Reader's Digest **269** ShutterStock, Inc **270** © Reader's Digest **270-271** © Reader's Digest **271** *R* © Reader's Digest **272** L © Reader's Digest **272-273** © Reader's Digest **273** © Reader's Digest **275** *T* © Reader's Digest **276** © Reader's Digest **277** © Reader's Digest **278** L © Reader's Digest, *R* © Reader's Digest **279** L © Reader's Digest, *R* © Reader's Digest **280** © Reader's Digest **281** © Reader's Digest **282** © Reader's Digest **283** *TR* Getty Images/David Pluth, *BL* © Reader's Digest **284** *T* © Reader's Digest, *B* © Reader's Digest **285** © Reader's Digest **286** © Reader's Digest **287** *T* iStockphoto.com, B © Reader's Digest **288-289** © Reader's Digest **290** © Reader's Digest **291** *T* © Reader's Digest, *BL* © Reader's Digest, *BR* © Reader's Digest **292** *TR* © Reader's Digest, *BL* © Reader's Digest **293** © Reader's Digest **294** *T* © Reader's Digest, *BL* © Reader's Digest, BR © Reader's Digest **295** © Reader's Digest **296** BL © Reader's Digest **296-297** *T* © Reader's Digest, *B* © Reader's Digest **298** © Reader's Digest **299** *T* © Reader's Digest, *B* © Reader's Digest **300** L © Reader's Digest, *R* © Reader's Digest **301** *TR* © Reader's Digest, *BL* © Reader's Digest **302** © Reader's Digest, *BR* © Reader's Digest **303** *T* © Reader's Digest, *BL* © Reader's Digest, *BR* © Reader's Digest **304-305** © Reader's Digest **306** © Reader's Digest **307** © Reader's Digest **308** © Reader's Digest **309** © Reader's Digest **332-333** © Reader's Digest **334** *T* © Reader's Digest, *BL* © Reader's Digest **335** *T* © Reader's Digest, B © Reader's Digest **337** © Reader's Digest **338-389** All © Reader's Digest

Acknowledgments

The publishers wish to thank the following individuals, companies and organisations for their help during the preparation of *The Ultimate Book of Herbs*.

Alex Jordan. Ambiance Interiors. Australia Post. Australia's Open Garden Scheme. Baytree. Beclau. Blooms the Chemist. British Sweets & Treats. Buds and Bowers Florist. Bulb. Bunnings. Chee Soon and Fitzgerald. Chinese Ginseng & Herb Co. Coles Supermarkets Australia. Darling Street Health Centre. Domayne. Dong Nam A & Co. Doug Up on Bourke. Dulux. Feed Ya Face. Flower Power Nursery. Freedom Furniture. Fruitique. Funkis Swedish Forms. Gardens R Us. Glebe Newsagency. Glenmore House. Gold's World of Judaica. Gundabluey. Herb Herbert. House of Herbs and Roses. Julie Pilcher Flowers. Mint Condition. Moss River. Mr Copy. Mrs Red and Sons. New Directions Australia. No Chintz. Oishi. Oxford Art Supplies. Paper Couture. Paper2. Pet City. Price War. Reln Plastics. Rococo Flowers. Ros Andrews. Royal Botanic Gardens, Sydney. Sally Stobo. Spotlight Australia. St. Vincent de Paul Society. Stark's Kosher Supermarket. Summers Floral Woollahra. Swadlings Timber and Hardware. The Barn Café and Grocery. The Floral Decorator. The Nut Shop. The Tegal Garden. Urban Balcony. Vicino. Wholefoods House. Yarrow's Pharmacy.

Special thanks to Fratelli Fresh for the supply of fresh herbs for photography. Herbie's Spices. Ici et La.

Craft project makers Irene Barnes – hanging herb ball. Georgina Bitcon – sewing and embroidery projects. Margaret Cox – garden dibbers. Julie Pilcher – herb and flower wreath; table centrepiece; tussie-mussie. Stephen Prodes – window boxes.

Photographers Andre Martin (cover; all chapters except Gardening); Chris L. Jones (Gardening)

Illustrator Margaret Cory (garden plan), Stephen Pollitt

Locations and animals Finckh/Talako house and Akira (the cat). Gibson/Chamberlain house and Pinky (the cat). Martin/Barnes house and Maxie and Saffron (the dogs). Ladkin house. Sarsfield house.

UK consultant and writer Deni Bown

UK medical consultants The National Institute of Medical Herbalists

Consultants and writers Pamela Allardice; Keran Barrett; Georgina Bitcon; Janine Flew; Lynn Lewis; Dr Judyth A. McLeod; Cathryn Rich; Jayne Tancred; Gabrielle Wheatley

Editor Lisa Thomas
Art Editor Julie Bennett
Designer Kate Harris
Picture Researcher Rosie Taylor
Proofreader Barry Gage
Indexer Marie Lorimer

READER'S DIGEST GENERAL BOOKS
Editorial Director Julian Browne
Art Director Anne-Marie Bulat
Managing Editor Nina Hathway
Head of Book Development Sarah Bloxham
Picture Resource Manager Christine Hinze
Pre-press Account Manager Dean Russell
Product Production Manager Claudette Bramble
Senior Production Controller Katherine Tibbals

The Ultimate Book of Herbs is published by The Reader's Digest Association Limited, 11 Westferry Circus, Canary Wharf, London E14 4HE

ISBN: 978 0 276 44540 8
Concept code: AU0612/IC
Book code: 400-425 UP0000-1
Oracle code: 250013207S.00.24